Word 2003 Bible

Word 2003 Bible

Brent Heslop, David Angell, and Peter Kent

Wiley Publishing, Inc.

Word 2003 Bible

Published by
Wiley Publishing, Inc.
10475 Crosspoint Boulevard
Indianapolis, IN 46256
www.wiley.com

Copyright © 2003 by Wiley Publishing, Inc., Indianapolis, Indiana

Published simultaneously in Canada

Library of Congress Card Number: 2003101910

ISBN: 0-7645-3971-X

Manufactured in the United States of America

10 9 8 7 6 5 4 3 2

1B/SV/QZ/QT/IN

About the Authors

Brent Heslop is an avid Word user. He has coauthored more than 15 books and written numerous magazine articles using Word. He also works as a consultant and teaches HTML publishing and interactive programming classes. His books include *Microsoft Word 2000 Bible* and *Word 97 Bible* (published by Wiley).

David Angell is a computer industry writer and consultant. He has used Word as his word processing workbench since the early days of Word for MS-DOS. David has authored and coauthored more than 14 books. His books include *Word 2000 Bible, Word 97 Bible,* and *DSL For Dummies* (all published by Wiley). David is also a principal in angell.com, an Internet and ISDN consulting and technical communications firm.

Peter Kent has used Microsoft Word for 14 years to write 50 books, scores of technical manuals, and literally thousands of magazine articles and corporate documents. He has worked in the software development business for nearly 22 years, designing and testing software, writing documentation, and training users. He is the author of the widely reviewed and praised *Poor Richard's Web Site.* Today, he is vice president of marketing for Indigio, an e-services firm.

Credits

Senior Acquisitions Editor
Jim Minatel

Senior Project Editor
Jodi Jensen

Development Editor
Kevin Kent

Technical Editor
Herb Tyson

Copy Editor
Kim Cofer

Editorial Manager
Mary Beth Wakefield

Vice President & Executive Group Publisher
Richard Swadley

Vice President and Executive Publisher
Bob Ipsen

Vice President and Publisher
Joseph B. Wikert

Executive Editorial Director
Mary Bednarek

Project Coordinator
Erin Smith

Graphics and Production Specialists
Elizabeth Brooks
Amanda Carter
Jennifer Click
Sean Decker
LeAndra Johnson

Quality Control Technicians
Laura Albert
John Tyler Connoley
John Greenough
Andy Hollandbeck

Senior Permissions Editor
Carmen Krikorian

Media Development Specialist
Angela Denny

Proofreading
TECHBOOKS Production Services

Indexing
Sherry Massey

Cover Image
Murder By Design

For Nick and Chris

Preface

Welcome to the *Word 2003 Bible*. As part of the Wiley *Bible* series, this book emphasizes "handiness" by giving you complete coverage of Word 2003 in an easy-to-use format. In this book, you find all the information that you need to successfully use Word, whether you're a new or experienced user. To make it as easy as possible to find, understand, and implement information, throughout the text the major tasks are clearly delineated. This guide is designed to facilitate your access to Word and get you quickly on your way to getting the most out of this truly exciting and powerful new product.

Who Should Read This Book

The *Word 2003 Bible* is both a tutorial for beginners as well as a complete reference for experienced Word users. If you're upgrading to Word 2003, you will find that this book fully integrates the new features with those that remain the same, so you can learn about new features in the context of features with which you are already familiar.

How This Book Is Organized

This book matches the way you work with Word 2003. Organized into seven parts, it starts with the fundamentals and builds on them as you progress through the book. Each chapter can stand on its own or point you to any additional information you need.

Part I: The Fundamentals

Part I explains mastering the rich assortment of Word's essential word-processing tasks. You learn the basics of working in the Word 2003 environment, how to create and edit documents, search and replace specific text or formatting, print documents, and manage document files.

Part II: Beyond the Basics

Part II covers working with Word's features that, though still related to the manipulation of text, are a little more advanced. You learn how to proof your work, check spelling and grammar, and even how to use Word as a research tool. You find out how to place text into tables, how to work with sections, columns, and page formatting. You can also find out about some extremely useful "linking" tools—bookmarks, cross-references, footnotes, indexes, and tables of various kinds.

Part III: Working More Effectively

In this part of the book you can find out how to use the tools that are intended to help you "speed up the process." This part looks at how styles and autoformatting can help you format text very quickly by automating the process and how templates, wizards, and themes can jumpstart new documents. We've also included a chapter that offers an understanding of document-layout principles—what looks good, what looks bad—and a chapter that explains how you can speak and Word will understand (perhaps) and convert your words to text.

Part IV: Inserting Pictures and Other Content

Part IV delves into Word's graphics capabilities to create dazzling documents as well as integrating content from other Office applications into your Word documents. You learn how to use Word's powerful graphics features, including choosing the right image file format, editing graphics, laying out your documents, and creating WordArt to add shaped text with special effects. You learn how to bring information from other Office applications, including Microsoft Access, Microsoft PowerPoint, and Microsoft Excel. This part also covers how to use Microsoft Graph Chart and Microsoft Equation, which are included with Office.

Part V: Complex Documents: Mail Merge, Forms, Outlines, and Web Pages

Part V covers creating more complex documents. By the time you finish this part of the book you will know how to use Word's mail merge tools to create and print form letters, envelopes, labels, and lists by merging information from a database. You also learn how to create your own interactive forms and tie them directly to a database, how to use outlines and master documents to organize your thoughts and text, and how to work with Word's HTML Web page features.

Part VI: Distribution and Collaboration

Part VI explains how to work with Word's workgroup collaboration tools. You may be surprised at what you find in this section—even many users who have been working with Word for a decade or more are unaware of some of the neat collaboration tools, and this version of Word has made them even better. In this part, you see how to share documents among colleagues—and even merge their changes back into the original. You find out how to fax and e-mail documents and how to use SharePoint services to build document areas online that incorporate document libraries with discussions, to-do lists, calendars, and more. And you learn about Word's comment and review features.

Part VII: Customizing and Troubleshooting Word

Part VII explains troubleshooting Word's idiosyncrasies, customizing Word to fit the way you work, and automating Word tasks. You learn how to overcome common and not-so-common Word problems, and then go on to tailoring Word's menus, toolbars, and shortcut keys to the way you work. In addition, you delve into how to master field codes and macros to simplify and automate Word tasks and learn how to secure your information so only approved people can view or edit it.

Appendixes

In Appendix A, you get a detailed survey of the new and improved features in Word 2003, as well as the changes that took place between Word 2000 and Word 2002 (for those of you who may be upgrading from Word 2000). Appendix B provides information about the bounty of software included on the book's companion CD-ROM.

How to Approach This Book

If you are starting out with Word for the first time, Chapters 1 through 12 lay out the word-processing essentials of Word. Read these chapters, and you'll know how to create attractive documents quickly and relatively efficiently. From this base, you can move through the ranks of more advanced topics as you need them. Even if you're an experienced Word user, you'll want to check out Chapters 1 through 12 because of the many changes in Word's basic word-processing capabilities. You can use Appendix A as your guide to what's new in this version of Word.

If you spend much time at all with Word, you'll want to read Chapters 13 through 16 because the information in those chapters can end up saving you many hours by helping you learn how to work more effectively using several advanced tools. Of course, if you eventually want to insert pictures and other content into your documents, you'll want to read Chapters 17 and 18. But consider also spending some time with Chapters 19, 20, and 21. They offer useful "secrets" that the average Word user may not know about.

Take a look at Chapters 22 through 24 if you need to create mail-merged labels, letters, and envelopes, if you want to create fill-in forms, or if you want to exploit the power of Word's fields. And anyone who works with large documents really should read Chapter 25, where you learn about Word's outlining feature and master documents.

If you are planning to build Web pages, read Chapters 26 and 27 to find out how Word can help you—and why you might not want to use Word! And if you work in conjunction with others, in workgroups or some other kind of collaboration, take a look at the chapters in Part VI, which offer information on tools that can save you a lot time in collaborative tasks.

Note   One thing to keep in mind as you use this book is that you may notice some differences in what you see depending on whether you're running Windows 2000 or Windows XP. You may also notice differences depending on whether you've kept the XP default settings or customized them, or if you're using the Windows XP Classic Windows settings, which lets you make XP look like Windows 2000. Taking all of these things into consideration, what you see on your screen may not be *exactly* what is described or shown here.

Using the companion CD-ROM and Web site

Wiley has provided so much add-on value to this book that we couldn't fit it all on one CD! With the purchase of this book, you not only get access to lots of bonus software programs and demos, you also get an entire eBook—free!

Please take a few minutes to explore the bonus material included on the CD:

✦ **Bonus software:** A plethora of programs (shareware, freeware, GNU software, trials, demos, and evaluation software) that work with Office. A ReadMe file on the CD includes complete descriptions of each software item.

✦ *Office 2003 Super Bible* **eBook:** Wiley created this special eBook, consisting of over 500 pages of content about how Microsoft Office components work together and with other products. The content has been pulled from select chapters of the individual Office *Bible* titles. In addition, some original content has been created just for this *Super Bible*.

✦ **PDF version of this title:** As always, if you prefer your text in electronic format, the CD offers a completely searchable PDF version of the book you hold in your hands.

After you familiarize yourself with all that we have packed onto the CD, be sure to visit the companion Web site at: www.wiley.com/compbooks/officebibles2003/. Here's what you'll find on the Web site:

✦ Links to all the software that wouldn't fit on the CD

✦ Links to all the software found on the CD

✦ Complete, detailed tables of contents for all the Wiley Office 2003 *Bibles: Access 2003 Bible, Excel 2003 Bible, FrontPage 2003 Bible, Office 2003 Bible, Outlook 2003 Bible, PowerPoint 2003 Bible,* and *Word 2003 Bible*

✦ Links to other Wiley Office titles

Conventions Used in This Book

To make this book as easy as possible to use, icons in the margins alert you to special or important information. Look for the following icons:

 Caution   Marks a warning about a particular procedure to which you should pay particular attention.

 Cross-Reference   Points you to another place where additional information on the current topic can be found.

 Note   Marks a special point or supplementary information about a feature or task.

 Tip   Marks a tip that saves you time and helps you work more efficiently.

 On the CD-ROM   Points you to helpful software provided on the accompanying CD.

To further assist you in reading and learning the material in this book, the following formatting conventions are used throughout:

✦ Text you are asked to type appears in **bold**.

✦ New words and phrases that may require definition and explanation appear in *italics*. Text that carries emphasis and single characters that may be easy to lose in the text also appear in italics.

✦ Menu commands are indicated in sequential order by using the command arrow. File ➪ Open, for example, indicates that you should click the File menu and then choose the Open command.

✦ Keyboard shortcut keys look like this: Alt+Tab.

✦ When instructed to *click* an item, press the left mouse button unless otherwise specified. When you should use the right mouse button instead, you are asked to *right-click*. Of course, this will be different for left-handed users.

Acknowledgments

We owe a debt of gratitude to numerous people who helped us make this book a reality. First, we want to thank Jim Minatel, our acquisitions editor at Wiley Publishing, who gave us the opportunity to work on this *Bible*.

We would like to thank our project editor, Jodi Jensen, who was instrumental in keeping the traffic moving. One person who carries a tremendous load in getting a book to press is the development editor. We are very grateful to have had Kevin Kent as our DE. Kevin did a great job encouraging us and sharing ideas to help us better organize and improve the text. We would also like to thank Herb Tyson, technical editor, who provided a great deal of information and expertise about a plethora of little details, and Kim Cofer, copy editor, for the essential clean-up work she did.

We also want to thank the companies that gave us permission to include their material on the CD-ROM that accompanies this book.

Contents at a Glance

Preface ix
Acknowledgments xiii

Part I: The Fundamentals 1
Chapter 1: Getting Started with Word 2003 3
Chapter 2: Navigating and Editing Documents 41
Chapter 3: Finding and Replacing Text and Formats 77
Chapter 4: Character Formatting and Fonts 93
Chapter 5: Paragraph Formatting 121
Chapter 6: Printing Documents 163
Chapter 7: Managing Documents 189

Part II: Beyond the Basics 221
Chapter 8: Proofing and Researching 223
Chapter 9: Working with Tables 251
Chapter 10: Sections, Columns, and Page Formatting 283
Chapter 11: Using Bookmarks, Cross-References, Footnotes, and Links 317
Chapter 12: Creating Indexes and Tables of Contents 337

Part III: Working More Effectively 365
Chapter 13: Styles and AutoFormatting 367
Chapter 14: Using Templates, Wizards, and Themes 389
Chapter 15: What Looks Good? 411
Chapter 16: Creating Documents Using Speech Recognition 425

Part IV: Inserting Pictures and Other Content 435
Chapter 17: Illustrating Your Documents with Graphics 437
Chapter 18: More Object Types—Drawings, Text Boxes, and More 465
Chapter 19: Advanced Graphics and Multimedia 505
Chapter 20: Linking Information from Other Applications 519
Chapter 21: Working with Microsoft Graph Chart and Microsoft Equation 539

Part V: Complex Documents: Mail Merge, Forms, Outlines, and Web Pages **555**

Chapter 22: Creating Form Letters, Envelopes, Labels, and Catalogs 557
Chapter 23: Creating Dynamic Documents Using Field Codes 585
Chapter 24: Creating Forms 609
Chapter 25: Getting Organized with Outlines and Master Documents 625
Chapter 26: Creating Basic Web Pages 643
Chapter 27: Advanced HTML and XML 663

Part VI: Distribution and Collaboration **683**

Chapter 28: Faxing and E-mailing with Word 685
Chapter 29: Comments and Reviewing 697
Chapter 30: Online Collaboration 717

Part VII: Customizing and Troubleshooting Word **733**

Chapter 31: Troubleshooting and Overcoming Word's Idiosyncrasies 735
Chapter 32: Customizing Menus, Options, Toolbars, and Keys 749
Chapter 33: Making the Most of Word Macros and VBA 785
Chapter 34: Securing Your Data 801

Appendix A: What's New in Word 2003 813
Appendix B: What's on the CD-ROM 821

Index 827
End-User License Agreement 873

Contents

Preface ix

Acknowledgments xiii

Part I: The Fundamentals   1

Chapter 1: Getting Started with Word 2003 3

Starting Word and Opening Documents 3
   Starting Word from the Programs menu 3
   Starting Word from a shortcut 3
   Starting Word with Windows 4
   Opening a document from Word 4
   Opening documents automatically with Word 6
   Controlling Word using startup switches 6
   Opening the last document 6
Touring the Word Environment 7
   The text area 8
   The menu bar 8
   Toolbars 8
The Task Pane 14
   The ruler 16
   The scroll bars 16
   The status bar 17
   Office Assistant 18
   Dialog boxes and control settings 18
Using the Mouse and the Keyboard 21
   Using the mouse 21
   Using the keyboard 22
   Right-click for shortcut menus 22
   Undo and Repeat 23
Working with Document Views 24
   Changing views 24
   Normal view 24
   Web Layout view 25
   Print Layout view 25
   Reading Layout view 25
   Outline view 26
   Document Map view 26
   Full Screen view 28
   Zoom 28
   Print Preview 29
   Adding Thumbnails 29

Creating a New Document 29
Starting a new document with a template 30
Using wizards to create a document 30
Saving a Document 32
Saving a document as a Web page 33
Getting Help in Word 34
Using the Office Assistant 35
Using the Microsoft Word Help task pane 35
Accessing Microsoft Office Help on the Web 36
Helping WordPerfect users 37
Closing a Word Document 39
Exiting Word 39
Summary 40

Chapter 2: Navigating and Editing Documents **41**

Editing Text 41
Displaying nonprinting characters 42
Inserting and overtyping text 43
Beginning a new paragraph 43
Adding a new line 43
Aligning text 44
Inserting the date and time 44
Splitting a document window for easier editing 45
Navigating Through a Document 46
Scroll bars move the insertion point 47
Moving the insertion point with the scroll bar 47
Using the keyboard to move the insertion point 48
Returning to the location of your last edit 49
Navigating using the Go To tab 50
Selecting Text and Graphics 51
Selecting text and graphics using the mouse 51
Selecting text and graphics using the keyboard 52
Making multiple selections 52
Using the Extend Selection mode 52
Deleting Text and Graphics 53
Undoing Actions 54
Moving and Copying Text and Graphics 54
Using the Clipboard 55
Using the Cut, Copy, and Paste buttons 55
Paste Options and Paste Special 55
Moving and copying with commands and keyboard shortcuts . . . 56
Moving and copying with the shortcut menu 57
Using the Office Clipboard 57
Cut and Paste options 59
Drag-and-drop editing 60
Document scraps and shortcuts 61
Using the Spike for multiple cut-and-paste operations 61
Pasting text into other documents 62
Inserting Symbols and Special Characters 63
Using the Symbol command 63
Entering a character code 64
Using the Symbol dialog box and shortcut keys 65
Using shortcut keys to insert a symbol 65

AutoCorrect and AutoText 67
   Working with AutoCorrect 67
   Saving time with AutoText 71
Summary 74

Chapter 3: Finding and Replacing Text and Formats 77

Finding Text Using the Find Command 77
   Adding Find to the Standard toolbar 79
   Find options 79
   The act of searching 80
Refining Searches 81
   Using wildcards 81
   Sounds Like searches 82
The Search Browse Object Button 83
Finding and Replacing Text 83
   Finding and replacing word forms 85
   Replacing special characters 85
   Automatically adding text to replacement text 87
   Replacing with images and large text blocks using the Clipboard 87
   Finding and replacing formats 87
Summary 90

Chapter 4: Character Formatting and Fonts 93

Applying Character Formats 93
   Boldfacing text 95
   Italicizing text 96
   Underlining text 96
   Using superscripts and subscripts 97
   Using All Caps and Small Caps 98
   Adding a drop cap 99
   Adding color to your text 99
   Striking through text 100
   Using other special effects 100
   Text animation 101
Word's Handy Character Formatting Tools 102
   Displaying character formatting 102
   Repeating character formatting 104
   Copying character formatting 104
   Undoing character formatting 105
   Highlighting text 105
Changing Character Spacing 106
   Expanding and condensing character spacing 106
   Adjusting spacing in character pairs 107
Changing the Case of Characters 108
Changing Fonts and Font Sizes 108
   Fonts in the Font list box 109
   Displaying font names in their font 110
   About font styles listed in the Font dialog box 110
   Choosing a font 111
   Changing fonts 111
   Changing font sizes 112

Changing Default Character Formatting 113
Hiding Text in Your Document 113
Using Fonts with Shared Documents 114
    Print/preview font embedding 115
    Editable font embedding 115
    Installable font embedding 115
    Substituting unavailable fonts 116
Managing Fonts in Windows 117
Summary 119

Chapter 5: Paragraph Formatting **121**

Applying Paragraph Formatting 121
    Checking paragraph formats 122
    Duplicating paragraph formats 123
    Removing paragraph formats 124
    Using line breaks 124
Aligning Paragraphs 125
Click and Type: Inserting Paragraphs 127
Adjusting Line and Paragraph Spacing 127
    Adjusting paragraph spacing 128
    Adjusting line spacing 128
Setting Tabs 130
    Setting tabs using the ruler 132
    Changing or clearing a tab stop using the ruler 133
    Setting tabs using the Tabs dialog box 133
    Changing and clearing tabs using the Tabs dialog box 134
    Changing the default tab stops 135
Setting Indents 135
    Setting indents using the Formatting toolbar 136
    Setting indents using the ruler 137
    Setting indents using keyboard shortcuts 138
    Setting indents using the Paragraph dialog box 138
Bordering and Shading Paragraphs and Pages 139
    Adding borders using the Borders toolbar 140
    Adding borders using the Borders and Shading dialog box 141
    Spacing between text and border 143
    Placing borders around individual lines 143
    Fitting a border within margins 144
    Removing or changing borders 144
    Adding shading 145
    Adding horizontal lines 147
Creating Bulleted or Numbered Lists 148
    Creating bulleted lists 148
    Customizing a bulleted list 149
    Creating numbered lists 151
    Customizing numbered lists 152
    Restarting and continuing numbering 153
    Adding unbulleted or unnumbered paragraphs to a list 154
    Ending bulleted or numbered lists 154
    Creating outline numbered lists 154
    Customizing outline numbered lists 155
    Creating list styles 157

Paragraphs and Pagination 158
Hyphenation 159
   Using automatic hyphenation 159
   Using manual hyphenation 160
   Using nonbreaking and optional hyphens 161
Summary 161

Chapter 6: Printing Documents 163

Printing Basics 163
   Printing selected text or pages 164
   Printing more than one document at a time 165
   Printing multiple, collated copies 165
   Printing in reverse order 165
   Printing other document information 166
   Drag-and-drop printing 166
   Printing a document using different printers 166
Printing in Color 167
Previewing Documents Before Printing 168
   Changing the Print Preview appearance 170
   Editing in Print Preview mode 171
   Adjusting margins in Print Preview 171
   Automatic pagination adjustment 171
Changing Your Printing Options 172
Printing to a File 174
Document Image Writer Files 175
Printing to a Fax Modem 176
Printing Envelopes and Labels 176
   Printing envelopes 176
   Including barcodes with addresses 180
   Adding graphics and logos 180
   Adding postage 182
   Printing labels 182
   Customizing labels 184
Printing Data from a Form in Word 185
Changing Printer Properties 185
Printing Documents on a Network 186
Summary 187

Chapter 7: Managing Documents 189

Managing Documents in Word 189
Opening Document Files 189
   Opening a document 190
   Opening recently used documents 191
   Using My Recent Documents to open documents 192
   Using Windows documents lists 192
   Adding a document to the desktop 192
   Thumbnails, Previews, and Properties 193
   Managing documents using the Open dialog box 194
Managing Folders 196
   Creating new folders with Word 196
   Changing the default folder 196
   Creating a new folder and making it the default folder 198

Saving Documents 198
   Saving a document with a new name 200
   Saving a document in a different format 201
   Using Batch Conversion 203
   Saving documents as Web pages 203
   Saving different versions of a document 204
   Sharing documents across different versions of Word 206
   Using Fast Save 207
Backing Up and Recovering Files 207
   Using AutoRecover 207
   Recovering from a crash 208
   Creating backup files 210
Creating Document Properties 210
Using Word Count 212
Using AutoSummarize 212
Finding Files 214
   Using File Search 214
   Using file indexes 217
   Advanced searches 217
   Searching through the File Open dialog box 218
   Using wildcards 219
Summary 220

Part II: Beyond the Basics   221

Chapter 8: Proofing and Researching 223

Correcting Spelling and Grammar While Working 223
Correcting Spelling and Grammar After Working 224
   Skipping selected text 226
   Checking spelling in other languages 227
   Spelling options 227
Using Custom Dictionaries 229
   Managing custom dictionaries 230
   Creating a new custom dictionary 230
   Adding new words to a dictionary 231
   Selecting dictionaries 231
   Creating exclude dictionaries 231
Using the Word Grammar Tool 232
   Changing grammar options 233
   Changing grammar and writing style rules 234
   Viewing document and readability statistics 235
Rechecking Documents 235
Proofing with AutoCorrect 236
   Working with AutoCorrect entries 236
   AutoCorrect options 236
   Adding AutoCorrect entries 237
   Editing and deleting AutoCorrect entries 238
   Adding AutoCorrect exceptions 238
   Correcting AutoCorrections 238

Using Research Tools 239
    The Research pane 240
    Using the thesaurus 241
    Using the dictionary 242
    Translating words 243
    Other information sources 244
    Research Options 247
Summary 248

Chapter 9: Working with Tables **251**

Understanding Tables 251
Adding Tables to Documents 252
    Using the Insert Table button 253
    Using the Insert Table command 253
    Using Table AutoFormatting 254
    Drawing a table 255
    Creating a table within a table 258
    Positioning tables in documents 258
Navigating within Tables and Adding Text 260
    Getting around in a table 260
    Adding text to a table 260
Selecting Parts of a Table 261
    Selecting with the mouse or keyboard 261
    Extending the selection 262
Modifying a Table Layout 262
    Resizing tables 262
    Inserting and deleting cells, rows, and columns 263
    Moving and copying cells, rows, and columns 264
    Column width and row height 265
    Splitting a table 270
Fine-tuning a Table 270
    Formatting text in a table 270
    Changing text alignment 270
    Changing text direction 270
    Aligning a table on the page 271
    Preventing page breaks 271
    Merging and splitting cells 271
    Table headings on each page 272
    Borders and shading 273
    Table gridlines 273
Using Tabs in Tables 273
Using Tables to Position Text and Graphics 274
Converting Text into Tables, and Vice Versa 274
Sorting Table Data and Numbering Cells 276
    Sorting in a table 276
    Numbering cells in a table 277
Table Calculations 278
    Calculating in a table 278
    Creating your own formula 278
    Number formats 279
    Bookmarks 280
Placing Captions on Tables 280
Summary 281

Chapter 10: Sections, Columns, and Page Formatting 283

Formatting Sections of a Document 283
   Inserting section breaks 284
   Copying section breaks 285
   Removing section breaks 286
Working with Columns 286
   Applying column formatting 287
   Calculating the number of columns 288
   Typing and editing text in columns 288
   Adding a line between columns 289
   Changing column widths and spacing between columns 289
   Removing columns 290
   Breaking a column 291
   Balancing column lengths 291
Formatting Your Pages 292
   Setting page margins 292
   Setting margins in the Page Setup dialog box 292
   Setting margins using the ruler 294
   Creating facing pages and gutters 295
   Changing paper size and orientation 295
   Changing pagination 297
   Inserting hard page breaks 297
   Turning off background pagination 298
   Aligning text vertically on a page 298
   Inserting line numbers 299
   Controlling line numbers 300
Adding Page Borders 301
Creating Headers and Footers 303
   Inserting page numbers 303
   Removing page numbers 304
   Changing the position of a page number 304
   Formatting page numbers 304
   Numbering pages for sections of a document 305
   Including sections and total page numbers 306
   Adding header and footer text 307
   Hiding text while working with headers and footers 308
   Adding headers and footers to sections 309
   Creating different first-page headers and footers 309
   Creating headers and footers for odd and even pages 310
   Positioning headers and footers 310
Backgrounds and Watermarks 311
   Adding background color 312
   Adding a pattern or image 312
   Adding a text watermark 315
Summary 316

Chapter 11: Using Bookmarks, Cross-References, Footnotes, and Links 317

Introducing Fields 317
Working with Bookmarks 318
   Inserting bookmarks 318
   Viewing bookmarks 319
   Moving to bookmarks 320

Manipulating bookmarks 321
Placing the contents of a bookmark in your document 322
Calculating with bookmarks 323
The problem with bookmarks 323
Working with Cross-References 324
Creating in-document cross-references 325
Keeping cross-references up to date 326
Types of cross-references 326
Working with Footnotes and Endnotes 328
Creating footnotes and endnotes 329
Keeping footnotes and endnotes in view 331
Moving to footnotes and endnotes 331
Modifying footnotes and endnotes 332
Manipulating footnotes and endnotes 332
Converting footnotes to endnotes, and vice versa 333
Moving footnotes and endnotes 333
Changing footnote and endnote separators 333
Placing Links in Your Document 334
Summary 335

Chapter 12: Creating Indexes and Tables of Contents **337**
Adding Indexes to Your Documents 337
Creating, formatting, and modifying index entries 337
Marking index entries automatically 338
Marking index entries manually 340
Using page ranges in index entries 342
Cross-referencing index entries 342
Creating multilevel indexes 343
Formatting index entries 344
Modifying index entry fields 344
Formatting and compiling an index 345
Customizing your index style 346
Updating an index 347
Editing the INDEX field 348
Deleting an index 351
Adding Tables of Contents to Your Documents 351
Preparing your document for adding a table of contents 351
Compiling a table of contents 352
Assembling a table of contents using
Word's heading styles 352
Assembling a table of contents using custom styles 354
Assembling a table of contents using TC entry fields 355
Creating tables of contents from Outline levels 357
Updating a table of contents 357
Creating Tables of Figures and Other Tables 358
Marking table entries with a TC field 359
Compiling a table of figures 359
Creating Tables of Authorities 360
Marking citation entries 360
Compiling a table of authorities 362
Updating a table of authorities 362
Creating and editing citation categories 363
Summary 363

Part III: Working More Effectively   365

Chapter 13: Styles and AutoFormatting 367

Styles Defined 367
    Four style types 368
    Styles and formatting together 368
    Styles, templates, and themes 368
Viewing and Using Styles 369
    Selecting a custom view 371
    Applying styles to paragraphs and text 372
    Viewing style information 373
    Selecting styles throughout your document 374
Creating and Modifying Styles 374
    Creating new styles 374
    Modifying and deleting styles 376
    Using shortcut keys 377
    Automatic style application 378
Copying Styles Between Documents 378
    Using the Organizer 378
    Copying text from another document 380
    Using the Style Gallery 380
    Displaying style names in the Style Area 381
    Renaming styles 382
    Printing a list of the styles in a document 382
Word's AutoFormat Tool 383
    Applying styles using AutoFormat 384
    Reviewing AutoFormat changes 385
    Setting AutoFormat options 386
Summary 388

Chapter 14: Using Templates, Wizards, and Themes 389

Introducing Templates, Wizards, and Themes 389
Working with Templates 390
    Template components 390
    Local and global templates 391
    Naming and finding templates 392
    Creating a new document 392
    Saving a document based on a template 395
    Previewing the styles in a template 396
    Creating your own templates 396
    Template attachments 397
    Linking a different template to a document 397
    Using components from different templates 399
Conjuring Up Documents with Word's Wizards 403
    Using the Letter Wizard 404
    Using Word's other wizards 407
Using Themes 408
Summary 409

Chapter 15: What Looks Good? **411**

Word Processor or Desktop Publishing Program? 411
The Number One Rule: Don't Be Too Clever 412
Function over form, or form over function? 412
Templates are not always good 413
Paragraph Formatting 414
Working with paragraph alignment 414
Indenting and adjusting margins 415
Using white space 416
Typefaces 417
Typeface combinations 418
Using typesetting characters 419
Font size 420
Bold, italic, underline, and color 421
Adding Images 421
Avoiding the Weird Stuff 422
Checking Your Work 422
Summary 424

Chapter 16: Creating Documents Using Speech Recognition **425**

Setting Up Speech Recognition 426
Adjusting the microphone 426
Training the speech system 427
Taking Dictation 429
Fixing problems 430
Continued training 431
Voice commands 432
More Voice Settings 432
Summary 433

Part IV: Inserting Pictures and Other Content **435**

Chapter 17: Illustrating Your Documents with Graphics **437**

Understanding Bitmap Pictures and Vector Drawings 437
Graphics File Formats Supported by Word 438
Where to Get Graphic Images 439
Commercial clip art and photographs 439
Free clip art 440
Inserting Pictures into Documents 440
Inserting clip art and pictures 441
Working with Microsoft Clip Organizer 443
Microsoft's online clip-art gallery 445
Scanning and digital cameras 446
Copying pictures into documents 446
Resizing and Cropping Pictures 447
Resizing and cropping using the mouse 447
Resizing and cropping using the Format Picture dialog box 448
Adding Borders to Pictures 449

Adding Shadow Borders 451
Adjusting Picture Characteristics 452
    Adjusting the contrast and brightness of an image 453
    Creating a transparent background for an image 453
Hiding Pictures 454
Object Layout and Position 455
    Choosing a layout 456
    High-resolution wrapping 458
    Positioning the object 459
    Using anchors 460
    Positioning with the Drawing toolbar 461
    Selecting objects 462
    Aligning objects using the Drawing Grid dialog box 463
    Aligning objects 464
Summary 464

Chapter 18: More Object Types—Drawings, Text Boxes, and More 465

Drawing in Word 465
    Beginning a drawing 465
    Working with the drawing canvas 466
Using the Drawing Toolbar 467
    Drawing lines and shapes 469
    Editing drawing objects 474
    Positioning drawing objects 477
    Layering drawing objects 478
Laying Out Text and Graphics with Text Boxes 480
    Inserting a text box 480
    Formatting text in a text box 484
    Changing between text boxes and frames 486
    Text boxes and publishing techniques 486
Adding Special Effects to Graphics with WordArt 490
    Editing WordArt graphics 491
    Shaping text 492
    Lengthening text and stretching letters 493
    Aligning WordArt text 493
    Kerning and adjusting spacing between characters 493
Using the Organization Chart Tool 494
    Changing layouts 495
    Changing formats 495
Adding Callouts to Objects 496
Attaching Captions to Objects 498
    Entering captions directly 498
    Adding captions with AutoCaption 500
    Updating your captions 501
    Editing caption labels 502
    Deleting labels and captions 502
    Changing the caption style 502
    Changing the caption numbering style 503
    Using chapter numbers in a caption 503
Summary 504

Chapter 19: Advanced Graphics and Multimedia 505

Image Editing Tools 505
    Image editors 505
    Image editor filters or plug-ins 506
Optimizing Images 506
    Choosing the right file format 506
    Changing your monitor resolution and color settings 507
    Changing the resolution of an image 508
    Avoiding the jaggies 509
    Compressing images 509
    Interlacing images 510
    Adding tiled and transparent backgrounds 511
    Converting pictures to Word Picture format 512
Protecting Your Images 513
Adding Animation, Sound, and Video 513
    Adding animated GIFs 513
    Sounding off with audio clips 514
    Inserting video clips 515
Summary 517

Chapter 20: Linking Information from Other Applications 519

Linking and Embedding Objects in Word 519
    Linked versus embedded objects 519
    OLE, COM, and ActiveX 521
Embedding Objects in Word Documents 521
    Embedding an object 522
    Embedding while working in another application 524
    Using drag-and-drop 527
    Editing embedded objects 528
    Converting embedded objects to different file formats 528
    Converting embedded objects to graphics 529
Linking Objects in Word 529
    Creating links 530
    Updating links 530
    Editing linked objects 533
    Breaking links 533
    Locking and unlocking links 533
Shading Linked and Embedded Objects 533
Inserting Data from Access 534
Inserting a PowerPoint Slide or Presentation 537
Summary 538

Chapter 21: Working with Microsoft Graph Chart and Microsoft Equation 539

Using Graph 539
    Starting and quitting Graph 539
    Working in the Datasheet window 540
    Working with charts 544
    Getting data and charts from other sources 549

Working with Microsoft Equation 550
   Positioning the insertion point 551
   Building a sample equation 552
   Adjusting spacing and alignment 552
Summary 553

Part V: Complex Documents: Mail Merge, Forms, Outlines, and Web Pages   555

Chapter 22: Creating Form Letters, Envelopes, Labels, and Catalogs 557

Merging Letter and Address Files 557
What Is Merging? 558
   The main document 558
   The database 559
   Putting the two documents together 559
Writing Form Letters 560
   Using the Mail Merge Wizard 561
   Working with existing documents directly 568
Using an Address Book 570
Creating Envelopes, Mailing Labels, and Lists 571
   Using Mail Merge to print envelopes 571
   Merging labels 573
   Merging catalogs and directories 574
Merging E-mails and Faxes 575
Editing Main Documents 576
   Deleting, inserting, and formatting merge fields 576
   Editing merge codes 577
Merging Specific Records 578
   Selecting records for one state 578
   Using other comparison operators 579
   Selecting with two rules 579
   Selecting with more than two rules 580
   Adding ranges to rules 580
   Removing rules 581
Setting the Record Order 581
Adding Special Word Fields to a Main Document 582
   Specifying text to appear in merged documents 582
   Using fill-in fields in merged documents 583
Summary 584

Chapter 23: Creating Dynamic Documents Using Field Codes 585

What Are Field Codes? 585
Working with Field Codes 586
   Finding fields 586
   Displaying field codes 587
   Updating fields 587
   Unlinking fields 588

Inserting Field Codes 588
   Using the Field dialog box 588
   Inserting field codes directly 589
Looking at Fields 590
   Taking a field apart 591
   Dissecting field instructions 591
Changing the Appearance of Field Results 596
   Using the format field switch (*) 597
   Using the number picture field switch (\#) 599
   Using the date-time picture field switch (\@) 601
Editing Field Codes 603
Protecting Fields 603
Working with Smart Tags 604
Summary 608

Chapter 24: Creating Forms 609

Understanding Word Forms 609
Creating a New Form in Word 609
Adding Text and Inserting Form Fields 611
Understanding Form Fields 612
   Defining text fields 612
   Defining check boxes 617
   Creating drop-down fields 617
   Attaching macros to fields 618
   Assigning bookmarks to fields 619
   Calculate on Exit 619
   Enabling fields 619
   Adding help text 619
   Drawing and inserting tables 621
   Adding frames 621
   Adding ActiveX controls 621
Locking and Protecting the Form 621
Filling Out a Form 623
Printing a Form 623
Summary 623

Chapter 25: Getting Organized with Outlines and Master Documents . . . 625

Using Outlines 625
   Understanding Outline View 626
   Creating outlines 627
   Rearranging your outline 630
   Printing an outline 632
   Copying an outline 633
Understanding Master Documents 633
   The Master Document view 634
   Building a master document 635
   Working with master documents 638
   Working with subdocuments 638
Summary 641

Chapter 26: Creating Basic Web Pages 643

Creating Web Pages 644
   Using a Web Page template 644
   Microsoft's template library 645
   Saving Word documents in HTML 645
Word and FrontPage 646
Working with Frames 648
   Creating frames 649
   Adding documents to frames 650
   Configuring frames 650
Using HTML Styles 652
Inserting Hyperlinks 653
   Linking between frames 654
   Creating hyperlinks using AutoFormatting 655
Adding Tables to Web Pages 655
Adding Visual Elements to Web Pages 655
Adding Multimedia Elements to Web Pages 656
   Adding images and drawing objects 656
   Adding sound and video objects 657
Previewing Web Pages 657
Using the Web Toolbar 658
Working with Web Folders 658
Publishing Your Web Documents 659
Summary 660

Chapter 27: Advanced HTML and XML 663

Understanding HTML, XML, Styles, and Word 663
The Web Tools Toolbar 666
Creating Forms 667
   Understanding form elements and properties 668
   Adding form elements to a Web page 668
Processing a Form 672
Adding a Script to a Web Page Using Word 672
Adding Multimedia 675
   Inserting movies 676
   Inserting sounds 676
   Inserting scrolling text banners 677
Working with XML 678
   Creating an XML document 679
   Saving in XML and WordML 682
Summary 682

Part VI: Distribution and Collaboration   683

Chapter 28: Faxing and E-mailing with Word 685

Faxing from Word 685
   Sending a fax from Word 685
   Using online fax services 686

Sharing Documents via E-mail 687
    Sending mail from within Word 688
    Routing a document 690
    Using Word as your Outlook Compose window 692
Setting Up E-mail Options 693
Summary 695

Chapter 29: Comments and Reviewing 697

Placing Comments in Documents 697
    Working with comments 699
    Inserting voice comments 700
    Changing and manipulating comments 701
    Highlighting text 704
Using Reviewing Tools 705
    Adding revision marks 705
    Viewing changes 705
    Reviewing, accepting, and rejecting changes 706
    Customizing revision marks 708
    Comparing and merging documents 709
    Comparing side by side 711
Reading Layout View 712
    Moving around in Reading Layout view 712
    Changing text size 714
    Editing in Reading Layout view 714
Summary 714

Chapter 30: Online Collaboration 717

SharePoint Team Services 717
    Sharing files 718
    The Document Library page 720
    Uploading files 722
    Checking out files 722
    Working with versions 723
    Document workspaces 724
    Web discussions 725
    Accessing file libraries directly from Word 727
    Online meetings 728
Exchange Folders 730
Summary 732

Part VII: Customizing and Troubleshooting Word   733

Chapter 31: Troubleshooting and Overcoming Word's Idiosyncrasies . . . 735

Installation and Interface Quirks 735
    Install on Word's demand 735
    Missing menu options 736
    Uncluttering the taskbar 737
    Persistent toolbars 738
Editing Quirks and Problems 738
    Deleting paragraph marks does strange things 738
    AutoCorrect and AutoFormat hell 739

Recurring and disappearing text 740
Having pictures appear where you want them 741
Resolving font problems 741
Optimizing Word and Reducing the Size of Files 742
Speeding up Word 742
Reducing the size of Word documents and Web page files 743
Saving Word Documents 743
Changing the default folder 743
File name extensions for Windows and Word 744
Recovering and Backing Up Files 744
What to do when a file will not open 745
Automatically repairing Word application files 745
Troubleshooting Problems from Outside Word 746
Peripheral devices and problems with files 746
What to do when Word will not save your file 747
Macro viruses: What to do if Word starts acting strange 747
Summary 748

Chapter 32: Customizing Menus, Options, Toolbars, and Keys **749**
Customizing Word 749
Changing Word's Options 750
View tab 750
General tab 753
Edit tab 755
Print tab 757
Track Changes tab 759
User Information tab 761
Compatibility tab 761
File Locations tab 763
Save tab 764
Spelling & Grammar tab 766
Security tab 767
Working with Toolbars 770
Using the Customize dialog box 770
Adding buttons to a toolbar 771
Moving and copying toolbar buttons 772
Deleting toolbar buttons 772
Restoring a toolbar to its original state 773
Editing buttons 773
Working with custom toolbars 775
Customizing Menus 776
Creating a new menu 776
Adding a command to a menu 776
Editing shortcut menus 777
Changing accelerator keys 777
Organizing commands into groups 777
Customization options 778
Customizing Keyboard Shortcuts 779
Creating a shortcut key for a style 781
Assigning keyboard shortcuts for other purposes 782
Restoring shortcut key assignments 783
Summary 783

Chapter 33: Making the Most of Word Macros and VBA **785**

Understanding Macros 785
Storing Global and Template Macros 786
Recording and Saving Macros 786
    Recording macros 786
    Assigning a macro to a toolbar or shortcut keys 788
    Saving macros 789
Running Macros 789
    Running macros from previous versions 790
    Running automatic macros 791
    Preventing automatic macros from running 792
    Running macros from a field code 792
Editing Macros 792
    Dissecting a macro 793
    Deleting unnecessary commands 794
    Adding remarks and comments to a macro 794
Managing Macros 794
    Copying or moving macros between templates 795
    Deleting and renaming macros 796
Introducing Visual Basic 796
    Using Visual Basic code for common Word tasks 797
    Examining the ANSIValue macro code 797
    Starting a new macro with Visual Basic 799
Summary 800

Chapter 34: Securing Your Data **801**

Collaboration Protection 801
    Open protection 801
    More advanced encryption 802
    Modification protection 803
    Specifying levels of protection 804
Additional Privacy Features 807
Restricting Permission 807
Digital Signatures 808
    Signing a document 808
    Viewing a certificate 809
Macro Security 810
Summary 811

Appendix A: What's New in Word 2003 . . . . **813**

Appendix B: What's on the CD-ROM **821**

Index 827

End-User License Agreement 873

The Fundamentals

P A R T

I

♦ ♦ ♦ ♦

In This Part

Chapter 1
Getting Started with
Word 2003

Chapter 2
Navigating and Editing
Documents

Chapter 3
Finding and Replacing
Text and Formats

Chapter 4
Character Formatting
and Fonts

Chapter 5
Paragraph Formatting

Chapter 6
Printing Documents

Chapter 7
Managing Documents

♦ ♦ ♦ ♦

Getting Started with Word 2003

✦ ✦ ✦ ✦

In This Chapter

Starting Word and opening documents

Touring the Word environment

Using the mouse and keyboard in Word

Creating a document

Saving a document

Getting help in Word

✦ ✦ ✦ ✦

Whether you've been using Microsoft Word for years, or are new to the program, this chapter helps you get started quickly. Long-term users will find a number of interesting new features, while newcomers should be able to get a feel for the program and what's available. This chapter provides a quick tour of the Word 2003 interface and then discusses basic document creation, editing, printing, and saving functions.

Starting Word and Opening Documents

You can start Microsoft Word 2003 and open documents in several ways. Learning the different methods of launching Word increases your flexibility with the program. For example, you can choose from a wide selection of predefined document templates and wizards to simplify the creation of standard documents such as memos, letters, faxes, newsletters, reports, and so on. You probably already know that, in Windows, you can create a shortcut icon to quickly start Word from your desktop. If you plan to work on the same document for several days, you also can modify the properties of the shortcut icon so that Word automatically starts and then loads the last document that you worked on each time you start Windows.

Starting Word from the Programs menu

In Windows, the most common way to start Word is to use the Start menu on the taskbar. Click the Start menu button, and then choose Microsoft Word from the Programs or All Programs menu. When Word starts, a "pressed" button appears in the taskbar, which indicates that Word is active. If you already have created a Word document, you also can start Word by choosing Start ➪ Documents and then selecting a Word document from the menu that appears.

Starting Word from a shortcut

You also can access Word from the desktop or any drive or folder by creating a *shortcut,* which is a link to a Windows program or device. Shortcut files end with the extension .lnk, which stands for *link*. A shortcut file icon looks similar to the program file icon, except that a small, curved arrow appears in the icon's lower-left corner.

Here's a quick way to place the Word program on your desktop using a shortcut:

1. Minimize all programs so that you can see the Windows desktop.

2. Click the Start button to open the Windows Start menu.

3. Click the Programs submenu, and find the Microsoft Word menu option.

4. Point at the Word option in the Programs menu.

5. Press and hold down the left mouse button as you drag the icon off the menu and over the desktop—don't release it yet.

6. Press the Alt key, and you'll see a little curved-arrow icon—the shortcut icon.

7. Release the mouse button, and a shortcut icon is placed on the desktop.

8. Release the Alt key.

You can also place this icon in the Quick Launch area of your Windows taskbar so that you can start the program quickly by clicking the button there. (The taskbar is the bar on which the Start menu sits.) Carry out the same dragging operation, but drop the icon onto the Quick Launch area instead of on the desktop. Alternatively, you can drag the icon off the desktop and drop it onto the Quick Launch area.

You can easily delete the Word shortcut by right-clicking the icon and choosing Delete.

Note   If you upgraded from Office 2000, you may still have the Office Shortcut bar installed, which gives you another way to start Word. If the Shortcut Bar is a feature that you like and use, you already know about it, so we won't waste time discussing it here. If you did a clean install of Office 2003, you won't see this feature.

Starting Word with Windows

If you want Word to run whenever you start Windows, add the Winword program file to the Startup folder in the Start menu. To add Word to the Startup folder using Windows, follow these steps:

1. Open the Windows Start menu.

2. Click the Programs submenu, and find the Word menu option.

3. Point at the menu option in the Programs menu.

4. Press and hold down the mouse button while you drag the icon off the menu and place it over the Startup menu—don't release it yet.

5. Press the Alt key, and you'll see a little curved-arrow icon—the shortcut icon.

6. Release the mouse button, and a shortcut icon is placed in the Startup menu.

7. Release the Alt key.

Opening a Document from Word

After you create and save a document, the file exists on your disk. To use Word to make changes to the file or to save a copy of it under a different name, you need to open that file. Word provides several methods for opening files. The easiest is to click the Open button on the Standard toolbar. Another is to choose File ➪ Open or press Ctrl+O. Both methods take you to the Open dialog box, where you can locate the file that you want (see Figure 1-1).

View button

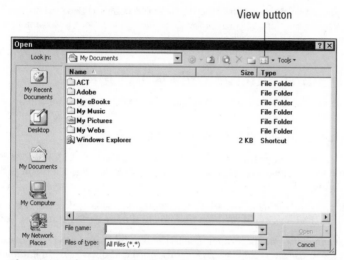

Figure 1-1: The Open dialog box, showing the Details view.

With the Views button (the little icon second from the right) on the Open dialog box toolbar, you can change the display of your files. Click the drop-down arrow on the right side of the button and play with the various views offered:

✦ **Large Icons:** Displays each file as a large icon with its name underneath. Quite frankly, this is a very inconvenient way to display files and makes it difficult to find things. We suggest you use a different view.

✦ **Small Icons:** Much the same as the prior choice but with smaller icons.

✦ **List:** An alphabetical list of files, which is much easier to work with.

✦ **Details:** A list showing each file's size and date of last modification.

✦ **Properties:** Select a file in this view, and a pane on the right displays the file's properties.

✦ **Preview:** Select a file, and you can actually read the contents of the file in the right pane.

✦ **Thumbnails:** Each file is displayed as a picture. This view doesn't work with Word document files unless the document author specifically saved a thumbnail image (see Chapter 7). The Thumbnail view does work with image files and Web pages, however.

If a document is selected, the Views button on the Open dialog box toolbar also displays details of the selected document and a window that allows you to see, as well as read, the document.

If you worked on a document recently, that document is listed at the bottom of the File menu. In this case, you only need to click its name to open it from the File menu. The default number of files listed is four, but Word 2003 can list as many as nine file names at the bottom of the File menu. You can choose how many files last opened to display by first choosing Tools ⇨ Options and then clicking the General tab. The Entries box across from the Recently Used File List option displays the number of recently used file names currently displayed in the File menu. To display the last seven files, for example, type **7** in the Entries box.

Tip   With Word 2003, you can quickly open any Word document by double-clicking the file name in Windows Explorer, on the desktop, or in a My Computer folder. Word is automatically launched, and the document is opened.

Opening documents automatically with Word

By creating a new shortcut, you can open a specified document at the same time you open Word 2003 itself:

1. Right-click the Windows desktop and choose New ⇨ Shortcut.

2. In the Create Shortcut box, click the Browse button and use the Browse for Folder dialog box to find the winword.exe file (probably in the C:\Program Files\Microsoft Office 2003\Office 2003\ folder).

3. Add a document path and file name—enclosed in quotation marks—after the text that appears in the Type the Location of the Item text box in the Create Shortcut text box.

Adding a document file name after the program name in the text box causes that document to load automatically whenever the shortcut is used. To start Word and open a document named Letter.doc stored in a folder named Docs on the C: drive, for example, add **"C:\Docs\Letter.doc"** in the Target text box.

You can also modify a shortcut to start Word and load multiple documents by separating the path names with a space. To load two documents named Letter.doc and Resume.doc in the Docs folder, for example, type **"C:\Docs\Letter.doc" "C:\Docs\Resume.doc"**.

Note   The shortcuts created during Word's installation cannot be edited. However, after you create a shortcut, as described in the preceding steps, you can edit it as described in the following section.

Controlling Word using startup switches

Using a startup switch lets you control how Word starts. A *switch* is a command-line parameter that is added after the Winword program. To add a switch, follow these steps:

1. Right-click a Word shortcut to display the pop-up menu and choose Properties. The property sheet for the shortcut is displayed.

2. Add the switch to the end of the Target settings command line.

For example, you can modify the command line to include the /n switch by typing **"C:\Program Files\Microsoft Office\Winword" "/n"**. (The /n switch instructs Word to start without a default document.) Typically, Word starts with a blank document named Document1, but you can start Word without loading that default blank document. Using this startup option displays Word faster than the startup option of loading it with a document.

Opening the last document

You can get Word to automatically open the last document you were working on by using the /mfile1 switch.

You might create an icon that you use only when you want to open the last file. Note also that you can open any of the last nine files in this manner. Typing **/mfile3**, for example, opens the third from the last file you worked on.

Touring the Word Environment

The Word 2003 environment includes the elements that make up your interface with it, and Figure 1-2 labels the main components of the Word screen. The title bar at the top of the screen displays the program name (Microsoft Word). The Document1 file name is the default file name assigned to a new document. The Word Control menu is represented by the letter *W*, located in the upper-left corner of the title bar. The Control menu provides the menu of commands for manipulating the Word program window.

A window displayed in full-screen size is called a *maximized window*. The three buttons in the top-right corner of the window minimize, maximize or restore, or exit your document, respectively. (The middle button is the Restore button when the window is maximized, and it is the Maximize button when the window is not full size.) The Restore button returns the window to the size and position it had before it was maximized.

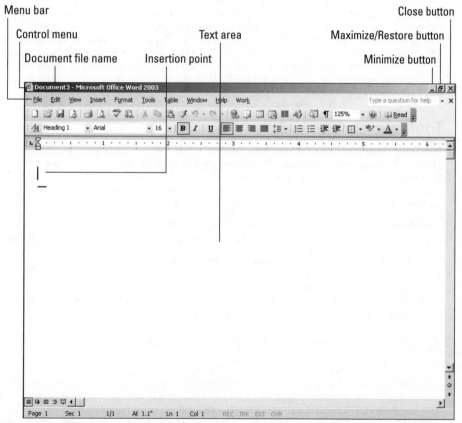

Figure 1-2: The parts of the Word window.

The text area

The text area of the window occupies the bulk of the screen; it is where you create, edit, format, and view your document files. The blinking vertical bar is called the *insertion point*. It indicates where text is to be entered into a document. You also use the insertion point to specify the point from which you want to select or edit text. In a window's text area, the mouse pointer appears in the shape of an I-beam.

The menu bar

Directly below the title bar is the *menu bar*, which contains pull-down menus that organize families of commands for working with documents. Word 2003's menus arrange together commands that perform similar actions. For example, the File menu contains a group of commands that manipulate your document files. Choosing a command tells Word what to do; for example, the File menu contains commands to open, print, and save your documents.

You can open menus by clicking them or by pressing Alt+underlined letter shown in the menu's name on the menu bar. Pressing Alt+A, for example, opens the Table menu. It's important to note that when you open a menu, it doesn't display all the menu options, so when we talk about menu options in this book and you can't find them, make sure you open up the menu completely. You can do this by clicking the little arrow buttons at the bottom of the menu. (You can change this behavior by choosing Tools ➪ Customize, clicking the Options tab, and selecting Always Show Full Menus.)

Toolbars

Word comes with a number of toolbars, each of which contains a series of buttons designed to perform common related tasks. To display a list of available toolbars, choose View ➪ Toolbars; a submenu of toolbars appears. Currently displayed toolbars have a checkmark next to them. An even quicker way to choose a toolbar is to display a pop-up toolbar menu by clicking the right mouse button anywhere on a toolbar.

Moving your mouse pointer over a toolbar button displays the name of the button, which often gives you a clue regarding its function. This pop-up button name is called a *ScreenTip*.

You can customize a toolbar by adding commands to it or by replacing the commands on the toolbar with those of your own choosing. You can create a customized toolbar for each type of document that you regularly produce. For example, you can create a toolbar with buttons to access a regularly used command, such as creating a Search and Replace button to replace the frequently used chart or columns buttons.

 Cross-Reference   For more information about customizing toolbars, see Chapter 32.

Word 2003 displays the Standard and Formatting toolbars by default. With these toolbars, you can access the most commonly used commands with the mouse instead of having to choose commands from the menus. For example, to print a document, click the printer icon instead of choosing the File ➪ Print command. This action immediately prints the document without displaying the Print dialog box.

Word may display other toolbars, depending on what you are doing at the time. If, for instance, you are working with a document that has revision marks in it (see Chapter 29),

Word automatically displays the Reviewing toolbar. If you are working on a picture or drawing, Word may display the Picture or Drawing toolbar.

The Standard and Formatting toolbars are normally anchored just below the menu bar. When you display other toolbars, however, they either appear stacked in the order that you display them or float on-screen like small windows. Some, like the Drawing toolbar, anchor themselves to the bottom of the screen (above the status line).

To move a toolbar, simply use the *drag bar* to drag the toolbar to where you want it to be displayed. The drag bar is indicated by four little dots on the left side of the toolbar or in the top-left corner (depending on where the toolbar happens to be). Point at this bar, press and hold down the mouse button, and drag the bar to the position you prefer. You can place a toolbar on any window edge—top or bottom, left or right—or let it float inside the window. You can also change a floating toolbar to an anchored toolbar by double-clicking the drag bar. Figure 1-3 displays several toolbars, both anchored and floating.

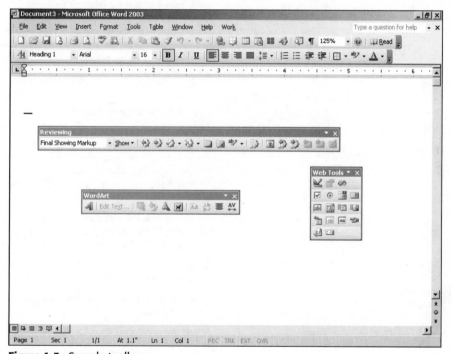

Figure 1-3: Sample toolbars.

The Standard toolbar

The Standard toolbar includes both frequently and infrequently used commands for working in Word 2003. Figure 1-4 shows the buttons on the Standard toolbar, and Table 1-1 describes what these buttons do.

Figure 1-4: The Standard toolbar.

Table 1-1: The Standard Toolbar Buttons

Button	Name	Action
	New Blank Document	Opens a new document based on the current default settings.
	Open	Opens an existing document or template. Word displays the Open dialog box, where you can locate and open the desired file.
	Save	Saves the active document or template under its current name. If you have not yet named the document, Word displays the Save As dialog box so that you can do so.
	Permission	If you have installed the Information Rights Management Service (see Chapter 34), you will see this button on the toolbar. It lets you restrict the use of the document by preventing recipients from copying, printing, or forwarding it.
	Print	Prints all pages of the active document.
	Print Preview	Displays the layout of a document as it will appear when printed.
	Spelling and Grammar	Checks the spelling and grammar of the entire document, or if you have selected text, checks the spelling of that selection. Word displays the Spelling dialog box when it does not find a word in the dictionary.
	Research	Opens the Research task pane, where you can find synonyms, look up words in a dictionary, consult an encyclopedia, and so on.
	Cut	Removes selected text and graphics from the document, and stores them on the Clipboard.
	Copy	Copies selected text and graphics and stores them on the Clipboard.
	Paste	Inserts the contents of the Clipboard at the insertion point or over the selection.
	Format Painter	Copies character formatting to other selected text.
	Undo	Reverses your last action. Clicking the down arrow attached to the Undo button lets you choose from a list of the most recently changed operations.
	Redo	Repeats the last change you made to a document. Clicking the down arrow attached to the Redo button lets you choose from a list of the most recently changed operations.

Button	Name	Action
	Insert Hyperlink	Opens a dialog box for inserting a URL in your document. You can create a link to a file on your own computer, the Internet, or an office-wide network.
	Tables and Borders	Opens the Tables and Borders toolbar.
	Insert Table	Inserts a table. To select the number of rows and columns, drag over or past the sample table that is displayed. The sample then expands as you drag the pointer.
	Insert Microsoft Excel Worksheet	Inserts a Microsoft Excel worksheet into your document.
	Columns	Formats the current section of your document with one or more newspaper-style columns. To select the number of columns, drag over the sample columns that are displayed. The number of sample columns then expands as you drag the pointer.
	Drawing	Displays the Drawing toolbar.
	Document Map	Opens a separate window to the left of your document that shows an outline of your document's headings. Jump to any heading in your document by clicking it in the Document Map.
¶	Show/Hide	Makes normally invisible, nonprinting characters such as tabs and paragraph marks visible for easier editing.
100%	Zoom	Determines how large or small a document appears. Choices include 500%, 200%, 150%, 100%, 75%, 25%, 10%, Page Width, Text Width, Whole Page, and Two Pages. The default setting is 100%, but you can type any integer value from 10% to 500%. Note that the contents of the menu depend on the view you have selected.
	Microsoft Word Help	Displays Office Assistant's Search dialog box or the Microsoft Word Help window.
Read	Read	Puts your document into Word 2003's new e-book reading mode, to make the document easier to read.
▼	More Buttons (down triangle)	The little down triangle at the end of the bar lets you quickly add or remove buttons on the toolbar or change settings.

Note Your toolbar may have other buttons; many programs automatically add buttons to the toolbar. (Some programs, such as Adobe Acrobat, even create their own toolbars.) Some label printers add an icon to the toolbar so that you can highlight text and click the button to send the text to a label. You can reset the toolbar or add and remove buttons by clicking the triangle at the right end of the toolbar and choosing Add or Remove Buttons ⇨ *toolbar name*. A menu opens and displays all the available buttons (click one to add or remove it), and at the bottom is the Reset Toolbar command.

The Formatting toolbar

The Formatting toolbar displays controls that affect the appearance of characters and paragraphs in your document. As you move the insertion point through the document text, the Formatting toolbar reflects the formatting applied to that text. Figure 1-5 shows the buttons on the Formatting toolbar, and Table 1-2 describes what these buttons do.

Figure 1-5: The Formatting toolbar.

Table 1-2: The Formatting Toolbar Buttons

Button	Name	Action
Normal ▼	Style	Determines the style to apply to selected text. A *style* is a collection of character and paragraph formatting instructions that are commonly used together. Word 2003 includes several styles and also allows you to create your own. The default style is Normal.
Times New Roman ▼	Font	Displays the Font list box for choosing different typefaces. The default font is Times New Roman.
12 ▼	Font Size	Displays a Font Size (Points) list box for controlling the size of characters. A point is $\frac{1}{72}$ inch. In addition to using the drop-down list box, you can directly enter any point size between 1 and 1,638, including half-point sizes such as 10.5 or 100.5. The default size is 12 points.
B	B (Bold)	Applies boldface to selected text. If no text is selected, but the insertion point is inside a word (and the When Selecting, Automatically Select Entire Word option has been selected in the Edit tab of the Options dialog box), Word applies bold to the word.

Button	Name	Action
I	I (Italics)	Italicizes text.
<u>U</u>	U (Underline)	Underlines words and spaces.
	Align Left	Aligns the current or selected paragraph along the left indent. Align Left is the default setting.
	Center	Centers the current or selected paragraph between indents.
	Align Right	Aligns the current or selected paragraph along the right indent.
	Justify	Distributes the current or selected paragraph text between the left and right indents.
	Line Spacing	Adjusts the spacing between lines.
	Numbering	Numbers the selected paragraphs sequentially by inserting an Arabic numeral (1, 2, 3, and so on) in front of each, and aligns the paragraph text ¼-inch to the right of the numbers.
	Bullets	Places a bullet in front of each selected paragraph, and aligns the paragraphs ¼-inch to the right of the bullets.
	Decrease Indent	Moves selected paragraphs left, to the previous default tab stop. The default setting is ½-inch.
	Increase Indent	Moves selected paragraphs right, to the next tab stop. The default setting is ½-inch.
	Borders	Displays the Borders toolbar, which you can use to add borders and shading to selected paragraphs, table cells, graphics, and frames.
	Highlight	Highlights words and spaces using a color that you specify.
	Font Color	Allows you to quickly change the color of the current font.
	More Buttons (down triangle)	The little down triangle at the end of the bar lets you quickly add or remove buttons on the toolbar or change settings.

The Task Pane

Word provides another, special form of toolbar called a *task pane*. This pane is displayed automatically under certain conditions, and a variety of commands also open it. You can choose View ➪ Toolbars ➪ Task Pane or Tools ➪ Research to open a particular task pane setting.

The task pane is actually a dozen or so specialized toolbars in one. Choosing Tools ➪ Research opens the Research task pane. But after the Research pane is open, you can choose a different pane. Figure 1-6 shows the Home task pane. If you click the black triangle to the right of the task pane title, a list of panes opens. Table 1-3 describes the available panes.

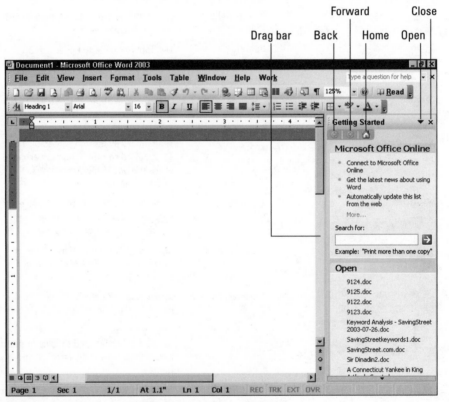

Figure 1-6: The task pane, with the Home pane displayed.

Table 1-3: The Task Panes

Task Pane Name	Purpose
Home	Provides a quick way to open existing or new documents, and links to Microsoft's Office Web site and online news.
Help	Provides a way for you to access information about Word, both in Help files on your computer and online.
New Document	Tools for starting new documents, including the ability to find templates on Microsoft's Web site.
Search Results	A tool for searching the Microsoft Web site for various types of information, including Assistance, Training, Templates, Clip Art and Media, and Office Marketplace.
Clip Art	Find clip art and other media files in a variety of locations.
Research	Use a thesaurus or dictionary, search an encyclopedia, carry out an Internet search, find a stock quote, and more.
Clipboard	Advanced clipboard functions let you save multiple items on the clipboard and paste them all together or in different locations.
Shared Workspace	A system that allows you to save documents centrally so that other users can collaborate with you.
Document Updates	Used in conjunction with the Shared Workspace to find updated documents.
Document Protection	Settings for protecting your document.
Styles and Formatting	A tool for working with paragraph and font styles and formats.
Reveal Formatting	Displays details about the formatting of the selected text.
Mail Merge	A wizard used for creating mail-merge letters, e-mail messages, envelopes, labels, and directories.
XML Structure	A tool for working with XML tags within your document.

Cross-Reference   XML tags are explained in Chapter 27. For now, all you need to know is that you probably don't need to know anything about XML.

As Figure 1-6 illustrates, the task pane gives you several tools for moving the pane and for navigating around inside it:

✦ **Drag bar:** Enables you to increase or decrease the area taken up by the task pane.

✦ **Open:** Opens the task pane list from which you can select another pane.

✦ **X:** Closes the task pane.

✦ **Left arrow (Back):** Displays the prior task pane.

✦ **Right arrow (Forward):** Displays the task pane from which you have just come after using the left arrow.

✦ **Home:** Displays the Home task bar.

The ruler

Word 2003's horizontal ruler shows and also adjusts the margin indent and tab settings of paragraphs. The ruler is displayed across the top of the window to provide you with a quick way to change paragraph indents, adjust margins, change the width of newspaper-style columns, change the width of table columns, and set tab stops using the mouse. To display and hide the ruler, choose the View ⇨ Ruler command. The measure, which by default is in inches, displays the available text area width, indent markers, and tab settings. The ruler also displays applied settings as you move the insertion point through your document. The zero point on the ruler aligns with the left boundary of the first paragraph of the selection.

With this ruler, you can adjust settings for selected paragraphs or for the paragraph that contains the insertion point. To change settings for one or more paragraphs using the ruler, move the insertion point into the paragraph or select the paragraphs you want to change. Then drag a marker on the ruler, and set tabs by clicking the ruler at various points along the horizontal ruler bar. Word also includes a vertical ruler, which appears only when your document is displayed in Print Layout view or Print Preview.

The scroll bars

At the far right side of the window is the vertical scroll bar. Clicking the arrow buttons located at the top and the bottom of the vertical scroll bar scrolls the document, one line at a time, in the direction of the arrow. The box within the scroll bar is called a *scroll box*. Its position in the scroll bar indicates the position of the insertion point relative to the size of your document as a whole. By dragging the scroll box with the mouse, you can move up or down (forward or backward) in your document. As you scroll through your document using the scroll box, a box appears to the left of the scroll bar that shows you the current page number.

Three additional buttons appear at the bottom of the vertical scroll bar as well. The double-headed arrows move you up or down in a unit defined by the middle button (the one with the circle on it, the Browse Object button). Clicking the Browse Object button allows you to choose how you want to move around the document. Most of the choices affect the double-headed arrows. For example, choose Browse by Heading and the double-headed arrows move you from heading to heading, up or down, depending on which you click. (Two of your choices, Go To and Find, open the appropriate dialog boxes and have no effect on the double-headed arrows.)

Note   Once in a while, you may find it convenient to split the window so that you can see two different areas of a document at one time. You can do this with the help of the *split bar*—the small, unobtrusive rectangle that sits at the top of the vertical scrollbar, above the up triangle. Click and drag it down to divide your window into two parts.

You can browse your document by moving between edits, headings, graphics, tables, fields, endnotes, footnotes, comments, sections, and pages. This sort of movement can be a real timesaver when you have a long document and want to review only editorial comments, headings and footers, and so on.

The window also has a horizontal scroll bar, allowing you to move the document right and left. On the left side of this scroll bar you'll find five buttons that allow you to switch quickly between the most common document views. (Word 2003's different document views are explained later, in the section "Working with Document Views.")

The status bar

At the bottom of the window is the status bar, which displays information regarding the status of the document and the task you are currently performing. For example, when you save a document, the status bar displays a dotted line that reflects the amount of the file that has been saved.

The first section of the status bar provides information about your location in the document based on the position of the insertion point. This section shows the number of the page—this is the number you have assigned to the page. So, for example, if this page is the first page in section 2, and that section begins numbering with 1, this page will be page 1 (1 will appear as the page number when you print the page), even though it may actually be the tenth page in the document. Next, you can see the section number (*sections* are specially formatted parts of a document), followed by x/n, where x is the page's sequence number; although when you print this page it will show 1, this is really the tenth page in the document. n is the total number of pages in the document, so if there are 25 pages, you would, in this case, see 10/25. By the way, you can double-click anywhere in this area to open the Go To dialog box.

The next portion of the status bar displays the precise location of the insertion point. It shows the distance (in inches) of the insertion point from the top edge of the page, followed by the line and column number of the insertion point's position. A *column* is the character position within the line of text; tabs and spaces are counted as characters.

The last items on the status bar indicate when certain Word features or modes are active. For example, when you press the Insert key on your keyboard, OVR (overtype) is displayed. When you press Insert again, the OVR indicator is dimmed. Double-clicking a mode indicator on the status bar also turns the mode either on or off. For example, double-clicking OVR switches you to overtype mode. In overtype mode, each character that you type replaces the character that lies to the right of the insertion point. When OVR is dimmed, however, insert mode is active. In insert mode, Word moves the existing text to the right to make room for the new text. You can modify the OVR behavior by choosing Tools ➪ Options, clicking the Edit tab, and selecting or clearing the Typing Replaces Selection check box. The following list identifies the status bar mode indicators:

- ✦ **REC:** Records macros
- ✦ **TRK:** Tracks changes in your text
- ✦ **EXT:** Extends selections
- ✦ **OVR:** Overtypes text

Two additional status indicators also appear to the right of OVR. These include the language being used with Word 2003 and the Spelling and Grammar Status indicator (the open book icon).

Note   You can right-click on some of these mode buttons to view pop-up menus.

By default, the status bar is displayed, but you can hide it to view more of your document. To remove the status bar, choose Tools ➪ Options, click the View tab, and click to uncheck the Status Bar box located in the Window section. To turn the status bar back on, choose Tools ➪ Options again, click the View tab, and click to place a checkmark in the Status Bar box.

Office Assistant

By now, you have probably met the animated Office Assistant icon that pops up whenever Word 2003 starts. The Word 2003 Assistant works out of the box, which means it has no window around it, so it takes up less screen real estate. Office Assistant is available to provide help with Word 2003 using a natural language interface. You enter your queries as sentences or questions, and the Assistant attempts to match them with the appropriate help information. If you choose not to use the Assistant, you can still access the Word Help system using the Microsoft Word Help window. If the Assistant is not your cup of tea for getting help, you can shut it off completely as explained later in the section "Getting Help in Word." Few Word users want the assistant to stick around once they've learned the program!

Dialog boxes and control settings

A command in a menu or a button followed by an ellipsis (. . .) displays a dialog box after you choose that command or button. For example, choosing Format ➪ Font. . . displays the dialog box with control settings, as shown in Figure 1-7. Note that some controls are already set or have text entered. These are the default settings, which you can change. Control settings vary depending on the type of information that Word needs to activate a feature. A label identifies each control setting. Related control settings are usually grouped together and placed inside a box with a group label. One control setting is always active in a dialog box. You can tell which control is active because it either has a dotted rectangle around the label or the setting is highlighted.

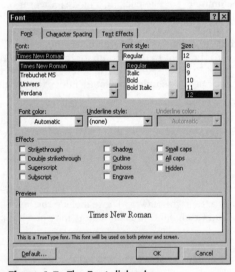

Figure 1-7: The Font dialog box.

Note   In each label, with the exception of the OK, Cancel, and Close buttons, one letter is underlined. You can press the underlined letter in conjunction with the Alt key to activate the control setting, regardless of which part of the dialog box is selected at that moment.

Press the Tab key to move, in order, through the control settings and buttons—from upper left to lower right in the dialog box. (Pressing Shift+Tab takes you through the options and controls in the opposite direction.) You also can use the mouse to choose a control setting by clicking the setting.

If a label for a setting, group of settings, or button is dimmed, that item is not available. When a control setting is available, it is black. You must either click the OK button to save your setting changes or click the Cancel button (or press Esc) to cancel the command before choosing another command or typing text in a document. If you try to do something outside some dialog boxes, Word beeps to remind you that you first must close the dialog box. (Some boxes, however, are designed to allow you to work in the document while the box remains available for further use.)

Many dialog boxes use a file folder metaphor to let you choose from sets of related options. You can organize and reference each set of options by clicking a tab. For example, note the tab labeled Character Spacing in Figure 1-8. Clicking this tab or pressing Alt+R displays the Font Character Spacing options, and clicking the Font tab or pressing Alt+N redisplays the Font options.

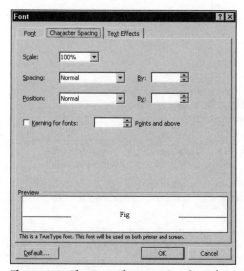

Figure 1-8: The Font Character Spacing tab.

With dialog box control settings, you can "converse" with Word 2003 by specifying how you want the program to affect your text. Word uses various types of controls in dialog boxes, including tabs, option buttons, check boxes, text boxes, list boxes, and command buttons. Figure 1-9 shows examples of two different dialog boxes. Table 1-4 describes each of the control types.

Check box

Tab   Drop-down list box

Text box

Option button

Help button

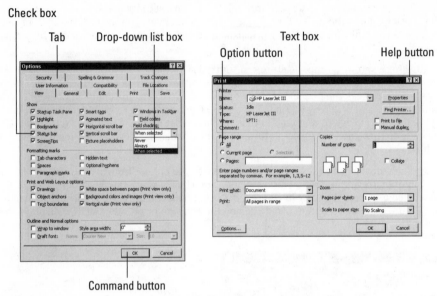

Command button

Figure 1-9: Two dialog boxes showing the various components.

Table 1-4: Dialog Box Components

Control Setting	Action
Tab	Separates groups of options. Clicking the tab or pressing Alt and the underscored character in the tab name displays the additional options.
Option button	Selects a single option from multiple options in a group. Displays a dot in the center when selected. (This is a round button, sometimes referred to as a *radio button*.)
Check box	Displays a check mark when the setting is selected. Check boxes often are clustered in groups, but unlike option buttons, choosing one does not prohibit you from choosing others.
Text box	Used to enter text, such as a file name or measurement specification. When you move the mouse pointer to a text box, the pointer changes to an I-beam, thus indicating that you can insert text. When you select a text box, the highlighted text is replaced with the new text that you type.
List box	Displays a scrolling list of alternatives. Also includes a text box with a list of options displayed under the text box. The drop-down list box has a down arrow displayed to the right of the text box. When you choose the down arrow, a list of available options appears. Word often uses drop-down list boxes to save space in dialog boxes. If the list is longer than the list box, a scroll bar appears at the right side of the list box. Many list boxes allow you to type your own entry or choose an option from the list. Some list boxes, however, require you to choose from the options in the list.

Control Setting	Action
Command button	Instructs Word to perform the appropriate task or display additional information. For example, the OK button saves your control setting changes and exits the dialog box. If the name on the command button is followed by an ellipsis (. . .), choosing this button either opens another dialog box related to that command and closes the first dialog box or opens a dialog box related to that command while leaving the first dialog box open. When the second dialog box is closed, you may continue to select options in the first dialog box. The active command button has a dotted rectangle around its label.
? button	Opens Help information for the dialog box.

Note When you perform certain options, you may find it confusing that the Cancel button changes to a Close button. When Word 2003 completes an action that cannot be canceled, the Cancel button changes to the Close button, which closes the dialog box without reversing any completed changes. Clicking the Cancel button discards the options that you selected, closes the dialog box, and returns you to your document. The keyboard equivalent to the Cancel and Close buttons is Esc. Double-clicking the Control menu icon in the upper-left corner also closes the dialog box.

Using the Mouse and the Keyboard

You can use the mouse or the keyboard to display and choose commands from Word's menus. Whether you use the keyboard or the mouse, some commands require that you first select the part of your document on which you want the command to act. These commands appear dimmed in a menu until you make such a selection. For example, you cannot choose Edit ➪ Cut until you select the item that you want to cut from your document.

Choosing some commands displays a bullet or checkmark next to the command name, which indicates that command is currently in effect. If more information is needed to complete a command, Word displays a dialog box, in which you select options to control how the command is performed. If you choose a command or feature that has not yet been installed, Word informs you that it cannot locate the command or feature.

Using the mouse

The mouse is an indispensable tool in Word's graphic point-and-click environment of buttons and icons. Simply by pointing to a button or icon with the mouse pointer and then clicking a mouse button, you can execute a command. Mouse use has its own special lingo in the Windows environment, and Table 1-5 lists the basic terms used throughout this book to define such operations. Working with the mouse quickly becomes second nature. As you become proficient with Word, you can use the mouse to integrate various keyboard shortcuts and to perform many tasks more quickly.

When you move the mouse pointer to different parts of your screen or perform certain commands, the shape of the pointer changes. The mouse pointer's shape indicates what kind of action is being performed. For example, the pointer is an arrow when you select commands from a menu, an hourglass when Word is processing a command, or an I-beam when the pointer is in a text-entry area. Additional mouse pointers can appear depending on the task being performed.

Table 1-5: Mouse Function Terms

Term	Meaning
Click	Quickly press and release the left mouse button while the mouse pointer is on an object, such as a menu command, an icon, or a button.
Right-click	Quickly press and release the right mouse button while the mouse pointer is on an object, such as a menu command, an icon, or a button.
Double-click	Quickly click the left mouse button twice while the mouse pointer is on an object, such as a menu command, an icon, or a button.
Drag	Move the mouse pointer to an object, press and hold the left mouse button while moving the mouse, and then release the button.
Point	Move the mouse pointer directly to a specific location, such as a menu command, an icon, or a button.

Using the keyboard

To choose a command from a menu using the keyboard, press the Alt key while also pressing the underlined letter in the menu that you want to open. Then press the underlined letter in the command that you want to execute. For example, press Alt+F and then *S* to execute the File ➪ Save command. You also can use the up- and down-arrow keys to highlight a command within an open menu, and then press Enter to execute the highlighted command. Pressing Alt alone places you in the menu bar, in which you can then use the right or left arrow to highlight a menu name and press Enter (or the down arrow) to open the menu. Once in a menu you can press the left or right arrow keys to move to the previous or next menu. You also can press Esc to exit a menu without selecting a command and return to your document.

You can choose a number of commands by pressing the shortcut keys listed on the menu to the right of the command. With shortcut keys, you can execute a command without opening a menu. For example, press Ctrl+S to save a document or Ctrl+B to apply bold formatting to selected text. Word provides many shortcut keys so that you can use the keyboard while you work. If a keyboard shortcut is available for a command, it usually is listed to the right of that command in the menu. Some keys also are assigned to Word commands that are not listed in menus. For example, you can execute the File ➪ Exit command directly from the keyboard by pressing Alt+F4.

Tip   For a list of the shortcut keys for different tasks, choose Help ➪ Microsoft Word Help (or press F1), type **shortcut keys**, and press Enter.

Right-click for shortcut menus

When you point to or select certain items in Word, such as a paragraph, graphic, or table, you can display a shortcut menu that contains commands related to that item. They appear in the document window exactly where you are working. For example, Figure 1-10 shows the shortcut menu for working with text in a document. To display a shortcut menu, position the insertion point on the text or item with which you want to work, and then click the right mouse button or press Shift+F10. When the shortcut menu appears, simply choose a command. To close a shortcut menu without choosing a command, click anywhere outside the shortcut menu or press Esc.

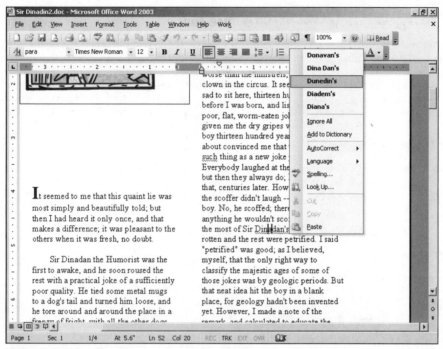

Figure 1-10: The shortcut menu for working with text in a document.

Undo and Repeat

As you work, it helps to keep the Undo command in mind. The Undo command is located in the Edit menu, and it cancels the most recent commands or actions that you've completed. Clicking on the arrow to the right of the Undo button on the Standard toolbar displays a drop-down list of the most recent actions that can be undone. Word tracks the editing and formatting changes that you make, so if you don't like the results of a command or accidentally delete some text, choose Undo. The fastest way to undo an action is to click the Undo button on the Standard toolbar, or to press Ctrl+Z. Some actions, such as saving a document, cannot be reversed, however. In this case, Undo changes to Can't Undo and appears dimmed on the menu, thus indicating this option is unavailable. You also can redo an action that you've undone, using the menu option or using Ctrl+Y.

The Repeat command in the Edit menu repeats the last command or action that you've completed. It often is easier to choose Repeat than to choose the same command several times, particularly when the previous command involved a complex formatting change that you applied using the Format ⇨ Font or Format ⇨ Paragraph command. You can select other text and then choose Repeat to apply the same formatting in one step. The Repeat command also duplicates typing, so choose Repeat when you type a long paragraph and want to include the same text elsewhere in your document. Both Ctrl+Y and the F4 key are keyboard shortcuts for the Repeat command.

Caution

Carefully observe to make sure that Word actually does repeat the action; in some cases you may find that it only *partially* repeats.

Working with Document Views

With Word, you can view your documents from several different perspectives. Changing views in Word does not change the document, however. It only changes your view of that document. Think of Word's different views as being similar to looking at an object through a magnifying glass. As you change the angle or the distance of the magnifying glass, the object appears to change as well. The five main views in Word are Normal, Web Layout, Print Layout, Reading Layout, and Outline; other views include Document Map, Full Screen, Zoom, and Print Preview.

Changing views

You manage Word's view options from the View menu, which allows you to change to any view. You also can use the buttons on the horizontal scroll bar to change views (see Figure 1-11). With these buttons, you can switch between Normal, Web, Print, Reading, and Outline views.

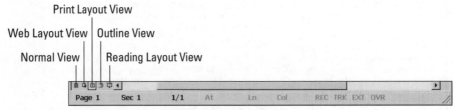

Figure 1-11: The View buttons on the horizontal scroll bar.

To use the View menu to change views, do the following:

1. Choose View (Alt+V) to display the View drop-down menu.

2. Select the view you want to use to display your document.

Normal view

Normal (View ➪ Normal) is the default view in Word, and the benefit of working in Normal view is speed. It is not a true WYSIWYG ("What You See Is What You Get") view, because you cannot see the headers and footers, footnotes, and annotations without issuing a command from the View menu, but you can see the formatting and layout elements of the document. This view is not appropriate when you are trying to see how the page will print, especially if you have images in the document. In fact in some cases pictures will not even be displayed in Normal view (pictures appear only if their wrapping styles is "inline with text").

To speed up text entry, display graphics as placeholders. This way, you don't have to wait for Word to redraw the screen. To customize the Normal view to speed Word's response time when entering text, follow these steps:

1. Choose View ➪ Normal.

2. Choose Tools ➪ Options.

3. Select the Draft Font and Picture Placeholders options in the View tab.

4. Click OK or press Enter.

Web Layout view

Choosing View ➪ Web Layout shows how any document would appear as a Web document. Unlike the Web Page Preview command (on the File menu), however, this view allows you to view how a document would appear as a Web page without starting Microsoft Internet Explorer. You can use the Web Layout command to check out a Word document before saving it as a Web document, thus seeing how the converted document would appear before you actually convert it.

Print Layout view

Print Layout view is the most accurate of all views in Word (with the exception of the Print Preview, which isn't really intended as an editing view). It also is the slowest. Depending on how fast your computer and graphics card work, scrolling and screen refreshing can slow down drastically when you include graphics in a document and use Print Layout view. The main benefit of Print Layout view is that it is a true WYSIWYG view. With it, you can see all the elements of your document on the page, just as they would appear on a printed page (or at least close, though for a closer-to-print-layout view Print Preview is better). It usually is most efficient to work in the faster Normal view and then switch to Print Layout view to see how the page would look if printed.

Tip   Print Layout view shows the vertical ruler along the left side of the document. You can change the left and right margins in Print Layout view using the horizontal ruler, and you can change the top and bottom margins using the vertical ruler.

You can customize Print Layout view a little. If you choose Tools ➪ Options, and then click the View tab, you'll find a check box labeled White Space Between Pages (Print view only). Clear this check box to squeeze pages together in Print Layout view to save screen space. Word removes the gray area around the pages, along with the headers and footers, and any blank space in the margins. This check box may be disabled. If it is, close the Options dialog box, change to Print Layout view, and return to the dialog box.

Reading Layout view

A new tool in Word 2003 is the Reading Layout view, shown in Figure 1-12, which is designed to make the document easier to read. It *does not* display the document as it would look when printed. Rather, it re-configures it into easy-to-read screen pages. You can move through a document very quickly in this view using the arrow keys and Page Up and Page Dn keys; these keys move you up or down one or two entire pages at a time. You can still edit in Reading Layout view, but it's very slow.

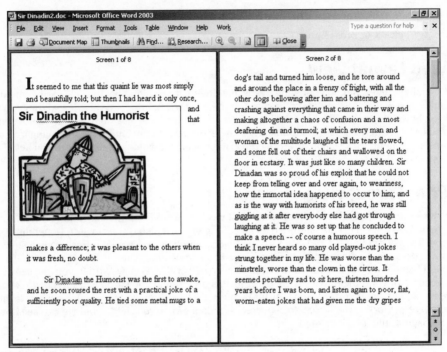

Figure 1-12: The Reading Layout view.

Outline view

Outline is a specialized view that you can use to organize a document. In Outline view, you can collapse and expand portions of the document so that you see only the headings of your choice. You also can quickly and easily move as well as copy large portions of a document in Outline view. The real key to using this view efficiently is to use Heading styles because Word recognizes these styles immediately in Outline view. Figure 1-13 shows a document in Outline view.

Document Map view

Choosing View ➪ Document Map or clicking the Document Map button on the Standard toolbar while in any document view displays a vertical pane along the left edge of the document window. An outline of the document's structure appears in this vertical pane. Figure 1-14 shows the Document Map as it appears in Normal view. Note the headings listed in the left pane. You can use Document Map to quickly browse a long document or an online document and to keep track of your location within it. The Document Map view works in conjunction with Heading Styles.

Tip　Using the Document Map is a good way to get an outline view of your document even if you haven't used heading styles (see Chapter 25 for a discussion of Word's Outline feature). If you are given a document, for example, that has been badly formatted, you can use the Document Map view in your clean-up process.

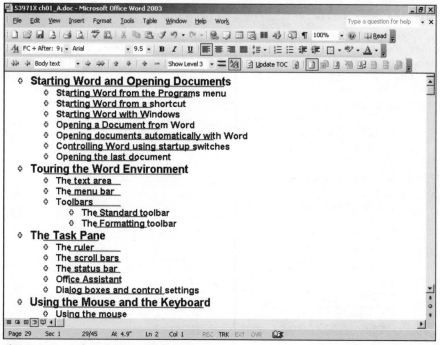

Figure 1-13: A document in Outline view.

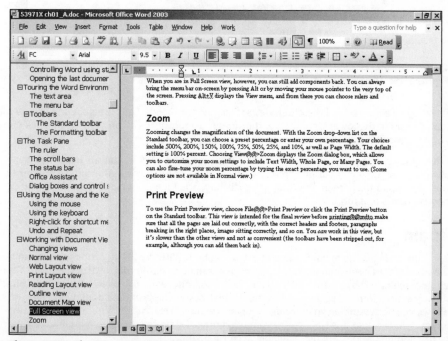

Figure 1-14: The Document Map view.

Full Screen view

Wish you could hide all Word's menus, toolbars, and rulers and have the whole screen for writing? If so, use the Full Screen view, shown in Figure 1-15. This view simply removes all the components around the document—the toolbars, menu bar, status bar, and, unfortunately, even the scroll bars.

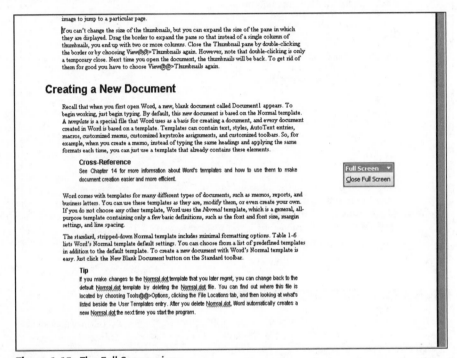

Figure 1-15: The Full Screen view.

Begin by selecting one of the other views; *then* choose View ➪ Full Screen. A one-button tool-bar appears in the lower-right area of the screen. To return to the previous view, click once on the Close Full Screen button or press Esc.

When you are in Full Screen view, however, you can still add components back. You can always bring the menu bar on-screen by pressing Alt or by moving your mouse pointer to the very top of the screen. Pressing Alt+V displays the View menu, and from there you can choose rulers and toolbars.

Zoom

Zooming changes the magnification of the document. With the Zoom drop-down list on the Standard toolbar, you can choose a preset percentage or enter your own percentage. Your choices include 500%, 200%, 150%, 100%, 75%, 50%, 25%, and 10%, as well as Page Width. The default setting is 100% percent. Choosing View ➪ Zoom displays the Zoom dialog box, which allows you to customize your zoom settings to include Text Width, Whole Page, or Many Pages. You can also fine-tune your zoom percentage by typing the exact percentage you want to use. (Some options are not available in Normal view.)

Print Preview

To use the Print Preview view, choose File ➪ Print Preview or click the Print Preview button on the Standard toolbar. This view is intended for the final review before printing—to make sure that all the pages are laid out correctly, with the correct headers and footers, paragraphs breaking in the right places, images sitting correctly, and so on. You *can* work in this view, but it's slower than the other views and not as convenient (the toolbars have been stripped out, for example, although you can add them back in).

When you first enter Print Preview view, there's no mouse-insertion I-beam. Rather, the mouse controls the zoom. Click on the document to zoom in. If you want to edit in this view, click the Magnifier icon in the toolbar and then click to place your insertion point appropriately in the document.

Adding Thumbnails

Choose View ➪ Thumbnails to add a column on the left side of your window that displays thumbnail images of each page. This is available for the Normal, Web Layout, Print Layout, Reading Layout, and Outline views. You can use the thumbnails as a navigation tool. Just click an image to jump to a particular page.

You can't change the size of the thumbnails, but you can expand the size of the pane in which they are displayed. Drag the border to expand the pane so that instead of a single column of thumbnails, you end up with two or more columns. Close the Thumbnail pane by double-clicking the border or by choosing View ➪ Thumbnails again. However, note that double-clicking is only a temporary close. Next time you open the document, the thumbnails will be back. To get rid of them for good you have to choose View ➪ Thumbnails again.

Creating a New Document

Recall that when you first open Word, a new, blank document called Document1 appears. To begin working, just begin typing. By default, this new document is based on the Normal template. A *template* is a special file that Word uses as a basis for creating a document, and every document created in Word is based on a template. Templates can contain text, styles, AutoText entries, macros, customized menus, customized keystroke assignments, and customized toolbars. So, for example, when you create a memo, instead of typing the same headings and applying the same formats each time, you can just use a template that already contains these elements.

 Cross-Reference See Chapter 14 for more information about Word's templates and how to use them to make document creation easier and more efficient.

Word comes with templates for many different types of documents, such as memos, reports, and business letters. You can use these templates as they are, modify them, or even create your own. If you do not choose any other template, Word uses the *Normal* template, which is a general, all-purpose template containing only a few basic definitions, such as the font and font size, margin settings, and line spacing.

The standard, stripped-down Normal template includes minimal formatting options. Table 1-6 lists Word's Normal template default settings. You can choose from a list of predefined templates in addition to the default template. To create a new document with Word's Normal template is easy. Just click the New Blank Document button on the Standard toolbar.

Tip   If you make changes to the Normal.dot template that you later regret, you can change back to the default Normal.dot template by deleting the Normal.dot file. You can find out where this file is located by choosing Tools ➪ Options, clicking the File Locations tab, and then looking at what's listed beside the User Templates entry. After you delete Normal.dot, Word automatically creates a new Normal.dot the next time you start the program.

Table 1-6: Word's Normal Template (Normal.dot) Default Settings

Option	Default Setting
Paper size	Letter (8½ x 11 inches)
Left and right margins	1.25 inches
Top and bottom document margins	1 inch
Line spacing	Single
Justification	Align left
Tabs	0.5-inch
Font	Times New Roman
Point size	12 points
View	Normal

Starting a new document with a template

Word includes several preconstructed templates for creating documents such as letters, resumes, memos, and so on. To create a new document and select one of Word's templates, choose File ➪ New; the New Document task pane opens (see Figure 1-16). You have a variety of options in this pane—you can select the default Blank document, a default Web document, an XML document, and so on.

Notice the On My Computer link? Click this to open the Templates dialog box, which includes tabs organizing the templates and wizards by document type: Legal Pleadings, Letters and Faxes, Memos, and so on. As you click the tabs in the Templates dialog box, note the variety of templates available in Word. You can preview a template by clicking the icon, which (in most cases) then displays the template layout in the Preview area.

Select a tab for the type of document you want, and then choose a template or wizard icon from the list. Make sure the Document radio button in the lower-right corner is selected, and click OK. Word then displays either the new document with the specified template's layout and formatting or the wizard's on-screen instructions for creating the document.

Using wizards to create a document

Wizards are easy-to-use programs supplied with Word that enable you to create documents by answering a series of questions. Icons for wizard files appear with a wand in the New dialog box. Word provides a collection of wizards for automatically creating letters, memos, resumes, newsletters, and other common documents. Wizards use templates and include step-by-step instructions to walk you through creating a document. They prompt you to fill in information, which the wizard inserts into the document. Creating a complex document—such as an agenda, an award, a newsletter, or a resume—from scratch could take hours, but using Word's wizards, these documents take only a few minutes.

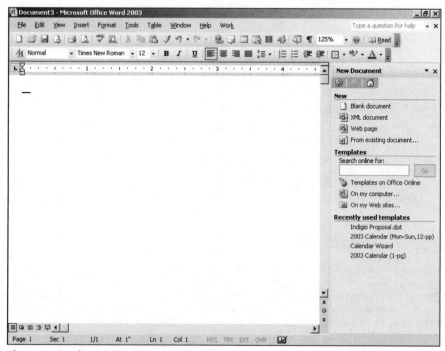

Figure 1-16: The New Document task pane.

To create a letter using the Letter Wizard, follow these steps:

1. Choose File ➪ New. The New Document task pane opens.

2. Click the On My Computer link. The Templates dialog box appears.

3. Click the Letters & Faxes tab.

4. Double-click the Letter Wizard, and a small dialog box appears.

5. Select whether you want to Send One Letter or Send Letter to a Mailing List. The appropriate wizard dialog box appears. Figure 1-17 shows a sample Letter Wizard dialog box.

6. Answer the questions in the dialog boxes, and then follow the instructions. Word then sets up the basic formatting and layout of your document.

7. To move to the next step, click the Next button. To return to the previous step, click the Back button.

8. To create the document and close the wizard, click Finish. Word then displays the new document, which includes text from the wizard.

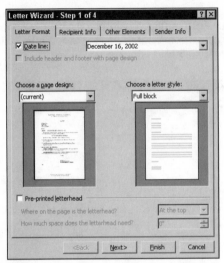

Figure 1-17: The Letter Wizard dialog box.

Saving a Document

Until you save a document to a disk (either hard or floppy), that document exists only in your computer's memory. When saving a new document, you must name the file and also specify where you want it to be saved. Word 2003 can store files using any number of formats. The most common are the .doc and .htm formats. The .doc format is the proprietary document format used by Word, and .htm is the universal format used for Web documents.

You can edit an existing Word file and create different versions in different formats by saving the file in a particular format—the original file will be untouched, so you'll end up with two separate files. This capability enables you to exchange files with others who are using different word processors or HTML authoring programs.

To save a document, follow these steps:

1. Click the Save button, or choose File ➪ Save (Ctrl+S). The Save As dialog box appears (see Figure 1-18). By default, the File Name text box lists the first sentence of the document in the text box.

2. Enter a name with as many characters as you want, within reason. The entire pathname, including all the directories and the file name, cannot exceed 255 characters. For ease of use and efficiency, however, keep your file names as concise as possible.

   A Word document file name can include letters, numbers, and spaces, as well as the following symbols: @ # $ % & ( ) [ ] _ { }. Word automatically adds the file name extension .doc for you, so you don't have to type it.

3. Click OK or press Enter to save your document. If you try to save a document with the name of a previously existing file, Word displays a dialog box asking you to confirm that you want to replace the existing document. Click No to type a different name for the document being saved, or click Yes to replace (or overwrite) the existing document.

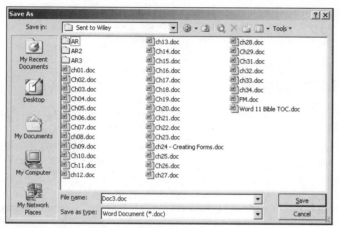

Figure 1-18: The Save As dialog box.

The next time you save your document, you won't have to type a name, of course. Pressing Ctrl+S will quickly save the file.

Caution   Get into the habit of pressing Ctrl+S frequently, to reduce the chance of losing work due to a computer problem!

Word helps you to save and protect your documents in many ways. The option settings determine how and when you save your documents. To see what options are available, choose Tools ➪ Options and then click the Save tab. You also can access the Save tab from the Save As dialog box by choosing Tools ➪ General Options. This lets you change the save settings for the current document, allowing you, for example, to define how auto-recovery works. (You can learn more about Word's AutoRecover feature in Chapter 7.)

Note   You can specify any given folder to be the one in which Word saves or opens documents. By default, Word uses the My Documents folder. To change this, choose Tools ➪ Options and click the File Locations tab. Select Documents, and then click Modify to select a new folder.

Saving a document as a Web page

Word 2003 provides a seamless interface for creating both Word (*.doc) and Web (*.htm) documents. Because the HTML (HyperText Markup Language) format is a native file format, you can save any .doc file as an .htm file, and vice versa. Word saves the .doc formatting as well as the .htm formatting. This allows you to create Web documents in Word for viewing in a Web browser. Word also reads those documents back in for editing, however. When any Word document is saved as a Web page, almost all the document's information, including its content, formatting, and document properties, are retained in the HTML document.

Saving a document as a Web page is easy. Choose File ➪ Save as Web Page, which displays the Save As dialog box with the .htm file name extension already selected. You can save the document by clicking Save. Clicking Change allows you to change the page title for the document, which appears on the title bar of the Web browser window. You also can save a Word document as a Web page from the Save As dialog box, just as you would any other file format—select the format from the Save As Type drop-down menu.

Cross-Reference Before you decide to dive right in and begin using Word to create Web pages, read Chapter 26. The bullet list near the beginning of that chapter provides some things you might want to consider when you're deciding how best to create Web pages.

Getting Help in Word

Word offers several types of help, as well as different help interfaces. Here's what you'll find on the Help menu:

✦ **Microsoft Word Help:** Opens the Help task pane, where you can type keywords to find information, view a table of contents, and find information on the Microsoft.com Web site.

✦ **Show/Hide the Office Assistant:** Turns the Office Assistant on and off. You can click once on the Assistant to ask a question, or right-click to view a menu from which you can set options. The Office Assistant incorporates *IntelliSense* Technology to provide a natural language interface to the system. The Assistant also automatically provides Help topics and tips on tasks that you perform as you work.

✦ **Office on Microsoft.com:** Loads the Office Web site into your Web browser. This is a site that provides updated help information and other technical resources. You also can download free service release updates and product enhancements, and purchase third-party add-on tools that let you print postage, translate documents, send faxes, and more.

✦ **Contact Us:** Displays the Contact Us page on the Office Web site.

✦ **WordPerfect Help:** This eases the transition for users switching from WordPerfect to Word. There is a separate Help dialog box for WordPerfect users, and you can even turn on an option that automatically tells you how to use a Word feature when you press a WordPerfect keystroke combination.

✦ **Detect and Repair:** Runs a utility that checks the Microsoft Office program files for problems and repairs any problems it finds.

✦ **Activate Product:** Turns on, or registers, the program.

✦ **Privacy Settings:** Allows you to modify your Customer Service Improvement Program. This is a system by which Word can transmit information, across the Internet, about your hardware and about how you use your computer. This is anonymous information that Microsoft is using to plan new software and determine problems with Word. It also allows Microsoft to upload new help information to your system, and a little program that tracks software errors. By default this system is turned on; you can turn it off if you prefer, as many users do. How do you decide? It all depends how paranoid (or careful) you want to be. Do you trust that your information will be used appropriately? If not, turn it off.

✦ **About Microsoft Word:** Displays a dialog box that includes information about Word's version number, the product's license, and the system information about your computer and Windows settings. You will most likely need this information when you call for technical support. If a Word feature doesn't seem to be working, click the Disabled Items button in this dialog box. Word sometimes disables components that are causing problems (restarting the program may restart the functions).

In addition, you'll find a Type a Question for Help text box on the right side of the menu bar; type keywords in here, press Enter, and the Help task pane opens.

Using the Office Assistant

By default, the Office Assistant is always on the screen. Click the icon to receive help on any subject, and a box appears that prompts you for a search phrase. Press Enter, and the Help task pane opens with the search results. Right-click the Office Assistant to display a pop-up menu of Office Assistant options. Choosing Hide hides the assistant, but only during the current session. The next time you open Word, the assistant will be back (although if you keep hiding it, eventually it will ask if you want to hide it for good).

If the Office Assistant is not your preferred way to get help—quite frankly, it can be very irritating—you can deactivate it. Right-click the icon and choose Options to display the Office Assistant dialog box (see Figure 1-19), which allows you to alter the situations in which Office Assistant offers help. Clear the Use the Office Assistant check box to permanently hide it. (Even with the Office Assistant shut off, you can display it anytime by choosing Help ➪ Show the Office Assistant.) In the Gallery tab, you can select a different assistant. You also can access the Gallery tab by choosing the Choose Assistant item in the pop-up menu.

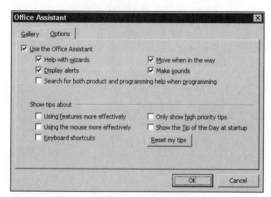

Figure 1-19: The Office Assistant dialog box.

The Office Assistant really isn't very necessary because you can reach the Help task pane any time by pressing F1.

Using the Microsoft Word Help task pane

If you would rather use the Windows-style Help system instead of the Office Assistant, you can turn off the Office Assistant, as previously mentioned. The Windows-style Help system uses a Web-like interface. You can click on hyperlinks to go to related help topics. After you turn off the Office Assistant, you can access the Microsoft Word Help task pane (see Figure 1-20) by choosing Help ➪ Microsoft Word Help or pressing F1.

The Microsoft Word Help task pane includes three areas:

✦ The Search area, where you type a search phrase and press Enter or click the Table of Contents link to open, yes, the Help Table of Contents

✦ The Office on Microsoft.com area, with links to Microsoft's Help Web site

✦ The See Also area, with a few additional links to more information

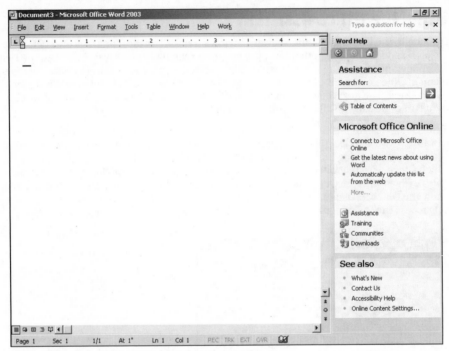

Figure 1-20: The Microsoft Word Help task pane.

Browsing the Help Contents

The Table of Contents link displays a Table of Contents for Help topics (see Figure 1-21). The book icons that appear in the Contents tab are referred to as *chapters*. Click a book to show all the Help pages in that topic. Click an entry with a ? icon to open a Help window displaying information about that subject.

Searching for Help

Type a search term into the Search box at the top of the task pane, and then click the green arrow or press Enter. You'll see the results. Click on one to open a window containing text about that topic (see Figure 1-22). Or you can click the category below an entry to display the Table of Contents, already open to that category, where you can browse similar subjects.

Accessing Microsoft Office Help on the Web

Word includes an option to connect automatically to an entire menu of online Help sites by clicking Help on the menu bar and then scrolling down to Office on the Web. This way, you have access to the entire wealth of the Internet in getting assistance with Word 2003 and with your document itself. Click Microsoft on the Web, and select an option from the submenu. These options connect you with a particular Internet site. You can load these sites through any Internet browser, such as Microsoft Internet Explorer or Netscape Navigator.

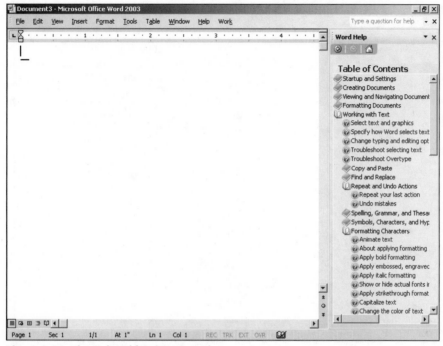

Figure 1-21: The Help Table of Contents box.

Helping WordPerfect users

Word 2003 goes out of its way to help ease your transition from WordPerfect to Word. There is a separate Help dialog box for WordPerfect users, and you can even turn on an option that automatically tells you how to use a Word feature when you press a WordPerfect keystroke combination.

Tip
Note, however, that Word is not necessarily very good at helping WordPerfect users. In fact, Word is more useful for users of *older* versions of WordPerfect than new. And because turning on WordPerfect features changes the behavior of Word, it can be a source of confusion and trouble leading to Help Desk calls.

If you are a WordPerfect user and new to both Word and Windows, choose Help ➪ WordPerfect Help to display the Help for WordPerfect Users dialog box (see Figure 1-23). In the Command Keys list, select a function or WordPerfect command to display to the right of the list information about how to carry out that function in Word. If there is an ellipsis after the selected item, double-click the item or choose Help Text to display a submenu of related items (unfortunately there's no way to *go back* without closing the dialog box and starting again!). If an arrow is next to the item, you can click the Demo button and have Word demonstrate that feature, though you should read the text first because it's not always apparent what is going on. If you click Demo when you have *not* selected an item with a Demo attached, the dialog box simply closes.

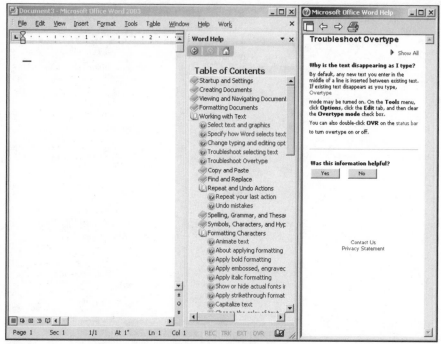

Figure 1-22: The Help task pane, along with a Help window containing explanatory text.

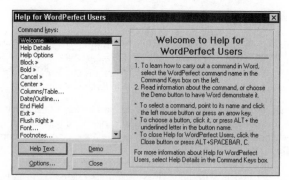

Figure 1-23: The Help for WordPerfect Users dialog box.

The Help Text button closes the dialog box and opens a message box carrying the help text for the item you selected. This box stays visible while you are working in the document, so you can follow the instructions as you work; if there's a Demo associated with the Help item, you'll see a Demo button in this message box.

Word formatting and WordPerfect Reveal Codes

The main conceptual difference between Word and WordPerfect involves how formatting is applied. Word is a paragraph-oriented system, and it does not use codes in the same way as WordPerfect. If you have used HTML, you'll understand how WordPerfect works—it *tags* text to define formatting. In Word 2003, you can view the paragraph and character formatting for specific text by pressing Shift+F1 to open the Reveal Formatting task pane. Click the text you want to inspect to change the contents of the Reveal Formatting pane.

You also can display various nonprinting characters in your document. Click the Show/Hide button in the Standard toolbar, or choose Tools ➪ Options and select the View tab. In the Formatting Marks group, click the All check box to display all nonprinting characters. Or you can select the check boxes for the specific nonprinting characters you want to view.

Closing a Word Document

When you've finished working with a Word document, you have several options for closing it. The following procedures all close a document while leaving the Word program itself running.

✦ Choose File ➪ Close.

✦ Press Ctrl+F4.

✦ Click the Close button on the right edge of the menu bar.

If you have not saved your document since the last time you made a change, Word will ask if you want to do so.

Exiting Word

Word creates numerous different files during the course of its operation, many of which are stored in memory until you quit the program. Some of these files are temporary files that are deleted when you exit Word. If you do not exit properly, however, some of these files may not close properly, and this can result in wasted space as well as hard disk problems down the road. Simply turning off the power switch also destroys any unsaved data. Use one of the following methods to exit Word correctly:

✦ Choose File ➪ Exit.

✦ Press Alt+F4.

✦ Click the Close button in the upper-right corner of the Word program title bar.

✦ Double-click the Control menu icon in the upper-left corner of the Word program title bar.

✦ Right-click the Microsoft Word button in the taskbar and choose Close from the pop-up menu. (This method allows you to close Word while you are using another application.)

When you use one of these techniques to exit Word, the program tells you whether you have unsaved data by displaying a dialog box (see Figure 1-24). This dialog box allows you to either save your work or cancel the Exit command.

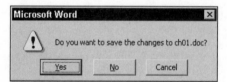

Figure 1-24: The Word message box asks
if you want to save your files.

Summary

This chapter has oriented you to the Word environment and shown you how to create documents quickly using the core Word tools. For example, you can now do the following:

✦ Start Word and create new documents in a variety of ways. Use File ⇨ New (Ctrl+N) to create documents using wizards and templates.

✦ Identify the essential elements of the Word 2003 environment, including document windows, menus, toolbars, the task pane, the ruler, scroll and status bars, and dialog boxes.

✦ Use the mouse and work with keyboard commands in Word.

✦ Display documents in different views using commands in the View menu.

✦ Save documents.

✦ Get help using the Office Assistant or the Microsoft Word Help window.

✦ Exit Word.

✦   ✦   ✦

Navigating and Editing Documents

◆   ◆   ◆   ◆

In This Chapter

Inserting and
overtyping text

Showing and hiding
nonprinting characters

Defining new
paragraphs

Selecting text
and graphics

Deleting, moving,
and copying text

Inserting symbols and
special characters

Inserting text
using AutoCorrect
and AutoText

◆   ◆   ◆   ◆

Most of the time, you probably are typing, navigating, or editing text. At first glance, these tasks may seem to be elementary, but numerous timesaving keystrokes and commands are at your fingertips, just waiting to be discovered. This chapter unveils methods to speed up entering text and navigating and editing a document. It teaches how to insert date, time, and special symbols and characters, and it explains how to use two of Word's powerful tools, AutoCorrect and AutoText, to insert and correct text automatically as you type.

Editing Text

When you first create a document using the Normal template (the New Blank Document button on the Standard toolbar), the insertion point rests at the top of the document, ready for you to start. To add text to a document, just begin typing. If you are new to word processing, you probably have the urge to press Enter at the end of each line. Fight this urge. The only time you need to press Enter is when you want Word to create a new paragraph. By default, Word automatically wraps your text to the next line when it reaches the right margin. If the wrap occurs within a word, that entire word is placed on the next line.

Note

Most users seem to press the spacebar *twice* at the end of each sentence. This is not necessary. The custom comes from the days of the typewriter—because typewriter characters are all the same size, adding two spaces between sentences made the text look better, providing more than just a space the size of a single character. But most of the time, you'll be typing using fonts that adjust for spacing. So when using a word processor such as Microsoft Word you do *not* need to follow this ancient custom.

Don't try to correct mistakes and apply formatting as you type. For now, just relax, because Word makes correcting text and applying formatting to text simple. In fact, Word includes AutoText, AutoFormat, and AutoCorrect features that automatically enter text, apply formatting, and correct mistakes for you as you type, so if you see Word suddenly change something you've typed, that's what's happening.

Cross-Reference

AutoCorrect and AutoText are both covered later in this chapter in the section "AutoCorrect and AutoText." For information on checking your spelling using AutoCorrect, see Chapter 8. For information on styles and using AutoFormat, see Chapter 13.

Displaying nonprinting characters

If you're new to Word, you may have trouble understanding how Word displays and handles text. This is largely because your text also includes nonprinting characters that affect how that text is displayed. One of the most revealing commands in Word is the Show/Hide button (the paragraph-icon button) in the Standard toolbar. Show/Hide displays *nonprinting characters,* which are characters that can be displayed on the screen but that do not print. When this option is toggled on, Word shows the invisible characters you include in a document, such as paragraph marks, spaces, and tabs.

Displaying nonprinting characters is sometimes a good idea because you can see at a glance whether you have typed an extra space or pressed Enter accidentally. On the other hand, you'll often find having all that extra information very distracting, so you may not want the feature turned on all the time. If you don't see the nonprinting characters in your document and would like to, click the Show/Hide button on the Standard toolbar. You can change which nonprinting characters appear by changing the settings in the View tab of the Options dialog box (Tools ➪ Options); to see all nonprinting characters while you work, select the All check box in the Formatting Marks group.

To specify which nonprinting characters are displayed, follow these steps:

1. Choose Tools ➪ Options.

2. Select the View tab in the Options dialog box (see Figure 2-1).

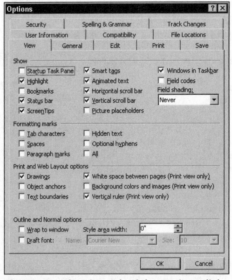

Figure 2-1: The View tab of the Options dialog box.

3. In the Formatting Marks group, select or clear the check box for the formatting marks that you want to display or hide.

4. Click OK.

We recommend that when you start learning how to use Word, you *do* display nonprinting characters. As you'll learn in a moment—and in more detail in Chapter 5—deleting a paragraph mark accidentally can have unexpected results. Unless you display nonprinting characters, you can't even see the paragraph mark, so inexperienced users sometimes have trouble figuring out where they are.

Inserting and overtyping text

When you insert text into a line, Word moves the existing text to the right to make room for the new text. To type over existing text, switch to Overtype mode by double-clicking OVR on the status bar at the bottom of the Word window or by pressing Insert on your keyboard. To switch back to Insert mode, double-click OVR or press Insert again. (You can change the behavior of the Insert key on the Edit tab of the Options dialog box.)

Beginning a new paragraph

To start a paragraph, simply press the Enter key. You can break an existing paragraph into two by positioning the insertion point where you want the new paragraph to begin and pressing Enter. Word then inserts a paragraph mark and moves the insertion point down to the first line of the new paragraph.

In Word, a paragraph is any amount of text and graphics that ends with a paragraph mark. Word even creates a paragraph mark if you press Enter without typing any text. Paragraphs are central to working with text and graphics in Word. They have meaning beyond a simple, grammatical definition because many types of formatting are applied to paragraphs as a whole. Here are some guidelines for working with paragraphs in Word:

✦ When you delete a paragraph mark, the next paragraph is merged into the first, so the second paragraph assumes the formatting of the first. If you select the paragraph mark and some text in the second paragraph, however, pressing Delete makes the first paragraph assume the formatting of the second.

✦ If you accidentally delete a paragraph mark, you can restore it by clicking the Undo button on the Standard toolbar or by pressing Ctrl+Z.

✦ Set your basic paragraph formats once. Then, when you press Enter to start a new paragraph, Word carries over the preceding paragraph's formatting to the new paragraph.

Cross-Reference   To find out more about formatting paragraphs, see Chapter 5.

Adding a new line

Word automatically wraps text to the next line when it reaches the right margin. In some situations, such as when typing a list, you might want to start a new line before reaching the margin to keep the line within the paragraph. New lines (called *line breaks*) are extremely helpful for keeping the format of several short lines the same, because the one paragraph mark that ends the list controls all of the new lines. Also, there is usually more space placed between paragraphs than between lines within a paragraph, so using the *manual line break* provides a way to start text at the beginning of a new line but not add extra space between lines.

To start a new line anywhere within a paragraph, position the insertion point where you want the new line to begin and press Shift+Enter. Word then inserts a line break character and moves the insertion point to the beginning of the next line. Line breaks appear as an arrow with a right-angle bend in it when you display nonprinting characters.

Aligning text

In Word, don't press the spacebar to align text. The spacebar method works on a typewriter because that type is *monospaced*, which means that every letter takes up the same amount of space. This method generally doesn't work with Word, however, because Windows uses *proportional fonts*. When you use a proportional font, letters occupy different amounts of horizontal space; for example, an i occupies a much narrower space than an M. (Some fonts are monospaced, but most of the fonts you'll be using are not.)

Align text using Word's tabs, indents, or other formatting options. This way, you can ensure the text is aligned properly, and Word can readjust the paragraph automatically when you add or delete text. (For more information on aligning text with tabs, see Chapter 5.) Also note that it's *much* easier to modify documents that have been properly formatted than trying to fix a document—adding and removing items, for instance—in which text is aligned using spaces.

Also, don't just rush in where angels fear to tread and start aligning text using the Tab key. Unless you understand how to use tabs (see Chapter 5), you can end up with a document that is hard to modify because you've pressed Tab multiple times to line things up on each line, rather than setting the tabs correctly and pressing just once. Such documents take a lot of work to modify, so if you are building a large, complex document that will require modification in the future, make sure you learn about tabs first!

Inserting the date and time

Using the Insert ⇨ Date and Time command, you can quickly insert the date and time in several different formats (see Figure 2-2). The date and time entry is tied to your computer's clock, so it always uses the current date and time—assuming that time is correct, of course!

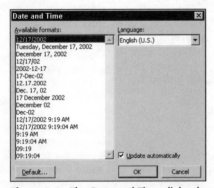

Figure 2-2: The Date and Time dialog box.

You can even enter the date and time into your document so that it automatically updates each time you print the document. To insert the date or time in a document, follow these steps:

1. Position the insertion point where you want to insert the date or time.

2. Choose Insert ➪ Date and Time. The Date and Time dialog box appears.

3. Select the Update Automatically check box in this dialog box to create a dynamic link to your computer's clock that updates the time or date entry.

4. Double-click the date or time format that you want in the Available Formats list, or select the entry and then click OK.

If you use *Update Automatically*, whenever you print the document or use Print Preview (see Chapter 6), the date fields update themselves automatically. You can also update a date field by right-clicking it and selecting Update Field, or by clicking it and pressing the F9 key. If you want to convert the automatic-update field to a non-update field, click in the field and press Shift+Ctrl+F9. You learn more about fields in Chapter 23.

Caution   There's a potential problem with these automatic dates. When you print an older document at a later date, you get the current date, not the original!

Note   If your computer's clock is not set correctly, double-click the time displayed in the Windows task bar or use the Date/Time utility in the Control panel to change the settings. (See Chapter 8 for information on searching the Internet from directly within Word. If you search for *correct time*, you'll find Web sites that can tell you exactly what time it is wherever you are.)

Splitting a document window for easier editing

With Word 2003, you can view different parts of a document at the same time by splitting the window into two panes. Perhaps you want to copy or move information from one area of the document to another, or simply refer to information in one part so that you can write something related to it in another. You can even work in a different view in each pane. For example, the document can be in Outline view in one pane and Normal view in the other.

Look carefully, and immediately above the upward-pointing triangle at the top of the vertical scrollbar you'll see the *split box*—a little gray rectangle. When you place the mouse pointer on this bar, a double-headed arrow divided by two short lines appears. The easiest way to split a document window is to double-click the bar. The document window is then split evenly into two panes with the split box at the top of the split (see Figure 2-3).

To adjust the size of the panes, drag the split box up or down. Or, instead of double-clicking and then readjusting, simply drag the bar down to the position you want. Note that each pane has its own scroll bar and ruler. To switch between panes, simply click in the pane you want to activate or press F6 to move the text-insertion bar between panes.

Split box

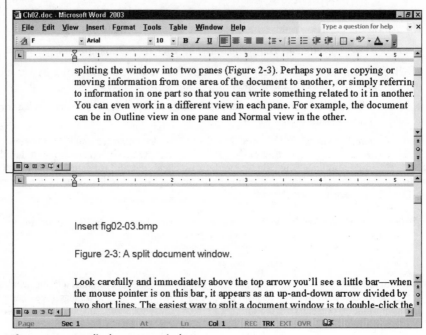

Figure 2-3: A split document window.

You can remove the split in the following three ways:

✦ Double-click the border between the two panes (the bar between the ruler at the top of the lower pane and the scroll bar at the bottom of the top pane); the split closes and the information in the upper pane remains visible in the full window.

✦ To close the split and leave the information in the lower pane visible, drag the border up to the top of the window and release.

✦ To close the split and leave the information in the upper pane visible, drag the border down to the bottom of the window and release.

You also can split a document window using the Window menu or the keyboard. Just choose Window ➪ Split or press Alt+Ctrl+S. Then use the up or down arrow to position the horizontal gray line where you want the split to be, and press Enter. After you split the window, the Split command in the Window menu changes to Remove Split. To remove the split using the Window menu or the keyboard, just choose Window ➪ Remove Split or press Alt+Ctrl+S again.

Navigating Through a Document

The insertion point shows where the text that you type will appear. As you type, Word scrolls the document to keep the insertion point visible in the window. To insert text in another part of your document, move the insertion point to that location and then insert the text. The following sections explain how to navigate through your document.

Commands for moving the insertion point and scrolling also are used in conjunction with keyboard commands for selecting text and graphics. This is explained later in this chapter.

Scroll bars move the insertion point

Word 2003 changes a very basic feature that you might not even think about but that is actually quite important. In earlier versions of Word, scrolling through a document using the scroll bar did *not* move the insertion point. For example, if you clicked on the scroll bar a number of times to view a lower part of the document, the insertion point would remain where you left it. Start typing and Word would jump back to the insertion point and place text there.

This actually confused many new users who assumed that when they saw a particular page on the screen, that would be where the insertion point was located. New users often lost the insertion point.

Word 2003 changes this behavior entirely. By default, when you scroll through the document, the insertion point moves to the page displayed. The cursor remains in the same position on the screen, regardless of which page or which part of a page is displayed.

However, if you prefer the old behavior, you can tell Word to switch back. Choose Tools ⇨ Options; under the Edit tab, look for the Use Smart Cursoring check box. Clear the check box, and Word 2003 works in the same manner as earlier versions.

Note As odd as the old insertion point behavior sounds, it's actually a very useful characteristic when you understand how it works. It allows you to view another part of the document to refer to information there, but then lets you begin typing and automatically continue working where you left off without having to navigate back to your original position.

If you do use the scroll bars to move down, using the old program behavior, and then decide you want to insert text at the new position, be sure to point and click with the mouse to position the insertion point at that new location.

Moving the insertion point with the scroll bar

To use the scroll bar to move the insertion point, you can use these methods:

✦ Click the triangle box at the top (to move up) or bottom (to move down) of the scroll bar to move one line (sometimes less!) at a time.

✦ Click inside the scroll bar, between the scroll box (the square that sits inside the scroll box) and one of the triangle boxes.

✦ Drag the scroll box up or down—this is especially useful because as you drag, Word displays a box showing which page, and even which heading, will be displayed if you release the box (see Figure 2-4).

✦ Click the double-headed arrows at the bottom of the vertical scroll bar to take you to the same position on the previous or next page. (See Chapter 3 for details on how this component works.)

✦ Press Shift and click on the scroll bar to move directly to the related position.

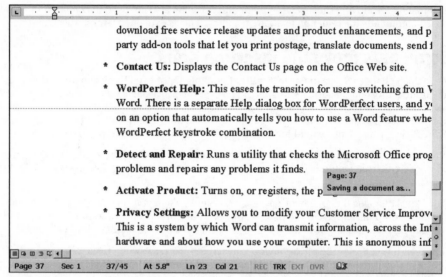

Figure 2-4: A page reference and header appears when you scroll through a document using the vertical scroll bar.

Remember, after displaying the page in which you want to work, click the specific location where you want to position the insertion point. The insertion point always stays within the margins. When you click outside the right margin or after the final paragraph mark of your document, the insertion point moves to the text closest to where you clicked. (When you click outside the left margin, however, you select a line.)

Of course there's also a horizontal scroll bar, and although you won't use it as much as the vertical one, you should know these functions:

✦ Use the triangle boxes, the scroll box, and the scroll bar, as with the vertical bar, to move left and right.

✦ Hold Shift and click the triangle box to move into the document margin.

Note   If the scroll bars are not visible, you can display them by choosing Tools ➪ Options, selecting the View tab, and then selecting the Vertical Scroll Bar and Horizontal Scroll Bar check boxes.

Using the keyboard to move the insertion point

Of course, you can also use the keyboard to move the insertion point. Table 2-1 describes the keyboard options for moving the insertion point within a document.

**Table 2-1: Keyboard Commands for Moving
the Insertion Point and Scrolling**

To Move	Press
One character to the left	Left-arrow key
One character to the right	Right-arrow key
One line up	Up-arrow key
One line down	Down-arrow key
One word to the left	Ctrl+left-arrow key
One word to the right	Ctrl+right-arrow key
To the end of a line	End
To the beginning of a line	Home
To the beginning of the current paragraph	Ctrl+up-arrow key
To the beginning of the preceding paragraph	Ctrl+up-arrow key twice
To the beginning of the next paragraph	Ctrl+down-arrow key
Up one screen	Page Up
Down one screen	Page Down
To the bottom of the screen (unless you've chosen something from the Select Browse Object menu, in which case it moves to the object — see Chapter 3)	Ctrl+Page Down
To the top of the screen (unless you've chosen something from the Select Browse Object menu)	Ctrl+Page Up
To the first character displayed in the window	Alt+Ctrl+Page Up
To the last character displayed in the window	Alt+Ctrl+Page Down
To the end of the document	Ctrl+End
To the beginning of the document	Ctrl+Home
To the preceding insertion point location	Shift+F5 or Alt+Ctrl+Z

Returning to the location of your last edit

When you work on a large document, finding the exact location where you performed your last edit can be tedious. Word makes it easy, however, by remembering the last three locations where you either entered or edited text. To return to the location of your last edit, just press Shift+F5. Word then moves the insertion point to the location where you last edited the document. The next two times that you press Shift+F5, Word moves to the previous two locations where you entered or edited text.

Note Shift+F5 even works when you open an existing document. Press Shift+F5 and you'll jump to the place at which the insertion point was positioned the very last time you saved the document before closing it.

Navigating using the Go To tab

You can use the Go To tab of the Find and Replace dialog box to move the insertion point anywhere in your document. Choose Edit ➪ Go To, press Ctrl+G or F5, or double-click in either of the first two sections of the status bar at the bottom of the Word window to display the Find and Replace dialog box with the Go To tab already selected.

The Go To tab contains the Go to What list that shows where you can move in the document (see Figure 2-5). You can go to just about any location: sections, lines, footnotes, annotations, graphics, tables, and so on.

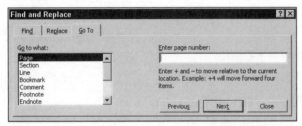

Figure 2-5: The Go To tab of the Find and Replace dialog box.

Cross-Reference For information on using the Find and Replace tabs and their respective dialog boxes located beneath the Go To tab, see Chapter 3.

To use the Go To tab, choose the item you are looking for from the Go to What list box. To go to the next selected item, choose Next. To go to a specific occurrence of the item that you selected, type a number in the Enter box. The Enter box changes its name in relation to the category you choose. For example, when you choose the Line option, the Enter box name changes to Enter Line Number.

The Go To tab also allows you to move forward or backward a specific number of occurrences for most of the options in the Go to What list. Select the item that you want and then type a plus or minus sign in the Enter box followed by the number of occurrences of the selected item that you want to move. (The plus sign is optional — omit it and Word assumes you want to move forward.) For example, to move forward seven pages, choose Page in the Go to What box and type **7** (or **+7**) in the Enter Page Number text box. To move back seven pages, choose Page in the Go to What box and type **–7** in the Enter Page Number text box.

With the Go To command, you can even specify a percentage of an item selected in the Go to What list box. For example, to move to a location 50 percent of the way from the beginning of the document, select the Page item in the Go to What list, type **50%** in the Enter box, and then click the Go To button.

The Edit ➪ Find command also allows you move to specific text quickly. This is discussed in Chapter 3.

Selecting Text and Graphics

Before moving, copying, deleting, or otherwise changing text and graphics, you must first select the item. The general rule is to *select* and then *do*, and this rule applies to nearly every action you perform in Word. You can select with the mouse or with the keyboard. Word highlights selected text or graphics. To cancel most selections, just click outside the selection or use the arrow keys to move the insertion point.

Selecting text and graphics using the mouse

You can select words, sentences, and areas of text by double-clicking, dragging, or pressing a key as you click. To select lines, paragraphs, or an entire document, use the *selection bar*, which is the invisible area along the left edge of the text area. You can identify the selection bar by moving the mouse pointer to the left side of your document; when the pointer is in the selection bar, it changes from an insertion point to a right-pointing arrow. Table 2-2 describes the different ways to select text and graphics using the mouse.

Table 2-2: Mouse Options for Making Selections

To Select	Do This
A word	Double-click the word.
A line of text	Click in the selection bar to the left of the line.
Multiple lines of text	Click and drag in the selection bar in the direction of the lines you want to select.
A sentence	Hold down Ctrl, and then click in the sentence you want to select.
A paragraph	Click three times, at the same speed as a double-click, on a word in the paragraph. Double-click in the selection bar to the left of the paragraph.
Multiple paragraphs	Drag the selection bar in the direction of the paragraphs you want to select.
Any item or amount of text	Click where you want the selection to begin, hold down Shift, and then click where you want the selection to end. Click and drag the mouse pointer across the text.
An entire document	Triple-click in the selection bar.
A vertical block of text	Hold down Alt, click the mouse button, and then drag.
A graphic	Click the graphic.

If you begin selecting in the middle of a word and drag to include part of a second word, Word will probably select both words and even the spaces after them. This is a feature that is called *automatic word selection*, and although it's often very useful, some people find it rather irritating. You can turn it off by choosing Tools ➪ Options and selecting the Edit tab. Under Editing Options, clear the When Selecting, Automatically Select Entire Word check box.

You can select text and graphics quickly by positioning the insertion point at the beginning of the text or graphic that you want. Then hold down the Shift key, and click where you want the selection to end.

Selecting text and graphics using the keyboard

If you know the key combination to move the insertion point, you can select text using that key combination while holding down the Shift key. For example, Ctrl+right arrow moves the insertion point to the next word, and Ctrl+Shift+right arrow selects the text from the insertion point to the beginning of the next word. Table 2-3 describes how you can select text or graphics using the keyboard.

Table 2-3: Keyboard Options for Making Selections

To Select	Press
One character to the right	Shift+right-arrow key
One character to the left	Shift+left-arrow key
To the end of a word	Ctrl+Shift+right-arrow key
To the beginning of a word	Ctrl+Shift+left-arrow key
To the end of a line	Shift+End
To the beginning of a line	Shift+Home
One line down	Shift+down-arrow key
One line up	Shift+up-arrow key
To the end of a paragraph	Ctrl+Shift+down-arrow key
To the beginning of a paragraph	Ctrl+Shift+up-arrow key
One screen up	Shift+Page Up
To the end of a document	Ctrl+Shift+End
To the beginning of a document	Ctrl+Shift+Home
To include the whole document	Ctrl+A or Ctrl+5 (on the numeric keypad)

Making multiple selections

Here's a neat little trick for selecting multiple, noncontiguous items. For instance, say you want to select paragraph A, skip paragraph B, and select paragraph C. Start by selecting paragraph A, using whatever method you want. Then press Ctrl, and while still holding down the key use the mouse to drag over paragraph C, selecting that paragraph. You'll now have two noncontiguous blocks of selected text.

Using the Extend Selection mode

The F8 key is called the *Extend Selection key*. This key is a great way to select text in Word because it allows you to take your finger off the Shift key while making your selection. When you are trying to select text from point A to point B and you're not quite sure where point B is in the document, this feature is very useful. While in Extend Selection mode, you can use any method for moving around in the document—Word highlights all the text between the original insertion point and the current insertion point.

To start and stop an extended selection, follow these steps:

1. Move the insertion point to the beginning of the text that you want to select.

2. Press F8 (Extend Selection), or double-click the EXT box in the status bar. You are now in Extend Selection mode.

3. Move to the end of the text you want to select using the method of your choice.

4. Press Esc to exit Extend Selection mode—the text remains highlighted, but if you move the cursor now you'll lose the selection. Or, press Shift+F5 to move back to the original position and "release" all the highlighted text.

You can use any method for moving around while in Extend Selection mode. For example, press F8 to start, press F5 to open the Go To box, and use it to go to any point in the document. Or turn on Extend Selection mode and use the scroll bar to move somewhere in the document; then click in the page to highlight text from the origination point.

You also can use the F8 key to select specific units of text, such as a word, sentence, or paragraph. For example, pressing the F8 key twice selects the word where the insertion point is. Table 2-4 lists the F8 options for selecting specific units of text. Before pressing F8, however, make sure the insertion point is in the unit of text that you want. To shrink a selection and make it smaller than the current one, press Shift+F8 as many times as needed to decrease the selection.

Table 2-4: Options for Selecting Specific Units of Text Using the F8 Key

To Select	Press F8
The current word	2 times
The current sentence	3 times
The current paragraph	4 times
The entire section	5 times
The entire document	6 times

Deleting Text and Graphics

With Word 2003, you can delete text and graphics quickly. To replace text, just select the text and begin typing. Once you press a key, Word replaces the selected text with the new text. If you don't want a selection to be replaced as you type, choose Tools ➪ Options, select the Edit tab, and then clear the Typing Replaces Selection check box (this is an unusual feature that most people do *not* use—it seems natural that if you type over something you replace it, and it can save you a lot of time). Table 2-5 describes Word's keyboard deletion options. Word also allows you to delete any selected text or graphics using the Edit ➪ Clear ➪ Contents command, which works in the same way as pressing the Delete key (and thus is not particularly useful).

Table 2-5: Deletion Options

To Delete	Press
Selected text	Backspace or Delete
Characters before the insertion point	Backspace
Characters after the insertion point	Delete
A word before the insertion point	Ctrl+Backspace
A word after the insertion point	Ctrl+Delete

Undoing Actions

When you make a mistake in Word, you can undo that action or command. For example, if you accidentally delete a word, you can easily bring it back. Then, if you decide to go through with the action or command after all, you can even redo it. Word provides three methods to undo or redo your most recent action:

✦ Click the Undo button or the Redo button on the Standard toolbar.

✦ Choose Undo or Redo from the Edit menu.

✦ Press the shortcut keys Ctrl+Z (undo) or Ctrl+Y (redo).

To undo or redo multiple actions, use the Undo or Redo command multiple times. Or click the arrow beside either the Undo or Redo button to display a list of actions. Figure 2-6 shows a sample list of previous actions that might appear after you click the Undo button. Click or drag to select the actions that you want to undo or redo. Undo and redo actions are performed in the sequential order of the original actions. You cannot undo certain actions, however, such as saving a document, and you can't undo an item several steps back without undoing the items that occurred *after* it.

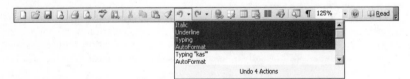

Figure 2-6: Clicking the Undo button displays a list of previously executed actions.

Moving and Copying Text and Graphics

At the heart of word processing is the ability to manipulate text. After you rapidly fire off your ideas, Word 2003 makes it easy to delete, copy, or move text. The following sections explain the essential Word tools for manipulating text and graphics in a document.

Using the Clipboard

Cutting differs from *deleting*, because text that is cut is stored in the *Clipboard,* which is a temporary storage area for cut or copied selections. After you have cut or copied a selection, you can *paste* (insert) it anywhere in your document, multiple times if you wish.

Cutting removes the original selection from the document and places a copy in the Clipboard; *copying* makes a copy of the selected text or graphic but leaves the original selection unchanged.

After you paste a selection that you have copied or cut, it remains on the Clipboard so that you can continue pasting the text into new locations as often as you want. But Word has a very useful feature. Whereas, in the past, most Windows programs held only one thing at a time in the Clipboard, Word now lets you store multiple items. The next few sections explain the basic copy and paste functions and then look at the Clipboard task pane.

Note When you quit Word after cutting or copying large amounts of text or graphics to the Clipboard, the program may display a dialog box that asks if you want to save the Clipboard contents. If you plan to use its contents with another application, save the Clipboard; if you don't, choose No to clear the Clipboard.

Using the Cut, Copy, and Paste buttons

Use the Cut, Copy, and Paste buttons on the Standard toolbar to move or copy text or graphics within a document, among different documents, or among most applications.

To move or copy text and graphics using the Standard toolbar, follow these steps:

1. Select the text or graphic that you want to move or copy.

2. Do one of the following:

   • Click the Cut button (the scissors) on the Standard toolbar to move the selection.

   • Click the Copy button (the two overlapping pages) on the Standard toolbar to copy the selection.

3. Word places the text on the Clipboard.

4. Position the insertion point at the new location. If the new location is in another document or application, open or switch to that document or application. If the new location is in a Word document that already is open, choose that document from the Window menu.

5. Click the Paste button (the Clipboard with a document in front) to paste the item.

Paste Options and Paste Special

One of the most overlooked editing commands is Paste Special. This is unfortunate because Paste Special can save you a lot of time by providing options not available with the standard Paste command. In the past, Paste Special was hidden away on the Edit menu; most users didn't even know it was there. However, Word 2003 now provides the Paste Options button that appears in the document when you paste, so it's hard to ignore.

If you're inserting text with special formatting, for example, you can control whether to insert the text with or without that formatting. Many times, people cut and paste formatted text into a document and then wonder why that text appears different from the existing text. The best way to make text match the current document's text is to choose Edit ➪ Paste Special and then choose the Unformatted Text option. To retain the formatting of the original text, choose Formatted Text (RTF). RTF stands for Rich Text Format, and it instructs Word to retain the text's basic format. You can even choose to insert text copied from another application as an image.

When you paste material into your document from another Word document or another application such as Microsoft Excel, use the Edit ➪ Paste Special command to link the pasted item to its original file. The item in your Word document is then updated whenever you make changes to the original file.

Cross-Reference For more information about exchanging information with other applications, see Chapter 20.

The Paste Options button appears when you paste something into a document. Point at the button and a triangle appears; click the triangle to open the menu, and select one of the following:

✦ **Keep Source Formatting:** To maintain its original formatting

✦ **Match Destination Formatting:** To format the text in the same way the paragraph you inserted it into is formatted

✦ **Keep Text Only:** To throw away all formatting, keeping the destination formatting, but also throwing away the paragraph break, if there is one

✦ **Apply Style or Formatting:** To select the formatting you want to use for this text

Cross-Reference See Chapter 13 for more information on styles.

Moving and copying with commands and keyboard shortcuts

You can use commands and keyboard shortcuts to copy and move selections as well. To copy a selection, choose Edit ➪ Copy, move the insertion point to the location where you want to insert the copied selection, and then choose Edit ➪ Paste. To move a selection, choose Edit ➪ Cut, move the insertion point to the location where you want to insert the cut selection, and then choose Edit ➪ Paste. Word's shortcut keys make copying and moving selections using the keyboard much faster. Table 2-6 describes these keyboard shortcuts.

 Tip Note the items in the table that have to do with moving paragraphs. You can move a paragraph by simply placing the cursor anywhere in the paragraph (no need to select it all); then press Alt+Shift+up-arrow to move it in front of the previous paragraph, for instance.

Table 2-6: Keyboard Shortcuts for Copying and Moving Selections

To Do This	Press
Copy selected text and graphics to the Clipboard	Ctrl+C
Move selected text and graphics to the Clipboard	Ctrl+X
Paste Clipboard contents in a document	Ctrl+V
Move a paragraph up	Alt+Shift+up-arrow key
Move a paragraph down	Alt+Shift+down-arrow key
Move a selection to another location	Press F2, place the insertion point in the new position, and press Enter.
Copy a selection to another location	Press Shift+F2, place the insertion point in the new position, and press Enter.

You may find it helpful to use mnemonics to remember the shortcut commands for cutting, copying, and pasting. For example, you might think of X as looking like scissors, C as standing for copying, and V as the insert text symbol in proofreading marks. One editor says that she uses the mnemonic *V is for vomit, spewing something forth* to remember the shortcut for pasting. Also, note the sequence of these three keys on your keyboard: X, C, and then V. They mirror the toolbar's sequence of Cut, Copy, and Paste, which are the commands to which these keys correspond.

Moving and copying with the shortcut menu

As if all these methods weren't enough, Word also includes a shortcut menu that allows you to cut, copy, or paste text. Simply right-click the mouse in the document area and the menu appears. Remember, however, that unless you have selected text, the menu item appears dimmed.

Tip

There are two other ways to open this shortcut menu. Most keyboards created for PCs over the last few years contain a shortcut-menu key—it generally has a picture of a little menu with an arrow pointing at it. Press this key to open the shortcut menu associated with the component or text on which your insertion point is placed. If you don't have this key, press Shift+F10.

You can mix and match keyboard and mouse methods to perform copy and move operations as well. For example, you can press Ctrl+C and then right-click and choose Paste from the shortcut menu.

Using the Office Clipboard

A nifty Microsoft Office tool that works well with Word is the Office Clipboard. In the past, you could copy and paste only the last item you placed on the Clipboard. When you copied or cut text or a graphic, the existing Clipboard entry was replaced. The Office Clipboard, however, is a tool that allows you to choose from any of the last 24 copied items. (The system collects items from any Windows application, not just those that are part of the Office suite). If you try to copy a 25th item, Word displays a message box informing you that there's no room for more items in the Clipboard. Continue copying, and Word removes the first item in the Clipboard to make room.

To display the Clipboard task pane, choose Edit ⇨ Office Clipboard, or press Ctrl+C twice rapidly (see Figure 2-7). Table 2-7 describes the Clipboard functions.

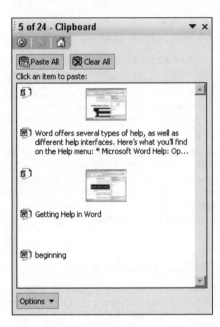

Figure 2-7: The Office Clipboard allows you to store as many as 24 copied or cut items.

Table 2-7: The Clipboard Task Pane Functions

Button or Procedure	Action
Paste All	Pastes all items in the Clipboard into your document at the current insertion point
Clear All	Removes all items from the Clipboard
Click on an item in the Clipboard	Pastes the item into the document
Point at the item and click the triangle; then select Delete	Removes just that item from the Clipboard

A number of options are related to the Clipboard. Click the Options button in the task pane to open a menu with the choices shown in Table 2-8.

Table 2-8: The Clipboard Options

Option	Purpose
Show Office Clipboard Automatically	The Clipboard opens automatically the *second time* you cut or copy something
Show Office Clipboard When Ctrl+C Pressed Twice	Pressing Ctrl+C twice opens the Clipboard task pane
Collect Without Showing Office Clipboard	Items are copied to the Clipboard without opening the task pane.
Show Office Clipboard Icon on Taskbar	Select this to put an icon on the Windows taskbar whenever the Office Clipboard task pane is open—you can right-click the icon to open a menu allowing you to clear or close the Clipboard
Show Status Near Taskbar When Copying	A status message will appear near the taskbar warning you if you are running out of space on the Clipboard—not so useful if you are in Word, but useful if you are copying from other, non-Office applications

Note   You can permanently store text and graphics as well, for use over and over again, with the AutoText command. This is explained later in this chapter.

Cut and Paste options

You can control the manner in which cut and paste works in a variety of ways. Choose Tools ➪ Options, select the Edit tab, and you'll see options under the Cut and Paste options area. The Settings button opens a box with more options. Table 2-9 explains these options.

Table 2-9: Cut and Paste Options

Option	Purpose
Show Paste Options buttons	If this isn't selected, you won't see the Paste Options button in your document when you paste something (as explained earlier).
Smart cut and paste	Clear this if you *don't* want to use the following options, displayed by clicking the Settings button.
Use default options for	You can make Cut and Paste work just as it did in Word 2002 or Word 97 through 2000; selecting one of these adjusts the Individual Options settings.

Continued

Table 2-9 *(continued)*

Option	Purpose
Adjust sentence and word spacing automatically	When you paste text, Word automatically inserts and removes spaces to make it fit properly.
Adjust paragraph spacing on paste	As with the preceding option, Word attempts to properly space a paragraph when you insert.
Adjust table formatting and alignment on paste	Word tries to clean up pasted tables to make them fit properly.
Smart style behavior	When the text you are pasting has the same style name as a style in the document into which you are pasting, the text takes on the formatting for the style in the new document.
Merge formatting when pasting from PowerPoint	When pasting from PowerPoint, Word will attempt to merge the formatting from that application into your document.
Adjust formatting when pasting from Microsoft Excel	When pasting from Excel, Word will adjust the text to the document's format.
Merge pasted lists with surrounding lists	If you paste a list of items into a list in your document, Word will attempt to merge the lists properly.

Drag-and-drop editing

Drag-and-drop editing with the mouse is an easy way to move or copy a selection. This feature is especially convenient for copying or moving text a short distance or between two documents that appear on the screen simultaneously. Drag-and-drop editing also allows you to scroll through a document to copy or move text and graphics over long distances, such as numerous pages. To scroll through a document when performing a drag-and-drop operation, drag the selected item beneath the horizontal ruler or above the horizontal scroll bar.

Note   If you cannot use the drag-and-drop feature, choose Tools ➪ Options and select the Edit tab. Then, under Editing Options, select the Drag-and-Drop Text Editing check box.

A quick way to gather several pieces of text and graphics for pasting is to use a second document window. Or, you can drag and drop selections onto the desktop to create scrap documents. To open and work with a new document window, choose File ➪ New and then Window ➪ Arrange All. Use drag-and-drop editing to move or copy text and graphics between the document windows.

To move or copy text and graphics between windows using drag-and-drop editing, follow these steps:

1. Select the text or graphics that you want to move.

2. Do one of the following:

   • To move a selection, point to the selection and hold down the mouse button until you see the drag-and-drop pointer.

   • To copy a selection, hold down the Ctrl key, point to the selection, and then hold down the mouse button until you see the drag-and-drop pointer.

3. Drag the pointer to the new location. Note that the object is inserted at the location of the insertion point, not at the pointer.

4. Release the mouse button to drop the text into place.

Tip   Here's another quick way to move text. Select the text, point at the place where you want to insert it, and then press Ctrl while right-clicking. To copy instead of just moving the text, press Ctrl+Shift while you right-click.

Document scraps and shortcuts

The drag-and-drop editing feature allows you to select text in the document window and then drag and drop the selected text on the desktop. This creates a document scrap that can be dragged into another document or into the existing document. By default, text is copied rather than moved from the current document. To move text from your document to the desktop, press the Shift key when you drag the selected text. On the desktop, the first part of the selected text appears after the icon labeled Document Scrap. Double-click the Document Scrap icon, and Word displays the document, just as it does any Word document.

A shortcut menu is also available for dragging text to the desktop. Using the right mouse button to drag selected text to the desktop displays a shortcut menu, which helps you to decide how to handle the scrap. Four options appear on the shortcut menu, allowing you to choose whether to copy the selection (Copy Scrap Here), to move the selection (Move Scrap Here), to create a document shortcut (Create Document Shortcut Here) to the selected text in the original document, or to cancel (Cancel) the drag-and-drop operation.

Instead of using the menu to move text to the desktop, you can use the left mouse button and simply press and hold down the Shift key. Alternatively, you can press and hold the Alt button to create a shortcut.

Dragging a scrap document from the desktop to a document copies the selection into the document and works the same way no matter which mouse button you use. To delete a Document Scrap, right-click the icon and then choose Delete from the shortcut menu.

Using the Spike for multiple cut-and-paste operations

When you want to remove several items from one or more documents and insert them as a group elsewhere, you can use the Spike. In most cases, you should use the new Clipboard to copy and paste multiple items, but the Spike can be useful in some cases because it's a very fast way to collect and paste items.

The Spike is a multiple cut-and-paste tool that collects, in order, each item that you delete. The first item you cut appears at the top of the Spike entry, the second item follows it, and so on. Word separates items with a paragraph mark. When you insert the contents of the Spike, you can choose either to clear the Spike or to save the items to use again. The Spike allows you to cut and paste data both to and from multiple documents.

To move selections using the Spike, follow these steps:

1. Select the text or graphic that you want to move to the Spike.

2. Press Ctrl+F3. Word removes the selected text or graphic and adds it to the Spike.

3. Repeat steps 1 and 2 for each item that you want to collect in the Spike.

4. Position the insertion point where you want to insert the contents of the Spike.

5. Do one of the following:

   - To paste the text and keep the contents of the Spike after pasting, type **spike** at the location where you want to paste and press F3.

   - To paste the text and clear the contents of the Spike, press Ctrl+Shift+F3.

Note   You cannot copy text to the Spike—the text is removed from the document and placed in the Spike. However, it is easy to get around this limitation, especially if you are moving a number of items but only want to copy some of them. Simply *spike* the item (select it and press Ctrl+F3), and then immediately press Ctrl+Z to Undo the action. The removed text is replaced, but it still remains in the Spike.

By the way, the Spike contents remain until you clear the Spike. Even if you close Word and come back a month later, the Spike contents are still there.

Pasting text into other documents

The formatting that Word applies to pasted text depends on whether the copied text includes a section break and whether the document to which you copy is empty. A section break contains all of the formatting for the section that precedes it. Section formatting includes margins, number of columns, line numbers, page size and orientation, and headers and footers. Each document has at least one section. The last paragraph mark in a Word document functions like a section break: It contains all of the section formatting for the last section of a document. If you include the last paragraph mark when you copy or move text, one of the following happens:

✦ If you include a section break when you copy or move text, you create a new section when you paste that text into another document. The formatting in the copied or moved section break then is applied to all text that precedes it, either up to an existing section break or to the beginning of the document.

✦ If the document into which you paste the text is empty, Word applies the section formatting of the document from which the text was copied. For example, any headers or footers in the document from which you copied the text now become part of the document into which you paste that text.

✦ If the document into which you paste the text is not empty, the pasted text takes on the section formatting of that document. For example, headers and footers copied with the section break are discarded, and Word retains the headers and footers of the document into which you paste the text.

✦ When you copy text without including either a section break or the final paragraph mark, the section formatting is not copied. The text then takes on the section formatting of the document into which it is pasted.

Inserting Symbols and Special Characters

In addition to the letters, numbers, and punctuation marks shown on the keyboard, numerous fonts include many other special characters, such as bullets, copyright and trademark symbols, curly quotes, foreign characters, and em as well as en dashes. (Em dashes are used to interrupt or highlight a thought in a sentence, and en dashes are used to represent the word *to* or *through* between words or numbers.)

You can insert these characters using the Symbol command or a unique key combination. Word includes several shortcut keys for symbols, and you can assign custom shortcut key combinations to symbols that you frequently use.

Word also includes an Equation Editor that allows you to insert mathematical symbols or create equations.

Cross-Reference   For more information on the Equation Editor, see Chapter 21.

Using the Symbol command

When you choose Insert ➪ Symbol, the Symbol dialog box (see Figure 2-8) displays those symbols available for the font that you're using. The fonts that ship with Word contain tens of thousands of alphabetic characters, ideographic characters, and symbols. Fonts that follow the Unicode standard contain characters for foreign languages, so you can insert special foreign characters and edit text in a variety of languages.

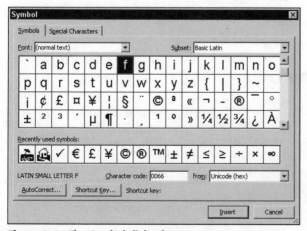

Figure 2-8: The Symbol dialog box.

All fonts installed in Windows that are based on the ANSI character set use the (normal text) entry in the Font drop-down list in the Symbol dialog box. Fonts that don't comply with the ANSI character set are listed by name on the Font drop-down list in the Symbol dialog box.

Note So what characters are part of the ANSI character set? You can find the character set online at various Web sites, such as www.fingertipsoft.com/3dkbd/ansitable.html or http://tatumweb.com/typerat/ansirodent.htm.

The Symbol dialog box remains open until you click Cancel or Close, thus allowing you to scroll through a document and insert symbols repeatedly without having to choose the Symbol command each time. When you're using AutoCorrect and you type certain characters, they automatically change into symbols. For example, type **(c)** and Word automatically changes it into ©. To give you more symbol creation abilities, the Symbol dialog box contains a button that takes you to AutoCorrect.

Note Symbols and special characters in non-ANSI fonts, such as those of the Symbol font, are protected if you insert them via the Symbol dialog box. Otherwise, when you change the font of a symbol, you also might change the symbol itself. For example, selecting the entire document and choosing an ANSI font that contains a Wingdings symbol does not change the Wingdings character to the ANSI font character. To change a protected character, you must delete it, choose the font that you want to use, and then insert the symbol again.

To insert symbols using the Symbol dialog box, follow these steps:

1. Position the insertion point where you want to insert the symbol.

2. Choose Insert ➪ Symbol.

3. Select the symbol you want. Either select from the list under the Special Characters tab, or on the Symbols tab select from the Recently Used Symbols, or select a Font and then pick a character. Although all fonts have characters that may be useful to you, take a particular look at the Wingdings and Webdings fonts.

4. Double-click the symbol you want, or click once and then click the Insert button. Word inserts the character in the point size of the text that precedes the insertion point.

5. To insert another symbol, position the insertion point in the document and repeat step 4. If you are using the keyboard, press Ctrl+Tab to move between the Symbol dialog box and your document.

6. After you finish inserting symbols, click Close.

Entering a character code

Every character in a character set has a unique three-number code. When you click a symbol in the Symbol dialog box, the Character Code box displays that code. For fonts that are ANSI-based, these codes are standardized. To insert a symbol into your document by typing its ANSI code, press Alt+0 and the code number with the numeric keypad; for example, pressing Alt+0153 inserts the trademark symbol (™) at the insertion point.

Tip If you use a laptop, you will probably have to turn on Num Lock and use the special numeric keypad keys to enter characters using character codes—you won't be able to use the number keys at the top of your keyboard. See your user manual for more information.

Don't confuse character codes, however, with the shortcut keys that Word assigns to commonly used characters. If a shortcut key is assigned to a symbol, that key appears after the Shortcut Key label in the Symbol dialog box.

To insert a symbol using the ANSI character code, follow these steps:

1. Position the insertion point where you want to insert the symbol.

2. Make sure that Num Lock is activated.

3. Hold down Alt, and press 0 (zero) on the numeric keypad followed by the appropriate ANSI character code.

The AutoCorrect command allows you to insert any symbol as you type, as is explained later in this chapter.

Using the Symbol dialog box and shortcut keys

The Special Characters tab (see Figure 2-9) in the Symbol dialog box (Insert ➪ Symbol) includes a collection of frequently used symbols and special characters. These special characters have been assigned to shortcut keys so that you can insert them quickly. For example, you can insert the copyright symbol © directly in your document and avoid displaying the Symbol dialog box by pressing Alt+Ctrl+C. Table 2-10 lists some of Word's default shortcut keys for special characters.

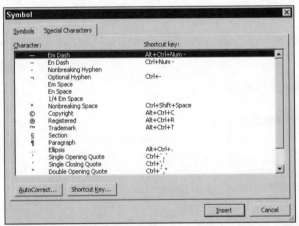

Figure 2-9: The Special Characters tab of the Symbol dialog box.

Using shortcut keys to insert a symbol

If you frequently insert a particular symbol, you can assign it a custom shortcut key and then insert the symbol simply by pressing that shortcut key rather than using the Symbol command. If the symbol is a non-ANSI font, inserting it with a shortcut key is advantageous, because the shortcut key inserts the symbol as a protected character.

Table 2-10: Shortcut Keys for Common Special Characters

Character	Shortcut Key
Em dash	Alt+Ctrl+– (minus sign on numeric keypad)
En dash	Ctrl+– (minus sign on numeric keypad)
Nonbreaking hyphen	Ctrl+Shift+- (hyphen)
Optional hyphen	Ctrl+- (not the numeric keypad)
Nonbreaking space	Ctrl+Shift+spacebar
Copyright	Alt+Ctrl+C
Registered	Alt+Ctrl+R
Trademark	Alt+Ctrl+T
Ellipsis	Alt+Ctrl+.

To assign a symbol to a shortcut key, follow these steps:

1. Choose Insert ➪ Symbol.

2. Select the Symbols or Special Character tab containing the character that you want.

3. Select the symbol or character that you want.

4. Click the Shortcut Key button. The Customize Keyboard dialog box then appears with the chosen symbol displayed (see Figure 2-10).

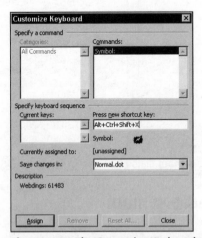

Figure 2-10: The Customize Keyboard dialog box.

5. In the Press New Shortcut Key box, type the key combination that you want to use for the symbol or character and click Assign.

6. Click the Close button to return to the Symbol dialog box.

7. Repeat steps 3 through 6 for each symbol you want to assign to a shortcut key combination.

8. When you finish assigning symbols to keys, click Close in the Customize dialog box and then click Close in the Symbol dialog box.

You can insert any symbol automatically with the AutoCorrect command, as explained in the following sections.

AutoCorrect and AutoText

The AutoCorrect and AutoText commands both allow you to insert frequently used boilerplate text and graphics. With AutoCorrect, Word inserts your previously created entries automatically as you type. For example, when you type **(r)**, Word inserts the registered symbol ®. You also can use AutoCorrect to correct misspelled words or insert a symbol not available on the keyboard. For example, AutoCorrect can replace *teh* with *the* automatically (see Chapter 8). AutoText entries are inserted after you choose the AutoText command or type the entry name and use a shortcut key.

Tip What's the difference between AutoCorrect and AutoText? AutoCorrect automatically makes changes to your typing—if you don't like the result you can undo, but Word doesn't ask your permission first. AutoText, on the other hand, is like a library of boilerplate text. Word may recognize something it has in the library when you type the right characters, but it won't insert it unless you give it permission.

Working with AutoCorrect

When you store an AutoCorrect entry, Word saves that entry with its original formatting if the selection contains fields, symbols, paragraph marks, imported graphics, or objects other than text. If the selection contains only text, Word stores the entry as plain text (without formatting). Whenever you type the name of an AutoCorrect entry followed by a space, Word inserts the entry. For example, suppose you create an entry called *ms* for the company name *Microsoft*. Whenever you type **ms** followed by a space, Word replaces *ms* with *Microsoft*. Word's AutoCorrect feature also can understand that if you add an apostrophe *s* ('s) to the entry, it should change the text to the possessive form. For example, if you type **ms's**, AutoCorrect changes the entry to a possessive form. So *ms's Style Guide* is changed automatically to *Microsoft's Style Guide*. In addition, AutoCorrect allows you to replace text with symbols automatically, as explained earlier. To undo an AutoCorrect entry, simply click the Undo button on the Standard toolbar or press Ctrl+Z.

Creating AutoCorrect entries

You can create an AutoCorrect entry in several ways, such as by entering text in the AutoCorrect dialog box or by selecting a block of text or graphics before choosing the Tools ⇨ AutoCorrect command.

Cross-Reference Chapter 8 looks at using AutoCorrect for spelling errors and mistyping.

The length of an AutoCorrect entry is limited only by the available memory. Word 2003 comes with a set of predefined AutoCorrect entries as well. After entering or selecting an AutoCorrect entry, you must give it a unique name. Here are some guidelines for naming an AutoCorrect entry:

✦ An AutoCorrect name can be as long as 31 characters.

✦ Don't use a common word to name an AutoCorrect entry unless you alter that word. For example, don't name an entry *address*. Instead, precede it with an asterisk or other character to make it unique, such as **address*. When you don't make the word unique, Word inserts the AutoCorrect entry whenever you type that word, whether you want it to or not.

To add an item based on existing text, follow this procedure:

1. Highlight the text and select Tools ➪ AutoCorrect Options. The AutoCorrect dialog box opens, as shown in Figure 2-11.

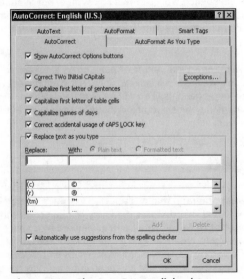

Figure 2-11: The AutoCorrect dialog box.

2. Select the Plain Text or Formatted Text option button. If you always want the text you insert to have the formatting of the original, pick the latter.

3. Type a name in the Replace text box.

4. Click Add.

You can create entries without selecting text first. Simply open the dialog box and type the replacements text in the With text box.

AutoCorrect options

The AutoCorrect dialog box also includes a variety of options under two tabs: The AutoCorrect tab and the AutoFormat as You Type tab. Table 2-11 explains the AutoFormat as You Type options.

Cross-Reference We explain the AutoCorrect tab in Chapter 8 because these are really correction tools intended to fix errors. The other tabs in the AutoCorrect dialog box control AutoText (discussed shortly), AutoFormat, and Smart Tags. We look at AutoFormat and Smart Tags in Chapters 13 and 23, respectively.

Table 2-11: AutoFormat as You Type Options

Option	Action
"Straight quotes" with "smart quotes"	Replaces straight quotation marks and apostrophes with more typographically correct *curly* quotes.
Ordinals (1st) with superscript	Replaces *st* and *rd* with superscript characters. For instance, 3rd becomes 3rd.
Fractions (1/2) with fraction character	1/2 becomes ½, for instance. Doesn't work with all fractions, though. 11/32 won't convert, for example, nor will 7/8. In fact, it doesn't even work with 1/3.
Hyphens (--) with dash (—)	Replaces two hyphens (--) with the more typographically correct em dash.
Bold and _italic_ with real formatting	Type *these words* and you'll get **these words**. People who write a lot of e-mails using e-mail systems that don't allow real formatting may like this feature.
Internet and network paths with hyperlinks	Type an Internet address, such as www.microsoft.com/ and Word creates an actual link that you can click on to open your browser.
Automatic bulleted lists	Type * followed by a tab and some text, press Enter, and Word assumes you want to create a bulleted list.
Automatic numbered lists	Same as the bulleted list, but start with a number.
Border lines	Type --- (three hyphens), press Enter, and Word inserts a line across the page.
Tables	Type + signs and hyphens to create a table. For example, type +-+-+-+-+ and press Enter, and Word creates a 4-column table. Increase the width of columns by increasing the number of hyphens between + signs.
Built-in heading styles	Word automatically applies headings to text it assumes is supposed to be a heading. This one can be a real nuisance.

Continued

Table 2-11 *(continued)*

Option	Action
Format beginning of list item like the one before it	Word watches how you format the first item in a list and then formats subsequent items the same. If the first word in the first list item is bold, all the items in the list will be formatted like that. In theory. Doesn't work well.
Set left- and first-indent with tabs and backspaces	This one can be very irritating. Press Tab, type some text, press Enter, and Word adjusts the margin on the next paragraph to match the tabbed margin you've just created.
Define styles based on your formatting	Creates new styles based on manual formatting you apply to a paragraph. Styles are covered in Chapter 13.

Changing or deleting AutoCorrect entries

You can rename, change, or delete any AutoCorrect entry. The method you use to change an entry depends on whether that entry was created from a formatted selection or was entered as plain text in the dialog box.

To rename or delete an AutoCorrect entry, follow these steps:

1. Choose Tools ➪ AutoCorrect.

2. Do one of the following:

  • To change the name of an AutoCorrect entry, select the AutoCorrect entry name in the list and then click Delete. Type a new name in the Replace box, and click Add.

  • To delete an AutoCorrect entry, select the entry you want to remove and click Delete.

3. Choose OK.

In addition to changing an AutoCorrect text entry, you can easily replace an existing entry. To do so, insert the existing entry in your document, make your changes, and then select the revised entry. Choose Tools ➪ AutoCorrect, type the existing AutoCorrect name in the Replace box, and click the Replace button. When Word displays a message asking if you want to redefine the entry, choose Yes. Finally, click OK to replace the entry and close the AutoCorrect dialog box.

The AutoCorrect Options button

When Word uses AutoCorrect, it displays a *button* in your document. For example, as previously mentioned, when you type **(c)**, Word converts it to ©. It then places a blue underline below the character. (If you can't see the line, it may be because you've moved the cursor away; place it immediately after the character.) Point at the line and a button appears. Click the triangle, and a small menu opens allowing you to change the character back to your original typing, tell AutoCorrect never to make this correction again, and open the AutoCorrect Options box.

You don't really need this menu in order to convert the text back to your original typing; just press Ctrl+Z to undo the change.

Tip   If you want to type something that AutoCorrect *usually* changes, but know that *this* time you don't want to change it, type it slowly. AutoCorrect assumes that you want it to remain the way you typed it.

Turning off AutoCorrect

To turn off AutoCorrect, choose Tools ➪ AutoCorrect. Clear the Replace Text as You Type check box, and then click OK.

Saving time with AutoText

AutoText provides a quick and easy way to store and insert frequently used text and graphics—not automatically, but when you choose to do so. When you create an AutoText entry, you can insert it using the Standard toolbar, the AutoText dialog box, or a keyboard shortcut. Word 2003 also allows you to manage AutoText entries so that you can update them by deleting, renaming, and editing them.

Creating AutoText entries

The first step in creating an AutoText entry is selecting the text or graphics from a document that you want to save as an entry. The quickest way to change this into an AutoText entry is to press Alt+F3—a small AutoText box opens, in which you type a name and press Enter. You can also use the New button on the AutoText toolbar, which we'll look at in a few moments. (Label your AutoText entries with names that are short and easy to remember; this way, you can insert them with a quick keyboard shortcut.)

Word saves AutoText entries exactly as they are formatted when you store them. If you want an AutoText entry to match the formatting of surrounding text, however, you can specify that it should be inserted without the formatting (as explained in the following procedure). To create an AutoText entry with full control over how it is handled, follow these steps:

1. Select the text or graphics that you want to store as an AutoText entry. To store formatting with the entry, include the paragraph mark with the selection.

2. Choose Insert ➪ AutoText ➪ AutoText. The AutoText tab of the AutoCorrect dialog box appears (see Figure 2-12). By default, the first words and any punctuation appear in the Enter AutoText Entries Here text box.

3. Accept the default name, or type a new name in the Enter Auto Text Entries Here box. An AutoText name can have as many as 32 characters, including spaces. Keep it as short as possible, however, and make it easy to remember.

4. Do one of the following:

    • If you want the AutoText entry to be available in any document, the Look In scrolling list should read All Active Templates. This list displays only the Normal document template and the template attached to the current document (if different from the Normal template).

    • If the document you're currently working on is based on another template, you may want to save the AutoText entry to the template so that it is available only to documents based on that template. To change the template, choose the template from the Look In box.

5. Click Add.

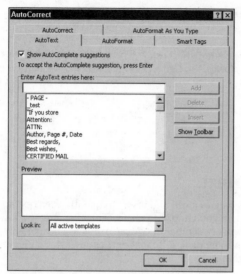

Figure 2-12: The AutoText tab of the AutoCorrect dialog box.

 Cross-Reference   For more information about templates and copying AutoText entries among them, see Chapter 14.

If you store a phrase that you intend to insert into a sentence, select one blank space after the phrase when you create the AutoText entry. Then, when you insert the phrase in a sentence, the blank space that you usually insert after typing a word is already there. You also can add punctuation, such as a period, when a phrase is usually inserted at the end of a sentence.

Inserting AutoText entries

You can insert an AutoText entry in several ways: using the AutoText button on the toolbar, choosing Insert ⇨ AutoText, or using the F3 keyboard shortcut. To insert the AutoText entry quickly and with its original formatting, use the AutoText button or the keyboard. Use the AutoText tab of the AutoCorrect dialog box, however, when you don't remember the name of the AutoText entry, when you want to preview its contents, or when you want to insert it as plain text if it is saved as formatted text.

To insert an AutoText entry using the AutoText tab of the AutoCorrect dialog box, follow these steps:

1. Position the insertion point where you want to insert the AutoText entry.

2. Choose Insert ⇨ AutoText, or click the AutoText button (the hand on the calculator) on the AutoText toolbar.

3. Select the entry directly from one of the submenus, and Word inserts it into your document. Or select AutoText to open the AutoText box.

4. In the Enter AutoText Entries Here box or list, type or select an AutoText name.

5. Click Insert to insert the item into your document.

To insert an AutoText entry using the keyboard shortcut, do the following:

1. Position the insertion point where you want to insert the AutoText entry. Make sure the insertion point is at the beginning of a line or is surrounded by spaces if you're inserting within text.

2. Type the name (or just enough letters to uniquely identify the name) of an AutoText entry. For example, if you have entries named *number* and *name*, type **nu**. If you type too few characters to specify a particular entry, Word displays a message in the status bar. If this happens, just type a few additional characters to specify which entry you want.

3. Press F3 and Word inserts the AutoText entry into the document.

To insert an entry when Word recognizes the entry, do the following:

1. Position the insertion point where you want to insert the AutoText entry. Again, you must be near a blank space or at the beginning of a line.

2. Begin typing the AutoText name. Once Word recognizes the name, it displays a little box above your typing with the name of the AutoText entry and the Words *(Press ENTER to Insert)*.

3. Press the Enter key and Word inserts the information for you.

To insert an AutoText entry using the AutoText toolbar, do the following:

1. Open the AutoText toolbar by choosing View ➪ Toolbars ➪ AutoText.

2. Position the insertion point where you want to insert the AutoText entry. Again, you must be near a blank space or at the beginning of a line.

3. Click the menu on the middle of the AutoText toolbar, which should say All Entries or show the name of a style or template being used. Simply scroll down, find the one you want to insert, and click on it. The entry then appears in your text.

If you use a specific AutoText entry frequently, you can assign it to a toolbar button, menu, or key combination.

Cross-Reference   For more information on customizing toolbars, see Chapter 32.

Managing AutoText entries

Over time, you may need to change your collection of AutoText entries. You can delete an entry, change the contents of an entry, or rename an entry.

Use the Style command in the Format menu to manage AutoText entries across templates, including moving them between document templates as well as renaming and deleting them.

Cross-Reference   For more information on styles, see Chapter 13.

Editing an AutoText entry

If you only want to make changes to an AutoText entry, you can change the existing entry's contents and then resave that entry instead of creating a new entry from scratch.

To edit an AutoText entry, follow these steps:

1. Insert the AutoText entry in a document.

2. Make your changes.

3. Select the entire revised entry. To store paragraph formatting with the entry, include the paragraph mark with the selection.

4. Use one of the methods for adding an AutoText entry, described previously.

5. Type or select the original name of the AutoText entry and then click Add. When Word displays a message asking if you want to redefine the AutoText entry, choose Yes.

Deleting an AutoText entry

To remove an AutoText entry that you no longer need, open the AutoText dialog box by choosing Insert ➪ AutoText ➪ AutoText. In the Enter AutoText Entries Here box, type or select the AutoText entry name that you want to remove and click Delete.

Renaming an AutoText entry

After you work with AutoText entries, you may want to rename an entry to make it easier to insert. To rename an AutoText entry, you must insert it into a document, save it as a new entry, and then delete the old entry.

Note   Changing the name of an entry also changes its location on the AutoText tab because AutoText entries are listed in alphabetical order in the Enter AutoText Entries here list box.

Printing AutoText entries

To help you manage your AutoText entries, you can print the names and contents of AutoText entries attached to the current document. Entries are printed in alphabetical order by AutoText name. Entries stored in the current template are printed first, entries stored in Normal.dot are printed next, and entries stored in add-in templates are printed last. AutoText entries are printed with their original formatting.

To print a list of AutoText entries, follow these steps:

1. Select File ➪ Print, or press Ctrl+P.

2. In the Print What drop-down list, select AutoText Entries.

3. Click OK.

Summary

Word provides many ways to get around your document and work with text. Some of the timesaving navigation and editing techniques explained in this chapter include the following:

✦ Displaying and using the Go To dialog box (F5) to move quickly to a specific location in a document.

✦ Using the mouse, selection bar, and Extend Selection mode key (F8) to select text.

✦ Pressing the right mouse button to display the shortcut menu for cutting, copying, and pasting selected text.

✦ Editing using drag and drop.

✦ Cutting and pasting multiple selections of text using the Office Clipboard.

✦ Inserting special characters and symbols using the Symbol dialog box.

✦ Using AutoCorrect and AutoText to speed up and automatically correct frequently mistyped words and phrases.

✦   ✦   ✦

Finding and Replacing Text and Formats

In This Chapter

Finding text using
Word's Find command

Finding and
replacing text

Replacing word forms

Finding and replacing
special characters

Finding and replacing
formatting

Refining searches using
wildcard characters and
operators

This chapter explains how to use the Find and Replace commands, two of Word's most powerful navigational and editing tools. The Find command quickly moves you to a specific point in your document, and the Replace command searches for and replaces text, with or without formatting. You also can search for nonprinting characters, such as spaces, paragraph marks, or tabs. You can search an entire document, including annotations, footnotes, endnotes, headers, and footers. Or you can limit searches to selected text or to the part of the document before or after the insertion point. Word also includes wildcard characters and several special characters, called operators, to refine your searches.

Finding Text Using the Find Command

The Find command searches a document for words, phrases, punctuation, and formatting. Perhaps you are looking for a name you need to change or formatting that you want to modify throughout the document, or perhaps you are simply looking for information that you know is somewhere in your document. If you're creating large documents, with scores or hundreds of pages, you'll discover the Find command to be invaluable.

To display the Find and Replace dialog box with the Find tab selected, choose Edit ➪ Find, press Ctrl+F, or click the Select Browse Object button in the vertical scroll bar (the little dot at the bottom, between the two double arrows) and then click the Find icon (the binoculars). Click the More button and the dialog box expands to show all the controls and options (see Figure 3-1).

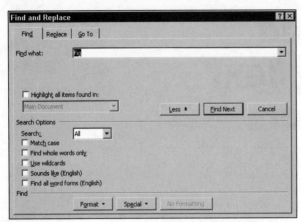

Figure 3-1: The Find and Replace dialog box with the Find tab selected.

Figure 3-2 shows the Find icon selected in the Select Browse Object menu. Don't worry if your icons appear in a slightly different order than how they appear in the figure.

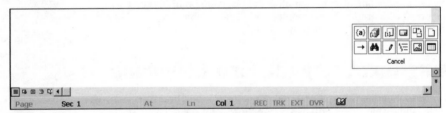

Figure 3-2: The Find icon selected in the Select Browse Object menu.

The Find Next button in the Find and Replace dialog box is dimmed until you enter text you want to locate in the Find What text box. (The last seven Find What text box entries are available for reuse when you click the down-arrow button, although the list is lost when you close Word.)

You can enter up to 255 characters in the Find What text box. If you enter more characters than fit in the text box, though, the beginning text scrolls out of view. To view this text, use the arrow, Home, or End keys. Standard text-editing keys work in the Find What text box. For example, you can use the Backspace or Delete key to erase text.

The Find command is a fast way to move to specific text. Entering a sequence of unique characters to mark a portion of text makes using the Find command an easy way to return to that part of your document. For example, two asterisks can be used to mark text that you want to revise later; you can then use the Find command to quickly move to any text marked with two asterisks. (The Edit ➪ Go To command also enables you to move directly to a specific line, page, section, table, and a variety of other places, as discussed in Chapter 2.) Before activating the Edit ➪ Find command, you can cut or copy text to the Clipboard and then paste it in the Find What text box by pressing Ctrl+V.

Adding Find to the Standard toolbar

Unfortunately, the Find command doesn't appear on the Standard toolbar, so do yourself a favor and add it. Follow these steps:

1. Click on the triangle at the right end of the Standard toolbar.

2. Choose Add or Remove Buttons ➪ Standard to see all the available buttons on a drop-down menu.

3. Click the Find button.

4. Click outside the drop-down menu to close it.

You can now begin a search for specific text by clicking the Find button on the toolbar.

Cross-Reference   For more information on customizing toolbars, see Chapter 32.

Find options

You can specify in a number of ways exactly *how* Word should search. When you first open the Find box, most of these options aren't available until you click the More button to expand the dialog box.

Finding versus highlighting

The first item you see is the Highlight All Items Found In check box. This box controls the result of your search. By default, Word uses the traditional form of searching by which you move from one item to the next. If you turn on the Highlight All Items Found In option, though, Word finds all the items you are looking for and highlights them all at the same time. The document jumps to the first one it finds, but *all* occurrences, quite likely ones you can't even see in other parts of the document, are now highlighted. This feature enables you to change formatting of text very quickly. For example, you could search on a name, highlight all occurrences, and change the formatting to bold and italic.

Caution   Be very careful with tools that allow you to select or modify information in your document without you seeing what is happening. One of those tools you learn about later in this chapter: Find and Replace All. This function lets you change all occurrences of a word or block of text to something different. Often such actions have unintended consequences. If you highlight all occurrences of *Smith*, for example, and change the name to bold and italic, you may also end up changing the name **Smith**town.

If you click on the check box, the drop-down list box is now enabled, and you can choose from several options: Current Selection (to search highlighted text—perhaps you are searching just one section of the document), Main Document (to search all of the body of the document), Headers and Footers (to search through just headers and footers), Comments (to search just the comments), and Footnotes and Endnotes (to search only the document's footnotes and endnotes).

Choosing where to search

The Search drop-down list box controls the direction of your search, and what is searched, beginning at the insertion point. (Note that if you have chosen to use the Highlight All Items Found In feature, the Search drop-down list is disabled.)

Choosing the All setting instructs Word to search the entire document, including comments, footnotes, endnotes, headers, and footers. The direction for All is down—Word searches from the insertion point to the end of your document or selected text and then begins at the top of your document and ends where you started the search.

Note   You can confine searches to a selection of text. Selecting a block of text before issuing the Find command confines the search to that selection. When Word has finished it asks if you want to search the entire document.

The Search list also includes two other options: Up and Down. Selecting Up or Down limits the search to the main document and excludes annotations, footnotes, endnotes, headers, and footers. Choosing Up instructs Word to search from the insertion point to the beginning of the document. When Word reaches the beginning of the document, it displays a dialog box asking if you want to continue the search from the opposite end of the document. If you search down and reach the end of the document, Word asks if you want to search from the top.

Searching by case

By default, the Find command locates each occurrence of your search text whether the characters found are uppercase or lowercase. Choosing the Match Case check box instructs Word to find only text that matches the uppercase and lowercase letters of your search text. As with selecting the Find Whole Words Only check box, selecting the Match Case check box focuses your search and saves time.

Searching for whole words

Selecting the Find Whole Words Only check box restricts a search to entire words that match your search text. Focusing your search this way saves time. For example, suppose that you're searching for the word *ate*. Choosing the Find whole words only check box instructs Word to find only that word and to skip words such as *congratulate, irritate, late,* and *substantiate.*

The act of searching

After entering text and setting any controls in the Find dialog box, click the Find Next button to start the search. Word then either finds and highlights the first occurrence of your search text or displays a dialog box informing you that the text was not found. If Word locates your search text, you can make changes to that text or continue searching for the next occurrence. You don't have to close the Find and Replace dialog box to make changes to your document. Just click outside the dialog box or press Ctrl+Tab. Then, after your changes are made, continue to use the Find and Replace dialog box by clicking the Find Next button to move to the next occurrence.

If you want to continue searching for the text in the Find What text box without using the Find and Replace dialog box, click the Cancel button or press Esc to close the dialog box. Then press Shift+F4 to move to the next occurrence of the search text. The found text is highlighted. To replace it, just type your new text. To move to the next occurrence of the search text without changes, press Shift+F4.

Tip Here's a very quick way to modify text. Suppose that you want to quickly find all occurrences of a word and change them to bold. You can use the Replace function, which is discussed later in the chapter. Another quick way is to search for the word, and when you find the word you want, close the Find box. Now press Ctrl+B to bold the word. Then press Shift+F4 to find the next one; press F4, the Repeat key, to convert that word. Press Shift+F4 again, then F4, and so on.

Alternatively, you can use the mouse to continue locating text without displaying the Find and Replace dialog box. At the bottom of the vertical scroll bar is the Previous Find button (the two up arrows) and the Next Find button (the two down arrows). Clicking the Previous Find button moves you to the previous occurrence of the search text. Clicking the Next Find moves you to the next occurrence of the search text.

Refining Searches

Several advanced tools are available for searching that are useful yet not often employed. You can use wildcard searches and *Sounds like* searches, as well as *Find all word forms*.

Using wildcards

Word lets you refine your searches using wildcard characters and operators. The question mark and asterisk are wildcard characters that represent characters in the search text. The question mark matches any single character; the asterisk matches any group of characters (commonly called a *text string*). Word looks past the asterisk to see whether the search is limited by any other characters. For example, searching for **wo*d** finds text such as *word*, *world*, and *worshipped*.

To use these wildcard characters, select the Use Wildcards check box in the Find and Replace dialog box. These wildcards are handy for finding words that you don't know how to spell. For example, if you are not sure how to spell *receive*, you can type **rec??ve**. Word then locates any word that begins with *rec* followed by any two characters followed by *ve*.

Just as parentheses are used in math to specify equations to be performed first, Word uses parentheses both to indicate the order of evaluation and to group expressions. An *expression* is any combination of characters and operators that specifies a pattern. An *operator* is a symbol that controls the search. Using operators, you can create specific search criteria. For example, you can find all words that start with a particular prefix and end with a specific suffix, such as all words that start with *dis* and end with *ed*. Using this search criteria, Word might find words such as *disinterested*, *disinherited*, *displaced*, and *distinguished*.

When you select the Use Wildcards check box, the Special menu (click the Special button) changes to include a list of operators at the top of the menu. Table 3-1 lists search operators and describes how each operator affects a search.

Note One other operator that you can use in the Replace With text box is \n—the \ character followed by a number. This operator rearranges expressions in the Find What text box to the order given in the Replace With text box. If you typed (Windows) (for) (Word) in the Find What text box and \3 \2 \1 in the Replace With text box, the text would change from *Windows for Word* to *WordforWindows* (without spaces). Of course another way to do this is by using a normal Find and Replace procedure.

Table 3-1: Search Operators

To Find	Operator	Examples
Any Character	?	*d?g* finds *dig*, *dog*, and *dug*
Character in Range	[-]	*[a-m]end* finds *bend*, *fend*, *lend*, and *mend* (the first character in this case is *a*, *m*, or any letter between)
Beginning of Word	<	*<tele* finds *telemarketing*, *telephone*, and *television*
End of Word	>	*tion>* finds *aggravation*, *inspiration*, and *institution*
Expression	()	Lets you "nest" search expressions within a search term. For instance, *<(pre)*(ed)>* to find *presorted* and *prevented*.
Not	[!]	Finds the text but excludes the characters inside the brackets; *t[!ae]ll* finds *till* and *toll* but not *tall* and *tell*
Num of Occurrences	{n}	Finds the specified number of occurrences of the letter immediately before the {; *to{2}* finds *too* and *tool* but not *to*
	{n,}	Adding a comma after the number tells Word to look for at least that number of occurrences; *a{4,}* finds four or more of the letter *a* in a row.
	{n,n}	*10{2,3}* finds *100* and *1000* but not *10*
Previous 1 or More	@	Finds one or more of the character immediately preceding the @ sign; *^p@^t* finds one or more paragraph break marks followed by a tab mark
0 or More Characters	*	Finds a word with one or more of the specified character, or words with none of the characters; *des*t* finds *descent*, *desert*, *dessert*, and *destruct*
One of the specified characters	[]	*b[aeiou]t* finds *bat*, *bet*, *bit*, and *but*
Any single character with the exception of the ones in the range inside the bracket	[!a-z]	*m[!o-z]st* finds *mast* and *mist* but not *most* or *must*

If you *want* to search for one of these special characters, yet at the same time search using wildcards, what do you do? You have to use the \ *escape character* in front of the special character. For example, suppose that you want to search for *recieve?* or *receive?* You could enter *rec??ve\?* If you haven't checked the Use Wildcards check box, though, you don't have to worry about that.

Sounds Like searches

Another method of searching for words that you aren't sure how to spell is the Sounds Like check box. Selecting this option instructs Word to consult a list of words that sound like each other, such as the names Cathy and Kathy and British spellings such as colour for color. There are other ways to specify exactly what you want to search, using the Format and Special buttons. These are most often used during Find and Replace procedures, so we'll cover them a little later in this chapter. There's also the Find All Word Forms check box; we'll look at that later, too, because there's a particular characteristic of this feature related to Replace we need to explain.

The Search Browse Object Button

The Search Browse Object button is the little circle at the bottom of the vertical scrollbar, between the up and down double-arrow buttons. Click the Search Browse Object button and the Search Browse Object menu pops up (refer to Figure 3-2).

You should understand that the Find command works, to some degree, in conjunction with the Search Browse Object menu and the double arrows. When you first open Word, before you use the Find command or select anything from the Search Browse Object button, these arrows move you between pages. If you click the down double arrow, you go to the next page; click the up double arrow to move to the previous page.

But eventually, these buttons start working differently. Press F5 (which moves you between recently edited text), and now the arrows are called Next Edit and Previous Edit. Do a search using Find, and the arrows become Next Find/Go To and Previous Find/Go To buttons.

You can reset the buttons by clicking the Search Browse Object button and selecting the Browse By Page button from the menu. Or select any of the other items to change mode (in some cases a dialog box opens). Select Go To, Find, Browse by Edits, Browse by Heading, Browse by Graphic, Browse by Table, Browse by Field, Browse by Endnote, Browse by Footnote, Browse by Comment, or Browse by Section.

If you select Browse by Comment, for example, each time you click the double down arrow you move to the next comment. Select Find, and the Find dialog box opens so that you can do a search. Then clicking the double arrows moves you up or down to the search term.

 See Chapter 29 to find out more about the Comments feature.

Finding and Replacing Text

The Edit ➪ Replace command, just like the Find command, also finds text that you specify. However, Edit ➪ Replace also automatically replaces each occurrence of search text with replacement text. For example, with the Edit ➪ Replace command, you can search for *stewardess* and replace each occurrence with *flight attendant*. You can also instruct Word to search for and replace each occurrence individually or all at once.

To display the Find and Replace dialog box with the Replace tab selected, as shown in Figure 3-3, choose the Edit ➪ Replace command or press Ctrl+H. The settings in the Replace tab are similar to those in the Find tab, except for the Replace With text box and the Replace and Replace All buttons.

After you enter the search text in the Find What text box, choose the Replace With text box and enter the replacement text. Clicking Cancel or pressing Esc cancels the current replace session but leaves any changes made during the session intact.

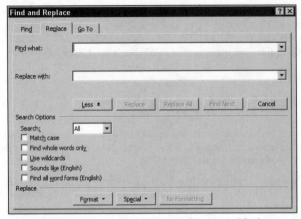

Figure 3-3: The Find and Replace dialog box with the Replace tab selected.

The Replace tab in the Find and Replace dialog box presents options to search for and replace text in one of three ways:

✦ Clicking the Find Next button finds the next occurrence of the search text.

✦ Clicking the Replace button replaces the currently selected text and moves to the next occurrence.

✦ Clicking the Replace All button instructs Word to replace all occurrences of the search text with the replacement text. When the session is completed, a dialog box and the status bar display the number of changes made.

Caution   Be careful using the Replace All button. Don't use it unless you are absolutely sure that you will be changing only exactly what you intend, and not words that contain your Find What text. If text was changed but you didn't mean to change it, choose the Edit ➪ Undo Replace All command or press Ctrl+Z after the replace session. Remember, you can undo your previous commands using the Undo button on the Standard toolbar.

To search and replace text in a document, follow these steps:

1. Choose Edit ➪ Replace. The Find and Replace dialog box appears with the Replace tab selected.

2. Enter the search text in the Find What text box.

3. Make sure the All option is selected in the Search list box. If you want to limit the search to text before or after the insertion point, choose the Up or Down option in the Search list box.

4. In the Replace With text box, enter the replacement text.

5. Do one of the following:

   • To confirm each replacement, choose Find Next, and then click Replace to replace the text or Find Next to skip to the next occurrence.

   • To change all occurrences of the search text without confirming each replacement, click Replace All. You can use the Replace All option any time during the replace session.

6. If you clicked the Replace All button, a dialog box informs you when the session is completed that the document has been checked in the direction you specified. It also tells you how many replacements were made. If you chose either the Up or the Down option, Word asks if you want to continue searching from the opposite direction. If you do, click Yes. To close the dialog box and return to the Find and Replace dialog box, click No. If you have searched the entire document or you have chosen the All option and are not using the Office Assistant, a dialog box appears to inform you that Word has searched the entire document; click OK to close the dialog box. If you're using the Office Assistant, a message appears to inform you that Word has searched the entire document.

7. Click Close in the Find and Replace dialog box to end the replacement session.

Finding and replacing word forms

The Find and Replace dialog box includes a check box labeled Find All Word Forms, which refers to the different grammatical versions of a word. For example, when you search and replace with the Find All Word Forms check box selected, the replace operation does its best to make the tense of the verb grammatically correct for the current sentence. When you enter the word *locate* in the Find What text box and the word *search* in the Replace With text box, Word replaces each form of the word *locate* with the proper tense of the word *search*. The word *locate*, for instance, might be replaced with *search*, *locates* with *searches*, *located* with *searched*, *locating* with *searching*, and so on.

Be careful when using this feature, because the changes are not always what you might want. Using the previous example, the sentence *Locating this book has not been easy* is changed to *Searching this book has not been easy*, a phrase with a very different meaning. In most cases, it's safest to use the Replace button to verify the changes rather than the Replace All button after selecting the Find All Word Forms check box. In fact, if you use this option and click Replace All, a dialog box informs you that Replace All is not recommended with Find All Word Forms and asks you to confirm if you want to continue the Replace All operation.

Replacing special characters

In addition to searching for and replacing text, you can search for and replace Word's special characters, such as paragraph and tab marks. This procedure is similar to that used for text, except that you use the Special menu button or enter the code representing the character in the Find What and Replace With text boxes. For example, ^p indicates a paragraph mark. Table 3-2 lists the special characters available in the Special menu and the respective codes for the Find What or Replace With text boxes. Some codes are only available for the Find What text box, however.

Tip   These codes only work if the Use Wildcards check box is *not* checked.

Use the lowercase letter when entering the code for a special character. If you enter an uppercase letter and try to execute the Find or Replace command, a message box informs you that the uppercase character is not a valid special character.

When replacing a symbol or special character, you can always copy and paste that symbol or character in the Find What or Replace With text box. If you know the shortcut key or ANSI code for a symbol, you can insert it directly into the Find What and Replace With text boxes. For example, to insert the copyright symbol (©), press Alt+Ctrl+C or the ANSI character code Alt+0169. Remember that you must use the numeric keypad to enter an ANSI character code. For more information on working with symbol shortcut keys and ANSI codes, see Chapter 2.

Table 3-2: Characters in the Special Menu

Special Character	Code	Available
Paragraph Mark	^p	Always
Tab Character	^t	Always
Any Character	^?	Find Only
Any Digit	^#	Find Only
Any Letter	^$	Find Only
Caret Character	^^	Always
Section Character	^u	Always
Paragraph Character	^v	Always
Clipboard Contents	^c	Replace Only
Column Break	^n	Always
Em Dash	^+	Always
En Dash	^=	Always
Endnote Mark	^e	Find Only
Field	^d	Find Only
Find What Text	^&	Replace Only
Footnote Mark	^f	Find Only
Graphic	^g	Find Only
Manual Line Break	^l	Always
Manual Page Break	^m	Always
Nonbreaking Hyphen	^~	Always
Nonbreaking Space	^s	Always
Optional Hyphen	^-	Always
Section Break	^b	Find Only
White Space	^w	Find Only

Note   You might want to turn on the Show/Hide button before you search for special characters because you can then see the nonprinting characters that Word locates. To view hidden characters, click the Show/Hide button on the Standard toolbar.

To find and replace special characters, follow these steps:

1. Choose Edit ➪ Replace. The Find and Replace dialog box appears with the Replace tab selected.

2. Click inside the Find What text box.

3. Click the Special button, and select the special character or item you want to find and any text for which you want to search.

4. Position the insertion point in the Replace With text box.

5. Click the Special button, and select the special character or item to add to the Replace With text box. You can add more than one special character to the text box, and you can also add text before or after a special character in the Replace With text box.

6. Make sure that the All option is selected in the Search list box. If you want to limit the search to text before or after the insertion point, choose the Up or Down option in the Search box.

7. Do one of the following:

- To confirm each replacement on a one-by-one basis, click Find Next. Then click Replace to replace the text or Find Next to skip to the next occurrence.

- To replace all occurrences of the search text without confirmation, click Replace All.

8. When the replace session for the entire document is complete, a dialog box informs you how many replacements were made. Click OK or press Enter to close the dialog box.

9. Click Close in the Find and Replace dialog box to end the session.

Automatically adding text to replacement text

The Find What Text option is added to the Special list when the insertion point is in the Replace With text box. Clicking the Special button and then choosing the Find What Text option inserts ^& in the Replace With text box. This instructs Word to include the text in the Find What text box as part of the replacement text. Using ^& is an easy way to add text before, after, or both before and after existing text. For example, suppose the Find What text box contains *July 19* and you want to replace the text with *Wednesday, July 19, 2000.* In the Replace With text box, you can type **Wednesday, ^&, 2000**.

Replacing with images and large text blocks using the Clipboard

When you choose the Replace With text box, the Clipboard Contents option is added to the Special list. With Clipboard Contents, you can insert graphics and other nontext elements stored on the Clipboard in conjunction with the Replace command. This option is helpful for inserting replacement elements such as text containing different formats, blocks of text larger than 255 characters, tables, and pictures. You can also use Clipboard Contents to insert text with mixed formatting, such as an italicized word and a word with a single underlined letter. For more information on working with the Clipboard, see Chapter 2.

Finding and replacing formats

Word can find and replace any kind of formatting, including character and paragraph formatting, styles, and even the language you assign to specific text for proofing. You can specify formatting two ways in the Find and Replace dialog boxes: using formatting dialog boxes or using shortcut key combinations.

Formatting dialog boxes become available when you click the Format button and select an option from the Format menu. Figure 3-4 shows the Format menu.

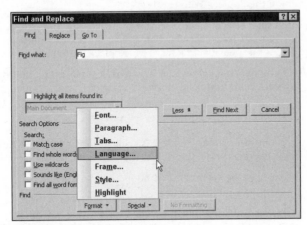

Figure 3-4: The Format menu.

The options in the Format menu open dialog boxes similar to those used to apply formatting from the Word menu bar. For example, the options you see in the Find Font dialog box (accessed when you choose Format ⇨ Font from the Find and Replace dialog box) are the same options you see when you choose Format ⇨ Font from the Word menu bar. After the Find Font dialog box is displayed (see Figure 3-5), you can choose the formatting you want to search for.

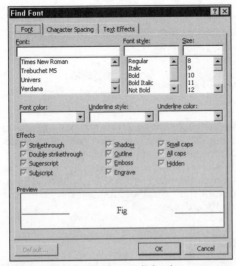

Figure 3-5: The Find Font dialog box.

Cross-Reference
For more information on working with the Font dialog box, see Chapter 4. For information on working with the Paragraph dialog box, see Chapter 5.

Table 3-3 shows the key combinations to enter in the Find What and Replace With text boxes for common character formats.

Table 3-3: Shortcut Keys for Locating Character Formats

Character Format	Key Combination
Boldface	Ctrl+B
Hidden	Ctrl+Shift+H
Italic	Ctrl+I
Subscript	Ctrl+=
Superscript	Ctrl+Shift++ (plus sign)
Underline	Ctrl+U
Word underline	Ctrl+Shift+W
Remove character formatting	Ctrl+spacebar

Be sure to clear the character formats or fonts from the Find What and Replace With text boxes after performing a find or a find and replace operation. If one or more character formats and a font name appear below a text box, press Ctrl+spacebar or click the No Formatting button to remove them.

For example, to find and replace underlined text with italic text, follow these steps:

1. Choose Edit ➪ Replace. The Find and Replace dialog box appears with the Replace tab selected.

2. Choose the Find What text box. Press Ctrl+U (the key combination for underlined characters).

3. Choose the Replace With text box. Press Ctrl+I (the key combination for italicized characters).

4. Make sure the All option is selected in the Search list box.

5. Do one of the following:

   • To confirm each replacement, click Find Next. Then click Replace to replace the search text, or click Find Next to skip to the next occurrence.

   • To replace each occurrence of the search text on a one-by-one basis without confirming each replacement, click Replace.

   • To replace all occurrences of the search text without confirmation, click Replace All.

6. If you click Replace All, a dialog box or an Office Assistant message appears when the session is completed and informs you that the document has been checked in the direction you specified. It also tells you how many replacements were made. If you chose either the Up or the Down option, the Office Assistant displays a message or a dialog box appears that asks if you want to continue searching from the opposite direction. If you do, click Yes. Otherwise, click No to close the dialog box and return to the Find and Replace dialog box. If you have searched the entire document or have chosen the All option and are not using the Office Assistant, click OK to close the dialog box.

7. Click Close in the Find and Replace dialog box to end the session.

If you want the replacement text to include different formats, such as one word in italics and one in normal text, see the section "Replacing with images and large text blocks using the Clipboard" earlier in this chapter.

To replace fonts, follow these steps:

1. Choose Edit ➪ Replace. The Find and Replace dialog box appears with the Replace tab selected.

2. With the insertion point in the Find What text box, click the Format button and select Font; then select the font you want to find.

3. Click in the Replace With text box. Click the Format button, select Font, and then select the replacement font for the existing font you selected in the Find What text box.

4. Make sure that the All option is selected in the Search list box. If you want to limit the search to text either before or after the insertion point, choose the Up or the Down option in the Search box.

5. Do one of the following:

   • To confirm each replacement on a one-by-one basis, click Find Next. Then click Replace to replace the search text or Find Next to skip to the next occurrence.

   • To replace all occurrences of the search text without confirmation, click Replace All.

6. If you chose Replace All, a dialog box informs you when the session is finished that the document has been checked in the direction you specified. It also tells you how many replacements were made. If you chose either the Up or the Down option, Word asks if you want to continue searching from the opposite direction. If you do, click Yes. Otherwise, click No to close the dialog box and return to the Find and Replace dialog box. If you have searched the entire document or have chosen the All option and are not using the Office Assistant, click OK to close the dialog box.

7. Click Close in the Find and Replace dialog box to end the session.

Summary

This chapter has given you several ways to save time when locating and replacing text and formatting. As you learned in this chapter, you can control searches to find or find and replace text quickly by doing the following:

✦ Limiting the search to a portion of your document.

✦ Highlighting multiple areas within the document at the same time.

✦ Specifying the formatting for the text that you want to find or replace.

✦ Instructing Word to automatically replace different word forms, such as nouns and verbs.

✦ Searching for and replace special characters, including nonprinting characters.

✦ Replacing text with multiple formats or with graphics by using the Clipboard.

✦ Using pattern matching and operators to refine your search.

✦　　✦　　✦

Character Formatting and Fonts

✦ ✦ ✦ ✦

In This Chapter

Applying character formatting

Using handy Word tools to display, repeat, copy, and undo character formatting

Changing the case of characters

Changing fonts and font sizes

Sharing documents with different fonts

Installing and managing fonts in Windows

✦ ✦ ✦ ✦

It's time now to enhance your message with character formatting and fonts. With basic character formatting, you can apply boldface, italic, and underlines to your text. Beyond these basics, Word includes several character formatting options to make your documents look professional.

This chapter doesn't explain character styles in detail—that's covered in Chapter 5. But you should at least understand one thing before we get started here. A paragraph has a *default character style*. As you learn later you can have many different paragraph styles—paragraphs with different characteristics. For instance, the default paragraph style is called *Normal*. The characters in a Normal paragraph use the Times New Roman typeface (a typeface is a particular look). The characters are 12 points tall (a point is a measure of size) and are not bold, italic, or underlined. Other styles look different. The Heading 1 style, for instance, uses the Arial typeface and 16 point text.

This chapter looks at how you change text from the default appearance—how you add bold, italics, underlines, and so on.

Applying Character Formats

Word includes a rich collection of character formatting options. You can easily apply formats to any selected text, from single characters to entire documents. You can change the format of text you have already typed by selecting the text and then choosing a formatting command, or you can choose the format *before* you enter the text. If you choose a formatting command without first selecting any text, Word applies that format at the insertion point; any text that you type from that point forward has the new format until you change the formatting again. Word includes three ways to change character formats:

✦ With the Formatting toolbar (see Figure 4-1), you can apply the three most common character formats by clicking the Bold, Italic, and Underline buttons. If you don't see the Formatting toolbar on your screen, choose View ⇨ Toolbars ⇨ Formatting, or right-click anywhere on a toolbar that is currently displayed and choose Formatting from the shortcut menu. You can add buttons that apply character formatting options to the Formatting toolbar.

Cross-Reference
For information on customizing toolbars, see Chapter 32.

✦ With the Font dialog box (see Figure 4-2), you can apply one or multiple character formats simultaneously. You can choose options from the Font tab or Character Spacing tab. Display the Font dialog box by selecting Format ⇨ Font or by pressing Ctrl+D. You can also select Font from the shortcut menu—right-click in the document window or press Shift+F10. (Note, however, that this shortcut menu does not always include the Font option, depending on where the cursor is placed when you open it.)

✦ With shortcut keys, you can apply a format as you enter text. For example, pressing Ctrl+B applies boldface text, and pressing Ctrl+I applies italic text. Pressing the shortcut keys again turns off the format. Word provides an extensive collection of such keys for applying most character formats. (These shortcut keys are described in the rest of this chapter.)

Figure 4-1: The Formatting toolbar provides easy access to commonly used formats.

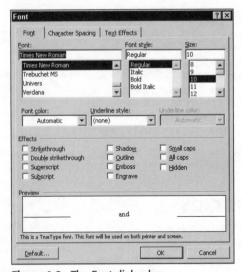

Figure 4-2: The Font dialog box.

To modify text that you have already typed into your document, simply select the text using one of the methods described in Chapter 2; then use one of the methods just discussed to apply the new format. For instance, select a word and then apply bold and italic, or select a sentence and apply a different typeface.

Note

In the Options dialog box (Tools ⇨ Options), under the Edit tab, there's a check box labeled When Selecting, Automatically Select Entire Word. This setting defines how Word handles formatting in many cases. For example, place an insertion point inside a word without selecting any text, press Ctrl+B, and what happens? If this check box has been selected, bold is applied to the entire word. If the check box is not selected, bold is not applied to the word. By default this check box is selected.

Suppose, however, that you want to change the appearance of the text that you are about to type from the appearance of the text you have just typed. Without any text selected, simply apply the formatting—bold, italics, underline, or whatever—then begin typing. The new words, as you type, will have the format you just specified.

It's important to understand that when you make changes to character format when no text is selected, you are applying that format *at the cursor position*, not to the cursor itself. So if you move the cursor somewhere else in the document, and *then* type, you will not see the format you just selected. You must place the cursor, select the format, and immediately begin typing without moving the cursor elsewhere. (In fact, if you even move the cursor away and then move the cursor back to exactly the same position, the formatting that you selected is lost.)

When you apply character formats in a document, these formats affect only the current document. With Word, however, you can save any changes you made in the Font dialog box as default settings, which Word then uses when you open a new document based on the current template. For example, if you're using the Normal template, which is the default template, the character formatting changes are saved to the Normal template. You can also create character styles, which can be attached to document templates to apply a collection of character formats simultaneously.

Cross-Reference   To learn more about working with character styles, see Chapter 13.

Note   You can find and replace character formatting using the Find or Replace command in the Edit menu. For more information on working with the Find or Replace command, see Chapter 3.

Boldfacing text

Boldfacing text makes the stroke weight of the characters heavier. Boldface text is commonly used for headers, headlines, or to bring out an important word or phrase. Different fonts offer different boldface options. The Bold button on the Formatting toolbar and the Ctrl+B short-cut key both apply the standard bold member of a font family. If the font you're using offers other boldface options, use the Font or Font Style settings in the Font dialog box or the Font drop-down list on the Formatting toolbar.

To format text in boldface using the Formatting toolbar or shortcut keys, follow these steps:

1. Select the text that you want in boldface, or, if you want the new text you are about to type to be boldfaced, position the insertion point where you want the boldfacing to begin.

2. Click the Bold button on the Formatting toolbar, or press Ctrl+B. Any selected text then appears in boldface.

3. If you didn't select any text before clicking the Bold button or pressing Ctrl+B, enter the text that you want to be boldfaced.

4. After you've finished typing, click the Bold button, press Ctrl+B, or press Ctrl+spacebar to return to regular text.

Note   Pressing Ctrl+spacebar removes any direct character formatting from selected text. If you select a bold word in a Normal paragraph, for example, and press Ctrl+spacebar, Word removes the bold. If you are typing an italic phrase and press Ctrl+spacebar, you will no longer be in italics when you continue typing.

Italicizing text

An italic format is a script version of a font style that slants the characters. Use italics instead of underlining or boldfacing to emphasize a word or phrase. Italics are often used to make the words of a book or movie title stand out in text, too. Be careful not to overuse italics, however, because if you do, italics lose their effect. The Italic button on the Formatting toolbar and the Ctrl+I shortcut key both apply the standard italic member of a font family. If the font you're using offers other italic options, use the Font or Font style settings in the Font dialog box or the Font drop-down list on the Formatting toolbar.

To italicize text, do exactly the same as you did for boldface in the previous section, except use the italics toolbar button, or press Ctrl+I.

Underlining text

With Word, you can format text with several types of underlining. Figure 4-3 shows examples of these options. Clicking the Underline button on the Formatting toolbar formats all selected text or any text at the insertion point, including spaces, with a *single* underline. To use another underlining option, use the Font dialog box or the shortcut keys to apply the standard underlining options as described next.

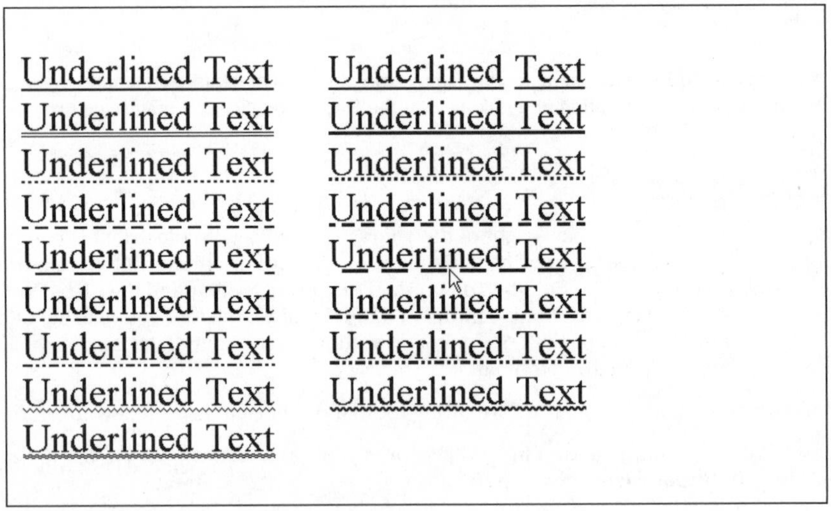

Figure 4-3: Examples of underlining in Word.

To underline text, follow these steps:

1. Select the text that you want to underline, or position the insertion point where you want the underlining to begin.

2. Do one of the following:

   • Click the Underline button on the Formatting toolbar.

   • Press one of the shortcut keys: Ctrl+U for a single underline, or Ctrl+Shift+D for a double underline.

- Choose Format ➪ Font, press Ctrl+D, or choose Font from the shortcut menu. Choose an underline option from the Underline style drop-down list, and then click OK.

3. If you didn't select text before selecting underlining, type the text that you want to be underlined. To return to regular text, click the Underline button, press the shortcut key, press Ctrl+spacebar, or choose None from the Underline style drop-down list in the Font dialog box, and then click OK.

The Font dialog box provides a number of underlining options from the Underline drop-down list box. You can create any of the following:

✦ Single underlines below words, but not spaces (select Words Only)

✦ Thick underlines

✦ Dotted underlines

✦ Wavy underlines and double wavy underlines

✦ Dashed underlines

Take a look at the Font dialog box to see all the underline formats you can use. You can also change the underline color; next to the Underline Style drop-down box you'll find an Underline Color drop-down box from which you can choose.

Using superscripts and subscripts

With superscript and subscript formats, you can change the location of characters, placing them above or below the normal line of text. Superscripts and subscripts are commonly used in mathematic and scientific formulas. For example, the number 2 is formatted as superscript in $E=MC^2$ or as subscript in H_2O. You can select superscripts or subscripts and make their point size smaller.

To format text as superscript or subscript, follow these steps:

1. Select the text to be formatted as either superscript or subscript.

2. Do one of the following:

- Press Ctrl+Shift++ (plus sign) to format text as a superscript, or press Ctrl+= (equal sign) to format text as a subscript.

- Choose Format ➪ Font, press Ctrl+D, or right-click and choose Font from the shortcut menu to display the Font dialog box. Then select the Superscript or Subscript check box in the Effects group, and click OK.

 Note Word also includes a powerful Equation Editor for creating and working with mathematical formulas. For more information on the Equation Editor, see Chapter 21.

Word provides more control over superscript or subscript in the Fonts dialog box, under the Character Spacing tab:

1. Select the text that you want to format as superscript or subscript.

2. Choose Format ➪ Font, press Ctrl+D, or choose Font from the shortcut menu to display the Font dialog box.

3. Click the Character Spacing tab (see Figure 4-4).

4. Click the up or down arrow on the By box on the Position line to enter a positive value (superscript) or negative value (subscript).

5. Click OK.

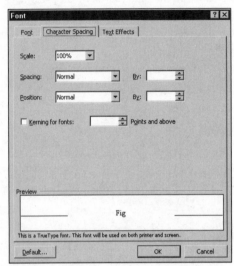

Figure 4-4: The Character Spacing tab in the Font dialog box.

To underline superscript text, select the superscript text—but not the surrounding text—to be underlined. If you apply underlining to selected text that includes superscript characters, Word underlines the text, including the superscripts, below the baseline of the regular text. When underlining is applied to text that contains subscript characters, the underlining is automatically placed beneath the subscripts, just below the baseline of regular text.

Note   In some cases, adding a subscript or superscript may cut off the top or the lower portion of a line. To correct this, choose the Format ➪ Paragraph command and then increase the spacing settings. Paragraph formatting is discussed in Chapter 5.

Using All Caps and Small Caps

The All Caps format displays text in all uppercase letters—similar to what you get when you press the Shift key or Caps Lock on your keyboard as you type a letter or word. But these features are not identical. When you use the Shift key or Caps Lock, the letters you type are actually entered as uppercase letters. When you apply All Caps formatting, however, either to selected text or by selecting All Caps and then typing, the text is simply formatted and displayed on-screen in all uppercase. The letters are not converted to uppercase letters. The important difference here is that you can always select text later that was formatted using All Caps, deselect the All Caps check box, and the original capitalization used for that text is reinstated. With All Caps formatting, Word doesn't care whether you have Caps Lock enabled on your keyboard or if you are pressing the Shift key as you type. All letters are displayed in uppercase.

The Small Caps format is similar to All Caps, in that all letters are shown in uppercase. The difference is that all letters typed in lowercase are displayed in a smaller point size than letters typed as capital letters. In the Small Caps format, Word *does* care whether the Caps Lock mode is turned on or whether you are pressing the Shift key. When you turn on Caps Lock or press Shift, Word creates normal capital letters. When Caps Lock is off and you are not pressing Shift, Word creates the mini capital letters.

To format text as Small Caps or All Caps, follow these steps:

1. Select the text that you want to format, or position the insertion point where you want to begin typing all capital or small capital letters.

2. Do one of the following:

    • Press Ctrl+Shift+K for Small Caps, or press Ctrl+Shift+A for All Caps.

    • Choose Format ⇨ Font, press Ctrl+D, or choose Font from the shortcut menu to display the Font dialog box. Then select Small Caps or All Caps from the Effects group, and click OK.

Adding a drop cap

Drop cap is short for *dropped initial capital letter*. Typically a drop cap is an oversized, single capital letter designed to stick up above a line of text or to stand out in a block of text. Drop caps commonly are used at the beginning of chapters or to start a new section in a book. Using a drop cap is a great way to add visual appeal to your page. To create a drop cap, follow these steps:

1. Click in the paragraph to which you want to add a drop cap.

2. Choose Format ⇨ Drop Cap to open the Drop Cap dialog box

3. Choose one of the drop-cap styles: Dropped or In Margin. The former places the image within the paragraph text, whereas In Margin places the drop cap in the margin outside the paragraph text.

4. From the Font drop-down list, select the typeface you want to use.

5. Choose a setting from the Lines to Drop box. This setting defines how high the letter will be.

6. Select the Distance from Text to define how much space you want to allow around the drop cap.

7. Click OK to close the dialog box. Word creates a text box with the drop cap inside.

Cross-Reference You learn more about text boxes in Chapter 18.

Adding color to your text

If you want to make your text stand out, you can add color. You can use different colors to add emphasis to a displayed document, such as formatting an urgent item in red. Some people use red text to mark areas of the document they want to come back to and finish off later. If you have a color printer, colored text also prints in color. When you use color text, though, consider what it may appear like when you print. Some colors when printing on a black and white printer will not appear well, or perhaps not at all.

The default Automatic setting in the Font color control in the Font dialog box generally displays text in black. (However, this is actually the Microsoft Windows *Message Box* color, which can be modified in the Appearance tab of the Display dialog box, which you can find in the Windows Control Panel.)

To colorize your text, follow these steps:

1. Select the text that you want to appear in a different color, or position the insertion point where you want the colorized text to begin.

2. Choose Format ➪ Font, press Ctrl+D, or choose Font from the shortcut menu.

3. Select a color from the Font Color list box, or click More Colors and select one from the Colors dialog box.

4. Click OK.

Tip

Don't forget the always-useful F4 key. It can help you apply the same formatting to various pieces of text. Select the first piece of text and apply the formatting. Move to the next piece and press F4. Move to the next piece of text and press F4 again, and so on. Note, however, that if you're applying formatting using keyboard shortcuts, only the last you applied is saved in F4. You can't press Ctrl+B to apply bold, Ctrl+U to apply underline, move to another word and press F4 to repeat both types of formatting. F4 repeats only the underlining in this case. To apply multiple formatting changes, use the Font dialog box and *then* use the F4 key to repeat the formatting.

Striking through text

To add a line through selected text, use the Strikethrough check box in the Effects group of the Font dialog box. The Font dialog box allows you to put a single strikethrough line through text, or double lines.

Some people use strikethrough to indicate areas of a document they want to remove when they are collaborating on a document with someone else. However, Word has a much more effective tool for revising documents, the Tools ➪ Track Changes command.

Cross-Reference

For more information on using Track Changes, see Chapter 29.

Using other special effects

Word provides a number of other interesting special effects, from shadowed text to engraved text, as described in the following list (see Figure 4-5):

✦ **Embossed text:** To make text appear to be slightly raised off the page, use the Emboss check box in the Effects group of the Font dialog box. Word puts a gray outline around the right side of each letter, with the letters themselves in white. However, if you apply another color, that color replaces the white and the text appears to have a shadow rather than be embossed. The amount of this embossing effect is preset and cannot be changed.

✦ **Engraved text:** To make text appear to be carved into or engraved on the page, select the Engrave check box in the Effects group of the Font dialog box. Word puts a gray outline around the left side of each letter. The depth of the engraving effect is also preset and cannot be altered.

✦ **Shadowed text:** To add a gray drop shadow to selected text, click the Shadow check box in the Effects group of the Font dialog box. Note that you cannot change the shadow's color or position. The effect is subtle, and works better with larger characters and in combination with a color if you're printing the document on a color printer.

✦ **Outlined text:** To create text with an outline effect—the text outlined and white space inside the letters—click the Outline check box in the Effects group of the Font dialog box. Note that the fill color of Outline text is always white.

Note

The mix combinations of these formats are limited. You can mix Shadow with Outline, but not Emboss or Engrave. And Outline, Emboss, and Engrave cannot mix in any combination.

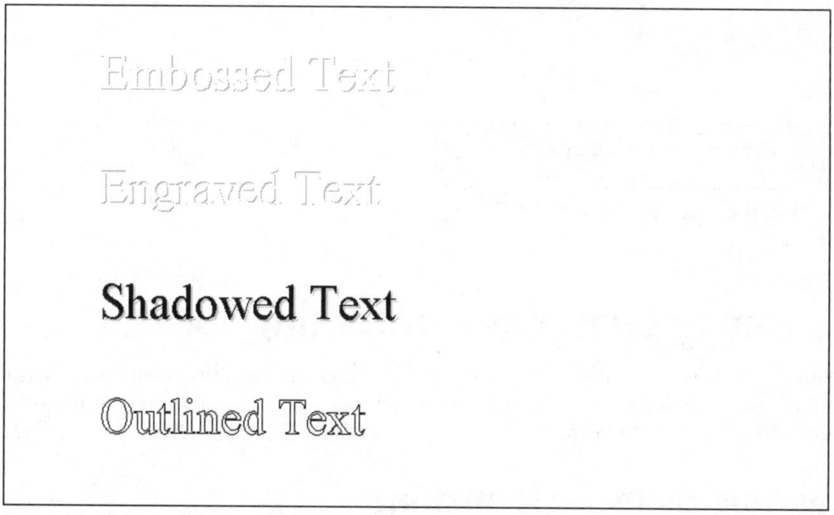

Embossed Text

Engraved Text

Shadowed Text

Outlined Text

Figure 4-5: Text with special formatting effects applied.

Text animation

The third tab in the Fonts dialog box is Text Effects (see Figure 4-6). This area allows you to give your text a blinking background, make it sparkle, and even create a light show or "marching ants" (a moving dotted line) around it. These special effects cannot be printed, but they can add some fun to a document displayed on a screen. They also *do* work in the Reading Layout view that you'll learn about in Chapter 29, so you could use some of these effects to make parts of the document stand out when you are distributing them to colleagues.

Tip

Be aware that professional designers cringe at these types of glitzy special effects, so it's a good idea to use them for personal and internal documents rather than for professional documents!

Click the tab labeled Text Effects, and select from several animations that appeal to you. You cannot mix animations. Look at the Preview box at the bottom of the Font dialog box for a quick peek at how the effect looks, and click OK. Any selected text then appears in your chosen animation's format.

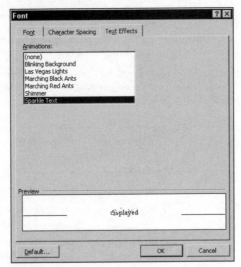

Figure 4-6: The Text Effects tab in the Font dialog box.

Word's Handy Character Formatting Tools

Word also includes some handy tools to work with character formatting efficiently. With these tools, you can display the formatting applied to a selection of text, repeat or copy formatting, and even undo formatting.

Displaying character formatting

With Word, you can view the character formatting applied to any existing text using the Reveal Formatting task pane (see Figure 4-7). This feature is helpful when you want to know what formatting is applied to a paragraph before you copy the formatting. To see which formats are applied to a given section of text, choose Format ➪ Reveal Formatting, or press Shift+F1.

Click on a piece of text you want to view, and Word displays information about the paragraph and font formatting, and even information about the document section (margins and so on).

Cross-Reference   For more on working with paragraph and character styles see Chapter 13; for information on working with sections, see Chapter 10.

Note that if you select a paragraph that contains text with varying formats, the information in this box may be misleading. If you simply place the insertion point inside a paragraph, you'll see the format of the text *at that point*. If, however, you select text, and the selection contains different formats, you'll be shown the format at the beginning of the text selection, the left-most edge.

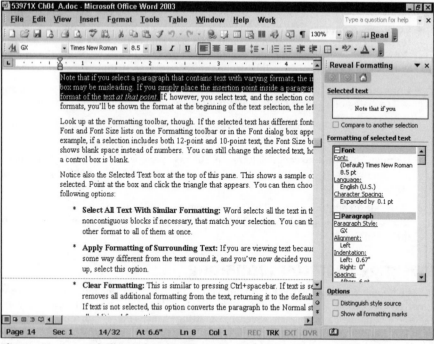

Figure 4-7: A sample formatting display.

Look up at the Formatting toolbar, though. If the selected text has different fonts or font sizes, the Font and Font Size lists on the Formatting toolbar or in the Font dialog box appear blank. For example, if a selection includes both 12-point and 10-point text, the Font Size box on the toolbar shows blank space instead of numbers. You can still change the selected text, however, even though a control box is blank.

Notice also the Selected Text box at the top of this pane. This shows a sample of the text you selected. Point at the box and click the triangle that appears. You can then choose one of the following options:

✦ **Select All Text With Similar Formatting:** Word selects all the text in the document, in noncontiguous blocks if necessary, that match your selection. You can then apply some other format to all of them at once.

✦ **Apply Formatting of Surrounding Text:** If you are viewing text because it appeared in some way different from the text around it, and you've now decided you want to clean it up, select this option.

✦ **Clear Formatting:** This is similar to pressing Ctrl+spacebar. If text is selected, it removes all additional formatting from the text, returning it to the default paragraph style. If text is not selected, this option converts the paragraph to the Normal style and removes all additional formatting.

Here are the other features of this pane you should know about:

✦ **Compare to another selection:** Click this check box and then click on another piece of text somewhere else in your document. The contents of the pane will change to show the differences between the text. For instance, *16 pt -> 10 pt* means that the first selection used a font size of 16 points, while the second uses 10 points.

✦ **Underlined headings:** Click on an underlined heading in the task pane and the appropriate dialog box opens. Click Font, for instance, and the Font dialog box opens.

✦ **+ and − boxes:** Click these boxes to view or remove information about that particular heading.

✦ **Distinguish style source:** Click here and the task pane will show you both formatting applied directly to the font, if any, and the formatting that is part of the paragraph style. (Remember, paragraph styles are covered in more detail in Chapter 5.)

✦ **Show all formatting marks:** This is the same as clicking the Show/Hide button on the Formatting toolbar. It displays spaces, tabs, paragraph marks, and so on, in your document.

Repeating character formatting

With the Repeat command in the Edit menu, you can copy formatting immediately after you've formatted characters. However, this method repeats only the most recent format. If you use the Repeat command after making several formatting choices using shortcut keys or the Formatting toolbar, the command repeats only the most recent choice. If you use the Font dialog box to apply several formatting choices at once, however, the Repeat command repeats all those choices because you made them as a single action. To copy character formatting with the Repeat command, select the text that you want to format and then choose Edit ➪ Repeat (last action) or press Ctrl+Y or F4.

Copying character formatting

The Format Painter is a very handy feature that you can use to copy all the character formats in a section of text to another section of text. Perhaps you want one paragraph, or maybe a heading, to exactly match a paragraph or heading elsewhere in your document. The Format Painter helps you do this very quickly.

To copy character formatting, follow these steps:

1. Select the text with the formatting that you want to copy. (You should select a block of text, not just place the cursor inside the text.)

2. Click the Format Painter button on the Standard toolbar, or press Ctrl+Shift+C. The mouse pointer changes to a paintbrush with an I-beam pointer.

3. Select the text you want to format. If you used the toolbar button, you just release the mouse button and the format is copied (the pointer changes back to an arrow). If you used Ctrl+Shift+C, press Ctrl+Shift+V to copy the format.

If you want to copy formats from one area to several others, use the Ctrl+Shift+C/V method. Or—and this is often easier—double-click the Format Painter button on the toolbar. The Format Painter remains enabled until you press the Esc key or click the button again.

Undoing character formatting

Word's formatting commands, buttons, and shortcut keys act as toggle switches, turning a formatting feature either on or off. For example, selecting text and clicking the Bold button boldfaces that text, and selecting that same text and then clicking the Bold button removes the boldface formatting from the text.

You can also quickly remove any character formatting and return to the regular text format (as defined in your Normal style) by pressing Ctrl+spacebar. Word then removes any character formats that you applied using the Formatting toolbar, shortcut keys, or Font dialog box. Word doesn't remove any character formats that are part of the paragraph style, however.

Cross-Reference   To find out more about styles, see Chapter 13.

If you mistakenly format the wrong text, you can reverse the action using the Undo command. With Word, you can undo the most recent action or command using one of three methods: clicking the Undo button on the Standard toolbar, choosing Edit ➪ Undo, or using the shortcut keys Ctrl+Z. To undo multiple actions, click the arrow beside the Undo button to display a list of recent actions and then select those that you want to undo. The actions are undone in the order in which they occurred.

Highlighting text

In the world of paper-based documents, one tool we've all used at one time or another is a highlighter pen. With these handy pens, you can highlight text in a document with just about any color—though yellow is the classic. Word also includes this handy tool, but in digital form. Using Word's highlighter pen button on the Formatting toolbar, you can highlight any text or graphic, and you can choose from many colors. To leave a comment about highlighted text, you use the Insert ➪ Comment command.

Cross-Reference   For more information on inserting and working with comments, see Chapter 29.

Note   It may be useful at this point to clarify what the word *highlight* means in this context. It's common in the computer business to talk about selected text as *highlighted text*. When you select a word, the background behind the word changes color. In this context, however, when we talk of Word's highlighting feature, we are talking about applying a sort of *permanent* highlight to the text. Even when the text is no longer highlighted using the mouse, the background remains a different color.

To highlight text, follow these steps:

1. Click the Highlight button on the Formatting toolbar. The mouse pointer changes to a highlight marker pen.

2. Click the arrow button next to the Highlight button to select a color. If you use the same highlighting color each time, you don't need to select the color again. Just clicking the button will apply the last color you used (the current color appears on the button).

3. Select the text that you want to highlight, and Word applies the background color.

4. Repeat with the next area of text that you want to highlight.

5. When you finish highlighting text, press Esc or click the Highlight button again.

Highlighting parts of a document works best when the recipients of that document review it online. If you highlight parts that you plan to print using a black-and-white printer, run a test print of the highlighted text to make sure the results are legible.

To remove highlighting, click the Highlight button, click the arrow next to the Highlight button, and then select None. You can then select highlighted text from which to remove the highlighting.

To search an entire document for highlighting and replace it on a one-by-one or an all-at-once basis, use the Replace command (click the Format button and you'll see Highlight at the bottom of the menu that appears). Simply search for Highlight, and then Replace with nothing. When you remove highlighting, the text is not removed; only the highlight is.

You can control if highlighting appears in your document from the View tab in the Options dialog box. Choose Tool ⇨ Options, and then click the View tab. Clicking the Highlight check box (removing the checkmark) hides the highlighting in your document.

Changing Character Spacing

The normal spacing between letters in a word is suitable for most situations. Sometimes, however, you may need to adjust this space. For example, in a newsletter headline using a large character size, you may need to adjust the space between a certain pair of characters (this is known as *kerning* to publishing professionals) or tighten the space between all characters in a sentence to fit the text into a tight space, such as a two-column newsletter. To change either kind of spacing, display the Font dialog box by pressing Ctrl+D, or choose Font from the shortcut menu, and then click the Character Spacing tab.

Note   You can save changes made in the Character Spacing tab as defaults for the template of your current document, as explained later in this chapter in the section "Changing Default Character Formatting."

Expanding and condensing character spacing

The Spacing control in the Character Spacing tab defines how much space appears between characters. This control changes the spacing between characters by the same amount for all characters in a selection. The default setting is Normal. Choosing the Expanded setting expands all of the spacing between all characters in your selected text. Choosing the Condensed setting condenses all of the spacing between all characters in your selected text. Figure 4-8 shows a sample of expanded and condensed text. By default, Word uses one additional point for expanded spacing and one less point for condensed spacing. You can also type a number (positive for adding space, negative for removing space), choose the By text box and click the up- or down-arrow buttons, or press the up- or down-arrow keys.

Note that you can have a little fun with this and reduce spacing so much that letters overlap each other.

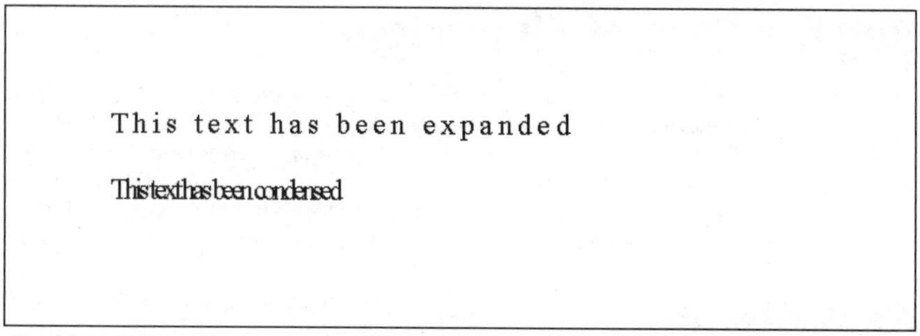

This text has been expanded

This text has been condensed

Figure 4-8: Expanded and condensed text.

Adjusting spacing in character pairs

You can use the Spacing format to kern character pairs—to increase or decrease the space between two individual letters. Kerning is most noticeable with large font sizes, such as those used in headlines, because the spacing allocated to some characters becomes too large when certain characters are paired with other characters. For example, when you have a capital T followed by a lowercase o, you can use kerning to nestle the o under the top of the T.

However, Word provides another tool that automatically applies kerning for you. You can use this to automatically kern a proportionally spaced TrueType or PostScript Type 1 font larger than a minimum size, which varies depending on the font. In a proportionally spaced font, the width of each character varies; for example, the characters *i* and *w* have different widths. If you select the Kerning for Fonts option in the Character Spacing tab, Word automatically adjusts the kerning for TrueType or PostScript Type 1 fonts that are larger than the font size you specify. In the Points and Above box, you can specify the point size to begin applying automatic kerning. To turn kerning on or off, press Ctrl+D or choose Font from the shortcut menu, select the Character Spacing tab, and then select Kerning for Fonts. The current point size appears in the Points and Above box. Click OK to close the Fonts dialog box.

To automatically adjust the spacing in character pairs, follow these steps:

1. Select the text that contains some character pairs that you want to change. You could select an entire document, for instance.

2. Choose Format ➪ Font, press Ctrl+D, or choose Font from the shortcut menu to display the Font dialog box.

3. Click the Character Spacing tab.

4. Click the Kerning for Fonts check box.

5. In the Points and Above box, type the point size at which you want to apply kerning. For instance, if your document has headings and titles that are 20 points and larger, typing 20 tells Word to automatically kern all those headings and titles.

6. Click OK to accept the change.

Tip　If the character spacing and kerning options are grayed out, you most likely are working on a document that was saved as a Web page. These options are not supported when working with Web pages. To enable character spacing and automatic kerning, save your document in the Word Document format.

Changing the Case of Characters

With the Change Case command, you can automatically change selected characters from uppercase to lowercase, or vice versa. Choosing Format ➪ Change Case displays the Change Case dialog box (see Figure 4-9). Table 4-1 describes the available options in the Change Case dialog box. You can choose only one option at a time, of course. Also, note that the Change Case command doesn't affect letters using the Small Caps format; you must remove this format to make these letters lowercase. (It does, however, work with All Caps.)

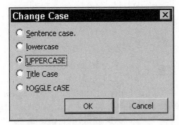

Figure 4-9: The Change Case dialog box.

You can also use the Shift+F3 keyboard shortcut to move through three options: Title Case, UPPERCASE, and lowercase. Each time you press Shift+F3, Word changes to the next case option. However, if you have selected a sentence, multiple sentences, or parts of multiple sentences (by selecting the ending punctuation of one sentence, and one or more characters of the next), Shift+F3 will move between Sentence case, lowercase, and UPPERCASE.

Table 4-1: Change Case Dialog Box Options

Option	Action
Sentence case	Changes the first character of the sentence to uppercase and all other characters to lowercase.
Lowercase	Changes all characters to lowercase.
UPPERCASE	Changes all characters to uppercase.
Title Case	Changes the first character of each word to uppercase and all other characters to lowercase.
tOGGLE cASE	Switches uppercase characters to lowercase and lowercase characters to uppercase.

Changing Fonts and Font Sizes

When you create or open a new document using the Normal template, Word begins working with the default font, 12-point Times New Roman. The current font name and size appear on the Formatting toolbar. You can choose from any font installed on your system to change the appearance of your text. The last ten fonts that you used appear at the top of the font list on the Formatting toolbar and are separated from the other available fonts by a line (see Figure 4-10). All of your installed fonts are listed alphabetically below the line.

Figure 4-10: The Font list box displays the last ten fonts used above the line.

Tip If you always create and print your documents, and never share them with anyone, you can use any font you want. But if you frequently share documents, you want to be careful which fonts you work with. Stick with the standard Windows fonts wherever possible. If you send a document to someone who does not have the fonts you used, the document won't look the same and will print differently on that person's computer unless you *embed* the fonts in your document. You learn more about embedding fonts later in this chapter in the section "Using Fonts with Shared Documents." Most people rarely need to use anything more than Times New Roman and Arial, fonts that are on all Windows computers.

The following sections explain the different types of fonts available with Word, how to change from one font to another, and how to change font size. You can also change Word's default font and font size, which is explained later in this chapter in the section "Changing Default Character Formatting."

Fonts in the Font list box

The two font standards for Windows are TrueType and PostScript Type 1. Both are *scalable* fonts, which are also called *outline* fonts. Scalable fonts are device-independent; in other words, they can be printed using any printer supported by Windows. A scalable font uses a single font file to display and print that font to give you true WYSIWYG (*What You See Is What You Get*). Windows comes with a basic collection of TrueType fonts and five symbol fonts (Symbol, Webdings, Wingdings, Wingdings 2, and Wingdings 3). The Symbol font character set includes the Greek alphabet, the four standard card suit symbols, and other mathematic, logical, chemical, and business symbols. The Webdings and Wingdings font character sets include many unique symbols not found in other sets, such as computer pictograms, astrologic signs, and clock faces.

Note Because Word is a Windows application, Windows does most of the font management work. Windows includes a Font Control Panel to install and manage TrueType fonts. To install and manage PostScript Type 1 fonts, you need the Adobe Type Manager.

The fonts and font sizes available for use in your documents depend on the fonts available from your printer and the fonts installed on your system. The Font list boxes on the Formatting toolbar and in the Font dialog box list the installed fonts.

Microsoft breaks fonts into two major divisions: TrueType (Microsoft's font standard) and every other type of font. TrueType fonts have a TrueType symbol (refer to Figure 4-10) to the left of the font name in the Font list. PostScript Type 1 fonts are lumped with other font formats and identified by a printer icon. Any printer fonts displayed in the Fonts list come from the print driver you're using to print your documents.

Any font without a TrueType symbol or a printer icon beside it is called a *Vector font*. Vector fonts are also known as *stroke* or *plotter fonts*, because they were designed for plotters. Plotters create fonts by drawing line segments between various points. Vector fonts can be printed on most printers, but you probably won't want to use these fonts instead of the available TrueType fonts.

Windows works with PostScript Type 1 fonts using the Adobe Type Manager, but Word doesn't display a helpful icon to identify PostScript Type 1 fonts. You can thank the ongoing font wars between Microsoft and Adobe for this; unfortunately, if you're using PostScript Type 1 fonts, you're the victim of this war.

Displaying font names in their font

The fonts in the Font drop-down list box on the Formatting toolbar are displayed in the style of the font itself. This is a great timesaver, because you no longer need to format text using a font just to see how that font appears (in the old days, you couldn't see what the font looked like until you selected it and typed some text). Referring back to Figure 4-10, you see that the font names in the drop-down list appear in the style of that font. If you want to display the font names in the list without applying the font style, you can turn off this feature by choosing Tools ⇨ Customize, clicking the Options tab, and then clearing the List Font Names in Their Font check box. But then, why would you? Most people are using computers that are fast enough to handle these fonts easily. If, however, you are using an older, slower computer, you may find that opening this drop-down list box is very slow. In that case, you may want to clear the List Font Names in Their Font check box. Note, by the way, that this control also defines the display of the Style drop-down box.

About font styles listed in the Font dialog box

A *font style* is a variation of a font's design. For the Times New Roman font, for example, there are different variations of the font's standard design, such as bold, italic, and bold italic. Each variation is a separate font style, and together, they make up a *font family*. Commonly, the italic, bold, and bold italic members of a font family do not appear in Word's font list, because Word uses the related format button on the Formatting toolbar for these font family members. In most cases, only the regular font name and any members of the font family other than italic, bold, and bold italic, such as expanded or condensed, appear in the font list.

About Font Names

Font names often have a direct relationship to the names of their designer, to places, and sometimes even to events in history. Some font names also include the name of the licenser. For example, font names licensed from International Typeface Corporation, a leading source for hundreds of font designs licensed to many font foundries, all have the letters ITC before their name. In addition, many font vendors also add a code in the name to identify the font as theirs. For example, Bitstream adds a BT to the end of the font name, AGFA Compugraphic adds ATT to their font names, and Monotype adds MT to many of their font names. Font names in your font lists are often abbreviated from the actual names of those fonts.

The Font Style control list of the Font dialog box displays all available variations of a font style. Different fonts have different styles associated with them. Within most font families, the standard font is usually referred to as *regular, roman,* or *medium.* Some font families are more extensive than others; for example, they might include several different weights and widths of a font, such as condensed, extra thin, expanded, extra bold, and so on. Different font designs use different descriptive terms for a font's weight. No standardization of font style terms exists.

Choosing a font

Windows and Office combined offer you more than 20 different fonts. It doesn't take long to accumulate more additional fonts, either, especially when software vendors frequently bundle fonts with their products. It's easy to get confused about which fonts came with Windows and Office and which fonts were installed with other applications. If you plan on sharing a document or publishing that document as a Web page, you most likely should stick to the standard fonts that most other users have. If you stick to Times New Roman for body text and Arial for headings, you can be pretty sure that anyone receiving the document will have those fonts.

Changing fonts

Word provides three methods to change fonts: the Font dialog box, the Font list on the Formatting toolbar, and shortcut keys. The easiest way to choose a font is using the Formatting toolbar or shortcut keys.

To change a font, follow these steps:

1. Select the text that you want to change to a different font. If you want to type new text in a different font, position the insertion point where you want the new font to begin.

2. Do one of the following:

   - Click the down arrow to the right of the Font list box on the Formatting toolbar, and select the font that you want.

   - Press Ctrl+Shift+F, and then press the up- or down-arrow keys to scroll through the list of fonts in the Font list box on the Formatting toolbar. Select the font that you want by pressing Enter.

3. If you didn't select text before choosing your font, any text that you type now is in the font that you just selected.

Tip

If you have a lot of fonts, you can quickly display them starting with a specific letter by clicking the down arrow associated with the Font drop-down list box. Once in the list box, enter the first letter of the font name that you want to locate. The list then displays all of the fonts beginning with the letter that you entered, and you can quickly click the font that you want to use.

Pressing Ctrl+Shift+Q automatically chooses the TrueType Symbol font, which is useful if you use a particular symbol often and know which letter creates that symbol. Type the letter and press Ctrl+spacebar to return to the default font.

Changing font sizes

The standard measuring unit for fonts is called a *point,* and there are 72 points in an inch. A font's point size is measured from the top of the highest ascender to the bottom of the lowest descender. Commonly used point sizes from 8 to 72 appear in the Fonts list box, but you can type any value into the box, from 1 to 1,638. Different fonts in the same point size can appear noticeably different in size, however, because of the relationship between the font's x-height and the ascenders and descenders (see Figure 4-11). The term *x-height* refers to the height of a font's lowercase x. Because the letter x sits squarely on the baseline, with no ascenders or descenders, it provides a point of reference for the height measurement of a font. Table 4-2 lists shortcut keys for changing font sizes.

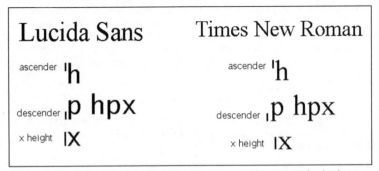

Figure 4-11: A font's point size is measured from the top of the highest ascender to the bottom of the lowest descender.

Table 4-2: Shortcut Keys for Changing Font Sizes

Key	Action
Ctrl+Shift+>	Increases the font to the next larger point size available in the Font size list box.
Ctrl+Shift+<	Decreases the font to the next smaller point size available in the Font size list box.
Ctrl+[	Increases the font size by one point.
Ctrl+]	Decreases the font size by one point.

To change a font size, follow these steps:

1. Select the text that you want to change to a different font size. If you want to type new text in a different font size, position the insertion point where you want the new font size to begin.

2. Do one of the following:

   • Click the down arrow to the right of the Font size list box on the Formatting toolbar, and select the font size that you want.

   • Press Ctrl+Shift+P, and enter the font size that you want. Alternatively, press the up- or down-arrow keys to scroll through the list of font sizes one at a time, and then select the font size that you want from the list by pressing Enter.

   • Press one of the shortcut keys listed in Table 4-2.

3. If you didn't select text before choosing your font size, enter the text that you want to appear in the font size that you selected. Then choose a different font size to end the task.

There's another way to change font size—this time horizontally. In the Fonts dialog box, under the Character Spacing tab, you'll find Scale setting. You can select from sizes between 33% and 200%. This setting squeezes and expands the font horizontally, but has no effect on how tall the font is.

Changing Default Character Formatting

When you begin typing in a new document, Word uses the font, font size, and other formats that are preset for the Normal style (the default text style). You can, however, change these default character formats. If you change the default character format, Word then uses the new formats in all new documents that you create using the current document's template. (You learn more about templates in Chapter 14.)

The default font formats affect most text in a document. To change the text formats for specific elements, such as body text, topic headings, bulleted lists, and headers or footers, modify the built-in styles. For example, to change the font and font size of header text, you must modify the formats of the built-in header style. For more information about modifying styles, see Chapter 13.

To change the defaults on character formatting itself, follow these steps:

1. Press Ctrl+D, or display the shortcut menu. Then choose Font to display the Font dialog box.

2. Set up the font the way you want it—choose a typeface, size, color, and any other effects you want.

3. Click the Default button.

4. Click Yes when Word displays a dialog box asking you to confirm if you want to change the default font for the current template. Word then immediately applies the new formats in the current document, and this changes the default font for all documents that you create using the Normal style template.

Tip To change default formatting quickly, select text with the formats that you want, display the Font dialog box, and click Default.

Hiding Text in Your Document

Any document text, such as notes, comments, or any kind of information that you don't want displayed or printed, can be formatted as hidden text. Hiding text doesn't make the text private. Anyone using the file in Word can still display the hidden text, so be careful not to hide any skeletons. Adding hidden text doesn't affect text formatting, either. You can toggle hidden text on and off using the keyboard shortcut Ctrl+Shift+H, but the text must be selected. You can see hidden text in normal, outline, page layout, and master document views if you choose to display hidden text—click the Show/Hide button on the Standard toolbar or press Ctrl+Shift+*.

To hide text, follow these steps:

1. Select the text that you want to hide, or position the insertion point where you want to enter hidden text.

2. Do one of the following:

   • Press Ctrl+Shift+H.

   • Choose Format ➪ Font, press Ctrl+D, or choose Font from the shortcut menu. Then select Hidden from the Effects group, and click OK.

3. If you don't select any text, enter the text that you want to hide. To return to regular text format, press Ctrl+Shift+H, press Ctrl+spacebar, or display the Font dialog box. Then clear the Hidden check box and click OK.

Word also uses the hidden text format to hide entries in tables of contents, index entries, and annotation marks. For more information on creating tables of contents and indexes, see Chapter12. For more information on adding notes and comments, see Chapter 29.

Note   You can format any character, even a page break or paragraph mark, as hidden text, but doing so affects the page numbering. Display hidden text if you intend to print hidden text; if you don't want to print hidden text, hide it. Otherwise, page breaks and page numbering may appear in odd places because no text is visible.

If you want to display hidden text in Print Preview or to print hidden text, choose File ➪ Print and click the Options button. Then select the Hidden Text check box in the Include With document group.

Using Fonts with Shared Documents

Word supports TrueType font embedding, so you can include TrueType fonts in your documents. With this feature, you can share your documents with other users or send a document out to be professionally printed at a service bureau. There are three types of font embedding: print/preview, editable, and installable. The type of embedding that you use affects the way that you can use the font on another system. If the TrueType font supports font embedding and you embed that font in the document, the embedded TrueType fonts display and print when other users open the document on their systems—even if the fonts aren't installed on their computers.

Some fonts don't allow embedding. For example, the MS Outlook font has restricted license embedding, so no font embedding is allowed. If an application doesn't support font embedding, Windows uses an internal font mapping system to substitute an available font for the unavailable TrueType font, and the font it picks may not be suitable in some cases.

To embed fonts in a Word document, follow these steps:

1. Make sure the document in which you want to embed the fonts is the active document.

2. Choose File ➪ Save As.

3. Enter the name of the document in the File Name text box. If necessary, change the drive and directory using the Drives and Directories list boxes.

4. Choose Tools ➪ Save Options to display the Save dialog box.

5. Select Embed TrueType Fonts. If this option is dimmed, you cannot embed TrueType fonts. If you want to save the document without embedding the entire font, choose the Embed Characters in Use Only check box (this saves a little space, but if the recipient wants to add some text he won't be able to use any characters you haven't used). You can also choose the Do Not Embed Common System Fonts option to tell Windows to save space by not bothering to embed fonts that are in common use but to only embed the unusual fonts.

6. Click OK to close the Save dialog box.

7. Click OK to save the file with the embedded TrueType file, and then close the Save As dialog box.

Note   How fonts are embedded in a document is determined by the font foundry and is not evident until you open the document on a system without those particular fonts, such as PostScript fonts. Remember, you cannot embed some fonts.

Print/preview font embedding

Using a font with print/preview embedding temporarily installs the embedded fonts on a computer not equipped with the embedded fonts when you open the document. You can then preview the document on the screen, and you can print it with the correct fonts. You cannot modify the document, however, and Windows doesn't share these temporary fonts with other documents or applications. Instead, the temporary fonts are deleted when you close the document. Most TrueType font foundries support print/preview font embedding.

Editable font embedding

Editable font embedding goes beyond print/preview font embedding. Editable fonts store enough font information in the file so that a recipient can modify your text, save changes under the original file name, and then print the document. This gives you more flexibility to start a document on one computer and then complete and print it on another. You cannot save the file with a different file name, however. If you cut or copy text to the Clipboard and then paste it into another document, Windows applies one of the fonts installed on the computer—but not the embedded font—to the pasted text. As with print/preview embedding, opening the file on a computer without the required fonts causes the embedded fonts to be installed temporarily in the file; when you close the document, the temporary fonts are deleted. Garamond, Lucida, Console Tahoma, Trebuchet MS, and Wingdings allow editable font embedding.

Installable font embedding

Installable font embedding offers all the flexibility of editable fonts, but this type of embedding goes one step further. When you open a document with embedded fonts, Word checks that the fonts are installed on your computer. If the fonts cannot be found, Word asks if you want to permanently install them. When you share a document containing installable TrueType fonts, it's as if the user already has those fonts installed. He or she can access the font in any other Windows application, add it to other documents, and even share it with someone else. The font remains installed even after the user closes the shared document. Most fonts that ship with Windows and Microsoft Office are installable fonts.

When you select to save a document with installable fonts, the document file increases in size, because the font files are literally embedded in that document. For example, if you create a document using the Lucida Fax font from the Microsoft TrueType font pack, the document file increases by approximately 50K because of the embedded font file.

Microsoft uses font embedding as part of its dynamic font strategy. Dynamic fonts are those that display on a Web page even if they aren't installed on the reader's system. Microsoft includes the Web Embedding Fonts Tool at its Web site as a free utility. With the Web Embedding Fonts Tool (commonly referred to as WEFT), you can create font objects that are linked to your Web pages. These font objects are compressed and contain only the characters used by that particular site or page. Because the font object doesn't contain the entire font, the file sizes are much smaller than those of regular TrueType fonts. When a person loads a Web page with a font object linked to it into Internet Explorer, the font object is downloaded and decompressed, and the font is installed. This font is privately installed, however, so that other applications cannot access the font. Unfortunately, Netscape Communicator doesn't support Microsoft's dynamic fonts. You can download Microsoft's WEFT at the following URL: www.microsoft.com/typography/web/embedding/weft2/.

Substituting unavailable fonts

Again, a common problem when switching printers or sharing documents is that fonts may be used on one configuration or system that may not be available on another. If the fonts used to format a document aren't available, Word tries to substitute a similar available font to display and print the document. For example, if you format text with the Helvetica font on a PostScript printer and then switch to a LaserJet printer, Word substitutes the Arial font. The substituted font is not actually applied to the text in the file itself. If you select text that is formatted with the unavailable font, the name of that font is displayed in the Font box on the Formatting toolbar and in the Font dialog box; however, the font is not included in the list of available fonts. You can apply the font by entering its name in the Font box. The original font is used whenever you print the document from a system on which that font is available.

Word tries to match missing fonts with similar fonts, but its choice may not be your choice. Not only can you view the names of fonts that are missing from a document and those that Word uses as substitutes, you can also specify which fonts Word should use as substitutions. With Word, you can even permanently change the font formatting to use the substituted fonts. If no font substitution is necessary, Word displays the message No font substitution is necessary. All fonts used in such a document are available, so click OK to continue.

To substitute unavailable fonts, follow these steps:

1. Open the document containing fonts that you need to substitute.

2. Choose Tools ➪ Options. The Options dialog box appears.

3. Click the Compatibility tab.

4. Click the Font Substitution button. Word displays the Font Substitution dialog box (see Figure 4-12).

5. Select the missing font in the Missing Document Font list box.

6. Select the font that you want to substitute for the missing font in the Substituted Font list box.

7. To permanently *replace* missing fonts with substituted fonts, click the Convert Permanently button, and then click OK when Word asks if you want to permanently convert all missing fonts to their current substitutes.

8. Click OK to close the Font Substitution dialog box.

9. Click OK to close the Options dialog box.

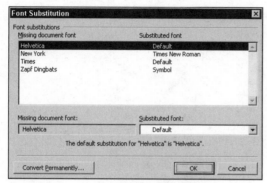

Figure 4-12: The Font Substitution dialog box.

Managing Fonts in Windows

The two scalable font formats used most often in Windows are TrueType and Adobe PostScript Type 1. You can use both scalable font formats simultaneously in Windows, and your Word documents can contain a mixture of the two formats. PostScript fonts have long been the standard in the professional desktop publishing industry and offer a richer library of available fonts. PostScript fonts are a good choice if you plan to send documents to a service bureau to create output at a resolution higher than the 600 dpi common with most home printers. The only drawback to PostScript Type 1 fonts is that you need to purchase Adobe Type Manager to work with these fonts.

Note   Microsoft and Adobe have joined forces to create a font format known as OpenType. OpenType is a superset of TrueType and PostScript Type 1 fonts, and the goal is to create a cross-platform font technology for publishing documents on the Web. With the OpenType font format, readers can see font formatting even if they don't have the font installed on their systems. OpenType also has a method of font compression that promises to make downloading the fonts used in Web pages faster.

Word takes advantage of a Windows feature called *font smoothing*. The font smoothing feature improves the readability of fonts on your screen. It also reduces the jagged effect that fonts sometimes get on the low resolutions of PC monitors. Font smoothing *anti-aliases* fonts, which involves the addition of colored pixels (based on the background and foreground color) that are strategically placed around the edges of a font to make that font appear less jagged.

You can install and manage TrueType fonts using the Fonts Control Panel in Windows. The Fonts Control Panel makes TrueType fonts available to Word and any other Windows application. To install and work with Adobe PostScript Type 1 fonts, you need to use the Adobe Type

Manager. Both TrueType and PostScript fonts are device-independent; in other words, they can be printed to any printer supported by Windows.

Fonts in Windows are stored in the Fonts subfolder in the Windows folder. You can access the Font Control Panel (see Figure 4-13) by double-clicking the My Computer icon on the Windows Desktop and then double-clicking the Control Panel and Fonts folders. The icons with the double Ts indicate that font is a TrueType font.

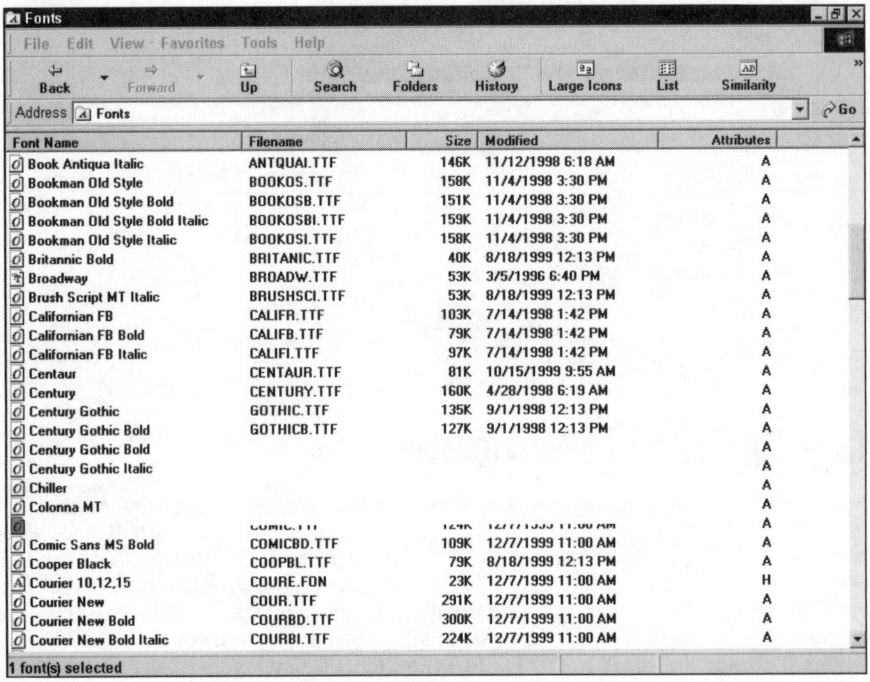

Font Name	Filename	Size	Modified	Attributes
Book Antiqua Italic	ANTQUAI.TTF	146K	11/12/1998 6:18 AM	A
Bookman Old Style	BOOKOS.TTF	158K	11/4/1998 3:30 PM	A
Bookman Old Style Bold	BOOKOSB.TTF	151K	11/4/1998 3:30 PM	A
Bookman Old Style Bold Italic	BOOKOSBI.TTF	159K	11/4/1998 3:30 PM	A
Bookman Old Style Italic	BOOKOSI.TTF	158K	11/4/1998 3:30 PM	A
Britannic Bold	BRITANIC.TTF	40K	8/18/1999 12:13 AM	A
Broadway	BROADW.TTF	53K	3/5/1996 6:40 PM	A
Brush Script MT Italic	BRUSHSCI.TTF	53K	8/18/1999 12:13 AM	A
Californian FB	CALIFR.TTF	103K	7/14/1998 1:42 PM	A
Californian FB Bold	CALIFB.TTF	79K	7/14/1998 1:42 PM	A
Californian FB Italic	CALIFI.TTF	97K	7/14/1998 1:42 PM	A
Centaur	CENTAUR.TTF	81K	10/15/1999 9:55 AM	A
Century	CENTURY.TTF	160K	4/28/1998 6:19 AM	A
Century Gothic	GOTHIC.TTF	135K	9/1/1998 12:13 PM	A
Century Gothic Bold	GOTHICB.TTF	127K	9/1/1998 12:13 PM	A
Century Gothic Bold				A
Century Gothic Italic				A
Chiller				A
Colonna MT				A
	COMIC.TTF	124K	12/7/1999 11:00 AM	A
Comic Sans MS Bold	COMICBD.TTF	109K	12/7/1999 11:00 AM	A
Cooper Black	COOPBL.TTF	79K	8/18/1999 12:13 PM	A
Courier 10,12,15	COURE.FON	23K	12/7/1999 11:00 AM	H
Courier New	COUR.TTF	291K	12/7/1999 11:00 AM	A
Courier New Bold	COURBD.TTF	300K	12/7/1999 11:00 AM	A
Courier New Bold Italic	COURBI.TTF	224K	12/7/1999 11:00 AM	A

Figure 4-13: The Windows Fonts Control Panel.

To add TrueType fonts using the Font Control Panel, drag the font icons from Windows Explorer to the Windows Fonts folder. You can also install a new font by choosing File ➪ Install New Font in the Font Control Panel. Deleting fonts is just as easy: simply select the font and then press Delete or choose File ➪ Delete.

Double-click any font icon to display a window containing sample text and other information about that font (see Figure 4-14). The typeface name, file size, version, and vendor appear at the top of the window, followed by the alphanumeric characters of the font. The remaining part of the window displays the font in several sizes. You can also change how fonts are listed in the Fonts Control Panel by choosing one of the options from the View menu, which are listed in Table 4-3.

Note   Choose View ➪ Toolbars to display a toolbar with buttons for the Large Icons, List, List Fonts By Similarity, and Details views.

Figure 4-14: A font sample.

Table 4-3: View Options in the Fonts Control Panel

Option	How It Displays Font Files
Large Icons	Displays a large icon for each font on your system, a very inconvenient way to sort through a list.
List	Lists font files as small icons in an alphabetical listing. This may be the best way if you're using a lot of fonts.
List Fonts By Similarity	Organizes fonts in the list according to their similarity. All fonts in the family are listed together, as are any other fonts that are similar.
Details	Lists fonts by font name, file name, file size, and last date modified.
Hide Variations	Displays font families rather than the members of those families.

Summary

Character formatting is the basic form of formatting in Word. It includes such essentials as boldfacing, italicizing, and underlining, but it also includes working with different fonts. With Word, you can format your text using the handy Formatting toolbar, the Font dialog box, or shortcut keys. In this chapter, you learned about formatting characters and working with fonts, including how to do the following:

✦ Use the Formatting toolbar and the Font dialog box to perform a variety of character formatting tasks. To display the Font dialog box, press Ctrl+D or choose Format ➪ Font.

✦ Display character formatting by pressing Shift+F1 and then clicking the text that you want to check. You can also simply place the insertion point in the text and see its formatting displayed on the Formatting toolbar.

✦ Use the highlighter pen to highlight text by clicking the Highlight button and then selecting the text.

✦ Change fonts and font sizes using the Formatting toolbar's Fonts and Font Size drop-down lists or the Fonts dialog box. You can also press Ctrl+Shift+> to increase the font size by one point and Ctrl+Shift+< to decrease the font size by one point.

✦ Change the default character formatting in the Font dialog box by choosing your setting and then choosing Default.

✦   ✦   ✦

Paragraph Formatting

In This Chapter

Aligning paragraphs

Adjusting line and paragraph spacing

Setting tabs and indents

Enhancing paragraphs using lines, borders, and shading

Creating bulleted, numbered, and outline numbered lists

Hyphenating your documents

Paragraphs—the basic building blocks of any document—have a special meaning in Word. Paragraphs can include any amount of text and graphics, or any other item, followed by a paragraph *mark* or *break*. Paragraph marks store the formatting applied to each paragraph. In this chapter, you learn the fundamentals of paragraph formatting in Word.

Each time you press the Enter key, Word begins a new paragraph. Click the Show/Hide button on the Standard toolbar or press Ctrl+Shift+* to display the paragraph marks—press the Enter key several times, and you'll see Word insert strange little backward *P* icons, with the semi-circle at the top of the *P* filled in. These are the paragraph marks, and they store the information about the paragraph.

Note   The paragraph ends at the paragraph mark. Thus formatting for a paragraph is held in the paragraph mark at the end of the text; delete that mark and the formatting for the preceding text is removed and replaced with the formatting held in the next paragraph mark.

Applying Paragraph Formatting

You can apply paragraph formatting using *styles*, which are in effect collections of formatting. We look at styles in more detail in Chapter 13. This chapter looks at how to apply paragraph formatting directly. In order to apply formatting to a paragraph, place the cursor inside the paragraph you want to modify—make sure you have not selected any text within the paragraph, though, but that the cursor is merely sitting in the paragraph. (In some cases if you've selected a few characters or words and you apply some kind of format, you'll be modifying just the selected text, not the entire paragraph.) You can also select an entire paragraph, or multiple paragraphs, and then apply formatting.

When you press Enter to start a new paragraph, that new paragraph will, in general, contain exactly the same formatting as the previous paragraph. There are some cases when this *won't* happen, though. Some styles may be set up such that when you press Enter, a new style, with different formatting, is used for the next paragraph. For instance, a heading style may be set up to automatically begin working with a body-text style when you press Enter.

Cross-Reference   See Chapter 13 to learn more about using styles in your documents.

You can apply paragraph formatting using buttons on the Formatting toolbar (see Figure 5-1), settings in the Paragraph dialog box (see Figure 5-2), or shortcut keys. By changing the formatting of a paragraph, you can change the alignment and spacing of the lines within that paragraph.

Figure 5-1: The Formatting toolbar.

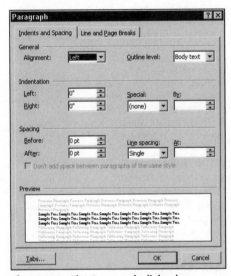

Figure 5-2: The Paragraph dialog box.

Checking paragraph formats

The formats applied to the current paragraph appear in the settings on the Formatting toolbar, the horizontal ruler, and in the Paragraph dialog box. If you select several paragraphs with different formats, the dialog box settings may appear blank or dimmed. Word cannot indicate different formats at the same time. On the ruler, dimmed indent and tab markers show the settings for the first paragraph in the selection.

With Word, you can display information about any paragraph formats that are applied to a given paragraph. To check the formatting of a paragraph, choose Format ➪ Reveal Formatting, or press Shift+F1 and the Reveal Formatting task pane opens (see Figure 5-3). You can now click in a paragraph to see what formatting has been applied to the paragraph.

Cross-Reference   See Chapter 4 for more information about working with the Reveal Formatting task pane.

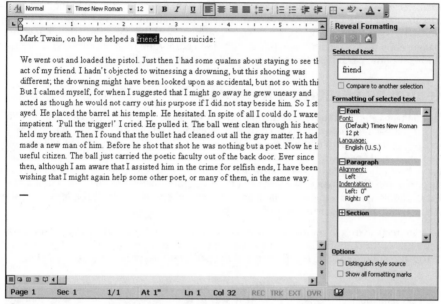

Figure 5-3: Paragraph formatting information.

Duplicating paragraph formats

The easiest way to duplicate paragraph formatting is to carry that formatting forward by pressing Enter. The current paragraph ends and a new one begins with the same formatting as the preceding one. If the formatting that you want to copy is in another part of your document or even a different document, use the Format Painter, with which you can duplicate all of the formatting in the selected text. To use the Format Painter, select the text with the formatting that you want to copy. Make sure that you select the entire paragraph, including the paragraph mark at the end. Click the Format Painter button (see Figure 5-4) on the Standard toolbar, and select the block of text to which you want to apply the formatting. Again, if you want to make sure that you transfer all the paragraph formatting, be sure to select the entire paragraph, including the end paragraph mark. Or, you can select several paragraphs at the same time.

 Figure 5-4: The Format Painter button.

If you want to copy formats and apply them to multiple non-contiguous paragraphs, select the paragraph with the formatting that you want to copy, double-click the Format Painter button, and then select, one at a time, the paragraphs that you want to change. Click the Format Painter button or press Esc to end the formatting.

You can also apply a formatting change to different paragraphs. Apply it once; then click the next paragraph and choose Edit ➪ Repeat, press Ctrl+Y, or press F4. Remember that these commands duplicate only the last action. So if you want to apply multiple formats at the same time—such as both bold and strikethrough—use the Format Font dialog box rather than keyboard shortcuts before using Edit ➪ Repeat.

Because formats are stored in the paragraph mark, you can copy and paste the paragraph mark itself to create new paragraphs with the same formatting. Use the Show/Hide button to display the paragraph marks, select the paragraph mark of the paragraph that you want to change, copy that mark, and then paste the copied paragraph mark immediately after the last character of the paragraph to which you wish to apply formatting.

Removing paragraph formats

You can use a shortcut to remove any paragraph's formats that have been applied, converting the format back to that which is used by the paragraph's style. We'd better clarify that: Every paragraph in your document has a style applied to it. For instance, most text will probably use the Normal style. The style defines how much space appears before and after the paragraph, how much space between lines, and so on. But you can apply formatting directly to the paragraph. For instance, say you used the Paragraph dialog box to specify that a block of text is double-spaced—there's a blank line after every line. That paragraph format has been, in effect, laid over the Normal style's settings.

You can press Ctrl+Q to remove any direct paragraph formatting and leave only the paragraph's style formatting. Thus, in our example, if you place the cursor in the text and press Ctrl+Q, the double-spacing is removed and the paragraph returns to the Normal style.

Tip   This doesn't change any direct *character* formatting applied to the paragraph's text, however. So remember Ctrl+Q; it's a very useful way to return a paragraph to its styles formatting, without removing character formats such as bold and italics.

You can also press Ctrl+Shift+N to apply the default Normal style formatting to the paragraph. (Again, the character formatting is not removed.) Almost the same as Ctrl+Q, but of course, Ctrl+Q doesn't change the style.

Some paragraph formatting commands and buttons act as toggle switches; using them, you can turn the formatting on or off. For example, with the insertion point in a paragraph, you can convert that paragraph to a bulleted item by clicking the Bullets button on the Formatting toolbar. With the insertion point in that same paragraph, clicking the Bullets button again removes the bullet formatting of the paragraph.

Tip   If you cut and paste text from another Word document or another application and have difficulty reformatting that paragraph, cut the text (Ctrl+X), select Edit ⇨ Paste Special, and choose Unformatted Text. All of the formatting is removed.

Using line breaks

We explained that when you press Enter, you start a new paragraph. But it's possible to create individual blocks of text, separated by a blank line if you wish, *within* a paragraph. Instead of pressing Enter to go to the next line, press Shift+Enter, and Word inserts a *line break* instead of a paragraph break—instead of the backward P, you'll see a little arrow with a right-angle bend in it (see Figure 5-5).

A line break is also known as a *soft return*. Using soft returns, you can break lines but keep them in the same paragraph. Line breaks can save you a lot of time when formatting. Line breaks are especially helpful for creating headings that you want to appear on more than one line and also for creating lists aligned with tabs. After you finish entering the line breaks, press Enter in the usual way to end that paragraph and begin the next.

Show/Hide button

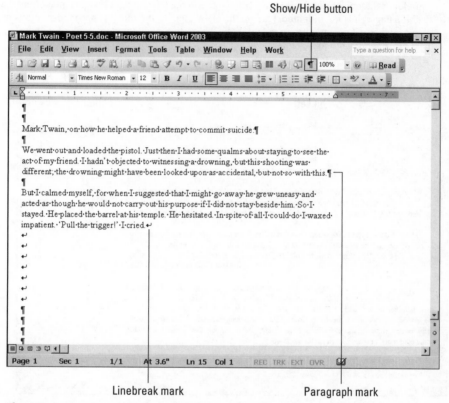

Linebreak mark   Paragraph mark

Figure 5-5: You can see both paragraph breaks and line breaks in this image.

Aligning Paragraphs

Word provides four ways to align paragraphs within your document's margin: left-aligned, right-aligned, center-aligned, and justified. By default, Word aligns text flush with the left margin (left-aligned), leaving a ragged right edge. Figure 5-6 shows the four different paragraph alignments. With Word, you can align paragraphs using the Paragraph dialog box, the align buttons on the Formatting toolbar, or shortcut keys.

To align paragraphs, follow these steps:

1. Position the insertion point in a paragraph, or select the paragraphs that you want to align.

2. Do one of the following:

- Click the alignment button on the Formatting toolbar for the justification that you want (see Table 5-1).

- Press one of the shortcut keys in Table 5-1.

- Choose Format ⇨ Paragraph, or choose Paragraph from the shortcut menu (Shift+F10), to display the Paragraph dialog box. Choose the alignment option from the Alignment list in the Indents and Spacing tab, and then click OK.

Note   Before centering or aligning a paragraph relative to the left and right margins, make sure that the paragraph is not indented. Paragraphs are aligned to the margins if no indentations are set for them; if paragraphs are indented, they align to the indentation. Working with indents is explained later in this chapter.

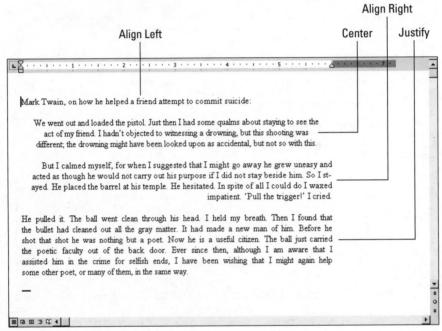

Figure 5-6: Four paragraph alignment options in Word.

Table 5-1: Paragraph Alignment Buttons and Shortcut Keys

Alignment Type	Button	Shortcut Keys	Description
Align Left		Ctrl+L	Text aligns with the left margin, and the right margin is ragged. This is the default setting.
Center		Ctrl+E	Text is centered between margins.
Align Right		Ctrl+R	Text aligns with the right margin, and the left margin is ragged.
Justify		Ctrl+J	Text aligns with both the left and right margins by adding extra spaces between words.

Click and Type: Inserting Paragraphs

Word has a little-known feature called *click and type* that you turn on under the Edit tab of the Options dialog box. When enabled, this feature lets you click, in Print Layout view, an area of a page without an existing paragraph to begin a new one.

Suppose you just opened a new document. The page has a single paragraph on the first line. Choose View ➪ Print Layout, and move the mouse pointer around the page. Notice that it changes as you move around the page. Depending on where you point, the insertion I-beam has an additional icon next to it—an icon that corresponds with one of the alignment buttons on the Formatting toolbar: Align Left, Center, or Align Right.

Click the Show/Hide button on the Standard toolbar so that you can see the first paragraph mark at the top of the page. Now move the mouse pointer down the page and point at the bottom-right corner of the page, but stay inside the margins set for the document. You should see an I-beam with an Align Right icon next to it. Double-click, and you've just inserted a right-aligned paragraph near the bottom of the page, along with a number of Normal paragraphs between the first line on the page and your newly inserted paragraph.

Note　　You can even tell Word what paragraph style you want to use when you use the click and type feature. Just choose a style from the Default Paragraph Style drop-down in the Click and Type area of the Option dialog box's Edit tab.

Adjusting Line and Paragraph Spacing

You can adjust the spacing between lines in a paragraph as well as the spacing between paragraphs themselves. By adjusting the spacing between paragraphs, you can control the white space around paragraphs that contain oversized graphics or fonts. Using paragraph spacing, you can manage the layout of your documents more precisely than you can just by pressing Enter to create paragraph breaks for spacing.

Spacing between lines in a document is called *leading* (pronounced *ledding*). With Word, you can control the leading to improve the readability of the text in paragraphs. For example, if your text appears in long lines, you may need more spacing so that the reader's eye doesn't lose its place when moving from the right margin back to the left. Alternatively, if you're using a font style with small letters, your text may require less spacing between the lines than that between lines containing larger fonts. Line and paragraph spacing makes it easy to use *white space* to make your documents easier to read quickly. Very dense blocks of text are harder to read than text separated by white space between paragraphs.

Tip　　Adjusting spacing in the way we've just discussed is an example of a case in which doing it *right* can save you a lot of time when making changes to a document. If you use paragraph spacing to adjust the space that appears between paragraphs, you can modify that spacing very easily later if you decide you want to adjust the document. If you used paragraph and line breaks to adjust the space between text and paragraphs, you have a lot of work to do if you want to change things. Also, paragraph formatting lets you adjust spacing in increments of 1 point, something you can't do easily by inserting paragraph and line breaks.

Adjusting paragraph spacing

Instead of pressing Enter to add blank lines before or after a paragraph, use the Format ➪ Paragraph command. Using the Paragraph dialog box, you can adjust the paragraph spacing precisely as well as keep any spacing changes for a paragraph if you copy, move, or delete that paragraph.

To adjust paragraph spacing, follow these steps:

1. Position the insertion point in a paragraph, or select the paragraphs that you want to adjust.

2. Choose Format ➪ Paragraph, or choose Paragraph from the shortcut menu. Click the Indents and Spacing tab in the Paragraph dialog box.

3. Do one of the following:

   • To change the space before the selected paragraph, click the up or down arrow in the Spacing Before box to increase or decrease the spacing amount in half-line increments. Alternatively, you can type a value in the box. The Preview section of the Paragraph dialog box shows the effect of your selected spacing.

   • To change the space after the selected paragraph, click the up or down arrow in the Spacing After box or type a value in the box.

Tip

You can use measurements other than points to specify spacing. To add a quarter-inch of spacing, type **.25** in the Before or After box. To add spacing of two centimeters, type **2 cm**. To add spacing of one pica, type **1 pi**. The Preview section of the Paragraph dialog box shows the effect of your selected spacing.

4. Click OK.

Note

If a paragraph has spacing before it and falls at the top of a page, Word ignores that spacing so that the top margins of your document pages always remain even. If the paragraph is the first paragraph in a document or a formatted section, however, Word always observes this spacing. Word also observes the spacing before a paragraph that follows a hard page break. For more on working with sections and hard page breaks, see Chapter 10.

Adjusting line spacing

The line-spacing feature in Word begins with automatic spacing, and with this feature, you can increase spacing, reduce spacing, permit extra spacing for a large character or super-script on the line, or even control the spacing exactly. Spacing is measured in terms of lines. Normal text has single spacing of one line, but you can choose from several line options or even specify line spacing based on points. Table 5-2 describes the line-spacing options in Word. You can apply line spacing using the Paragraph dialog box or shortcut keys, but the Paragraph dialog box offers the most options.

Table 5-2: Line Spacing Options

Option	Spacing
Single	Single-line spacing. (Line height automatically adjusts to accommodate the size of the font and any graphics or formulas in a line.)
1.5 Lines	Line-and-one-half spacing (an extra half-line of space between lines).
Double	Double-spacing (an extra full line of space between lines).
At Least	At least the spacing that you specify in the At box—the line won't be shorter than what you specify, but it may be taller because Word will add extra spacing for tall characters, big graphics, and superscript or subscript text.
Exactly	The exact spacing that you specify in the At box. All lines are exactly the same height, regardless of the size of the characters in the line; Word doesn't add extra spacing. Note that some text may be cut off if enough space is not available.
Multiple	Multiples of single-line spacing, such as triple (3) or quadruple (4), as specified in the At box.

To adjust spacing between lines, follow these steps:

1. Position the insertion point in a paragraph, or select the paragraphs that you want to adjust.

2. Do one of the following:

   • Choose Format ⇨ Paragraph, or choose Paragraph from the shortcut menu. The Paragraph dialog box appears. Click the Indents and Spacing tab, and in the Line Spacing list box, choose one of the options listed in Table 5-2. To specify your own line spacing, type the spacing amount that you want in the At box. For example, enter **1.25** for an extra quarter line of space between lines, or click the up or down arrow to increase or decrease the amount in half-line increments. When you finish, click OK.

   • Press one of the shortcut key combinations in Table 5-3.

Table 5-3: Shortcut Keys for Line Spacing Options

Shortcut	Action
Ctrl+l	Single-spacing
Ctrl+5	1.5-line spacing
Ctrl+2	Double-spacing
Ctrl+0 (zero)	Add or remove 12 points of space before a paragraph

Note   Notice the Don't Add Space Between Paragraphs of the Same Style check box below the Spacing controls in the Paragraph dialog box. This is not usually enabled; it's enabled when you open the dialog box from the Modify Style dialog box, which we examine in Chapter 13. Check this box and Word adds extra space below the last paragraph of a series of paragraphs of the same style. So, for instance, if you have a style you use for bulleted lists, you can press Enter at the end of each bulleted item, creating a new paragraph for each. But it's not until you press Enter and start a new style that Word inserts extra space.

Tip   Do you ever have to create documents that are double-spaced (a blank line between every line of text)? Students often do, for instance. Do *not* create this double spacing by pressing Enter or Shift+Enter at the end of each line. (We've seen this many times, so we *know* a lot of you are doing this!) If you do, you'll find it a nightmare to readjust everything when you insert or remove text during editing. Use Paragraph formatting and save yourself hours of work.

Setting Tabs

A *tab stop* is the position at which the text-insertion point stops when you press the Tab key. Pressing the Tab key moves the insertion point to the right, shifting the position at which you will insert text. If there's any text to the right of the insertion point when you press Tab, that text is shifted, too.

Word documents are set up with default tab stops every ½ inch across the document, but you can set your own tab stops, too, wherever you want them. In fact, there are several different types of tab stop that you can use (left, centered, right, decimal, or bar) and a variety of other options, too. When you set a custom tab, all the default tabs to the left of the custom tab are cleared—that is, when you press Tab, Word will ignore the default tabs and go to the first custom tab.

There's an advantage to using tabs rather than spacing. After the tabs are in your document, you can move or change the tab stops and then the selected text moves or realigns with those stops. Remember, however, that tabs belong to paragraphs. If you set tab stops as you type text and press Enter, the tab settings carry forward to the next paragraph.

Note   One of the most common word-processing mistakes is using spaces to align text. In most cases, the text is in proportional font. Because proportional-font characters take up different amounts of space, however, the text in that font cannot align correctly with this method. Using tabs ensures that your text is aligned perfectly and makes it *much* easier to modify settings.

You can set tabs using the horizontal ruler or the Tabs dialog box. To display the Tabs dialog box, choose Format ➪ Tab or click the Tabs button in the Paragraph dialog box (Format ➪ Paragraph). Table 5-4 describes the tab options available in Word, and Figure 5-7 shows how left-aligned, center-aligned, right-aligned, and decimal tab settings affect a paragraph.

Table 5-4: Tab Options

Type of Tab	Ruler Tab Indicator	Action
Left-aligned	⌞	Begins text at the tab stop. (This is the default tab setting.)
Center-aligned	⊥	Centers text on the tab stop.
Right-aligned	⌟	Ends the text at tab stop.
Decimal	⊥•	Centers text over decimal point for a list of numbers.
Bar	I	Runs a vertical line through a selected paragraph at the tab stop.

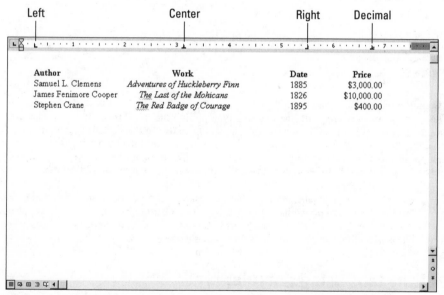

Figure 5-7: Tabs aligned using the Left, Center, Right, and Decimal tab settings.

Figure 5-8 shows columns divided using the bar tab.

Bar tabs

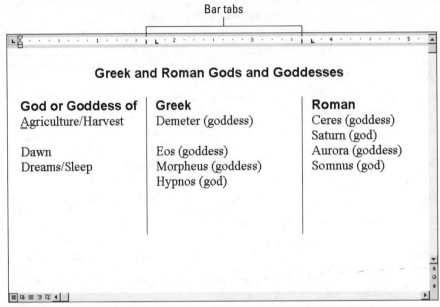

Figure 5-8: Bar tabs dividing text.

Use line breaks rather than paragraph breaks between lines of short text within columns. This way, you can realign the information, by adjusting the tab settings, very quickly without needing to select the paragraphs (just click anywhere within the paragraph and make your changes). Press Shift+Enter to insert the new line. If you add tabs later using new lines, the tab applies to all of the lines before the next paragraph mark. If you want to align large columns of text, use Word's powerful table feature, which is explained in Chapter 9.

Note Bar *tabs* are not real tabs! Placing a bar tab inserts a vertical line in your document, down through the paragraph, at the bar-tab position. But a bar tab has no effect on text position. Pressing the Tab key does not move text to the bar-tab position. Bar tabs are usually combined with other types of tabs that set the text alignment.

Setting tabs using the ruler

A convenient way to set tabs is to use the ruler. If your ruler is not displayed, choose View ➪ Ruler to display it. At the left of the ruler is the Tab Alignment button, with which you can quickly change tab styles. Using the mouse and the ruler, you can set, move, and remove the left-aligned, center-aligned, right-aligned, decimal, or bar tabs with a precision of as much as ¹⁄₁₆-inch. The ruler displays Word's default tab stops (set every ½-inch, unless you change the interval, which we look at later in this chapter) as tiny vertical lines along the bottom of the ruler. (You may have to look closely to see these thin black lines on the gray bar under the ruler.) When you set your own tab stops, all of the default tab stops to the left are removed.

To set tabs using the ruler, follow these steps:

1. Position the insertion point in a paragraph, or select the paragraphs that you want to adjust.

2. Click the Tab Alignment button at the far left of the ruler until the symbol for the tab style you want is selected (see Table 5-4).

3. Position the pointer just below the mark on the ruler where you want the tab stop to appear. Click the left mouse button to place the tab stop on the ruler. The tab stop marker then appears for the tab style that you selected (see Figure 5-9).

4. Do one of the following:

   • Repeat step 3 to add more tab stops of the same style.

   • Repeat steps 2 and 3 to add other types of tab stops to the ruler.

Figure 5-9: The ruler with tab stops displayed.

Changing or clearing a tab stop using the ruler

To change a tab marker on the ruler, place the insertion point in the paragraph you want to work on. Then point to the tab marker with the mouse pointer, hold down the left mouse button to select that marker, and drag the marker to its new position. When you release, the marker is dropped into its new position.

To clear a tab stop quickly using the mouse and ruler, drag that marker all the way off the ruler and onto the document—when you release, the marker is removed.

Setting tabs using the Tabs dialog box

Using the Tabs dialog box (see Figure 5-10) to set tabs offers some advantages over using the ruler and mouse. With the Tabs dialog box, you can precisely set each tab's position by typing decimal numbers (in inches).

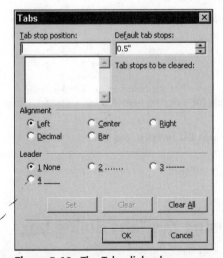

Figure 5-10: The Tabs dialog box.

You can also add dotted, dashed, or underlined tab leaders. A *tab leader* links related but separate items across a page, such as entrées and prices in a menu or chapters and page numbers in a table of contents (see Figure 5-11).

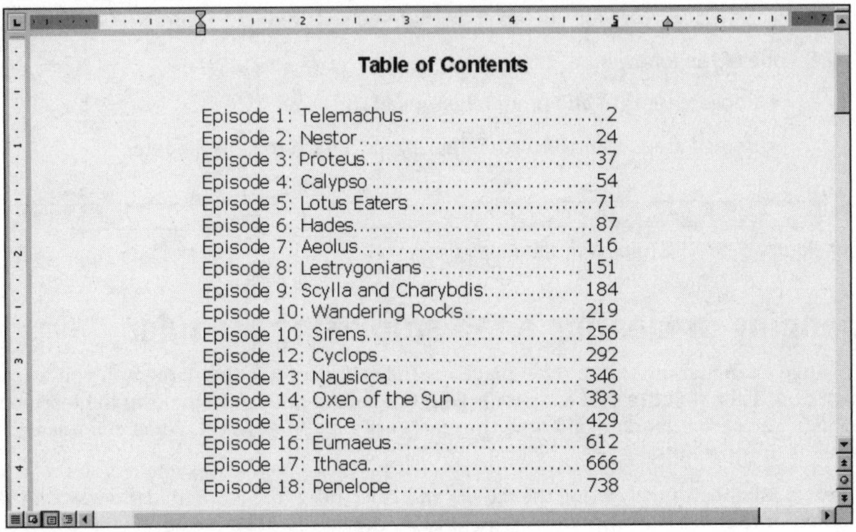
Table of Contents

Episode 1: Telemachus....................2
Episode 2: Nestor....................24
Episode 3: Proteus....................37
Episode 4: Calypso....................54
Episode 5: Lotus Eaters....................71
Episode 6: Hades....................87
Episode 7: Aeolus....................116
Episode 8: Lestrygonians....................151
Episode 9: Scylla and Charybdis....................184
Episode 10: Wandering Rocks....................219
Episode 10: Sirens....................256
Episode 12: Cyclops....................292
Episode 13: Nausicca....................346
Episode 14: Oxen of the Sun....................383
Episode 15: Circe....................429
Episode 16: Eumaeus....................612
Episode 17: Ithaca....................666
Episode 18: Penelope....................738

Figure 5-11: Leader tabs link related but separate items.

To set tabs using the Tabs dialog box, follow these steps:

1. Position the insertion point in a paragraph, or select the paragraphs that you want to adjust.
2. Choose Format ➪ Tabs. The Tabs dialog box appears.
3. Using decimal numbers, type the position of the tab stop that you want to set in the Tab Stop Position box.
4. In the Alignment group, select the tab style that you want: Left, Center, Right, Decimal, or Bar.
5. If you want a leader, select the tab leader style that you want in the Leader group: 1 None for no leader (the default setting), 2 for a dotted leader, 3 for a dashed leader, and 4 for a solid underlined leader.
6. Choose Set to set the tab stop. The Tab Stops list box displays your tab stops after you set them.
7. Repeat steps 3 through 6 to set additional tab stops.
8. Click OK to close the Tabs dialog box.

Changing and clearing tabs using the Tabs dialog box

To change existing tab stops using the Tabs dialog box (Format ➪ Tabs), select the tab stop that you want to change in the Tab Stops list box. Select the new formatting options for the selected tab stop in the Alignment and Leader groups, and then click Set.

You can clear tab stops either individually or as a group. You can also clear tabs using the Tabs dialog box whether you originally set the tabs using this dialog box or the ruler.

To clear tabs, follow these steps:

1. Position the insertion point in a paragraph, or select the paragraphs that you want to adjust.

2. Choose Format ➪ Tabs to display the Tabs dialog box.

3. Do one of the following:

   - Click Clear All to clear all of the tab stop settings.

   - Select the tab that you want to delete from the Tab Stops list, and then click Clear. Repeat this process to clear additional tab stops. As you select tab stops to clear and then click Clear, the tab stops that you remove are listed in the Tab Stops to be Cleared area at the bottom of the dialog box.

4. Click OK.

Changing the default tab stops

By default, Word has preset tabs every ½-inch. When you set a custom tab, however, all of the preset tabs to the left of that custom tab are cleared. Use the Tabs dialog box to change the default tab stop interval if you routinely use the preset tabs but don't like the default setting. Note that custom tab stops that you may have set for existing paragraphs aren't affected.

To change the default tab stops, display the Tabs dialog box. In the Default Tab Stops box, type a new default tab interval or click the up or down arrow to change the number in the box. Then click OK. Note that this changes the default for the current document only, not for all documents.

Setting Indents

With indenting, you can set off a paragraph from other text. Figure 5-12 shows paragraphs formatted with different indents. Don't confuse page margins with paragraph indents, however. *Margins* specify the overall width of the text and the area between the text and the edge of the page, whereas *indents* move the paragraph's text in or out from the left and the right margins. You can indent paragraphs in the following ways:

✦ Indent paragraphs from the left, right, or both margins to set those paragraphs off from other text.

✦ Use negative indents to run text into the left or right margin.

✦ Indent only the first line of a paragraph, which is commonly used as a substitute for pressing Tab at the beginning of each new paragraph.

✦ Create a *hanging indent,* which hangs the first line of a paragraph to the left of the rest of the paragraph. (In other words, every line except the first line is indented.) Hanging indents are often used in bulleted and numbered lists, footnotes, and bibliographic entries.

✦ Create *nested indents,* which are indentations within indentations.

First-line indent   Left and Right indent

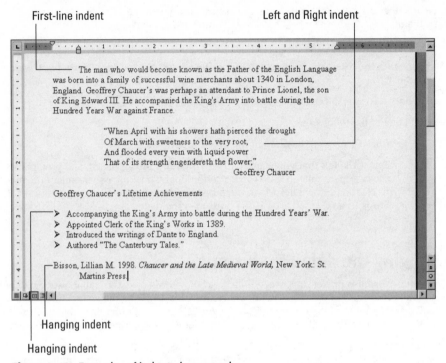

Hanging indent

Hanging indent

Figure 5-12: Examples of indented paragraphs.

Word provides several ways to create indents. You can indent paragraphs using the Formatting toolbar, the ruler, shortcut keys, or the Paragraph dialog box. Indenting with the Formatting toolbar or shortcut keys, however, depends on tab-stop settings. If you haven't changed Word's default ½-inch tab stops, you can create indents at ½-inch intervals using the Formatting toolbar or shortcut keys.

Note   You can use hanging indents to create a bulleted or a numbered list, but with Word's bullets and numbering features, you can create such lists automatically—including the bullets and the numbers. Working with bulleted and numbered lists is explained later in this chapter.

Setting indents using the Formatting toolbar

The Formatting toolbar includes two buttons for indenting paragraphs to the next tab stop: Decrease Indent and Increase Indent (see Figure 5-13). Use these buttons to create left indents only; you cannot create first-line or hanging indents with these buttons. To indent or to remove indents from paragraphs using the Formatting toolbar, position the insertion point in the paragraph or select the paragraphs that you want to adjust. Click the Increase Indent button to indent text to the next tab stop, or click the Decrease Indent button to un-indent text to the previous tab stop. You can click either button as many times as you want to continue moving the indentation to the next tab stop.

Figure 5-13: The Decrease Indent and Increase Indent buttons of the Formatting toolbar.

Setting indents using the ruler

You can create any kind of indent using the ruler, which contains triangular *indent markers* at the left and right margins. Table 5-5 shows and describes each of these indent markers. You can drag them in either direction along the ruler to set indents. At the left margin, the top triangle represents the first-line indent and the bottom triangle represents the left indent. Both the top and bottom triangles move independently, but you can use the square below the bottom triangle to move the first-line and left-paragraph indents at the same time. At the right margin, the triangle represents the paragraph's right indent.

Table 5-5: Indent Markers on the Ruler

Drag	To Set
▽	First-line indent
⬠	Left indent
⯆⬠	First-line and left indents
△	Right indent

To set indentations using the ruler, follow these steps:

1. Position the insertion point in a paragraph, or select the paragraphs that you want to indent.

2. Do one of the following:

   • To set a first-line indent, drag the First Line Indent marker to the position where you want the indentation.

   • To set a left indent, drag the square below the Left Indent marker to the position where you want the indentation. (Note that the top triangle moves as well.)

   • To set a right indent, drag the Right Indent marker to the position where you want the indentation.

   • To set a hanging indent with the first line at the left margin, drag the Left Indent marker to a new position on the ruler.

You can press and hold the Alt key while dragging to get more control; you'll be able to move the controls smoothly and drop them at any position rather than the default gradations. You can also see exact measurements on the ruler as you drag.

Tip When you drag the Left Indent or First Line Indent marker to the left of the left margin, the ruler automatically scrolls to the left. If you want to scroll into the left margin on the ruler without moving the indent markers, first make sure that you're in Normal view (View ⇨ Normal). Then hold down the Shift key as you click the left scroll arrow on the horizontal scroll bar.

Setting indents using keyboard shortcuts

You can create indents using keyboard shortcuts as well. Keyboard shortcuts rely on existing tab settings to determine the position of the indents. To create indents using keyboard shortcuts, position the insertion point in a paragraph or select the paragraphs that you want to indent. Then press one of the keyboard shortcuts listed in Table 5-6.

Table 5-6: Keyboard Shortcuts for Indenting Paragraphs

Keyboard Shortcut	Type of Indention
Ctrl+M	Moves the left indent to the next tab stop.
Ctrl+Shift+M	Moves the left indent to the preceding tab stop.
Ctrl+T	Creates a hanging indent.
Ctrl+Shift+T	Moves the left indent to the previous tab stop, but the first line remains in its current position.

Tip   Here's another way to set indents, although one that's a little irritating to some users. Choose Tools ⇨ AutoCorrect Options and click the AutoFormat as You Type tab. Make sure that the Set Left- and First-Indent With Tabs and Backspaces check box is selected. Now, when you press Tab and then type a paragraph, you'll be setting the indent for that paragraph.

Setting indents using the Paragraph dialog box

You can use the Paragraph dialog box to set any type of indent. One advantage of using this dialog box is that you can enter precise measurements instead of just eyeballing the text alignments with ruler measurements. You can also create indents using measurements other than decimal inches. To create a six-point left indent, for example, type **6 pt** in the Left Indentation box. To create a left indent of two centimeters, type **2 cm**. To create a left indent of one pica, type **1 pi**. (There are six picas in one inch and 12 points in one pica.)

To set indentations using the Paragraph dialog box, follow these steps:

1. Position the insertion point in a paragraph, or select the paragraphs that you want to indent.

2. Choose Format ⇨ Paragraph, or choose Paragraph from the shortcut menu (Shift+F10), to open the Paragraph dialog box. Then click the Indents and Spacing tab.

3. Do one of the following:

   • To create a paragraph indent, type or select a value in the Left or Right Indentation text box. The Indentation group in the Paragraph dialog box lists three options: Left, Right, and Special. (Table 5-7 describes these indentation options.) The Preview box shows the effect of your choice.

   • To create a first-line or a hanging indent, select First Line or Hanging from the Special list box. Then type or select a value in the By text box to specify the first-line or hanging-indent measurement.

4. Click OK.

Table 5-7: Indentation Options

Option	Action
Left	Indents selected text from the left margin. If the amount to indent is a positive number, the paragraph is indented inside the left margin; if the amount is a negative number, the paragraph is indented outside the left margin (sometimes called *outdenting*).
Right	Indents selected text from the right margin. If the amount to indent is a positive number, the paragraph is indented inside the right margin; if the amount to indent is a negative number, the paragraph is indented outside the right margin.
Special	Indents the first line (or lines) of selected text from left indent used by subsequent lines (or from the left margin if no indent is made). Click the down arrow to select First Line or Hanging. First Line shifts the first line to the right of subsequent lines, while Hanging moves the first line to the left of subsequent lines. The default indent is ½-inch. Change the indent by typing a new number or by using the up- or down-arrow key.

Bordering and Shading Paragraphs and Pages

A *border* can be a box surrounding a paragraph on all sides or lines on one or more sides of the block of text. *Shading* fills a paragraph (with or without borders) with a background pattern. If you're planning to print on a black and white printer, you'll probably want to stick to black, white, and gray for your lines and backgrounds, but Word does allow you to use different colors. Figure 5-14 shows samples of different borders applied to paragraphs.

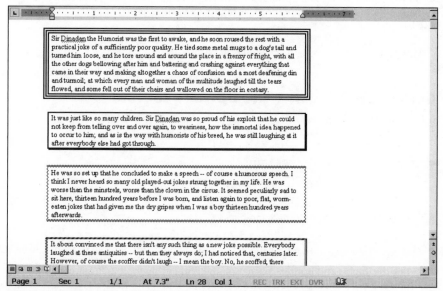

Figure 5-14: Examples of borders.

Like all forms of paragraph formatting, borders belong to the paragraphs in which they are applied. In other words, they carry forward when you press Enter at the end of a paragraph. If a group of paragraphs is formatted with a box around them and you press Enter at the end of the last paragraph, your new paragraph falls within the same box as the previous paragraph. To create a new paragraph outside of the border, move the insertion point outside the border before you press Enter, or just press Enter and then press Ctrl+Q to return the new paragraph to the default paragraph setting.

The width of a paragraph box, or of the line if you just created a horizontal line rather than a box, is determined by the paragraph indent and margins. The line or box begins at the left text position—the left margin or, if set, the left indent—and ends at the right text position—the right margin or indent.

To place several paragraphs in a single box or to give them the same background shading, make sure that all of the paragraphs have the same indents. If you select and then box or shade several paragraphs with different indents, each paragraph appears in its own separate box or shading. To make paragraphs with different indents appear within a single box or background shade, you must create a table, put each paragraph in a row by itself, and then format a box around the table.

For more information about creating tables and adding borders to a table, see Chapter 9.

Sometimes the screen inaccurately shows text as extending beyond borders or shading. This situation results from screen fonts and screen resolutions, which differ from printer fonts and resolution. Your printed text does format within the border or shading even if it doesn't display correctly on the screen.

The same border and shading options for paragraphs can be applied to an entire page as well. Tools for creating paragraph borders and page borders are located in the same dialog box.

You find out how to create page borders in Chapter 10.

Adding borders using the Borders toolbar

Word includes a Tables and Borders toolbar, as shown in Figure 5-15, for applying borders, lines, and shading.

Figure 5-15: The Tables and Borders toolbar.

To add boxes or lines to paragraphs using the Tables and Borders toolbar, follow these steps:

1. Click the Tables and Borders button on the Formatting toolbar, or choose View ➪ Toolbars and select the Tables and Borders toolbar. You can also right-click on any toolbar and select Tables and Borders.

2. Position the insertion point in a paragraph, or select the paragraphs that you want to enclose. Remember that if you create a box for more than one paragraph, that box encloses those paragraphs as a group (unless they have different indents) with no borders between them.

3. Click the Line style box down arrow, and choose a line style. If the Line style box is not visible, drag the Tables and Borders toolbar so that you can see all of the options.

4. Choose the border that you want to add by clicking the Outside Border button and then selecting one of the border buttons that appears in the drop-down box (see Figure 5-16).

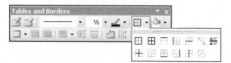

Figure 5-16: Border options in the Tables and Borders toolbar.

Adding borders using the Borders and Shading dialog box

You can also add borders using the Borders and Shading dialog box (see Figure 5-17). Table 5-8 explains the options in the Border tab. The Borders and Shading dialog box includes the Options button, which displays a dialog box in which you can change the distance from a box line to the surrounded text precisely. You can also specify a shadow or a three-dimensional (3-D) border option. Special options for placing a border on an entire page are found here as well.

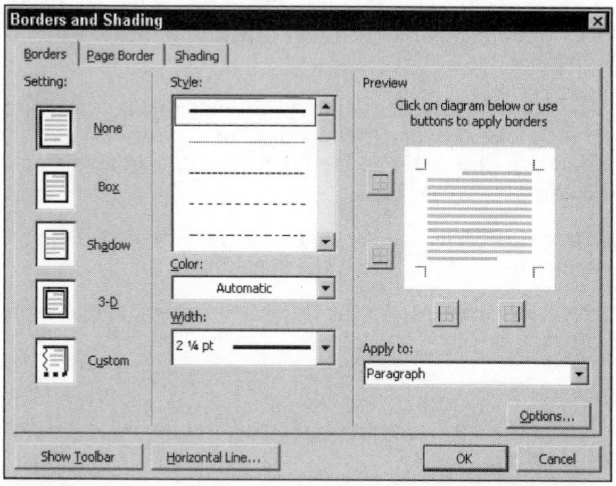

Figure 5-17: The Borders tab of the Borders and Shading dialog box.

Table 5-8: The Borders and Page Borders Tab Options

Option	Effect
None	Removes an existing box.
Box	Creates a box with identical lines on all four sides.
Shadow	Creates a box with a drop shadow on the bottom and right sides.
3-D	Creates a border with a 3-D effect.
Custom	This button really isn't very useful; in theory it combines any of the previous effects with non-boxed border options, but in practice you should probably ignore it.
Apply to	Defines where the border will be applied, and the options vary between the Borders and Page Borders tabs—in the Borders tab you will see *Paragraph* and, if you highlighted text within a paragraph first, *Text*.
Style	Provides a variety of lines styles for you to choose from. Select a Style first and then a line Width, and the Style list box changes to show that style in the selected thickness.
Width	This should probably be called *Thickness*, a less ambiguous term. Allows selection of various line thicknesses, ranging from ¼ to 6 points.
Color	Creates a line or a box in the selected color. Sixteen colors and gray shades are available. If you select the Auto option, the default color for text is used, generally black.
Art	Allows selection of various page borders, including over 150 different icons and ornamental designs. The Art list box appears only on the Page Border tab.

To add a border using the Borders and Shading dialog box, follow these steps:

1. Position the insertion point in a paragraph, or select the paragraphs that you want to enclose. Remember that if you create a box for more than one paragraph, that box encloses those paragraphs as a group (unless they have different indents) with no borders between them.

2. Choose Format ➪ Borders and Shading. The Borders and Shading dialog box appears. Click the Borders tab. If you plan to apply a border to a page or a group of pages (rather than to paragraphs), click the Page Border tab in the Borders and Shading dialog box and select from the Apply To drop-down list box.

3. Select one of the line styles from the Styles list, or click one of the Settings boxes to select a style and apply the lines around the box at the same time.

4. If you wish you may also select a line color from the Color drop-down, and a line thickness from the Width drop-down.

5. Do one of the following:

   - Click one of the buttons to the left and underneath the Preview image to place a line in the associated position.

   - Click inside the Preview image itself to place a line on one of the edges.

   - If you selected multiple paragraphs, you'll notice that the Preview image shows two paragraphs, separated by a blank line; you can create a line between paragraphs by clicking this blank line in the Preview image.

6. Click OK.

Tip You can use different lines on different edges. Select your first line style, color, and thickness. Then click on an edge of the square in the Preview box inside the Borders and Shading dialog box; select another line and click on another edge; and so on.

Spacing between text and border

When you place a border around text, Word drops the border into place very close to the text all around. This is sometimes very inconvenient, especially if you want to shade an area below a heading or place a border around an entire page—the text sits so close to the border it looks bad in some cases.

You can adjust spacing between the text and the border, though. While working in the Borders and Shading text box, click the Options button to see the Border and Shading Options dialog box (see Figure 5-18). You can set the spacing here precisely.

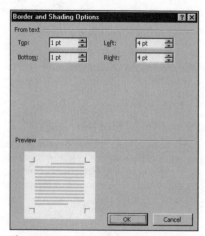

Figure 5-18: Set spacing between borders and text here.

You can also use the mouse to change a border directly within your document. Move the mouse pointer to the border line you want to adjust, and carefully place it directly over the line—the mouse pointer will change from an arrow to two lines with up and down arrows (or left and right arrows if you are adjusting a vertical border). Drag the border to change the space between the text and that border.

Placing borders around individual lines

Word allows you to place borders around individual lines of text. Select the text you want to place the border around, and then create your borders using the Borders and Shading dialog box. Notice that the Apply To drop-down list box shows the word *Text*, meaning that Word will create a text border rather than a paragraph border.

When you click OK, Word creates the border, placing a left border in front of the first character you selected, and a right border after the last one. If you selected multiple lines of text, each line has its own border around it.

Fitting a border within margins

When you create a box around a paragraph, the left and right edges of the box are placed slightly outside the page margins (assuming the text hasn't been indented, of course, in which case the margins are slightly to the left and right of the indent positions).

You may want the borders to fall within, or exactly at, the page margins. To make a border fit within the margins, indent the paragraph on both the left and the right side by the width of the border. You can use the ruler, but you can be more precise using the Borders and Shading dialog box.

To make borders fall on the margins using the Borders and Shading dialog box, follow these steps:

1. Position the insertion point in a paragraph, or select the paragraphs that you want to adjust.

2. Choose Format ➪ Borders and Shading.

3. On the Borders tab, note the width (the thickness) of the border line in the Width control.

4. Click Options. The Borders and Shading Options dialog box then appears. Note the spacing in the From Text boxes labeled Left and Right.

5. Click OK or Cancel twice to close both dialog boxes.

6. Choose Format ➪ Paragraph. Then click the Indents and Spacing tab.

7. In the Left and Right boxes of the Indentation group, type the number of points equal to the combined width of the border and the spacing specified in the Left and Right values in the Border and Shading Options dialog box. For example, if the border is three points thick and the entry in the From Text box is one point, enter four points in the Left and Right boxes.

8. Click OK.

Removing or changing borders

You can remove borders either all at once or line by line. You can remove or change a border using the Borders toolbar or the Borders and Shading dialog box.

To remove or change borders using the Borders toolbar, follow these steps:

1. Position the insertion point in the paragraph containing the borders, or select the paragraphs that you want to adjust.

2. Display the Tables and Borders toolbar by clicking the Borders button on the Formatting toolbar.

3. Do one of the following:

   • Click the Outside Borders button, and choose no borders.

   • Choose a new line style.

   • Click the buttons for the boxes or borders that you want to add.

To remove or change borders using the Borders and Shading dialog box, follow these steps:

1. Position the insertion point in the paragraph containing the borders, or select the paragraphs that you want to adjust.

2. Choose Format ⇨ Borders and Shading, and click the Borders tab. If you're removing borders applied to an entire page or to a group of pages, click the Page Border tab.

3. Do one of the following:

   • To remove a box border, select the None button in the Setting group.

   • To remove individual border lines, click the button representing the line you want to remove in the Preview image.

   • To change a line, select the line that you want from the Style scroll box.

4. Click OK.

Adding shading

Shading in Word comes in various percentages of black (grays) and different colors, as well as in various patterns. For each shade or pattern, you can select a foreground or a background color. Colors are converted to shades of gray or patterns on a black-and-white printer. You can use shading with borders so that a paragraph is surrounded by a line and filled with shading, or you can use shading alone so that a paragraph is shaded but has no border.

Working with shading requires playing with different configurations to find the one that is most readable. As a general rule, however, the smaller the font size, the lighter you need to make the paragraph shading. Applying bold to text may also help. To change the color of text with a background shading, use the Font dialog box (Format ⇨ Font).

For more information on working with the Font dialog box, see Chapter 4.

Fill versus pattern

Word lets you apply two forms of shading: *fill* and *pattern*. You can think of these as the fill being the foundation, and the pattern being laid on top. Or the fill is the background color, while the pattern is the foreground pattern or color. The fill is always a solid shade or color. The pattern can be solid, but also may be an actual pattern of dots or lines.

Thus, you can have one color as a fill, and another color for the pattern—a fill of light yellow with a pattern of black lines on top, for instance. Of course, if you use a solid pattern you won't see the fill underneath.

Note also the difference between a fill for which you have selected No Fill and one for which you have selected the color white. These are *not* the same thing. No Fill means the paragraph has no background color; you can see through the text to the watermark below, for example. If you use a white fill, the watermark would not be visible under that paragraph.

To find out more about watermarks, see Chapter 10.

The same goes for the pattern. If you have any kind of pattern, even a white pattern, the document background cannot be seen below the paragraph. Thus a Clear pattern is not the same as a white pattern. Select Clear if you want to use a fill, but with no pattern or color sitting on top.

Applying shading

You can apply shading using the Shading tab of the Borders and Shading dialog box (see Figure 5-19) or using the Tables and Borders toolbar.

To shade paragraphs using the Tables and Borders toolbar, position the insertion point in a paragraph or select the paragraphs that you want to shade. Click the Tables and Borders button on the Formatting toolbar to display the Tables and Borders toolbar, and then click the down arrow next to the Shading button to display a palette of fill colors. Choose the color of shading and the pattern that you want.

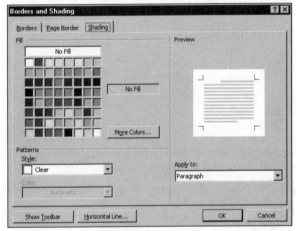

Figure 5-19: The Shading tab of the Borders and Shading dialog box.

To shade paragraphs using the Borders and Shading dialog box, follow these steps:

1. Position the insertion point in a paragraph, or select the paragraphs that you want to shade.

2. Choose Format ➪ Borders and Shading.

3. Click the Shading tab.

4. Select a Fill color (click the More Colors button if you don't see the one you want to use).

5. Select a Pattern Style. Style options include Clear (no pattern), Solid (completely blocks both the Fill color and the document background), percentages (the density of the Color shading), and striped as well as checkered patterns such as Dk Horizontal (for dark horizontal stripes) and Lt Grid (for a grid made of light cross-hatching). You can also apply light and dark trellises.

6. Select from the Color list to specify a color for the pattern you selected. The result of your selection appears in the Preview box. Automatic is selected by default—this means that the pattern will be created using black or gray.

7. Click OK.

Adding horizontal lines

You can also place horizontal lines, also known as *horizontal rules,* on your pages. You may want to use these lines in documents intended for printing, although the horizontal-line feature really grew out of the Web. Because Web pages are not divided like typical printed pages, horizontal lines are frequently used to divide Web pages. Word includes several clip-art images that can be used as lines.

To insert a horizontal line, choose Format ➪ Borders and Shading. The Borders and Shading dialog box appears. Click the Horizontal Line button, and the Horizontal Line dialog box appears (see Figure 5-20). The box will fill with images of horizontal lines, but it may take a little while. These are being drawn from an online library (so if you are not connected you may not see any, or many). If the box remains blank, try clicking on the scroll bar to move down the list and the box may suddenly fill.

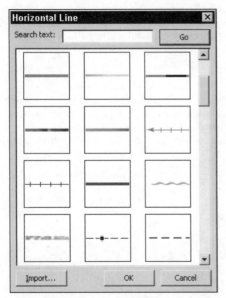

Figure 5-20: The Horizontal Line dialog box.

There's a search box, too. In theory, you can type a word—*star* or *arrow*, for example—and then click Search to find a matching horizontal line. In practice, it may not be worth the trouble. You can also click the Import button to load a file on your hard disk into the list of lines.

When you see a horizontal line you like—scroll down through the box to see more—click on it and click OK, or simply double-click it. The line will be placed into your document at the insertion-point position.

Double-clicking the line image in your document displays the Format Horizontal Line dialog box, which you can use to change the width, height, and alignment of the line.

Creating Bulleted or Numbered Lists

Bulleted lists help to distinguish a series of important items or points from the rest of the text in a document, and numbered lists are often used for step-by-step instructions. Word provides flexible, easy-to-use methods for creating bulleted and numbered lists with a variety of formats. You can type the text for the bulleted or numbered list and then apply the list formatting to the text, or you can place the insertion point in a blank line, apply the bulleted or numbered list format to that line, and then type the list. Either way, Word sets a ½-inch hanging indent after you select a list format, and Word adds the bullet or number in front of each paragraph, in the selected text, or in each new paragraph that you type.

Tip   You can create a numbered or bulleted list automatically as you type. At the beginning of a new paragraph, type a number or an asterisk followed by a space or a tab. Then, when you press Enter to add the next item in the list, Word automatically inserts the next number or bullet. To finish the list, press Enter followed by Backspace. This feature only works, however, if Automatic Bulleted Lists and Automatic Numbered Lists are selected in the AutoFormat As You Type tab of the AutoCorrect dialog box—choose Tools ➪ AutoCorrect.

Creating bulleted lists

Word offers seven standard bullet shapes: solid circle, empty circle, solid square, 3-D box, diamond, arrow, and checkmark. If you want to use a heart, pointing hand, or other symbol, you can select these bullets from any of your installed symbol fonts, such as Symbol, Wingdings, Webdings, and Monotype Sorts. You can even select a bullet image from a library of hundreds.

You can create a bulleted list using the Bullets and Numbering dialog box (see Figure 5-21) or the Formatting toolbar.

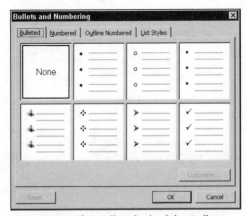

Figure 5-21: The Bulleted tab of the Bullets and Numbering dialog box.

To start a new bulleted list, simply place the insertion point where you plan to begin and then click the Bullets button on the Formatting toolbar—Word automatically inserts a bulleted-list entry using the solid black circle as a bullet. (To be more precise, it uses the type of bullet you used the last time you created a bulleted list during the current session, or, if it's the first bulleted list in this session, it uses the solid circle.) Now simply start typing, and each time you press Enter, Word moves the text to the next line and puts a bullet at the beginning of that line, too.

If you want to specify a different bullet symbol, place the insertion point where you plan to begin. Then choose Format ⇨ Bullets and Numbering, click the one you want to use, and click OK. (We look at how to use a different bullet image, one that doesn't appear in this dialog box, in the next section).

You can also convert text that you have already typed to bulleted text. Simply place the cursor in the paragraph you want to convert, or select several paragraphs, and click the Bullets button or use the Bullets and Numbering dialog box.

When you want to end a bulleted list, type the last entry, press Enter, and then press the Delete key.

Note Note that when Word creates a bulleted list, it automatically sets up a hanging indent—now you can see the purpose of the hanging indent. You want the bullet to appear to the left of the text, so the first line has to hang out to the left. Take notice that if you right-click on a bulleted list entry, the shortcut menu that appears has two extra commands, Decrease Indent and Increase Indent; use these to adjust the position of the bulleted list on the page.

Customizing a bulleted list

You can customize a bulleted list in several ways:

✦ Picking another bullet image

✦ Modifying the position of the bullets

✦ Modifying the position of the text in the list

Picking another bullet image

To use another bullet image, open the Bullets and Numbering dialog box and click one of the bullet-styles boxes. This is the style that you will be replacing with your new bullet. Click the Customize button and the Customize Bulleted List dialog box opens (see Figure 5-22).

Tip Notice the Reset button in the Bullets and Numbering box. This button is enabled if the bullet-style box you click on has been modified. Clicking Reset changes the box to the default.

You now have three ways to select another bullet image. You can select a Bullet Character and modify the character's font, you can select a special character, or you can select a bullet image.

Modifying a bullet's font

Click on one of the Bullet Characters at the top of the Customize Bulleted List dialog box (this may be a character that was already there when you opened the dialog box, or a character you placed there using the Character button, which we'll look at shortly). The Font dialog box, which you learned about in Chapter 4, opens.

You can now modify the character—change the size, make it bold or italic, use a different font, even use one of the animation styles under the Text Effects tab. When you are finished, click OK to close the Font box; then click OK again to close the Customize Bulleted List box and place your selected character into your bulleted list.

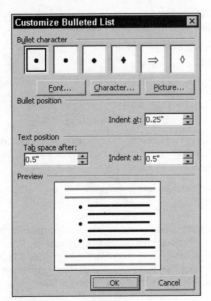

Figure 5-22: The Customize Bulleted List dialog box.

Selecting a special character

If you click the Character button in the Customize Bulleted List dialog box the Symbol dialog box, which we look at in Chapter 4, opens. You can select a symbol from any of the typefaces on your system; in particular, look at the Symbol, Webdings, and Wingdings typefaces.

Selecting a bullet picture

Click the Picture button, and the Picture Bullet dialog box opens (see Figure 5-23). This functions in the same way as the Horizontal Line dialog box we looked at earlier in this chapter. It slowly loads (it's loading off the Internet) literally hundreds of bullet images. As with the horizontal lines, these are really a Web feature, but there's no reason you can't use the images in your print documents.

Changing list positions

You can modify the position of the bullet and the text in the list. In the Customize Bulleted List dialog box, modify the settings in the Bullet Position and Text Position boxes.

The Bullet Position setting defines how far to the right of the left margin the bullet should be placed. The Tab Space After value defines at which point the text begins on the first line—that is, how far Word tabs to the right after the bullet before starting the text. And the Indent At value defines where subsequent lines of text appear. For example, if you set the Bullet Position Indent At to 1" and the Text Position Indent At to 1", the bullet and the subsequent lines of text are on the same vertical line.

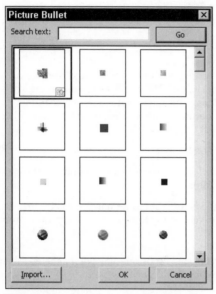

Figure 5-23: The Picture Bullet dialog box.

Creating numbered lists

Numbered lists are created in a manner similar to bulleted lists, except that instead of bullets Word places sequential numbers. This is a very useful feature, because if you add a paragraph in the middle of a numbered list or rearrange the order of the paragraphs in a list, Word automatically renumbers the paragraphs so that they retain their sequence. The Numbered tab in the Bullets and Numbering dialog box (see Figure 5-24) offers seven standard numbering formats and the ability to customize them. You can create a numbered list in two ways: using the Bullets and Numbering dialog box or using the Numbering button on the Formatting toolbar.

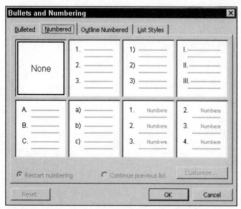

Figure 5-24: The Numbered tab in the Bullets and Numbering dialog box.

To create numbered lists, follow these steps:

1. Type your list, and then select it.

2. Do one of the following:

   • Choose Format ➪ Bullets and Numbering, or choose Bullets and Numbering from the shortcut menu. Click the Numbered tab. Then select the numbering style that you want from the predefined choices. Your choices include Arabic numbers, Roman numerals, and letters, with periods, parentheses, or double parentheses to separate the numbers from the list text. Click OK.

   • Click the Numbered List button on the toolbar.

3. To add additional numbered items to your list, move the insertion point to the end of a line formatted with a number and press Enter.

4. Move the insertion point to the end of the last numbered item in your list. Press Enter and then Del, or press Enter and click the Numbering button on the Formatting toolbar, to turn off the number formatting.

Tip   You can quickly convert a numbered list to a bulleted list by selecting the numbered list and then clicking the Bullets button on the Formatting toolbar, and vice versa.

Customizing numbered lists

You can customize an existing numbered list or apply your own specifications to the number format using the Customize button in the Numbered tab of the Bullets and Numbering dialog box. Click on one of the number-style boxes and then click the Customize button to display the Customize Numbered List dialog box (see Figure 5-25). Table 5-9 explains the Numbered List options in this dialog box.

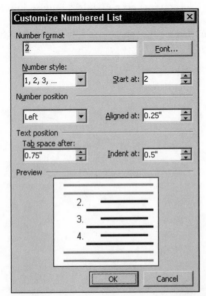

Figure 5-25: The Customize Numbered List dialog box.

Table 5-9: Numbered List Options

Option	Action
Number format	Types the characters, if any, that you want to come before each number. If you want each number enclosed in parentheses, for example, type an opening parenthesis before the number in this box. *Do not type over this number in this box!* If you do so, even replacing it with another number, you will break the automatic numbering; each number in the list will be the same.
Number style	Specifies the numbering style that you want. Choices include Arabic numerals, uppercase and lowercase Roman numerals, uppercase and lowercase alphabet letters, and word series (1st, One, and First). You can also choose no numbers at all, killing the sequential numbering. (Why? So that you can retain the indentation without the numbers.)
Font	Specifies the special font or font attributes (such as bold, italic, and underline) and the point size for the numbers. A standard Font dialog box appears when this button is chosen.
Start at	Indicates the starting number for your list. If you're using a series of lists, the starting number may be something other than 1.
Number position	Chooses the alignment of the number at the Aligned At position. For instance, if you select Left, the number begins at the Aligned At position; if right, the number ends there.
Aligned at	Sets the distance from the left margin that Word places the number.
Tab Space after	The distance between the Aligned At number position and the text on the first line.
Indent at	The left-most position of the text on subsequent lines.

Restarting and continuing numbering

You can tell Word whether to restart or continue numbering. Notice, in the Bullets and Numbering dialog box on the Numbered tab, the Restart Numbering and Continue Previous List option buttons. When you use the dialog box to create a list, or when you open the box while the list is selected, these option buttons are enabled and one is selected:

✦ **Restart Numbering:** Starts the numbering sequence over from 1. You might use this to place two numbered lists one after the other. Word will want to continue the second list with the next number in sequence from the previous list; this option tells it not to. Also, there are times when Word gets a little confused and starts a brand new list, many paragraphs away from the last list, with the next number in sequence. This option slaps its hand and tells it not to.

✦ **Continue Previous List:** Tells Word you want to begin your list where the last one left off. For instance, you may want to create a very long procedural description, with paragraphs of unnumbered text within the list. This allows you to create lots of individual numbered lists, but link them all together.

Tip

Another way to use these commands is to right-click the first entry in the list and select from the pop-up menu Restart Numbering or Continue Numbering.

Adding unbulleted or unnumbered paragraphs to a list

Sometimes the topic of a bulleted list or a numbered item cannot be discussed conveniently in a single paragraph. If you require more than one paragraph to describe a single topic in a bulleted list, only the first paragraph for that topic should have a bullet. The remaining subordinate paragraphs for that topic don't need bullets, but they do need the same hanging indent as the bulleted paragraphs in the list. There are a couple of ways in which you can create these indented subordinate paragraphs:

✦ Press Shift+Enter to make a line break (press twice if you want a blank line between the blocks of text) and continue typing. The new block of text will not be preceded by a bullet or number because Word regards it as part of the same paragraph (and only places a bullet or number at the beginning of each paragraph).

✦ Click on a line from which you want to remove a bullet or number; then click the Bullets or Numbering button on the toolbar to do so. Then use the Left Indent marker on the ruler to line up the text of the subordinate paragraph with the text of the previous paragraph.

Ending bulleted or numbered lists

As mentioned previously, the formatting for a paragraph is stored in the paragraph mark. Therefore, as with other paragraph formatting, the bulleted or numbered list format carries forward each time you press Enter to begin a new paragraph. If you create a bulleted list by pressing Enter, you need to end the bullet or numbered list formatting when you finish with the list. To end a bulleted or numbered list, press Enter at the end of a list and take one of the following actions:

✦ Press Delete to remove the number and bullet, leaving the insertion point on the line immediately below the last list entry and moved back to the style's left margin.

✦ Press Enter again. The same as pressing Delete, except that you'll get a blank line between the list and the line on which the insertion point is placed.

✦ Press Backspace to remove the bullet and place the insertion point on the line below the last entry, at the bullet position.

✦ Press Ctrl+Shift+N return to the Normal style.

✦ Press Ctrl+Q to return to whatever style was applied to the text immediately before you began the bulleted or numbered list.

✦ Click the Bullets button to remove the bullet or the Numbering button to remove the number from the paragraph, returning the insertion point to the style's left margin.

Creating outline numbered lists

Outline numbered lists are similar to numbered or bulleted lists, but in these multilevel lists, the number or bullet of each paragraph changes according to its level of indention. With outline numbered lists, you can mix numbered and bulleted paragraphs based on the indentation level. You can create multilevel lists with as many as nine levels. Use the outline numbered list format if you want your list to have numbered items with indented, bulleted subparagraphs; for example, many types of technical and legal documents require each paragraph and indentation level to be numbered sequentially. Multilevel lists are created using the Outline Numbered tab in the Bullets and Numbering dialog box (see Figure 5-26).

Note *Outline Numbered* is a misnomer. In fact these outline lists may be either numbered or bulleted.

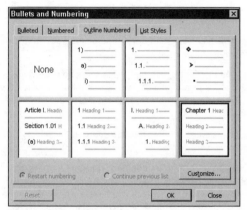

Figure 5-26: The Outline Numbered tab in the Bullets and Numbering dialog box.

As with bullets and numbering, you can set the outline numbering first and then begin typing, or type and then select the text and apply the formatting. To create subordinate paragraphs, simply increase the indentation using the Increase Indent button on the Formatting toolbar, or by pressing Shift+Alt+right arrow—Word automatically switches to the subordinate numbering system. To switch back to a higher level, use the Decrease Indent button or Shift+Alt+ Left Arrow.

Customizing outline numbered lists

You can customize an outline numbered list format by clicking Customize in the Outline Numbered tab, which displays the Customize Outline Numbered List dialog box (see Figure 5-27). You can see additional options by clicking More. Table 5-10 describes the available options in the Customize Outline Numbered List dialog box.

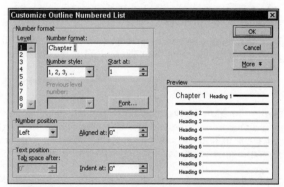

Figure 5-27: The Customize Outline Numbered List dialog box.

Table 5-10: Options in the Customize Outline Numbered List Dialog Box

Option	Description
Level	Determines which level to modify.
Number format	Determines which characters (if any) come before each number or bullet at this indentation level.
Number style	Determines the numbering or bullet style used. Choices include a combination of the numbering choices available for numbered lists and the bullet choices available for bulleted lists or even no number or bullet at all.
Start at	Determines the starting number for paragraphs at the selected level of indentation.
Previous level number	If you selected Level 2 or lower, and have chosen a numbering format (rather than a bullet), this drop-down list box is enabled. It displays a list of the levels for which you have customized a format. If you select a previous level number, Word will include that level number along with the level number for the selected format. (More explanation of this point follows the table.)
Font button	Determines any special font or font attributes (such as bold, italic, and underline) or the point size for the numbers or bullets used at this indentation level.
Number position—Aligned at	The indentation at which the number is placed.
Text position—Tab space after	How far Word tabs before beginning the text on the first line after the number.
Indent at	The left position of the subsequent lines.
Link level to style	Applies the selected style to the text used at this numbering level; see Chapter 13 for information on styles.
Follow Number With	Tells Word to place a Tab after the number, to use spaces, or to place nothing between the text and the number (in which case the Tab Space After setting is disabled).
Legal style numbering	Converts Roman numerals (IV, V) to Arabic numerals (4, 5)—the Number Style box is disabled.
Apply Changes To	If you are modifying an existing numbered list, you can choose to modify the Whole List, from This Point Forward, or the Current Paragraph.

The Previous Level Number tells Word to include the number of the previous level along with the number of the level you are modifying. For instance, the first level would be 1, the next level down would be 1.1, the next 1.1.1, the next at the same level 1.1.2, and so on. This is a common outlining style for many government and military documents, for instance.

Creating list styles

Word also lets you customize lists by creating special list styles. Click the List Styles tab in the Bullets and Numbering dialog box (see Figure 5-28). This dialog box lists all the outline list styles that have been created—select one and click OK to apply that style to your Outline list.

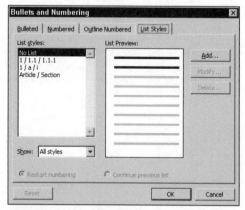

Figure 5-28: The List Styles tab of the Bullets and Numbering dialog box.

You can use the Add button to add another style, or Modify to change one you've selected. When you click one of these buttons, you see the New Style or Modify Style dialog box (see Figure 5-29). You learn more about these dialog boxes in Chapter 13 when we discuss the larger issues of styles. For now, just know that you can create a style that encompasses all levels of an outline list, defining exactly what font should be used, how much indentation, whether to use a bullet or number, what number to start with, and so on. Simply provide the style a name, select a starting number, select the level you want to define, and then make all your selections. Then go back and do the next level.

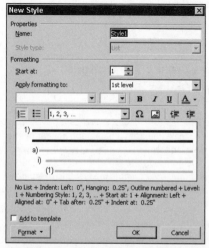

Figure 5-29: The New Style dialog box.

Paragraphs and Pagination

Word automatically creates page breaks as you write, but you can control how paragraphs are positioned relative to these page breaks. For example, you may want to prevent page breaks within boxed or shaded paragraphs. To control paragraph positions relative to page breaks, use the Line and Page Breaks tab in the Paragraph dialog box (see Figure 5-30). Table 5-11 describes the options in the Line and Page Breaks tab.

Note   The page breaks created by Word are very different from the page breaks you can create yourself using Ctrl+Enter or the Insert ⇨ Break command. Word's page breaks are placed according to how much text is on the page, the page margins, and so on. On the other hand, the breaks you enter are fixed. If you place a break immediately before a paragraph, it doesn't matter how much text you add before the paragraph, the break remains there.

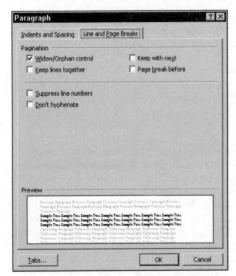

Figure 5-30: The Line and Page Breaks tab in the Paragraph dialog box.

Table 5-11: Line and Page Breaks Tab Options in the Paragraph Dialog Box

Option	Action
Widow/Orphan control	Instructs Word not to let a single line from a paragraph appear by itself at the top or bottom of a page. This option is on by default. A *widow* is the final line of a paragraph that jumps to the top of the next page because it doesn't fit on the current one. An *orphan* is the first line of a paragraph that falls at the end of a page with the remainder of the paragraph appearing on the next page.
Keep lines together	Instructs Word not to split the paragraph into separate pages. This is useful when working with lists.

Option	Action
Keep with next	Instructs Word to keep the paragraph with the next paragraph. This is useful when working with captions and lists.
Page break before	Instructs Word to place the paragraph on top of the next page. This is useful when working with figures, tables, and graphics.
Suppress line numbers	Instructs Word to remove line numbers from the selected text if your document displays line numbers.
Don't hyphenate	Instructs Word to exclude the selected paragraph from automatic hyphenation.

Hyphenation

Speaking of hyphenation, it's time to cover that subject. Hyphenation reduces ragged right edges on blocks of text (it also allows you to get more words on a page, though only slightly). Hyphenation is the process of breaking words between lines, so part of a word appears on the right side of one line, with a hyphen placed after it, while the rest of the word appears on the left side of the next line. Why not use paragraph justification to create nice straight right edges? Because justified text is hard to read. But hyphenation can even be used with justified text, to reduce the amount of white space inserted between words.

The following sections look at four types of hyphenation:

✦ Automatic hyphenation

✦ Manual hyphenation

✦ Optional hyphenation

✦ Nonbreaking hyphenation

Using automatic hyphenation

Automatic hyphenation inserts optional hyphens. An optional hyphen is a hyphen that Word uses only when a word or a phrase appears at the end of a line. If the word or phrase moves to a different position because of editing, the optional hyphen is removed.

Note   Normally, optional hyphens are not visible in your document. You can view optional hyphens by choosing Tools ➪ Options and then clicking the View tab. Under Formatting Marks, select the Optional Hyphens check box.

To select automatic hyphenation, follow these steps:

1. Choose Tools ➪ Language ➪ Hyphenation to open the Hyphenation dialog box (see Figure 5-31).

2. Select the Automatically Hyphenate Document check box.

3. If you do not want to hyphenate words in uppercase letters, leave the Hyphenate Words in CAPS check box blank.

4. Set a value in the Hyphenation Zone. This value is the distance in inches between the end of the last complete word in a line of text and the margin—in other words, the degree of raggedness Word should allow. Word uses this measurement to determine if a word should be hyphenated. Large values decrease the number of hyphens; low values increase the number of hyphens but reduce the raggedness of the right margin.

5. If you don't want consecutive lines to have hyphens—it can make a document look a little strange—set a limit in the Limit Consecutive Hyphens To box.

6. Click OK.

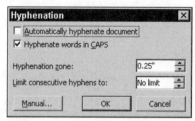

Figure 5-31: The Hyphenation dialog box.

Tip

If you don't want certain paragraphs to be hyphenated automatically, select those paragraphs and then choose Format ➪ Paragraph. In the Paragraph dialog box, select the Line and Page Breaks tab and then the Don't Hyphenate check box.

Using manual hyphenation

Using manual hyphenation, you have more control over what is hyphenated and how it is hyphenated. You can select which parts of the document are hyphenated and where a hyphen appears in specific words. This is a huge hassle for a large document, but it does allow you to do a better job than Word might do automatically—Word sometimes hyphenates words in positions that don't look good.

To select manual hyphenation, follow these steps:

1. Select the text you want to hyphenate manually. If you want to hyphenate manually the entire document, don't select anything.

2. Choose Tools ➪ Language ➪ Hyphenation to open the Hyphenation dialog box.

3. Click the Manual button, and Word immediately begins scanning the selection or the document for words to be hyphenated. When such a word is located, Word displays the Manual Hyphenation dialog box (see Figure 5-32).

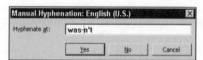

Figure 5-32: The Manual Hyphenation dialog box.

4. To hyphenate the word at a point other than that suggested in the Hyphenate At box, click where you want the hyphen to appear.

5. To accept the suggestion, click Yes.

6. To skip the word and move on, click No.

7. To stop the manual hyphenation, click Cancel.

Using nonbreaking and optional hyphens

Use nonbreaking hyphens to hyphenate phrases or terms that you don't want to wrap to another line (for example, 02-12-03). With nonbreaking hyphens, the entire phrase or term wraps to the next line instead of breaking.

To insert a nonbreaking hyphen, do the following:

1. Position the insertion point where you want to place the nonbreaking hyphen.

2. Press Ctrl+Shift+- (hyphen).

Use an optional hyphen when you want to break specific lines of text. For example, if a lengthy word wraps to the next line and leaves a large amount of white space, you can insert an optional hyphen in that specific word so that the first part appears on the first line. If the word later moves to a different position because of editing, the optional hyphen does not print. If further editing moves the word back into a hyphenation zone, the hyphen reappears.

To insert an optional hyphen, do the following:

1. Position the insertion point where you want the optional hyphen to appear.

2. Press Ctrl+- (hyphen).

Summary

Mastering paragraph fundamentals is essential for creating just about any document in Word. Even when you work with graphics, basic paragraph formatting is used to place the images. Because of the importance of paragraphs, Word provides several ways to apply paragraph formats. In this chapter, you learned the key elements of formatting paragraphs, including the following:

✦ Apply paragraph formatting using the Formatting toolbar or Format Paragraph dialog box (Format ➪ Paragraph).

✦ Remove paragraph formatting by pressing Ctrl+Q to return the text to the current style's default settings or Ctrl+Shift+N to apply the Normal style to the paragraph.

✦ Align paragraphs using the following shortcut keys: Ctrl+L for left-align, Ctrl+R for right-align, Ctrl+E for center-align, and Ctrl+J for justified text. You can also use the alignment buttons on the Formatting toolbar.

✦ Set tabs using the horizontal ruler by clicking the Tab Alignment button at the far-left end to choose the tab style that you want and then clicking the ruler at the point where you want to insert the tab. You can also use the Tabs dialog box (Format ➪ Tabs) to set tabs.

✦ Add borders and shading to paragraphs by clicking the Border button on the Formatting toolbar to display the Border toolbar or by choosing Format ➪ Borders and Shading to display the Borders and Shading dialog box.

✦ Insert horizontal lines using the Horizontal Line button in the Borders and Shading dialog box (Format ➪ Borders and Shading).

✦ Create bulleted and numbered lists using the Bullets and Numbering buttons on the Formatting toolbar, or the Bullets and Numbering dialog box (Format ➪ Bullets and Numbering).

✦ Use the Hyphenation dialog box to automatically or manually create hyphens (Tools ➪ Language ➪ Hyphenation).

✦　　✦　　✦

Printing Documents

Many Word documents are destined to end up in printed form. Previous chapters have discussed how to create well-written, well-formatted documents. Now you're ready to print them. With Word's impressive array of printing tools, you can print everything from business letters with envelopes to entire collated manuscripts. This chapter teaches you how to transform your documents into printed materials.

Printing Basics

With one click, you can print your Word document: just click the Print button in the Standard toolbar, and the document goes directly to the default printer. Word prints the entire document using default settings—such as page margins, paper size, and orientation—that define the layout of the document. You can easily change these settings using the Page Setup command in the File menu.

To format pages using the Page Setup command and other tools, see Chapter 10.

Installing a printer is a function of Windows, not of Word. When you install one or more printers in Windows, any Windows software application can use the printers, and they can generally use them without any other action on your part. Printers are set up in Windows using the Printers folder, which you can access by opening the Control Panel (Start ⇨ Settings ⇨ Control Panel) and double-clicking the Printers icon.

You can tell Word exactly what you want to print using the File ⇨ Print command to display the Print dialog box (see Figure 6-1). With the Print dialog box, you can print the entire document, selected text, or a range of pages. You can also specify how many copies of the document to print.

Always save your document before printing. This way, you can ensure that you're able to return to your document without losing any changes if a printing problem occurs.

In This Chapter

Printing basics in Word

Changing Word's printing options to match your individual needs

Printing a document to a file

Printing to a fax modem

Changing printer properties to get more from your printer

Printing documents on a network

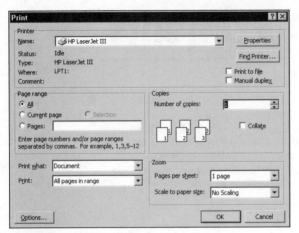

Figure 6-1: The Print dialog box.

Printing selected text or pages

You have two choices when you want to print part of a Word document: you can print specific pages, or you can print a specific selection of text. If you do not select anything in a document before opening the Print dialog box, the Selection option is not available in the Print dialog box. When you select text to print and choose the Selection option, nothing else in the document but the selected portion will print.

Note   To print a selection of text, you must open the Print dialog box and choose the Selection option. You cannot just select text in a document and then click the Print button on the Standard toolbar.

To print a portion of a document, follow these steps:

1. Select the text that you want to print. If you want to print one whole page of your document, move the insertion point to the page that you want.

2. Choose the File ➪ Print command, or press Ctrl+P.

3. Do one of the following:

   • To print selected text, choose the Selection option.

   • To print only the page that is displayed in the document window, select the Current Page option. The current page is the one that your pointer is located on.

   • To print a page other than the current one, enter the page number in the Pages text box.

   • To print multiple pages, enter the page numbers, separated by commas, in the Pages box. For example, entering **3,7,21** prints pages 3, 7, and 21. The page numbers must be in numeric order.

   • To print a range of pages, enter the number of the first page that you want, a hyphen, and then the last page that you want in the Pages box. For example, entering **25-30** prints pages 25 through 30.

- To print a mixture of specific pages and continuous pages, combine the two previous actions. For example, enter **3,7,21,25-30** to print these pages all at once.

- To print only the odd or even pages, choose either Odd Pages or Even Pages from the Print list box.

4. Click OK.

Printing more than one document at a time

Printing multiple documents is different from printing a single document because with multiple documents you do not open them first in Word. Instead of using the File ➪ Print command, you use the File ➪ Open command to locate the files. Select the files you want to print from the list in the Open dialog box, click the Tools button on the Open dialog box toolbar, and select Print.

You can also print multiple files from within Windows Explorer. Select the files, right-click on them, and select Print.

Printing multiple, collated copies

If you print more than one copy of a document, you can also collate the copies. When you collate copies, Word prints one complete copy of the document before starting to print the next copy. If you choose not to collate, Word prints the number of copies you specify for each individual page before it starts printing the next one. To collate multiple copies, place a check in the Collate box, which is located in the Copies group of the Print dialog box.

Tip

In some cases collating can dramatically slow down your printing. When Word collates, it sends multiple copies of the document to the printer. When it prints without collating, it sends a single copy, with instructions to print multiple times. If a document has a lot of large images in it, collating can mean the difference between printing in five minutes and printing in 30 minutes.

Printing in reverse order

All printers typically print your documents from the first page to the last, but some printers stack the printed pages with the first page under the second page, the second page under the third page, and so on. For example, many ink-jet printers, such as HP DeskJets, print pages in this fashion. This means that you must collate them back into the right order by hand. With Word, however, you can print in reverse order by rearranging the pages before downloading the job to your printer.

To print your document in reverse order, choose File ➪ Print to display the Print dialog box, and then click Options, click the Reverse Print Order check box, and click OK twice. When you print your document in this way, Word prints your document backwards, so it ends up in the correct order.

Note

The settings in the Print dialog box are the same as those in the Print tab of the Options dialog box (Tools ➪ Options). Any changes that you make in the Options dialog box affect all documents, however, not just the current document (as is the case when you use the Options button in the Print dialog box).

Printing other document information

You can print information about your document other than its text. Using the Print What list box in the Print dialog box, you can print styles, AutoText entries, keyboard shortcuts that you assigned while working in the document, the document's comments, and even the document's properties, such as the file name, title, author, and specific information about the number of words and total editing time.

Some of these options create useful references: Styles, AutoText Entries, and Key Assignments are sometimes useful to print and give to members of a team working on collaborative documents.

The Document Showing Markup and List of Markup printouts could be useful for reviewing changes to a document. The latter may also be useful for producing addenda or correction lists.

Drag-and-drop printing

You can also print Word document files by dragging and dropping them on the printer icon in the Printers folder. You can drag files from a folder window, from Windows Explorer, or from the Windows desktop to the printer's icon or its queue window. If you drag more than one file to the printer icon, a message box appears and asks if you're sure that you want to print multiple files. Click Yes. When you drag and drop a Word document file, Windows starts Word to spool the document to the printer. The Word document is closed once it has been sent to the printer.

The queue window appears when you double-click the printer icon in the Printers folder or in the Windows taskbar—where it's placed during printing. It shows which documents are being sent to the printer and their status: Printing, Deleting, Paused, and so on. It also provides other information, such as the user who sent the document to the printer (useful for network printers), the size, how many pages have completed, and so on. It has several commands you can use to pause and cancel printing and to configure the printer.

Tip   If you create a shortcut on the Windows desktop for your printer, you can quickly print files by dragging and dropping those files on the printer icon. To place the printer icon on your desktop, drag the printer icon from the Printers folder to the desktop. When you release your mouse button to drop the icon, a message box may appear (depending on the version of Windows you are using) and tells you that you cannot copy or move the printer icon, but asks if you want to create a shortcut. Click Yes, and the shortcut is created.

Printing a document using different printers

You may have multiple printers to work with, especially if you are using Word in an office. For example, you may have a color printer for presentation materials and a laser printer for everyday black-and-white printing. A large office may have printers in various locations around the building. Word lets you choose between these different printers. You can use the Find Printer button in the Print dialog box to locate the appropriate networked printer.

Note   One printer is always defined as the default printer for your system. A printer can be set as the default printer in the Windows Printers folder by right-clicking the printer icon and then choosing Set As Default from the shortcut menu. The default printer always appears as the first choice in the Printer Name drop-down list in the Print dialog box. When you click the Print button on the Standard toolbar to print a document, Word uses the default printer.

Changing printers often affects the layout of your documents—usually when it's a document being sent to a really important client, for some reason. These problems can occur because different printers have different capabilities—they have different minimum margins, for instance. If you create a document using an old HP LaserJet 4 as the printer, for example, and then print it on a PostScript printer, the page breaks and word-wrapping formatting may change. Problems can also occur when you open a document created on a system that used fonts that are unavailable on your current printer. Word will substitute a similar, available font, but you can also specify a specific substitution font (as discussed in Chapter 4).

When you are working in a document, Word lays out the document using the currently selected print driver. If you use more than one printer, make sure that the selected printer matches the type of printer you'll be printing the document on before you begin creating a new document; or, at least, before printing select the print driver, come back to the document, and check the document's margins and pagination.

To select a different printer in Word, follow these steps:

1. Choose File ➪ Print. The Print dialog box appears.

2. Click the Printer Name drop-down arrow.

3. Select an installed printer from the list. If you want to install a new printer, go to the Windows taskbar and choose Start ➪ Settings ➪ Printers. (Some users may have to right-click Printers and Faxes and choose Open.) The Printers window appears and displays the Add Printer icon. Double-click the Add Printer icon. In most cases, you need either your Windows disk (or CD) or a driver disk from the printer manufacturer to install a new printer.

Tip

Differences among printers can be a particularly irritating problem when you are sending important documents to clients at other companies. You have no idea what printer will be used to print the document, so you have no way to be sure it will look correct when printed. That's why many companies no longer send Word documents. Instead, they create an Adobe Acrobat PDF file. The layout of a PDF file is always the same, regardless of the printer used to print the file. If you have a copy of Adobe Acrobat, you can create your documents in Word and export them to PDF format. (Acrobat itself is not a word processor.) See www. Adobe.com/ for more information.

Printing in Color

Color printers are cheap and plentiful these days. (Well, the printers themselves are often cheap; it's the supplies that are going to cost you!) More documents than ever are being printed in color, so it's quite likely that you will, at least now and then, shoot your documents off to a color printer. Before you do so, however, here are a few things to consider.

Perhaps the first thing to remember is that you're not a designer. (Well, maybe *you* are, but most readers are not.) The problem with providing sophisticated design tools to non-experts is that they really don't know how to use them well. Which colors go well together? How much color, and where? How do you balance whitespace, text blocks, and color images and fonts?

Our advice is to try not to be too clever. Use a little color here and there, but don't overdo it just because you can. Real graphic designers generally have a natural aptitude for this sort of thing and on top of that are trained. They know how to use color well; many of the rest of us really don't.

Having said that, though, color can be very useful. It can make documents more interesting, and thus easier to read. In the same way that pictures and whitespace can be used to break up big blocks of text and make them less intimidating, color can be used in headings and *pull quotes* to do the same. (You've seen pull quotes in magazines a million times—the little blocks of text pulled out of the main article and formatted in larger type.) Coloring headings in particular can really make a document easier to work with, allowing the eye to scan from section to section more smoothly.

Here are a couple of things to keep in mind when using color so that your documents remain clean and easy to read:

✦ Word allows you to place things in the background of a document. You can put watermarks in a document, and even have garish backgrounds similar to those you run across on the Web all the time. Be careful. Backgrounds underneath text can be very distracting, making your documents much harder to read and thus less likely to be read. We suggest you use very light, uncluttered images underneath text.

Suppose that you want to put a watermark saying *PRELIMINARY* under the text. You could, perhaps, create an image with a small word repeated over and over again, and use a bright color or maybe a very dark gray to make sure it stands out. Your readers won't thank you for it! It will make any long document almost impossible to read, and even short ones uncomfortable. On the other hand, you could use a single, large *PRELIMINARY*, angled across the page, and displayed with a *very* light gray. This way, the document is much easier to read and readers will still know that the document is preliminary.

✦ Another thing to watch out for is the use of color in documents that will be copied or faxed. If the primary purpose of printing your document is to create an original that can be photocopied a hundred times or faxed to someone else, avoid using color. What looks great on your screen and in your printout will look different once copied or faxed. And if you used color to differentiate bars in a bar chart, pies in a pie chart, or anything similar . . . sorry, but your black-and-white charts are now illegible.

Use color where it makes sense. If you're fairly certain that the document won't be copied or faxed, and you can use color to make it attractive, then sure, go ahead. But don't use color for color's sake. It often causes problems, and those ink and toner cartridges are very expensive anyway!

Previewing Documents Before Printing

Print Preview is an important tool that Word offers. Using the Print Preview toolbar, shown in Figure 6-2, you can view your document in a variety of ways to check out how each will look in printed form.

It's important to check any document that's more than a page or two long very carefully. Large documents generally need to be *paginated* before printing. That is, you check the document to ensure that page breaks appear in the right places. Word automatically places page breaks in your document, of course, but it can't always make the right choice. It may, for instance, push an image down onto the next page because it won't fit on the previous page, leaving a large white space on the previous page. To fix this problem you could change the size of the image, or perhaps move some text down below the image.

Multiple Pages

One Page   Shrink to Fit

Magnifier   View Ruler   Full Screen

Print   Zoom   Close

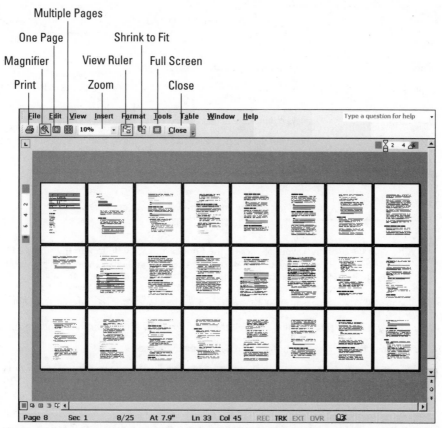

Figure 6-2: Print Preview can show a thumbnail view of how multiple pages will appear when they print.

So viewing in Print Preview mode is, for most who create large Word documents, the last stage before printing. In some cases, you may want to go through the Print Preview twice: the first time to adjust page breaks to make sure that everything looks okay, and then one more time to ensure that your changes didn't mess something else up.

Table 6-1 describes the buttons on the Print Preview toolbar.

Table 6-1: The Print Preview Toolbar Buttons

Button	Action
Print	Prints the document using the default print options (also indicates the current printer).
Magnifier	Enlarges or reduces the document view.
One Page	Displays the document in single-page view.

Continued

Table 6-1 *(continued)*

Button	Action
Multiple Pages	Displays one or more pages of the document.
Zoom Control	Selects different magnifications from 10 to 500% (also includes Page Width, Whole Page, and Two Pages options).
View Ruler	Displays or hides the horizontal and vertical rulers.
Shrink to Fit	Adjusts your document's font and line spacing so that lines will not spill over if the last page of your document contains only a few lines of text.
Full Screen	Removes the title bar and toolbars to show a full-screen display of the document.
Close	Closes Print Preview and returns you to your document.

Note   Choosing View ⇨ Print Layout or clicking the Print Layout View button on the status bar is a way to check quickly the layout of a document before printing. This way, however, doesn't include all the bells and whistles available in Print Preview.

To preview a document in Print Preview, follow these steps:

1. Choose File ⇨ Print Preview, or click the Print Preview button on the Standard toolbar.

2. To close Print Preview, choose the Close Preview button.

You can move around a document in Print Preview the same way that you can in the document window: using the arrow keys, the scroll arrows, and the PgUp and PgDn keys. If you are viewing multiple pages, the PgUp and PgDn keys move through the document one page at a time.

Changing the Print Preview appearance

Print Preview has several options for viewing documents. You can show the page width, display the whole page, or magnify part of a page. Print Preview can also simultaneously display as many as 24 pages, organized in three rows. In addition, you can configure how the pages are displayed. For example, if your document has 12 pages, you can display two rows of 6 pages or three rows of 4 pages. You can change your view of a document in Print Preview by using one of the following methods:

✦ To display only the width of a page, one whole page, or two pages, click the Zoom Control down arrow to the right of the magnification percentage in the Print Preview toolbar. At the bottom of the drop-down list, you can choose Page Width, Text Width, Whole Page, or Two Pages. Alternatively, to display a single page, click the One Page button on the Print Preview toolbar.

✦ To display more than two pages, click the Multiple Pages button to the left of the magnification percentage. A drop-down box appears, showing six pages arranged in two rows. Place the mouse pointer inside the drop-down box; then click and drag into the main Print Preview window. You can drag the boundaries of this box down and to the right to increase how many pages are displayed (to a maximum of 24). For example, if your display shows two rows of three pages and you want to see one row of four pages, drag the mouse to the right to highlight the pages that you want, and then release the mouse button.

✦ To reduce or enlarge the previewed document, change the Zoom Control percentage, or click the Magnifier button and then click within your document.

Editing in Print Preview mode

You can edit your document directly in Print Preview mode, which can save time by avoiding those annoying little errors that seem to appear on every other printed page. You can also edit with one or more pages displayed in Print Preview, but if you are viewing multiple pages, the text may be too small to see clearly. If the text is too small to read, change to Page Width or increase the magnification percentage. Click the drop-down list box to see the magnification options.

To edit in Print Preview mode, follow these steps:

1. Display a page with a size at which you can read the text.

2. Click the Magnifier button to turn off magnification mode. By default, each time you click on a page, you zoom in or out. So you have to turn this feature off.

3. To begin editing, click within your document and make your changes.

Adjusting margins in Print Preview

You can change margins in Print Preview mode using the horizontal and vertical rulers. Remember that margin changes in Print Preview apply to the entire document, not just to one portion. To apply margin changes to specific portions of your document, you must use File ➪ Page Setup instead.

To change a document's margins in Print Preview, follow these steps:

1. If the rulers are not displayed, click the View Ruler button to display them. The horizontal ruler shows the width of the entire page; the vertical ruler shows the height of the entire page. The margin areas are displayed in gray on the rulers, and the text areas are displayed in white.

2. Position the mouse pointer in the margin boundary (the spot where the white portion of the ruler meets the gray portion). The mouse pointer then changes to a double-headed arrow.

3. Press and hold down the left mouse button. A dashed line appears through the page indicating the margin position. Drag to adjust the selected margin, and then release the mouse button. You can repeat this step for each remaining margin, if desired.

Automatic pagination adjustment

As discussed earlier, you can use Print Preview mode to check on pagination, to make sure the pages are laid out correctly. If only a few lines of your document appear on the last page, you might try clicking the Shrink to Fit button in the Print Preview toolbar.

This command shrinks font size and the spacing between the lines so that the lines will not spill over onto that short, final page. When you click the Shrink to Fit button, Word calculates what changes are needed; the status bar reflects the repagination process for each attempt to shrink your document. If you are working with a long document, Word can shrink your font and spacing so that the document shrinks by more than one page. However, Word often is unable to carry out this operation. And in any case, if it does succeed you should check to see if it has changed other page breaks in a way that you don't like. (If clicking the Shrink to Fit button shrinks the font size and line spacing too much, press Ctrl+Z to undo the changes.) This is a nice feature in theory, but in practice it probably has limited use, because you'll spend more time checking a long document to see what Word has done than you would fixing the problem manually.

Changing Your Printing Options

Word provides a variety of options for tailoring your printed output. You can access these options from the Print dialog box by clicking the Options button, which displays another Print dialog box with a Print tab (see Figure 6-3). You can also access these settings by choosing Tools ➪ Options and clicking the Print tab.

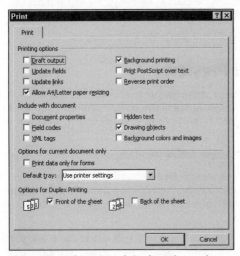

Figure 6-3: The Print tab in the Print options dialog box.

Notice, by the way, that most of the options in this box apply to all Word documents. Two, though, apply to just the current document. Table 6-2 describes the settings in the Print tab of the Print dialog box.

Table 6-2: Print Options

Option	Action
Draft output	Specifies to print the document without formatting or graphics, in order to speed up printing (often very useful for large documents with many images). The result of Draft output depends on your printer.
Update fields	Updates all the fields in your document before printing. (Chapter 23 covers fields.)
Update links	Updates all the links in your document before printing. (Chapter 20 covers linking information from other applications.)
Allow A4/Letter paper resizing	Automatically adjusts documents created with another country's standard paper size, such as A4, to letter size. This affects the printout only, not the document itself.
Background printing	Prints in the background so that you can continue with your work. This option uses memory, however, and slows the program's overall performance. However, turn it off and you can't use Word until it's finished printing.
Print PostScript over text	Prints PostScript code, such as a watermark, in a converted Word for Mac document on top of the text rather than underneath it. This affects only documents containing PRINT field codes. (Chapter 23 covers working with field codes.)
Reverse print order	Prints the first page last (useful for printers that lay the paper down face up on the output tray, so that the first page out is at the bottom of the pile). This is not used when printing envelopes.
Document properties	Prints the document summary information on a separate page when printing your document. These properties include the author, subject, print date, and number of pages, words, and characters.
Field codes	Prints the field codes themselves rather than the results of the field codes. (Chapter 23 covers working with field codes.) Sometimes useful for troubleshooting a complicated document.
XML tags	Check this to print XML tags in your documents; these are discussed in Chapter 27.
Hidden text	Prints any hidden text, such as table-of-contents entries or text you intentionally placed as hidden, in the location where it appears in your document.
Drawing objects	Prints drawing objects that you created. Drawing objects are vector images, such as lines and circles, in a Word drawing. Clear this check box to print only a blank box in place of a drawing, which speeds printing of a draft document. (For more information on drawing objects, see Chapter 18.)

Continued

Table 6-2 *(continued)*

Option	Action
Background colors and images	As you can see in Chapter 10, you can apply backgrounds to your documents, including watermarks. If this box is not checked, however, the backgrounds won't print. Keep in mind that some background components are designed purely for Web use and don't print anyway.
Print data only for forms	Prints the data entered into an online form without printing the form itself. (Chapter 22 covers creating forms.) This affects only the current document.
Default tray	Selects the print tray. To set different paper sources for different sections of the document, choose File ➪ Page Setup to open the Page Setup dialog box, and then select the Paper Source tab. This affects only the current document.
Front of the sheet	*Duplex printing* is the term given to printing on both sides of the paper, as many modern printers can do. In theory, this check box and the next one define the order in which Word prints your duplexed documents. In practice, we have been unable to get these check boxes to have any effect on duplex printing whatsoever.
Back of the sheet	As with the Front of the Sheet option, this check box appears to have no effect on Duplex printing.

Printing to a File

Printing to a file means that Word sends printing instructions with the document to a file rather than to the printer. This print file can then be used to print a document from another computer, even if it doesn't have Word installed on it. These files have the .prn file name extension.

The important thing about this procedure is that you need to select the printer that will ultimately print the file. Otherwise, you will encounter formatting problems when the file prints. So even if you don't have that printer available to *you*, you must still install the print driver for that printer on your computer.

Printing to a file isn't as useful as it was in years past—and it was never used all that much. Word is just about everywhere these days, so it's rare that you'll have to send a file to be printed to someone that doesn't have the program. More commonly people use Adobe Acrobat these days for this purpose, anyway (see www.Adobe.com/). As Adobe provides a free Acrobat reader, just about anyone can view and read an Acrobat file. These files are often inconvenient, because they're large—they contain not just the document contents but printer instructions—and because not one computer user in a hundred knows how to use them. To print to a file, follow these steps:

1. Choose File ➪ Print, or press Ctrl+P. The Print dialog box appears.

2. Click the Printer Name drop-down arrow.

3. Select the printer name from the drop-down list.

4. Select the Print to File check box, and then click OK. The Print to File dialog box appears (see Figure 6-4).

5. Type a file name in the File Name box. Word automatically adds the .prn extension to the file name.

6. Choose Printer Files (.prn) as the Save As type.

7. If necessary, select the drive and directory where you want to save the file.

8. Click OK.

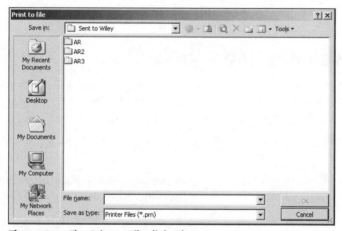

Figure 6-4: The Print to File dialog box.

How, then, do you use a printer file after you've created it? You have to copy it to the printer port using a DOS command. And let's face it, how many people know how to find DOS, let alone use it anymore? If you need to print to a file and you feel comfortable with DOS, here's a quick rundown of what to do. Open a DOS window by choosing Start ⇨ Accessories ⇨ Command Prompt.

In the Command Prompt window, move to the drive and directory containing the .prn file (use the change directory command, cd, to change directories). Type **copy *filename*.prn lpt1** to send the print file to the LPT1 printer port.

Document Image Writer Files

You can also print to a Microsoft Office Document Imaging file by selecting Microsoft Office Document Image Writer from the Name drop-down list box before you print. These files can be opened in the Microsoft Office Document Imaging program, a system designed to compete with Adobe Acrobat.

Document Imaging lets you view documents in a variety of ways, from a variety of sources, convert text in an image document to raw text using OCR (Optical Character Recognition), add comments and notes, insert pictures, and so on. It's not intended to create documents, but to view, manage, and modify documents from different programs. You can find this program on the Windows Start menu, under Programs ⇨ Microsoft Office Tools ⇨ Microsoft Office Document Imaging.

Printing to a Fax Modem

If you have a fax modem installed on your PC or network, you can print your document to a fax printer, which means the document is sent as a fax transmission via the fax printer driver. Fax software installs into Microsoft Windows as a printer, which you can see for yourself in the Printers folder. With the fax modem method, you send the fax electronically, without having to print the hard copy, go to a fax machine, and manually send it. Microsoft Windows comes with Microsoft Fax—although in some versions you have to choose to select it, it's not installed by default—or you can use third-party software, such as WinFax.

Cross-Reference   Chapter 28 explains how to use Microsoft Fax to send documents as faxes.

Printing Envelopes and Labels

Word makes printing envelopes easy. You can print mailing and return addresses directly on an envelope, and you can print addresses on a mailing label (or on a sheet of mailing labels) as well.

Cross-Reference   To print mailing labels for multiple addresses, such as you would for form letters, see Chapter 22.

Word offers wizards that help you to create and print both envelopes and labels. With these wizards, you can create a single envelope label or multiple envelopes and labels for form letters.

Cross-Reference   For information on using the Envelope Wizard and the Labels Wizard, see Chapter 22.

Word automatically locates the mailing address in the document, or you can select it. The return address is entered automatically from information entered in the User Information tab of the Options dialog box—fill in this information once and it will be used by default for every envelope (see Figure 6-5). If you ever want to change your default return address, you can just add the new default return address here.

You can also change the default return address for any envelope or label when you create it using the Envelopes and Labels dialog box. Changing the return address in the Envelopes and Labels dialog box affects only the current envelope, however. The next time you open the Envelopes and Labels dialog box, the default return address appears.

Tip   Word asks if you want to save the changed return address as the default return address before printing an envelope. Clicking Yes changes the return address information in the User Information tab of the Options dialog box.

Printing envelopes

You can print a return address and a delivery address directly on an envelope, or you can add the envelope to a document and print it later (with the letter itself). Word provides predefined envelope styles and sizes, but you can also customize your own envelope formatting.

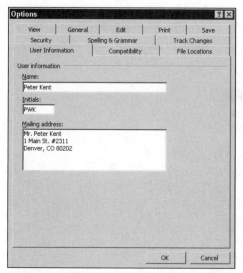

Figure 6-5: The User Information tab of the Options dialog box.

To create and print an envelope, follow these steps:

1. Select the mailing address in the document. (If the address is a contiguous block of three to five short lines near the beginning of the letter, Word *may* automatically select the address for you when you choose the Tools ➪ Letters and Mailings ➪ Envelopes and Labels command. But it may not.)

2. Choose Tools ➪ Letters and Mailings ➪ Envelopes and Labels. The Envelopes and Labels dialog box appears (see Figure 6-6).

3. Click the Envelopes tab and check that the mailing address, placed into the Delivery Address box by Word, is correct. If it is not, correct it.

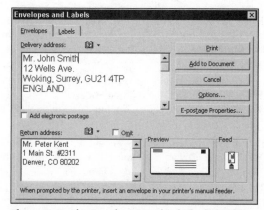

Figure 6-6: The Envelopes and Labels dialog box.

4. If you want to omit the return address from your envelope, select the Omit check box. Use this option, for example, if your envelopes are preprinted with your return address.

5. Click the Options button; then click the Envelope Options tab to open the Envelope Options dialog box (see Figure 6-7).

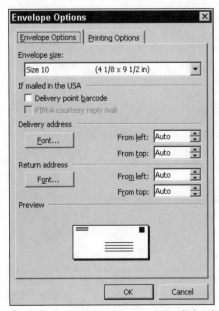

Figure 6-7: The Envelope Options dialog box.

6. Do any of the following in the Envelope Options dialog box:

- Add a Delivery Point Barcode and FIM-A markings, if you are in the U.S. We look at this subject in more detail in the next section.

- To change the envelope size, choose a size from the Envelope Size drop-down list. If you want to define your own custom size, choose the Custom option from the list, which displays the Envelope Size dialog box (see Figure 6-8). Enter the Width and Height measurements, or use the increase or decrease button, and then click OK.

- To change the font size for either the delivery or the return address, click the appropriate Font button. The Font dialog box then appears, where you can select the font and attributes you want to use. For more information on working with fonts, see Chapter 4.

- To change the position of the addresses on the envelope, use the From Left and From Top settings. You can see how your changes look in the Preview box.

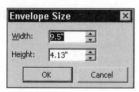

Figure 6-8: The Envelope Size dialog box.

7. Click OK to return to the Envelopes and Labels dialog box.

8. Do one of the following:

- To print the envelope now, insert the envelope in the printer and click the Print button. You can see how to insert the envelope in your printer by clicking the Options button and then clicking the Printing Options tab. Figure 6-9 shows the Printing Options tab in the Envelope Options dialog box. The recommended envelope feed method is the highlighted option in the Feed Method group.

- To add the envelope to the document, click the Add to Document button. If you select this option, the envelope is added to the beginning of the document, and Word inserts a section break directly after the envelope information. Figure 6-10 shows an envelope added to a Word document. The envelope information becomes page 0, so you must print page 0 to print the envelope. If an envelope is already attached to the document, the Change Document button will be available; choose this button to replace the old envelope with the new one.

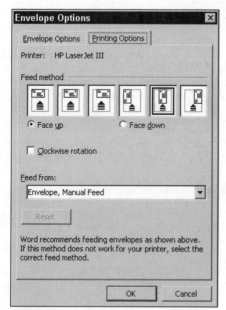

Figure 6-9: The Printing Options tab of the Envelope Options dialog box.

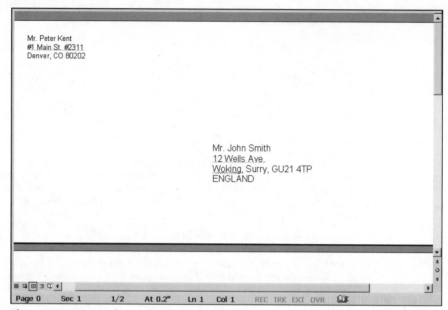

Mr. Peter Kent
#1 Main St. #2311
Denver, CO 80202

Mr. John Smith
12 Wells Ave.
Woking, Surry, GU21 4TP
ENGLAND

Page 0   Sec 1   1/2   At 0.2"   Ln 1   Col 1   REC TRK EXT OVR

Figure 6-10: An envelope added to a document.

Including barcodes with addresses

There are two types of postal barcodes: POSTNET and Facing Identification Marks (FIMs). POSTNET codes are simply ZIP codes that are translated into barcode language for the U.S. Postal Service's computers to read. FIMs are used in the United States on courtesy reply mail to identify and orient the front of the envelope during presorting. Figure 6-11 shows both types of barcodes on a single envelope—one just above the addressee, and one near the stamp area. Adding barcodes to your envelopes can speed the delivery of your mail as well as lower the postage costs of mass mailings that qualify.

To add this information to your envelope, use the Delivery Point Barcode and FIM-A Courtesy Reply Mail check boxes in the Envelope Options dialog box.

Adding graphics and logos

You can add graphics or some form of logo to your envelope, making your envelopes look professional without the cost of printed stationary. Figure 6-12 shows a graphic added to the return address of an envelope.

Tip   Once created and added to the envelope design, a graphic can be saved as AutoText and used repeatedly. For more information about AutoText, see Chapter 2.

Figure 6-11: The two types of barcodes on a single envelope.

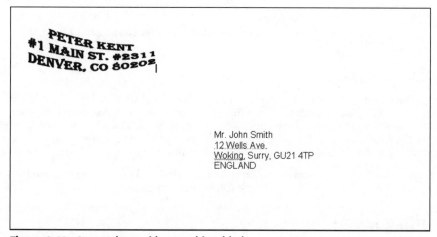

Figure 6-12: An envelope with a graphic added.

To add graphics to an envelope, follow these steps:

1. Select the mailing address in the document.

2. Choose Tools ➪ Letters and Mailings ➪ Envelopes and Labels. The Envelopes and Labels dialog box appears. Be sure the Envelopes tab is selected, and if necessary, modify the mailing and return addresses.

3. Click the Add to Document button. Word inserts the envelope at the beginning of your document and changes to Print Layout view.

4. Insert a graphic by choosing Insert ➪ Picture. You might also use WordArt to create a special text image.

5. Position and then resize the item on the envelope. If you choose an item of clip art or create a drawing using Word's drawing tools, you can just drag it to a new position and then drag the sizing handles to resize it. Otherwise, you must insert a frame to position the item.

Cross-Reference   For more information on working with Word's graphics tools, see Chapters 17 and 18.

Adding postage

Notice the E-postage Properties button in the Envelopes and Labels dialog box? This button takes you to an e-postage utility . . . if you have one installed, which you don't unless it's been added (Word doesn't currently come with such a utility). Stamps.com provides a utility that allows you to print your own stamps and mailing labels with postage already applied from within Word. Other companies may provide similar utilities.

These new print-your-own-postage services really do work and can be very convenient if you do a lot of mailing. Visit www.Stamps.com/ for more information.

Printing labels

With Word, you can print a single label or a full page of the same label with either your delivery or your return address. (Chapter 22 explains how to print mailing labels for multiple addresses.)

To print a single label or the same address on a sheet of labels, follow these steps:

1. Choose Tools ➪ Letters and Mailings ➪ Envelopes and Labels. The Envelopes and Labels dialog box appears.

2. Click the Labels tab (see Figure 6-13).

3. Do one of the following:

   • To change the address, choose the Address box and then enter the new address text.

   • To print your return address instead of the delivery address on a label, check the Use Return Address check box. You can accept what appears, or modify it if you want.

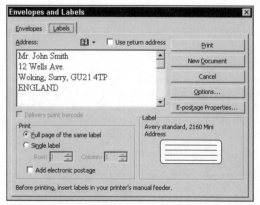

Figure 6-13: The Labels tab in the Envelopes and Labels dialog box.

4. Select the type of label that you want to print; click the Options button to open the Label Options dialog box (see Figure 6-14). Choose Dot Matrix or Laser and Ink Jet (the default) printer and the desired paper tray.

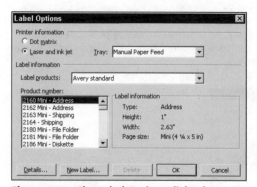

Figure 6-14: The Label Options dialog box.

5. Open the Label Products drop-down list to select the manufacturer of the labels that you're using. You can choose from a wide range of options, including some that are probably quite familiar, such as Avery.

Tip

You can see details about the size and margins of each label by clicking the Details button. Or you can configure your own labels, if they're not in the list, using the New Label button.

6. Select the Product number for the type of label that you're using.

7. Click OK to close the Label Options dialog box.

8. Do one of the following:

- To print a full page of identical labels, use the Full Page of the Same Label print option, which is selected by default.

- To print a single label, select the Single Label print option. You must also specify the row- and column-number position of where you want the label to print. For example, the Avery Address 5160 label sheet has three columns and ten rows of labels. To print a label in the second row, fourth column, type **2** in the Row text box and **4** in the Column text box. You can also use the increase or decrease buttons to set these values.

9. Insert a sheet of labels in the printer and click the Print button.

Instead of printing the labels, you can save a document with the labels already laid out. You can use this document in the future to print more, without going through this procedure.

As discussed earlier, you can add postage to your mailings if you've installed an e-postage utility. You can add postage directly to mailing labels, including delivery confirmation information.

Customizing labels

If none of the predefined labels matches your requirements, you can create your own. Word offers two ways to create custom labels: start with a predefined label and then make changes to its specifications or start from scratch. To see the specifications of a predefined label, click Details in the Label Options dialog box. An information dialog box appears with the name of the selected label type in the title bar, as shown in Figure 6-15. The information this dialog box shows varies with the label type.

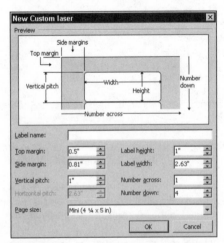

Figure 6-15: The New Custom Laser dialog box.

To start a new label design, choose New Label. This information dialog box is the same as the one that appears when you click Details. In addition to the illustrated label layout, this dialog box shows the exact label specifications.

✦ The Top Margin and Side Margin settings tell Word how close the first label should be to the upper and left edges of the page.

✦ The Horizontal Pitch and Vertical Pitch settings indicate the space between the beginning of one label and the beginning of the next.

✦ Labels often have a space between one label and the next or between adjacent labels in the same row. To set the label's height and width, use the Label Height and Label Width settings.

✦ The Number Across and Number Down settings tell Word how many labels to place on each row and how many rows to place in each column.

When you make changes, note how the Preview box adjusts the picture of the label to show its current size and location.

If you make changes to a predefined label layout, that layout then becomes a custom label and Word asks you to name it. After you have created and named a custom label, that name (followed by "- custom") appears at the top of the Product Number list. To remove the custom label design, select it on the list and then click Delete. Word asks for confirmation, however, before deleting the label.

To ensure that your labels print correctly, you can choose New Document, which creates a new document that contains the labels as they will print. This way, you can preview how the labels will appear. You can also save the document and print it later.

Tip   It is a good idea to print a sheet of labels on plain paper first to check the layout rather than risk an expensive sheet of labels.

Printing Data from a Form in Word

If you're using Word as a front end for working with forms, you can specify to print only the data in the form without the form itself. This comes in handy if you want to print out data on to a preprinted form such as a company invoice or a standard 1040 tax form. By coordinating the online form with the printed form, the data in the form fields appear in the same locations on the printed forms. To print just the data in a form, choose Tools ➪ Options, and then click the Print Tab. Select the Print Data Only For Forms check box. You can then use the standard ways to print a form document and only the data appears on the printed document.

Cross-Reference   For information on working with forms in Word, see Chapter 24.

Changing Printer Properties

Each printer has a driver with its own icon in the Printers folder. And attached to each printer icon is a Properties dialog box with properties that you can customize for that printer. Figure 6-16 shows an example of a Properties dialog box.

You can get to a printer driver's properties by right-clicking its icon in the Windows Printers (or Printers and Faxes) folder and then clicking Properties in the context menu. You can also get to a Properties box through Word's Print dialog box by clicking the Properties button in the top-right corner. However, note that the properties that you access through Word (or through any Windows application) will not exactly match those connected to the Printers icon in the Printers folder. In fact, in some cases the properties are very different.

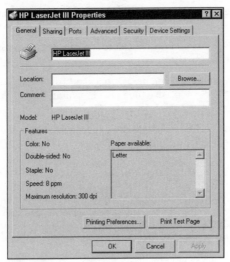

Figure 6-16: The printer Properties
dialog box for the HP LaserJet III printer.

Note Settings that you make in Word, such as the number of copies to print, will override any settings that you make in the printer's Properties dialog box.

You can quickly access your printer's properties by creating a shortcut on the Windows desktop for your printer icon. You can simply drag the printer icon from the Printers folder. A
message box then appears and states that you cannot copy or move the printer icon, but it
also asks if you want to create a shortcut. Click Yes to create the shortcut. Then right-click
the shortcut icon for the printer on your desktop and click Properties.

Printing Documents on a Network

Small offices with light printing demands can often share a printer by attaching that printer to
a computer on the office's network. That computer acts as a *print server*, even if it also doubles
as someone's workstation. All printing jobs are routed to that computer through the network,
and then from the computer to the printer through the printer cable.

Heavy printing traffic affects the performance of the workstation and requires that the computer always be up and running to support printing for the entire office. The solution to this
problem is using a network-ready printer with a network adapter already built in for connecting to the network. Or you can use a print-server device that connects to your printer and
also connects to the network as a network node. (Many companies choose to use a PC not
needed as a workstation as a print server rather than using a special print-server device.)
Printing is routed by all users on the network to the print-server device, which is connected
to one or more printers.

Note Many print-server devices are available, some for under $100. Devices that connect single
printers to a network can often be purchased for as little as $60; devices that connect two
printers are available for as little as $75.

If you're printing documents on a network printer, you may want to add a separator page to your document. A separator page prints before your document is printed, and it identifies the document's owner. In a network-printing environment, many print jobs are stacked one on top of the other on the printer, and a separator page helps people to find their printed documents at the printer.

You specify a separator page through the printer properties. Choose File ➪ Print, select the printer you want in the Name drop-down list box, and click the Properties button to open the Properties dialog box for that printer. Somewhere you should see a Separate setting. You may have to click the Advanced button—each dialog box is different, depending on the printer type.

Summary

Printing is the final step in producing your document, whether that document is a book, letter, envelope, or mailing label. The following list highlights the main topics covered in this chapter:

✦ You can use the Print dialog box (File ➪ Print) to print any number of copies of a complete document, or only a few pages or part of a document, to a selected printer.

✦ You can collate multiple copies so that they print as complete documents by choosing the Collate check box in the Print dialog box.

✦ You can print in reverse order to ensure the printed document is stacked in the correct sequence on your printer's output tray by clicking the Options button in the Print dialog box and then checking Reverse Print Order.

✦ You can print Word documents by dragging and dropping the files on the Windows printer icon.

✦ You can easily switch between different printers in Word's Print dialog box so that you can print specific documents on specific printers.

✦ Print Preview (File ➪ Print Preview) gives you a preview of how single or multiple pages will look when they print. (You can also choose View ➪ Print Layout.)

✦ You can print envelopes and mailing labels with your choice of size, feed method, added barcodes, and in the case of labels, the label layout by choosing Tools ➪ Letters and Mailings ➪ Envelopes and Labels.

✦ You can click the Options button in Word's Print dialog box to change a variety of print settings for the current document, or you can use the Print tab in the Options dialog box (Tools ➪ Options) to change print settings for all Word documents.

✦ You can access your printer's properties via the Printers folder in the Control Panel or via the My Computer folder. Right-clicking the printer icon displays the printer's Properties dialog box.

✦ If you're printing documents to a network printer, you may want to use a separator page to identify your documents at that printer. Setting up a separator page is handled via the printer Properties dialog box for the printer, which is located in the Printers folder.

✦   ✦   ✦

Managing Documents

In This Chapter

Managing documents
in Word

Saving documents

Saving documents
as Web pages

Sharing documents
across different
versions of Word

Backing up files
and recovering
damaged files

Finding files

So far, you've learned the main techniques for creating, editing, and printing documents in Word. All these activities occur in the foreground of word processing. Other important operations, such as document management, distribution, and protection, occur in the background. This chapter teaches you about these operations, and it also provides some valuable insight regarding file recovery. We also look at how to find files, which may not seem important when you first start working with Word; but once you've created a few hundred documents, finding files becomes pretty significant.

Managing Documents in Word

When you turn your documents over to Word, you can be sure that you can create, store, and retrieve your documents at any time. All you need to learn are a few file management principles to use the powerful tools in Word.

With Word, a document is considered to be a file, so when you create and save a new document, you are actually creating a new computer file. The three basic file activities are creating, modifying, and deleting.

After you create a file, you can open and close it as often as necessary. You can even make changes and save the modified document with a new name so that you still have both versions.

Word's AutoRecover feature can protect your files in case of an abnormal shutdown, such as a power failure or software crash. You can also automatically create backup copies of any file that you save.

Opening Document Files

After you create and save a document, the file exists on your disk. You can preview the contents of a file, or you can print the file without opening it. To use Word to change the file or save a copy of it under a different name, you need to open the file. Word's primary method for opening files is the File Open dialog box. Click the Open button on the Standard toolbar, choose File ⇨ Open, or press Ctrl+O. The Open dialog box (see Figure 7-1) includes the following buttons in the left pane:

✦ **My Recent Documents:** Displays a listing of shortcuts to recently used documents, with the most recent at the top.

✦ **Desktop:** Displays a list of document files located on the Windows desktop.

✦ **My Documents:** Opens the My Documents directory, which many people use to store all their work.

✦ **My Computer:** Displays all your computer's drives; you can now work your way down to the folder containing the document you need.

✦ **My Network Places:** A list of your network connections so you can find files out on the network somewhere.

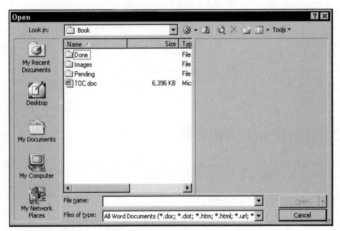

Figure 7-1: The Open dialog box.

With the Views menu on the Open dialog box toolbar, you can change the display of your files using the List or Details command. The Details listing displays the name, size, type, and date and time of the last modification for the files in the current folder. The List view displays only the names of these files. If a document is selected, the Views button on the Open dialog box also displays details of the selected document and a window allowing you to see and read the document.

Opening a document

If the file you want to open is not listed on the File menu as a recently used file (we discuss this in the next section), use the Open dialog box to browse through your drives and directories and to select the file you want to open. The Open dialog box displays a list of all Word files in the selected folder. You can also look in a different drive or folder for the document you want. With the dialog box buttons, you can move to the next-higher folder and even change the way you view the listed items.

To open a file, follow these steps:

1. Display the Open dialog box.

2. Click the Look In down arrow to select a different drive.

3. If you see the name of the file that you want in the list, select it and click the Open button, or double-click it.

You can open more than one file at a time from the list displayed in the Open dialog box. To select contiguous files, click the first file that you want and then press and hold Shift while you click on the last file that you want. To select noncontiguous files, press and hold Ctrl while you click each file.

If you don't see the file you want in the list after you select the correct drive and folder, the file may not be a Word document. To change the file type being viewed, click the down arrow of the Files of Type list box. The top choice in the list is All Files. Select this option to see all files (regardless of their type) in the current folder. Unfortunately, more recent versions of Windows, by default, hide the file extension—the three characters after the dot in the file-name. But you can determine the file type by the accompanying icon.

Tip   Hiding the file extension, many of us believe, is a bad idea. It sometimes makes it hard to recognize a file type, although the accompanying icon is a good indicator in most cases. (Be aware, however, that some virus files carry the wrong icon to intentionally mislead the computer user.) You can change the Windows default setting so that the file extension is always displayed in Windows and in Word's Open dialog box. Open Windows Explorer (right-click the Start button and choose Explore) and choose Tools ➪ Folder Options. In the Options dialog box, click the View tab, clear the Hide File Extensions for Known File Types check box, and click OK.

If Word doesn't recognize a file you select from the Open dialog box when you try to open it, the Convert File dialog box may appear. You can choose the file format of the document (if it's available in the Convert File From list) and then convert the file to a Word document. (The Convert File dialog box appears if you have checked the Confirm Conversion at Open check box under the General tab of the Options dialog box.) For more information on file formats supported by Word, see "Saving a document in a different format" later in this chapter.

Note   In some cases, if Word can't recognize the file you've selected, it will display a box in which you can select the *text encoding* so that Word can convert the file. However, if this happens, it's most likely that you've selected a file that is not a document file—you may have selected a database or image file, for example.

Opening recently used documents

If you've worked on the file recently, that file is listed at the bottom of the File menu. In this case, you need only click its name to open it. The default number of files listed is four, but Word can list up to nine file names at the bottom of the File menu. To change the number of files listed here, follow these steps:

1. Choose Tool ➪ Options.

2. Click the General tab in the Options dialog box (see Figure 7-2).

3. In the Entries box opposite the Recently Used File List check box, type or select the number of documents (as many as nine) that you want to appear at the bottom of the File menu. If you don't want *any* recently used files to appear, disable this option.

4. Click OK, or press Enter.

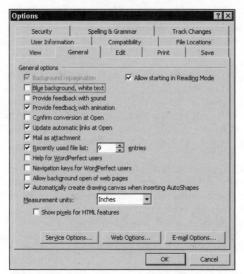

Figure 7-2: The General tab in the Options dialog box.

Using My Recent Documents to open documents

You can also use the My Recent Documents button in the Open dialog box to select shortcuts to recently used documents beyond the last nine that the File menu shows. Choosing File ➪ Open displays the Open dialog box, and in the Open dialog box, click the My Recent Documents button in the left pane. A list of recently opened document file names then appears as shortcuts. Select the file name, and click Open or double-click the file name.

Using Windows documents lists

Microsoft Windows keeps track of the last 15 documents you've opened. These documents can be any file that you worked on, including files from other applications, not just Word. If you primarily use Word, you may find that all the Word files you've worked with during the last few days are automatically being tracked by Windows. To open a document without opening Word first, choose Start ➪ Documents. A list of files then appears. Click the one you want to open, and Windows starts Word and opens the selected document.

Adding a document to the desktop

If you expect to work on a document over a long period of time, you can create a shortcut on your Windows desktop. Once the shortcut is on the desktop, simply double-click the shortcut to open Word and the document simultaneously.

To create a document shortcut on the Windows desktop, follow these steps:

1. Right-click on the Windows desktop.

2. Choose New ➪ Shortcut from the shortcut menu.

3. In the Create Shortcut dialog box, click the Browse button and browse to the file that you want to place on the desktop.

4. Select the file and choose Open.

5. Click Next.

6. If you want to change the name of the shortcut to something other than the document file name, enter the new name in the Select a Name for Shortcut box and click Finish.

Here's another, in some cases quicker, way to create a shortcut:

1. Position the Word window so you can also see the desktop.

2. Open the File Open dialog box, and find the file.

3. Click the file and drag it to the desktop.

4. Before releasing the mouse button, press and hold the Alt key.

5. Release the mouse key and then release the Alt key. The shortcut is placed on the desktop.

The Alt+drag method works from any Windows Explorer or My Computer folder, although it doesn't work from the My Recent Documents list.

Thumbnails, Previews, and Properties

From the Open dialog box you can view information about any file you click on. That way, you can be pretty sure it's the file you want before you open it. Word lets you view files in the Open dialog box in various ways, including the typical Windows Explorer type views: Large Icons, Small Icons, List, and Details. But in addition you have these three options:

✦ **Properties:** Displays the file's properties in a pane to the right of the list of files (see Figure 7-3).

✦ **Preview:** Displays a preview image in the pane (see Figure 7-4). You can actually scroll down through the Preview pane and see the entire document if you wish.

✦ **Thumbnails:** Replaces the file list with icons of files and, where available, thumbnail images of the files. If you selected the Save Preview Image check box in the Summary tab of the Properties dialog box before saving a file, Word will be able to display that file's thumbnail image.

✦ **Webview:** This is a little-used Windows feature that may not work on your system. If it's functioning, Webview lets you view folders as Web pages.

To move among these views, choose a particular view from the Views button drop-down list at the top of the Open dialog box.

Tip

Keep Preview turned off most of the time. It can be very useful now and then, but it really slows things down—especially when you're trying to preview large files.

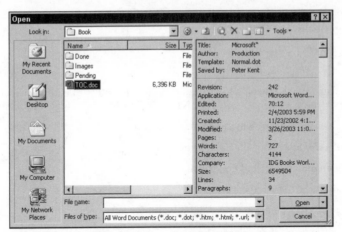

Figure 7-3: Previewing a document's properties.

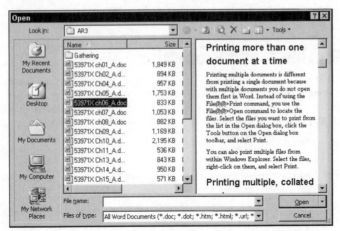

Figure 7-4: Preview of a document file in the Open dialog box.

Managing documents using the Open dialog box

You've already seen how to open and preview a file. With the Open dialog box, you can also perform many other file-management operations on one or more files, all without leaving Word. To do so, you first need to find the files that you want to manage and then list them in the Open dialog box. Once the documents are in the Open dialog box, you can work with them using the shortcut menu.

To manage documents using the Open dialog box, follow these steps:

1. Choose File ⇨ Open to display the Open dialog box.

2. Select the file with which you want to work.

3. Right-click the file name, and then select the appropriate command from the shortcut menu. Table 7-1 lists these commands and the actions they perform.

Table 7-1: Open Shortcut Menu Options

Command	Action
Open	Opens the selected file.
Print	Opens the Print dialog box, where you can select the options you want before printing the file.
Open With	Lets you send a file to a particular program. For instance, you might have selected, say, a Web page and decide that you want to send it to Microsoft FrontPage.
Send to	Copies the file to a floppy disk, creates a shortcut on the desktop, places it in an e-mail message, or opens it in another application.
Cut	Removes the document to the Clipboard.
Copy	Copies the document to the Clipboard.
Paste	Pastes a document that you have Cut or Copied into the directory. This allows you to move or copy a file in one directory, switch to another, and drop the file into that directory.
Create Shortcut	Creates a shortcut to the document that you can later move to the desktop or another folder.
Delete	Deletes the selected file.
Rename	Highlights the file name for editing.
Properties	Opens the Properties dialog box, where you can view any of the general, summary, or statistical properties. You can also edit summary properties or change the file attributes. Note that this is *not* the same as the Properties dialog box available within Word; rather it is the generic file-management Properties dialog box.

Other menu options may be available, too, such as a command that sends a file to a virus checker or to a file-compression utility. Such menu options are added by the program's installation procedure.

You can use many of the commands in the Open shortcut menu to manage groups of files. First, select all the files on which you want to perform the same operation. Then select the command you want to perform. Most of the shortcut menu commands apply to all selected files. The Properties command, however, applies only to the first file in the selected group.

To select multiple adjacent files, click the first file that you want, press and hold the Shift key, and then click the last file in the series. The two files you clicked and all of the files in between are now selected. (You can also go from last to first, if you want.) Note, however, that the Print option no longer works with multiple files in this way. Instead, you must select the multiple files and choose Tools ➪ Print from the toolbar in the Open dialog box.

To select multiple nonadjacent files, click the first file that you want, press Ctrl, and then click the additional files one at a time to select them as well. To deselect a selected file, press Ctrl and then click the file.

When you delete a file, Windows doesn't actually erase it from the disk. Instead, the file is sent to the Windows Recycle Bin. You can recover this file at any time—at least until you empty the bin. To recover such a file, minimize the active windows until you can see the Recycle Bin icon. Double-click the icon to open the Recycle Bin dialog box. Select the file that you want to recover, and then choose File ⇨ Recover. Windows places the file back in its original folder.

Managing Folders

Before you begin saving your own new files, you'll probably want to create one or more document folders for storing your files. You can use Windows Explorer to create new folders, or you can create new folders with Word. You can also change the default folder, which Word automatically displays whenever you open or save a document.

Creating new folders with Word

In either the Open or the Save As dialog box, you can easily create a new folder in any directory by clicking the Create New Folder button on the toolbar. In the New Folder dialog box, enter the name for your new folder and then click OK. The new folder becomes a subfolder of the current folder.

Changing the default folder

Word uses the My Documents folder as the default folder for new documents if you do not specify another. In other words, when you use the File Open dialog box the first time during a session, Word assumes you want to look into the My Documents folder. And the first time you save a new document during a session, it assumes that's where you want to place it.

To keep your documents in one or more different folders, you need to pick a different folder name from the list before opening or saving a file. It's usually a good idea, especially if you create many documents, to create multiple folders—perhaps a folder for each project or each client, for instance. Once you create your own folders, you can specify the one that you use most often as the default folder.

To change the default folder, follow these steps:

1. Choose Tools ⇨ Options, and then click the File Locations tab (see Figure 7-5).

2. Select Documents in the File Types list. Then click Modify.

3. In the Modify Location dialog box (see Figure 7-6), navigate to the folder that you want to use as the default.

4. Click OK, or press Enter, to return to the File Locations tab of the Options dialog box.

5. To change the default locations of any other file types, select the appropriate file type and then click Modify.

6. When you finish, click OK.

Tip   Changing the name of the default My Documents folder in Windows Explorer also changes the My Documents icon label in the Open dialog box to the new name of the folder.

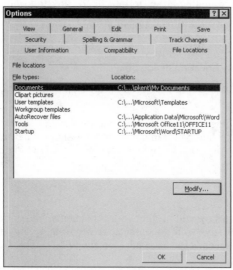

Figure 7-5: The File Locations tab in the Options dialog box.

Figure 7-6: The Modify Location dialog box.

Creating a new folder and making it the default folder

You can also create a new folder and make it the default folder using the File Locations tab of the Options dialog box. To create a new folder in the Options dialog box, follow these steps:

1. Choose Tool ➪ Options, and then click the File Locations tab.

2. Select Documents in the File Types list.

3. Click Modify to open the Modify Location dialog box.

4. To create a subfolder of the current folder, click the Create New Folder button to open the New Folder dialog box.

5. Enter the name for your new folder in the Name box, and then click OK. The Modify Location dialog box reappears, where you can immediately assign the new folder as the default (as explained in the previous section, "Changing the default folder").

Saving Documents

Word includes many ways to help you save and protect your documents. The options that you set determine how and when you save your documents. To see what options are available, choose Tools ➪ Options, and then click the Save tab (see Figure 7-7). Table 7-2 explains these options.

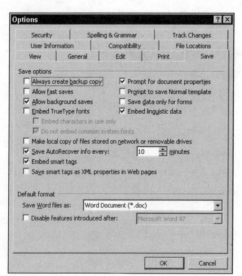

Figure 7-7: The Save tab in the Options dialog box.

Caution   The Fast Save option is reputed to cause many problems. Some users believe that it's the number one cause of file corruption for Word users and should never be used. In earlier versions of Word, Fast Save was turned on by default. In Word 2003, however, it's turned off by default. Some would say that it should stay that way.

Table 7-2: Save Options

Option	Action
Always create backup copy	Creates a complete backup copy of the previous version of the file. Each time you open the file, Word updates the backup copy.
Allow fast saves	Adds the changes that you make to the file instead of updating the entire file—information you deleted actually remains in the document hidden away from view. This option is quicker than a full save, but your files can become substantially larger. Also, it means that the document may contain information that you would never want anyone to see. This information won't be visible in Word, but a knowledgeable person could open the document in another kind of program and view this content. This option is an alternative to the Always Create Backup Copy option; you cannot use both.
Allow background saves	Saves the document in the background without disrupting your work. The status bar shows a pulsating disk icon during background saves.
Embed TrueType fonts	Embeds any TrueType fonts in the document so that other users who open it can view the document with its original fonts even if they don't have TrueType fonts. (See Chapter 4.)
Embed characters in use only	Embeds only the TrueType fonts used in the document. This option decreases the file size, but it is available only when Embed TrueType Fonts is checked.
Do not embed common system fonts	Tells Word not to bother embedding fonts that are present on every Windows system.
Make local copy of files stored on network or removable drives	Tells Word to save a copy of the file on your own hard disk when you save a copy on a network or removable drive.
Save AutoRecover info every	Automatically saves a copy of the active document at the specified time interval. You probably won't notice this happen. We discuss AutoRecover later in this chapter.
Embed smart tags	The Smart Tags you've used in your document will be embedded in the document so other users can work with them. (See Chapter 23 to find out more about Smart Tags.)
Save smart tags as XML properties in Web pages	When you save a document containing Smart Tags in a Web page, Word will save them as XML tags. (See Chapter 27 for information about XML.)
Prompt for document properties	Displays a prompt for the document properties, including title, subject, author, and key words, which are added to the Word file, when saving a document for the first time. You can use these properties to search for a file and to keep track of details about a file. A very good idea for workgroups that use Properties a lot—this forces people to remember to enter the information.

Continued

Table 7-2 *(continued)*

Option	Action
Prompt to save Normal template	Displays a prompt when you close Word that asks if you want to save any changes made to the Normal template file (Normal.dot). This prompt appears only if you made such changes (margin settings, AutoText items, and so on).
Save data only for forms	Applies to data entered in a form on the monitor. Enabling this option saves the data as a single tab-delimited record in Text Only format so that you can use it in a database.
Embed linguistic data	Word will embed information about the language used in the document.
Save Word files as	Allows you to select a file format to use as the default. You have a lot of choices, which we look at in detail later in this chapter.
Disable features introduced after	Pick a version of Word (Word 97 or Word 6.0/95). Word will not save any features that were introduced in versions of Word later than these. This is useful for people sharing documents with others who are working with older versions of Word. But of course, it also means that features you use in Word 2003 may not be saved.

Saving a document with a new name

Saving a file with a different name uses extra disk space, but there are several reasons for doing just that. For example:

✦ You want to track modifications made by others.

✦ You want to save a copy in a different folder than the original.

✦ You want to change the original document but also keep that version intact so that you can compare the different versions.

✦ You want to save the file in a different format to use on another application.

Tip   You can also use Word's versioning feature to save each version of a document in a single file, as explained later in this chapter.

When applied to an open document, the Save As command from the File menu can create a copy of the current document and allow you to select a new name, a new storage location, and a different file format.

To save a document with a new name, follow these steps:

1. Choose File ➪ Save As. The Save As dialog box appears (see Figure 7-8).

2. Type the new name in the File Name box—there's no need to include the .doc extension. Word automatically adds it to the file.

3. Select the appropriate drive from the Save In drop-down list if you want to save the new file in a different location.

Figure 7-8: The Save As dialog box.

4. To save the document in a different file format, click the down arrow to the right of the Save As Type box and select the desired format. (File formats that you can use when converting Word documents are discussed in the next section of this chapter.)

5. Click Save, or press Enter.

When you use the File ➪ Save As command to save an existing document under a new name, Word creates a copy of that document and makes it the new current document. In addition, Word automatically closes the original document and stores it in the original folder. Any changes made to the original document after the last time you saved the document using the old name are not saved in the original document, though, of course, they are contained in the new file. Therefore, if you want to ensure the original file has all of your changes, save it before using the File ➪ Save As command. If you want to continue working on the original, you have to open it again.

Saving a document in a different format

You can convert Word documents into other file formats for use on older versions of Word, Word on the Macintosh, and other programs. Table 7-3 lists the file formats that Word can open and save. (Note that it can't use all formats for both saving and opening.)

Table 7-3: File Format Converters in Word

File Format	Description
Word Document	This is the default Word 2003 format, containing all the features of this program.
Document Template	A file used as a template to begin new files. (Templates are discussed in Chapter 14.)

Continued

Table 7-3 *(continued)*

File Format	Description
Other Word Formats	Word lets you save in older Word formats, so people using older versions of the program can use it. Of course if you used features in your document that are not present in those earlier programs, the features will be lost.
XML Document	Saves the file in eXtensible Markup Language format (see Chapter 27).
WordPerfect	Word can save in a variety of WordPerfect formats, so WordPerfect users can open your work.
Works 4.0 for Windows	Works is another Microsoft suite, a sort of MS Office "Lite."
Rich Text Format	Rich Text Format was designed for transferring files between word processors. It's a kind of generic word-processing format that many programs can open.
Plain Text	Saves text without formatting. Converts all section breaks, page breaks, and new line characters to paragraph marks, and uses the ANSI character set. Select this format if the destination program cannot read any other available file format.
MS-DOS Text with Layout	Saves as ordinary text, not word processing format, but preserves line breaks, and inserts spaces to approximate indents, tables, line spacing, paragraph spacing, and tab stops, and converts section breaks and page breaks to paragraph marks. Use this format to convert a document to a text file format if you also want to preserve the page layout.
MS-DOS Text Only	Converts files the same way as Plain Text format. Uses the extended ASCII character set, which is the standard for MS-DOS–based programs. Use this format to share documents between Word and non-Windows–based programs.
Web Page	There are several Web-page formats, as discussed in Chapter 26.

Tip   The Microsoft Web site offers other file converters. Go to `www.microsoft.com/` and go to the Download Center. (At the time of writing, you could select All Products ➪ Downloads to get to the Download Center. But the menu options or links may change.) From the Download Center, search for Word converters.

To save a document in a format other than the current Word format, follow these steps:

1. Display the Save As dialog box (File ➪ Save As).

2. Click the arrow button in the Save As Type drop-down list box.

3. Scroll to the file type that you want, and then click it. If the file type uses a different extension, Word automatically changes the extension in the File Name text box.

4. Click Save to save the file in the new format.

In addition, Word can *open* many different file formats. In addition to most of the above formats, Word can open files that have been saved in Lotus 1-2-3, Microsoft Excel, Outlook phone book, Windows Write (Windows' built-in word processor), Schedule+ contact lists (Schedule+ is a pre-Outlook scheduling program), WordPerfect, and Works.

Tip   Word has a special open feature called Recover Text From Any File. Word attempts to extract text from any file you open with this feature, even if the file is not a word-processing file.

Using Batch Conversion

Word includes the Batch Conversion Wizard. With this wizard, you can convert multiple files into a different file format instead of simply one file at a time using the Save As dialog box.

To perform a batch file conversion, follow these steps:

1. Place the documents you want to convert into a single folder.

2. Choose File ⇨ New.

3. In the New Document task pane, click the On My Computer link.

4. In the Templates dialog box click the Other Documents tab and then double-click the Batch Conversion Wizard.

5. Click Next and select one of the following two options: Convert From Another Format to Word, or Convert From Word to Another Format.

6. Select the format, from the associated drop-down list box, that you want to convert from or to.

7. Click Next and choose the source folder of the files that you want to convert and the destination folder for the converted files. Click the Browse button to navigate to the folder that you want.

8. Click Next and select the files you want to convert. Double-click the individual files, or click the Select All button, to specify the files that you want.

9. Click Next. The wizard is now ready to perform the batch conversion.

10. Click Finish. A message box appears and informs you of the status of the file conversions, file by file.

11. After the file conversions are complete, a message box appears and asks if you want to convert more. Click Yes or No.

Saving documents as Web pages

At the heart of Word is a seamless integration between Word (*.doc) and Web (*.htm) documents. Word not only creates Web documents for viewing in a Web browser, it also reads these documents back in for editing. When you save any Word document as a Web page, almost all of the document's information, including its content, formatting, and document properties, are retained in the HTML (HyperText Markup Language) document.

 Tip   Web designers *hate* Web pages created by Word, and generally won't accept them. Word's Web pages are bloated, much bigger than they need to be, because they carry all that extra information. If you have to create text to pass on to a Web designer, don't save them as Web pages. Leave them as Word files and let the designer convert them.

Saving a document as a Web page is easy. Choose File ⇨ Save as Web Page, which displays the Save As dialog box with the .htm file extension selected. You can save the document by clicking Save. You change the page title for the document, which appears on the title bar of the

Web browser window, by clicking Change Title. You can also save a Word document as a Web page from the Save As dialog box (just as you would for any other file format).

Tip   You can view any Web page in a Web browser using the **Web Page Preview** command (File ➪ Web Page Preview) in Word. Word automatically launches Internet Explorer.

You can also save Web pages directly to a Web server (a process referred to as *publishing* your Web pages) using the Office Web Folders feature. Your pages are published to an intranet or Internet Web server. When you install Office, if you have a Web server running on your network or PC, a Web Folders icon is added to your system as a separate drive. You can view this folder in the Windows Explorer or My Computer window on the Windows desktop.

Cross-Reference   To learn more about publishing to Web pages, see Chapter 26 and 27.

Saving different versions of a document

If you are in the habit of using File ➪ Save As to save a copy of every new draft of a document, you may want to use Word's versioning feature. This enables you to store each version of your document in the same file so that older versions can't get lost, misplaced, or confused with the current version.

Note   In a file containing multiple versions of a document, Word's document statistics apply only to the current version.

To save a new version of an existing file, follow these steps:

1. Choose File ➪ Versions. The Versions dialog box appears (see Figure 7-9).

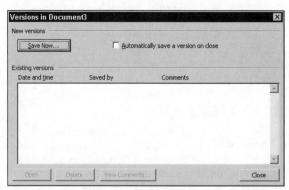

Figure 7-9: The Versions dialog box.

2. Click Save Now. The Save Version dialog box appears (see Figure 7-10).

3. Enter your comments on the version. Word automatically adds the current date and time.

4. Click OK. Word saves a new version of the document in the same file as the original.

Tip   You can also save a new version by choosing Tools ⇨ Save Version in the Save As dialog box.

Figure 7-10: The Save Version dialog box.

Working with versioning files

After you create one or more additional versions of a file, you can choose File ⇨ Versions to reopen the Versions dialog box and work with these files (see Figure 7-11). To open any version, select that version and then click Open—Word will open another window with the selected version, but keep the current version open, too. To delete an old version, select that version and then click Delete. Word asks you to confirm the deletion, and it reminds you that you can't undo this action. In the Versions dialog box, you can see the first few words of your comments about the file; if you want to see more, click View Comments. These comments are read-only—you can't modify them.

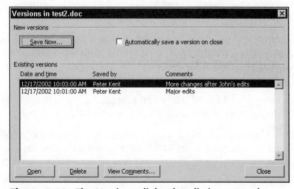

Figure 7-11: The Versions dialog box listing several versions of a document.

Saving a version as a separate file

When you open an older version of a file, Word displays the document in a separate editing window, which splits the screen. The version you have opened has a save date and time in its title bar—a reminder that you're not working with the current version.

If you make changes to the older version, Word won't save this document in the same file. When you choose File ➪ Save, Word displays the Save As dialog box and shows the file name (as it appears in the title bar) with the version creation date. When you click Save, you get a new file containing only the version you just edited.

Note   You can't use Word's Compare Documents feature to compare two versions of a document within the same file. For more information on working with the Compare Documents command, see Chapter 29.

Automatically saving new versions

You may want to save a snapshot of your document each time another editor or reviewer finishes working with it. To enable this feature, check the Automatically Save A Version On Close check box in the Versions dialog box (File ➪ Versions).

Tip   This feature works best if you don't expect each reviewer to open the file several times before completing his or her work on it. If you expect people to open and close the file several times during an editing session, you should not use this feature because you'll end up with a lot of unnecessary versions.

Sharing documents across different versions of Word

You can open documents created in Word 6.x, Word 95, Word 97, Word 2000, and Word 2002 inside Word 2003. All data and formatting created in these previous versions of Word are fully supported in Word 2003.

You can quickly create new documents or modify existing documents specifically for use in earlier versions of Word by turning on the Disable Features Introduced After feature and selecting a version in the Save properties of the Options dialog box (Tools ➪ Options).

Word 2003 files can actually be opened in Word 2000 and Word 2002, but not in Word 95 and Word 6.x. Even so, if your workgroup uses a combination of versions, your workgroup can still exchange documents and templates among these versions. Here are guidelines for managing workgroups using different versions of Word:

✦ If your workgroup includes many Word 6.0/95 users and you plan a gradual upgrade to Word 2003, save Word 2003 documents in Word 6.0/95 (*.doc) format.

✦ If your workgroup includes many Word 6.0/95 users and you plan a one-time upgrade to Word 2003, install the Word 2003 converter on computers using the older versions. With this converter, you can open Word 2003, Word 2000, and Word 2002 documents in Word 95 or Word 6.x.

✦ If you want to retain most features unique to Word 2003 in the documents, and Word 95 or Word 6.x users only need to view these documents, save Word 2003 documents in Word 97 & 6.0/95-RTF format. Remember, people using Word 95 and Word 6.x cannot make any changes to these documents.

✦ If you want to open a Word 2003 document in multiple programs, save the document in Rich Text Format (RTF) (*.rtf).

Tip   Several different converters and viewers are available from the Microsoft site at www.microsoft.com/word/. With the help of these converters and viewers, you can share your Word files with people who don't have Word or who have older versions of Word.

Using Fast Save

The Allow Fast Saves option in the Save tab of the Options dialog box (Tools ➪ Options) instructs Word to save only the changes to a document. That is, when you save the document, the process is very fast—it takes less time than a normal save, in which Word saves the complete document. That doesn't normally matter, but is much more noticeable if you are working with very large documents containing images (such documents can take a long time to save).

Ironically, however, full saves require less disk space than fast saves. Fast saves are larger than full saves because when Word uses fast saves, it keeps track of all your changes to a document by appending those changes to the end of the document file. Using full saves preserves the document without keeping track of your changes.

Caution   As mentioned earlier, Fast Saves have a very bad reputation and are considered by some to be a primary cause of file corruption in Word. You may want to avoid using this feature.

Backing Up and Recovering Files

One of the most frustrating events when working with a computer is opening a program after your computer has crashed and remembering that you hadn't saved your work for an hour or two. That time has just been thrown into the trash bin of time—it's gone, and you've got to go back through it again, rebuilding the work you've lost.

So you need to spend a little time understanding—and using—the tools Word provides you for protecting and recovering your data. Word helps you create backups and has a great AutoRecover feature, too.

Using AutoRecover

If you're working with a file that you've already saved, another temporary file is stored in the folder where you saved your document. While you're editing the file, the name of this temporary file appears with an initial tilde followed by a dollar sign; for example, a file named Proposal appears as ~$Proposal.doc. When you close the file or exit Word, the program prompts you to first save or discard your changes to the file, and the temporary file is then deleted. If Word crashes, though, these files get left over, undeleted. You can delete old versions of the temporary files, though you shouldn't try to delete temporary files from the current session if Word is still open.

The AutoRecover feature protects you from power failures or inadvertently turning off your computer without saving your work—or, let's be honest, those all-too-often occasions on which Word locks up or crashes. The AutoRecover feature creates and updates a copy of the current file. These files are different from the ~*.doc temporary files, though. The AutoRecovery files are saved as AutoRecovery*.asd files (or AutoRecovery.as$ if you haven't named the file yet).

Tip   AutoRecover is not a substitution for saving your file periodically yourself! AutoRecover cannot recover all your changes—it will miss changes you made after the last time it created its AutoRecover file but before the program crashed. Get into the habit of pressing Ctrl+S periodically. Eventually it becomes automatic, so you do it without even thinking about it.

Note that AutoRecover does *not* save the current file itself; it saves a copy. This contrasts with some other applications, in which an automatic save actually saves your work periodically and in which you cannot "unsave" these changes.

When you close Word normally, the temporary copy that AutoRecover creates is deleted. If Word is not closed normally, however, such as during a power failure or a crash, that temporary copy remains on the hard disk. The next time you open Word, any saved temporary files are automatically opened as recovered files, but you must still choose whether to save the previous changes to the original document.

When Word is first installed, the AutoRecover feature is set to save the open files every ten minutes by default. This way, you cannot lose more than ten minutes of work because of a power failure or some other inadvertent shutdown. You can change the interval between automatic saves to a value between 1 and 120 minutes anytime that you want. You can also turn off AutoRecover, but there isn't any solid reason to disable this powerful and friendly safety feature.

To save files automatically as you work, follow these steps:

1. Choose Tools ➪ Options.

2. Click the Save tab.

3. Select the Save AutoRecover Info Every option.

4. Select or type the number of minutes that you want between automatic saves in the Minutes box.

5. Click OK, or press Enter.

Word saves the AutoRecover files in a folder hidden away somewhere. Choose Tools ➪ Options and then click the File Locations tab. Click AutoRecover Files in the File Types list box. You can select this entry, and then choose Modify to change this location if you wish. If possible you should place these files on a disk other than the one on which you generally save your Word files. Then, if that disk fails for some reason while you are working on a Word file, you can still recover the file.

Recovering from a crash

The Word AutoRecover feature in the most recent versions of Word works very well—much better than in earlier versions. In the past AutoRecover has been a hit-and-miss type of thing. Maybe Word would recover your file, maybe it wouldn't. But now Word does such a great job at saving AutoRecover files and actually recovering from problems that you may find when your system crashes your stress level is much lower than it might have been in the past!

Tip   As discussed in the previous section, Word is set by default to save AutoRecover files every ten minutes. That means the most work you are likely to lose is ten-minute's worth. You might consider changing this to every two or three minutes, even. AutoRecover saves seem to happen quickly, without you even noticing, so why not? If you are working with very large files, with many images for instance, saving that frequently may be a problem, but for most situations, it's probably not.

When you reopen Word after a crash, it opens with the Document Recovery task pane open, as shown in Figure 7-12.

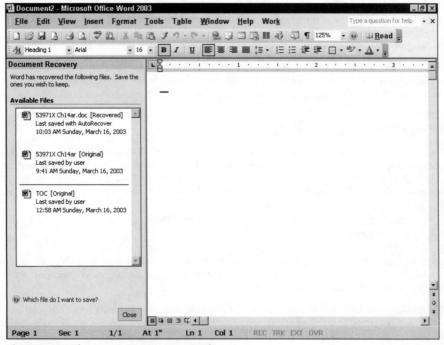

Figure 7-12: The Document Recovery task pane.

A list of files is displayed in this box. For each file, you can see the name, Last Saved By/With information (telling you that the file is an AutoRecover file or that it was saved by the user), and the time and date of the last save. Point at the file, and a triangle appears to the right of the name. Click the triangle, and a menu opens with these options:

✦ **Open:** Opens the file.

✦ **Save As:** Opens the file and then opens the Save As dialog box so you can save it with another name.

✦ **Delete:** Deletes the file and removes it from the list.

✦ **Show Repairs:** Opens a dialog box showing you what repairs Word made to the file. Sometimes, when your system crashes, the file is damaged. When Word opens the file, it repairs the file. This option lets you view what changes have been made to the file. However, the box is often not so helpful, so you may not be able to really understand what Word has done.

Now, which file do you keep, and which do you delete? The AutoRecover file is not always the most recent. Think about this sequence of events:

1. Word automatically creates an AutoRecover file.

2. You carry on working.

3. You save the file using Ctrl+S or File ⇨ Save.

4. Your system crashes.

In this case your original file is the most recent. The recovered file probably won't do you any good because you saved the file more recently than AutoRecover did. On the other hand, it's possible that Word had to make repairs to your original, but didn't fix it well. Use the Show Repairs option to see if you can figure out what it did.

If you're paranoid about losing data, you may even want to open each file, check the recent changes, and see which file seems to be the better one. Either choose the Open menu option, or simply click on the file name and Word will open the file for you.

Creating backup files

You can choose to have Word create a backup file for every document file you create. If you choose to keep backup files, Word creates a duplicate of the document you're opening and names it *Backup of filename*.wbk. When you update the file and save your updates, you then have two files: the current document and the backup document (which is one version old).

Note   This option requires a full save, so when you select it, Word clears the Allow Fast Saves check box. You cannot have both.

If a problem such as a power failure occurs, open the file ending with the .wbk extension to restore the latest version. Any changes that you made since the last save operation are missing, but at least you have most of your file.

The only disadvantage of this option is that each file you save in Word has a complete backup copy, so the amount of disk space required by your files may double. Many Word users turn off this option as they gain confidence in their file-handling abilities.

To create backup files, follow these steps:

1. Choose Tools ➪ Options.

2. Click the Save tab.

3. Select the Always Create Backup Copy option.

4. Click OK, or press Enter.

Creating Document Properties

You can certainly work with documents without entering any additional properties information beyond the file name, but when you're trying to find that elusive document, document properties can be quite useful. You can create a search based on the author, any of the keywords, the subject, or even a longer title than the document name itself. We discuss how to use Properties to find files a little later in this chapter.

To enter property information for a new or existing document, open the file and then choose File ➪ Properties. The Properties dialog box opens. Click the Summary tab to enter or modify summary information (see Figure 7-13).

The author name is filled in automatically from the User Information page of the Options dialog box. Enter any additional information that may help to identify the document in a search, such as a longer title, the main subject, and any other keywords or comments that could help you to remember what the document contains.

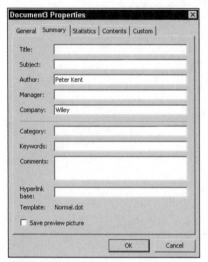

Figure 7-13: The Summary tab of the Properties dialog box.

Notice the Save Preview Picture check box in the corner of the Summary tab. When this box is checked, Word creates a thumbnail image that can be viewed from the File Open dialog box when you select Thumbnails from the View button.

You can also view statistics about the current document by clicking the Statistics tab in the Properties dialog box. Word counts not only characters but also characters combined with spaces to give you a more accurate estimate of the total space required to print the document.

You can also add more specific information from a large list of options under the Custom tab (see Figure 7-14). You can enter a Department, Destination, or Disposition name; the name of someone who has checked the document; an Editor, Group, or Publisher name; a Mailstop; a Language; or even a telephone number. Take a look at this list to see what is available to you.

To enter information, simply select the item you want to add, select a Type—Text, Date, Number, or Yes or No—type the information into the Value box (or click the Yes or No option button if you selected that data Type), and click Add.

The Custom tab in the Properties dialog box lets you add all sorts of additional information. Property information is tedious to create, and it is easy to ignore. When you're searching for that lost document, however, you'll be glad that you took the time to enter this information completely.

Tip   If you want to be reminded to create a summary for a new document, select Prompt For Document Properties on the Save tab of the Options dialog box.

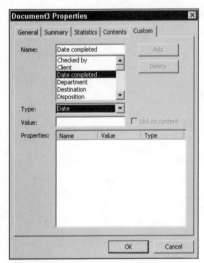

Figure 7-14: The Custom tab of the Properties dialog box.

Using Word Count

Word 2003 has a nice Word Count feature, especially useful for writers who are paid by the word! Whether you care about the number of characters in your document or the number of words, Word Count will help. (As Mark Twain said, "I never write 'metropolis' for seven cents, because I can get the same price for 'city.'")

Choose Tools ➪ Word Count, and a little dialog box opens showing you all the stats: the number of pages, words, characters (excluding spaces), characters with spaces, paragraphs, and lines in your document. There's a Footnotes and Endnotes check box in this dialog box. Turn it on to include those elements in the count.

Also, notice the Show Toolbar button. Click this to open the Word Count toolbar (which can always be opened using the View ➪ Toolbars ➪ Word Count command, too). This toolbar contains a Recount button and a drop-down list box. Click the Recount button at any time and open the drop-down list to see the latest statistics. (Recount actually works *very* quickly.)

Using AutoSummarize

Word has an interesting AutoSummarize feature you can use to create, yes, a summary of the document. To create an autosummary of a document, use the AutoSummarize command in the Tools menu. When you choose Tools ➪ AutoSummarize, Word takes a few moments (depending on the length of your document) to read it through and prepare a summary. Then the AutoSummarize dialog box opens (see Figure 7-15).

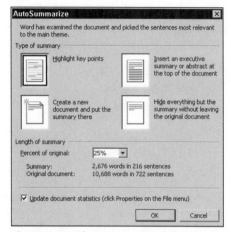

Figure 7-15: The AutoSummarize dialog box.

You have a choice of four ways to create the document summary and to specify how much detail you want in that summary:

✦ Highlight key points. Significant words in your document are highlighted with a yellow background; when you save the document, though, the highlighting is lost.

✦ Insert an executive summary or abstract at the top of the document.

✦ As a separate document, in a separate Word window, which you can then save.

✦ Word hides all the text in your document, but displays the summary. This form of summary is also lost when you save or close the document.

The dialog box shows an example of each option. Be sure to have the Show Highlight option selected (which it is by default) in the View tab of the Options dialog box if you want the summary elements to be highlighted. The second option is useful for condensing the subject matter for an introductory section of the document. The third option is handy for creating a summary to include in a separate document.

You can also set the length of the summary to specify how much detail you want. Click the Percent of Original down arrow to display a drop-down list of options: 10 (or 20) sentences, 100 (or 500) words or less, 10%, 25%, 50%, or 75%. As you change the length of the summary, the number of words and sentences in the Summary line changes accordingly.

The final option in the AutoSummarize dialog box automatically updates your document statistics with the number of words, sentences, and so on. Click OK when you finish setting these options.

Figure 7-16 shows a document with a 19% summary highlighted in the text.

The AutoSummarize toolbar that appears when you choose to highlight the key words contains tools to change the view of the summary, from highlighting the summary elements to hiding the original document and displaying only the summary elements. With the scaling bar, you can change the level of detail in your summary by dragging the vertical line. You can also see the percentage of the original change as you drag the line. Click Close when you have finished reviewing the summary elements, and you return to your original document.

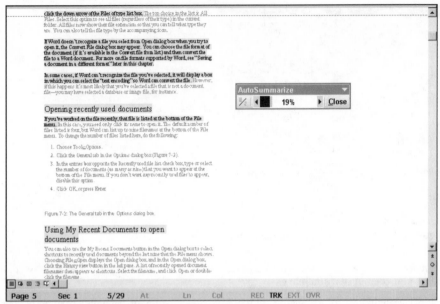

Figure 7-16: A summary highlighted in a document.

Note Just how useful is this feature? Let's just say we know very few people who actually use it. *Very* few.

Finding Files

Sometimes, it seems to be impossible to locate that file you created six months ago but need to review now. Searching every folder to find the file is tedious. Fortunately, however, Word provides a number of features for just such occasions. In fact, Word 2003 has a new search function you can use from within the application itself (in the past a Find File system was build into the Open dialog box). You can use this feature to search using just about any criteria—the file name, date, the information under the Summary tab of the Properties dialog box, the various Custom entries in the Properties dialog box, and so on. You can even search for a word inside a document.

Using File Search

Open the File Search task pane by selecting File ➪ File Search (see Figure 7-17). The simplest way to use this system is to type in the Search Text box at the top a piece of text you know to be in the file you are looking for. Click Go, and Word begins searching all the Word files it can find on your computer and on any networked drives you have mapped in Windows Explorer.

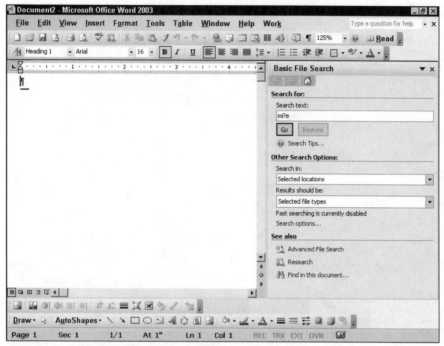

Figure 7-17: The Basic File Search task pane.

You can narrow the search to a great degree using the Search In and Results Should Be boxes. Search In allows you to specify *which* drive to look on, or even which directory on which drive. Click the triangle at the end of the box to open a drop-down list; then click the check box next to My Computer twice to clear all selections. Then you can navigate through the "tree"—by clicking on the + boxes to open up branches—until you find the directory you think the file is stored in (or the branch it's stored in; Word can search subdirectories, too).

Now, watch carefully! Click the check box to select that directory. Word will search inside that directory, but *not* in subdirectories. Click again, and you'll see that the check box changes—there's still a checkmark inside it, but now it looks like three check boxes stacked. That means Word will search inside that directory *and* inside subdirectories. Click somewhere outside this drop-down directory listing to close it once you've finished.

The Results Should Be box lets you specify what types of files you want to search. By default Word searches for Office files and Web pages, but you can click on the Anything check box and Word will search all the files it finds. For instance, you could use this option if you are looking for something stored in a text file.

When you are ready, click Go, and Word begins its search. Word now changes the task pane, displaying the Search Results pane, as you can see in Figure 7-18. You can now carry out various actions on these files. Just point at a file name, click the little triangle that appears to the right of the name, and pick one of the commands described in Table 7-4.

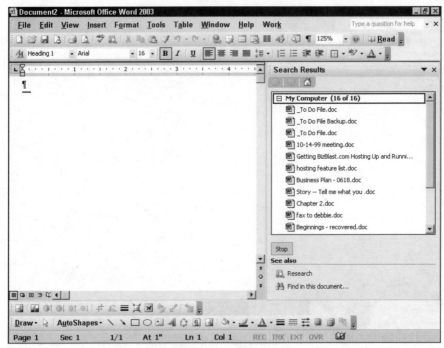

Figure 7-18: File Search displays the files it has found.

Tip   If you want to modify your search criteria and search again, click the Modify button at the bottom of the Search Results box. (When the search has stopped, the Stop button changes to Modify.)

Table 7-4: File Search Actions

Menu Name	Action
Edit with Microsoft Word	Opens the document in Word so you can review or edit it. (You can also left-click on the file name to quickly open it.)
New from this file	Opens a copy of the file, so you can save it with a new name.
Copy link to clipboard	Places a link in the Clipboard, a directory path to the file. You could save this somewhere so you'll know where to find the file next time you need it. Then you can copy the path into Windows Explorer's Address box and press Enter to open it.
Properties	Opens the files Properties dialog box so you can see if it's the file you need before you open it.

Using file indexes

In the File Search task pane, notice the Search Options link under the Results Should Be drop-down list. Immediately above this link you see either *Fast searching is currently disabled*, or *Fast searching is enabled*. Click the Search Options link to open the Indexing Service Settings dialog box, where you can turn on file indexing (select the first option button). The Indexing Service allows Word to search files much more quickly. Instead of starting a completely new search each time you try to find a file, Word creates a special index of all your files. So when you search, it looks through the index rather than searching each individual file.

Click the Advanced button in this dialog box to open the Microsoft Indexing Service window. This is a Windows component, not an Office component, so we won't go into too much detail. But note that when you turn on this feature, Microsoft begins indexing. You can use this window to start and stop indexing, view the progress, and specify what type of files should be indexed.

Indexing is a useful feature, but note that the index takes up hard-drive space—in fact the more useful the index (that is, the more files you have), the more space you're going to need. On most newer PCs, the space is not really a consideration. However, indexing can dramatically slow down even fast computers. It also has a reputation for unreliability; the system may tell you it can't find a document even if the document exists.

Advanced searches

Full-text searches are often very useful, but Microsoft probably shouldn't have made full-text searches the default search type. Most people want to search by file name, and full-text searches are very slow. In order to search for a file by the file name, you need to go to the Advanced File Search task pane (see Figure 7-19). To get to this task pane, click the Advanced File Search link under the See Also heading in the Basic File Search task pane.

Begin by making the Property selection. You can search for just about anything you can imagine by selecting from this list: Author, Company, Creation Date, File Name, Last Printed Date, Number of Characters + Spaces, and so on. Note that many of these values are from the file's Properties dialog box, as described earlier in this chapter.

After picking a Property, select the Condition. The Condition drop-down list box changes depending on your Property choice. For instance, if you are searching for Number of Characters + Spaces, the Condition drop-down contains these options: equals, not equal to, more than, less than, at least, at most. Note that some conditions are, in most cases, totally useless. For instance, few people know, to the exact character, how many characters and spaces are stored in a file—so rarely is the *equals* condition of any use. However, they may know that they have a large file with over, say, 500,000 characters and spaces, so *more than* might be useful.

Note also that in some cases, the contents of the Condition box actually complete the search criteria. Select the Last Modified property, choose Yesterday from the Condition list, and you're ready to search. Word will look for files created yesterday. In most cases, though, after selecting a Condition, you must enter a Value. Select the Property of Author, the Condition of Includes, and then type part of an author's name into the Value box.

Now, click the Add button, and your criteria are placed in the list. Now you can add another criteria. Suppose that you just added a criteria saying that you are looking for the Author named *Kent*. You could now add another criteria specifying the author *Hesl*. You could add other criteria, too, such as creation dates, the Subject, the Title, and so on.

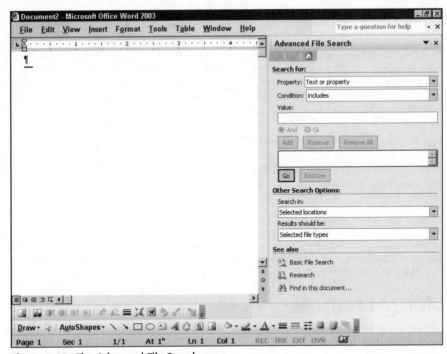

Figure 7-19: The Advanced File Search pane.

The And and Or option buttons at the top of the list tell Word what to do with these entries. And means "find a file that matches all of the criteria in the list" (the first *and* the second *and* the third, and so on). The Or option button means "find a file that matches *any* of the criteria" (the first *or* the second *or* the third, and so on).

So you could search, for instance, for any file that was authored by Kent *or* Heslop, or any file that was authored by *both* Kent or Heslop (both names would have to appear in the Author box in the Properties dialog box).

Finally, select the Search In and Results Should Be information, as described earlier in the chapter, and click the Go button.

Searching through the File Open dialog box

You can also search for files while you are in the File Open dialog box. Choose Tools ⇨ Search to open the File Search dialog box (see Figure 7-20). Although it looks different from the File Search task pane, the controls are almost exactly the same.

In Basic Search the default is to search text within documents. Type the words you are looking for, select the Search In and Results Should Be criteria, and click the Search button. To do more advanced searches—the same as within the File Search task pane—click the Advanced tab.

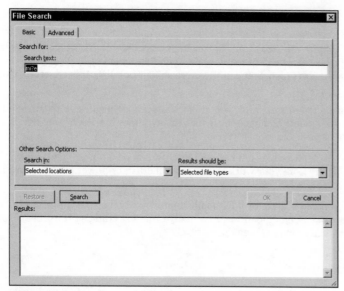

Figure 7-20: The File Search dialog box, opened from within the File Open box.

Using wildcards

If you don't know the exact spelling of the value that you're looking for, you can use special wildcard characters and search operators when specifying summary information in search criteria. Table 7-5 explains these special characters.

Table 7-5: Special Search Characters and Operators

Character	Action
? (question mark)	Matches a single character.
* (asterisk)	Matches any number of characters.
" " (quotation marks)	Matches all characters within the quotation marks.
\ (backslash)	Means the next character should be treated as a normal character instead of as a special character. Used with a question mark or asterisk, for example.
~ (tilde)	Logical NOT operator indicating that the document must not match this criterion.

Tip

The more criteria you specify, the longer it takes to find your files. In addition, if you specify incorrect criteria, you probably won't find your files. For example, if you misspell a key word, Word cannot find the file. It is usually better to specify fewer criteria than to specify too many and risk not finding any matches.

Summary

Windows and Word 2003 provide many tools for managing documents. This chapter has taken you on a tour of Word's file management features, from finding, opening, and saving files to recovering files from a system crash. Some of the more salient points in this chapter include the following:

✦ When managing documents in Word, you are actually managing files. With Word, you can create new documents and save these files in any folder in the system, even in one that you created as your personal folder.

✦ Word restores AutoRecover files after you have experienced a power failure or system crash. You can also restore your work after a system crash or power failure from a backup file.

✦ To locate a file, you can search for it by its file name, by a text string within the document, by the date of last modification, or by many other criteria. Use File ➪ File Search, or select Tools ➪ Search in the Open dialog box.

✦   ✦   ✦

Beyond the Basics

P A R T

II

♦ ♦ ♦ ♦

In This Part

Chapter 8
Proofing and
Researching

Chapter 9
Working with Tables

Chapter 10
Sections, Columns, and
Page Formatting

Chapter 11
Using Bookmarks,
Cross-References,
Footnotes, and Links

Chapter 12
Creating Indexes and
Tables of Contents

♦ ♦ ♦ ♦

Proofing and Researching

♦   ♦   ♦   ♦

In This Chapter

Correcting
spelling errors

Creating a custom
dictionary

Checking grammar
using the Word
grammar tool

Using AutoCorrect to fix
mistakes automatically
as you type

Working in the
Research pane

Using the thesaurus
and dictionary and
translating words

Searching the Internet
and encyclopedias

Finding stock quotes

♦   ♦   ♦   ♦

It's a fact of life: people make errors in spelling and grammatical syntax when writing a new document, either because they focus more on the ideas and concepts they're writing about or because they make simple typographical errors. By carefully reading a finished document, you can catch most or even all such errors, but this takes time. Instead, you can use the Word spell checker, which compares all words in the document to those words in a dictionary that you specify. In addition, the Word grammar checker detects possible errors in word usage, and the AutoCorrect catches misspelled words and other errors as you go. Using this chapter, you can master Word's essential proofing tools.

This chapter also looks at the research tools that Word puts at your fingertips. Use the built-in thesaurus to pick just the right word, or the dictionary to make sure a word means what you think it does. Look up stock quotes, translate words between languages, and even do Internet searches, all from within Word.

Correcting Spelling and Grammar While Working

Word looks for spelling errors while you are working. Each time you type a word it checks its dictionary to see if it can find the word; if it can't, it displays a wavy red line underneath the word. It also checks for problems with your grammar. Type **He watch him very carefully.** and Word will underline the word *watch* with a green wavy line. Why? Because it realizes that the word should be *watched* or *watches*, so it marks the word as a grammar mistake.

Caution   Be careful! Word is not always right. Some things it thinks are misspelled are not, and some—many—grammatical mistakes it finds are not mistakes at all. And Word often overlooks real grammar mistakes. Automatic spell checking and grammar checking are no substitute for professional editing when necessary, but they're great tools for most documents.

To correct an error immediately, right-click the offending word to open a shortcut menu, which contains the following options (the actual menu options vary depending on the type of mistake):

✦ **One or more suggested changes:** Offers corrections that Word thinks may fix the problem. Click on a suggestion to replace the mistake with the correction.

✦ **Grammar ... / Spelling ...:** Opens the Spelling and Grammar dialog box (which we explain in the next section).

✦ **Ignore Once:** Lets you close the menu without making a change.

✦ **Ignore All:** Tells Word to ignore all occurrences of this error in your document.

✦ **About This Sentence:** Displays the Office Assistant, which explains why Word thinks the text may be an error. This option is disabled if you have disabled the Office Assistant.

✦ **Add to Dictionary:** Adds the word to Word's dictionary, so Word doesn't think the word is a mistake the next time it sees it.

✦ **AutoCorrect:** Provides a list of words that you can set up as automatic corrections. The next time word sees the word *nezt*, for instance, it will automatically change it to *next*.

✦ **Look Up:** Looks up the word in the dictionary.

The status bar also displays icons at the right end that indicate the current spelling and grammatical status of your document.

✦ An icon showing a book with a pen writing on it means that spell and grammar checking are underway (you see this while you are typing).

✦ An open book with an X indicates that checking is complete and that errors have been found.

✦ If this icon shows an open book with a checkmark, however, checking is complete and Word has found no errors.

Tip   Double-click the icon showing a book with an X, and Word will jump to the first error after the cursor position and open the pop-up menu.

Many professional writers do not use the proofing-as-you-type tools, because they are a very inefficient way to proof long documents. They're not so bad for short documents; but for very long documents, it's far more efficient to ignore all errors as you type and then fix them all at once when you're finished.

Correcting Spelling and Grammar After Working

In order to check spelling and grammar for an entire document at the same time, press F7, choose Tools ➪ Spelling and Grammar, or click the Spelling and Grammar button on the Standard toolbar. The Spelling and Grammar dialog box opens (see Figure 8-1), and the tool begins checking your document, stopping on the first error it finds.

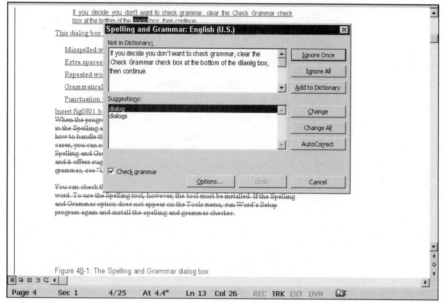

Figure 8-1: The Spelling and Grammar dialog box showing a misspelled word.

It really doesn't matter where the cursor is when you begin spelling. The tool begins at the cursor point, goes all the way to the end of the document, and then continues from the top of the document. Alternatively, you can select a block of text first and then start the tool. Word checks the selected text and then asks you if you want to continue checking the entire document.

Note
If you decide you don't want to check grammar, clear the Check Grammar check box at the bottom of the dialog box and then continue.

This dialog box actually displays a variety of different errors:

✦ Misspelled words

✦ Extra spaces between words

✦ Repeated words

✦ Grammatical mistakes

✦ Punctuation mistakes

During a spell check, Word stops automatically each time it finds what it considers to be an error. The Spelling and Grammar dialog box shows the error, which is highlighted in red, with the text around it (so you can see the word in context). Table 8-1 describes the dialog box options that appear when Word finds a spelling error.

Table 8-1: Spelling Error Options

Option	Action
Not in Dictionary	Displays the error in context.
Suggestions	Displays a list of suggested corrections.
Ignore Once	Continues the spell check without changing the selection. Word displays additional instances of the same error.
Ignore All	Continues the spell check without changing the selection. Word does not display additional instances of the same error during the current session, which means this option applies to all open documents and not just the active one.
Add to Dictionary	Adds the selected word to the active dictionary. To see the name of the active dictionary, click the Options button.
Change/Delete	Accepts the highlighted suggestion in the Suggestions box. Instead of choosing one of the suggestions, you can also edit the error in place and then click Change. If the error is a repeated word, this button changes to Delete, which removes the repeated word.
Change All/Delete All	Changes all instances of the selection in the current document (unlike Ignore All) to whatever you select in the Suggestions box or type in the text. If the error is a repeated word, this button changes to Delete All.
AutoCorrect	Adds the error and its correction to the AutoCorrect list (see "Proofing with AutoCorrect," later in this chapter).
Options	Opens the Spelling & Grammar tab of the Options dialog box, in which you can specify various spelling options. (You find out more about this tab in the "Spelling Options" section later in this chapter.)
Undo	Undoes the last action made during the current spell-check session. Clicking this button a second time undoes the second-to-last action, and so on. This button is not available until you make at least one change.
Cancel/Close	When you first open the Spelling and Grammar dialog box, the Cancel button is displayed. When you make the first change, the Cancel button changes to the Close button. Clicking either button closes the dialog box and saves any changes you've made.

Skipping selected text

Sometimes you may want to skip parts of your document during a spell check. Memos and letters, for example, have headings and address blocks with names and other text that slow down the spell checker, or perhaps you have inserted a block of programming code or a foreign language. Word provides a way for you to skip such text while checking your document.

To skip selected text during a spell check, follow these steps:

1. Select the text you want to skip.

2. Choose Tools ➪ Language ➪ Set Language. This opens the Language dialog box (see Figure 8-2).

Figure 8-2: The Language dialog box.

3. Click the Do Not Check Spelling or Grammar check box.

4. Click OK.

Checking spelling in other languages

The English (U.S.) version of Microsoft Office comes with proofing tools for English, Spanish, and French. Word can also run spell checks for text written in other languages; however, you must buy and install a separate dictionary for each language that you want to check. You can also purchase the Microsoft Proofing Tools Kit separately from a Microsoft reseller. The Proofing Tools Kit CD includes the proofing tools for all the languages supported in the Microsoft MultiLanguage Pack for Office. The Microsoft MultiLanguage Pack for Office provides the translated text for the user interface and help system for all of the Office programs in more than 80 languages. The MultiLanguage Pack also includes the Microsoft Proofing Tools Kit, which includes the proofing tools for the languages.

You can also purchase supplemental medical and legal dictionaries from third-party vendors.

To check selected text in another language, follow these steps:

1. Select the text you want to format in the other language.

2. Choose Tools ⇨ Language ⇨ Set Language. This opens the Language dialog box as before.

3. Select the language from the Mark Selected Text As list.

4. Click OK.

Note   You can create a style that includes a language format and the appropriate dictionary for each language that you use. For more on styles in Word, see Chapter 13.

Spelling options

Customizing, fine-tuning, and many dictionary-handling options are found in the Spelling & Grammar tab of the Options dialog box. The choices in this dialog box are very important if you write or edit using many different styles of documents.

To customize spelling options, follow these steps:

1. Choose Tools ➪ Options. The Options dialog box appears.

2. Click the Spelling & Grammar tab to display the Spelling & Grammar Options dialog box (see Figure 8-3).

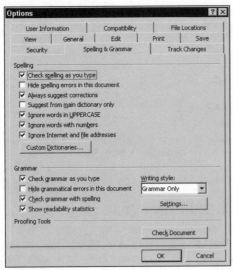

Figure 8-3: The Spelling & Grammar tab of the Options dialog box.

3. Select the options that you want (see Table 8-2).

4. Click OK.

Tip If you are working in the Spelling and Grammar dialog box, click the Options button to display the Spelling & Grammar tab of the Options dialog box.

Table 8-2: Spelling Options

Option	Action
Check spelling as you type	Checks for spelling errors as you type the words and underlines misspelled words with a wavy red line.
Hide spelling errors in this document	Shows or hides the wavy red underline, which indicates a possible spelling error.
Always suggest corrections	Shows suggested replacements for all misspelled words found during the spell check.
Suggest from main dictionary only	Shows suggestions from the main dictionary but not from other open, custom dictionaries.
Ignore words in UPPERCASE	Skips words with only uppercase characters.

Option	Action
Ignore words with numbers	Skips words that contain numbers.
Ignore Internet and file addresses	Skips Internet as well as e-mail addresses and file names.
Custom Dictionaries	Opens the Custom Dictionaries dialog box, in which you can create a new dictionary, add an existing dictionary to the list, edit or remove an existing dictionary, and apply a different language format to your document.

Using Custom Dictionaries

When you install the spelling option in Word, it includes a dictionary known as the main dictionary. Word always uses this dictionary during a spell check. In addition to this standard dictionary, however, you can create specialized dictionaries. For example, if you frequently create documents with industry-specific words and acronyms, you can add these special words and terms to a custom dictionary. With a custom dictionary, the spell checker won't highlight those words or terms unless they are not spelled correctly in the document.

Custom dictionaries act as supplemental word databases for specialized needs. With Word, you can use as many as ten custom dictionaries simultaneously. When you create a new dictionary, Word automatically activates it, so it is available during any spelling check. If you decide that you no longer want to use a particular custom dictionary, you can always deactivate it.

A custom dictionary is a list of words that you don't want to add to the main dictionary but that you do want the spell checker to skip in some situations. Word automatically starts its own custom dictionary the first time that you spell check your document. The Change All and Ignore All selections are added to that dictionary. Word uses any additional custom dictionaries that you activate in conjunction with the main dictionary to perform the spell check.

To open the Custom Dictionaries dialog box, follow these steps:

1. Choose Tools ➪ Options. The Options dialog box appears.

2. Click the Spelling & Grammar tab to display the Spelling & Grammar properties.

3. Click the Custom Dictionaries button to display the Custom Dictionaries dialog box (see Figure 8-4).

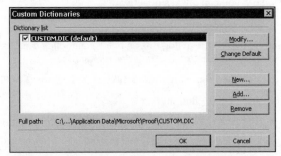

Figure 8-4: The Custom Dictionaries dialog box.

The Custom Dictionaries dialog box contains all the options needed to create and modify dictionaries in Word. Table 8-3 describes the custom dictionary options.

Table 8-3: Custom Dictionary Options

Option	Action
Modify	Opens the selected custom dictionary where you can add, delete, and edit words in the list.
Change Default	Lets you change the dictionary that Word will add words to when you ask it to add to the dictionary.
New	Opens a dialog box where you can create a new custom dictionary.
Add	Opens a dialog box where you can select existing dictionary files to add to the Dictionary list.
Remove	The Remove option deletes the selected dictionary from the Custom Dictionary list. Selecting this option does not physically delete the custom dictionary from your drive. Rather, it simply removes the dictionary from the list so that it no longer appears when you open the Spelling & Grammar Options dialog box. **Caution:** Do not remove the first dictionary (Custom.dic) in the list because it is used by other Microsoft applications.

Managing custom dictionaries

Activating and deactivating custom dictionaries tells Word which ones in the list to use when spell checking. If the dictionary that you want exists on your computer but is not on the Custom Dictionary list, you can add it to the list. If you want an entirely new set of words in a custom dictionary, you can create a new custom dictionary and then add it to the Custom Dictionary list. When you remove a dictionary from the list, it still exists on your disk; to delete the dictionary file, you must use the normal file management process.

Creating a new custom dictionary

A custom dictionary is a list of words, each on its own line, in a document with the .dic extension. (These are simply text files.) When you create a new dictionary, Word automatically activates it, so it is available during any spell check. If you decide that you no longer want to use a particular custom dictionary, you can always deactivate it.

To create a custom dictionary, follow these steps:

1. Open the Spelling & Grammar Options dialog box as before, and click the Custom Dictionaries button to display the Custom Dictionaries dialog box.

2. Click the New button to open the Create Custom Dictionary dialog box (see Figure 8-5).

3. Enter a file name for the new custom dictionary.

4. Click Save. The name you entered in step 3 now appears in the Custom Dictionary list.

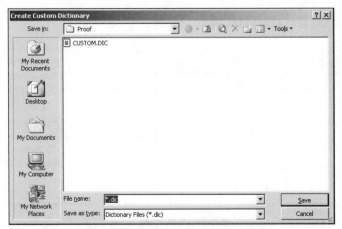

Figure 8-5: The Create Custom Dictionary dialog box.

Adding new words to a dictionary

You can add words to a custom dictionary in several ways:

✦ Right-click on a misspelled word in your document and select Add to Dictionary

✦ During a spell check operation, click the Add to Dictionary button

✦ Click a dictionary name in the Custom Dictionaries dialog box and then click Modify. Word displays a dialog box in which all the words in the dictionary are listed. Type a word and press Enter or click Add. (Select a word and click Delete to remove it.)

Selecting dictionaries

To add a custom dictionary to the Dictionary List, simply open the Spelling & Grammar Options dialog box, choose Custom Dictionaries, and then click the Add button. Word displays the Add Custom Dictionary dialog box, which lists the dictionary files in the current folder. You can switch drives and directories to find the dictionary that you want to add. When you add the dictionary, Word automatically places a checkmark next to it to indicate that it is active.

You can have as many dictionaries in the list as you want, but only ten can be *active* (indicated with a checkmark) at any one time.

Creating exclude dictionaries

You can also create *exclude* dictionaries, words that you want Word to skip. For example, if you are using the U.S. English dictionary, but still prefer some of the British spellings of words— such as theatre and colour—you can tell Word to ignore these words.

Create a text file, name it the same as the main dictionary you are working with, and give it an .exc extension. Save this file in the same directory as the main dictionary. In the file, you can type all the words you want to be excluded, one on each line.

Using the Word Grammar Tool

Word's grammar checker identifies sentences that contain possible grammatical or stylistic errors, and it also suggests corrections. The grammar checker has four predefined style levels: standard, formal, technical, and casual. You can further customize each style to observe or to ignore certain rules of grammar or style. You can also create custom grammatical styles that contain rules you specify.

When you run a spell check, the grammar check will be run at the same time. As each possible error is caught, it is displayed in the Spelling and Grammar dialog box, with the offending words displayed in the upper box and highlighted in green (see Figure 8-6). Select the appropriate option. See Table 8-4 for an explanation of the various grammar options in the Spelling and Grammar dialog box.

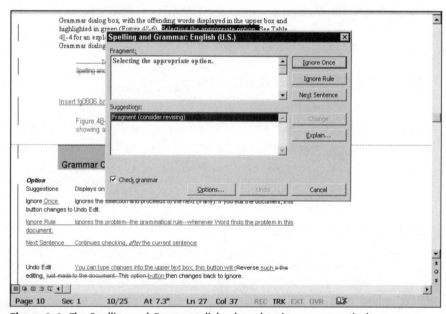

Figure 8-6: The Spelling and Grammar dialog box showing a grammatical error.

Table 8-4: Grammar Options in the Spelling and Grammar Dialog Box

Option	Action
Suggestions	Displays one or more suggested corrections (if any) for the selection in the upper box.
Ignore Once	Ignores the selection and proceeds to the next (if any). If you edit the document, this button changes to Undo Edit.
Ignore Rule	Ignores the problem—the grammatical rule—whenever Word finds the problem in this document.

Option	Action
Next Sentence	Continues checking, *after* the current sentence.
Undo Edit	You can type changes into the upper text box; this button will reverse such editing. This button then changes back to Ignore Once.
Resume	Displays in place of the Ignore Once button when you click outside the Spelling and Grammar dialog box. Clicking Resume restarts the Grammar Checker from the point at which you stopped.
Change	Makes the correction.
Explain	Displays an explanation of why Word thinks it has found a grammatical error.
Check Grammar	Clear this check box to tell Word not to check grammar while running a spell check.
Options	Displays the Spelling & Grammar Options dialog box.
Undo	Undoes the last actions made during the current grammar check one at a time. Clicking this button a second time undoes the second most recent action, and so on.
Cancel/Close	Closes the dialog box. The Cancel button becomes the Close button after you make at least one change.

Changing grammar options

You can specify what level of rules to include in the grammar check, and you can choose to display the readability statistics after the check is complete. You can also choose whether to check grammar while checking spelling.

To check grammar without checking spelling, follow these steps:

1. Choose Tools ➪ Options. This displays the Options dialog box. (Or click the Options button in the Spelling and Grammar dialog box.)

2. Click the Spelling & Grammar tab to display the Spelling and Grammar properties.

3. Select the options that you want (see Table 8-5).

4. Click OK.

Table 8-5: Grammar Options

Option	Action
Check grammar as you type	Checks grammar and marks with wavy green underlining any possible errors as you enter text.
Hide grammatical errors in the document	Hides the wavy green lines in your document. Word still checks while you are typing, but won't indicate them. (When you do a Spelling and Grammar check Word will be able to run it more quickly than if you didn't check as you type.)

Continued

Table 8-5 *(continued)*

Option	Action
Check grammar with spelling	Each time you spell check, Word checks grammar, too.
Show readability statistics	Specifies if readability statistics are displayed after a complete grammar check (more about this later).
Writing style	You can choose to check Grammar, or both Grammar and Style (see the next section "Changing grammar and writing style rules").
Recheck Document	Tells Word to clear all the information it has gathered during spelling and grammar checking. See the "Rechecking Documents" section later in the chapter.
Settings	Displays the Grammar Settings dialog box.

Changing grammar and writing style rules

Word lets you specify what rules it should check against during a grammar check. For example, the Comma Required Before Last List Item option enables you to tell Word to always check for a *serial comma*. This means that when you have a list of items (such as *red, green,* and *blue*), a comma must appear before the *and*. If you don't check for this option, Word allows you to type *red, green* and *blue*. You can tell Word to check for clichés, to ignore sentence fragments and capitalization errors, and so on. To change grammar rules, follow these steps:

1. Click the Settings button in the Spelling & Grammar tab of the Options dialog box to open the Grammar Settings dialog box (see Figure 8-7).

2. Select the Writing Style that you plan to use: Grammar or Grammar & Style. (If you installed Word 2003 over some earlier versions of Word, you may also see other Writing Style options, such as Casual and Formal.)

3. Select the options that you want to change in the Grammar and Style Options list. The Reset All button restores all the default settings for the selected writing style.

4. Click OK.

Figure 8-7: The Grammar Settings dialog box.

Viewing document and readability statistics

When you grammar check an entire document, a Readability Statistics dialog box (see Figure 8-8) may display when the grammar check is complete (if you have selected Show Readability Statistics in the Spelling & Grammar tab of the Options dialog box). After the grammar check is complete, Word displays a message box telling you that the checking has been completed. Click OK.

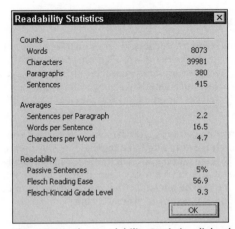

Figure 8-8: The Readability Statistics dialog box.

Document statistics displayed in this dialog box include the number of characters, words, sentences, and paragraphs in the document. They also include the average number of sentences per paragraph, of words per sentence, and of characters per word.

The readability of a document is often measured in terms of a grade level, and various algorithms can be used to estimate a document's ease of reading. The Readability Statistics dialog box includes the results of three such commonly accepted estimates.

The readability estimates in Word consist of the following:

✦ **Passive sentences**, or the percentage of sentences written in the passive voice. Active voice is considered to be more readable, so a high number of passive sentences means higher difficulty.

✦ **Flesch Reading Ease**, or readability based on the average number of syllables per word and the average number of words per sentence. Standard writing averages 60 to 70 on a 100-point scale. The higher the score, the more people can readily understand the document.

✦ **Flesch-Kincaid Grade Level**, or readability based on the average number of syllables per word and the average number of words per sentence. This score indicates a grade-school level. For example, a score of 6 means that a sixth-grader can understand the document. Standard writing is approximately seventh- to eighth-grade level.

Rechecking Documents

On occasion you may want to completely recheck a document. Perhaps you are working with a document that has been worked on for an extended time, perhaps even by multiple people.

It may have been checked several times by several people using their own ideas of what's right and wrong. If you run the Spelling and Grammar checker again, Word is going to ignore all the text that has been checked before.

You can tell Word to start over and check everything. In the Spelling & Grammar options, click the Recheck Document button. Word will clear all its information; the next time you check Spelling & Grammar, everything will be rechecked.

Proofing with AutoCorrect

AutoCorrect is a database of common spelling, typographical, and other mistakes that follows along as you type and fixes these mistakes as you make them—you'll notice that something you've just typed suddenly changes. AutoCorrect also replaces character strings with symbols. For example, when you type (c), AutoCorrect automatically changes those characters into the copyright symbol (©). Type (r) and you'll get ®; type (tm) and you'll end up with ™. You can add your own entries in AutoCorrect.

Because AutoCorrect automatically inserts text as you type, you can use it to correct your most common typing and spelling errors, which are contained in a table along with their corrections. You can also use it to correct your capitalization and punctuation. You can easily add entries directly to the AutoCorrect table or, as you've already seen in this chapter, during a spell check. An AutoCorrect entry doesn't have to be a mistake that you want Word to correct, however. You can add any entry to change any text or character string.

Working with AutoCorrect entries

AutoCorrect has its own extensive database of common mistakes (for instance, it changes *hte* and *teh* to *the*), but you'll probably want to add your own entries to reflect your own most common errors. As mentioned, you can add AutoCorrect entries during a spell check or using the AutoCorrect dialog box.

To work with AutoCorrect entries, choose Tools ➪ AutoCorrect. The AutoCorrect dialog box appears, and the AutoCorrect tab displays the properties for managing AutoCorrect entries (see Figure 8-9).

AutoCorrect options

AutoCorrect actually does two things. It has a library of corrections that you can add to or remove from—when it recognizes something you type, it replaces the typing with whatever is specified in the library. For instance, you could type *address123* and AutoCorrect would automatically replace the text with your street address. It also looks for common errors and automatically replaces those. These are the types of errors that AutoCorrect fixes:

✦ **Correct TWo INitial CApitals:** With this turned on, Word assumes that if you type a word with the first two letters capitalized, you made a mistake, so it replaces the second one with a lowercase letter.

✦ **Capitalize first letter of sentences:** If you don't capitalize the first letter in a sentence, Word does it for you.

✦ **Capitalize first letter of table cells:** Same thing; if you don't do it, Word does it for you.

✦ **Capitalize names of days:** Type *monday* and Word replaces it with *Monday*.

✦ **Correct accidental usage of cAPS LOCK key:** If you type the first letter of a sentence in lowercase, all other letters in uppercase, Word assumes you have accidentally left the CAPS LOCK key on your keyboard turned on; it turns it off for you.

✦ **Replace text as you type:** With this check box cleared, Word will still fix the problems defined by the check boxes above this one, but will *not* automatically replace text with the corrections in the AutoCorrect list.

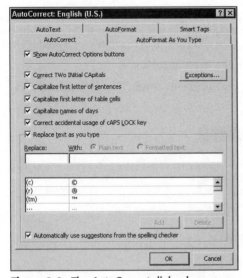

Figure 8-9: The AutoCorrect dialog box.

Adding AutoCorrect entries

To add entries in the AutoCorrect dialog box, follow these steps:

1. Choose Tools ⇨ AutoCorrect. This displays the AutoCorrect dialog box.

2. In the AutoCorrect properties tab, type the word that you commonly misspell in the Replace box.

3. In the With box, type the correct spelling of that word.

4. Click Add.

In the AutoCorrect dialog box, the Automatically Use Suggestions from the Spelling Checker check box tells AutoCorrect to add the spell-checker suggestions as replacement entries for the misspelled word. Adding AutoCorrect entries during a spell check is one of the best ways to systematically add common errors that pop up during these checks.

To add entries to AutoCorrect during a spell check, follow these steps:

1. Run the spell checker.

2. When Word finds an error and you select a correct spelling in the Spelling & Grammar dialog box, select the correct spelling.

3. Click the AutoCorrect button.

Editing and deleting AutoCorrect entries

You can change an AutoCorrect entry by selecting that entry, entering your text in the With box, and then clicking the Replace button. You can delete any entry in the AutoCorrect database by selecting it from the list and then clicking the Delete button.

Adding AutoCorrect exceptions

AutoCorrect lets you specify exceptions to its rules. You can tell it, for instance, that although you do want to use the "two capital letters at the start of a word is a mistake" rule, you don't want it to fix the name *EXchange*, because your company uses that form for a product name.

To specify exceptions to the AutoCorrect rules, follow these steps:

1. In the AutoCorrect dialog box, click the Exceptions button. The AutoCorrect Exceptions dialog box appears (see Figure 8-10).

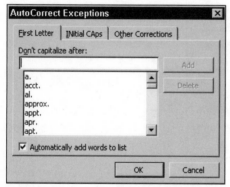

Figure 8-10: The AutoCorrect Exceptions dialog box.

2. Click one of the tabs to specify the rule for which you want to specify an exception.

3. Type the exception.

4. Click OK twice to return to your document.

Correcting AutoCorrections

Notice that at the bottom of the AutoCorrect Exceptions dialog box is a check box labeled Automatically Add Words to List. If you leave this checked, when you change a word back to its original form, after AutoCorrect has modified it while you are typing, AutoCorrect automatically adds the word to the AutoCorrect Exceptions list.

Here's how to change a word back. Suppose you are typing the word *EXchange*, and AutoCorrect automatically converts it to *Exchange*. Press Ctrl+Z to undo the operation (or choose Edit ➪ Undo), and AutoCorrect converts it back to the way you typed it and automatically adds it to the Exceptions list.

Note   AutoCorrect will *not* do this every time you fix one of its changes—only if it matches the Correct TWo INitial CApitals or Capitalize First Letter rules.

You can also use a pop-up menu to specify how you'd like to handle an AutoCorrection. When you notice that Word has automatically changed something you type, point at the word and you'll see a small blue bar appear underneath the word. Point at the bar, and a small menu pops up, with the words AutoCorrect Options. Point at the little triangle, and a pop-up menu appears (see Figure 8-11). This menu lets you change the word back, stop automatically modifying the word, or open the AutoCorrect Options dialog box.

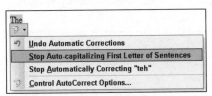

Figure 8-11: The AutoCorrect pop-up menu.

Cross-Reference   AutoCorrect is discussed in more detail in Chapter 2.

Using Research Tools

Word has had very basic research tools for some time—the ability to look up a word in a thesaurus or dictionary. But Word 2003 extends the research feature set with the addition of a new Research task pane.

You can still look up words in a thesaurus—you can now choose from several, in fact. But suppose that you want to insert a stock price into a document. You can use the Research pane to find the stock you're interested in, its latest price, the amount and percentage change, the previous high, and so on, and then quickly drop the stock price into your document. Of course, you need Internet access for features like this, but most corporate users have always-on access, and many small office and personal users can quickly connect, too.

The Research pane

Most of the research results are displayed in the Research pane, which you can see in Figure 8-12. You can open the pane in several ways:

✦ Choose Tools ➪ Research.

✦ Choose Tools ➪ Language ➪ Thesaurus or Tools ➪ Language ➪ Translate.

✦ Click the Research icon button (usually on the Standard toolbar).

✦ Click the Research text button (usually on the Reading Mode toolbar).

✦ Point at a word in your document, press Alt, and click on the word; the Research pane opens, the word you clicked on is loaded into the Search For box, and the thesaurus is searched.

✦ Right-click on a word and select Look Up or Translate or Synonyms ➪ Translate.

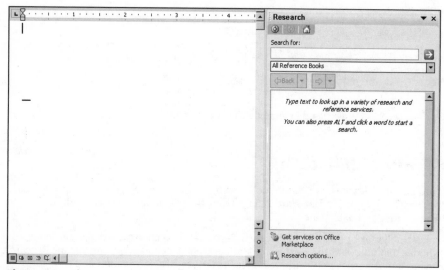

Figure 8-12: The Research pane.

You can navigate the Research pane using the Back and Forward buttons below the Show Results From box, similar to using Back and Forward buttons in a Web browser.

✦ Click the Back button to move back to the previous search.

✦ If you've used the Back button, you can use the Forward button to move forward to the search you just came from.

✦ Click the little black triangles on the Back or Forward buttons to see a list of searches; select from the list to return to the selected search.

At the top of the pane you'll find a little gray Back arrow and a Home button; these are used to change to different panes.

Using the thesaurus

Stuck for a word? Already used one word multiple times and need a little variety? Word's thesaurus can help you find the word you need. A thesaurus can help you by finding words related to the one you search for; synonyms (a word that means essentially the same thing as the word it replaces); and antonyms (a word that means the opposite of the selected word), though Word's thesaurus primarily finds synonyms.

Here's the quickest way to use the thesaurus:

1. Right-click on the word you want to look up.

2. Select Synonyms from the pop-up menu. A drop-down menu opens, displaying a list of words similar to the one you clicked.

3. Click on one of these words to replace the one in your document.

If you didn't find what you want, and you need to explore the thesaurus a little more, you need to open the Research pane. The quickest way to do this is directly from the thesaurus pop-up menu you saw when you right-clicked on the word. Simply choose Synonyms ⇨ Thesaurus.

The thesaurus (see Figure 8-13) loads the word into the Search For box and automatically searches the default thesaurus, displaying the matches.

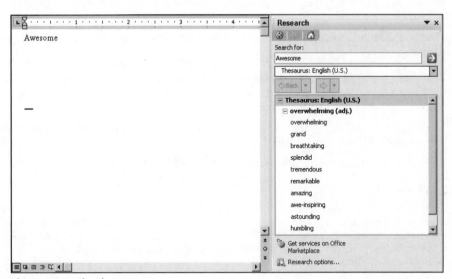

Figure 8-13: The thesaurus.

Note What is the default thesaurus? It's the one set as default in the Language box. Choose Tools ⇨ Language ⇨ Set Language and click on the language you want to use as the default. Click the Default button, and then click OK. For instance, if English (U.S) is selected as the default, the default thesaurus you'll see in the Show Results From box is Thesaurus: English (U.S.).

You can get to the thesaurus quickly in the following ways, but only if the thesaurus was the last reference tool you used:

✦ Right-click on a word and select Look Up.

✦ Point at a word in your document, press Alt, and click on the word; the Research pane opens, the word you clicked on is loaded into the Search For box, and a search is performed.

When you use one of these methods, Word searches using the last-used information source. If, for example, you just searched for a word using MSN Search, Word will search for the word you clicked on using MSN Search.

Note   The Alt+click method can take a few seconds to work, particularly if it's the first time in your Word session that you've used the feature or if your computer is doing something else in another program.

Working in the thesaurus

Now that you've got your matches, you can carry out a number of actions. First, notice that some words are bold—these are the major matches. Search for *evasion*, for instance, and the thesaurus may find *avoidance* and *prevarication*. Below the bold words are other, non-bold words. These are words similar to the bold ones. Under *avoidance* you may find *dodging*, *elusion*, and *fudging*, for example. You can use the little – icon next to a bold word to close the list below it.

When you've found a word you are interested in, there are several actions you can take:

✦ Click on a word to search for that word in the thesaurus.

✦ Point at a word and click the little down-triangle that appears to the right of the word; select Copy (to place the word in the Clipboard) or Paste (to replace the word in the document with the selected word).

✦ Type a word directly into the Search For box, and click the arrow button to the right to search for that word.

✦ Select another research option under Can't Find It?

Can't Find It?

Sometimes you'll see options under the Can't Find It? heading, at the bottom of the thesaurus matches. You may see a spelling alternative—a word that Word thinks might be close to what you want. Click that word, and Word will search for it in the thesaurus. You may also see a list of Other Places to Search. Clicking on one of those links will carry out a search on the word in those other information sources—all the Reference Books, for instance, or Research Sites.

Using the dictionary

The Research pane also contains one or more dictionaries—you'll probably find the Encarta World Dictionary, in both U.S. and U.K. editions. In the Search For text box, type the word you want to look up and then select the dictionary from the Show Results From drop-down list box. (Don't worry if you're not quite sure how to spell the word; the encyclopedia will help you.)

When you click the arrow button, the Research pane searches the dictionary and displays the matches it has found. It also displays alternative spellings under Can't Find It? (see Figure 8-14).

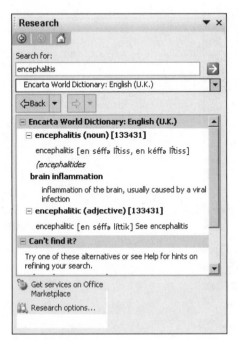

Figure 8-14: Encarta's dictionary is built into Word.

Translating words

Word's Research pane can help you translate words, and it really works pretty well.

Caution   Translation tools are often very unreliable and should not be used for critical work. You should never use the translation tool to help you write an entire letter in a language you don't understand. It simply won't work because the tool can't translate syntax; it can translate only single words. This tool is sometimes useful for figuring out a foreign word you find in a document, but if you are working on something really important, you should check the meaning of a word with someone who understands the language.

Here's how to translate a word that appears in a document:

1. Right click on the word.

2. Select Translate from the pop-up menu. The Research pane opens (see Figure 8-15).

3. If necessary, select the From and To languages you want to use (Word automatically uses the last settings you worked with). You'll see the translation below the selection boxes.

Of course, you can also type a word you want to translate directly into the Search For box and click the arrow button.

Figure 8-15: Translating words in the Research pane.

Other information sources

Word's research tool also allows you to search a variety of other information sources, including an encyclopedia and Internet search sites. In fact, the tool was created to allow other companies to create their own information sources. So don't be surprised if you find third-party tools you can connect to and information sources set up on corporate intranets.

You can search these other information services by opening the Research pane, entering a word into the Search For box, selecting an information source from the drop-down list box below the Search For box, and clicking the arrow button. The next time you want to search the same information source, you can simply right-click a word and select Look Up. (You learn how to add information sources later in this chapter in the section "Adding, removing, and updating services.")

Searching the Internet

You can search the Internet directly from within Word, without bothering to open a browser first. Select one of the Internet searches from the drop-down list box below the Search For box—Word comes with several MSN searches already configured. These are the search services at Microsoft Network, Microsoft's Internet service.

Enter a word, or words, you want to search for and then click the arrow key. You'll see a page with information that MSN found for you (see Figure 8-16), but notice also that you may have multiple pages available—at the top of the list you may see something like *1–5 of 894*, meaning the page you can see is showing you the first five matches out of 894 that MSN found. (Click Next at the top of the list to display the next few matches.)

For each entry you'll find a title, a short description, and a link. Click the link to open your browser and display the page.

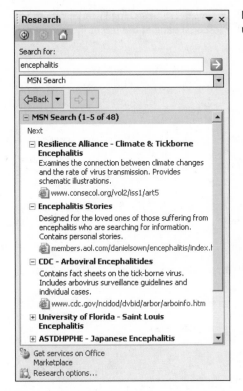

Figure 8-16: The Research pane can be used to search the Internet.

Searching the encyclopedia

The Research pane can also be used to search through Microsoft's Encarta encyclopedia. Type a word, or several words, select the encyclopedia, and click the arrow button. You'll see a number of entries, with plus sign icons next to them. If you see one you think may have the information you're looking for, click the plus sign (+) to display a description and a link to the encyclopedia article. After you click the plus sign, it changes to a minus sign (–), as shown in Figure 8-17. Click the link to open your browser and load the article. These articles are loaded from the Encarta Web site.

Retrieving stock quotes

Here's a neat feature. Type a company name or a stock ticker symbol into the Search For text box and then select Stock Quote from the Show Results From drop-down list. Click the arrow button, and the Research pane searches online for stock information. The results are shown in Figure 8-18. (Note that you'll probably have to turn on this reference source, as described in the section "Turning on Reference Sources.")

This information comes from the CNBC part of the MSN Web site. You'll get the basics—the price, change, high and low, and volume—but you'll also get links to more detailed information, including a 1-year, 3-year, and 5-year chart. Clicking one of these links loads the appropriate page in your browser.

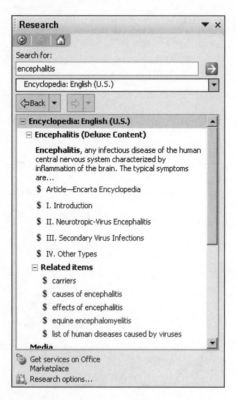

Figure 8-17: Searching Encarta, with the Research pane at the top of the window.

Figure 8-18: Stock quotes are just a click away.

You can also click the gray button with the down-pointing triangle below the stock quote to open a small menu. Select Insert Stock Price to place the ticker symbol and current price into your document at the cursor position—for example, *MSFT 58.22*.

Sometimes you'll see links to other companies. For example, if you type Johnson into the Search For box, the Research pane has no way of knowing *which* Johnson you are referring to. Is it Johnson Controls, Inc. (JCI), Johnson Electric Holdings, Limited (JELCY), Johnson Outdoors, Inc. (JOUT), or one of several others? The Research pane displays the first one's stock information, but you can quickly view information for the others by clicking on the plus sign icon next to a stock name.

Research Options

You can modify the manner in which the Research pane operates in several ways. You can select which services you want to use, add research-source providers, and even set up parental controls. Click the Research Options link at the bottom of the Research pane to open the Research Options dialog box (see Figure 8-19).

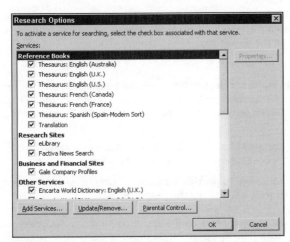

Figure 8-19: The Research Options dialog box lets you add, remove, and control reference sources.

Turning on reference sources

The large list box in the Research Options dialog box displays all the reference sources currently available to you. The ones with the checkmarks next to them are available to the Research pane. Check a service to activate it, or clear the check box to remove it from the Research pane.

Note   If you have turned on Parental Controls some of these reference sources may not be available.

Click on a reference source and then click the Properties button to open a box that displays information about that particular reference source—a description and copyright notice perhaps, a provider name, and the path to the resource. This is typically *internal*, meaning it's built into Word, or a Web URL, which is a link to a file on the Web.

Adding, updating, and removing services

If you know of other service providers you can add them quickly by clicking the Add Services button, typing the Web address of the service, and clicking the Add button. Word will access the address and find out what reference sources are available.

Where would you find such services? Your company might have created something—perhaps an industry-specific dictionary or technical documentation related to your products. Also note the Get Services on Office Marketplace link at the bottom of the Research pane. Click this to launch a browser and load the Available Research Services page, where you can find commercially available services.

You can also update services to see if new reference services have been added. Click the Update/Remove button, and you'll see all your reference sources grouped by the different services—click on a group of sources (they'll all be selected at once) and click the Update button. You can also click the Remove button to get rid of all the sources provided by that provider.

Implementing parental controls

The parental controls let you limit access to the reference sources, something many parents may want to do if they have included the Internet-search reference sources in particular. Click the Parental Control button to open the dialog box.

You have two options:

✦ **Turn on content filtering to make services block offensive content.** Select this to automatically stop offensive content being returned when you search. But note that this option does not help if the reference source you are searching makes no attempt to block offensive content.

✦ **Allow users to search only the services that can remove offensive results.** This option simply blocks the services that don't attempt to block offensive content.

If you turn on parental controls, you'll have to provide a password. *Don't forget it!* You won't be able to change parental controls without entering the password first.

Note   Even if you try to block offensive content, and even if a service claims it can block offensive content, remember there's no such thing as perfection. So now and then, offensive content may get through. (After all, how do you define *offensive?*)

Summary

Automatic spelling and grammar checking and correction make it quick and easy to improve the quality of your documents. Word provides a standard dictionary that you can customize with your own special terms, and you can document statistics to estimate the reading level of the resulting document. The Research pane is a really neat little tool that can help you with your writing in many different ways. Other highlights from this chapter include the following:

✦ Word quickly scans the entire document and picks words that are apparently misspelled or repeated, and the program often suggests a correction.

✦ You can create a custom dictionary with words and acronyms that are specific to your work.

✦ The grammar checker finds errors in syntax and style, and it also offers alternatives. You can ask for an explanation of the rule violation, accept the suggested change, or ignore the apparent violation.

✦ The Word thesaurus helps you to create more interesting documents by suggesting synonyms and antonyms for selected words.

✦ You can open the Research pane by clicking one of the Research buttons or by choosing Tools ➪ Research.

✦ The thesaurus can help you find just the right word; using the right-click method is very quick.

✦ If you don't find what you're looking for in the Research pane, make sure you look under the Can't Find It? heading, where you may find useful alternatives.

✦ You can search through two or more dictionaries; Word provides the British and American versions of Encarta.

✦ The Translation feature provides a quick way to do simple translations, but shouldn't be used for anything complex.

✦ You can also search the Internet, Encarta encyclopedia, and stock quotes.

✦   ✦   ✦

Working with Tables

◆ ◆ ◆ ◆

In This Chapter

Understanding tables

Adding tables
to documents

Modifying and
fine-tuning tables

Adding graphics
to tables

Converting text to
table, and vice versa

Sorting table data
and numbering cells

◆ ◆ ◆ ◆

Tables provide an efficient, concise way to present related data in a document. You can use tables to arrange columns of numbers, lists of information, and side-by-side paragraphs of different sizes. You also can place graphics combined with text in tables, allowing you to use tables as a simple page-layout tool. Tables are easy to create and modify in Word, and you can insert them anywhere in a Word document. This chapter teaches you how to harness the power of tables to deliver all kinds of information.

Understanding Tables

Tables are grid-like structures similar to spreadsheets, and they consist of cells arranged in rows and columns. A cell is the box in which a row and a column meet. You can enter text, numbers, or even images in a cell. Text wraps in a cell just as it does in a paragraph of regular text. Rows expand vertically to accommodate text that wraps in a cell. You can change the width of a cell as needed, and in some cases cells will also widen automatically to accommodate the text you are typing.

You can create a new table structure and enter text, or, in some cases, you can convert existing text to a table layout. After creating a table, you can format it in several ways. You can merge and split cells, format some or all of the gridlines to print, add borders and shading to selected cells, adjust the column width and spacing, adjust the row height, and even add or delete rows and columns. You can also specify if page breaks can occur in a cell and designate one or more rows as headings so that they appear at the top of the table on each new page. You can even add formulas to perform calculations using the table data, in effect turning a table into a simple spreadsheet.

Tip You can create forms based on Word tables that act as front ends for databases and spreadsheets, as explained in Chapter 24.

Adding Tables to Documents

The basic method of adding a table to a document is to insert the table grid and then to add the text. You can also convert text to a table, which is explained later. When first inserting a table, you select the number of columns and rows to match your data. The table initially occupies all of the space between the margins, and each column is the same size. You can modify this, however, after you add the text, see how much space you need, and judge how the table looks in your document. Figure 9-1 shows a table inserted into a document.

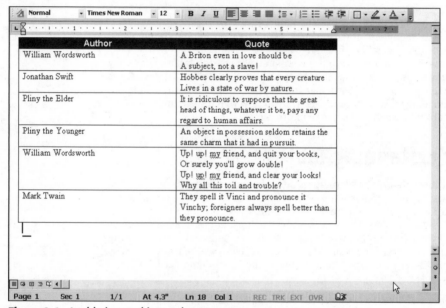

Author	Quote
William Wordsworth	A Briton even in love should be A subject, not a slave!
Jonathan Swift	Hobbes clearly proves that every creature Lives in a state of war by nature.
Pliny the Elder	It is ridiculous to suppose that the great head of things, whatever it be, pays any regard to human affairs.
Pliny the Younger	An object in possession seldom retains the same charm that it had in pursuit.
William Wordsworth	Up! up! my friend, and quit your books, Or surely you'll grow double! Up! up! my friend, and clear your looks! Why all this toil and trouble?
Mark Twain	They spell it Vinci and pronounce it Vinchy; foreigners always spell better than they pronounce.

Figure 9-1: A table inserted into a document.

Note   Don't confuse columns used in tables with Word's newspaper columns feature, which formats a document into newspaper-like columns. The Format ➪ Columns command and the Columns button on the Standard toolbar are used for newspaper column features; they are not used for tables.

You can choose from several methods to create a table. If your table is relatively simple, with evenly spaced rows and columns, use the Insert Table button on the Standard toolbar, or you can choose Table ➪ Insert ➪ Table to use the Insert Table dialog box or the Tables and Borders toolbar. If your table is more complex, with irregularly sized rows and columns, use the Draw Table feature in the Table menu.

Note   If you make a mistake when creating or editing a table, you can use the Edit ➪ Undo command (or press Ctrl+Z) to undo it. You can also use the Edit ➪ Repeat command (or press Ctrl+Y) to repeat a Table command.

Using the Insert Table button

With the Insert Table button on the Standard toolbar, you can quickly create a table by speci-fying how many rows and columns you want:

1. Position the insertion point where you want to insert the table.

2. Click the Insert Table button on the Standard toolbar. This displays a drop-down grid in which you can drag the pointer to select the number of columns and rows to create (see Figure 9-2).

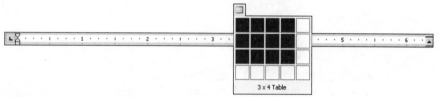

Figure 9-2: The Insert Table drop-down grid.

3. After you drag the pointer to select the number of columns and rows, release the mouse button for Word to insert the table.

Using the Insert Table command

Using the Insert Table dialog box, you can create tables with as many as 63 columns and what seems like an unlimited number (32,767) of rows. With this method, you can also add format-ting options to your new table. Clicking the AutoFormat button lets you choose from a collec-tion of ready-made table templates, each using a different formatting scheme.

To use the Table menu to create a table, follow these steps:

1. Choose Table ➪ Insert ➪ Table to display the Insert Table dialog box (see Figure 9-3).

2. Enter the number of rows and columns in the dialog box.

3. Click OK.

Note
You can specify the number of rows when you first create a table, but it may be more effi-cient to begin with only one row. If you begin with a single row when you start adding your text, you can move from cell to cell by pressing Tab. When you press Tab in the last cell, a new row is then added to the table. This method saves you the time of trying to count or pre-dict how many rows your table needs; the table creates itself as you type in your text. You should probably specify the number of columns when you create the table, however, because columns are not quite so easy to add.

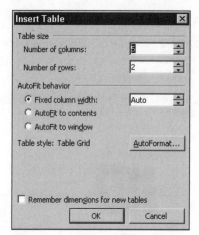

Figure 9-3: The Insert Table dialog box.

Using Table AutoFormatting

Just as you can use pre-made templates and styles for documents and paragraphs, you can also use pre-made templates for tables. Using Table AutoFormatting, you can apply a format to an entire table uniformly. The Table AutoFormat feature provides an extensive list of pre-made table formats that incorporate many formatting features, including table formats for Web pages. You can use a table format as it is, or you can customize it.

Simply place the cursor where you want to put the table, and choose Table ➪ Table AutoFormat, and the Table AutoFormat dialog box opens, as shown in Figure 9-4. (You can also get here by clicking the AutoFormat button in the Insert Table dialog box, but if you do so, some of the buttons in the Table AutoFormat box will not be functional.) This dialog box is described in Table 9-1.

Table 9-1: The Table AutoFormat Dialog Box

Component	Purpose
Category	Displays All Table Styles by default, but you can choose to view Table Styles in Use or User-Defined Table Styles.
Table Styles	Enables you to click on a style name and view the results in the Preview area. Word provides dozens of different styles, combining different colors, shading, borders, text, and so on.
New	Creates a new table style.
Delete	Deletes the selected table format (of course, you can't delete the formats provided by Word—only ones you have created).
Modify	Modifies the selected table format—opens the Modify Style dialog box.
Default	Makes the selected table the default for the document—or for the template that created the document (you are asked which to apply it to). Each time you create a table, the selected table style is used automatically.

Component	Purpose
Apply Special Formats to:	
Heading Rows	Treats the heading row differently from the body of the table—makes the text bold or italic, perhaps, or uses a different background, depending on the selected style.
First Column	Treats the first column differently from the body of the table.
Last Row	Treats the last row differently from the body of the table.
Last Column	Treats the last column differently from the body of the table.

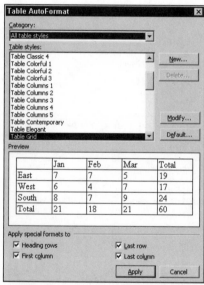

Figure 9-4: The Table AutoFormat dialog box.

Word lets you create your own table formats. Click the New button in the Table AutoFormat dialog box (or select a table format you want to modify and then click Modify), and the New Style dialog box opens (see Figure 9-5). We look at this dialog box in more detail in Chapter 13. Note for now that it allows you to modify a table's font, border size, background colors, and so on.

Drawing a table

With the Draw Table feature, you can create a non-uniform table. The cells can be of varying sizes, and the rows can have different numbers of columns. You can use Draw Table just as you would draw a table by hand with a pencil. You can create quite complex tables using this tool, even nesting tables within each other, as shown in Figure 9-6. (You can also nest tables using Table ➪ Insert ➪ Table.)

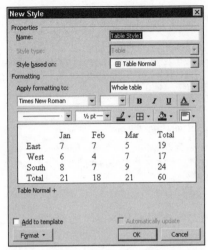

Figure 9-5: The New Style dialog box, in which you can create a new table format.

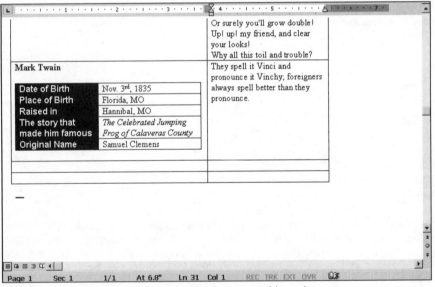

Figure 9-6: A complex table created using the Draw Table tool.

First you drag the table boundary to where you want the table to appear in the document, and then you draw the lines that divide the table into cells. After configuring the table, you can use the buttons on the Tables and Borders toolbar to customize your table with formatted lines and borders and with shading. You can even change the orientation of the text in a cell.

To create a table with Draw Table, follow these steps:

1. Choose Table ➪ Draw Table, or click the Tables and Borders button on the Standard toolbar. The Tables and Borders floating toolbar appears (see Figure 9-7), and the pointer changes to a pencil icon. Table 9-2 describes the Tables and Borders buttons.

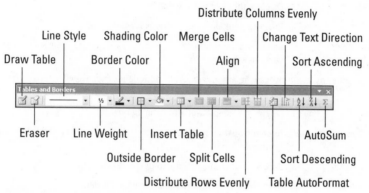

Figure 9-7: The Tables and Borders toolbar.

2. Click in the document where you want one of the corners of the table to be, and then drag to the opposite corner and release the mouse button.

3. Use the pencil to draw the row and column gridlines in the table. You can draw lines that cross several rows or columns, but do not go all the way across the table, allowing you to create quite complex tables.

4. To remove a line, click Eraser on the Tables and Borders toolbar, move the pointer over the line that you want to remove, and click.

After you complete the table structure, you can begin adding text and graphics. You can also use the Tables and Borders toolbar to customize the appearance of either selected cells or the entire table.

Table 9-2: Buttons on the Tables and Borders Toolbar

Button	Description
Draw Table	Toggles the Draw Table feature on and off.
Eraser	Removes table lines.
Line Style	Displays a drop-down list of line styles, including solid, dotted, and dashed.
Line Weight	Displays a drop-down list of line weights, from ¼ to 6 points.
Border Color	Displays a color palette for border lines.
Outside Border	Lets you define where borders should be placed (which edges).
Shading Color	Displays a color palette for background shading.
Insert Table	Displays the Insert Table dialog box.

Continued

Table 9-2 *(continued)*

Button	*Description*
Merge Cells	Removes the dividing lines between selected cells.
Split Cells	Displays the Split Cells dialog box.
Align	Provides nine alignment options for text in cells.
Distribute Rows Evenly	Moves the inner horizontal cell boundaries to make all selected rows the same height.
Distribute Columns Evenly	Moves the inner vertical cell boundaries to make all selected columns the same width.
Table AutoFormat	Opens the Table AutoFormat dialog box.
Change Text Direction	Reorients text direction to one of three ways—Left to Right, Top to Bottom, Bottom to Top.
Sort Descending	Sorts rows of table content in descending order.
Sort Ascending	Sorts rows of table content in ascending order.
AutoSum	Automatically adds the contents of all cells above or to the left of the current cell and then places the total in the current cell.

Creating a table within a table

Word lets you can create *nested* tables, which are tables within tables. Nested tables are particularly useful for presenting related information. For example, you may create a table showing your company's sales and then insert a nested table to show your company's net revenue on those sales.

Creating a nested table is easy. Within an existing table, click the cell in which you want the nested table to appear and then choose Table ➪ Insert ➪ Table. Specify your table settings in the Insert Table dialog box, and click OK. The table gridlines then appear in the table cell. You can also use the Table ➪ Draw Table command, the Draw Table button, or the Insert Table button on the Standard toolbar to create a nested table. Once you create a nested table, you can format it just as you can any other table.

Positioning tables in documents

A cool feature of Word is the capability to position a table anywhere in your document. Whenever your pointer moves over a table—in the Print Layout, Print Preview, or Web Layout views—a drag handle appears in the upper-left corner of the table.

Dragging the handle—pointing to the handle and then holding down the left mouse button as you move the mouse pointer—allows you to position the table anywhere in your document. You can place the table within text—so the text wraps around the table—or you can place the table before or after text or other objects, such as graphics or other tables. You have to adjust the table's Positioning settings to get the table to sit just where you want it.

Begin by opening the Table Properties dialog box (see Figure 9-8) by doing one of the following:

✦ Right-click anywhere in the table and choose Table Properties from the shortcut menu.

✦ Click anywhere in the table and choose Table ➪ Table Properties.

✦ Double-click the table's drag handle in the top-left corner.

You can choose one of the three settings in the Alignment group: Left, Center, or Right. The default setting is Left, and you can use the Indent From Left box to specify how many inches from the left margin you want the table.

If you want the text to wrap around the table, click Around in the Text wrapping group—the None setting means that the table sits before or after text, rather like a paragraph; that is, the text will not flow around it. You can fine tune your table positioning within text by clicking Positioning (this button becomes active when you click Around), which then displays the Table Positioning dialog box (see Figure 9-9).

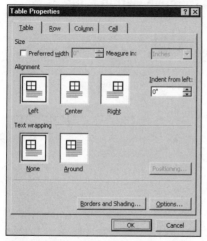

Figure 9-8: The Table tab of the Table Properties dialog box.

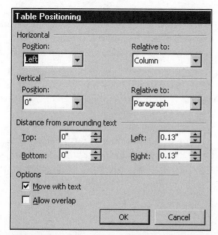

Figure 9-9: The Table Positioning dialog box.

Navigating within Tables and Adding Text

You can use the mouse, arrow keys, and Tab key to move the insertion point within a table. The column marks in the ruler indicate the current position of the insertion point. When you create a table, the insertion point is positioned in the first cell so that you can enter text immediately.

Getting around in a table

Moving around in a table using the mouse is as simple as clicking the cell that you want. Table 9-3 shows the keystrokes used to move within a table.

Table 9-3: Keystrokes Used to Move Within a Table

Movement	Keystroke
Next cell	Tab or, if the insertion point is at the end of the cell content, right-arrow key
Preceding cell	Shift+Tab or, if the insertion point is at the beginning of the cell content, left-arrow key
Next row	Down-arrow key (if the insertion point is on the last line of the content)
Preceding row	Up-arrow key (if the insertion point is on the first line of the content)
First cell in a row	Alt+Home
Last cell in a row	Alt+End
Top cell in a column	Alt+PgUp
Bottom cell in a column	Alt+PgDn

Adding text to a table

Whether you're typing text or entering numbers, you can create new paragraphs in a cell by pressing Enter. To move to the next cell, press Tab. If you press Tab while the insertion point is in the last cell of the last row, Word creates a new row with the same formatting as the preceding one.

There is no trick to entering text in a table. It's the same as entering text in a document. The only difference is that each cell has its own "margins," so as text fills a line, the text wraps in the cell. You can format text in a cell just as you format text in a document: select the appropriate text, and then apply the formats.

Tip   Of course, the Tab key doesn't work the way it normally does. It doesn't push the text insertion point over in the paragraph in which you're working, it moves the insertion point to the next cell. To duplicate the effect of using Tab in a normal, non-table paragraph, press Ctrl+Tab.

Selecting Parts of a Table

You can use the mouse and keyboard to select cells, rows, and columns, as described in Chapter 2. You can also use the Table ⇨ Select menu to select the table, column, row, or cell that contains the insertion point or to select the entire table. After you make a selection, you can perform many operations, modifying the text within the cells or the cells themselves.

Note

There is a subtle but important difference between selecting text in a cell and selecting the cell itself. If you select the text within the cell, you cannot modify the cell's properties, such as the distance between text and the cell border. When a cell has been selected, the entire cell is black; when just the text within the cell has been selected, there is still white space around the text within the cell.

Selecting with the mouse or keyboard

If you're unfamiliar with tables, take a moment to move the mouse pointer slowly around a single cell. (Enlarge the document view so the cell is displayed large.) As you move around in the cell, you'll notice that the mouse pointer changes shape:

✦ **The I-beam shape:** The normal cursor; click to place the insertion point in the cell

✦ **A black arrow:** When you point near the top-left corner, the arrow appears; click to select the cell

✦ **Parallel lines with arrows:** When you place the pointer over a cell border, you can drag the border to enlarge or reduce the row or column

Table 9-4 shows how to select the parts of a table with the mouse; Table 9-5 shows how to select parts of a table with the keyboard.

Table 9-4: Using the Mouse to Select in a Table

To Select	Do This
Cell	Point to the top left of the cell and click.
Row	Point to the top left of any cell in the row and double-click; or place the pointer to the left of the leftmost cell in the row and, when the arrow turns into a large white pointer, click.
Column	Position the pointer above the top gridline of the first cell in the column until it changes to a down arrow, and then click.
Multiple cells, rows, or columns	Drag across the cells, rows, or columns. Alternatively, click in the first cell, row, or column; press and hold the Shift key; and then click in the last cell, row, or column. (This method may take some practice, but it is quick and efficient for selecting cells, rows, and columns.) If you're selecting rows, be sure to include the end-of-row mark—that is, the highlighting should extend *past* the last gridline.
Entire table	Click the table's drag box at the top-left corner of the table (in Print Layout, Print Preview, or Web Layout). Or position the mouse pointer on the top border line or the top-left cell—when it turns into a downward arrow, drag horizontally across the table.

Table 9-5: Using the Keyboard to Select in a Table

To Select	Do This
Column	Press and hold Alt, and then click anywhere in column.
Partial column	Place the insertion point in the beginning cell of your selection, and then press Shift+Up or Down Arrow key.
Row	Place the insertion point in the first or last cell in the row. Then press Alt+Shift+End (if the insertion point is in the first cell) or Alt+Shift+Home (if the insertion point is in the last cell).
Partial row	Place the insertion point in the beginning cell of your selection, and then press Shift+left- or right-arrow key.
Entire table	Press Alt+5 (numeric keypad with Num Lock off).

Tip   Another quick way to select a row, column, or entire table is to position the insertion point in a cell within the row or column that you want (or anywhere in the table to select the entire table). Choose Table ➪ Select, and then choose Table, Column, Row, or Cell.

Extending the selection

After you select a cell or block of cells, you can include additional adjacent cells by entering the Extend Mode rather than by starting again. To enter the Extend Mode, press F8. At this point, EXT appears in bold letters in the status bar. To leave the Extend Mode, press Esc. You can use the mouse to extend your selection simply by clicking the outermost cell in the new block of selected cells, or you can use the keyboard by pressing Shift and one of the arrow keys.

Modifying a Table Layout

Modifying a table layout means altering the structure of that table. This includes resizing the table as well as copying, moving, inserting, and deleting rows, columns, and cells. It also includes merging and splitting cells, changing the spacing and column width, changing the row height, and even splitting a table.

Resizing tables

You can easily resize your entire table using a resize handle, which appears at the lower-right corner of the table when you point at the table (it only appears in the Print Layout, Web Page Layout, and Print Preview views, though).

Dragging the handle—moving the pointer to the drag handle and then holding down the left mouse button as you move the pointer—resizes the table. You can also resize a table by choosing Table Properties from the Table menu or the shortcut menu. In the Table tab of the Table Properties dialog box, enter a Preferred Width setting, which can be in inches or a percentage of the document.

Inserting and deleting cells, rows, and columns

Before inserting a cell, row, or column, you must select an existing cell, row, or column so that Word knows where you want the new addition to appear. In fact you should select the number that you want to insert; if you want to insert five rows, for instance, select five rows, if you want to insert two cells, select two cells. If you want to insert more rows or columns than currently exist in the table, you'll have to perform the task more than once.

Then choose Table ⇨ Insert. (You can also click the Insert Table button on the Tables and Borders toolbar.) You can now choose what you want to insert: Columns to Left, Columns to Right, Rows Above, Rows Below, or Insert Cells.

If you select a cell, Word inserts a new row of cells at the location you specify relative to the selected cell. A new column is inserted to the left or right of the selected column, and a new row is inserted either above or below the selected row. All inserted cells, rows, and columns adopt the same formatting as the selected cell, row, or column.

Inserting cells

When you insert cells, you can choose whether to shift the existing cells to the right or down to make room for the new cells (see Figure 9-10). If you shift the existing cells to the right, an extra cell (or more if you select more than one cell initially) is added to the right end of that row. The cell contents move with the cells. If you choose to shift the existing cells down, an extra row (or more if you select more than one cell initially) and not just a cell is added to the bottom of the table. The contents of the selected cell or cells also move to the corresponding cell or cells in the new row.

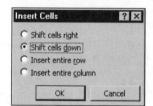

Figure 9-10: The Insert Cells dialog box.

Inserting rows and columns

As opposed to choosing Table ⇨ Insert and inserting rows and columns directly, you can also insert a new row or column using the Insert Cells dialog box. To do this, select the cell either to the right or below where you want the new column or row to be, and then choose the Insert Cells button on the Standard toolbar or Table ⇨ Insert ⇨ Cells. This displays the Insert Cells dialog box. Select either Insert Entire Row or Insert Entire Column.

Deleting cells, rows, and columns

You can delete the contents of a cell or even the cell itself. To delete the contents of a cell, simply select the contents and then press Delete. To delete a cell, select the cell and then choose Table ⇨ Delete ⇨ Cells to display the Delete Cells dialog box (see Figure 9-11). The choices in the Delete Cells dialog box are similar to those in the Insert Cells dialog box. Make the appropriate choice, and click OK. You can also display the Delete Cells dialog box by right-clicking a cell and then choosing Delete Cells from the shortcut menu. The Delete commands in the Table or shortcut menu vary according to the current selection in the table.

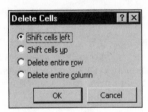

Figure 9-11: The Delete Cells dialog box.

Deleting rows and columns is the same as inserting rows and columns. You must choose Table ➪ Delete ➪ Rows (or Columns). You can also choose Delete Columns from the pop-up shortcut menu.

You can also delete a row or column by selecting that row or column and then pressing Shift+Del (pressing Del alone merely deletes the contents of the cells).

Caution   Unfortunately the Shift+Del method is a little buggy sometimes, especially when deleting rows. To delete an entire row, you must include the end-of-row marker in the selection; that is, the selection must extend past the right of the rightmost cell border in the row. On the other hand, even if you do this it may still not work properly. If you use the keyboard to select the row, for instance, it may not work; whereas, if you place the mouse pointer to the left of the row and click, selecting the entire row, it probably will. This idiosyncrasy can be very frustrating, but you can always fall back on the Table ➪ Delete ➪ Rows command. Also, note that Shift+Del places the cut row into the Clipboard.

To delete an entire table, place the cursor anywhere in the table and choose Table ➪ Delete ➪ Table. You can also select the paragraph immediately before a table, the paragraph after, and press Del to delete the table. Or select the entire table and press Del.

Moving and copying cells, rows, and columns

You can move and copy the contents of one cell to another just as you can move and copy any text or graphic. Select the contents of a cell, cut or copy, and then paste the contents elsewhere. You can also use the drag-and-drop method for moving cell contents. When moving or copying contents to a different location, you have two options:

✦ Add to the text already in the target location without changing it—that is, insert the contents of a single cell.

✦ Replace the existing text, placing the copied or cut cells over the existing ones in effect.

To move and copy the contents of cells, rows, and columns using drag-and-drop, follow these steps:

1. Select the cells, rows, or columns that you want to move or copy.

2. Place the pointer over the selection until the pointer becomes an arrow pointing to the upper left.

3. To move the selection, click and drag. You can move the selection to anywhere you want, including out of the table entirely. If you move the selection out of the table, the selection remains in the table format—that is, a new table is created to hold the contents.

4. To copy the selection, press and hold Ctrl and then click and drag. As before, you can copy the selection to anywhere, including out of the table.

5. Drop (release) the mouse button when you reach the location where you want the text to be placed.

To move or copy a row from its original location to a different one in the same table, include the end-of-row marker in the row selection. Otherwise, the drag-and-drop row selection will overwrite the row in which you drop the selection—and leave the selected row empty—instead of shifting the original row down. Also, be sure to drop the selection in the cell that is in the same column as the leftmost selected cell. Otherwise, when the entire selection is moved or copied it is offset to the right, even pushing cells out to the right of the table.

Column width and row height

You can modify both the width of a column and height of a row; the distance between the vertical and horizontal gridlines, respectively. When you first insert a table, Word divides the horizontal space automatically by the number of columns that you specify, so that each column has the same width. Row height is set initially to Auto, which means that a row expands to accommodate text that wraps. Several other row height options are available after you create the table, and you can make many changes to column as well as row dimensions.

Changing column width manually

You can change the column width of a table in several ways. One method is to drag either a column's vertical gridline or border in the table or one of the Move Table Column markers in the ruler (see Figure 9-12) to adjust the column's width visually. (To display the horizontal ruler, choose View ➪ Ruler.) Using this method, the vertical border moves, left or right, but all other vertical borders remain in the same positions. Thus, the columns to the left and right of the border change size. The overall width of the table doesn't change.

If you press and hold Shift and *then* drag the vertical border or gridline, only the column to the *left* of the border changes size—to the right, all columns move. Move the border to the right, for example, and you are pushing all the columns to the right; the table actually gets bigger. Note that you must press and hold the Shift key before you click on the border. If you hold the Shift key after you've clicked and begun moving the mouse pointer, the Shift key has no effect. The Alt and Ctrl keys also have a special effect. All four options are explained in the following list:

✦ **Drag without pressing any key:** The selected border moves, while the borders to the left and right do not.

✦ **Press Shift while dragging:** The border to the left of that selected does not move; all borders to the right move so that all cells to the right retain their original sizes—the overall table size either contracts or expands.

✦ **Press Ctrl while dragging:** The border to the left of that selected does not move; all borders to the right move so that the overall table size remains the same — the individual cells either contract or expand.

✦ **Press Alt while dragging:** Displays measurements in the horizontal ruler as you drag, showing the size of each column. Combine this with Shift or Ctrl if you wish.

Consider two other points about this dragging feature. First, it's sometimes difficult to grab the border with the mouse. You may have to try several times to get it. Try positioning the pointer over the border (the icon changes to two vertical bars), pressing the mouse button, and holding for a couple of seconds before you begin moving. Second, if some, but not all, cells are selected, you will be moving the vertical border only for the rows on which you have selected cells, not for the entire table.

Tip   Double-clicking a border automatically adjusts the column, allowing enough room for the contents of the column to the left. If double-clicking doesn't work, try triple- or even quadruple-clicking. This feature is a little flaky at times.

Author	Quote
William Faulkner	"If I had not existed, someone else would have written me, Hemingway, Dostoevski, all of us."
Jack Kerouac	"It is not my fault that certain so-called bohemian elements have found in my writings something to hang their peculiar beatnik theories on."
Ernest Hemingway	"We are all apprentices in a craft where no one ever becomes a master"
James Joyce	"No pen, no ink, no table, no room, no time, no quiet, no inclination."

Figure 9-12: Move Table Column markers on the ruler.

Changing column width using the Table menu

The advantage of using the Table menu to change column width is that you can enter precise values. To change column width from the Table menu, follow these steps:

1. Select the column that you want to adjust.

2. Choose Table ➪ Table Properties, or choose Table Properties from the shortcut menu, and click the Column tab in the Table Properties dialog box (see Figure 9-13).

3. Enter a value (inches is the default) for the column width in the Preferred Width box. (You can also select Percent from the Measure In drop-down to set the column to a percentage of the table width.)

4. To move to another column, click Previous Column or Next Column.

5. Adjust the next column.

6. When you have finished, click OK.

Changing column width automatically

Word provides two ways to adjust the width of selected columns automatically. One is the AutoFit option, in which Word resizes the selected columns according to their contents. The other is an automatic sizing option, in which Word proportionally resizes the selected columns regardless of their contents.

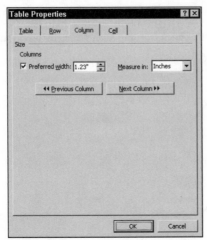

Figure 9-13: The Column tab in the Table Properties dialog box.

Place the insertion point in the table and then choose Table ➪ AutoFit. The menu that appears has the commands described in Table 9-6.

Table 9-6: The AutoFit Commands

Command	Action
AutoFit to Contents	Adjusts column widths depending on the contents—as you type you'll see the column widths adjust.
AutoFit to Window	Adjusts the table to extend from the left margin to the right margin and fixes the column widths.
Fixed Column Width	Fixes the column widths—similar to the previous, except that it does not extend the table to fit between margins.
Distribute Rows Evenly	Spaces rows evenly throughout the table.
Distribute Columns Evenly	Spaces columns evenly throughout the table.

Changing cell spacing and margins

Although you don't often see this characteristic of tables—few people use this feature—you can actually create a space between cells. In other words, instead of having cells separated by gridlines, you see a gridline, a space, and another gridline. The space between the gridlines cannot carry any text or images—it's like a *wall* between the cells. You can also adjust the space inside a cell, the space between the gridline and the content. Experiment with these two settings, and you'll quickly see how they work.

To adjust cell spacing—the distance between gridlines—choose Table ⇨ Table Properties, click the Table tab, and click the Options button to open the Table Options dialog box (see Figure 9-14). Click the Allow Spacing Between Cells check box and then enter the size of the space you want to see.

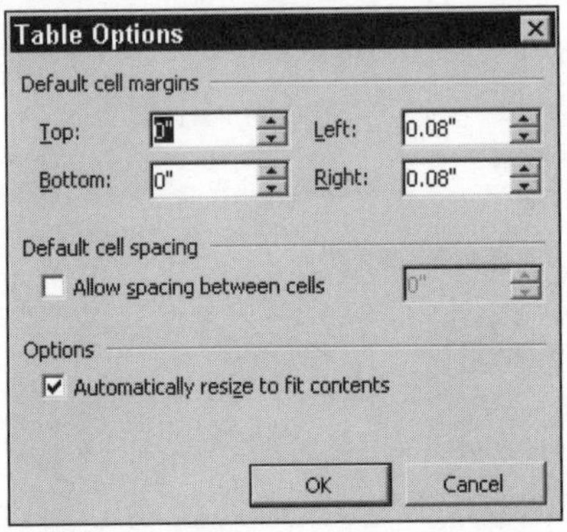

Figure 9-14: The Table Options dialog box.

To adjust the margins within cells, modify the settings in the Default Cell Margins boxes.

You can also modify the cell margins—but not the spacing—for specific cells. Select the cells you want to work on; then either drag the margin controls on the ruler or choose Table ⇨ Table Properties, click the Cell tab, and click the Options button to open the Cell Options dialog box (see Figure 9-15). Clear the Same as the Whole Table check box and enter specific settings.

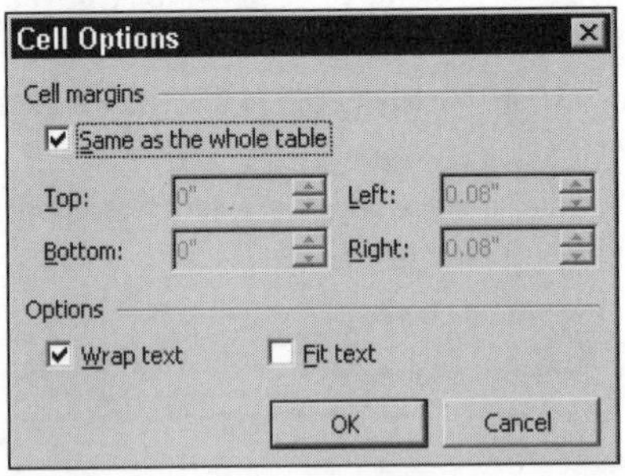

Figure 9-15: The Cell Options dialog box.

Notice the other settings in this dialog box:

✦ **Wrap Text:** Wraps the text onto multiple lines to make it fit.

✦ **Fit Text:** Squeezes the font size so the text fits inside the cell.

Changing row height and spacing

When you create a table, the row height is set to Auto, so although the row is initially one line high it will expand to fit text that wraps in any cell of that row. Word also provides two ways to specify row height. You can set a minimum height and let the row expand if the contents of a cell exceeds that minimum height, or you can specify a fixed row height in which the row doesn't change even if the contents of a cell exceeds that height. Word then displays and prints only the contents that fit within the cell space.

To change row height and spacing, follow these steps:

1. Choose Table ➪ Table Properties, or choose Table Properties from the shortcut menu. The Table Properties dialog box appears.

2. Click the Row tab (see Figure 9-16).

3. Check the Specify Height check box.

4. In the Specify Height box, enter the height that you want and then choose At Least or Exactly in the list box to the right. The At Least setting allows you to set a value that specifies the minimum row height, but the row still expands as necessary. If you specify Exactly, the row doesn't expand beyond the value you entered in the Specify Height box.

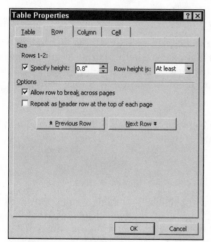

Figure 9-16: The Row tab of the Table Properties dialog box.

You can change the height of an individual row using the vertical ruler. (The document must be in the Print Layout view, however, to display this ruler.) Rows are indicated by light gray lines in the ruler. Dragging one of these lines changes the row height to the At Least setting and allows you to select the row height visually. To see the actual measurement as you drag, press and hold the Alt key. You cannot reduce a row height to less than that needed for the existing text.

If you want the selected rows to be equal in height, choose Table ➪ Distribute Rows Evenly. Alternatively, click the Distribute Rows Evenly button on the Tables and Borders toolbar.

Splitting a table

Splitting a table, as the name implies, breaks the table horizontally into two separate tables. To split a table, do the following:

1. Position the insertion point in the row that you want to be the top row of the lower table segment.

2. Choose Table ➪ Split Table. Alternatively, press Ctrl+Enter, but this keyboard action adds a page break in your table split. (You can type and then delete the page break.)

After splitting a table, you can move the table down and add plain text between the tables. To reunite the split tables, click the Undo button on the Standard toolbar.

Fine-tuning a Table

After creating your table, you can improve its visual appeal by changing the text format and appearance, aligning text in the cells, creating column headings, formatting the gridlines to print, and adding shading to the cells. Word also includes an AutoFormat feature with which you can select a preset table format.

Formatting text in a table

Formatting text in a table is the same as formatting ordinary text. For character formatting, select the text and then apply the formats. For paragraph formatting, place the insertion point in the paragraph and then apply the formats. You can also apply styles to a table to automate the formatting. The table shortcut menu has options for formatting paragraphs and changing text fonts as well.

Cross-Reference

We look at styles in Chapter 13, including Word's Table style that was introduced in Word 2002. You can use the Table style to quickly create tables of a specific layout.

Changing text alignment

You have several options for aligning text within cells. By default, text in table cells is aligned with the top of the cell. To change the text alignment, first select the cells that you want to change. Then right-click on the table, choose Cell Alignment from the shortcut menu, and select any of the nine alignment options (top left, top center, top right, middle left, and so on.). You can also use the Tables and Borders toolbar (click the Tables and Borders button on the Standard toolbar).

Changing text direction

Normally, text entered in a table cell reads from left to right. You may want some cells to read from the top down, however, or from the bottom up. You have three choices for text orientation: horizontally from left to right, vertically reading down, and vertically reading up.

To change text orientation, follow these steps:

1. Select the cells that you want to change.

2. Choose Format ➪ Text Direction, or click the Change Text Direction button on the Tables and Borders toolbar. The Text Direction dialog box appears (see Figure 9-17).

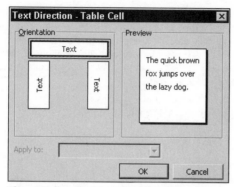

Figure 9-17: The Text Direction dialog box.

3. Select one of the three choices for text orientation. When you click any of these options, the Preview area shows the selected orientation.

4. Click OK, and Word adjusts the text.

Aligning a table on the page

As with a paragraph, you can adjust the position of a table on the page—it can be placed on the left side of the page, centered, or moved to the right. Select the table and choose Table ⇨ Table Properties to display the Table Properties dialog box; then click the Table tab.

Select one of the Alignment settings. If you choose Left, you can also force the table away from the left margin by entering an Indent From Left setting.

Tip   You can also align a table by selecting the entire table and then clicking the Left, Center, or Right button on the Formatting toolbar.

Preventing page breaks

The Row tab of the Table Properties dialog box has an option called Allow Row To Break Across Pages, which is selected by default. However, this often looks a little messy, so you may want to ensure that Word does *not* break a row—it puts the page break at the top of the row, rather than inside the row. Simply clear the Allow Row to Break Across Pages check box.

Merging and splitting cells

Word allows you to both merge cells—join adjacent rows into one—and split a row into two. You can merge cells either horizontally (so that they form fewer columns) or vertically (so that they form fewer rows). When you merge cells, Word converts the contents of each merged cell into separate paragraphs within the new, merged cell. To merge cells, simply select the cells you want to join together—you can select any number, not just two—then choose Table ⇨ Merge Cells.

Note Word lets you split a single cell into multiple smaller cells, both horizontally and vertically. It also allows you to split multiple cells at a time, not just one. (However, when you select cells on multiple rows it won't let you split the cells into a larger number of rows, only split them into multiple columns.) Select the cells you want to split and choose Table ➪ Split Cells. In the Split Cells dialog box (see Figure 9-18) select the number of rows and columns you want to create within the area you have selected, and click OK.

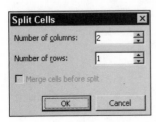

Figure 9-18: The Split Cells dialog box.

Notice also the Merge Cells Before Split check box in the Split Cells dialog box, which is enabled if you have selected multiple cells. This allows you to join the contents of the selected cells and distribute them across the new cells. Suppose you selected an area 2 columns by 3 rows and are splitting this into 3 columns (remember, you can't add rows in this case, only columns). Word merges the cells on the first row together, those on the second row together, and those on the third row together. Word then places the first merged contents in the first new cell, the second merged contents in the second cell (on the first row, also), and the third merged contents in the last cell on the first row.

Tip The Pencil and Eraser tools on the Tables and Borders toolbar offer quick and easy ways to split and merge cells. To split a cell, click the Pencil button and then draw a line either across or down the cell. You needn't split the cell into equal parts—simply draw the line wherever you want to divide the cell. To merge cells, simply click on borders with the Eraser tool.

You can also create headings that span several columns by merging several cells into one wide cell.

Table headings on each page

If you have built a long table that extends across two or more pages, you can create a table heading from the text appearing in the first row of the table, and have Word automatically repeat that row at the top of each page.

Note These rows repeat only when that table is split by a *soft* page break (one that is inserted by the system). If you insert a *hard* page break in the table (by pressing Ctrl+Enter) you are, in effect, breaking the table into two, so the heading is not repeated automatically.

To add column headings for each page, simply select the row or rows that you want to repeat, and choose Table ➪ Heading Rows Repeat. You can also select a check box labeled Repeat as Header Row at the Top of Each Page in the Table Properties dialog box.

Tip If you change a table heading on the first page, the table headings on all other pages change as well. And you won't be able to modify any but the first header row—the automatically generated rows are locked.

Borders and shading

To apply custom border and shading formats to any table, use the features on the Tables and Borders toolbar. From this toolbar, you can select a variety of colors, line thicknesses, and fill patterns, and you can even apply the formatting to selected cells in the table. In addition, you can use the Borders and Shading dialog box by choosing Format ⇨ Borders and Shading, or by right-clicking a table and selecting Borders and Shading from the shortcut menu. (For more information on working with borders and shading, see Chapter 5.)

 Tip To apply preset border and shading formats to a table quickly, use the Table AutoFormat feature.

 Note When choosing from the Format menu or the Tables and Borders toolbar buttons, any border or shading format that you select is applied only to your selection. Thus, if the insertion point is in a paragraph in a cell but the cell itself isn't selected, the formatting applies only to that paragraph. It doesn't apply to the cell. In this case, the formatted border appears only around the paragraph text and doesn't extend to the cell gridlines.

Table gridlines

If you remove all borders from your table, the table structure disappears on the document page. This can actually be quite useful because you can use the table to lay out images and pictures in a particular configuration. The problem, however, is that the table structure is difficult to see. That's why Word let's you turn on table *gridlines*. These are light-gray lines that appear where the table borders *would* appear were the borders present. If you want these gridlines to display on-screen, choose Table ⇨ Show Gridlines. The menu option then changes to Table ⇨ Hide Gridlines in case you want to turn them off later.

Using Tabs in Tables

One of the nicer features of tables is that they usually provide an alternative to lining up multiple columns of text or numbers using tabs. Using a table is far easier than figuring tab settings for multiple columns.

Cross-Reference See Chapter 5 for more information about using tabs.

In ordinary text, you enter a tab by pressing the Tab key. Pressing Tab in a table, however, moves the insertion point to the next cell. To enter a tab in a table cell, press Ctrl+Tab instead. The insertion point then moves to the next tab stop in the cell.

If your table consists of text, you probably don't need to worry about creating custom tab stops or entering tabs in the cells. Even if you want to add bullets or numbers to text within a cell, you can use the Bullet or Numbering button on the Formatting toolbar. Word then inserts the bullets or numbers and automatically applies a hanging indent to the text.

If you need to insert a custom tab stop for a cell, there are a few things to keep in mind. First, you can enter a tab stop for many cells at once by selecting those cells before entering the tab stop in the ruler. Second, if you select cells in multiple columns, you must enter the tab stop in the ruler above the leftmost selected. (For example, if you select cells in the second, third, and fourth columns of a table, you must enter the tab stop in the ruler over the second column.) The leftmost column is the active column, and it is indicated by the indent markers in the ruler above it (you'll notice that the rulers above the other columns *don't* have these). Word doesn't allow you to enter a tab stop in the ruler above any other column, whether it is selected or not.

Left, center, and right tabs work the same way in tables as they do in ordinary text, except that you must press Ctrl+Tab to move the insertion point to a tab stop in a cell. Decimal tabs, however, work differently in tables, because decimal tabs are most commonly used in tables with columns of numbers.

When you enter a decimal tab in the ruler above a selected column, the decimal tab takes effect immediately. There is no need to press Ctrl+Tab when you enter data in these cells. As with ordinary text, decimal tabs align numbers on the decimal point. Any number without a decimal point aligns to the right. Text in cells also aligns on the decimal tab.

If you have alignment problems with decimal tabs, the quickest and easiest way to correct them is to select the table, choose Format ➪ Tabs, and then choose Clear All. This removes all tab stops for the table from the ruler. You can easily reapply the tab stops that you want.

After you enter decimal tabs for a table, adjusting a column of numbers is simple. Select the column (or multiple columns), and drag the tab marker in the ruler to the left or to the right. The column then aligns beneath the tab.

Using Tables to Position Text and Graphics

Tables are useful when you need to position text and graphics together. A common method is to create a one-row table with two columns and then copy and paste the graphic objects into one of the two cells. Type the text in the other cell, and then use paragraph formatting to add spacing before the text to make it appear to be centered vertically on the graphics. Figure 9-19 shows an example of text and graphics in a table. As you can see in Chapter 17, though, you can position text and graphics in other ways; but using tables is often quicker and more predictable and allows you to do more complex layouts.

Cross-Reference   You can also add multimedia objects, such as sound bites or video clips, as well as files from other Office applications and other programs to your table. This is explained later in this book, in Chapters 18 through 21.

Converting Text into Tables, and Vice Versa

You may decide that you need to convert text in your document to a table format or that you no longer want your information in a table layout. You can quickly convert from one format to another.

To convert text into a table, use one of these methods:

✦ Highlight a paragraph and click the Insert Table button on the Standard toolbar; your paragraph is broken into two cells on a single row. Or you can select multiple paragraphs to place each in a separate cell on multiple rows.

✦ Select the text you want to convert and then choose Table ➪ Convert ➪ Text to Table to open the Convert Text to Table dialog box. Choose the number of columns and rows, and select a Separate Text At setting. For instance, to put each paragraph in a different cell, select Paragraph. As you can see in Figure 9-20, you can also click the AutoFormat button to format the table at the same time.

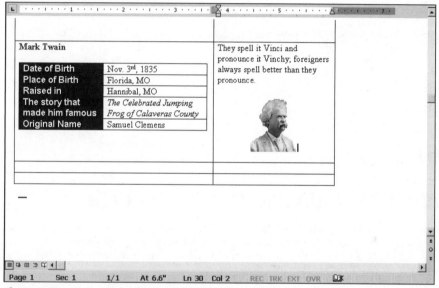

Figure 9-19: An example of text and graphics in a table.

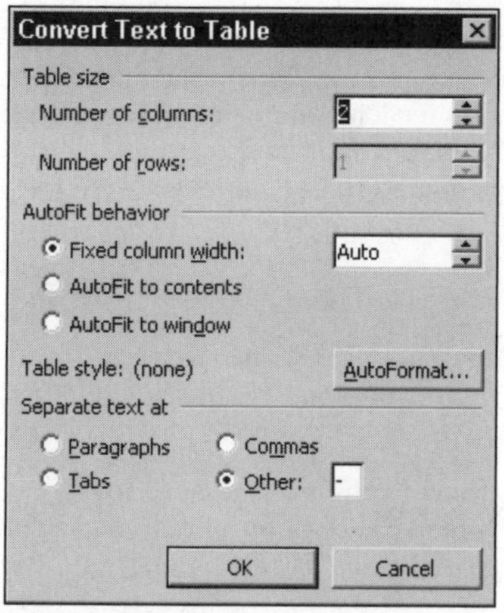

Figure 9-20: The Convert Text to Table dialog box.

Converting table text to ordinary text is the opposite of converting ordinary text to table. You can convert all or part of a table, but if you want to convert only part of a table, you must convert entire rows (otherwise Word will convert the entire table anyway). Select the rows or entire table that you want to convert and then choose Table ⇨ Convert ⇨ Table To Text to open the Convert Table To Text dialog box (Figure 9-21). Select how you want to separate the text (tabs are best for columns of numbers; paragraph marks are best for straight text) and click OK.

Figure 9-21: The Convert Table To Text dialog box.

Sorting Table Data and Numbering Cells

Sorting and numbering cells in a table is easy. You can sort by the contents of any column—alphabetically, numerically, or by date and in ascending or descending order. Adding numbers to table cells (for example, to the first cell in each row) or to every cell in the table is just as simple.

Sorting in a table

With Word, you can sort rows according to the contents of as many as three columns at once. For instance, suppose one column contains a State, another contains a City, and yet another contains a Last Name. You'll be able to sort rows according to the State—Alabama, followed by Arkansas, followed by Arizona, and so on. Then, within each state you could sort by City, and within each city by name. Now all the entries related to Arizona are together, all the entries related to Phoenix are together, and all entries related to Phoenix are sorted by Last Name.

To sort a table, follow these steps:

1. Select the entire table, or just the rows that you want to sort.

2. Choose Table ⇨ Sort, or use the Sort button on the Tables and Borders toolbar, to open the Sort dialog box (see Figure 9-22).

3. Note the My List Has option buttons at the bottom. If you have a header row—containing State, City, Last Name, for example—then Header Row should be selected. (This row won't be sorted and will be used to load the Sort By drop-down list boxes.)

4. In the Sort By drop-down list box, select the first column by which you want to sort. If you have a header row, the text in the header appears in the drop-down list box; otherwise, a column number appears.

5. In the Type drop-down list, select Number, Text, or Date. (Word automatically selects a data type matching the content of the column.)

6. Select Ascending or Descending order for the sort.

7. To sort with more criteria, repeat steps 4 through 6 using the Then By boxes.

8. Click OK.

Figure 9-22: The Sort dialog box.

You can sort table data quickly by the value in a single column with the Tables and Borders toolbar. Select the column that you want to sort and then click the Sort Ascending or Sort Descending button. The top row is assumed to be a header row and is not included in the sort.

Tip   You can also sort tabular text that is not in a table, either by paragraphs or by fields; that is, by columns of numbers or text that are separated by tabs or other characters instead of being in a table. As long as each line has the same number of separators, Word sorts the selection correctly. Click the Options button to specify other separation characters for columns of numbers and to specify other sort options for text. If you select text that is not in a table, the Table menu shows Sort Text instead of Sort.

Numbering cells in a table

To number cells in a table, select the cells that you want to number and choose the Numbering button on the Formatting toolbar or Format ➪ Bullets and Numbering. Word then numbers the selected cells from left to right, beginning in the first row. If you want to number only the first cell in each row, select only the first column in the table. Word then numbers all of the selected cells, whether or not they have text.

The cell numbers adjust automatically if you sort or otherwise change the order of the table, or if you insert rows or columns. If the selected cells contain more than one paragraph, Word numbers each paragraph separately.

To remove numbering from a table, select the cells with numbers. Then click the Number button on the Formatting toolbar.

Table Calculations

In tables with columns of numbers, you can add, subtract, multiply, and divide numbers in cells. You can also calculate averages, percentages, and minimum as well as maximum values. If you must perform complex calculations in a table, you can create that table in Excel and then link or embed the table in your Word document so that you can update it using Excel.

Cross-Reference   Chapter 20 tells you all about how to link information from other applications.

You can also use a table as a simple database to store information such as a list of names and addresses for use with form letters. The table then becomes an online form for working with a database or spreadsheet. A table is also an efficient way to store lists of names and addresses; you can sort, edit, and retrieve such information easily in a table. If your table consists of names and addresses, you can use the table as a database for mail-merge operations.

Cross-Reference   For more information on using a table as the data source for a mail merge, see Chapter 22.

Calculating in a table

Word can carry out calculations for you in a table, similar to the manner in which a spreadsheet works. And, similar to a spreadsheet, Word uses a simple code to refer to the cells, rows, and columns. In this code, letters refer to columns and numbers refer to rows. Therefore, a letter-number combination indicates a specific cell. For example, the first column in a table is column A, the second column is column B, and so on. The first row is row 1, the second row is row 2, and so on. Thus, the cell in the second column and third row is cell B3.

Note also that Word can automatically make calculations for you—when you use the AutoSum button on the Tables and Borders toolbar, or when you choose Table ➪ Formula and click OK, Word assumes you want to sum all the values in the columns immediately above the cell in which you placed the insertion point.

If you enter your own formula directly, however, rather than letting Word create formulae for you, you can not only select a Word function but also enter specific cell addresses in the formula.

Creating your own formula

To create a more complex formula, place the insertion point where you want the formula and choose Table ➪ Formula to open the Formula dialog box (see Figure 9-23). Word generally suggests a formula when you begin a calculation. If Word doesn't suggest a formula, it places an equal sign in the Formula box. All Word formulas begin with an equal sign, so you can enter whatever formula you want after that symbol.

If Word suggests a function through its built-in analysis of the surrounding cell data, you can still select a different formula or enter one of your own. Word stores additional formula components in the Paste Function box of the Formula dialog box. Additional functions include averaging, counting, rounding, and others.

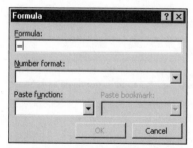

Figure 9-23: The Formula dialog box.

You can enter your own simple formula with specific cell references. For example, to add the third and fourth cells in the second column, type **=B3+B4**. To divide the first cell in the table by the cell in the third column of the fourth row, type **=A1/C4**.

You can specify groups of non-contiguous cells with a comma. For example, if you want the average of the values in cells A1, B3, and D5, type **=average(a1,b3,d5)** in the Formula box. In addition, you can specify a range of cells using a colon, so if you want the average of the values in all of the cells from A1 to C5, type **=average(a1:c5)**. If you've worked much with spreadsheet programs such as Excel, you'll be familiar with these conventions.

Number formats

You can tell Word how to display the number resulting from the formula by selecting an option from the Number Format drop-down list box (see Table 9-7). If the format that you want to apply to your result is not in Table 9-7, you can create your own. For example, to display the result with a single decimal place rather than with none or with two, you can type **0.0** directly in the Number Format box. If you want to display leading zeros for two-digit numbers, type **000.00**.

Table 9-7: Number Formats in the Formula Dialog Box

Format Code	Meaning
#,##0	The pound signs represent number placeholders so that numbers with four or more digits have a comma separator and no decimal places. The zero ensures that the formatted number displays at least 0, even if that number is less than 1. For example, 4321223 is displayed as 4,321,223, and .22 is displayed as 0.
#,##0.00	This is the same format as the preceding one, except that the formatted number always shows two decimal places. For example, 4321223 is displayed as 4,321,223.00, and .22 is displayed as 0.22.
$#,##0.00; ($#,##0.00)	This is a two-part format: the first part is for positive numbers, and the second is for negative numbers. For example, 4321223 is displayed as $4,321,223.00, and .22 is displayed as $0.22. However, −12345.6 is displayed with parentheses as ($12,345.60).

Continued

Table 9-7 *(continued)*

Format Code	Meaning
0	This format ensures that at least one positive digit is displayed. For example, .002 is displayed as 0, and 12345.09 is displayed as 12345.
0%	This formats a number as a percentage. For example, 104 is displayed as 104%.
0.00	This format ensures that at least one digit is displayed as a positive number with two decimal places. For example, 123 is displayed as 123.00, and .0987 is displayed as 0.09.
0.00%	This formats the number as a percentage with two decimal places. For example, 104 is displayed as 104.00%, and .79 is displayed as 0.79%.

Bookmarks

Word provides a little shortcut for specifying data. You can insert a bookmark on the data and use the bookmark in your formula. For instance, if you bookmark one value and name it *valueone*, and then bookmark another value and name it *valuetwo*, you could create a formula such as this: **=valueone/valuetwo**. (Note that you couldn't call them *1stvalue* and *2ndvalue*, as bookmarks cannot begin with digits.)

Highlight the number you want to bookmark and choose Insert ⇨ Bookmark. Type a bookmark name and press Enter. You can now use this name by typing it into a formula, or by selecting from the Paste Bookmark drop-down list box in the Formula dialog box.

If you change the value in any of the fields included in a formula, the calculated value must be updated. To update that result with the new values, move to the cell containing the formula and press F9. You can also right-click the number (but not the cell) and choose Update Field from the shortcut menu.

Unfortunately, you cannot copy the formula from the first cell to the other cells and expect the cell references to be changed accordingly. For that kind of help, you need to use Excel.

Cross-Reference   You can create a table in Excel, copy it, and then paste it into your Word document. Several options are available when you do this. For more on this topic, see Chapter 20.

Placing Captions on Tables

Word has the capability to create and place captions for your table. Once you've created a table, you may want to place a caption somewhere—on top, underneath, or on one side. This is easily done. In fact, you can even have Word automatically add captions as you add tables (and images, too).

Note, however, that the way the caption is treated depends on whether the object—in this case, the table—has been set up as an inline object or whether it has be converted to have text wrap around it, as you saw earlier in this chapter. If it's an inline object, ordinary text is inserted as the caption. If it has text wrapping around, the caption is placed in a text box.

Choose Insert ⇨ Reference ⇨ Caption to see the Caption dialog box (see Figure 9-24). Table 9-8 explains how to use this dialog box.

Figure 9-24: The Caption dialog box.

Table 9-8: The Caption Dialog Box Components

Button Name	Action
Caption	You can type caption text here.
Label	You can select from a number of pre-configured caption types— selecting modifies the Caption text.
Position	Determines where, in relation to the table, the caption appears— above, below, left, or right.
Exclude Label from Caption	Removes the label from the caption; only includes the text you type.
New Label	Click here to add a new label type to the Label drop-down list box.
Delete Label	Select a label you created and click Delete Label to remove it from the list.
Numbering	Click this button to open the Caption Numbering dialog box, and specify how Word will number your captions.
AutoCaption	Allows you to tell Word to automatically add a caption when inserting various object types. Select Microsoft Word Table to have Word automatically add captions to all your tables.

Summary

This chapter has discussed some of the ways that tables can enhance your documents. Tables include a lot of information in a small space. Through the examples in this chapter, you should be able to take advantage of Word's valuable table features. Highlights of this chapter include the following:

✦ Word provides several ways to insert tables in documents. You can use the Insert Table button on the Standard toolbar, choose Table ⇨ Insert ⇨ Table, or use the Draw Table feature. You can also choose a pre-made table format using the Table AutoFormat feature.

✦ You can position a table within a document using the table drag handle, which appears in the upper-left corner of the table in the Print Layout or Web Page Layout views.

✦ To move around within a table, enter text in the cells, or select blocks of cells, you can use the mouse, arrow keys, or various keystroke combinations.

✦ After the table is inserted in the document, you can change the row height and column width or spacing, and you can move or copy cells, rows, and columns. You can also split a cell into two or more cells and even merge two or more cells into one.

✦   ✦   ✦

Sections, Columns, and Page Formatting

In This Chapter

Formatting sections
of a document

Creating, editing, and
removing columns

Changing margin
settings and page setup

Inserting page breaks
and controlling
pagination

Inserting line numbers
and page numbers

Creating and editing
headers and footers

Creating document
backgrounds and
watermarks

You have already learned about the most basic parts of a document: characters and paragraphs. This chapter introduces the next level of formatting: individual sections of a document. Working with sections is essential for creating a page with multiple columns, which is the format used in most newsletters. This chapter also covers how to change various kinds of page formatting, such as margins, headers, footers, page numbers, and so on.

Formatting Sections of a Document

When you create a document using the Blank Document (Normal.dot) template, Word treats the entire document as a single section. When you insert a section break, however, the document then has two sections. With Word, you can divide a document into any number of sections and format each section separately. Think of each section as its own sub-document with its own formatting—different headers and footers, for instance, and perhaps different margins. Sections are especially important when creating desktop publishing documents, in which you often need different formatting on the same page. For example, you may want one section to have two columns and another to have a single column.

Sections are needed if you want to include changes for any of the following types of formatting:

Columns	Page numbering
Margins	Paper size and paper source
Headers and footers	Footnotes
Page orientation	Vertical alignment

Inserting section breaks

Section breaks are always visible in Normal view. To see them in Print Layout view, click the Show/Hide button on the Standard toolbar. Section breaks appear as double-dotted lines containing the words *Section Break* followed by the type of break (see Figure 10-1). A section break marks the point in your document where new formatting begins. You can insert a section break anywhere in a document. The text following the section break (along with its new formatting) can begin at the cursor, on the next page, or on the next even- or odd-numbered page.

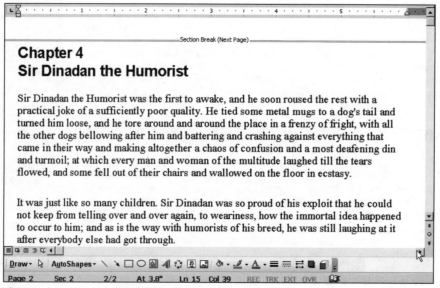

Figure 10-1: A section break in a document.

To insert a section break, follow these steps:

1. Position the cursor where you want a new section to begin.

2. Choose Insert ⇨ Break. The Break dialog box appears (see Figure 10-2).

3. Choose one of the options in the Section Break Types group. See Table 10-1 for a description of each option.

4. Click OK.

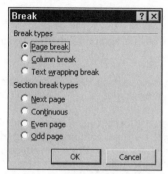

Figure 10-2: The Break dialog box.

Table 10-1: Section Break Options

Option	Action
Next page	Starts a new page and inserts a section break at the top of the page.
Continuous	Inserts the section break at the insertion point without adding a page break.
Even page	Inserts the section break and starts a new page; the page will always be an even-numbered page (usually a left page) and may leave an odd-numbered page blank.
Odd page	Starts a new page and inserts a section break at the top of the page. The page will always be an odd-numbered page.

Copying section breaks

Similar to how a paragraph mark stores paragraph formatting, a section break mark stores the formatting of the preceding section. To duplicate section formatting quickly, copy and paste the section break. After you paste the section break, the preceding text then takes on the formatting of the copied section break. (For more information on copying, cutting, and pasting, see Chapter 2.)

Tip Another way to duplicate section formatting is to copy and store a section break as an AutoText entry. This way, the section break and its special formatting are available in all new documents, and you can apply the break quickly and easily. For example, you can create sections for various column layouts, landscape mode, different margins for various purposes, and so on. Chapter 2 tells you more about working with AutoText.

Removing section breaks

Just as removing a paragraph break changes the format of one paragraph to another, removing a section break changes the formatting of one section.

Cross-Reference   When you remove a paragraph mark, what formatting the paragraph takes on depends on various things. See Chapter 31 for more about Word's idiosyncracies.

When you delete a section break, the first section takes on the formatting of the second. For example, if Section 1 is a one-column section and Section 2 has three columns, deleting the section break merges the content from the one-column section into the three-column section. So all the text is now in a three-column format. If you accidentally delete a section break marker, immediately click the Undo button or choose Edit ➪ Undo (or Ctrl+Z) to restore the break. To remove a section break, place the insertion bar immediately before the section break and press Delete. (It's a good idea to click the Show/Hide button on the Standard toolbar first so that you can see the section break that you're removing.)

To remove all section breaks in a document using the Replace command, follow these steps:

1. Choose Edit ➪ Replace, or press Ctrl+H. The Replace tab of the Find and Replace dialog box appears.

2. Place the insertion point in the Find What box.

3. Click the Special button, and then choose Section Break. (You may need to click More to see the expanded dialog box.)

4. Check that the Replace With text box is empty, and then click the Replace All button.

5. Click OK in response to the information box, and then click Close to close the Find and Replace dialog box.

Working with Columns

Word allows you to create newspaper-style columns that make text more appealing and readable. Newspaper-style columns are also called *snaking columns,* because the text wraps continuously from the bottom of one column to the top of the next. Figure 10-3 shows a document formatted with newspaper-style columns (this is Word's Brochure template). Word provides you two methods of creating columns: choosing Format ➪ Columns, or clicking the Columns button on the Standard toolbar.

The first method opens a dialog box in which you can select the desired formatting. With the second method, you can select only the number of evenly sized and spaced columns that you want (as many as six). Both methods automatically switch to Print Layout view.

You can include as many columns in a document as you have space for on your page. In addition, you can include different numbers or styles of columns in different parts of the document—as long as you divide your document into sections. For example, you can create newsletters that have two or more sections with a different number of columns in each.

Depending on which view you are in, columns appear differently on the screen. Normal view is faster for text entry, but it doesn't display the columns side by side (as they appear when printed). In Normal view, the text appears in the same width as the column but in one continuous column (even though the horizontal ruler shows columns). To display columns side by side, change to Print Layout view or Print Preview.

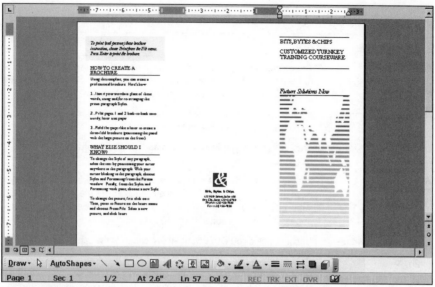

Figure 10-3: Word's Brochure template, a three-column document in landscape page setup.

Applying column formatting

You can apply column formatting to a selection, section, multiple sections, or even the entire document. When you format using the column commands, Word automatically inserts a section break if needed. When you use the Columns dialog box to apply column formatting, the Apply To list box displays the option to apply the formatting to based on the position of the insertion point or your selection (see Figure 10-4). The options shown in the Apply To list box change depending on whether text is selected or your document contains multiple sections. Table 10-2 explains how to use this dialog box.

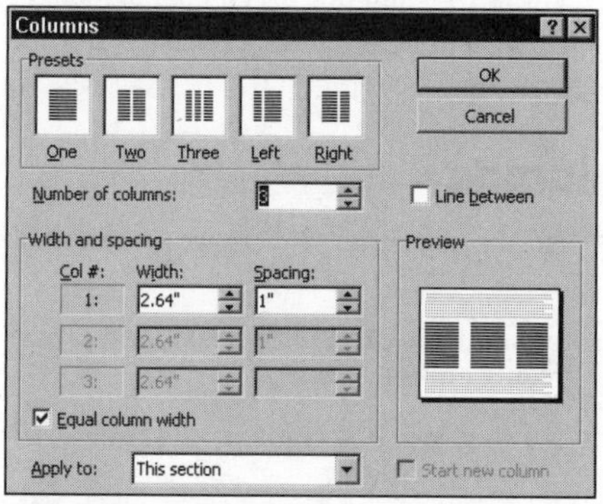

Figure 10-4: The Columns dialog box.

Table 10-2: The Columns Dialog Box Options

Component Name	Action
Presets	The default is One column, of course, a normal document. You can choose to have two or three columns, and also special two-column Left and Right settings (one thin column and one thicker column).
Number of Columns	If the Presets don't work for you, enter or select a specific number here, up to 30 columns depending on the page size.
Line Between	Check this box if you want Word to add a vertical border line between columns.
Width and Spacing	Set the width of the first column, and the space between columns. If you have unchecked Equal Column Width, you can set the width and spacing for subsequent columns, too. If you have more than three columns, a scroll bar appears so you can adjust them all.
Equal Column Width	Uncheck this if you don't want all the columns the same size.
Apply To	Defines which part of the document should be modified to multicolumn format, depending on where the cursor was or what was selected; the Whole Document, This Point Forward, Selected Text, Selected Sections, and so on.
Start New Column	If you selected This Point Forward, you can check this box if you want to begin a new column, at the insertion point, on the top of a new page.

Calculating the number of columns

Word determines the number of columns available on a page based on four factors: the page width, margin widths, the width of the columns, and the spacing between columns. For example, a wide landscape-oriented page has more room for columns than on portrait-oriented page. Similarly, a page with narrow margins has room for more columns. Columns must be at least ½-inch wide in Word. If you try to fit too many on a page, Word reverts to ½-inch columns with no spacing between them, which means a maximum of 12 columns in portrait or 18 columns in landscape orientation. If you want more columns, you'll need a bigger paper size or, perhaps, will have to change your page margins or orientation or change the spacing between your columns.

Typing and editing text in columns

You can type, edit, and format text in columns just like any other text. However, the following options are available for navigating column text:

✦ Press Alt+down arrow to move from one column to the top of the next, and press Alt+up arrow to move to the top of the previous column.

✦ Press Ctrl+down arrow to move to the next paragraph in a column, and press Ctrl+up arrow to move to the previous paragraph.

The selection bar that normally is available at the left margin of a page is now available at the left margin of each column in Print Layout view. You can see the column area markers in the horizontal ruler. When you move the mouse pointer into the area between the columns and next to the column's text, the insertion point becomes an arrow pointing to the right. By dragging the mouse, you can select lines and paragraphs within a column (see Figure 10-5).

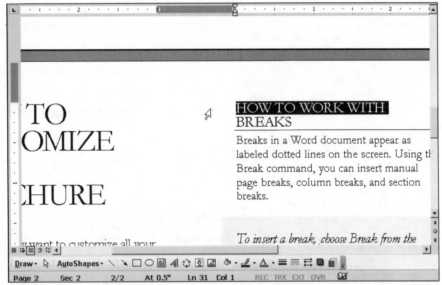

Figure 10-5: The selection bar exists at the left margin of each column in Print Layout view.

If text seems to be narrower than the columns, that text may be indented. Use the ruler or choose Format ➪ Paragraph to eliminate or change the indentation settings for selected text.

Cross-Reference For more information on formatting paragraphs, see Chapter 5.

Adding a line between columns

A vertical line between columns can add a visual element to help break up your page and make multicolumn text easier to read. Such lines are the length of the longest column in the section. You also can add vertical lines on your page by choosing the Format ➪ Borders and Shading command. (For more information, see Chapter 5.) For columns, the Line Between option in the Columns dialog box is a better choice, however, because it creates lines of uniform length in the section even if one column of text is shorter than the others.

Changing column widths and spacing between columns

With Word, you can change the width of columns or the space between columns in two ways: using the ruler, or using the Columns dialog box. If your columns are currently equal-width because the Equal Column Width check box in the Columns dialog box is checked, and you want to change them to unequal-width, you must first clear that option in the Columns dialog box. If you try to change the width of one column using the ruler, and the Equal Column Width check box is still checked, you end up adjusting all columns at the same time.

To change column widths and spacing using the ruler, follow these steps:

1. Switch to Print Layout view, and position the insertion point inside the section containing the columns that you want to change. The gray column markers in the horizontal ruler indicate the spaces between columns. When columns have different widths, the gray area on the ruler contains a grid-like icon. Figure 10-6 shows how the ruler appears when columns have unequal widths.

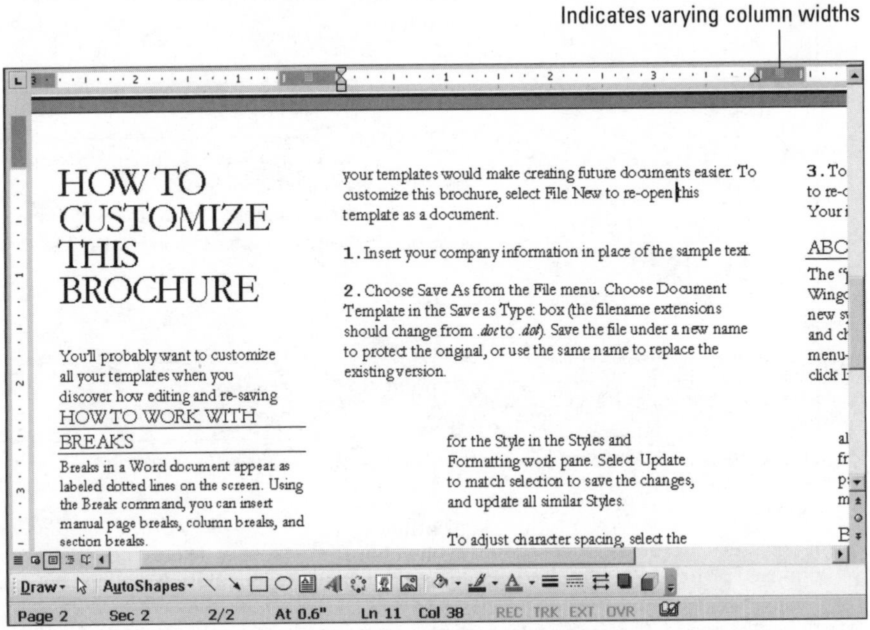

Indicates varying column widths

Figure 10-6: The ruler display for unequal-width columns.

2. Move the mouse pointer to the column marker over the column that you want to change.

3. If your columns are of equal width, drag the edge of the marker away from the center to add space between columns or drag it toward the center to remove space between columns.

4. If your columns have different widths, drag either edge of the marker to change the spacing between two columns. Only the column that contains the insertion point and the one to the left change. Drag the Move Column marker (the small grid icon that appears in the center of the gray area between columns in the horizontal ruler) to change the column width and keep the spacing unchanged.

Tip Hold Alt while dragging to see the column-width measurements displayed on the ruler as you move the column borders.

Removing columns

Both the Columns button and the Columns dialog box can be used to remove columns easily. Position the insertion point or select the sections in which you want to remove columns. You can use the Columns button on the Standard toolbar to specify a single column, or you can choose One in the Presets group of the Columns dialog box. Then click OK.

Breaking a column

When Word creates columns, it automatically breaks the columns to fit on the page. Sometimes, however, the column may break inappropriately. For example a column may end with a heading that should be at the top of the next column. Inserting a column break directly before the heading shifts that heading to the top of the next column, which keeps the heading and its following text together.

To insert a column break, follow these steps:

1. Position the insertion point at the beginning of the line in which you want the new column to start.

2. Do one of the following:

   • Choose Insert ⇨ Break, and the Break dialog box appears. Choose Column Break, and then click OK.

   • Press Ctrl+Shift+Enter.

If you want a column to start on a new page, insert a page break by pressing Ctrl+Enter. To remove a break, position the insertion point at the beginning of the text where you created the break and press Backspace.

Balancing column lengths

On pages where the text in columns continues to the next page, Word automatically lines up the last line of text at the bottom of each column. When a column's text runs out on a page, however, you may be left with two full-length columns and a third column that's only partially filled. You can balance column lengths so that the bottom of all columns are within one line of each other. Figure 10-7 provides examples of both unbalanced and balanced columns.

To line up the length of multiple columns, follow these steps:

1. Position the insertion point at the end of the text in the last column of the section that you want to balance.

2. Choose Insert ⇨ Break.

3. Choose Continuous in the Section Break Types group.

4. Click OK.

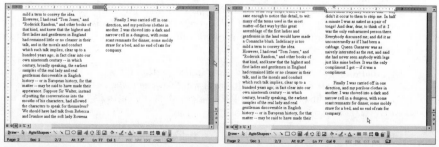

Figure 10-7: Unbalanced columns (left) and balanced columns (right).

Tip   If the preceding procedure doesn't work, look in the Options dialog box (Tools ➪ Options) under the Compatibility tab and make sure the Don't Balance Columns For Continuous Section Starts option is not checked.

To add a page break after the balanced columns, place the insertion point after the continuous section break marker. Then choose Page Break from the Break dialog box.

Formatting Your Pages

Page formatting encompasses formatting choices that affect the page, such as margins, headers, and footers. Word lets you apply page-setup formatting options to a selection, a section, multiple sections, or even the entire document. What you format depends on the position of the insertion point or the selection that you make *before* you select the Page Setup command.

The default measurement in Word is the inch. As with most measurement entries in Word, however, you can also specify centimeters (cm), points (pt), or picas (pi) by entering the two-letter code after a measurement value. Then, after you close the dialog box, Word automatically converts your entries to inches. The default unit of measure can be specified in the General tab of the Options dialog box, but in most cases, you should use inches as the default.

Cross-Reference   You can save page and section formatting as templates, and you can use these templates as a basis for new documents. For more on how to work with document templates, see Chapter 14.

Setting page margins

Margins are the borders on all four sides of a page within which the text of your document is confined. Figure 10-8 shows the margin areas of a document. Margins aren't necessarily blank, however. They may contain headers, footers, page numbers, footnotes, or even text and graphics. Different views give you different perspectives on your margins. In Normal view, you don't see them, but in Print Layout view, you see the page as it will print, margins and all. Choose Print Layout view if you want to see the headers, footers, page numbers, footnotes, and anything else that appears within the margins.

The default margins in Word are 1-inch at the top and bottom and 1¼-inches on the left and right. You can use the Page Setup dialog box or the ruler to change the margins for the entire document or for sections of the document. You can also change settings in Print Preview mode.

Setting margins in the Page Setup dialog box

Use the Margins tab in the Page Setup dialog box (File ➪ Page Setup) to set margins; this dialog box provides the greatest number of options for setting margins. You can set the margins to precise measurements, establish facing pages (mirror margins) and gutters for binding, set varying margins for different sections of your document, and apply your margin settings to the current template.

To set margins, either position the cursor in the section for which you want to set the margins or select the text or sections that you want to affect; then choose File ➪ Page Setup. The Page Setup dialog box appears. Table 10-3 describes the settings in the Margins tab of this dialog box (see Figure 10-9).

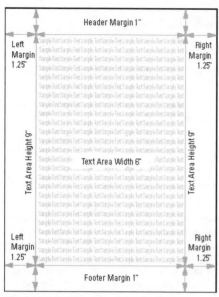

Figure 10-8: The margins of a document.

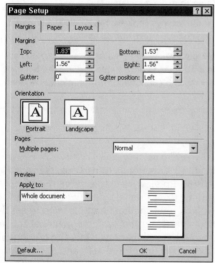

Figure 10-9: The Margins tab of the Page Setup dialog box.

Table 10-3: The Page Setup Margins Tab

Component Name	Action
Margins—Top, Left, Bottom, Right	Set the distance between the text and the edge of the page.
Margins—Gutter	An extra space to allow for binding on one side of the page. This gutter will switch from side to side between pages to allow for even and odd pages.
Gutter position	You can place the gutter on the Left of the page, or the Top of the page. This is the edge that will be bound or stapled together.
Orientation	Select Portrait (long side is vertical) or Landscape (long side is horizontal).
Multiple pages	Select Normal for most documents. The other options are Mirror Margins (the document will be printed double-sided like a book, so the inside margin switches sides each page); 2 Pages Per Sheet (yes, two pages will be printed on each sheet); and Book Fold (Word will print the pages so that you can fold the pages and bind, and end up with a booklet).
Sheets per booklet	If you selected Book Fold, you can now specify how many sheets in the booklet, so Word can figure out how it needs to print the pages to make it foldable.
Apply to	Define what the settings apply to: the Whole Document, This Point Forward, Selected Text, and so on.
Default	Click this button if you want to make the settings you have just created the default for all documents that use the template you are working with (see Chapter 14 for information about templates).

Setting margins using the ruler

A convenient way to set margins for your document or a section is to use the ruler and the mouse. Display the document in Print Layout or Print Preview view to change the margins on all four sides of your document. In Print Layout or Print Preview view, Word displays two rulers: a horizontal ruler, which appears at the top of your document and is used to set the left and right (or inside and outside) margins; and a vertical ruler, which appears at the left side of your document and is used to set the top and bottom margins. Only the horizontal ruler is available in Normal view. Each ruler shows a gray or colored area and a white area. The gray or colored area indicates the margins; the white area indicates the text area. The edge between the gray area and the white area is the margin boundary. Rest the mouse pointer on the edge to display a ScreenTip describing the margin that the marker represents.

Note   If only the horizontal ruler appears in Print Layout view, choose Tools ➪ Options, click the View tab, and choose the Vertical ruler (Print view only) option in the Print and Web Layout options group.

To change margins with a ruler, follow these steps:

1. Position the cursor in the section where you want to set the margins.

2. Choose View ➪ Print Layout. If your rulers don't appear, choose View ➪ Ruler to display them.

3. Position the pointer over the margin boundary that you want to change. The pointer then turns into a two-headed arrow, and a ScreenTip tells you which margin this marker will change.

4. Drag the margin boundary toward the edge of the page to make the margin smaller or toward the center of the page to make the margin wider. A dotted line then appears across the text to show you where the new margin will be. By holding down the Alt key as you drag, you can see margin measurements in the ruler. If you change your mind about changing a margin, press Esc before you release the mouse button or click the Undo button (or choose Edit ➪ Undo) after you release the mouse button.

Creating facing pages and gutters

As in a book, facing pages in a document are the left and right pages of a double-sided document. You create facing pages in Word with *mirror margins.* Using facing pages, you can have different headers and footers on each page, and you can also position page numbers on opposite sides of the facing pages.

A *gutter* adds extra space to allow for the binding of a document at one side or at the top of the page. A gutter doesn't change your document's margins, but it does reduce the printing area. Whether you're working with normal pages that have left and right margins or with facing pages that have inside and outside margins, you can add a gutter to leave extra space for binding. On normal pages, a gutter adds space at the left edge of the page; on facing pages— using *mirror margins*—a gutter adds space at the inside edge of each page. To leave an extra ½-inch for binding, for example, include a gutter of ½-inches. As you saw earlier, you can set mirror margins and a gutter in the Page Setup box under the Margins tab.

Changing paper size and orientation

By changing the paper size, you can create documents other than the standard 8½ x 11 inches. Word provides several predefined standard paper sizes, such as legal, executive, and envelope. Word also provides the option of defining your own custom paper size. In addition, you can even change the orientation of a page from the default portrait to a landscape orientation. Landscape orientation is useful for presenting charts and tables, creating brochures, or creating certificates. Figure 10-10 shows a document in landscape orientation.

As discussed earlier, Landscape is set under the Margins tab of the Page Setup dialog box. The page size is set under the Paper tab (see Figure 10-11). The components of this box are described in Table 10-4.

Note   Your page layout is to some degree affected by the printer you have selected in the Print dialog box. When creating documents you should always have the printer with which you intend to finally *print* the document selected, even if you don't often use that printer, as it affects margins and the paper source. You can change the printer by choosing File ➪ Print, choosing the printer from the Name drop-down list box, and clicking Close.

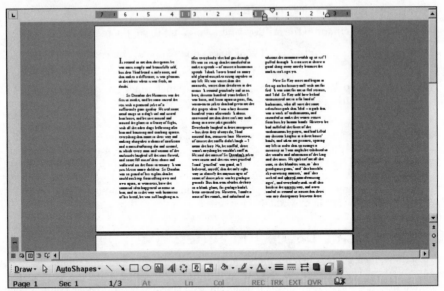

Figure 10-10: A document in landscape orientation.

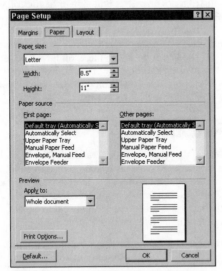

Figure 10-11: The Paper tab of the Page Setup dialog box.

Table 10-4: The Page Setup Dialog Box's Paper Tab

Component Name	Action
Paper size	Select a preset paper size, such as Legal or Letter, or an Envelope size.
Width	If you want to set up your document for a size that isn't covered by the preset sizes, enter the width here.
Height	If you want to set up your document for a size that isn't covered by the present size, enter the height here.
Paper source	Defines where the paper comes from—this depends on the printer you have selected in the Print dialog box. You can select a different tray or feeder for the first page and subsequent pages. Perhaps, for instance, you want to use letterhead paper for the first page, and blank paper for subsequent pages.
Print Options	Click here to open the Print Options dialog box (see Chapter 6).

Changing pagination

Word starts a new page automatically when the current page is full. These page breaks are called *soft breaks*. By creating your own page breaks, however, you can manually control when new pages begin. As you edit and reformat, Word continually recalculates the amount of text on the page, and it adjusts the soft page breaks accordingly. This process is called *background repagination*. When you're working with large documents, you can shut off background pagination to speed your editing.

Inserting hard page breaks

If you want to force a page to break at a particular place in your document, insert a *hard page break*. Word always starts text after a hard page break at the top of the next page. In Normal view, a soft page break appears as a dotted line and a hard page break as two dotted lines, one of which includes the words *Page Break*. In Print Layout or Print Preview view, however, you see the page as it prints. You can insert a hard page break using a command or a keyboard shortcut. After you insert a hard page break in Normal view, you can delete, move, copy, or paste it just like any other text.

To insert a hard page break, follow these steps:

1. Position the cursor at the beginning of the text that you want to begin on a new page.

2. Do either of the following:

   • Choose Insert ➪ Break, choose Page Break, and click OK.

   • Press Ctrl+Enter.

Tip

Generally, it's a good idea not to add hard page breaks until you have finished with the document and are ready to print it. You should use hard page breaks during final layout, to adjust how everything sits on each page.

Turning off background pagination

Background pagination is always turned on in Print Preview and Print Layout view, but it's easy to turn off for Normal or Outline view. Turning off background pagination may slightly improve the performance of Word. Even if background pagination is turned off, however, Word still paginates when you print your document, when you switch to Print Preview or Print Layout view, or when you compile an index or table of contents.

To turn off background pagination, follow these steps:

1. Choose the View menu, and then choose the Normal or Outline command.

2. Choose Tools ⇨ Options.

3. Click the General tab.

4. Clear the Background Repagination option.

5. Click OK.

Aligning text vertically on a page

Word provides three options to align text vertically on a page: top, center, and justified. These options determine how Word aligns a partial page of text between the top and bottom margins. This feature is useful in formatting single-page documents and title pages. If text fills each page, however, changing its vertical alignment doesn't make a difference. Figure 10-12 shows pages based on these vertical alignment options.

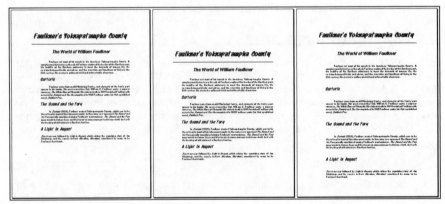

Figure 10-12: Sample pages showing top, center, and justified vertically aligned text.

To align text vertically on the page, follow these steps:

1. Position the cursor inside the section containing the text that you want to align.

2. Choose File ⇨ Page Setup.

3. Click the Layout tab (see Figure 10-13).

4. Choose one of the options in the Vertical Alignment list box (see Table 10-5).

5. Click OK.

If the section contains only one paragraph, the Justify option doesn't apply.

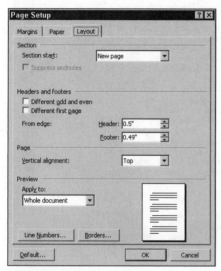

Figure 10-13: The Layout tab of the Page Setup dialog box.

Table 10-5: Options for Vertical Alignment

Option	*Action*
Top	Aligns the top of the first paragraph with the top margin. This is the default page alignment.
Center	Aligns the paragraphs in the center of the page, midway between the top and bottom margins.
Justified	Aligns the top of the first paragraph with the top margin, aligns the bottom of the last paragraph with the bottom margin, and spaces the intervening paragraphs evenly between the top and bottom margins.

Inserting line numbers

Numbered lines are frequently used in legal documents to make referencing easier. Word enables you to number some or all of the lines in a document. Word also provides options for controlling how these line numbers appear. Numbers can start at 1 or some other number, and they can appear on each line or only on some lines. They can be continuous, or they can restart at each section or page. You can even specify the distance between text and the line numbers as well as suppress line numbers for selected paragraphs. Line numbers appear either in the left margin of your page or to the left of text in columns (see Figure 10-14).

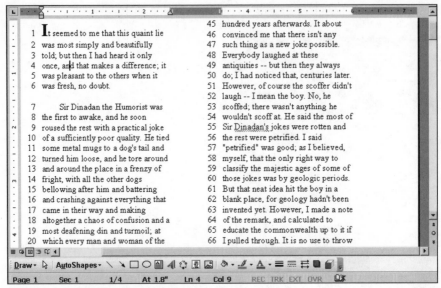

Figure 10-14: Line numbering in a document.

To insert line numbers, follow these steps:

1. Position the cursor in the section where you want to set the line numbers, or select the text or sections that you want to affect.

2. Choose File ➪ Page Setup. The Page Setup dialog box appears.

3. Click the Layout tab.

4. Click the Line Numbers button. The Line Numbers dialog box appears (see Figure 10-15).

5. Choose Add Line Numbering.

6. Enter a Start At number to specify the first line number.

7. Select a From Text value to specify how far from the text the number should appear (make sure your margins are wide enough for this spacing).

8. To change the increment in which the lines are numbered, enter a Count By value.

9. Select Restart Each Page, Restart Each Section, or Continuous, to define whether, and how, numbering should restart.

Controlling line numbers

What if you don't want a particular line or section to be numbered? In this case, you can remove line numbers for a section or the entire document, or you can suppress the line numbers for any selected group of paragraphs. To remove line numbers for a section or document, position the cursor in that section or select the sections in which you want to remove the line numbers. In the Page Setup dialog box (File ➪ Page Setup), click the Layout tab and then click the Line Numbers button. In the Line Numbers dialog box, clear the Add Line Numbering option. Finally, click OK twice to return to your document.

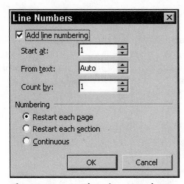

Figure 10-15: The Line Numbers dialog box.

To suppress line numbers for paragraphs, follow these steps:

1. Select the paragraphs in which you want to remove the line numbers.

2. Choose Format ➪ Paragraph. The Paragraph dialog box appears.

3. Click the Line and Page Breaks tab.

4. Check Suppress Line Numbers.

5. Click OK.

Adding Page Borders

As discussed in Chapter 5, you can add borders around paragraphs. You can also add borders around pages, around every page in a document or section, in fact. Applying a border to a page is much the same as applying it to a paragraph. The major difference, however, is that Word includes scores of different border styles from which to choose—not just the line styles that are discussed in Chapter 5, but special image borders, too.

To add a page border, choose Format ➪ Borders and Shading, and the Borders and Shading dialog box appears. Click the Page Border tab (see Figure 10-16), and select a border option from the Art list box. To add a border to one or more sides of a page, choose the Custom option and then click on the button in the Preview group indicating the line that you want to add. By default, the border is set to the Box setting and at 24 points from the edge of the page.

To change the space between the border and the margin or to specify the amount of space between the border and the text, click the Options button in the Borders and Shading dialog box. To change the space between the border and the text, select the Text option in the Measure From list box. Once you've selected the Text setting, the Surround Header and Surround Footer options then become available (see Figure 10-17). Use these options to choose whether the border should surround the header or footer. You can enter a size from 0 to 31 points in the Top, Bottom, Left, and Right text boxes to specify a margin between your text and the page border. In most cases, you should probably leave the Align Paragraph Borders and Table Edges With Page Border option cleared, because if you select this option, your borders and table edges can run into your page border. If you'd like to have text or an image appear over the border in some cases, make sure to clear the Always Display In Front check box.

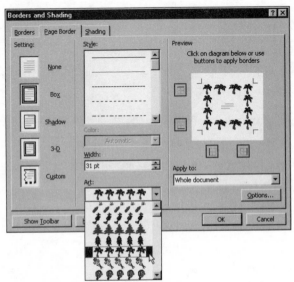

Figure 10-16: The Page Border tab in the Borders and Shading dialog box.

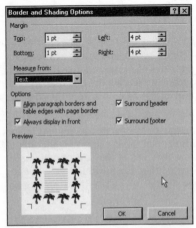

Figure 10-17: The Border and Shading Options dialog box.

Creating Headers and Footers

Headers and footers contain information that is repeated at the top or the bottom of pages in a document. The simplest header or footer is a page number. More elaborate headers or footers can be just about anything, such as the document title, date and time, fields, symbols, cross-references, frames, pictures, and objects. You can format headers and footers just like any other text in a document.

Headers and footers are placed within a page's top and bottom margins. The header and footer can also be different on the first page of a document or section than on subsequent pages. In addition, Word provides the option of creating different headers and footers on even and odd pages. This feature is especially useful for chapter headers in books and manuscripts. For example, each section of a document's chapter can have its own header and footer identifying the topic being discussed, and the position of page numbers may vary between even and odd pages.

Inserting page numbers

Documents are easier to read and to reference when their pages are numbered. There are two ways to insert page numbers: Insert ➪ Page Numbers, or View ➪ Header and Footer. The Insert ➪ Page Numbers command inserts a page number header or footer automatically, whereas with the View ➪ Header and Footer command you are manually placing the page numbers into the header or footer (you have more control over position and format, but it's more complicated).

Page numbers can appear at the top or the bottom of the page, and they can be aligned to the center or to either side of that page. Word doesn't display page numbers in Normal view, however. Therefore, to view page numbers, choose View ➪ Print Layout or View ➪ Header and Footer.

When you use the Insert ➪ Page Numbers method, Word actually creates a frame, places the frame in the header or footer, and places the page number inside the frame.

Cross-Reference　You learn more about frames in Chapters 18 and 24.

Note　If you see {PAGE} instead of the page number, choose Tools ➪ Options, click the View tab, and clear the Field Codes check box.

To insert page numbers, follow these steps:

1. Position the cursor in the section to which you want to add page numbers.

2. Choose Insert ➪ Page Numbers. The Page Numbers dialog box appears (see Figure 10-18).

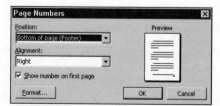

Figure 10-18: The Page Numbers dialog box.

3. In the Position list box, choose Bottom of Page (Footer) to position your page number at the bottom of the page as a footer. Alternatively, choose Top of Page (Header) to position your page number at the top of the page as a header.

4. In the Alignment list box, choose one of the options (Left, Center, Right, Inside, or Outside) to position the location of the page number. Inside positions the page numbers close to the inside edge of opposing pages; Outside positions the page numbers close to the outside edge of opposing pages. The Preview box shows your choice as it appears on the printed page.

5. Choose Show Number on First Page if you want a page number to appear on the first page of your document. Clear this option to prevent a page number from appearing on the first page.

6. Click OK, and Word automatically switches you to Print Layout view.

Removing page numbers

To remove page numbers from headers or footers, follow these steps:

1. Position the insertion point in the section from which you want to remove page numbers.

2. Choose View ➪ Header and Footer. Word displays the document in Print Layout view and shows the Header and Footer toolbar. The header and footer areas are enclosed by a nonprinting, dashed line, and text and graphics in the document are visible but dimmed. To switch to the footer or header, click the Switch Between Header and Footer button on the toolbar.

3. Select the page number. If you used the Insert ➪ Page Number to insert the page number, Word will have created a frame, so select the actual frame, not the number.

4. Press Delete. Word removes the page numbers from the selected section.

5. Click the Close button on the Header and Footer toolbar, or double-click the text in your document.

Changing the position of a page number

To move a page number, double-click that number to activate the Header and Footer toolbar. (You can also choose View ➪ Headers and Footers.) Select the page number, drag it to a new position, and click Close on the Header and Footer toolbar or double-click the text in your document.

If you used the Insert ➪ Page Number to insert the page number, Word will have created a frame with the number inside it. You can drag the frame into a new position. See Chapters 18 and 24 for more information about frames.

Formatting page numbers

Page numbers can appear in several formats, including numbers, uppercase or lowercase letters, and uppercase or lowercase roman numerals. The Page Number dialog box contains a Format button with which you can easily change the format of the page numbers at the same time that you insert them. To change the font or character formatting of a page number, select that page number and then use the buttons on the Formatting toolbar or choose the Format ➪ Font command.

To format page numbers, follow these steps:

1. Position the cursor in the section containing the page number that you want to change.

2. Choose Insert ➪ Page Numbers.

3. Click the Format button. The Page Number Format dialog box appears.

4. In the Number Format list box, choose the format that you want (see Figure 10-19). Then click the OK button to close the Page Number Format dialog box.

5. Click the Close button to close the Page Numbers dialog box.

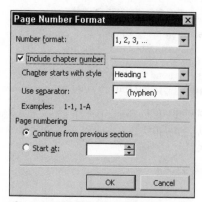

Figure 10-19: The Page Number Format dialog box.

Numbering pages for sections of a document

If you plan to divide a document into several sections, it's easiest to add page numbers before you add the section breaks. If you decide to add page numbers after you've added section breaks, position the cursor in the first section of the document and then insert the page numbers. Even if your document contains more than a single section, page numbering applies by default to your entire document, and the numbers are continuous throughout that document. You can start page numbering in any section and at any number you specify. For example, you can have the page numbering restart at 1 for each section.

To change the starting page number in a section, follow these steps:

1. Position the cursor where you want to change the starting page number.

2. Choose Insert ➪ Page Numbers.

3. Click the Format button.

4. Type or select a new starting page number in the Start At box in the Page numbering group. Then click the OK button to close the Page Number Format dialog box.

5. Click OK to close the Page Number dialog box and return to your document.

If you select the Continuous section break option in the Break dialog box to create two or more sections, the new header or footer doesn't appear until the page after the page that actually contains the section break. In other words, a new header or footer doesn't take effect until after a page break. To make the new header or footer appear on the same page as the beginning of the new section, move the section break to the top of the page. Position the cursor at the top of the page with the current section break, choose Insert ➪ Break, and in the Section Breaks Types group, choose the Next Page option. Then delete the section break that appears inside the section—Word then applies the formatting (including the new header or footer) that followed the deleted section break to the current page.

Cross-Reference

If you're creating a long document with several sections, you can save time using Word's Master Document feature. For more information on using Master Documents, see Chapter 25.

Including sections and total page numbers

When you insert a page number in a document, you're actually using a *field*. The page number is inserted as a {PAGE} field, which adds the page number to the header or footer of a document. In some cases, you might want to include the current section number as well as the total number of pages in a section or document using the {SECTION} field. The {NUMPAGES} field inserts the number of pages in the document, using the information in the Document Statistics tab of the Document Properties dialog box (File ➪ Properties). Using the {NUMPAGES} field along with the {PAGE} field, you can include the total number of pages with your page numbering. For example, you can include the total number of pages along with the current page number. A typical result using fields might display Page 10 of 20.

Cross-Reference

To find out more about fields, see Chapter 23.

To include section numbers or total page numbers:

1. Place the insertion point where you want to place the number, in the header or footer.

2. Choose Insert ➪ Field.

3. Do one of the following:

   • To include the total number of pages, highlight Document Information in the Categories list and then choose NumPages in the Field Names list box.

   • To include the number of the current section, highlight Numbering in the Categories list and then choose Section in the Field Names list box. This inserts the {SECTION} field and displays the number of the current section. The {SECTION} field inserts the section number on each page. For example, by adding the {SECTION} field after the page field in the third section of the document, you can create an entry that shows both the page and section number, such as *Page 2 of Section 3*.

   • To include inserts showing the total number of pages in a section, highlight Numbering in the Categories list and then choose SectionPages in the Field Names list. The {SECTIONPAGES} field inserts the total number of pages in the section. For example, on page 3 in a section with a total of 25 pages, you can add a footer that reads *Page 3 of 25*.

Note

The brackets that surround fields are not the brackets on your keyboard. You can use the Insert ➪ Field to insert a field, but a more direct way is to press Ctrl+F9. This displays the special brackets with a gray highlight for entering a field name. To add the total number of pages to a header of footer, for example, press Ctrl+F9 and type **NUMPAGES** within the brackets.

To display the result of the field code, press Alt+F9. If the field code itself appears rather than the number, choose the Tools ➪ Options command and check that the Field Codes setting is not checked in the Show group on the View tab. (For more information on field codes, see Chapter 23.)

Adding header and footer text

When you add headers and footers, Word switches to Page Layout view, activates a pane in which you can enter your header text, and displays a special Header and Footer toolbar. When you're creating or editing headers or footers in Page Layout view, your document is grayed; in turn headers and footers are grayed when you're working on your document. To see both your document and its headers and footers, choose File ➪ Print Preview.

In addition to the buttons with which you can insert the page number, date, and time fields, you can also use the AutoText button on the Header and Footer toolbar to insert predefined fields containing additional relevant information, such as the file name and author. Table 10-6 shows the available AutoText entries, most of which are acquired from the document properties.

Table 10-6: AutoText Entries for Headers and Footers

Entry	Example
-PAGE-	-1-
Author, Page #, Date	John Irving Page 1 6/15/03 (the three items are spread across the page)
Confidential, Page #, Date	Confidential Page 1 6/15/03 (the three items are spread across the page)
Created by	Created by John Irving
Created on	Created on 6/15/03 9:53 am
Filename	Writer's Association Newsletter
Filename and path	C:\Docs\Irving\Writers Association Newsletter
Last printed	Last printed 6/10/03 10:45 am
Last saved by	Last saved by John Irving
Page X of Y	Page 5 of 26

To add a header or footer to your entire document, follow these steps:

1. Choose View ➪ Header and Footer. Word displays the document in Print Layout view and also displays the Header and Footer toolbar (see Figure 10-20). The header and footer areas are enclosed by a nonprinting, dashed line, and the text and graphics in the document are dimmed. To switch to the footer or header, click the Switch Between Header and Footer button.

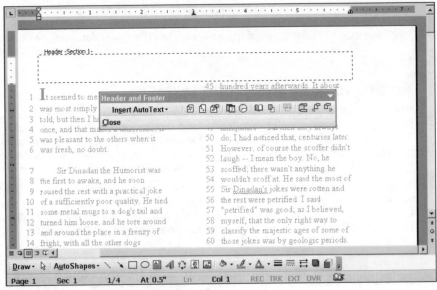

Figure 10-20: Inserting a new header or footer.

2. Type the text for your header or footer within the dashed line that surrounds the header or footer area, or select one of the AutoTexts. Note that you can add more than one line of text. Format the text just like any other text, and use the Tab key and spacebar or the alignment buttons on the Formatting toolbar to position it.

3. Use the Header and Footer toolbar buttons to insert any fields that you want in the header or footer.

4. Click Close or double-click your document to close the Header and Footer toolbar and return to the document itself.

Tip   To display and edit an existing header or footer quickly, double-click the dimmed header or footer in Print Layout view.

Another way to include the date or time in a header or footer is to insert a date or time field using the Insert ➪ Date and Time command. With this command, you can also select a format for your date or time.

Hiding text while working with headers and footers

The document text appears dimmed while you're working with headers and footers. If you want to hide the document text completely, click the Show/Hide Document Text button on the Headers and Footers toolbar. The document text is hidden only while you're working on the header or footer, however. To redisplay the dimmed document text, click the Show/Hide Document Text button again.

Adding headers and footers to sections

You can apply headers and footers to all of the sections in a document. If you then divide the document into sections, those headers and footers are the same for each section. To have a different header or footer in a section, go to that section, unlink the existing header or footer, and then create the new header or footer.

The new header or footer applies to the current section and to all of the following sections. Later, if you want the new header or footer to be the same as the preceding header or footer, you can relink it. If you change one header or footer without unlinking it, all the headers and footers in all linked sections change. To create a different header or footer for a section, follow these steps:

1. Position the cursor inside the first section in which you want to change the header or footer.

2. Choose View ➪ Header and Footer. Word displays the header for the current section. To change the footer for that section, click the Switch Between Header and Footer button.

3. Click the Same as Previous button to unlink the header and footer in the current section from those in the preceding section.

4. To remove the contents of an existing header or footer, select the contents and press Backspace or Delete.

5. Enter the new header or footer contents that you want for the current section. Word also inserts the same header or footer in all of the following sections, unless you go to the next header or footer and unlink it first.

   To use different header or footer contents in following sections, click the Show Next button to move to the next section. Then repeat steps 3 through 5 for each section.

6. Click Close on the Header and Footer toolbar or double-click the document to close the Header and Footer toolbar and return to the document.

To relink a header or footer with the preceding header or footer, simply open that header or footer and click the Same As Previous button. You'll see a message asking if you want to delete the header or footer and connect it to the preceding section.

Tip   Headers and footers are treated separately. You could have a header that's linked but a footer that is not in the same section, for instance. Note also that if a header or footer *is* linked, Same As Previous appears above the header or footer on the right side.

Creating different first-page headers and footers

Many documents have a different header or footer on the first page, or perhaps no header or footer on the first page at all. So Word lets you create a different header or footer at the beginning of each section in a document. To create a different header or footer for the first page of a document or section, follow these steps:

1. Choose View ➪ Header and Footer.

2. Click the Show Previous or Show Next button to locate the section in which you want a different first-page header or footer to appear. To change the footer for that section, click the Switch Between Header and Footer button.

3. Click the Page Setup button on the Header and Footer toolbar. The Page Setup dialog box appears.

4. Click the Layout tab.

5. In the Headers and Footers group, choose Different First Page.

6. Choose This Section from the Apply To list box.

7. Click OK. The title First Page Header or First Page Footer then appears at the top of the header and footer editing pane.

8. If you don't want any header or footer text, leave the header or footer editing area blank. If you want a different header or footer on the first page of the section, enter the text for your header or footer in the editing area.

9. Click the Close button on the Header and Footer toolbar or double-click in the document to close the Header and Footer toolbar and return to the document.

You can remove a first-page header or footer in the same way that you create one. Just navigate to the section, click the Page Setup button, click the Layout tab, and then clear the Different First Page option in the Headers and Footers group.

Creating headers and footers for odd and even pages

You may sometimes want different headers and footers for the odd- and even-numbered pages in your document. In a document with facing pages (mirror margins), odd-numbered pages appear on the right side and even-numbered pages on the left. You may want left-aligned headers on even-numbered pages and right-aligned headers on odd-numbered pages; this way, the headers always appear on the outside edges of your document. You can even create different odd and even headers and footers for each section in your document.

To create different headers and footers for odd and even pages, simply select Different Odd and Even in the Headers and Footers area under the Layout tab in the Page Setup dialog box.

Positioning headers and footers

Depending on what you enter in a header or footer, you may want to change the position of that text or even its location on the page. For example, you may want to change the horizontal text alignment. If so, you can center it between the left and right margins, align it with the left or right margin, or create a header that places its text in the right or left margin outside the document text area. In addition, you can change the vertical position by increasing or decreasing the distance from the top or the bottom edge of the page. You can also adjust the amount of space between the header or footer and the text in the main document.

The header and footer areas have two preset tab stops: one centered between the left and right margins, and one right-aligned at the default right margin (6 inches). These tab stops make it easy to center a chapter title or to place a page number flush with the right margin. The alignment buttons on the Formatting toolbar can also be used to align text in a header or footer.

If you want your headers or footers to run into the left or right margin, set a negative indent using the Format ➪ Paragraph command. For example, to create a header that starts in the left margin, type –1 in the Left box (located in the Indents and Spacing tab of the Paragraph dialog box). Printers usually cannot print all the way to the edge of the page, though; for example, many printers cannot print in the outermost ¼-inch of a page. If you specify a setting that invades this nonprinting zone, that text doesn't print.

Headers and footers are printed in the top and bottom margins. You can also specify how much space is left on the page above a header or below a footer in the top or the bottom margin.

To change the distance of a header or a footer from the edge of the paper, follow these steps:

1. Choose View ➪ Header and Footer.

2. Click the Show Previous or Show Next button to locate the section containing the header or footer that you want to affect.

3. Click the Page Setup button to display the Page Setup dialog box.

4. Click the Layout tab.

5. In the From Edge group, do one of the following:

   • Choose the Header box, and then type or select the distance that you want your header to be from the top edge of the page.

   • Choose Footer, and then type or select the distance that you want your footer to be from the bottom edge of the page.

6. Click OK to close the Page Setup dialog box.

7. Click the Close button on the Header and Footer toolbar or double-click in the document to close the Header and Footer toolbar and return to the document.

If your header or footer is larger than your top or bottom margin, Word moves your document text to make room for the header or footer. The page margin, however, is not changed. If you don't want Word to move your text, make your header or footer smaller or use Page Setup to move it closer to the edge of the page.

The final adjustment that you can make to the position of headers and footers is to set the amount of space between a header or footer and the document text. You can change the top and bottom margins in the Page Setup dialog box to increase the space, or you can drag the margin boundary marker (the line between gray and white) on the vertical ruler. Using the second method, you can see the exact margin measurement by holding down the Alt key as you drag the marker.

Backgrounds and Watermarks

Word provides a neat little tool for placing backgrounds and watermarks in your documents. In earlier versions users had to play a trick to place watermarks into documents (by placing a large image inside the header or footer), which was a little awkward. Microsoft realized this was a useful feature, and added a special document-background feature.

Select Format ➪ Background to see a drop-down menu (see Figure 10-21). This allows you to do three things:

✦ Add background colors

✦ Add background patterns and images

✦ Add text watermarks

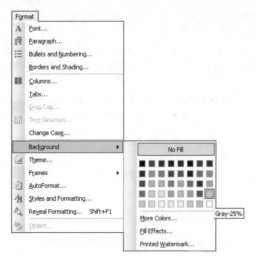

Figure 10-21: The Background drop-down menu.

Adding background color

To select a background color, simply select that color from the Background menu that appears when you select Format ⇨ Background. If you don't see the color you want, select More Colors and select or create another one.

Note that any choice you make here is overruled by a fill effect. That is, Word uses the last color or fill-effect choice you make. The watermark, however, sits on top of whatever color or fill effect you choose.

In earlier versions of Word, it wasn't possible to print most of these background patterns and colors. But now you can. Choose Tools ⇨ Options, click the Print tab, and select the Background Colors and Images check box. This is *off* by default, so by default the colors and backgrounds you select will not print. They are really intended for Web-based documents.

Should you print background colors and patterns? Maybe sometimes, probably not often. They use a lot of ink and generally make documents hard to read.

Adding a pattern or image

To add a pattern or image, select Format ⇨ Background ⇨ Fill Effects, to see the Fill Effects dialog box. This has four tabs: Gradient, Texture, Pattern, and Picture.

The Gradient tab (see Figure 10-22) lets you create a smooth gradient between shades and colors. Table 10-7 describes your choices here.

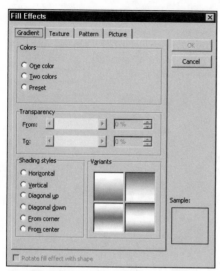

Figure 10-22: The Gradient tab of the Fill Effects dialog box.

Table 10-7: The Fill Effects Gradient Tab

Component Name	Action
One Color	Creates a gradient using varying shades of one color. You'll be able to select the color and a light or dark shade that the chosen color should fade to.
Two Colors	Creates a gradient using two colors that you can select.
Preset	Allows you to select from a list of pre-built (and ugly) color combinations (but then, this feature is probably one that shouldn't be used too much!).
Transparency	Lets you define the degree of transparency, or how much the colors are screened back, how light the colors are. This applies only to drawing objects, such as AutoShapes, inserted using the Drawing toolbar (see Chapter 17). Confusingly, this feature is *not* for use with background colors.
Shading Styles	Defines the direction of the fade between the colors.

The Texture tab allows you to select from a series of pre-built texture backgrounds, or even select one of your own if you have one. You can see some of the options in Figure 10-23.

Note Many of these fill effects are pretty ugly, and should rarely be used! They make reading a document very difficult, so don't get carried away!

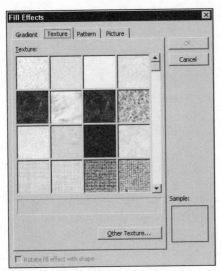

Figure 10-23: The Texture tab of the Fill Effects dialog box.

On the Pattern tab, you can select a foreground and background color and then select from a wide variety of rather ugly patterns (see Figure 10-24).

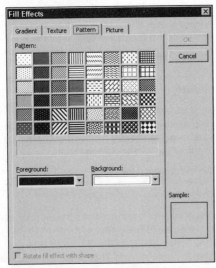

Figure 10-24: The Pattern tab of the Fill Effects dialog box.

Finally, in the Picture tab, you can select a picture that you have saved on your computer or a network drive, and use that as the background. Note that if the picture isn't big enough, it will be *tiled* across the page, that is, repeated multiple times to fill the page.

Adding a text watermark

A watermark is something subtle that sits underneath the text on your document. Traditionally it was a very light image impressed into the paper itself, almost unnoticeable. In recent years, though, the term watermark has come to mean something, generally text, that is placed below the text to carry some kind of message . . . perhaps informing readers that the document is *Confidential* or *Preliminary*, for instance.

To add a watermark, select Format ⇨ Background ⇨ Printed Watermark, and the Printed Watermark dialog box opens, as described in Table 10-8 and illustrated in Figure 10-25.

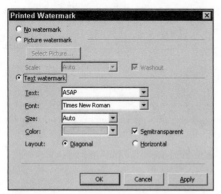

Figure 10-25: The Printed Watermark dialog box.

Table 10-8: The Printed Watermark Dialog Box Options

Component Name	Action
No Watermark	Removes the current watermark.
Picture Watermark	Inserts an image as a watermark.
Select Picture	Displays a File Open dialog box from which you can select the image you want to use.
Scale	Sizes the image so that it fits properly on the document background.
Washout	Ensures that the image is washed out or screened back so that it doesn't overwhelm the document and prevent the document text from being readable. Even if you clear this check box, the image will be screened back a little. But with this checked, it's very washed out.
Text Watermark	Enables you to use text rather than an image for a watermark.
Text	Provides several text options, including ASAP, Confidential, and Draft, or you can type your own.
Font	Enables you to select the font you want to use.
Size	Provides sizes for you to choose from.

Continued

Table 10-8 *(continued)*

Component Name	Action
Color	Provides colors for you to choose from.
Semitransparent	Screens back the text so that it doesn't overwhelm the document (similar to the Washout control). Even without this checked, however, it's still pretty light.
Layout	Enables you to designate the position of the watermark: diagonally across the page, bottom left to upper right, or horizontal.
Apply	Enables you to apply the watermark to your document while you are working so that you can experiment with various settings without continually closing and opening the dialog box.

Summary

Knowing how to create and work with sections and columns as well as how to specify formats for the pages in your document gives you tremendous power. You can

✦ Create and change the formatting for new and existing documents.

✦ Work with columns.

✦ Create complex documents, such as reports, newsletters, and brochures.

✦ Enter page numbers and other information into headers and footers.

✦ Work with background patterns and colors and watermarks.

✦   ✦   ✦

Using Bookmarks, Cross-References, Footnotes, and Links

♦ ♦ ♦ ♦

In This Chapter

Inserting bookmarks

Creating
cross-references

Creating footnotes
and endnotes

Adding links to
your documents

♦ ♦ ♦ ♦

In this chapter, we look at a few dynamic features that can make your documents a lot more sophisticated and useful. You learn how to create cross-references that automatically update. Want to refer someone to another chapter, to a particular page, or even a particular block of text? You can create a cross-reference (such as "See 'Gerbil Racing in the New Millennium' on Page 32"), and then forget about it. Even if you modify your document and "Gerbil Racing in the New Millennium" is now on page 38, Word figures that out and updates the cross-reference for you.

You also find out how to add footnotes and endnotes and automatically number them, too. And finally, you learn how to add hyperlinks to your documents.

Introducing Fields

Several of the features discussed in this chapter use fields. Chapter 23 covers fields in detail, but the following general pointers should help as you work your way through this chapter:

♦ By default, most fields look like any other document text unless they are selected, so you may have trouble telling what is a field and what isn't. If you want, Word can identify your document fields by shading them. Choose Tool ➪ Options, click the View tab, and then select Always from the Field Shading drop-down list. Now all of your fields are shaded and easy to spot.

♦ Fields are displayed as either codes or results. For example, a date field's result is the actual date, but a date field's code looks something like { DATE \@ "M/d/yy" }. The code is a set of instructions that tells Word what to do.

♦ To toggle between displaying field codes and field results for any particular field, place your insertion point in that field and press Shift+F9. You can also click the right mouse button when your insertion point is in the field and then choose Toggle Field Codes in the shortcut menu.

✦ To toggle field codes for the entire document, press Alt+F9. Alternatively, you can choose Tools ➪ Options, click the View tab, and select Field Codes from the Show area of the View tab.

✦ To update a field, place your insertion point in that field and press F9. You can also right-click and choose Update Field from the shortcut menu.

✦ To update all fields in a document, select the entire document (the fastest way is to press Ctrl+A) and then press F9. (However, note that if you put fields into the headers, footers, or footnotes, they won't be updated.)

✦ To move your insertion point to the next field, press F11. Press Shift+F11 to move to the preceding field.

✦ To edit a field's results, move your insertion point inside that field. If the Field Shading When Selected option is active in the View tab of the Tools ➪ Options dialog box, the field results are a lighter shade of gray when the insertion point is simply placed within the field than when the entire field is selected. Select the text that you want to edit, or format the text using any of Word's character formatting options.

✦ To delete a field, select the entire field, including the opening and closing brackets, and press Delete. Deleting fields is easier when the field codes are displayed. Alternatively, you can click in the field and press Delete twice. The first time you press Delete, Word selects the field, the second time Word deletes it.

Working with Bookmarks

Forget about those ratty old pieces of paper that you use—and lose—to mark your place in printed books. Word's electronic bookmarks give the term bookmark a whole new meaning. You can have a virtually unlimited number of bookmarks in any document. Don't let the name deceive you, either, because Word's bookmarks do much more than simply mark your place. They can mark any item or selection in a Word document, including text, graphics, tables, or any combination. If you select items and then create the bookmark you are marking the entire selection. The bookmark feature thus enables you to mark items for cross-referencing, indexing, moving, and copying.

Bookmarked items can also be used in fields and macros. You can even use bookmarks in calculations, which is similar to using a range name in a spreadsheet, as you saw in Chapter 9.

How to use bookmarks when creating cross-references is covered later in this chapter. How you can use bookmarks to mark page ranges for indexes is covered in Chapter 12.

Inserting bookmarks

Creating a bookmark involves two steps: choosing the location that you want to mark, and assigning a name for the bookmark so that you can identify it later. To create a bookmark, follow these steps:

1. Position your insertion point at the location to be marked. If you want the bookmark to mark an entire block or area of text—multiple pages if you wish—select everything before you proceed.

2. Choose Insert ➪ Bookmark, or press Ctrl+Shift+F5. The Bookmark dialog box appears, as shown in Figure 11-1.

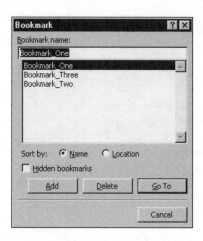

Figure 11-1: The Bookmark dialog box shows a list of existing bookmarks in the current document.

3. Enter a name for the bookmark in the Bookmark Name text box.

A bookmark name may contain as many as 40 characters, and though the first character must be a letter, you can use both letters and numbers after that. A bookmark name cannot include spaces, however, and you cannot use any symbol except the underscore character to separate words.

4. Click Add. The dialog box closes.

Note

If the Add button is dimmed after you enter the bookmark name, that name may be invalid. Word dims the Add button if the name includes any characters that are not allowed. As mentioned, the name cannot include any characters other than letters, numbers, or underscores, and though you can use numbers in a bookmark name, the first character must be a letter.

Viewing bookmarks

You can control the display of bookmark markers in your document. Choose Tools ➪ Options, and then select or clear the Bookmarks check box on the View tab. When this check box is selected, bookmarks are displayed, as shown in Figure 11-2. If you select a block of text before creating a bookmark, the selected text will be surrounded by square brackets. If you select no text before creating the bookmark, an I-beam symbol is displayed at your insertion point location. The I-beam looks like a plumper version of the mouse pointer that Word uses inside a text entry area. You can see the bookmarks in most views, but not Print Preview or Reading Layout, if they are checked on the View tab.

Note that bookmarks don't print, even if you can view them on the screen. It's probably a good idea to turn on the display of bookmarks, and leave them on, despite the fact that Word hides them by default. If you use bookmarks it's useful to be able to see where they are, so you know if you are adding information to a bookmark or moving one, or even accidentally deleting one. If your insertion point is placed immediately after bookmarked text, but before the bookmark's closing marker, everything that you type is included in the bookmark. As you learn later in this chapter, in the section "The problem with bookmarks," you can run into problems with bookmarks if you can't see them.

> [The first sentence of this paragraph was selected before creating the bookmark.]This
> sentence was not included in the selection. Notice the square brackets enclosing the first
> sentence.
>
> [This entire paragraph was selected before creating the bookmark. Notice the bracket only
> at the beginning of the paragraph.
>
> [This bookmark was created with the insertion point at the beginning of the paragraph. No
> text was selected. Notice the I-beam at the beginning of the paragraph.

Figure 11-2: The first bookmark on this screen was created with one sentence selected, the second bookmark with an entire paragraph selected, and the third without any text selected.

Moving to bookmarks

You can use the Bookmark dialog box (Insert ⇨ Bookmark) or the Go To tab of the Find and Replace dialog box (Edit ⇨ Go To) to jump to a specified bookmark. Both methods are covered in this section, but the Bookmark dialog box is the most direct route. (Using the Go To dialog box involves at least one extra step or keystroke.) If, however, you know the exact name of the bookmark that you want, the fastest way to jump to that bookmark is to press F5 to open the Go To tab, type the bookmark name, and then press Enter—you don't even have to select a Go To What entry first.

If several bookmarks are in a particular area, you may have difficulty telling where one bookmark ends and the next one begins. You can quickly identify the bookmark that you want, however, using one of the methods described in the following two exercises. Either method selects the entire bookmarked area.

To find a bookmark using the Bookmark dialog box, follow these steps:

1. Choose Insert ⇨ Bookmark.

2. Select the bookmark that you want to go to from the Bookmark Name list (refer to Figure 11-1).

3. Click Go To, or press Enter.

   Note that Go To is the default button: all you need to do is select a bookmark and press Enter. You can also move to a bookmark directly after opening the Bookmark dialog box by double-clicking the bookmark's name. You may need to drag the dialog box aside, however, to see the insertion point at the bookmark.

Note   You can sort your bookmarks alphabetically or by their location in the document. Sorting by location allows you to easily identify bookmarks based on their relative positions in the document. By default, however, bookmarks are sorted by name. To sort bookmarks by location, select the Location radio button near the bottom of the Bookmark dialog box. You can also display hidden bookmarks, such as cross-references, by selecting Hidden Bookmarks in the Bookmark dialog box.

To find a bookmark using the Go To dialog box, follow these steps:

1. Choose Edit ➪ Go To, or press Ctrl+G.

2. Choose Bookmark from the Go To What list.

3. Select the bookmark that you want to go to from the Enter Bookmark Name drop-down list, or type the bookmark name in the text box (see Figure 11-3). Note that the bookmarks are listed in alphabetical order by name.

Figure 11-3: The Enter Bookmark Name list in the Go To tab of the Find and Replace dialog box.

4. Click Go To, or press Enter.

Manipulating bookmarks

Table 11-1 describes what happens when you move, copy, or delete bookmarked items.

Table 11-1: Moving, Copying, and Deleting Bookmarked Items

Action	Result
Add text inside the bookmark brackets or in a paragraph marked with a single opening bracket.	The text is included in the bookmark.
Move text containing a bookmark to another location in the current document.	The bookmark moves with the text.
Move text containing a bookmark to another document.	The bookmark moves with the text unless the recipient document already contains a bookmark with the same name.
Copy text containing a bookmark to another location in the same document.	The bookmark stays in the original location. The copied text contains no bookmark.
Copy text containing a bookmark to another document.	Both documents contain the same text and bookmarks. If the other document already contains a bookmark with the same name, however, the bookmark isn't copied.

Continued

Table 11-1 *(continued)*

Action	Result
Delete all text or objects between two bookmark brackets or a paragraph marked with an opening bracket.	The bookmark is deleted.
Delete a portion of the text or objects in a bookmark selection.	The remaining items retain the bookmark.

To delete a bookmark from the list in the Bookmark dialog box without deleting any of the items that it references, follow these steps:

1. Open the Bookmark dialog box (Insert ⇨ Bookmark).

2. Select the bookmark that you want to delete.

3. Click Delete.

4. Close the Bookmark dialog box.

Caution   When you delete a bookmark, Word won't warn you that you may break something elsewhere in the document. Unlike in another Office Suite program, FrontPage, which keeps track of links, Word doesn't watch out for broken links. If you have referred to the bookmark in a cross-reference, for example, the cross-reference will be replaced with *Error! Reference source not found.*

Placing the contents of a bookmark in your document

You can insert the contents of a bookmark field anywhere in a document. Press Ctrl+F9 to insert the opening and closing field characters, type the name of the bookmark between the brackets, and press F9. Word creates a copy of the bookmarked contents and displays it at the new field position.

If your bookmark name is the same as one of Word's built-in field names, type **REF** in front of the bookmark name inside the field. For example, to insert the contents of a bookmark called MY_BOOKMARK, type **MY_BOOKMARK** in the field. If you have a bookmark called AUTHOR, however, which is also the name of a Word field, type **REF AUTHOR** in the field.

You can use the techniques just described to insert bookmark contents anywhere in the current document or even in documents linked in a master document (which you'll learn about in Chapter 25). To insert the contents of a bookmark in a different document, use the INCLUDEPICTURE or INCLUDETEXT fields. To replace the field with the contents of the bookmark, right-click and then choose Toggle Field Codes from the shortcut menu. For more information about using fields to refer to other documents, see Chapter 23.

When you insert the contents of a bookmark field, the object or text that is marked by that bookmark is actually inserted into your document. Unless the bookmarked text includes a paragraph mark, inserted items take on the paragraph formatting of the insertion point location. If you include a paragraph mark in the selected area, the bookmark's formatting takes precedence.

Calculating with bookmarks

You can also use bookmarks to identify values that you want to use in calculations, and you can insert the bookmarked items into formulas anywhere in a document. If the numbers change, you can recalculate the results simply by updating your fields. To create a bookmark for use in calculations, select the number that is used in the calculation and create the bookmark using the techniques covered earlier in this section.

To insert a formula to calculate numbers in bookmark fields, position your insertion point where you want the result of the formula to appear and then choose Insert ⇨ Field. Select Equations and Formulas from the Categories list box and =(Formula) from the Field Names list box, as shown in Figure 11-4. Click the Field Codes button (the button's name changes depending on what is selected in the Field Names box), and create a formula using the bookmark names in place of numbers. Depending on whether you're displaying field codes or results, you see either the formula or the result. For information about creating formulas and other expressions, see Chapter 23.

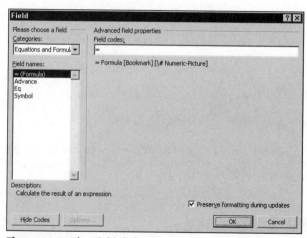

Figure 11-4: The Field dialog box with the Formula field selected.

Word has two special bookmarks that help you to address envelopes. If you have more than one address in a document, select the one that you want for the delivery address and create a bookmark called EnvelopeAddress. Then select the address that you want for the return address and create a bookmark called EnvelopeReturn. This way, when you choose Tools ⇨ Envelopes and Labels, the text included in these bookmarks is placed in the delivery and return address windows, respectively.

The problem with bookmarks

Perhaps the most irritating problem with bookmarks that you can't see is adding text to the bookmark without realizing you are doing it. Suppose you create a bookmark and then create a cross-reference to the bookmark. Later, you go to the bookmark and add more text immediately after it. In some cases you may actually be typing the text *inside* the bookmark, if you can't see the bookmark marker.

Later, when you update the fields in your document, your cross-reference will change. You may end up pulling in much more text than you intended. This is particularly a problem with headings, though unfortunately headings are hidden bookmarks. (Remember the Hidden Bookmarks check box in the Bookmarks dialog box? If you have created cross-references to headings, when you check this box you'll see a lot of strange numbers; these are the automatically created hidden bookmarks.) When you create a cross-reference to a header, Word creates a special bookmark around that header, but it *doesn't* mark them like real bookmarks, so regardless of the View settings you can never see the start and end of the bookmark. This has two effects:

✦ First, when you modify the heading by adding text to it, you may not be modifying the bookmark, so the cross-references will not update with the modifications. You can get around this problem by only modifying bookmarked headers by typing *inside* the header, never at the end. For instance, if you want to change the heading *Managing Your Document* to *Managing Your Documents*, don't simply type the *s* on the end; there's a good chance it won't be included in the bookmark. Rather, place the insertion point after the *n* in *Document*, type **ts**, and then delete the *t* at the end.

✦ The other problem is the opposite. When you add text after a heading, but you *don't* want to include that text in the bookmark on the heading, sometimes Word, just to be contrary, does so. This doesn't happen often, but it does happen. You may find that Word has duplicated a large block of text in your document, and when you go to the first few words of this duplicated block you discover that it begins with a cross-reference you set . . . but that the bookmark has extended paragraphs, perhaps pages, longer. Fixing the problem is easy. Delete the cross-reference and reset it. To avoid this problem is more difficult, because you can't see what's going on. Try not to add text immediately after a bookmarked heading; it usually isn't a problem, but sometimes it is.

Tip   Here's another thing you may want to avoid — automatically numbering headers throughout the document. These have been a long-term problem with Word. It's safer to manually number major headings in a document.

Working with Cross-References

Cross-references tell readers where to look for more information. For example, placed throughout this chapter are several cross-references that direct you to other chapters for more details on a subject. To direct you to the chapter that discusses sections, you can just type **See Chapter 10**. But what if a chapter gets added or deleted, and the chapter on sections is no longer Chapter 10? Going back and changing every reference to that chapter—as well as to any other chapter—could be a major headache.

Cross-referencing comes to the rescue. If, instead of typing **See Chapter 10**, you type **See** and then insert a cross-reference code that links to the heading of the chapter that you want to reference, Word can update the reference number automatically—no matter how many times that number changes. You can even create a cross-reference to a particular section name, on a particular page, and Word will update the section name and the page number if necessary.

You can cross-reference the following items:

✦ Numbered items (paragraphs in numbered lists—see Chapter 5)

✦ Headings that use one of Word's built-in heading styles

✦ Bookmarked items

✦ Footnotes and endnotes

✦ Captions associated with equations, figures, and tables

Cross-references are inserted as fields, so all the field information discussed earlier in this chapter applies.

Creating in-document cross-references

Creating a cross-reference is a simple matter of typing some fixed text and then inserting a reference to the item.

A cross-reference can include multiple references. For example, you could say "See Chapter 10 on page 263." In this example, you would type **See**, insert a reference to the chapter number, and then type **on page** and insert a reference to the page number on which the chapter heading appears.

You can also use cross-referencing to insert a chapter name or number inside your header or footer. Open the header or footer area, place your insertion point where you want to insert the reference, and follow these steps:

1. Place your insertion point where you want the cross-reference to appear. Make sure that your insertion point ends up at the exact spot where you want the cross-reference inserted.

2. Choose Insert ⇨ Reference ⇨ Cross-reference. The Cross-reference dialog box, as shown in Figure 11-5, appears.

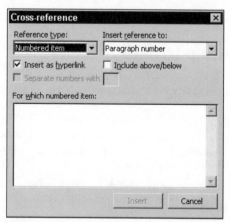

Figure 11-5: The Cross-reference dialog box lets you choose from several reference types.

3. Select the Heading category in the Reference Type drop-down list.

The For Which and Insert Reference To lists are modified depending on the Reference Type that you select. For example, if your Reference Type is Heading, the For Which list includes all of the headings in your document (assuming they were created using Word's default styles), while the Insert Reference To list displays different types of information that you can insert at the bookmark point—the Heading Text or Page Number, for instance.

4. Select an option from the Insert Reference To drop-down list to specify the information that should be inserted in the cross-reference. Note that each reference category contains a Page Number option, with which you can refer to the page where the referenced item occurs.

5. Specify the exact reference that you want from the For Which list. For example, if you choose Bookmark as the reference type, the For Which Bookmark list then contains a list of all bookmarks in the document.

6. Click Insert. The Cross-reference dialog box remains open so that you can add additional information to your reference or even additional references. (You can click in the document and move around, while the box remains open.)

7. When you are finished, close the Cross-reference dialog box.

Another option in the Cross-reference dialog box, Insert As Hyperlink, allows you to jump quickly to the referenced item in the same document. You'll be able to point at the cross-reference, press Ctrl, and click the mouse button to jump to the referenced information (a very useful feature, so you'll probably want to leave it turned on).

The Include Above/Below option adds the word *above* or *below* to refer to the location of the referenced item relative to the cross-reference (for example, *See Table 4 above*).

Tip   To create cross-references across document boundaries, all of the involved documents must be part of a master document. For more information about working with master documents, see Chapter 25.

Keeping cross-references up to date

Cross-references are inserted as fields. They are updated automatically whenever you print your document. You can also update them at any time using standard field updating techniques. With your insertion point in a cross-reference field, press F9 to update that field. Or, select the entire document and then press F9 to update all fields in that document.

The introductory text for a cross-reference can be revised just like any other text. If your fields are shaded, as suggested at the beginning of this chapter, you can easily tell where the introductory text ends and the cross-reference field begins.

You can change the reference information for a particular reference by selecting that reference, choosing Insert ➪ Reference ➪ Cross-reference, and then making any changes that you want in the Cross-reference dialog box.

Note   When you insert a cross-reference, Word creates a bookmark at the reference's location. For more information about bookmarks, see the "Working with Bookmarks" section earlier in this chapter.

Types of cross-references

Table 11-2 shows the types of information to which you can cross-reference using the Insert Reference To list.

Table 11-2: The Insert Reference To List

Choice	Action
For Numbered Items:	
Page Number	The number of the page on which the numbered item is found.
Paragraph Number	The number of the numbered item, taking into consideration the relative position of the cross-reference to the numbered item. For instance, if the cross-reference to the numbered item is 2.(b)(iii), and is placed in numbered item 2.(b)(i), the reference will be to (iii). If the cross-reference is in 2.(c)(i), the reference will be to (b)(iii).
Paragraph Number (no context)	The cross-reference will have no context whatsoever. If referring to paragraph 2.(b)(iii) the cross-reference will simply show (iii), regardless of where the cross-reference is placed.
Paragraph Number (full context)	The cross-reference will always show the full paragraph number, regardless of where the cross-reference is placed.
Paragraph Text	The text appearing in the referenced numbered item.
Above/Below	The word *above* or *below*, depending on the direction to the referenced numbered item.
For Heading Text:	
Heading Text	The actual heading text.
Page Number	The number of the page on which the bookmark is found.
Heading Number	Works in the same way as for Numbered Items. The actual cross-reference shown depends on the position of the cross-reference in relation to the header.
Heading Number (no context)	Works in the same way as for Numbered Items. The cross-reference always shows the sub-heading number, regardless of the position of the cross-reference in relation to the header.
Heading Number (full context)	Works in the same way as for Numbered Items. The cross-reference always shows the full heading number, regardless of the position of the cross-reference in relation to the header.
Above/Below	The word *above* or *below*, depending on the direction to the referenced heading.
For Bookmarks:	
Bookmark Text	The text within the bookmark markers.
Page Number	The number of the page on which the bookmark is found.

Continued

Table 11-2 *(continued)*

Choice	Action
Paragraph Number	See Paragraph Number above, under Numbered Items.
Paragraph Number (no context)	See Paragraph Number (No Context) above, under Numbered Items.
Paragraph Number (full context)	See Paragraph Number (Full Context) above, under Numbered Items.
Above/Below	The word *above* or *below*, depending on the direction to the referenced bookmark.
For Footnotes and Endnotes:	
Footnote/Endnote Number	The footnote or endnote number.
Page Number	The number of the page on which the footnote or endnote is found.
Above/Below	The word *above* or *below*, depending on the direction to the referenced footnote or endnote.
Footnote/Endnote Number (formatted)	The footnote or endnote number, displayed using the normal small font used for footnote and endnote numbers.
For Captions (Equations, Figures, Tables):	
Entire Caption	All the caption is transferred—label, number, and text.
Only Label and Number	Only the caption label and number is transferred.
Only Caption Text	Only the caption text is transferred.
Page Number	The number of the page on which the caption is found.
Above/Below	The word *above* or *below*, depending on the direction to the referenced caption.

Working with Footnotes and Endnotes

Footnotes and endnotes are additional explanatory information added to the bottom of the page, or the end of a section or document, related to something in the document's main text. For instance, you might mention a newspaper article in the main text and use a footnote to provide more details about the article. If you do any academic or business writing, you probably deal with footnotes and endnotes. Word cannot help you to compose your text, but it can streamline every other aspect of the process.

Every footnote and endnote includes a reference in the document text as well as the footnote or endnote itself. The reference in the text is usually a number, but it can also be a letter or any other symbol. The only difference between footnotes and endnotes is that footnotes appear on the same page as the material they reference, whereas endnotes appear at the end of a section or document.

Creating footnotes and endnotes

Creating a footnote or endnote involves two steps: inserting the reference in your document text, and writing the note itself. You can change many footnote and endnote options (such as positioning, formatting, numbering style, and so on), but the basic technique for inserting a footnote or endnote is always the same.

To create a footnote or endnote, follow these steps:

1. Either place the insertion point exactly where you want the footnote/endnote reference to appear—probably after the text you want to explain—or select text (in which case Word will place the reference immediately after the text anyway).

2. Choose Insert ⇨ Reference ⇨ Footnote.

   Note that you make the same menu selection whether you're creating a footnote or an endnote. The resulting Footnote and Endnote dialog box, as shown in Figure 11-6, allows you to specify which type of note to insert.

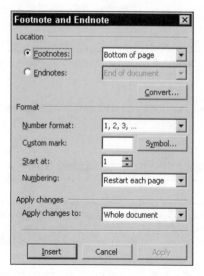

Figure 11-6: The Footnote and Endnote dialog box helps to define the note and to set the numbering style.

3. Select Footnote or Endnote.

4. Press Enter.

5. Word inserts a reference number and moves you to the position at which you will type your footnote or endnote (if you are in Normal view, Word opens a special footnotes pane, as shown in Figure 11-7).

6. Type the text for your note.

7. Click Close to close the note pane.

Tip   Double-clicking a footnote or endnote mark in any view displays the note.

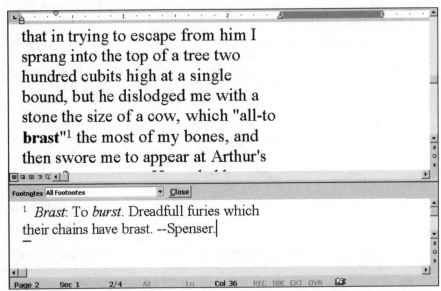

Figure 11-7: In Normal view, you enter footnote or endnote text in the note pane at the bottom of the screen.

As you saw, the Footnote and Endnote dialog box provides various options for creating your notes. These are explained in Table 11-3.

Table 11-3: The Footnote and Endnote Dialog Box

Component Name	Action
Convert	Click this button and you'll see a small dialog box in which you can choose to convert all footnotes to endnotes, all endnotes to footnotes, or to swap them—footnotes become endnotes and endnotes become footnotes.
Number Format	Select from a variety of different numbering formats for your footnote and endnote references: roman numerals, small letters, capital letters, symbols, and so on.
Custom Mark	You can type a character in here if you wish to specify a character to be used for the footnote or endnote you are creating.
Symbol	Click this button to select a symbol for the reference character.
Start At	If using one of the numbering formats for the references, you can specify which number, letter, or symbol Word should begin with.
Numbering	You can choose whether to use continuous numbering throughout your document, or whether to restart numbering at the beginning of every section or page.
Apply Changes To	Define where your changes should apply—in most cases you'll want to select Whole Document.

Note Word doesn't update custom reference marks. For example, if you change a footnote reference mark to an asterisk, that footnote mark remains an asterisk no matter how many footnotes are later added or deleted. In addition, the custom setting applies only to that individual footnote. If you want to assign a custom mark to additional footnotes or endnotes, you must do so individually.

By the way, Word's footnotes and endnote formats do not follow any kind of industry standard; but then, that's a pretty gray area anyway. Each publisher has its own preferences for the way these things are laid out. If you are using footnotes and endnotes for internal use, use whatever you want. If you are submitting to another organization, you should check with them to see what format they use.

Keeping footnotes and endnotes in view

One way to work with footnotes or endnotes is to keep the note pane open (View ➪ Footnotes) as you work on the document. The note pane then scrolls with your document so that you can always see any notes that are referenced in the visible portion of your document. You can switch back and forth between your document and the note pane by clicking in either pane or pressing F6.

When the note pane is open, you can specify whether to view footnotes, endnotes, or both by choosing the appropriate option from the drop-down list in the note pane menu bar. If the note pane isn't open, you can use one of the following methods to view your notes:

✦ Double-click any footnote or endnote reference mark to open the pane and view the note. Double-clicking any note reference in the note pane closes the pane and returns your insertion point to the location of the reference mark for that particular note in your document.

✦ Hold the Shift key as you drag the split box on the vertical scroll bar. This opens the note pane so that you can view or edit your notes. Close the note pane by double-clicking the split box or dragging the split bar up until the pane disappears.

✦ Choose View ➪ Footnotes.

If your document includes both footnotes and endnotes, you can switch between the two types in the note pane by selecting All Footnotes or All Endnotes from the Notes drop-down list in the note pane menu bar.

Moving to footnotes and endnotes

With or without the note pane being open, you can scroll through all of your footnotes or endnotes using the object scroll buttons at the bottom of the vertical scroll bars. Click the Select Browse Object button, and select Browse by Footnote (or Endnote) from the pop-up palette (see Figure 11-8). Then click the Next or Previous buttons to scroll through the notes sequentially. If the insertion point is in the document pane, it moves to the next (or the previous) note mark; if the insertion point is in the note pane, it moves to the next (or the previous) note.

Figure 11-8: The Select Browse Object pop-up palette with Browse by Footnote selected.

What if you want to locate a particular note or return to a particular reference location in your document? The following exercise answers the first question. As for the second, double-click any note reference, either in the note pane or in the note area in Print Layout view, and Word returns you to the reference mark for that note in your document.

To find footnotes or endnotes using the Go To command, follow these steps:

1. Choose Edit ⇨ Go To.

2. Select Footnote or Endnote in the Go to What list.

3. Do one of the following:

   • To jump to the next or the preceding footnote or endnote, click Next or Previous.

   • To move to a specific footnote or endnote, type a number in the Enter Footnote Number text box.

4. Click Close.

You can also choose Edit ⇨ Find to locate footnotes and endnotes. In the Find dialog box, select Footnote Mark or Endnote Mark from the Special pop-up list. (To see the Special button, you may need to click the More button.) You cannot use this method to find a specific footnote number, but you can keep clicking Find Next to cycle through all of the footnotes or endnotes in your document until you find the one that you want.

Modifying footnotes and endnotes

Unless you specify otherwise, all footnote and endnote text is formatted in a 10-point font. Footnotes use a built-in style called Footnote Text; endnotes use a built-in style called Endnote Text. The default font size for reference marks is also 10 points, and the style names are Footnote Reference and Endnote Reference. To modify any of these styles, choose Format ⇨ Style, select the style that you want to change, click Modify, and then click Format. Make your desired changes, and click OK. Click Apply in the Style dialog box to make your changes to the style. For more information about working with styles, see Chapter 13.

Modifying a footnote or an endnote style affects all of the footnotes or endnotes for a particular document, but you can also edit the text or change the formatting of specific footnotes or endnotes just as you can for any other text in Word. With your insertion point in the note pane, scroll to the note that you want to work with and then change it using the toolbars, ruler, or any of Word's menus or keystroke commands.

Manipulating footnotes and endnotes

Deleting a footnote or an endnote is as simple as selecting the reference mark in the document and then pressing Delete or Backspace. Moving or copying a selected reference mark also moves or copies the associated footnote or endnote text. You can use any of Word's cut, copy, and paste commands. When you move, copy, or delete footnotes or endnotes, Word automatically renumbers the notes in your document to reflect these changes.

Note   You *cannot* simply select everything in the footnote/endnote pane and press Delete to get rid of them.

You can delete all of the footnotes or endnotes in a document using the Replace feature. Choose Edit ⇨ Replace, select Endnote Mark (^e) or Footnote Mark (^f) from the Special pop-up list, leave the Replace With text box blank, and then click Replace All.

Converting footnotes to endnotes, and vice versa

With any electronic document, everything is subject to change. All of your carefully positioned footnotes may look great, but what happens when the powers-that-be decide that all footnotes should appear at the end of your document as endnotes? Simple. Just open the Footnotes and Endnotes dialog box, click the Convert button, choose what you want to convert (footnotes to endnotes, endnotes to footnotes, or swap), and click OK. But what about converting notes one at a time? To convert individual footnotes or endnotes, follow these steps:

1. Make sure that the note text is visible, either through the note pane in Normal view or on the page in Print Layout view.

2. With your insertion point anywhere in the note that you want to convert, click the right mouse button to open the Footnotes shortcut menu.

3. Choose Convert to Footnote or Convert to Endnote, as applicable.

Moving footnotes and endnotes

You can make two changes to the placement of footnotes and endnotes. First, you can tell Word that you want your footnotes to follow right after the last text on the page instead of appearing at the bottom of the page. Second, you can direct endnotes to appear at the end of each section instead of all together at the end of the document.

To change the placement of footnotes and endnotes, follow these steps:

1. Right-click in the footnote or endnote and choose Note Options from the shortcut menu.

2. Select a position from the drop-down list box near the top of the dialog box.

3. Click the Apply button.

Note When you use the master document feature (as described in Chapter 25), Word automatically numbers footnotes and endnotes consecutively across subdocuments.

Changing footnote and endnote separators

You can change the appearance of separators and continuation separator lines—and you can even get rid of them altogether. These lines appear between the main text and the footnote and endnote texts (the continuation separator is a line that appears above a footnote or endnote that is continued from the previous page). In addition, you can modify the continuation notice, text that appears at the bottom of a footnote or endnote explaining that the text is continued on the next page.

Note that these changes must be made in Normal view. You cannot edit separator lines in Print Layout view.

To change footnote and endnote separators and continuation notices, follow these steps:

1. Switch to Normal view.

2. Choose View ➪ Footnotes to open the notes pane.

3. Choose All Footnotes or All Endnotes, as applicable, from the notes drop-down list to view your footnotes or endnotes.

4. Choose one of the following from the notes drop-down list:

    • Footnote Separator or Endnote Separator to edit the separator line.

    • Footnote Continuation Separator or Endnote Continuation Separator to edit the continuation separator line.

    • Footnote Continuation Notice or Endnote Continuation Notice to edit the continuation-notice text.

5. Do one of the following:

    • Edit the separator by making any changes you want.

    • Delete the separator by selecting it and pressing Delete or Backspace.

    • Add a continuation notice.

6. Close the notes pane when you finish.

You can return to the default separators at any time by clicking the Reset button at the top of the notes pane.

Note   When you save a document with footnotes or endnotes in HTML, Word automatically converts them to hyperlinks and places footnotes at the end of the HTML file. Any endnotes are placed immediately after the footnotes. Short, horizontal lines separate the main text from the footnotes and the footnotes from the endnotes. Custom separators appear on the Web page.

Placing Links in Your Document

Although this is mainly a Web-page feature, Word lets you place links in your documents, a feature that you may find useful if you are in the habit of sharing documents mainly electronically rather than on paper.

Simply choose Insert ➪ Hyperlink and the Insert Hyperlink box opens (see Figure 11-9). The large list box displays all your headings and bookmarks. Select one of these, and click OK, to copy the heading into your text in the form of an active hyperlink—clicking on the link takes you to that part of the document.

Alternatively, you can specify the text that appears in your document as the link. For instance, you might type **Click here to go to the calculations, Joe!** in the Text To Display box at the top of the Hyperlink dialog box and then select a heading. Joe will be able to click on that text to get to the referenced area of the document.

Why use this feature rather than a cross-reference? It's simply quicker and easier if all you want to do is create an active link within your document.

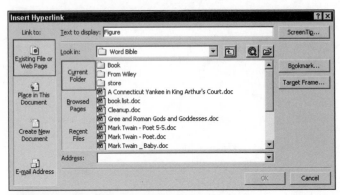

Figure 11-9: The Insert Hyperlink dialog box.

Summary

This chapter has covered many of the tools operating in the background of the document preparation process and taught you how to do the following:

✦ Add reference bookmarks and cross-references to your documents.

✦ Include and customize footnotes and endnotes in your documents.

✦ Quickly create links within your documents.

✦ ✦ ✦

Creating Indexes and Tables of Contents

In This Chapter

Creating indexes

Creating tables of contents

Creating tables of figures, tables of authorities, and other tables

Indexes and tables of contents are valuable additions to long documents. Readers can thumb through the table of contents to determine which sections interest them, and readers can zero in on a specific topic with a well-planned index. You can also create tables that list figures, charts, equations, or any other document items. The indexing and tables features in Word make it easy to add these important finishing touches to your documents.

Adding Indexes to Your Documents

In global terms, creating an index involves two steps. First, you mark all of the items in your document that you want included in the index. Second, you instruct Word to assemble the index from the marked entries. Index entries are contained in the XE field, and the information for the index itself is contained in the INDEX field. (You don't have to know a lot about fields at this stage, but you can learn more about them in Chapter 23.)

Tip

If you're creating your index from a master document, doing your index work in the master document itself is easier than doing the work in the individual documents. Working in the master document helps to ensure that index items are marked consistently and that the page number references in the index are accurate. You learn more about master documents in Chapter 25.

Creating, formatting, and modifying index entries

Before Word can assemble your index, you first must specify which items you want to be referenced in that index. The easiest way to mark index entries in your document is with a concordance file, which is a standard, two-column Word table containing all of the words or phrases that you want to include. You type all of the words or phrases, tell Word how you want those items to be listed in the index, and then let Word use the concordance file to search through your document and mark all occurrences of the items that you listed.

No matter how thorough you are in creating your concordance file, however, you cannot avoid the tedious task of combing through your document and individually marking those items that you may have missed. For example, even if you include *banned in Boston* and *Banned in Boston* in your concordance file, your document may include a reference to the event without using one of these precise phrases. You may have used the word *banned* in a paragraph and the word *Boston* somewhere later in that paragraph. But because the phrase *banned in Boston* is not used, no reference to this paragraph appears in your index unless you mark it separately.

In addition, because the concordance file marks every occurrence of the listed items, you may end up with some items being marked that really shouldn't be. There may be places in the document where a word or a phrase is used without relating to the topic that you want to index.

The best indexing technique is to start by creating a concordance file that's as inclusive as possible. Then add manual index entries as necessary while deleting any unneeded ones.

Tip   Plan your index carefully. Indexing is an art: no automated indexing feature, regardless of its power, can replace careful planning and design. You must go through your document and determine which index layout best serves your readers, so ask yourself some of the following questions: How detailed does the index need to be? Should cross-references be included to refer readers to other topics? Would multilevel categories make it easier for readers to find information? After settling these issues, make a list of all the index topics and then decide how you want each item to appear in that index. This chapter describes how to accomplish your goals using Word's indexing tools, but the more clear your goals are at the outset, the more useful your index will be.

Marking index entries automatically

Using a concordance file involves two steps: creating the file, and using the file to mark entries. Don't worry about alphabetizing the items as you create your concordance file. Word takes care of that job when it creates the index itself.

To create a concordance file, follow these steps:

1. Open a new document window by choosing File ➪ New and then Blank Document in the New Document task pane or by clicking New on the Standard toolbar.

2. Choose Table ➪ Insert ➪ Table to open the Insert Table dialog box.

3. Type **2** in the Number of Columns box and any number other than zero in the Number of Rows box. Then click OK.

4. In the first column of the new table, type the word or phrase that you want to index and then press Tab to move to the second column.

   The word or phrase in the first column must be the exact word or phrase, capitalized and punctuated exactly as it appears in your document, for which you want Word to search. For example, if *Up in Michigan* and *up in Michigan* are both used in your document and you want them both to be indexed, you must include them as two separate entries in your concordance file.

5. In the second column, type the index entry exactly as you want it to appear in the index. Then press Tab to move to the next row or to create a new row.

   The main index entry may not be the same as the item in the first column. Proper names are one area in which your document text (the first column entry) probably differs from the resulting index entry (the second column entry). In an index, proper names are usually listed with the last name first. Therefore, you can list *Ernest Hemingway* in the first column and *Hemingway, Ernest* in the second.

The document text may also differ from the index entry in the case of subentries. For example, you may want *Kansas City Star* to appear in your index as a subentry under *Hemingway, Ernest*. To do this, type **Hemingway, Ernest:Kansas City Star** in the second column. The colon tells Word to insert the second item as a subentry. You can have as many as nine levels of subentries, and you separate each level with a colon.

6. Repeat steps 3 and 4 for each index reference and entry.

7. After you complete your entries, you should spell check and proofread the file before you use it to mark your document.

8. Save the file as a standard Word document. Figure 12-1 shows a sample concordance file.

Three Stories and Ten Poems	early years first published work
Kansas City Star	early years Kansas City Star
Up in Michigan	early years first published work
The Torrents of Spring	first novel
Key West	in Key West
To Have and Have Not	political awakenings
war correspondent	political awakenings war correspondent
World War I	political awakenings war correspondent
Pulitzer Prize	Old Man and the Sea
Nobel Prize	Nobel Prize
A Moveable Feast	posthumous works
Dangerous Summer	posthumous works

Figure 12-1: A sample concordance file.

Tip You can streamline the creation of a concordance file by copying and pasting document text that you want to index instead of typing the text directly in the concordance table. Copying text can also reduce the potential for errors. Whenever you type new text, you open yourself to the possibility of typographical errors. With a concordance file, even something as seemingly insignificant as a lowercase letter that should really be an uppercase letter can prevent Word from finding and marking that text for your index entry.

If you plan to copy text from an existing document into your concordance file, the easiest way is to open both files and then choose Window ➪ Arrange All. With this command, both document windows are visible, and you can copy text from one document to the other.

After you create a concordance file, you can use it to mark index entries in a document automatically:

1. Open the document that you want to mark.

2. Choose Insert ➪ Reference ➪ Index and Tables, and then select the Index tab. The Index and Tables dialog box appears (see Figure 12-2).

3. Click AutoMark. The Open Index AutoMark File dialog box appears.

4. Select the name of the concordance file that you want to use.

5. Click Open.

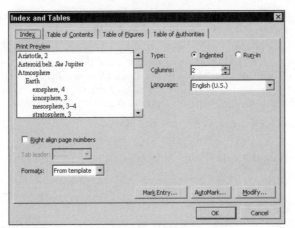

Figure 12-2: The Index tab in the Index and Tables dialog box.

Word proceeds to insert each marked index entry as an index entry (XE) field. Click the Show/Hide button on the Standard toolbar to see the field codes. Go through the document and check to see that the entries have been added in the manner you wanted, and remove any that you feel are not correct or necessary.

Marking index entries manually

After you create your concordance file and use it to mark your document, go through the document to find any items that you missed. If the entry that you want to mark is exactly the way that you want it to appear in the index, just select the text before you create the entry. Alternatively, simply place your insertion point at the location of the text and then type the entry directly in the Mark Index Entry text box, following this procedure:

1. Select the text that you want to mark, or position your insertion point where you want to insert the index entry.

2. Press Alt+Shift+X to open the Mark Index Entry dialog box (see Figure 12-3), or choose Insert ➪ Reference ➪ Index and Tables and then click Mark Entry in the Index tab in the Index and Tables dialog box.

Figure 12-3: The Mark Index Entry dialog box.

3. If you selected text before accessing the Mark Entry dialog box, Word places that text in the Main Entry text box. Type any new text or edit the existing text as needed. You can add character formatting to any portion of the entry by selecting the text that you want to format and then pressing Ctrl+B for bold, Ctrl+I for italic, or Ctrl+U for underline.

Tip You can press Ctrl+D while in this dialog box to open the Font dialog box so that you can have further control over the font format used.

4. To create a subentry, type it in the Subentry text box. (Working with subentries and with sub-subentries is discussed later in this chapter.)

5. By default, the index entry refers only to the current page. Select one of the other choices in the Options area if desired:

   • Select Cross-reference to create a cross-reference for the entry. (See the section "Cross-referencing index entries" later in this chapter for instructions on creating index cross-references.)

   • Select Page Range and then a bookmark name (or type a new bookmark name) if you want the entry to refer to a range of pages. (See the section "Using page ranges in index entries" later in this chapter for instructions on referencing page ranges.)

6. Select Bold or Italic from the Page Number Format area to define how the number will be formatted.

7. Do one of the following:

   • Click Mark to mark the entry.

   • Click Mark All to have Word mark every place that it finds the text. (It won't mark more than one occurrence of an item in each paragraph, so you don't have to worry about a bunch of extra entry codes.) If you choose this option, the status bar tells you how many entries were marked. Note that this option is case-sensitive: Word marks only instances that match your entry exactly. If, for example, you specify the index entry as *book sales,* clicking Mark All doesn't mark any instances where the phrase appears as *Book Sales.*

8. Mark additional entries by repeating steps 1 through 7. You can move between the Mark Index Entry dialog box and the document editing area by clicking in either area.

9. When you complete marking index entries, close the Mark Index Entry dialog box.

Note If the text that you select for an index entry contains a colon, Word adds a backslash in front of that colon in the Main Entry box. Because Word uses a colon to indicate an index subentry, the backslash tells Word that the colon should be inserted in the index as regular text. If you type the entry from scratch, be sure to type a backslash in front of any colons that you want to include. In addition, if your index entry includes quotation marks, Word adds backslashes in front of each mark in the entry field. (The backslash doesn't appear in the Main Entry box, however.) Field text is enclosed in quotation marks, so the backslash is necessary to direct Word to insert the quotation marks as text.

When you click Mark All, Word displays all of the hidden text as well as any other nonprinting characters in your document, and it doesn't close the dialog box when it finishes marking. This quirk isn't a real problem, but it could be confusing if you don't know what's happening. To stop displaying hidden text and nonprinting characters after clicking Mark All, just click the Show/Hide button on the Standard toolbar.

In some cases, you may want to include an individual symbol in the document index. To mark a symbol, select it and press Alt+Shift+X to open the Mark Index Entry dialog box. Then, in the Main Entry box, type the symbol and then type ;# (semicolon followed by a number sign) immediately after it. Finally, click Mark and OK. Word then places symbols in the index first (before any alphabetical entries).

Using page ranges in index entries

In many cases, you may want an index entry to reference a range of pages, such as *Hemingway in Spain, 33–38*. Before you can have such an entry, however, you must create a bookmark that refers to the specified pages. Steps 1 to 3 below lead you through the process of creating a bookmark for your page range; if you've already created a bookmark, skip to step 4.

Cross-Reference   For more information on creating bookmarks, see Chapter 11.

To use a range of pages in an index entry, follow these steps:

1. Select the pages with the text that you want to refer to in the index entry.

2. Choose Insert ➪ Reference ➪ Bookmark.

3. Type a name for the bookmark in the Bookmark Name box of the Bookmark dialog box, and then click Add.

4. Select the text that you want to mark as an index entry, or position your insertion point where you want to insert the index entry.

5. Press Alt+Shift+X to open the Mark Index Entry dialog box.

6. If necessary, type any new text or edit the existing text in the Main Entry text box.

7. To create a subentry, type it in the Subentry text box.

8. Choose Page Range and then type the name of the bookmark in the Bookmark text box, or select the bookmark's name from the drop-down list.

9. Click Mark and then Close if you're through marking index entries. The text now shows the XE field code followed by the text that you entered, an \r *switch*, and the name of your bookmark. (Switches are discussed later in this chapter.) Click the Show/Hide button on the Standard toolbar to remove the field code from the display.

Cross-referencing index entries

Use the following steps to insert text that directs a reader to another location in the index. When you use a cross-reference, the cross-reference text replaces the page number that normally appears in the index.

To create a cross-reference for an index entry, follow these steps:

1. Follow steps 1 through 4 in the earlier task, "Marking index entries manually."

2. In the Mark Index Entry dialog box, select Cross-reference.

3. Type the text for the cross-reference in the Cross-reference text box. Word automatically inserts the word *See* in italics because in most cases you want the reference to begin with *See* (for example, "*See* Hemingway's early years"). You can add your text after *See*, or you can delete *See* and start from scratch.

4. Click Mark to mark an individual entry, or click Mark All to mark all occurrences of the entry text.

Creating multilevel indexes

In many cases, breaking an index entry into levels can make it easier for readers to locate specific topics. Look at the following entry that lists all of the references to Ernest Hemingway:

> Hemingway 5, 33, 59, 160

These references don't give the reader any information beyond Hemingway being mentioned on each of the referenced pages. Now look at this entry:

> Hemingway
> > early years 5
> > > first published work 26
> > in Key West 33
> > as war correspondent 59
> > Nobel Prize 160

The second example uses multiple levels to more clearly delineate the topics. Creating multilevel entries is not difficult. As with the entire indexing process, however, it requires some planning. You must decide exactly how your entries should appear: what the main headings should be, and how detailed the subheadings should be. You must also be consistent as you mark the headings or create your concordance file.

To create a multilevel entry when marking an index entry manually, insert text in both the Main Entry and Subentry text boxes in the Mark Index Entry dialog box. To create the index entry for Hemingway's early years, type **Hemingway** in the Main Entry text box and **early years** in the Subentry text box.

You can have as many as nine levels of subentries. You can add additional subentries in the Subentry text box by separating each entry with a colon. For example, to add a subsubentry of *first published work* under *early years*, type **early years:first published work** in the Subentry text box.

You can create multilevel entries in a concordance file, too, by placing colons between the main entry and each level of the subentries. To insert the entry in the previous paragraph into a concordance file, type **Hemingway:early years:first published work** in the second column next to the first-column item containing the document text that you want to index.

Note You must make sure your spelling is correct throughout. If you misspell the Main Entry for some of the cases in which you create Subentries, you will end up placing Subentries under multiple Main Entries.

Formatting index entries

As you create an entry, you can select text in the Main Entry or Subentry text boxes in the Mark Index Entry dialog box and apply character formatting to that text. You can also apply formatting directly to the text within an existing XE (index entry) field. If you format the text in the Mark Index Entry dialog box, however, you're limited to the Ctrl+B (bold), Ctrl+I (italic), and Ctrl+U (underline) shortcut keys. You cannot access menus or toolbars from within a dialog box.

To make character formatting changes beyond the addition of bold, italic, or underline, select the text in the XE field and then select the formatting options that you want. If your index entries are not visible, you can display hidden text by clicking the Show/Hide button on the Standard toolbar or by choosing Hidden Text in the Formatting Marks area of the View tab in the Options dialog box.

When you edit text in the index entry field, you can access all of Word's standard character-formatting options that are accessible through the Formatting toolbar or when choosing Format ⇨ Font. Any character formatting that you add to an individual index entry is retained when you update the index or change its style.

Modifying index entry fields

An XE field contains all of the information defining an index entry and how it appears in the index. Table 12-1 lists *switches* that can modify the field to customize your entries. A switch is a *modifier,* a way to provide additional information. Each switch is preceded with the \ symbol—this is simply a way of telling Word that what follows is a switch.

Many of these switches are inserted automatically when you mark an index entry. Table 12-1 also helps you recognize switches that may already be present in your index entry fields, and it provides options for modifying these switches. Note, however, that you cannot use general switches that modify the format of, or prevent changes to, the field results in XE fields.

Table 12-1: Switches for the XE Field

Switch	What It Does
\b	Applies bold formatting to the page number for the index entry.
\f	Allows you to create subindexes containing only one type of index entry. This is used in conjunction with the \f switch for the INDEX field (which is the field that creates that actual index rather than the index entries). Add a space followed by a letter enclosed in quotation marks after this switch in some XE fields, and the same thing in an INDEX field, to compile an index consisting of only those XE fields.
\i	Applies italic formatting to the page number for the index entry. If the index style for the entry is already set to italic, this switch *removes* the italic formatting for that entry.
\r	This switch is followed by a space and a bookmark name enclosed in quotation marks, and directs Word to include the range of pages marked by the specified bookmark in the index entry. Word inserts this switch when you select Page Range and specify a bookmark name in the Mark Index Entry dialog box.

Switch	What It Does
\t	This switch is always followed by text and directs Word to use the specified text instead of a page number for the index entry. The text following this switch must be enclosed in quotation marks. Word inserts this switch when you add a cross-reference in the Mark Index Entry dialog box.
\y	This is a barely documented switch designed for use with Yomi (far east) languages. It's placed into the field by itself, with no additional information, and tells Word to use different sorting rules for these languages.

You can modify switches or insert new ones within a field just as you can add or edit any other text. To add switches or modify existing switches in an index entry field, place your insertion point anywhere in that field. Word inserts index entry fields as hidden text, so if you don't see any XE fields, click the Show/Hide button on the Standard toolbar or choose Tools ➪ Options and select Hidden Text on the View tab. Then you can move your insertion point inside the field and add or delete any text or switches as desired.

Formatting and compiling an index

After you mark your index entries, either manually or with the help of a concordance, you're ready to format and compile the index itself. Follow these steps:

1. Position your insertion point where you want the index to appear. If you're indexing a master document, switch to Master Document view and make sure that your insertion point is not inside a subdocument (see Chapter 25). If you want the index to begin on a new page, insert a page break in front of your insertion point.

2. Choose Insert ➪ Reference ➪ Index and Tables, and then click the Index tab.

3. Make one of the following selections in the Type area:

   - Indented to indent subentries under main entries.

   - Run-in to place subentries on the same line as the main entry (entries wrap to a second line as required).

4. Select a format from the Formats list. The Print Preview box displays a sample of the selected format so that you can see how your index appears in that format.

5. Make selections in the following areas as desired:

   - Type a number in the Columns text box if you want the index to be formatted in more than the default, two-column layout (enter **1** if you don't want the index formatted in multiple columns).

   - Select Language to choose a different language if necessary. The list includes the enabled editing languages and the languages installed with Word.

   - Select Right Align Page Numbers if you want the page numbers to be aligned with the right edge of each column (or with the right margin if the index is not formatted in columns).

   - Select the Tab leader style if you want to place a line between the text and the right-aligned page number. You can choose a dashed, dotted, or solid line. This option is dimmed unless Right Align Page Numbers is selected.

6. Click OK. Word repaginates the document and creates the index at the location of your insertion point. The index is formatted as a separate section, so you can use any of Word's section formatting options to work with it. Figure 12-4 shows a sample index with the section marker displayed.

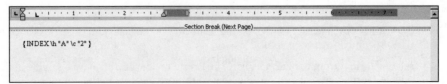

A

Africa, *See Green Hills of Africa*

E

early years
    first published works, 2
    Kansas City Star, 4

F

first novel, 7

I

in Key West, 12

P

political awakenings, 17
    war correspondent, 25

Figure 12-4: A sample index with the section marker displayed.

The entire index is actually a field (INDEX). If you press Shift+F9 with your insertion point anywhere inside the index, you can view the field code (see Figure 12-5). The INDEX field switches are described later in this chapter.

{ INDEX \h "A" \c "2" }

Figure 12-5: The field code for the sample index.

Tip   Don't bother manually formatting an index—or a table of contents—until you have finished the document. Any time you do a complete rebuild of an index or table, all manual formatting is lost (if you just update page numbers, manual formatting remains).

Customizing your index style

Each index level uses a built-in Word style (Index 1 through Index 9). To create your own index format, you can modify these styles as you can any other style:

1. Choose Insert ➪ Reference ➪ Index and Tables, and then click the Index tab.

2. Select From Template in the Formats list.

3. Click the Modify button. The Style dialog box appears and displays a list of the nine index styles, one for each entry or subentry level (see Figure 12-6).

Figure 12-6: The Style dialog box showing the nine built-in index styles.

4. Select the index style that you want to modify from the Styles list, and then click Modify.

5. Edit the style to meet your needs and then click OK.

Cross-Reference

For more on working with styles, see Chapter 13.

6. Click OK or Close until all of the dialog boxes are closed. If you're modifying the style for an index that you've already created, answer Yes when Word asks you if you want to replace the selected index.

Note

One built-in style, called Index Heading, doesn't appear in the Styles list when you click the Modify button in the Index and Tables dialog box. But Word uses it to format the area separating alphabetical groups of entries. To modify this style, choose Format ➪ Styles and Formatting, select Custom from the Show drop-down at the bottom of the task pane, and check the Index Heading entry in the Styles to be Visible list.

Updating an index

Because the index is actually a field, you can update your index at any time by updating the field. You should update the index when you add new index entries, when you make any editing or formatting changes to XE fields, or when you make changes to your document that might affect its pagination.

Any formatting changes that you make in the index itself are lost when you update it. Therefore, you may want to change the index's appearance by editing the field code rather than by editing the field result (the index text). If, however, you're certain that the document's pagination isn't about to change and that no further entries will be added to the index, you can convert an index field to text by placing your insertion point anywhere in the index and then pressing Ctrl+Shift+F9. (It doesn't matter if the field code or the index is displayed when you issue this command.) Note that after you convert a field to text, however, the index can no longer be updated—to update your index you would have to re-create it.

Tip   You could save the index field as an AutoText entry before unlinking so that you can re-use it later. (See Chapter 2 for more information on AutoText.) Of course, the problem we just described illustrates why it's a good idea to use styles and index commands and options rather than working with manual formatting.

To update an index, do the following:

1. If the index is displayed, place your insertion point anywhere inside it. (Because the index is a field, placing your insertion point inside the index selects the entire field.) If the index *field* is currently displayed, select the field.

2. Press F9, or choose Update Field from the shortcut menu.

Editing the INDEX field

The INDEX field contains information defining how the index should be built, and Table 12-2 lists the switches that modify this field and customize your index in various ways. Many of these switches are inserted automatically when you make selections in the Index and Tables dialog box. Table 12-2 helps you to recognize switches that may already be present in your field code, and provides options for modifying these switches.

You can modify switches or insert new ones within a field just as you can add or edit any other text. To add switches or modify any of the existing switches in your index field, place your insertion point anywhere in the index. If the field code is not currently displayed, press Shift+F9. Move your insertion point to the location in the field that you want to edit, and then add or delete text as desired.

When adding separator characters, be sure to put spaces before and after them within the quotation marks. Otherwise, these separate characters run in with the entry text and the page number.

Table 12-2: Switches for the INDEX Field

Switch	What It Does	Example
\b	Instructs Word to index only the portion of the document marked by the specified bookmark. Use this switch to create separate indexes for different parts of a document.	`{ INDEX \b hemingway }` builds an index using the index entries in the range designated by the bookmark named *hemingway*.
\c	Instructs Word to divide the index into a specific number of columns.	`{ INDEX \c 3 }` builds a three-column index. By default, an index contains two columns, but can contain up to four.

Switch	What It Does	Example
\d	Designates the separator characters used between a chapter number and a page number. This switch is used with the \s switch. The separator can contain as many as five characters, and you must enclose the characters in quotation marks.	`{ INDEX \s chapter \d ":" }` builds an index in which the entries look like the sequence *Twain, 3:5*. In this example, *3* is the chapter number and *5* is the page number within the chapter. The default separator is a hyphen.
\e	Designates the separator characters used between index entries and page numbers. The separator can contain as many as five characters, and you must enclose the characters in quotation marks.	`{ INDEX \e "--> " }` builds an index in which the entries look like *Twain-->5*. The default separator is a comma followed by a space.
\f	Creates an index that uses only the entry type that you specify.	Corresponds to an entry type used in some of your XE fields, allowing you to build an index that indexes only a subset of index entries.
\g	Used to designate the separator characters between the limits of the page range. You can have as many as five separator characters, and you must enclose the separator characters in quotation marks.	`{ INDEX \g " to " }` builds you an index in which the entries for page ranges look like *Twain, 25 to 32*.
\h	Inserts headings between index groups. There are two versions: \h "" inserts a blank line between groups in the index, and \h "A" inserts a heading letter between groups.	`{ INDEX \h "*** A ***" }` separates each alphabetical group with a line that looks like `"*** A ***."` The `"A"` in the field is actually a code that tells Word to move to the next letter of the alphabet for each group, so that your second group's heading would be `"*** B ***,"` and so on.
\l	Used to designate the separator characters between page numbers for entries that refer to more than one page (but not a page range). You can have as many as five separator characters, and you must enclose the separator characters in quotation marks.	`{ INDEX \l " and " }` builds an index in which multiple page references are separated as follows: *Twain, 25 and 32 and 51*. The default is a comma followed by a space, such as *Twain, 25, 32, 51*.
\p	Creates an index from entries for only the specified characters or that includes special characters. You can use an exclamation point with this switch to include special characters.	`{ INDEX \p a-c }` builds an index for entries beginning with the letters *a*, *b*, or *c*. `{ INDEX \p ! }` includes entries that begin with nonalphabetical characters. `{ INDEX \p !-f }` compiles an index for entries beginning with letters *a* through *f* as well as any special characters.

Continued

Table 12-2 *(continued)*

Switch	What It Does	Example
\r	This switch is added automatically when you choose Run-in in the Index tab of the Index and Tables dialog box to have subentries follow right after the main entries on the same line.	{ INDEX \r } builds a index such as *Hemingway: early years 5; in Key West 33; as war correspondent 59.*
\s	Use this switch in conjunction with the SEQ field to include chapter or other numbers along with the page numbers in your index (5-1, 5-2, and so on). First, format each segment in a separate section and instruct Word to restart the page numbering at 1 for that section. Then insert a SEQ field at the beginning of the section.	Assume that you insert a { SEQ chapter } field at the beginning of each chapter to assign the name *chapter* to the SEQ field. Then { INDEX \s chapter } includes the chapter-page number sequence in your index. Use the \d switch to specify a separator character other than the default hyphen.
\y	This switch enables the use of Yomi text, as described earlier in the chapter.	
\z "*####*"	This switch specifies an ID number of a language, so Word knows which sorting system to use (different languages having different sorting methods, of course). How do you know which ID to use for which language? A good question, for which Microsoft apparently has no ready answer. Here are a few switches: Spanish (Spain) 3082, English (US) 1033, Japanese 1041, French 1036. Look in C:\Program Files\ Microsoft Office\Office\, and you'll see subfolders with numbers as names—these correspond to the languages that have been installed.	{ INDEX \z 3082 } sorts the index assuming it is in French.

By default, the From Template index format doesn't insert any separators between groups of letters. Therefore, your index becomes one long, unbroken list unless you use the \h switch to add a heading between groups. The basic separator is a blank line between each alphabetical group (all of the entries starting with a same letter). To insert a basic heading separator into your index field, add the \h switch to your index field code and then follow the switch with a space enclosed in quotation marks:

```
{ INDEX \h " " }
```

This example shows only the heading switch. Your field code may contain several other switches in addition to this one, however.

Deleting an index

You can delete an index just as you can delete any other field. Simply select the entire field, and then press Delete. The quickest way to select the field is (with the field code displayed) to click anywhere in the field and then drag the mouse pointer a short distance. If the index itself is displayed, click in the left margin on one of the section breaks at the beginning or the end of the index. Remember that you must be in Normal view to see the section breaks. You can delete individual index entries by deleting the fields that mark the index entry text.

Adding Tables of Contents to Your Documents

A table of contents contains a list of headings in the document that provide a quick summary and overview of the topics covered, along with the page numbers where the topics can be found. When you switch to Web Layout view, the headings become hyperlinks on which you can click to jump to that topic in the document. And in other views, you can press Ctrl and click on a link to jump to the referenced heading.

Note The Ctrl+Click feature works if you have Use CTRL + Click to Follow Hyperlink selected in the Options dialog box (Tools ➪ Options—under the Edit tab). If this is turned off, there's no need to press the Ctrl button while clicking.

As with creating an index, creating a table of contents is a two-step process. First, mark the items in your document that you want to list in the table. Second, instruct Word to assemble the table of contents from the marked entries. The TC field contains table of contents entries, and the TOC field contains the assembled and formatted information for the table of contents. However, note that the process is, in most cases, much easier, because Word can add table of contents entries for you. If you use Word's Heading styles, you can crate the table based on those heading entries; there's no need to go through your document defining where table of contents entries should appear.

Tip If you plan to read the document online, on a Web site, you can create the table of contents as a set of hyperlinks displayed in a scrollable frame in the left side of a frame set. When you click a hyperlink in the left frame, the document in the right frame jumps to the heading referenced by the hyperlink. See Chapter 26 for more information.

Preparing your document for adding a table of contents

You can prepare a document for a table of contents in several ways:

✦ Use Word's built-in heading styles (Heading 1 through Heading 9) as you create the document. Word automatically recognizes these styles when it compiles a table of contents, so applying the styles to your headings is all the preparation that you need.

✦ Type your document without worrying about styles and let AutoFormat apply them for you.

Cross-Reference For more information on applying styles manually and using AutoFormat to apply them automatically, see Chapter 13.

✦ Build your document in Outline view. This way, as you promote and demote outline levels, Word automatically applies the appropriate heading style.

✦ Use your own custom styles. If Word's built-in heading styles cannot meet your needs, you can create any set of styles you that choose and assign them to headings or other text that you want to include in your table of contents. How to make Word recognize your custom styles when it compiles the table of contents is discussed later in this chapter.

✦ Mark items for the table of contents with the TC entry field. You can mark any document text for inclusion in a table of contents by inserting a field code. (See "Assembling a table of contents by using TC entry fields" later in this chapter for more on how to mark text as a table of contents entry and use the field entries to build your table of contents.)

Compiling a table of contents

The techniques for compiling a table of contents vary somewhat depending on the method used to prepare your document. The following sections discuss all four methods.

Note   Remember to turn off the display of hidden text and field codes. Both of these text elements can affect your document's pagination, and thus the page numbers in your table of contents.

Assembling a table of contents using Word's heading styles

Before you begin building the table of contents, make sure that you've applied one of Word's built-in heading styles (Heading 1 through Heading 9) to all of the headings that you want to include. You learn about styles in detail in Chapter 13. But all you need to know right now is that when you create a chapter title or subheading, you should apply one of Word's Heading styles to it. Simply place the insertion point on the line you want to convert and select one of the styles from the Style drop-down list box on the Formatting toolbar.

To assemble a table of contents from built-in heading styles, follow these steps:

1. Position your insertion point where you want the table of contents to begin. If you're using a master document to create your table of contents, switch to Master Document view and make sure that your insertion point is not in a subdocument.

2. Choose Insert ➪ Reference ➪ Index and Tables, and then click the Table of Contents tab (see Figure 12-7).

3. Select a format from the Formats list. As you select the different formats, the Print Preview and Web Preview boxes display samples of those formats.

   If you select From Template, you can click Modify, which opens the Style dialog box that displays a list of the TOC styles (1 through 9). Each style refers to the heading level of the same number. You can change the appearance of any heading level in your table of contents by modifying the applicable style. For example, to modify all your first level headings, modify the TOC 1 style.

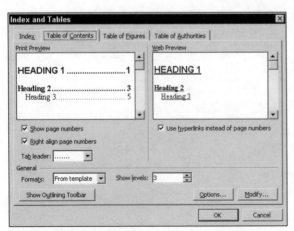

Figure 12-7: The Table of Contents tab of the Index and Tables dialog box.

4. Make selections in the following areas of the Table of Contents tab as desired (the default settings for some of these options vary depending on which table of contents format is selected):

   • By default, all of the table of contents formats display page numbers in both Normal and Print Layout views. Clear the Show Page Numbers check box if you want a table of contents without page numbers. (If you plan to use this document in purely electronic form, not printed, you really don't need page numbers—readers can Ctrl+Click on a table of contents entry to move to the referenced area.)

   • Select Right Align Page Numbers if you want the page numbers to be aligned with the right margin.

   • By default, all of the table of contents formats build a table using only the first three heading levels. To display a different number of levels, enter that number in the Show Levels text box.

   • Select Tab Leader if you want a line between the headings and the page numbers. You can choose a dashed, dotted, or solid line. Different formats show different or no tab leaders. This option is dimmed unless Right Align Page Numbers is selected.

Tip   Clear the Use Hyperlinks Instead of Page Numbers check box if you are planning to save the document as a Web page, but don't want the table of contents to be hyperlinks.

5. Click OK. Word then repaginates the document and creates the table of contents at the location of your insertion point. The table of contents is formatted as a separate section, so you can use any of Word's section formatting options to work with it. Figure 12-8 shows a sample table of contents.

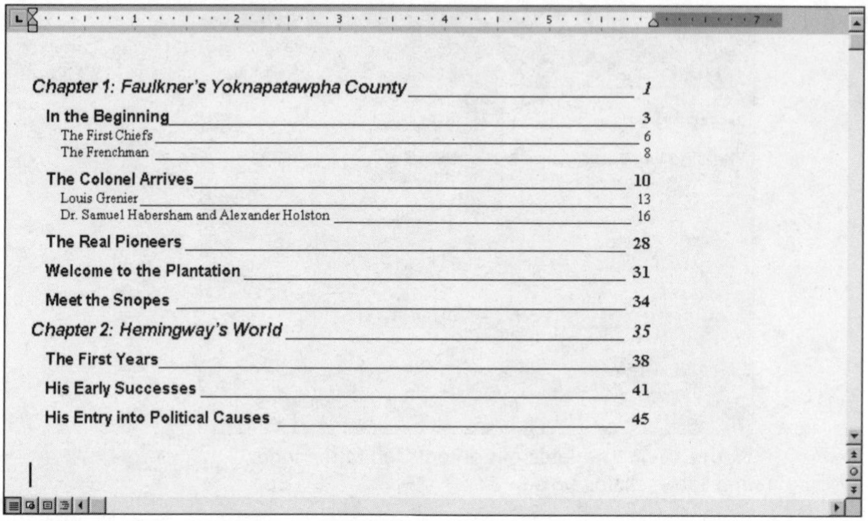

Chapter 1: Faulkner's Yoknapatawpha County _____ *1*

In the Beginning _____ 3

The First Chiefs _____ 6
The Frenchman _____ 8

The Colonel Arrives _____ 10

Louis Grenier _____ 13
Dr. Samuel Habersham and Alexander Holston _____ 16

The Real Pioneers _____ 28

Welcome to the Plantation _____ 31

Meet the Snopes _____ 34

Chapter 2: Hemingway's World _____ *35*

The First Years _____ 38

His Early Successes _____ 41

His Entry into Political Causes _____ 45

Figure 12-8: A sample table of contents.

The entire table of contents is actually a single field. To see the field code for this table of contents field, click in the margin next to the first line in the table to select the table. Then press Shift+F9. Figure 12-9 shows the field code for the sample table of contents in Figure 12-8.

{ *TOC* \o "*1-3*" \h \z }

Figure 12-9: The field code for the sample table of contents in Figure 12-8.

Each line in the table of contents is a hyperlink that jumps to that topic in the document. To see the hyperlink field code, click in the left margin next to the line to select it. Then press Shift+F9.

After you compile a table of contents or a table of figures (using any method), you can use that table to navigate through your document quickly. Just press the Ctrl key and click any heading in the table to move your insertion point to the referenced location.

Assembling a table of contents using custom styles

If you've used styles other than Heading 1 through Heading 9, you can still create a table of contents. Before you begin, however, make sure that you've applied styles to all of the headings that you want to include in your table of contents. Also, make sure that you've applied all of the styles in a consistent fashion. If, for example, you've created a style for level-one headings called Chapter Title, each level-one heading must be formatted with this style or it won't be included in the table of contents correctly. To assemble a table of contents from custom styles, follow these steps:

1. Choose Insert ➪ Reference ➪ Index and Tables, and then click the Table of Contents tab.

2. Select a format from the Formats list, and then select other options as before. As you select the different formats, samples are displayed in the Preview boxes.

3. Click Options. The Table of Contents Options dialog box opens (see Figure 12-10). This dialog box lists all of your available styles, including any captions, comments, footnotes, and other styles in the current document. A checkmark appears to the left of each heading style used in your current document.

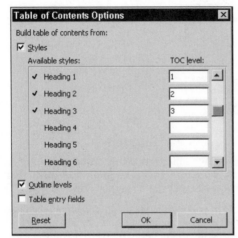

Figure 12-10: The Table of Contents Options dialog box.

4. Find the style you want to use as the level 1 in your table of contents, and type **1** in the text box next to it.

5. Repeat the process for each style that you want to include.

   Make sure that the TOC Level text box is blank for any styles that you don't want to include. To return to the default settings at any time, just click Reset.

6. Unless you've added some TC entry fields that you want to include in your table along with your custom styles, make sure that the Table Entry Fields check box is cleared. (See the next section for more information on TC fields.)

7. Click OK. Note that the Preview boxes in the Table of Contents tab now display your custom styles.

8. Click OK to compile the table of contents.

You can also use the Table of Contents Options dialog box to trick Word into formatting the built-in heading styles for a level different than the one for which they were designed. Suppose, for example, that you want all of the headings to which you applied the Heading 4 style to be formatted as level two in your table of contents. Just type **2** in the TOC Level box next to Heading 4. This changes the heading format only for your table of contents, however. It doesn't affect the formatting in your document text itself.

Assembling a table of contents using TC entry fields

To create a table of contents using TC entry fields, first mark the text that you want to include in the contents list and then assemble the table to add the marked entries. To use a TC field to mark a table of contents entry, follow these steps:

1. Select the text that you want to include in the table of contents, or place your insertion point at the location of the text that you want to mark for inclusion.

2. Press Alt+Shift+O to open the Mark Table of Contents Entry dialog box (see Figure 12-11).

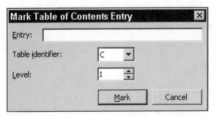

Figure 12-11: The Mark Table of Contents Entry dialog box.

3. If you selected text before pressing Alt+Shift+O, that text now appears in the Entry text box. If necessary, edit the text as you want it to appear in the table of contents. If you didn't select text, type your table of contents entry in the Entry text box.

   The text is displayed in your table of contents exactly as it appears in the Entry text box, including any capitalization and character formatting. You can add character formatting to the text in the Entry box by selecting the portion of text that you want to format and then pressing Ctrl+B (Bold), Ctrl+I (Italic), or Ctrl+U (Underline). And, as with the Mark Index Entry box we saw earlier, you can press Ctrl+D to open the Font dialog box.

4. Make a selection from the Table Identifier list.

   The table identifier instructs Word about the table in which to place the entry. By default, a table of contents entry uses the C identifier and a table of figures entry the F identifier. (This information is placed after the \f switch, as explained in Table 12-3).

5. Type or select a heading level in the Level box.

   The Level designation instructs Word how to treat the entry when it compiles your table of contents (level one, level two, and so on). If you use the built-in heading styles, Word takes care of this setting for you, but if you create a table of contents entry with the TC field, you need to give Word some help.

6. Click Mark. Word then places a TC entry field at your insertion point location (or at the end of your selected text). Figure 12-12 shows a sample TC entry field.

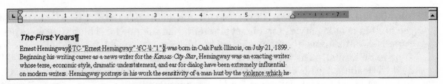

Figure 12-12: A sample TC entry field.

A TC field contains all of the information for a table of contents entry, and Table 12-3 lists the switches that modify the field to customize your entries. Many of these switches are inserted automatically when you mark a table of contents entry. Table 12-3 helps you to recognize switches that may already be present in your table of contents entry fields, and it also provides options for modifying these switches.

Table 12-3: Switches for the TC Field

Switch	What It Does
\f	Defines an entry type, such as illustrations. This switch works in conjunction with the \f switch for the TOC field. You can add a letter enclosed in quotation marks after this switch in a TC field and then add the same letter following a \f switch in a TOC field to compile a table of contents including only those TC fields with the same entry type.
\l	Designates the heading level. Level 1 is assumed if none is specified.
\n	Keeps the page number for a table of contents entry from displaying.

After you've created TC fields at each location to be included in your table of contents, the procedure for compiling the table is much the same as that for compiling a table when using styles. In the Index and Tables dialog box, under the Table of Contents tab, click the Options button. Then select the Table Entry Fields check box, and clear the Styles and Outline Levels check boxes.

Creating tables of contents from Outline levels

Selecting the Outline Levels check box in the Table of Contents Options dialog box allows you to create tables of contents using the Outline. Clear the Styles check box to make sure Word doesn't base the table of contents on any of your paragraph styles. Note also that the Show Outlining Toolbar button opens an abbreviated version of the Outlining toolbar.

Cross-Reference   See Chapter 25 for more information about document outlines.

Updating a table of contents

Because the table of contents is actually a field, you can update your table of contents at any time by simply updating the field itself. You should update the table of contents whenever you make changes to your document that may affect its pagination. You should also update the table of contents whenever you add new table of contents entries, either by marking entries with TC fields or by adding new headings to which you've applied built-in or custom styles.

Any formatting changes that you make to the table of contents itself are lost when you update it. Therefore, the best way to change the table's appearance is by editing the field code rather than by editing the field text. If, however, you're certain that the document's pagination isn't going to change and that you won't be adding any entries to your table of contents, you can convert the TOC field to text by selecting the table and then pressing Ctrl+Shift+F9. (It doesn't matter whether the field code or the index is displayed when you issue this command.) Note that after you convert a field to text, you can no longer update or revise that text as a field.

To update a table of contents, follow these steps:

1. Select the table of contents field.

2. Press F9, or choose Update Field from the shortcut menu. Word may display the Update Table of Contents dialog box (see Figure 12-13).

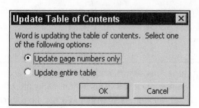

Figure 12-13: The Update Table of Contents dialog box.

3. Do one of the following:

- Choose Update Page Numbers Only if you want to update the page numbers in your table without updating any of the entries. This way, your formatting is preserved.

- Choose Update Entire Table if you want to update the names of the entries or any other options in addition to the page numbers. This way, any formatting that is applied directly to the table (rather than in a field code) is lost.

4. Click OK.

Creating Tables of Figures and Other Tables

In addition to a table of contents, you can also include tables listing figures, equations, charts, or other elements. In this section, all such tables are referred to as tables of figures. Remember that a table of figures can include many different document elements, and that you can have many different tables in one document.

You can prepare figures (or other document items) for inclusion in a table of figures using three different methods:

✦ You can mark items for the table of figures with the TC entry field. This field code is the same as that used to mark text for a table of contents; marking text or an object for inclusion in a table of figures is just a matter of changing a few options. The following steps teach you how to mark an item as a table of figures entry. (See "Assembling a table of figures using styles or TC fields" later in this chapter for more information on how to use the field entries to build your table of figures.)

✦ You can add captions to the items using Word's Insert ➪ Reference ➪ Caption command. Adding captions to items automates the process of creating a table of figures in the same way that using Word's built-in heading styles automates the process of creating a table of contents. Word automatically recognizes any captions created with the Caption command when it compiles a table of figures.

See Chapter 18 to find out more about using captions.

✦ You can apply styles to the items that you want to include in a table. As long as you apply the same style to all of the items that you want included in a particular table— and don't use that style for anything that you *don't* want in the table, of course—you can use any style that you want. If, for example, you want to create a table listing all of the drawings in your document, you can create a style called Drawing and then apply that style to every drawing. How to get Word to recognize your custom styles when it compiles a table of figures is discussed later in this chapter.

Cross-Reference For more information about working with styles, see Chapter 13.

Marking table entries with a TC field

To use a TC field to mark a table of figures entry, use the Mark Table of Contents Entry dialog box, as you saw earlier in this chapter (press Alt+Shift+O). But this time, to indicate that this is going to be included in a table of figures, select *F*. If you are creating a table of something else—a table of tables, a table of quotations, a table of just about anything—pick another letter. The actual letters don't really matter. Just make sure you use the same identifier for all of the items in a specific table.

In most cases you won't need to select a level—just leave it set to level 1—because in most tables other than tables of contents, all entries are at the same level.

Compiling a table of figures

Once you mark your entries or apply styles to your figure captions, you're ready to compile them. The following sections explain how to assemble a table of figures using styles, TC fields, or captions.

Assembling a table of figures using styles or TC fields

To assemble a table of figures from styles or TC fields, open the Index and Tables dialog box, and display the Table of Figures tab (see Figure 12-14). This is very similar to the Table of Contents tab, of course, so we won't describe the entire box—choose your table format and other settings as you learned earlier.

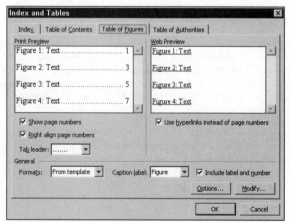

Figure 12-14: The Table of Figures tab in the Index and Tables dialog box.

Then click the Options button to open the Table of Figures Options dialog box (see Figure 12-15).

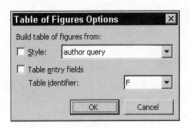

Figure 12-15: The Table of Figures Options dialog box.

Do one or both of the following:

✦ To build the table of figures from styles, check the Style check box and then select the style that you applied to your list items from the Styles drop-down list.

✦ To build the table of figures from TC entry fields, check the Table Entry Fields check box and then select the table identifier that you used in the TC fields from the Table Identifier drop-down list.

Assembling a table using captions

To create a table from figure captions—or from Equation or Table captions—open the Table of Figures tab in the Index and Tables dialog box; then select the label type you want to compile from the Caption Label list. The label type is the same one that you selected (or created) when you first added the captions.

Note also the Include Label and Number check box—check this if you want the caption label (not just the caption itself) to be included in the table.

Creating Tables of Authorities

Unless you work in the legal profession or have some other reason to work with legal documents, chances are that you can safely skip this section. A table of authorities is a highly specialized tool that most lawyers cannot live without—and that other mere mortals can survive quite nicely without ever encountering. A table of authorities lists legal citations, such as rulings and precedents. (The feature was added to Word as part of Microsoft's strategy to capture some of WordPerfect's legal market.)

Previously, compiling citations in a table of authorities was a tedious, time-consuming, and error-prone proposition. Word, however, makes marking a citation as easy as marking text for inclusion in any table. Compiling the table of authorities is much like compiling a table of contents or table of figures. Just tell Word where you want the table to go, and then choose from several style formats or create your own custom style.

Marking citation entries

The first step in creating a table of authorities is to mark your citations. There are two types of citation entries:

✦ A long citation is always used the first time the reference appears in your document. The long citation contains the full reference to the case, statute, or rule, such as *Twain v. Alcott, 352 Win 2d 901 (4th Cir. 1952)*.

✦ A short citation is used for each subsequent appearance of the reference. The short citation for the earlier example may simply be *Twain* or, if more than one case in your document involves Twain, *Twain v. Alcott.*

To mark citations for a table of authorities, follow these steps:

1. Select the citation that you want to mark.

2. Press Alt+Shift+I to open the Mark Citation dialog box (see Figure 12-16); you can also select Insert ➪ Reference ➪ Index and Tables, click the Table of Authorities tab, and click the Mark Citation button. Note that your selected text is displayed in both the Selected Text and Short Citation boxes.

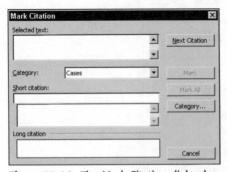

Figure 12-16: The Mark Citation dialog box.

3. Edit and format the text in the Selected Text box as necessary. You can use the following shortcut keys to add character formatting to the citation: Ctrl+B (Bold), Ctrl+I (Italic), or Ctrl+U (Underline). You can also press Ctrl+D to open the Font dialog box.

4. Choose a category from the Category drop-down list box. (To modify these categories or to create your own, see "Creating and editing citation categories" later in this chapter.)

5. Edit the text in the Short Citation box as you want it to appear in the table of authorities.

6. Do one of the following:

   • Click Mark to mark the individual entry. Word then marks the text with the TA (Table of Authorities Entry) field code.

   • Click Mark All if you want Word to search through your document and mark each occurrence of the same citation. Note, however, that Word marks only those occurrences that are precise matches for the long and the short citation entries in the Mark Citation dialog box.

7. Word marks the citation, and puts the text from the Selected Text box into the Long Citation box at the bottom of the dialog box.

8. Click Next Citation. Word then tries to find the next citation in your document by searching for words that are typically found in citations, such as *in re* or *v.* Next Citation is not foolproof, however. Some of your citations may not include the buzzwords for which Word scans. Be sure to check for unmarked citations before finalizing the table of authorities.

Compiling a table of authorities

After you mark the citations, all that remains is to format and compile the table of authorities. Compiling a table of authorities is similar to compiling an index or a table of contents. Just tell Word how you want the table of authorities to look and where you want it to be inserted.

Open the Index and Tables dialog box (Insert ➪ Reference ➪ Index and Tables) and click the Table of Authorities tab (see Figure 12-17). Select the category of citations that you want to compile from the Category list box. The default selection is All, so you don't need to do anything if you want to include all of the citation categories in your table.

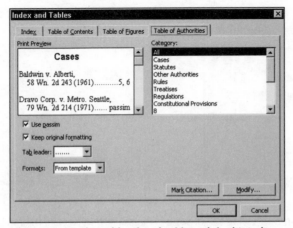

Figure 12-17: The Table of Authorities tab in the Index and Tables dialog box.

You'll also find a couple of check-box options:

✦ Check the Use Passim check box if you want Word to use the term *passim* in place of page numbers for each citation that is referred to on more than five different pages. (Passim means *throughout* or *frequently*. In this context it means that the citation appears frequently throughout the text, and is commonly used in legal documents.)

✦ Check the Keep Original Formatting check box to retain any character formatting that you applied to the citation in the document.

When Word compiles the table of authorities, it creates a separate section for each category. It also arranges the citations alphabetically within their sections.

Updating a table of authorities

You should update your table of authorities whenever you make changes to your document that may affect its pagination. You should also update your table of authorities when you make changes to any citation that should be reflected in this table.

To update a table of authorities, open the Table of Authorities tab in the Index and Tables dialog box, and click OK. Or simply select the table of the field and press F9. Word selects the existing table of authorities and displays a dialog box that asks if you want to replace the selected category. Click Yes to update the table of authorities. If you click No, Word keeps your old table of authorities and adds a new one. This way, you can add new categories or sections to your table.

Creating and editing citation categories

Word includes most commonly used citation categories, but you can add your own and even edit the existing ones. You can have a maximum of 16 categories in a table of authorities. Of these 16 categories, 8 are named (including All) and 8 are only numbered. To create and edit citation categories, follow these steps:

1. Press Alt+Shift+I to open the Mark Citation dialog box.

2. Click the Category button to display the Edit Category dialog box (see Figure 12-18).

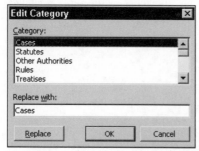

Figure 12-18: The Edit Category dialog box.

3. Make a selection from the Category list as follows:

   • Select the name of one of the seven existing categories that you want to replace, or

   • Select a number from 8 to 16 to create a new category.

4. Type the name of the new or modified category in the Replace With text box.

5. Click Replace.

6. Click OK, and then close the Mark Citation dialog box.

Tip   You can easily include chapter numbers along with page numbers in an index or a table. Just use the Insert ➪ Page Numbers command and choose Format. Check the Include Chapter Number check box in the Page Number Format dialog box, and then select the style that you applied to your chapter numbers.

Summary

This chapter discussed working with Word's tools for creating indexes and tables of contents and authorities. Both of these features are essential in creating long documents such as a manuscript or term paper. You can create a table of contents, table of figures, or table of citations—or a table of anything else. You can also choose from several formats to create impressive-looking indexes and tables of contents. In this chapter, you learned how to do the following:

✦ Create index entries using two methods. The first is creating a concordance file, which is a table of index entries, and then instructing Word to search the document for all of the entries in that file. The other is manually marking each index entry in a document by selecting the text and pressing Alt+Shift+X.

✦ Create and format an index using the Insert ➪ Reference ➪ Index and Tables command.

✦ Create a table of contents from heading styles in a document by choosing Insert ➪ Reference ➪ Index and Tables, clicking the Table of Contents tab, and then specifying the formatting of your table of contents.

✦ Create a table of figures based on figure caption styles in a document by choosing Insert ➪ Reference ➪ Index and Tables and then clicking the Table of Figures tab.

✦ Create a table of citations by choosing Insert ➪ Reference ➪ Index and Tables and then clicking the Table of Authorities tab.

✦   ✦   ✦

Working More Effectively

P A R T

In This Part

Chapter 13
Styles and
AutoFormatting

Chapter 14
Using Templates,
Wizards, and Themes

Chapter 15
What Looks Good?

Chapter 16
Creating Documents
Using Speech
Recognition

Styles and AutoFormatting

In This Chapter

Using styles
and templates

Creating new styles

Applying styles to text

Copying, renaming,
displaying, modifying,
and deleting styles

Adding shortcut
keys to styles

Using Word's automatic
style formatting features

Perhaps the single most time-consuming task when creating a document is formatting. Formatting a document involves several issues, including the document's appearance, consistency of formatting, adherence to your organization's guidelines, and so on. Using styles, however, you can reduce dramatically the amount of time and effort needed in formatting. In this chapter, you learn how to master Word's powerful style features.

Styles Defined

Simply put, a *style* is a collection of formats that you apply to text in a document. For instance, a style contains information related to the text's typeface and font size, the paragraph margins, how much space appears before and after the paragraph, and so on. Instead of applying each component directly to the text, however, you build this collection of formatting information, give it a name—the *style name*—and then apply the style to the text. It takes a while the first time, but now you can apply that style over and over again, taking just moments each time. This approach has two major benefits: applying formatting is simple and ensures uniformity, and reformatting is both quick and easy.

When you apply a style to text, all of that text immediately becomes formatted according to those formats defined in the style. (Well, with one exception—see the note following this paragraph.) Later, if you need to change some of the formatting, you just redefine the style with the new formats instead of searching for the text that you want to reformat, and all text that has that style applied to it changes instantly to match the new definition. Because direct formatting always overrides a style, however, anyone can change the formatting, regardless of whether he or she is familiar with using styles.

Note
There are two types of formatting—that applied with a style and that applied directly. For instance, if you place the insertion point in text and then select the Normal style, you are applying the Normal style to the text. If you select a word and press Ctrl+B, you are directly applying bolding to the word. Direct formatting overrides style formatting. So if you now change the style to something different, the word to which you applied bolding *remains* bold, even if the new style does not apply bold text.

Four style types

Word used to differentiate between two types of styles: paragraph and character. Now Word has four different style types:

✦ **Paragraph** styles format the entire paragraph at once, including font and font size, other character formatting, indentation, text alignment, pagination (as it applies to a paragraph), line spacing, tab stops, borders, frame, numbering, and language. (As discussed in Chapter 8, you can even define text as a particular language, to use the right spelling and proofing dictionaries if available.)

✦ **Character** styles format only the selected text, and include only character and language formatting.

✦ **Table** styles are used to set up the way in which table rows, columns, and cells appear. Applying a table style to non-table text actually places the text into a table (see Chapter 9).

✦ **List** styles define the way in which numbered and bulleted lists are formatted (see Chapter 5).

We look mainly at Paragraph and Character styles in this chapter, as tables and lists are covered in the chapters mentioned in the bulleted list.

Styles and formatting together

There's another important change between Word 2003 and versions of Word before Word 2002. Earlier versions kept styles and formatting as separate things, so long-term users of Word need to understand that Word is now mixing these things together. For instance, the Style drop-down list box doesn't just show the applied style; it also, in some cases, shows the formatting. If you bold a word in a Normal-style paragraph, for example, click on that word and look in the Style drop-down list box in the Formatting toolbar, you'll see that the entry now says *Normal + Bold.*

Also, the Pick Formatting to Apply list box—which we look at later in this chapter—shows you the formatting of the text, not just the style applied to the text.

Styles, templates, and themes

Styles, templates, and themes are closely related. We look more closely at templates and themes in the next chapter, but for now you should at least understand what these things are and how they relate to styles:

✦ **Theme**—A collection of design elements for a document. Originally intended for Web pages—and originally added to Microsoft FrontPage before being added to Word—themes contain styles along with a variety of other elements, such as navigation bars, bullet images, background images, and horizontal lines.

✦ **Template**—A template is a file that is used as a starting point for a document. When you open a template you are opening a document to which you can enter your text and other content, a document that already has the exact styles and document formatting that you need for that document (or perhaps something close that you can quickly modify). Templates can contain many other things, too, such as customized menus, toolbars, and keyboard shortcuts, macros, AutoText entries, and so on.

So a *template* is a blank document waiting for you to work on, containing styles and, perhaps, a theme. *Styles* are used to quickly format text (in paragraphs, tables, and elsewhere). All documents contain styles . . . many of them. *Themes* are overall design layouts, containing many elements including styles. A document may use no theme or one theme, but it cannot use more than one at any time.

Viewing and Using Styles

Every document contains styles. So whenever you open a template file to start a new document, you already have styles available to you; whether they are the ones you want or not is another matter. You can use these styles, you can create new ones, or you can copy styles from another document or template.

When you choose File ⇨ New and click the Blank Document link, or when you click the New Blank Document button on the Standard toolbar, you are making a copy of the Normal document template, Word's basic template designed for generic documents.

Cross-Reference   As discussed in Chapter 14, Word offers many more specific templates that you can use for letters, memos, faxes, and so on.

This document contains styles ready for you to use. Click the triangle on the right side of the Style drop-down list box on the Formatting toolbar, and a list of styles drops down (see Figure 13-1).

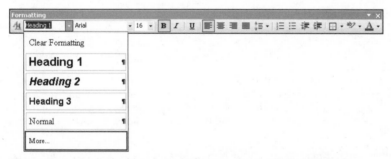

Figure 13-1: The Style drop-down list box on the Formatting toolbar.

This toolbar contains a very small number of basic styles: three Heading styles, and the Normal style. The Heading styles are intended for, well, headings. (As you learned in Chapter 12, these heading styles provide more than just formatting for headings; they are also used by Word when generating tables of contents and outlines.) The Normal style is intended for the normal text, often known as *body text*, within your document.

Note   You will see the Clear Formatting entry at the top of the list box, but this is not really a style. It's simply a command that clears any text formatting from selected text. If you have changed some words to bold or italic, selecting the paragraph and then selecting Clear Formatting returns those words to the default text format for that paragraph's style.

These styles, however, are only a small selection of what is available to you. You'll see the More entry at the bottom of this drop-down list box. Select this and the Styles and Formatting task pane opens (see Figure 13-2). You can also open this task pane by choosing Format ➪ Styles and Formatting.

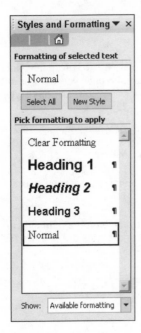

Figure 13-2: The Styles and Formatting task pane.

Initially, you see exactly the same entries as you saw in the Style drop-down list. But notice the Show drop-down list box at the bottom of this task pane. Open this list, and you'll see a few choices for what will be displayed in the large Pick Formatting to Apply list box. Unfortunately, these choices are not particularly clear, so read the following carefully! Here's what these choices mean:

✦ **Available Formatting:** Shows you the basic styles for the document you are working in (the basic styles in the template used to create this document) whether you have used them or not, plus any additional styles you have used (see All Styles later in this list), plus any text formatting you have applied on top of a style (bold or italic, for instance).

✦ **Formatting in Use:** Shows you any styles you have used in your document, plus any text formatting you have applied on top of a style (bold or italic, for instance).

✦ **Available Styles:** This is really misnamed. It *doesn't* show the styles that are available to you. Rather, it lists the basic styles for the document you are working in, plus any other styles you have applied anywhere in the document. It *doesn't* show any text formatting.

✦ **All Styles:** Shows you a much larger list of styles that you can use. For instance, rather than just three Heading levels, you see nine levels. This choice also does not show any text formatting.

✦ **Custom:** Defines very specifically what should be shown in the list box.

Tip   Point at the Formatting of Selected Text box at the top of the Styles and Formatting task pane and you'll see a triangle appear to the right of the style or format name. Click this triangle and select Reveal Formatting to see the Reveal Formatting task pane that we looked at in Chapter 4. To return to the original task pane, click the Reveal Formatting name at the top of the task pane and select Styles and Formatting.

Selecting a custom view

You can define very specifically what you want to see in the Pick Formatting to Apply list box, though you probably shouldn't mess with this setting until you have used styles for a while (if then). Select Custom from the Show drop-down at the bottom of the list, and the Format Settings dialog box opens (see Figure 13-3).

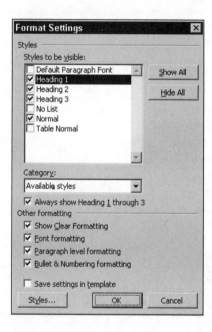

Figure 13-3: The Format Settings dialog box.

This dialog box modifies how the other Show choices work, making the titles—Available Formatting, All Styles, and so on—meaningless (or rather, even more meaningless than they were in the first place). Table 13-1 explains the available options in this dialog box.

Caution   The Custom selection from the Show drop-down list is very confusing; it's also hard to return to the original settings. (This is a dialog box crying out for a Reset button!) Note that you are also adjusting what you see in the Style drop-down list box if you make changes here.

Table 13-1: The Format Settings Dialog Box

Component Name	Action
Styles to be visible	A list of styles from which you can select the ones you want to see in the Styles and Formatting task pane.
Category	Select from Available Styles (again, a misnomer; it really means the basics), Styles in Use (the ones you've used in your document), All Styles (the entire list of available styles), User Defined Styles (styles you have created, which you learn about later in this chapter), and Do Not Show Styles (Word will remove all styles from the list).
Show All	Selects all the entries in the list box, so all will appear in the Pick Formatting to Apply list.
Hide All	Deselects all the entries in the list box.
Always show Heading 1 through 3	You might think this means that regardless of your choices in the list box, Word will always include Headings 1 through 3 in the list. It doesn't.
Show Clear Formatting	If checked, the *Clear Formatting* entry appears at the top of the Pick Formatting to Apply list.
Font formatting	Includes formatting you have applied directly to text in your document—bold, italic, and so on.
Paragraph level formatting	Includes paragraph formatting that you have applied directly in your document.
Bullet & Numbering formatting	Includes bulleted and numbered lists that you have applied to your document.
Save settings in template	Tells Word to save your changes in the document template, so other documents created with the same template will use the same settings.
Styles	Click here to open a dialog box in which you can create and manage styles; we look at this later in this chapter.

Applying styles to paragraphs and text

Okay, now that you know how to view all your available styles, it's time to look at how to apply a style to text. This won't take long.

Place the insertion point in the paragraph to which you want to apply the style—*do not select any text!* Click the triangle on the right side of the Style drop-down list box on the Formatting toolbar, select the style you want, and Word applies that style to the paragraph.

If you don't see the style you want in the list, click the More entry at the bottom of the list or choose Format ➪ Styles and Formatting to open the task pane. Then display the style you need using the Show drop-down list box and click on it. If necessary, click Custom at the bottom of the Show drop-down list and select the style you need in the Format Settings dialog box.

Now you've just applied a paragraph style. Say you *did* select text within the paragraph, as we told you not to do. (There's no reason you shouldn't, we just wanted to show you how to apply paragraph styles.) What happens? Well, you've just applied the style to the selected text, not the paragraph itself. The text now has the text formatting that the style defines, though of course not the paragraph formatting. For instance, if you applied Heading 1 text to a word in a Normal paragraph, the word would be bold, but of course it would not have the normal Spacing After setting defined for Heading 1.

You can also add keyboard shortcuts and even toolbar buttons to styles to let you quickly apply the ones that you use frequently. We look at shortcuts later in this chapter, in the section "Using shortcut keys."

Tip   To reset a paragraph to the formats defined in the style, click inside the paragraph and press Ctrl+Q.

There is another way to apply a style. You can use the Style dialog box. This is left over from earlier versions of Word, and isn't really needed anymore. However, as you'll learn later in this chapter, it's possible to display a Style Area on the left side of your document in Normal and Outline views, in which Word displays the name of the style next to each paragraph. If you double-click in this area, the old Style dialog box opens. You can select a style and click Apply.

Viewing style information

What sort of formatting comprises a particular style? You can quickly find out in the Styles and Formatting task pane. Just point at a style and wait for a second, and a pop-up box appears by the mouse pointer, describing the style: *Heading 3: Normal + Font: (Default) Arial, 13 pt, Bold, Space Before 12 pt*, and so on.

You can also view the details in the Modify Style dialog box. When you point at a style in the Styles and Formatting task pane you'll see that a triangle appears on the right side; click this triangle to open a pop-up menu. Select Modify, and the Modify Style box opens (see Figure 13-4), where you can find all the details. We'll be looking at this box in more detail later, when we discuss creating and editing styles.

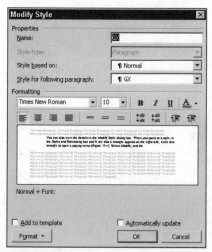

Figure 13-4: The Modify dialog box.

Selecting styles throughout your document

Word helps you modify the styles you have applied. On the pop-up menu you'll notice an option that says Select All: *x* Instance(s). Click on this option and Word highlights all the paragraphs or words that are using the selected style. You can now apply another style or formatting.

For instance, suppose you have decided that wherever you have used Heading 4 you really should have used Heading 3. You can click on the triangle to the right of the Heading 4 entry, choose the Select All: *x* Instance option, and then click the Heading 3 entry. Instantly all Heading 4s become Heading 3s. Or say someone working in one of your shared documents has used underlines to indicate the names of books referred to in the text, but you want to use italic. Use Select All: *x* Instances to select all the underlined text throughout the document; then use any formatting tool to convert it. You could press Ctrl+U to turn off underlining and Ctrl+I to make it italic, for instance. Or, if Italic appears in the Pick Formatting to Apply list box, simply click that and Word will remove underlines and apply italics all at once.

Here's another way to select all the text of a particular format. Click on that text somewhere in the document; then click the Select All button at the top of the Styles and Formatting task pane.

Creating and Modifying Styles

You don't have to use Word's styles. In fact any Word power user will eventually find the need to change something in a style, or even create styles from scratch. There are several ways to do this. We'll start by looking at how to create a brand new style.

Creating new styles

When you want to create a new style, click the New Style button at the top of the Styles and Formatting task pane, and the New Style dialog box opens (see Figure 13-5). Though this may look a little confusing at first glance, you'll see that much of what is in here you've learned before. Table 13-2 explains how you use this box.

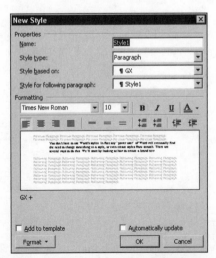

Figure 13-5: The New Style dialog box.

Table 13-2: The New Style Dialog Box

Component Name	Action
Name	Give your new style a name that you'll remember.
Style type	Select the type of style you are creating: Paragraph, Character, Table, or List; your choice will determine what components are available for creating the style.
Style based on	You may, if you wish, select a style on which to base this style, a starting point. However, note that this can cause problems in some cases. If you later change the style on which you based your new style, your new style may also change. For instance, if the base style is Arial, and your new style does not define a different typeface, if you later change the base style to Times New Roman, your new style will also become Times New Roman. In particular be very careful about changing the Normal style, because so many styles are based on it.
Style for following paragraph	This determines what happens when you press Enter while this style is in use. Most styles simply continue with the same style, but some styles assume that if you press Enter you have finished using the styles. For instance, if you select the Heading 1 style, type some text, and press Enter, the next line is automatically converted to Normal style.
Formatting	The Formatting area of the dialog box is where you actually create the style. If you are creating a Paragraph style, you can define paragraph and character formats. If you are creating a Character style, the paragraph formatting tools are disabled. And if you are creating a Table or List style, the tools for creating tables or bulleted and numbered lists appear.
Add to template	Select this check box if you want to add the new style to the document template you are currently using. That way, the next time you create a document using that template, the new style will be available.
Automatically update	Leave this check box unchecked unless you are *really* sure you want it! If you select it, each time you adjust the formatting of a paragraph that uses this style, *all* the paragraphs in the document using the style are modified too. *And* all styles based on this style. In most cases this is not a useful tool.
Format	Click this button to open a menu from which you can select a variety of formatting options: Font, Paragraph, Tabs, and so on.

Tip

It's important to remember that a style is attached to a document or template. If you create a style and don't select Add to Template, the style is only available in that single document. Make sure you select Add to Template so that the style is available to all documents created with the current template. You learn how to copy styles between documents later, in the section "Copying Styles between Documents."

Creating a style is really quite easy. Use the components in Table 13-2 to set up the style—give it a name, define what type it is and what it is based on, and so on—then format the style using the tools provided. If you are creating a Character style, for instance, you can see that the box provides the tools discussed in Chapter 4: the Font and Font Size drop-down list boxes from the Formatting toolbar and the Bold, Italic, Underline, and Font Color buttons. If that's not enough, you can click the Format button to get to more detailed tools that let you modify the Border and Language. The tools for formatting a style are described elsewhere in this document, as indicated in Table 13-3.

Table 13-3: The Style Formatting Tools

Format Type	Find Information Here
Font	Chapter 4
Paragraph	Chapter 5
Tabs	Chapter 5
Border	Chapters 5 and 10
Language	Chapter 8
Frames	Chapters 18 and 24
Numbering	Chapter 5

Tip   Here's a very quick way to create a new style. In your document, format a paragraph exactly the way you want your new style to look. Then click once in the Style drop-down list box on the Formatting toolbar—you'll see the entry is highlighted—and type a new style name. Press Enter, and your style has been created. Make sure you select the paragraph mark if you want to create a paragraph style; otherwise you'll be creating a character style.

Modifying and deleting styles

Modifying a style is the quickest way to change formatting in a document. When you modify a style, all of the text formatted in that style immediately becomes reformatted with the modified style. This is perhaps the single most compelling reason for using styles—it allows you to change the appearance of a document very quickly and easily. (This assumes that you are not using direct formatting throughout the document but are only applying styles to change the appearance of the text.)

There are two ways to modify an existing style. Point at the style in the Styles and Formatting task pane's Pick Formatting to Apply list box, click the triangle that appears to the right, and select Modify. You'll see the Modify Styles dialog box, which is the same as the New Styles dialog box. Simply make changes here in the same way you create a style.

But here's a way that is often quicker. Make your changes to a paragraph or text of the style you want to change, directly inside your document. For instance, if you want to convert Heading 2 from bold and italic to bold *without* italic, find a Heading 2 in your document and make the change. Then click inside this changed text, point at Heading 2 in the Pick Formatting to Apply list box, click the triangle, and select Update to Match Selection. Using existing text to modify a style in this manner allows you to see the new formatting applied to the text in your document before you actually change the style itself.

You can often simply click the style name in the Pick Formatting to Apply list or in the Style drop-down list box on the Formatting toolbar, and Word will display a dialog box asking if you want to update the style (see Figure 13-6). You can update the style or reapply the formatting of the style to the modified text.

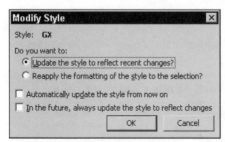

Figure 13-6: The message box that appears when you reapply a style to text that you have modified.

Note also that there are check boxes in here that allow you to Automatically Update the Style from Now On, and to Always Update the Style to Reflect Changes. The first check box tells Word that if you select an entire paragraph and make changes, it should assume that you want to change the style, and should change all the text of the matching style throughout the document, automatically.

The second check box, though, is misnamed. It should more properly be named *Don't bother to ask next time*. If you select In the Future, Always Update the Style to Reflect Changes, you are turning off the Prompt to Update Style check box in the Edit tab of the Options dialog box (Tools ➪ Options). From now on, Word won't bother asking whether you want to update the style; it simply reapplies the style. This probably isn't a good idea, of course, because you can accidentally change things throughout your document without noticing.

 Note   You can also delete a style—except for the built-in styles—by selecting Delete from the pop-up menu that appears when you click the triangle.

Using shortcut keys

You may want to add shortcut keys to your styles, so you can apply them very quickly while typing, without having to touch the mouse. For instance, Ctrl+Alt+1 applies the Heading 1 style and Ctrl+Alt+2 applies Heading 2. You can add these shortcuts to any style, or modify existing shortcuts.

In the New Style or Modify Style dialog box, click the Format button and select Shortcut Key to display the Customize Keyboard dialog box. Press the shortcut keys you would like to use, and Word will place them in the Press New Shortcut Keys text box. If the shortcut you chose is already in use, you'll see what it is used for displayed below this box. Often the shortcut is used for something you rarely do, so you can simply use your choice; otherwise try another shortcut combination. When you have the combination you want, click Assign.

Automatic style application

Word automatically applies styles for you in some situations. When you use Outline view, Word automatically assigns the style as you promote and demote paragraphs (see Chapter 25). When you create a table of contents or index, Word also applies styles to the entries, and it applies header and footer styles, too.

Table 13-4 lists those styles that Word applies automatically when you use the appropriate command. As with all styles, you can change the definition of these styles as needed.

Table 13-4: Styles That Word Applies Automatically

Style	Applied To
Annotation Text	Text entered in annotations
Annotation Reference	Annotation reference marks (the initials of the person entering the annotations)
Caption	Text entered using the Caption command
Comment Text	Comments (created using Insert ➪ Comment)
Footnote Text or Endnote Text	Text entered in a footnote or endnote
Footnote Reference or Endnote Reference	The footnote or endnote reference mark
Header	Text in headers
Index 1–9	Index entries
Line Number	Automatic line numbers from the Page Setup command
Macro Text	WordBasic macro text
Page Number	Automatic page numbers
TOC 1–9	Table of Contents entries
Table of Authorities	Table of Authorities text
Table of Figures	Table of Figures text

Copying Styles Between Documents

If you want to use a style that is in another document or template, you don't have to create the style again in the current document. Instead, you can use the Organizer. The Organizer differs from the Style Gallery in that the Organizer can copy individual styles, whereas the Style Gallery copies all styles from a document or template. The Style Gallery, however, offers you a preview of the styles before you copy them, which the Organizer doesn't.

Using the Organizer

To open the Organizer, choose Tools ➪ Templates and Add-Ins, and click the Organizer button (see Figure 13-7). With the Organizer, you can copy styles, macros, toolbars, and AutoText from one document or template to another. Make sure the Styles tab is selected in this case, of course.

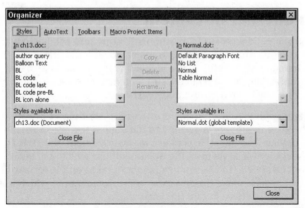

Figure 13-7: The Organizer dialog box.

The Organizer dialog comprises two list boxes placed side-by-side. Beneath each list box is a drop-down list box that displays the current document or template for the list box above. You can choose a different document or template in each list box, which then shows the styles in that document or template. Here's how to copy styles from one document to another:

1. The document you have open will be listed in the Styles Available In drop-down list box on the *left* side of the dialog box. You could pick another document if you wish, but we're assuming in this case that you are copying from a template or document into the one that is currently open, so there's no need to change anything.

2. The document or template from which you are going to copy is listed in the Styles Available In drop-down list box on the *right* side. If the one you want is not already listed (it probably isn't, as it shows the Normal template styles when you first open this box, regardless of which template the current document is based on), click the Close File button underneath. The button changes to an Open File button.

3. Click the Open File button and find the document or template from which you want to copy. When you first click this button, Word displays the contents of the User Templates directory, defined under the File Locations tab of the Options dialog box. You can navigate to another directory if you prefer.

4. When you've found the document or template you want to use, click it and click the Open button, or simply double-click on it. The Open dialog box closes, and Word loads a list of the styles stored in the selected document into the In *filename* box above the Styles Availble In box.

5. Select all the styles you want to copy in this right-side In *filename* box. You can hold Ctrl while you click on names to select multiple non-contiguous names, or drag the mouse down the list.

6. Click the Copy button. If any of the names match names of styles in the open document, Word will ask if you want to overwrite them. You can selectively choose to do so one by one, or simply say Yes to All.

That's about it; you've copied styles from one template to another. Note, however, the Delete and Rename buttons. You can delete or rename styles in *either list box*, so be careful. If you rename a style in the box listing styles in the document from which you are copying, you are literally renaming them in that document; this is not merely a tool for renaming while copying.

Copying text from another document

Another way to copy a style from one document to another is to copy text and paste it into another document. When you do this, the text's style is transferred with the text itself. (If you are transferring text with a Character style applied, the text will carry the style with it. If you are trying to transfer a Paragraph style, you must make sure you include a paragraph mark—see Chapter 5 for a discussion of how the paragraph mark carries the paragraph formatting.)

When you copy text with a style applied to it from one document to another, you need to consider several factors. If the style name that is applied to the copied text also exists in the document to which you are copying, and the style is in use in the document, the style is not transferred. The copied text picks up the style from the document into which it is being pasted. If the style isn't in use, the style in the receiving document takes on the formatting of the text being pasted. And if the style name doesn't exist in the document to which it is copied, the style is added to the list of styles in that document.

Actually, this method for copying styles is hugely frustrating to many people. Companies that routinely share and collaborate on documents find those documents accumulate garbage styles, as every Tom, Dick, and Helen dumps text into it using their own cute ideas of what makes a good paragraph or text format. We've seen this many times, as documents grow over months and years, as they are used to begin new documents, which also have more styles copied in . . . gradually they turn into a bloated mess.

Note   Word 2003 has a great new feature that many of us are going to love. You can limit formatting changes and keep others from importing and modifying your styles by locking the styles. We look at this feature in Chapter 34.

Using the Style Gallery

You can use the Style Gallery to copy an entire set of styles—but not individual ones—from a different template into the current document. The benefit of the Style Gallery is that you can preview styles before you actually copy them. If a style from the template that you choose to copy from has the same name as a style in the current document, the template style redefines and overwrites the current style. Again, the Style Gallery copies all of the styles from that template; if you want to copy selected styles, use the Organizer feature instead.

To use the Style Gallery to copy styles to your document, following these steps:

1. Choose Format ➪ Theme, and then click Style Gallery to open the Style Gallery dialog box (see Figure 13-8).

2. Select the template that you want from the list beneath the Template box.

3. Select the type of preview you want to see: the active document formatted with the styles from the selected template (Document), a sample document (Example), or a list of style names formatted with the style format (Style Samples).

4. Click OK to copy the styles from the selected template to the active document. (Word may have to copy off the Microsoft Office disks.)

Tip   In step 2 of these instructions, you select a template from the list of templates by clicking it. If you double-click instead, the styles from that template are added immediately to the current document and the dialog box is closed. This is a shortcut that you can use instead of selecting a style and then clicking OK. If you inadvertently double-click the template and don't want those styles to be added to your document, click the Undo button on the Standard toolbar before doing anything else.

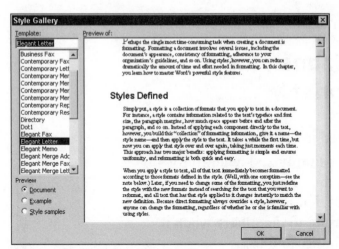

Figure 13-8: The Style Gallery dialog box.

Displaying style names in the Style Area

You can display the style names that you use as you work. The only disadvantage to this is that you also reduce the amount of screen space available for your document. If you work with styles to any degree, however, you may find it quite helpful to see the style names as you work. The area in which the style names are displayed is known as the *Style Area*.

Note   The Style Area is displayed only when you are in Normal or Outline view. You won't see it in Print, Reading, or Web Layout views.

To display style names, follow these steps:

1. Choose Tools ⇨ Options to open the Options dialog box.

2. Click the View tab.

3. In the Style Area Width box in the lower-left portion of the View tab, enter a value or use the arrows to select a value. The style area width is an area on the left side of your document that shows the paragraph style names next to each paragraph. A good starting value is 0.5" width.

4. Click OK. The Style Area appears to the left of your document (see Figure 13-9).

Tip   You can quickly display the Style dialog box by double-clicking anywhere in the Style Area.

You can adjust the Style Area's width by changing its value in the View tab of the Options dialog box, of course, but it's easier simply to use your mouse. The Style Area is separated from the text by a solid vertical line. If you carefully place the mouse pointer on this line, that pointer changes shape to show two opposing, horizontal arrowheads. When the pointer has this shape, drag the line to the left or the right as you want. To close the Style Area quickly, drag the line off the page to the left.

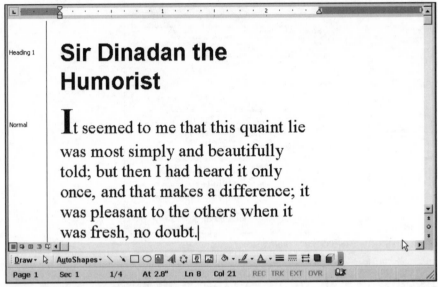

Figure 13-9: The Style Area in a document.

Renaming styles

You can rename a style in several ways. The easiest is to simply select the name that is currently displayed in the Style box on the Formatting toolbar and then to type a new name. Actually you haven't really renamed the style, you've just created an exact duplicate of it with a new name.

The other way to rename is to use the Organizer dialog box. Choose Tools ➪ Templates and Add-Ins and click the Organizer button to open this box. Select the style you want to rename, and click the Rename button. You can't actually rename built-in styles. If you try to, you end up with an *alias* for the original style.

Printing a list of the styles in a document

You can print a list of the styles in the template on which the current document is based. When you print this list of styles, the style name is followed by all of the formatting included in that style. This feature provides a handy way to check the makeup of all your styles currently available for the current document.

To print a list of the styles in a document, follow these steps:

1. Choose File ➪ Print, or press Ctrl+P, to open the Print dialog box.

2. Click the Print What box to see a list of elements that you can print.

3. Choose Styles from the list.

4. Click OK to print the styles.

Word's AutoFormat Tool

The automatic formatting feature in Word is called *AutoFormat,* and this feature can save considerable time and effort when formatting documents. When using the AutoFormat feature, Word analyzes each paragraph in the document to determine what kind of formatting should be applied: body text, bullets, heading styles, and so on. If you've already begun formatting the document, Word uses the formatting that you've applied as a guide to which styles it applies. Any styles that you applied are left unchanged.

When using AutoFormat, Word immediately begins the process of formatting the document. Once Word finishes, you can review all of the changes individually, reject them all at once, or accept them all at once. After the styles are applied, it's relatively easy to refine the document's appearance by changing the definition of a style or applying a different style to a particular paragraph, such as changing a Heading 2 style to a Heading 1. You can also change the overall design of the document using the Style Gallery to copy styles from a different template.

In addition to automatically applying styles to all of the paragraphs in a document, the AutoFormat feature can do the following:

✦ Indent paragraphs when it finds tab characters or spaces at the beginning of a paragraph.

✦ Remove extra paragraph marks at the end of each line of body text.

✦ Replace straight quotes and apostrophes with *smart* (curly) quotes and apostrophes.

✦ Replace (C) with ©.

✦ Replace (R) with ®.

✦ Replace (TM) with ™.

✦ Replace asterisks, hyphens, or other characters typed as bullets with real bullets (•).

✦ Replace :-(with ☹ or :-) with ☺.

You can view all of the available AutoFormat options in the AutoCorrect dialog box (see Figure 13-10). Remember, you can review each change and either accept or reject it. In addition, you can enable or disable different AutoFormat options in the AutoCorrect dialog box before using the AutoFormat feature.

You can also format text automatically as you type using the AutoFormat As You Type feature, which is also accessed in the AutoCorrect dialog box. Using this feature, Word automatically formats headings, numbered and bulleted lists, borders, and numbers as you type specific configurations of text and punctuation. We discuss this feature in Chapter 2.

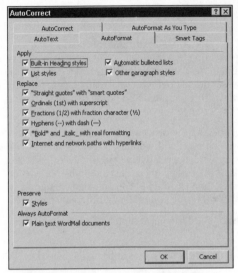

Figure 13-10: The AutoFormat tab of the AutoCorrect dialog box.

Applying styles using AutoFormat

You can use AutoFormat to apply styles to each paragraph in your document, or you can select the text that you want to format. To apply styles using AutoFormat, follow these steps:

1. Select the text that you want to format automatically. If you want to format the entire document automatically, don't select any text.

2. Choose Format ➪ AutoFormat to display the AutoFormat dialog box (see Figure 13-11).

Figure 13-11: The AutoFormat dialog box.

3. To review and change the AutoFormat options, click Options. The AutoFormat tab in the AutoCorrect dialog box opens. Enable the options that you want, and then click OK to return to the AutoFormat dialog box.

4. Choose the AutoFormat and Review Each Change option button. This allows you to double-check the formatting once it has been applied, and selectively approve or reject changes. Choosing AutoFormat Now automatically applies all formatting without giving you the chance to review changes.

5. Click OK, and Word begins autoformatting. After Word completes the formatting process, another AutoFormat dialog box appears (see Figure 13-12), in which you can review, accept, or reject the changes made.

Figure 13-12: The second AutoFormat dialog box.

6. You can scroll through the document to review it—leaving the dialog box open. Clicking Accept All accepts all of the AutoFormat changes without review, and clicking Reject All rejects all of these changes without review.

7. If you wish, you may apply a different set of styles; click Style Gallery to open the Style Gallery dialog box.

8. You can also click Review Changes to open the Review AutoFormat Changes dialog box (see Figure 13-13) in which you can review each change one by one; reviewing AutoFormat changes is explained in the next section.

Figure 13-13: The Review AutoFormat Changes dialog box.

Reviewing AutoFormat changes

As described, when using the AutoFormat feature to apply styles to your document, Word gives you the choice to accept or reject all of these changes at once or to review each change. When you review these changes, Word uses temporary revision marks to indicate the changes. You can also choose to hide the revision marks if you want to see the text as it appears with the AutoFormat changes. Table 13-5 lists the revision marks used with AutoFormatting in Word. (We look at using revision marks and the entire Reviewing process later, in Chapter 29.)

Table 13-5: Revision Marks Used in AutoFormatting

Revision Mark	What It Means
Blue paragraph mark	Word applied a style to the paragraph
Red paragraph mark	Word deleted the paragraph mark
Strikethrough character	Word deleted the text
Underline	Word added the underlined text
Vertical line in the left margin	Word changed the formatting in that line

To review AutoFormat changes, follow these steps:

1. In the AutoFormat dialog box, click Review Changes. This opens the Review AutoFormat Changes dialog box.

2. To review the AutoFormat changes, use any of the following methods:

   • To move from change to change, use the Find Next and Find Previous buttons, which are indicated by right-pointing and left-pointing arrows, respectively.

   • Scroll through the document. The dialog box remains open, but you can move the dialog box out of the way by dragging its title bar. As you scroll, you can reject a change by selecting the particular paragraph and then clicking Reject in the dialog box.

   • To apply a different style while in the Review AutoFormat Changes dialog box, click in the paragraph that you want to change and then select the style that you want from the Style drop-down box on the Formatting toolbar.

3. Each time you select a paragraph that has been changed, a description of the change appears in the Description box. To undo the change, click Reject in the Review AutoFormat Changes dialog box. To undo the last rejected change, click the Undo button. To display the document without revision marks, click Hide Marks.

Setting AutoFormat options

You can select which options the AutoFormat feature uses. For example, you may not want to apply styles to your headings, or you may want to replace straight quotes with smart quotes. You can specify these options by choosing the Options button in the AutoFormat dialog box to open the AutoFormat tab. You can also access these options by choosing Tools ➪ AutoCorrect Options and clicking the AutoFormat tab (see Figure 13-14). Table 13-6 explains each setting on the AutoFormat tab.

Note   It's easy to get confused about AutoFormatting because there are two places to control it. The settings in the AutoFormat tab are applied only when you run AutoFormat from the AutoFormat dialog box. The settings in the AutoFormat As You Type tab apply when you're editing a document. The settings in each tab are similar but not identical, and changes that you make to settings in one tab are not automatically reflected in the other. As a result, it's easy to clear a check box in the AutoFormat settings tab and then wonder why Word continues making AutoFormat changes automatically as you type.

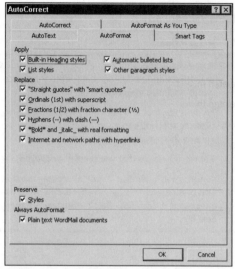

Figure 13-14: The AutoFormat tab in the AutoCorrect dialog box.

Table 13-6: AutoFormat Tab Options

Option	What It Does
Built-in Heading styles	Applies Word's built-in styles (Heading 1 through Heading 9) to headings.
List styles	Applies numbering and bullet styles to lists. If you select this option, Word first removes any manually inserted numbers or bullets.
Automatic bulleted lists	Adds bullets to lists.
Other paragraph styles	Where appropriate it automatically applies a paragraph style other than the styles for headings and lists, such as Body Text, Inside Address, or Salutation styles.
Straight quotes with smart quotes	Changes the usual straight quotes and apostrophes to curly quotes and apostrophes.
Ordinals (1st) with superscript	Replaces regular *st*, *nd*, or *rd* text in ordinals with superscript text.
Fractions (1/2) with fraction character (½)	Replaces fractions with formatted fractions.
Hyphens (--) with dash (—)	Replaces typed characters that represent symbols with the actual symbols. For example, if you typed (R) in place of a registration symbol, this option replaces that text with ®, two dashes with a true em dash character.

Continued

Table 13-6 *(continued)*

Option	What It Does
Bold and _underline_ with real formatting	Applies bold character formatting to words enclosed in asterisks and underline character formatting to words enclosed in underscores.
Internet and network paths and hyperlinks	Formats Internet and network paths as hyperlink fields so that you can jump directly to an item by clicking the hyperlink.
Styles	Retains any styles that you previously applied.
Plain text WordMail Documents	AutoFormats plain-text WordMail messages when you open them. This option affects only WordMail messages; it does not affect pasted text or other text files.

Summary

Paragraphs may be the building blocks of Word, but styles define what those blocks look like. Many of Word's formatting commands are simply pre-made styles. Word also includes a sophisticated kit of style-building tools to help you create styles for just about any type of formatting. With Word's AutoFormat tool, you can even apply your styles automatically to save time when formatting, which lets you concentrate on your document's content. This chapter explained working with both of these powerful features, including how to do the following:

✦ Master both how styles work and their relationship to document templates, which are styles at the document level rather than at the paragraph level.

✦ Apply styles by choosing the paragraph and then choosing the style from the Styles and Formatting task pane (Format ➪ Styles and Formatting) or the Styles list on the Formatting toolbar.

✦ Create your own styles from scratch using the Styles and Formatting task pane.

✦ Modify a style by selecting a paragraph with the style that you want to change, clicking in the Style box and pressing Enter, and then clicking OK in the Reapply Style dialog box to redefine the style.

✦ Apply styles for an entire document using the Format ➪ AutoFormat command.

✦ ✦ ✦

Using Templates, Wizards, and Themes

✦ ✦ ✦ ✦

In This Chapter

Saving time
with templates

Creating and
modifying templates

Attaching templates
to documents

Copying, renaming,
and deleting template
components

Creating documents
with wizards

Using themes to add
a consistent design to
documents

✦ ✦ ✦ ✦

By now, you already know quite a bit about Word's powerful formatting capabilities. Earlier chapters have looked at how to format characters, how to format paragraphs, and how to use styles to automate the process. When creating a complicated document from scratch, however, you can save yourself a good deal of time by using a template, wizard, or theme—tools that provide preformatted documents that you can build on.

This chapter explains how to create documents using the wizards, templates, and themes that come with Word, and how to modify those documents.

Introducing Templates, Wizards, and Themes

A good place to start is by describing what these three elements:

- ✦ **Template:** A file used as a starting point for a document. When you open a template you are opening a document to which you can enter your text and other content, a document that already has the exact styles and document formatting that you need for that document (or perhaps something close that you can quickly modify). Templates can contain many other things, too, such as customized menus, toolbars, and keyboard shortcuts, macros, AutoText entries, and so on.

- ✦ **Wizard:** A small program that runs within Word. It leads you through the process of creating a document by asking questions about how you want the document formatted and what you want in it. It then creates the document for you.

- ✦ **Theme:** A collection of design elements for a document. Originally intended for Web pages—and first added to Microsoft FrontPage before being added to Word—themes contain styles along with a variety of other elements, such as navigation bars, bullet images, background images, and horizontal lines.

In Word, you use templates frequently. Every time you start a new a document, in fact, you are opening a template. When you select Blank Document from the New Document task pane, you are using Word's Normal template. Templates can be very simple or quite complex. As for wizards, you most likely use them less frequently, but they're extremely useful when you need them. And themes—well, themes are designed for creating Web pages (ugly Web pages, in some cases), so you will likely use them less frequently than templates or wizards.

Working with Templates

Every Word document is based on a template. You can think of a template as a framework, boilerplate, or a master pattern that defines a document's appearance. A template may define some of a document's contents, as well as basic formatting. When you first create a document using the Normal template and begin typing, text appears in the default font: 12-point Times New Roman. The margins, meanwhile, are set to particular values for Word's Normal template, and the template contains various Heading styles, toolbars, menus, keyboard shortcuts, and so on.

You don't have to use the Normal template. Word has numerous other templates, each suitable for a specific type of document. You can also modify any of the supplied templates, including the Normal template, and even create your own templates.

Many Word users make the mistake of ignoring templates; they always use Normal. Using templates, however, can save you a great deal of time and effort, produce consistently formatted documents with ease, and ensure that all documents of the same type always contain the required components. You can create templates suitable for any type of documents, such as stationery (letters, memos, and faxes), forms and reports, proposals, and presentations.

Template components

A template contains many components—when you create a new document based on a template, the document uses these components. What sort of components? A template contains the following:

✦ Document layout information, such as margins and headers and footers.

✦ Paragraph and text layout information, as defined by the styles stored in the template (see Chapter 13). Everything that you type is initially formatted according to the styles defined in the template. You can, of course, change the formatting of individual parts of a document to override what the template specifies, as you've seen in earlier chapters (in particular the chapter on character formatting, Chapter 4, and on paragraph formatting, Chapter 5).

✦ Boilerplate text can be added to a template. For instance, a template used for letters may include your return address and your company logo, and a template used for proposals may include several paragraphs that summarize your organization's capabilities. Each new document based on a template opens with all of the boilerplate text and graphics in that template. As with formats, however, you can delete or change any boilerplate text or graphic that you don't need in a particular document.

✦ Field codes may be included, too. For example, a field code can represent the current date. Every document based on a template with that field code will replace the field code with the date on which that the document was created. For more information about field codes, see Chapter 23.

✦ AutoText entries (see Chapter 2) are included, too. When typing or editing a document, you can access all the AutoText entries in the template on which that document is based.

✦ Templates may include macros. A macro is a set of instructions that Word follows to accomplish a specific task, a little program that runs within the word processor. For information about macros, see Chapter 33.

✦ Templates also include menu bars, toolbars, and keyboard shortcut keys. Chapter 32 explains how to add menus to the menu bar, commands to existing menus, buttons to toolbars, and how to create shortcut keys.

Local and global templates

Templates may be *local* or *global*. Local refers to something that applies to a restricted area; global refers to something that applies to a wide area. The switch on the wall of your kitchen is local, for example. It controls only the light in your kitchen. The main switch in the breaker box where electricity enters your home, however, is global. It controls everything that uses electricity in your home.

Most Word templates are local. All of the components in a local template are available in only those documents based on that template or to which that template is attached. The Normal template, however, is global. Components of the Normal template may affect in some way, or be available to, documents based on *other* templates.

Note   The Normal template is thus named because it's saved as Normal.dot. However, Microsoft has, in recent years, taken to also calling this template the Blank Document template (that's what you see in the New Document task pane that we look at later, in the section "Creating a new document"). The Normal template and the Blank Document template are the same thing: different names for Word's most basic, global word-processing template.

If you want a certain template component, such as an AutoText entry, to be available to all documents, place it in the Normal template. This way, you don't have to repeat that entry in other templates. If an AutoText entry is useful only in a particular type of document, however, create a suitable template and place the AutoText entry in it.

A local template always has priority over a global template. When a document is based on a local template, Word looks for template components in that template first. If Word doesn't find a necessary component there, it looks in the global Normal template.

Suppose that the Normal template has an AutoText entry named CoName that contains the complete name of your organization. Now suppose that the Memo template also has an AutoText entry named CoName, but in this template, CoName contains an abbreviated version of your organization's name. In this situation, when you base a document on any template other than Memo, a reference to CoName provides the complete organization name. When you base a document on the Memo template, however, a reference to CoName provides the abbreviated organization name.

By default, the Normal template is global and all other templates are local. As you learn later in this chapter, however, you can make any template act as a global template so that documents based on other templates can have access to its components.

Naming and finding templates

Template file names end with the .dot extension. All templates that you create must have this extension for Word to recognize them. (Wizards, which are a form of template, use a different extension, .wiz.)

When you ask Word to show you a list of templates—you see how in the next section—Word looks in several places. First, it assumes that most of its templates are in subfolders of the Template folder it created during the installation process, which is a subfolder of the Microsoft Office folder. So, if you install Office in a folder named Program Files\Microsoft Office, templates are stored in subfolders inside the Program Files\Microsoft Office\Templates\ folder.

Word looks in two other places, as well. Open the Options dialog box (Tools ➪ Options), and click the File Locations tab. Notice the two template locations: User Templates and Workgroup Templates. These are folders that you can specify. So you can store templates you create in one folder, and templates that your company workgroup shares in another (perhaps on a network server). You'll find Normal.dot in the User Templates folder, by the way.

Tip   If you ever want to return to Word's default Normal template—perhaps you've made a lot of changes, and you want to revert to the original—it's a simple thing to do. Simply close Word, find the Normal.dot file (look in Tools ➪ Options, click File Locations, and see the folder name listed under User Templates), and rename or delete the file. Reopen Word, and the program automatically creates a new Normal.dot file for you.

Place any templates you create in the User Templates folder, and Word can find them. By the way, if you decide to create a templates folder elsewhere, follow this simple rule. Make sure that you store only templates in the folder, and that the folder contains few, if any, subfolders. If you point User Templates to a folder that has a few templates, plus lots of other files and subfolders, Word has to figure out what all the clutter is each time it opens the Templates dialog box, which takes time and may fill the dialog box with files you don't want to see.

Note also that Word provides other sources of templates. You can use one of your existing documents as a template, find a template online in Microsoft's Web-based template library, or access other Web sites containing templates.

Creating a new document

To choose and open a template, choose File ➪ New, and the New Document task pane opens, as shown in Figure 14-1.

The New Document task pane provides the following ways to access templates:

✦ **Several Basic Templates:** The Blank Document, Web Page, XML Document, and E-mail Message provide the most basic templates, for word processing, HTML, XML documents, and for creating an e-mail message (which requires Microsoft Outlook).

✦ **From Existing Document:** Word lets you choose a document that it will duplicate exactly, including all the contents, and you can then save it with a new name.

✦ **Templates on Microsoft.com:** Either type a name and click Go or click the Templates Home Page link to find a template in Microsoft's online library.

✦ **Recently Used Templates:** Under Other Templates you'll see several of your most-recently used templates (unless you haven't used any template other than Normal.dot recently).

✦ **On My Computer:** Click here to see the Templates dialog box, from which you can select from a wide range of templates stored on your computer or, in some cases, on the Microsoft Office disks.

✦ **On My Web Sites:** Click here to display a box in which you can open a Web site that stores templates and to which you have access. Your company, for instance, may set up a Web page containing templates.

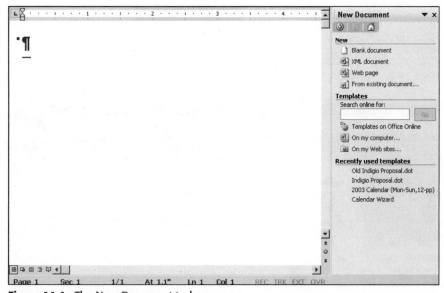

Figure 14-1: The New Document task pane.

To open a new template directly from the task pane, click one of the basic templates at the top, click From Existing Document, or click one of your recently used templates.

You can also select a template from a large library stored on your computer. Clicking On My Computer displays the Templates dialog box shown in Figure 14-2. This box provides access to dozens of different templates, categorized under various tabs. The first tab, General, contains the three basic documents (Blank Document, XML Document, and Web Page), plus the documents stored in your User Templates folder, as explained earlier (possibly dozens of templates, depending on what ones were chosen when Word was installed).

You'll find templates for letters, resumes, faxes, legal pleadings, and plenty of others. You can get an idea of what each looks like by clicking the template and examining the image that appears in the Preview box to the right. You can find more templates, too, by clicking the Templates on Office Online button, digging around until you find a template you like, and then clicking the Edit in Word link at the top of the template (see Figure 14-3). The template transfers to your computer and, in most cases, opens in Word. (In some cases, you may have to save it on your computer and then open it directly.)

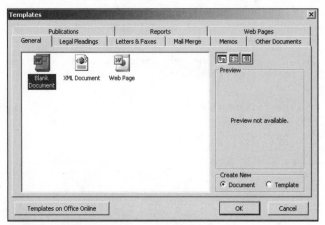

Figure 14-2: The Templates dialog box.

Figure 14-3: The Microsoft Templates home page.

When you've found the template you want, double-click it or click once and click the OK button. A few things happen now:

✦ Word creates a new document based on the template—it does not actually open the template. That is, if you now click the Save button on the Standard toolbar, Word asks you to provide a name for the file.

✦ Word places all the text and contents of the original template, if any, into the new file.

✦ Word attaches the template to the document, and at the top you see the name of the template file. With the template attached, you can use the template's styles, AutoText entries, toolbars, menus, and macros.

Tip   Now and then, you may want to open the actual template, rather than making a copy, so that you can modify the content of the template. Use Word's File ➪ Open command to open the actual .dot file. When you close and save the file, modifications are saved into the .dot file, and you won't be prompted to provide a new name.

Figure 14-4 shows you an example of a new document created from the Contemporary Fax template. We have not added or changed anything in this document, it's exactly as it opened. As you can see, the new document contains boilerplate text, lines across the page, and background shading. It also contains a number of Click Here and Type fields, blocks of text that you have to replace with your own. Go ahead and make any other changes to this document that you require.

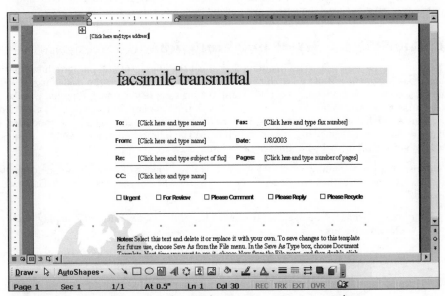

Figure 14-4: A document created using the Contemporary Fax template.

In new documents based on some templates, you'll find *fields* in the document. For instance, some of the letters contain the current date (which is based on your computer's date). For now, however, just understand that you can enter certain codes in a template or document that cause your computer to perform certain actions.

Cross-Reference   See Chapter 23 to find out more about field codes.

Saving a document based on a template

When you save a file, Word saves the boilerplate text copied from the template with any changes that you made to it. Word also copies the styles defined in the template and saves a record of the template to which the document is attached (see Tools ➪ Templates and Add-Ins).

The next time you open the document, you'll see the text as it was when you saved the document. In addition, all of the styles defined in the template are available—even those not used in the document itself. Because Word knows which template was used to created the document, you can also access any AutoText entries, macros, toolbars, or custom menus in that the template.

Note As you learn later in this chapter, you can easily modify the template so that it contains your own address rather than markers as boilerplate text. Then you won't have to type this information whenever you write a letter.

Of course, Word can reattach a document to its template only if that template is available. Suppose that you have a specialized template on one computer and you create a document based on that template. After saving the document, you then open it on a computer that doesn't have that template. The second computer displays the document, and you have access to the styles defined in the template because these styles are saved with the document. You do not, however, have access to the other AutoText entries, macros, and customized command settings contained in that specialized template.

Previewing the styles in a template

You can preview how the styles in a template affect the character and paragraph formatting in an existing document. If you're thinking about using a template as the basis for a new document, you can look at the effect of that template on a sample document supplied with Word. Of course you can also open a new document with the template, but this doesn't always do you any good. If the template contains boilerplate text and images you'll get a good idea, but if not, if it's more or less blank, it's not much help. The following method provides a quick way to get a good idea of what the template looks like.

Suppose that you're about to write a letter and you're thinking of basing it on one of the letter templates supplied with Word. To see how your letter will look, access the Style Gallery dialog box:

1. Choose Format ⇨ Themes, and then click the Style Gallery button to display the Style Gallery dialog box.

2. In the Template list box, choose the template that you want to view. For example, select Elegant Letter.

3. In the Preview section at the bottom left of the dialog box, choose Example. After a few seconds, the top part of an example letter with formatting based on the Elegant Letter template appears.

4. You may also view the document you currently have open as if the styles were applied to it (select Document), or samples of the styles (select Style Samples).

5. Click Cancel.

You can actually use this system to copy the styles in the template into the document that is currently open. Click OK to copy the styles from the selected template to your document. As discussed in Chapter 13, the styles you are copying will overwrite the ones in your document.

Creating your own templates

The templates supplied with Word provide a good basis to get started with typical office documents. However, you may find that you need other templates as well. Some may be similar to those supplied with Word, but others may be quite different. For instance, why open a letter template and type your address five times a day, when you could create a template that contains your address? You can create a new template by modifying an existing template or by converting a document to a template.

Using one template to create another

Suppose that you like the general style of the Contemporary Letter template but want to add your address and logo? You can easily modify the supplied template and save this modified version for future use. To create a template using an existing template, open the Templates dialog box, find the template, and click the Create New Template option button at the bottom of the dialog box. When you click OK, Word creates a new document, but it knows that you plan to create a template.

So once you have made your changes to the document and clicked the Save button, Word displays the Save As dialog box with the User Templates folder displayed, and the document in the File Name text box shown with a .dot extension. Save the file, and the next time you open the Templates dialog box you'll see your new template listed under the General tab.

Using a document to create a template

Instead of creating a new template by modifying an existing one, you can also create a new template from an existing document. Perhaps you created a letterhead document some time ago, and you want to use that as a template now. Simply save the file as a template in the User Templates folder (remember, the templates location is defined under the File Locations tab in the Tools ➪ Options dialog box). Choose File ➪ Save As, select Document Template in the Save As Type list box, and Word automatically switches to the User Templates folder for you, assuming that's where you'll want to save the file. Click OK, and you've got a new template that will appear under the General tab of the Templates dialog box.

Template attachments

A template can contain a number of items that, unlike styles, are not directly copied to a document created from the template. The template remains linked to the document, so the AutoText entries, toolbars, menus, and macros are available.

You can tell which template is attached by opening the Templates and Add-Ins dialog box (see Figure 14-5). Choose Tools ➪ Templates and Add-Ins, and look at the text box at the top of the dialog box. This shows the name of the template linked to the document.

Notice also the Automatically Update Document Styles check box. If this is checked, Word converts the styles in the document to match the styles in the template; furthermore, it checks to see if the styles in the template are ever modified and out of sync, and updates the document's styles as necessary.

Linking a different template to a document

After you create a document, it remains linked to its original template unless you attach a different one, move the template so Word no longer knows where it is, or move the document to a machine on which the template is not available.

You may want to change the template attached to a document to modify that document's appearance. For example, after creating a letter based on the Contemporary Letter template, you may decide it needs a more sophisticated look. You could modify the styles used by attaching the Elegant Letter template to that letter.

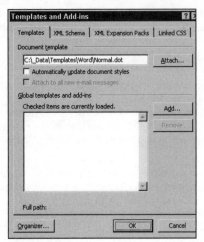

Figure 14-5: The Templates and Add-Ins dialog box.

To attach a template to a document based on a different template, follow these steps:

1. Open the document to which you want to attach a different template.

2. Choose Tools ➪ Templates and Add-Ins to display the Templates and Add-Ins dialog box. The Document Template text box at the top of the dialog box shows the name of the template to which the document is currently attached.

3. Check the Automatically Update Document Styles check box. (Think seriously about the consequences before you check this. If the document template is ever changed, this new document will change its styles when it is opened.)

4. Click the Attach button to display the Attach Template dialog box, which lists the available templates. Change to the folder containing the template that you want to attach.

5. Double-click the name of the template that you want to attach to the document, or click once and click OK, to return to the Templates and Add-Ins dialog box. The Document template text box now shows the name of the template that you want to attach.

6. Click OK, or press Enter, to attach the new template to the document. After a few seconds, Word displays the document in the new format.

Note   Attaching a different template to a document doesn't always reformat the document in the way that you want. Some styles and formatting don't change automatically, and in these cases, you need to reapply the style for that new style to take effect.

Attaching a new template to a document has the following effects on components in the document to which it is being attached:

✦ Text appearance may change, as Word applies different typefaces, sizes, and so on.

✦ The boilerplate text in the new template is *not* copied to the document. Any text and images in the document remains unchanged.

✦ Margin settings, page dimensions, and page orientation in the document remain unchanged. The document does not pick these things up from the template when it is attached to the document.

✦ Styles stored in the template are copied into the document. Each style in the document is replaced with a style of the same name in the new template; if the document uses a style that the new template doesn't have, the style in the document is unaffected.

✦ AutoText, toolbars, menus, and macros defined in the template become available, replacing those defined in the template originally linked to the document.

When you attach a new template to a document, the original template and the new template must be compatible. In the example presented here, you changed from one letter template to another, so everything worked well. If you had changed to an incompatible template, however, such as the Invoice template, you would have seen strange results, because the Invoice template is not designed for letters.

Note

Why *wouldn't* you check the Automatically Update Document Styles check box? Perhaps you want to make AutoText entries available, but do not want to modify the text formatting of the document. Or perhaps you did check this check box initially so that the styles are copied over, but you can go back and clear the check box so that the styles are not updated when the template's styles are.

Using components from different templates

You've already seen how documents based on any template can access components of the Normal template, because the Normal template is always global. For this reason, you should keep widely used template components in the Normal template. This way, you don't have to repeat them in other templates.

You also have access to components stored in any other global template, and to the single template that is linked to the document, as was just discussed.

Changing a template from local to global

Another way to use components in a different template is to change that template from local to global. Earlier in this chapter, you read that the Normal template is always global and that other templates are usually local. However, you can make any template global so that a document attached to any other template can access its components.

To provide global access to a template, follow these steps:

1. Choose Tools ➪ Templates and Add-Ins to open the Templates and Add-Ins dialog box. (If you haven't made any templates global already, the Global Templates And Add-Ins list box is empty, though some installation programs add features to Word by automatically creating global templates.)

2. Click Add to display the Add Template dialog box, which contains a list of available templates.

3. Select the name of the template that you want to make global, and click OK. The Global Templates And Add-Ins list box now displays the template chosen.

After you make a template global, you can use its AutoText entries, macros, menus, and toolbars—as well as those in the Normal template—in a document to which any template is attached.

Using the components

Well, there's one more step. After you attach the template, you can get to the AutoText entries, macros, menus, and toolbars. However, in the case of AutoText entries and macros, you have to tell Word you want to use them, as described here:

✦ To use an AutoText entry from the global template, choose Tools ➪ AutoCorrect Options, click the AutoText tab, and select either the new template or All Active Templates from the Look In text box. Click OK. If another template is selected, the AutoText entries in the new one won't work.

✦ To use a macro (see Chapter 33), choose Tools ➪ Macro ➪ Macros and select the template name or All Active Templates and Documents in the Macros In drop-down list box.

Menus and toolbars are different. Word makes all the menu options available from the template linked to the document and from all the global templates. When you choose View ➪ Toolbars, you see all the toolbars stored in the document, the template attached to it, and all the global templates. (See Chapter 32 for information on customizing menus and toolbars.)

Automatically opening global templates

It's important to note that if you close Word and then re-open it, the template you just defined as global is no longer global. It's still in the list, but the check box is now unchecked.

Global templates are loaded into your computer's memory. You can make any number of templates global, but as they occupy memory you probably shouldn't open more global templates than you actually need.

The Word installation procedure automatically creates an empty folder named Startup. You can use the Startup folder for templates that you want to become active and global immediately after you start Word. The Word startup folder is a subfolder of the Office directory in which Word was installed.

Suppose that you created a template called Main.dot that contains all of your frequently used components. You can use the Windows File Manager to copy this file to the Startup folder. Don't *move* Main from the template folder; rather, copy the template to the Startup folder. If you move the template file from the template folder, Word cannot access this file as a template. Now that the Startup folder contains a copy of Main.dot, this file automatically becomes an open global template the next time that you start Word. In fact there's no need to even add the template to the list in the Templates and Add-Ins dialog box—Word does that for you automatically.

Note   You can copy more than one template file to the Startup folder. All templates in the Startup folder become global and open when you start Word.

AutoText entries

AutoText entries, unlike menus, toolbars, and macros, cannot be stored in documents. That is, while toolbars and macros may be stored in documents or templates, AutoText items can be stored only in templates, not inside documents themselves. The only way a document has an AutoText item available is if the item is stored in a global template (we discussed this concept earlier in this chapter) or in the template that is attached to the document.

See Chapter 2 for details on creating AutoText entries. But we'll give a quick review here. When you create an AutoText item (under the AutoText tab in the AutoCorrect dialog box—see Figure 14-6), you can select a Look In option underneath the Preview box. Your selection at the point at which you click the Add button defines what is done with the AutoText item you are creating:

✦ **All Active Templates:** All the AutoText entries, in all the templates listed below, are displayed in the list of AutoText entries; but your new item will be saved in Normal.dot.

✦ **Normal.dot:** Word's basic global template, Normal.dot is always listed here. Selecting this displays just the AutoText items in Normal.dot, and when you click Add the new item is saved in Normal.dot.

✦ ***Templatename*.dot:** If other templates are attached to the document, they are also listed. Selecting a template displays the AutoText items stored by that template, and when you click Add, the AutoText is saved in that template.

Note   What about when you select text and use the Alt+F3 method for quickly creating an AutoText item—where is it saved? It's saved in the template currently selected in the Look In drop-down list box.

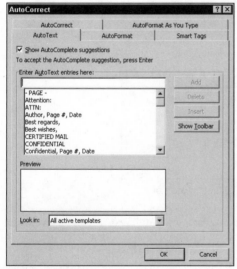

Figure 14-6: The AutoText tab of the AutoCorrect dialog box.

Copying, deleting, and renaming template components

Word includes an Organizer dialog box in which you can copy components between templates and between a document and a template. You also can rename and delete template components in the Organizer dialog box.

Copying components between templates

Suppose that you have a document based on one template and that you have made another template global so that you can access its components. Now you want to access this same document on another computer. Instead of making sure that the second computer has the same global template, it's often easier to copy the components of the global template that you're using into the template on which the document itself is based. Then you simply copy one template to the other computer.

Tip   It's not just templates—you can copy styles, toolbars, and macros between documents, too.

Or perhaps you want to create a document that you can send to someone with all the components it needs, without worrying about templates. You could copy menu options, toolbars, macros, and styles to the document. (As noted earlier, you can't copy AutoText items into the document, though.)

To open the Organizer dialog box, follow these steps:

1. Open a document based on the template containing the component that you want to copy, or open the template itself.

2. Choose Tools ⇨ Templates and Add-Ins to display the Templates and Add-Ins dialog box.

3. Click Organizer to display the Organizer dialog box, as shown in Figure 14-7.

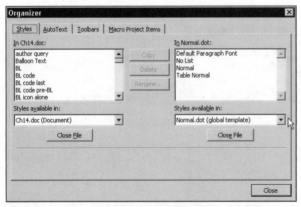

Figure 14-7: The Styles tab of the Organizer dialog box.

The Organizer dialog box is divided into four tabs: Styles, AutoText, Toolbars, and Macro Project Items. You saw how to work with the Styles tab in Chapter 13, and it's the same in the other tabs, too (the only difference is that under the AutoText tab you can't open documents—only templates).

You simply select the document or template to which you want to copy in one of the *Item* Available In drop-down list boxes or by using the appropriate Close File/Open File button. Then select the document from which you want to copy in the other drop-down list. (The drop-down on the left already displays the current document or, in the case of the AutoText tab, the linked template.) Then you can view items in templates or documents and use the Copy button to copy them from one to the other.

Tip   Macros can be assigned to toolbars. If you use the Organizer to copy a toolbar with a Copy button, remember to transfer the macro itself!

Deleting template components

If you experiment extensively with templates, some templates eventually become quite large, because they contain components that you don't use. To delete unwanted components from a template, select the appropriate tab in the Organizer dialog box, display the template's components in either list box, select a component that you want to delete, and then click Delete. When Word asks you to confirm, click Yes or No.

Renaming template components

Working with predefined templates, you may come across a component, such as a style, that you want to rename. For example, you may want to change *salutation style* to *greeting* or *signature style* to *name*. With the Organizer dialog box, you can rename template components as follows:

1. Select the appropriate tab in the Organizer dialog box. Then select the component that you want to rename.

2. Click Rename to display the Rename dialog box.

3. Type the new name for the template component, and click OK. The Organizer dialog box then reappears with the new name displayed.

Conjuring Up Documents with Word's Wizards

Wizards are easy-to-use programs that help you create documents by answering a series of questions. They are, in effect, templates on steroids. Not only do they provide you with a ready-to-go document, they actually help you build the document with our own information and choices. Icons for wizard files appear with a wand, and the files themselves end with the .wiz extension; you'll see these wand items in the Templates dialog box.

Word includes a variety of document types. For example, Figure 14-8 shows a calendar that you can create using the Calendar Wizard. Creating a complex document—an agenda, an award, a newsletter, or a résumé—from scratch could take hours; using Word's wizards, however, creating these documents takes only minutes. Table 14-1 lists the available wizards in the different tabs.

Table 14-1: Wizards Supplied with Word

Tab	Name	Description
Legal Pleadings	Pleading	Creates legal pleading papers
Letters & Faxes	Envelope	Addresses envelopes automatically
Letters & Faxes	Fax	Creates fax cover sheets
Letters & Faxes	Mailing Label	Allows quick creation of several mailing-label styles
Letters & Faxes	Letter	Allows stylizing of all letter components
Memos	Memo	Creates interoffice memos
Other Documents	Agenda	Creates organized meeting agendas

Continued

Table 14-1 *(continued)*

Tab	Name	Description
Other Documents	Batch Conversion	Not really a template wizard; it performs a batch conversion of selected files to or from Word's document format
Other Documents	Calendar	Creates monthly calendars
Other Documents	Résumé	Creates entry-level, chronologic, functional, and professional résumés
Web Pages	Web Page	Allows quick creation of Web pages

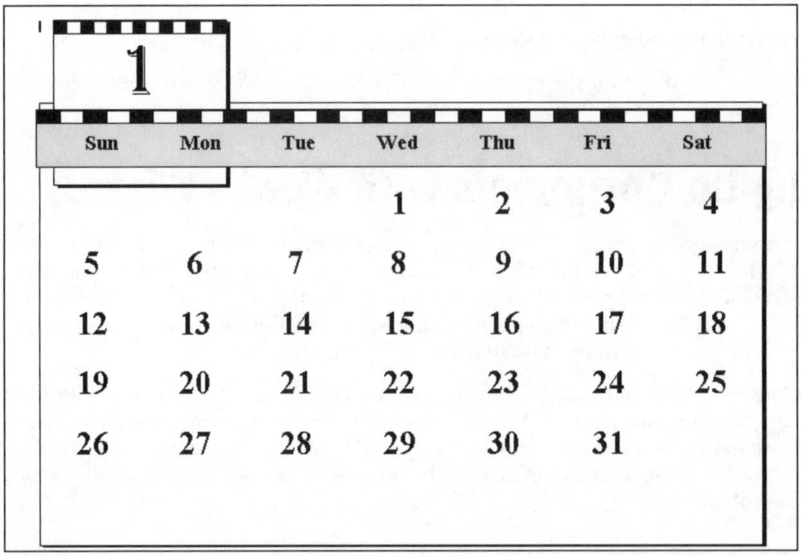

Figure 14-8: A calendar created using the Calendar Wizard. As you finish using the Calendar Wizard, the Office Assistant automatically appears with more options.

Using the Letter Wizard

You can use all Word wizards in much the same way; this section explains how to use the Letter Wizard. With this wizard, you can create a letter based on various page designs and styles, including personal, business, contemporary, or elegant. You can choose a block, modified, or semiblock style for your letter.

Adding your return address

The Letter Wizard can place your return address at the top of the page automatically. The wizard refers to the User Information tab of the Options dialog box (Tools ➪ Options) to find your return address, so to save time, make sure that this information is correct before opening the wizard.

Starting the Letter Wizard

To create a letter, you open the Letter Wizard and make choices in a series of dialog boxes. To open the Letter Wizard, follow these steps:

1. Choose File ⇨ New to see the New Document task pane.

2. Click the On My Computer link near the bottom of the options to open the Templates dialog box.

3. Click the Letters & Faxes tab.

4. Double-click the Letter Wizard icon or select the Letter Wizard icon and click OK.

At this point, you see a dialog box asking if you want to send one letter or send letters to a mailing list. Select Send One Letter to display the Letter Wizard dialog box (see Figure 14-9). This dialog box contains a miniature preview of a letter and asks that you choose a letter type. As you make your choices, the preview changes to show the current selection.

 Cross-Reference
Selecting Send Letters to a Mailing List in the Letter Wizard dialog box displays the Mail Merge Helper dialog box. See Chapter 22 to find out more about the Mail Merge Helper.

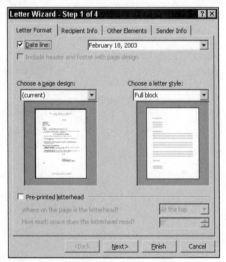

Figure 14-9: The Letter Format tab of the Letter Wizard dialog box.

Each Letter Wizard tab governs the appearance of your letter's Format, Recipient Info, Other Elements (such as a special Subject line), and Sender Info:

✦ **Letter Format:** Allows you to choose a page design, letter style, and date line style and to create space for a preprinted letterhead. By selecting Pre-printed Letterhead, you can set aside space on your page for a return address and company logo; this space can be set aside anywhere on your page.

✦ **Recipient Info:** Allows you to type in the recipient's name or to use Microsoft Outlook's Address Book for storing address data used in Word mailings. You can also pick a Salutation style.

✦ **Other Elements:** Allows you to place a Reference, Subject, Attention, or Mail Instructions line in your document. You can also select who should receive courtesy copies (cc); a path to the Address Book is provided to select these recipients.

✦ **Sender Info:** Allows you to type the sender's name or to choose the Address Book and to select a Complimentary closing. You can create a reference to Enclosures in your document, Job Title, and Company, and you can include the writer's or typist's initials.

Choosing a letter style

You can choose a Professional, Contemporary, Elegant, or Normal page design for your letter in the Letter Format tab of the Letter Wizard dialog box. Professional uses Arial, a sans serif font, Contemporary uses the serif font Times New Roman, and Elegant uses a serif font such as Garamond. Which font the wizard chooses for the Elegant letter style depends on which fonts are installed on your computer.

Addressing the letter

The Recipient Info tab (see Figure 14-10) contains the name and address used in your most recent letter; if this is your first time using the Letter Wizard, it either holds a dummy address or is blank. In either case, you can delete the existing text and type the new recipient's name and address. If you've set up an Address Book with Office using Outlook or Microsoft Exchange, click the Address button and then use an existing address from your Address Book.

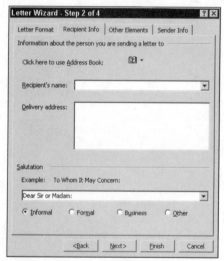

Figure 14-10: The Recipient Info tab of the Letter Wizard dialog box.

The Other Elements tab contains special addressing components such as mail instructions (CERTIFIED MAIL, CONFIDENTIAL). Components from the Other Elements tab are optional; you can skip this tab entirely and move directly to the Sender Info tab.

The Sender Info tab (see Figure 14-11) contains the address that you entered earlier in the User Information dialog box. You can also include options such as the typist's initials and references to enclosures in this tab. (Any changes that you make here, however, don't affect the

User Information data in the Options dialog box itself.) After you've finished with this dialog box, click Finish.

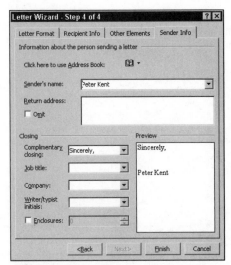

Figure 14-11: The Sender Info tab of the Letter Wizard dialog box.

After Word has created your letter, you can edit it to add the actual body of the letter and to replace any text that still remains in brackets (for example, if you didn't enter a recipient address into the wizard).

You can also change formatting, but think carefully before altering what the wizard suggests. In general, wizards provide suitable character, paragraph, section, and page formats, so change these formats only if you have a good reason. If you modify the letter extensively, you should generally create a template instead. After you've made all the necessary changes, save the letter as you would any other Word document and then print. Note also that the letter in Figure 14-12 has a little envelope icon. If you double-click this icon the wizard opens again, allowing you to modify the information you provided earlier.

Using Word's other wizards

All wizards work in a similar fashion to the Letter Wizard. Each wizard presents a series of dialog boxes or, in some cases, task-pane steps, in which you make choices and in some cases type text. Just follow the instructions. The first time that you use a particular wizard, you must work through quite a few steps, but each wizard remembers the choices that you make. So, when you use the wizard subsequently, you can usually accept your previous choices, making the process both fast and convenient.

You don't have to perform each step of a wizard. After entering your information, you can click Finish to skip any subsequent questions. The wizard then uses the default settings for any options that you skip. Figure 14-13 depicts the Résumé Wizard dialog box, which offers three styles and a flow chart to show where you are in the creation process. Résumé Wizard offers quick choices for résumé type, address, and heading appearances.

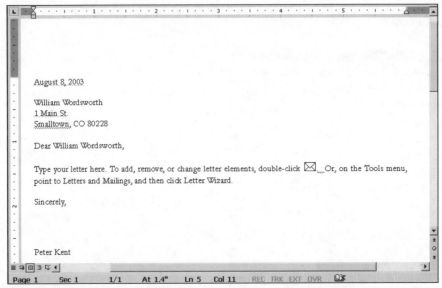

Figure 14-12: A business letter ready to edit. Some of the Letter Wizard options are already included in this example.

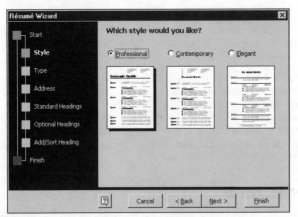

Figure 14-13: The Résumé Wizard dialog box.

Using Themes

A theme is a set of unified design elements and color schemes for background color or graphics, body and heading styles, bullets, horizontal lines, hyperlink colors, and table-border colors. Unlike a template, a theme doesn't provide AutoText entries, custom toolbars, macros, menus, or shortcut keys. A theme does provide a "look" for your document, however, using colors, fonts, and graphics.

Themes were originally intended for Web pages, and that's probably where they should stay in general. Themes provide a way for you to make your documents incredibly ugly and difficult to read with just seconds of work. Okay, some themes are okay, but this tool really comes from the *ransom-note school of desktop publishing,* providing cool tools that allow non-expert users a lot of control over graphic design. Remember, just because a Microsoft employee created a theme and loaded it onto the Word CD, that doesn't mean it's well designed or something that looks good.

Still, you can apply a new theme if you wish, change to a different theme, or even remove a theme by choosing Format ➪ Theme, which displays the Theme dialog box (see Figure 14-14). Before applying a theme, you can preview sample page elements in the Theme Preview pane by selecting the theme from a list, and you can also select options to apply brighter colors to text and graphics, animate certain theme graphics, or add a background image to your document. (Please, *remove* the background!) You can remove a theme from a document by opening the Theme dialog box (Format ➪ Theme) and then selecting (No Theme) from the Choose a Theme list box.

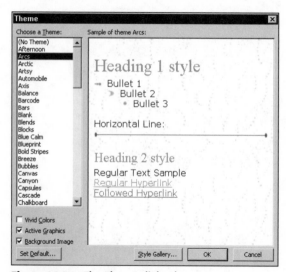

Figure 14-14: The Theme dialog box.

Note A variety of themes are available from Word, and if you have FrontPage 98 or a later version installed, you can use the FrontPage themes in Word documents as well. Additional themes are also available on the Web from the Microsoft Web site. Choose Help ➪ Office on the Web.

Summary

This chapter explored ways to format entire documents quickly using Word's wizards and predefined templates. Highlights of this chapter include the following:

✦ Using predefined styles in templates. This is one of the great, timesaving, formatting features available in Word.

✦ Creating a template. You can create a new template by modifying an existing template or by converting a document (created by you or a wizard) to a template.

✦ Using components from different templates and documents. You can use components from different templates by attaching another template to your document or creating a global template. You can also copy components between templates and documents.

✦ Creating documents using wizards. Select the wizard you want to use by choosing the File ➪ New command, clicking the On Your Computer link, clicking the tab in which the wizard is located, and then double-clicking the wizard's icon.

✦ Using Themes (Format ➪ Theme) to add a consistent page design to documents by using color, fonts, and graphics combinations.

✦   ✦   ✦

What Looks Good?

Word provides you with tremendous publishing power and tools that do all sorts of neat things. However, all that power is perhaps too much for mere mortals—non-designers, that is. It's all very well putting these tools into the hands of untrained people, but what are they going to do with it? All too often, something horrible.

Here is a phrase that has been around for about 15 years now: *ransom-note desktop publishing*. In the early days of desktop publishing, people with no graphic design or layout experience or education were suddenly given professional publishing tools. The results were often terrible. These programs were just so *cool*—the way you could lay out text in different sizes, different positions, different fonts, different formats, and different colors. The result was that all too often users mixed all sorts of things together, just because they *could*. A single page might have five or six different fonts mixed together, along with different sizes, bold, italics, various orientations, and multiple colors. In other words, ugly stuff.

Consider this chapter a support to all the features discussed in the rest of the book. It offers a few tips to help you create decent-looking documents. It is not the purpose of this book, or this chapter, to teach great desktop-publishing design, so don't expect to end up creating award-winning layouts. But by following a few simple guidelines, you *can* create professional-looking documents that avoid overusing the features at your disposal.

Word Processor or Desktop Publishing Program?

Word is a word processor and a desktop-publishing program. These two genres of software have merged. A decade or so ago if you wanted to lay out pages that looked professional—pages for newsletters, books, magazines, and so on—you needed a desktop-publishing program. Back then, there was a big difference between desktop-publishing programs and word-processing programs.

The former were good at placing text on pages in many different ways: you could use different positions and orientations, many colors, varying fonts, and so on. They weren't so good at some of the things that word processors did well. Word processors managed large amounts of *words*, with less regard to how they actually *looked*. They had great spell checkers, search-and-replace features, cross-indexing and tables of contents, and so on.

In This Chapter

Reviewing basic layout rules

Making paragraphs look good

Using the right typefaces

Working with images and other non-text elements

Microsoft Word, however, is now also a good desktop-publishing program. In fact, it has been pretty good for at least a decade. Although most publishers lay out their books using programs such as Quark or PageMaker, many could easily have been laid out using Word. We have been using Word to lay out technical manuals for at least the past ten years.

Note
So what's the difference? The term *word processor* applies to a program designed to manage words well—to help you put your thoughts into words, check for mistakes, find things in the text, create indexes, and so on. A *page-composition* or *page-layout* program is one that helps you lay words and images on a page so that they *look* good. Of course, there is a tremendous amount of overlap. After all, for many years word processors have allowed users to change the format of the text and paragraphs. And in recent years, the page-layout capabilities of word processors have grown tremendously. The opposite is not so true, however. Although you can often use word processors for page layout, page-layout programs are generally not as competent with word-processing tasks.

Now, Word is not a *great* desktop-publishing program—you wouldn't want to use Word for complicated magazine layouts, for example, because it doesn't handle placing images on the page as well as a true page-layout program. As you've seen in this book, however, there is an awful lot that you *can* do with Word.

The Number One Rule: Don't Be Too Clever

That's right, don't try to be too clever with your layouts. Document layout is a form of graphic design. Yes, we're talking text documents, but *layout* refers to the way everything sits on a page—how it *looks*. Words can be placed on a page in many different ways. This is a designer's job.

So what does *don't be too clever* mean, exactly? It means don't try to do too much, don't use too many cool layout tricks and tools, don't try to push your design skills further than they really should be pushed. Being too clever hurts in two ways:

✦ If you're not a real designer, you may find that your design skills don't match the capabilities of the tools you're using. You may mix the wrong colors together, for example, simply because you don't have the training to work with colors, or you may end up choosing fonts that aren't compatible.

✦ Even professional designers sometimes try to be too clever. They end up creating documents that look cool in some ways but that are so distracting that they are difficult to read. And we're betting that in most cases your goal is to create a document that someone will want to *read*.

Function over form, or form over function?

Before you start a document, think about what it is you really want. What is most important—that the document is easy to read or that it looks good? No, don't say you want *both*. Which of these two choices is *more* important? We're going to assume, and continue from here under this assumption, that readability is most important. Sure, you want the document to look good, too, and we'll show you how to do that. But after making the decision that readability is paramount, it should be easier to make some other decisions. You first have to understand that *cool* and *readable* are often two different things.

Here's a classic example. White text on a black background has become popular over the last few years, in particular on Web sites. Yet white on black is very difficult to read, far more difficult than the more traditional and less cool black on white.

Tip   Sometimes traditions become traditions because they *work*. A number of new document style guides became popular over the last few years, during the dotcom madness. We suggest that you stay away from these non-traditional guides. In many cases, they focus far more on form than function, more on the look of the document than on readability.

Templates are not always good

You might think that one way to ensure that your documents look good is simply to stick with using templates—the templates that come with Word, templates that you find on the Microsoft Templates Web site, and templates that you download for free or buy from other sites.

Cross-Reference   See Chapter 14 to find out more about using templates and themes.

Unfortunately, using a template doesn't always ensure a solid, readable document. Many of these templates are very good, but many are not. In particular, templates designed for Web pages, such as the themes you find in Word's Themes dialog box (Format ⇨ Theme), are often terrible. Some use white text on dark backgrounds of various colors, distracting backgrounds with thin fonts, documents designed to be printed that use sans serif fonts for body text, and so on. Many of these templates—again, in particular those designed for Web pages—are created to look nice, not actually be read. And, unfortunately, in many cases, they don't even look nice!

Take a look at Figure 15-1. Does the document with a theme applied (on the right) actually look better in any way? It's certainly harder to read, and it's hard to argue that it's more attractive.

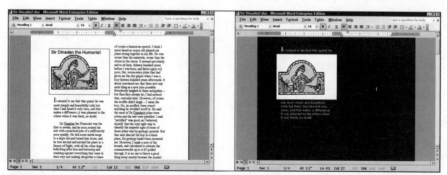

Figure 15-1: A document without a theme (left), and with a theme applied (right).

Paragraph Formatting

This next section looks at some things you can do to make your paragraph formatting look good. We examine these simple concepts:

Alignment

Indenting

Margins

White space

Cross-Reference See Chapter 5 to learn about the paragraph-formatting tools.

Working with paragraph alignment

It's popular these days to use *justified* text. Click the Justify button on the Formatting toolbar, and your text is spread across the page, between the margins, equally. You get nice straight lines along the edge of the text on both the right and left sides of the paragraph.

Unfortunately, you also get uneven spacing *within* each line. Word has to add a little space between some words in each line to force the line to stretch all the way across to the right margin (see Figure 15-2). It's not a lot, but in some cases, it's enough to make your text harder to read. The alignment does look neater, but justified text can take a little more work on your part. You have to hyphenate the text carefully to ensure that the spacing doesn't get so odd that it's actually more difficult to read. You also have to watch for *snakes* of white space that can work their way down through paragraphs.

Tip Columns that are very narrow don't work well with justified text. Either Word has to do very strange things to get the text to spread across to the right margin, leaving lots of big gaps, or you have to hyphenate a word on just about every line to get it to work.

Is it best, then, to use ragged edges and left-justify your text? In some cases. Both ragged edges and straight edges can be used in different circumstances. Generally, straight edges give a more formal (some would say even *stodgy*) look, while ragged edges are more informal. Perhaps the best choice comes down simply to what looks right for the document and your answer to the question, "Are you willing to take the time to hyphenate words to make a straight edge look good?" (Hyphenation can also improve the look of a ragged edge, but it's less critical in most cases.) In some cases, a straight edge simply will not work without a lot of hyphenation, in which case you should probably be using a ragged edge.

Tip Remember, you don't need to press the spacebar twice after a period at the end of a sentence. Word processors, using most typefaces, do not require an additional space. This is an old custom from the days of the typewriter, and it has remained even as use of typewriters dies out.

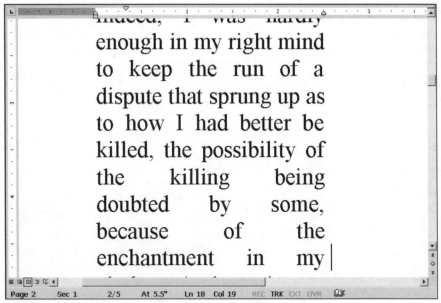

Figure 15-2: Sometimes justifying text causes odd-looking spaces; this text really needs hyphenating.

Indenting and adjusting margins

You can get lots more text on a page if you just narrow the margins and don't indent anything. (You can also reduce paragraph spacing.) Cram it in—just don't expect people to read your documents.

Word uses one-inch top and bottom margins in the default document, and one-and-a-quarter-inch margins on the side. They're not bad, though perhaps you could bring the side margins down a little. But don't reduce margins too much for most documents. Folks often use very thin margins for reference documents on which they are trying to get as much information as possible onto each page. For documents that have to be *read*, however, err on the side of large margins rather than small.

As for indenting, it can be used to set text apart—notes and quotes, for instance, can be indented to make them stand out a little, and to add a little white space to the document.

You may also want to indent the first line of a paragraph a little. Newspapers, for example, start the first line of text in each paragraph about two characters in from the left margin. Many documents, however, don't use this convention. Here's the rule, though: If you don't leave space before each paragraph—a blank line or so—you should indent the first line of each paragraph. You have to give the reader some way to recognize when one paragraph ends and another begins, and that's done using either a line between paragraphs or by indenting the first line of the new paragraph.

Using white space

What is *white space*? The area of the paper *not* covered by text and images. White space makes documents easier to read; it's as simple as that (see Figure 15-3). White space is especially important for documents that may be skimmed or read quickly. It's true, most books—novels, for example—don't include much white space. But white space is not necessary for the type of reading experience in which the reader has decided to become absorbed by the text, to focus on nothing but the text, for an extended period of time.

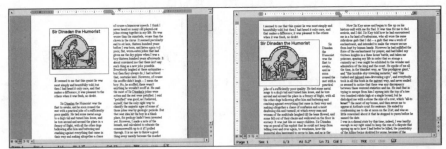

Figure 15-3: The document with white space (left) is easier to read; it's as simple as that.

Most documents you work with these days, from articles in popular-culture magazines to business memos, from sales proposals to technical documentation, work differently. For these documents, the aim is to help the reader get as much out of the document as quickly as possible, with as little mental investment as necessary. White space, in conjunction with a good layout of text and images, allows the eye to skim through a document, jumping from area to area, identifying the areas of the document containing the required information. White space allows a reader to get into the document, retrieve the information, and get out again, as quickly as possible.

So where can you use white space?

  Margins

  Between paragraphs

  Additional indentation of some text or paragraphs

  Around graphics and images

  Before and after headings

Use white space to make things stand out. When you place a quotation into your document, leave a line or two above, a line or two below, and indent from the left, for example. Make sure headings have more than the usual space above them, and a little space below. Don't cram images tightly into text—leave a little space around.

Typefaces

Text formatting, as discussed in Chapter 4, is a huge problem these days. And the biggest mistake people make is not a surprising one because few even understand the terminology. Here is the basic rule that is so often violated:

✦ Serif typefaces are good for body text.

✦ Sans serif typefaces work for headings.

Note The terms *font* and *typeface* are often used interchangeably, and the meanings are very similar. Strictly speaking, a *font* is a full set of characters of the same design and size. A *typeface*, sometimes known as a *type style*, is a particular character design. Thus, a font is a typeface of a particular size. The term *typeface* comes from a printing block with the shape of a character on it.

A *serif* typeface is one that has little decorative lines—*serifs*—at the end of the main strokes of a character. Look in Figure 15-4 at the *T* of *typeface*. Instead of just a vertical line with a horizontal line across it at the top, the capital serif *T* has extra pieces—the horizontal line has a down stroke at each end, and the vertical line has a small horizontal line attached at the bottom. These lines are additional in the sense that they are not necessary to help you identify the letter.

This is a Serif Typeface—
Times New Roman
This is a Sans Serif
Typeface—Arial

Figure 15-4: Serif and sans serif typeface.

Note that these extra lines are not completely decorative. For some reason, the human eye likes these little things, it makes characters easier for us to read. This is especially true when your document has lots of text close together, in body text.

A *sans serif* typeface (often simply referred to as a *sans* typeface) doesn't have these additional lines. *Sans* means *without* in French; thus, *sans serif* means without serifs. Look at the sans serif *T* in the illustration, and you can see that all it has is the vertical and horizontal lines.

Next time you go to a bookstore, look at a dozen or so books. Almost invariably, most of the text is printed using a serif typeface. (Headings may be printed with sans serif, and that's fine, but we're talking about the body text here.) Now and then, you may run across a book that uses a sans serif typeface, but it's generally one of two types of book: a self-published book published by someone without layout and publishing experience, or a book going out of its way to be intentionally modern and stylish (another example of form over function). The fact that the great majority of books use serif typefaces tells you something—that serif typefaces are much easier to read.

In most cases, you'll want to use a sans serif typeface for headings. They have a cleaner look and are very readable in small amounts. And using a sans serif typeface for headings and a serif typeface for body text helps the headings stand out a little more.

Note You may experience some resistance in your company or workgroup to this concept. Sans serif typefaces for body text has become so common that many people simply assume that it must be acceptable. So you may have some educating to do. Come back to the "readability versus coolness" argument and point out that the vast majority of books use serif typefaces for a good reason—a serif typeface is easier to read in large blocks of text.

As is often the case, there is an exception to this "rule." If you are creating Web pages, you may want to use a sans serif font throughout. Because of the low resolution of computer screens compared to the printed page, serif fonts don't look very good—they appear grainy. It can actually be more difficult to read a serif font on-screen, especially when the font is displayed small (and on a Web page you can't always control the way fonts are displayed), than it is to read a sans serif font. That's why most Web sites these days use sans serif fonts for body text instead of serif fonts.

Tip There are other things to consider when choosing a typeface. After you have applied a face to a block of text, read it through carefully to make sure it works well. Sometimes you notice things that you really hadn't thought of before. For example, some typefaces make it hard to distinguish between the number *1* and the letters *l* (el) and *I* (eye). In some documents, that can be a real problem, particularly documents using many numbers.

Typeface combinations

Okay, so you're going to use serif for body text and sans serif for headings. But *which* ones? MS Windows comes with some basics. Times New Roman is the default serif typeface, and Arial is the default sans typeface. These are good choices, too, and look quite reasonable. You may want to use other choices—Verdana is a very popular sans serif typeface, for instance. However, remember these simple rules:

✦ Don't get too fancy. There are hundreds of different and interesting-looking typefaces available, but some are appropriate for very specific uses and won't look good in most documents. Alegerian, for instance, is an interesting and rather ornate serif typeface, but can be very distracting.

✦ Pick a typeface for headings, and stick with it. Don't switch between typefaces, one for Heading 1, a different one for Heading 2, and so on.

✦ Don't use too many typefaces on a single page, or even in a single document. More than three on a page can look strange. In fact, if you want to use more than three or four typefaces in an entire document, make sure that you have a good reason! The more typefaces you use, the more likely you are to run into technical problems, such as having to embed fonts into the document.

✦ If you are sharing documents, you should use only common fonts to ensure that recipients see what you see. If you really want to use an uncommon font, you can embed the font (see Chapter 4).

Using typesetting characters

You can make a document look much more professional by simply using the correct characters. For example, use © instead of using (c) for the copyright symbol, use *curly* quotation marks and apostrophes instead of straight ones, and use a real em dash character (—) instead of using two dashes.

Note

Where *is* the hyphen key? Your keyboard has a key showing two horizontal lines next to the zero (0) key above the character keyboard (not on the numeric keypad). Press this without pressing the Shift key to type a hyphen. If you press the Shift key at the same time, you are typing an underline character. You also have a hyphen key on the numeric keypad, above the 9 key. This works as a hyphen whether or not Num Lock is turned on.

How do you create these special typesetting characters? First, choose Tools ⇨ AutoCorrect Options, and click the Auto Format As You Type tab. Make sure that the appropriate Replace As You Type options are turned on. Then refer to Table 15-1 to see what to type to insert the various characters in your document.

Table 15-1: Using Typesetting Characters

Character	Action
Curly quotes	Simply type quotation marks and apostrophes, and Word automatically replaces the straight ones with curly.
©	Type (c) and Word replaces it with the character.
®	Type (r) and Word replaces it with the character.
™	Type (tm) and Word replaces it with the character.
Em dash —	Immediately after typing a word, type two hyphens, followed by the next word (no spaces). Finish typing the word that follows the hyphen. When you type the next period or press the spacebar, Word converts the hyphens to an em dash.
En dash –	The same as the em dash, except that you should include a space before the two hyphens.
Hyphen -	Simply press the hyphen key.
½	Type 1/2 and press the spacebar.
¼	Type 1/4 and press the spacebar.
¾	Type 3/4 and press the spacebar.
Ellipsis . . .	Used inside or at the end of a sentence, an ellipsis indicates a thought that trails off. Simply type three periods, one after the other, and Word creates a real ellipsis character.

The Em Dash, En Dash, and Hyphen

It's worthwhile at this point to clarify the misunderstanding that exists about the em dash, the en dash, and the hyphen— three greatly misused typesetting characters. Here's what these things are and how they are used:

✦ **Em dash:** A long dash used inside a sentence to create a break in the flow, as in the sentence: "A serif typeface is one that has little decorative lines—*serifs*—at the end of the main strokes of a character." Traditionally, this dash was the width of the letter *M*, thus the name *em dash*. Microsoft fonts, however, typically have oversized em dashes and undersized en dashes.

✦ **En dash:** A shorter stroke used to indicate a range: 100–120. Traditionally, this dash was the length of the letter *N*, thus *en dash*.

✦ **Hyphen:** A stroke that's shorter still, used to hyphenate words. For example, *document-management system,* or *e-mail.*

Whatever you do, do *not* use a hyphen as an em dash; it slows down reading because it's confusing and looks unprofessional.

Not all fractions are available in the nicely typeset format shown in Table 15-1: ½, ¼, and ¾. So if your document calls for some fractions for which no typeset character is available, you should probably be consistent and *not* use the typeset characters at all. It looks a little unpolished to use ½ and ¼, and then have to use 6/7.

Tip   Word has some other AutoCorrect characters. You can type :) to create ☺, :(to create ☹, and :| to create ☺. However, don't use these characters too frequently; you run the risk of creating documents that go beyond cute to just plain corny.

Font size

There is no one perfect font size. It all depends on who is reading the document and how the text appears in relation to the rest of the page. Here are a few guidelines to help you:

✦ Word uses 12-point text as default, and that's a pretty good size in most cases.

✦ However, older readers may appreciate a larger font, perhaps as large as 14 or 15 points in some cases.

✦ Use larger fonts for faxes and forms, where possible. (Sometimes it's not possible if you want to get everything onto a single page.) They will be easier to work with and read.

✦ Headings should be larger than body text, of course. Look at the various headings in conjunction with body text and decide whether the change in size is enough to differentiate them.

✦ If you are using thin columns, you can often use a smaller font size; but small fonts on long lines are difficult to read.

Bold, italic, underline, and color

Some Word users employ different typefaces for emphasis. This is often distracting. In general, you should use bold, italic, underlines, and possibly color to emphasize words. Bold is good for emphasis, and italic fonts are often used for quotes and publication titles.

Underlines are a different issue. They should be used sparingly. They make text hard to read, and in some ways, they appear rather *retro*, harking back to the days of the typewriter when the underline was used frequently because you couldn't create italic text.

Color often works well for headings, and perhaps even a few words within body text to emphasize them. However, the main rules with color are to not use too many colors and to not color too many things. Often one color is more than enough, although you may get away with two in some cases. But once you start sprinkling your documents with three, four, or five different colors, you risk creating a jarring visual layout that is hard to read. Color is much more effective when you use it for just a few things—for headings, for example. Used too frequently, color loses its effect. The eye gets used to seeing it everywhere, and the brain no longer identifies the colored text as somehow special. (Oh, and some readers are colorblind!)

Adding Images

Images can add pizzazz and excitement to a document. But as with everything else in your layout, you have to be careful. Avoid filling every page with images. Apart from the obvious utility of illustrating concepts being described in the text, a few images sprinkled here and there can also help break up the text and make it more readable. A couple of visual elements on a page is usually more than enough, and you may want to avoid putting images on *every* page.

Note   Having warned you about overusing images, we do recognize that some documents are primarily image documents. Just be careful when you use images to illustrate what are primarily textual documents.

Cross-Reference   See Chapters 17 through 19 to find out more about working with images.

There are really two reasons for adding images to your document:

✦ One, as mentioned earlier, is to illustrate what you are writing about—a picture, they say, is worth a thousand words (a gross generalization, of course, but you get the idea).

✦ The other reason is the same reason you should use white space in your documents—to break up the text. Images can give the eyes a rest and can help the eyes scan and skim the page.

Images can be many different things. Little curly swirls marking the end of a chapter, fancy drop caps on the first letter of a chapter, even *pull quotes*. A pull quote is a piece of the document's text pulled out and set separately in a different font—usually larger, sometimes bold italic. Pull quotes can be placed into boxes, for instance, with the body text wrapping around the box, perhaps with a gray background.

Tip You have plenty of clip art available to you, but watch out for two things. First, try to pick clip art that doesn't scream out, "Hey, look at this corny cartoonish clip art." And second, avoid picking images that everyone else is using or that come from the same set and look almost the same.

Avoiding the Weird Stuff

Now let's get to the weird stuff—things that Word lets you do that in most cases you probably shouldn't: document backgrounds, animated text, fancy bullets and horizontal lines, and ornate borders around boxes.

Be very careful with these things. The fact that ugly Web pages have become common doesn't mean that they're okay. They're still ugly. And it definitely doesn't mean that the authors of paper documents should adopt some of the worst mistakes of Web authors.

Here are a few guidelines to help you avoid the weird stuff:

✦ If you plan to use a background, ask yourself *why*. If you can't come up with a good answer (better than "because I can," or "because it will look kinda cool"), don't do it!

✦ If you have to have a background, pick one as uncluttered as possible, print it, and ask other people if the document is hard to read.

✦ Remember that light-colored text on a dark background is hard to read.

✦ Dark-colored text on a dark background is also difficult to read. In fact, text and background colors require contrast, with the text having the darker color.

✦ Animated text is fun. On the printed page, though, it may not look quite as neat.

✦ Many of the templates and themes available use strange mixes of obtrusive bullet and horizontal-line images. These can be very distracting. In fact, be careful about combining too many colorful or unusual elements in a document. While one or two can work well, scattering the document with everything you can find looks merely amateurish.

✦ Ornate anything is distracting if overdone. An ornate border around every page may be okay for a single-page invitation, but it will look horrible on a fifty-page booklet. And an ornate page border, combined with ornate quotation boxes on each page, combined with lots of little images, combined with a very ornate heading font will look horrible even on a one-page document.

Checking Your Work

Don't forget to check your work once you're finished! The following shows a process that many people use to ensure that a document looks good (especially long documents). When you're sure that you're finished creating the document, take the following steps:

1. Run the spell checker (see Chapter 8 for information on checking your spelling and grammar).

2. Include the grammar checker, but be very careful. The grammar checker sometimes overlooks real grammar mistakes while making suggestions that are incorrect. On the other hand, the grammar checker can find a lot of little things that do need fixing.

Tip

The grammar checker often misses common mistakes such as a confusion between *its* and *it's*, *too*, *to*, and *two*, *which* and *that*, and *they're*, *there*, and *their*. Consider using the Edit ➪ Find command to track down and check these words.

3. Re-read the document, on paper not on-screen, marking up things that need fixing.

4. Make the changes to the document.

5. Run the spell checker and grammar checker again. (It will run very quickly because Word will check only things that have changed.)

6. Print and give the document to someone else to read and mark up. Seldom will you find all the mistakes yourself, even if you are a very good writer. Ideally, have a professional editor read the document, too.

7. Go through the changes provided by the reviewers and decide which are valid. Make those changes to the document.

8. Run the spell checker and grammar checker again.

9. Run hyphenation, if you wish by choosing Tools ➪ Language ➪ Hyphenation.

Cross-Reference

See Chapter 5 for more information on hyphenation.

10. Make sure that the correct print driver is attached to the document. Choose File ➪ Print, select the printer from the Name drop-down list box, and click Close. If you don't have the right printer selected, you can't properly paginate the document.

Cross-Reference

See Chapter 6 if you need help with printing.

11. Place the document into Print Preview view; then scroll from the first page to the last looking for the following pagination issues:

- Widows and orphans—a line of text sitting by itself at the top or bottom of a page, with the rest of the paragraph sitting on the preceding or following page.

- A heading sitting by itself at the bottom of a page—a paragraph or so of text should follow each heading before a page break.

- Large blank areas on a page—check for an unnecessary hard page break or an image that was too large and got pushed to the next page. Remove the hard page break or resize the image.

Use the following techniques to fix pagination issues:

- Add and remove the page breaks (Ctrl+Enter creates a hard page break).

- Resize images.

- Modify a paragraph's Spacing Before and After settings, usually to reduce spacing and pull text onto a preceding page. Changing every paragraph on a page by one or two points is often enough to make the change you want, without being noticeable.

- Modify a paragraph's Line Spacing setting by selecting Exactly and entering a value. Changing an entire page by one point can often pull a paragraph back onto a page from the next one, without being obvious.

- Adjust font sizes slightly. Reducing a heading font by one or two points, for example, might do the job, and most readers won't notice the difference.

Cross-Reference

Check out Chapter 10 if you need help with the items in the preceding list.

12. When you get all the way to the end of the document, having fixed pagination, go back to the beginning of the document and quickly check again. You can place several pages on the screen at once to speed things up. If you find problems, repeat steps 11 and 12.

13. Press Ctrl+A to select the entire document.

14. Press F9 to update fields, such as a table of contents, index, and cross-references. If you see a message asking if you want to update the entire field, or just update page numbers, update the entire field.

15. Okay, one more time . . . go through the document in Page Layout view checking pagination! If you find problems, fix them; then repeat steps 13–15.

Summary

It's not hard to make your documents easy to read with a very professional appearance. The most important thing to do is avoid doing everything. Don't get into the "I'll do this because I can" mindset because Word gives you way too much power to be used all at once. Highlights of this chapter include the following:

✦ Using white space—through the use of margins, indentation, spacing before and after paragraphs, and so on—to make your documents easier to read and skim.

✦ Using a serif typeface for the document's body text and a sans serif typeface for headings.

✦ Learning not to use too many typefaces on one page or in a document.

✦ Using Word's typesetting characters to make your documents look much more professional.

✦ Learning to use images to make a document look good and discovering that if you overdo it, the document appears cluttered.

✦ Specific steps you can follow to check your document before publishing it.

✦   ✦   ✦

Creating Documents Using Speech Recognition

✦   ✦   ✦   ✦

In This Chapter

Setting up your computer for voice recognition

Speaking into your computer

Correcting problems

✦   ✦   ✦   ✦

Should this chapter be in a part titled *Working More Effectively*? Or are we jumping the gun? If you absolutely hate typing, or are very, very bad at it, you may find voice dictation to be the proverbial godsend. On the other hand, if you type well, you may try it once and never return. This chapter talks about a feature of Word that allows you to talk to your computer and have the computer convert your words into text on a page—all thanks to a technology known as *speech recognition*.

Here are two things you should know about speech recognition:

- ✦ Like ending world hunger, the quest for speech recognition has gone on for a long time.

- ✦ And, like ending world hunger, the quest is not yet over.

Speech recognition has not reached *2001: A Space Odyssey* or *Star Trek* levels of accuracy. In fact, it's unlikely to do so for some time. Speech-recognition research is actually several decades old, but it has not yet achieved a technology that is, let's face it, very good. Oh, sure, speech-recognition technology gets a fair bit of praise, even from reviewers. But only a small fraction of computer users who try it continue using it.

Scientific American did a recent survey of writers who had reviewed speech-recognition programs of various kinds in the press and given the software good reviews. The magazine sought out these writers and asked them, "Are you using this software now?" The answer, invariably, was *No*!

Speech-recognition technology is currently at the "Wow, isn't this cool" stage of development. It is not yet at the "Everybody should use this!" stage. Having said that, speech-recognition technology can be hugely beneficial for some people. If, due to a disability, you are unable to type, it may well be worth investing the time and effort to train Microsoft Office's speech-recognition system to convert your speech as accurately as possible.

We've left this chapter in the *Working More Effectively* part of the book because speech recognition *will* be a truly fantastic tool one day, perhaps in the not-too-distant future (three to five years?), and because for some people, who really do need help, it already is a great tool.

Setting Up Speech Recognition

First, you have to set up your system for speech recognition. Before you start, however, you need to make sure of a few things:

✦ You need a microphone.

Tip

Be sure to buy a decent microphone! If you are serious about using speech recognition, it's worth getting a good microphone to increase the quality of the sound being input into your computer. Don't expect to use the computer's built-in microphone. You may even want to consider buying a headset microphone to leave your hands free to use the mouse or keyboard. (You discover why as we move on.)

✦ Your computer must have a sound input port. Most computers on which you are likely to be running Microsoft Office do have such a port, although certainly not all. Somewhere on your computer, you should find a small hole with a picture of a microphone next to it. Make sure that your microphone can plug into this hole. You may require an adapter depending on the type of microphone you have.

✦ Your computer must have speakers. If you are working on a laptop, they are probably built in to your system. Although you can also plug in external speakers. If you are using a desktop computer, look for a socket next to the microphone socket, or on the back somewhere. Of course, your computer may already be—and most likely is—set up to work with sound.

✦ Make sure that sound is turned on. You should see a little microphone or speaker icon in the system tray of your Windows taskbar. (The system tray is the area near the clock.) If the sound icon has a red circle around it with a line through it, the sound is muted. Click once on the icon, clear the Mute check box on the Volume Control box that appears, and then click outside the Volume Control box to close it.

If you don't have this control, it could be that it has been turned off. Open the Windows Control Panel (Start ➪ Settings ➪ Control Panel) and double-click the Sounds and Multimedia or Sounds and Audio Devices icon. At the bottom of the box that appears is a check box labeled Show Volume Control on the Taskbar. If this dialog box is unchecked, your sound settings are not properly configured. Click to place a checkmark in the box and click OK to close the Control Panel.

Adjusting the microphone

The first time you try to open the Language bar, Word tells you that you have to configure the system first. Choose Tools ➪ Speech and a little message box opens explaining this. Click OK and the first page of the Microphone Wizard opens.

Note

The Language bar is used by Word's speech-recognition system, which we're looking at now, its handwriting-recognition system, and an IME (Input Method Editor), a system used for entering the thousands of different Asian characters with a standard western 101-key keyboard. These features are all known as *text services* because they are all used to enter text. The Language bar's buttons vary depending on what application is running and what service is in use.

This message box simply explains briefly what we've already told you. It also states that the microphone should not be too close to your mouth and that you should not be breathing into it. Click Next and the wizard begins working (see Figure 16-1). Speak into your microphone (read the sentence above the status bar in the middle of the box), and try to keep the volume bar up within the green area of the color bar above it. The wizard listens and adjusts the volume accordingly.

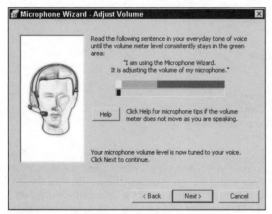

Figure 16-1: The Microphone Wizard begins by checking your microphone volume.

If the volume bar is not moving while you talk, you've got a problem. Make sure the microphone is properly plugged in, in the correct socket, too. Make sure it's turned on, if it has a volume control. If you have another microphone, try that one. Does the microphone require a battery? Some do. Try changing the battery. Still can't get the bar to move? You're going to have to figure out your computer's sound configuration and get it working before you can continue.

Note If the microphone doesn't seem to be working, make sure it's not turned off in the Volume Control properties. Right click on the volume control in the system tray, and choose Open Volume Controls. Choose Options ⇨ Properties, place a check next to Microphone, and click OK. Back in the Volume Control dialog box, make sure that the Mute box under Microphone isn't on, and that the volume is set near the middle of the range.

When you click the Next button, the wizard asks you to speak into the microphone again. Do so and this time the wizard plays back what you say. If it doesn't sound too good, try adjusting the microphone and trying again, or go Back and re-adjust the volume.

Training the speech system

When you click Finish, the Microphone Wizard closes and the Voice Training Wizard begins. Click Next on the first page to see a page with a Sample button. Click this to listen to how you should speak during this training; then click Next to move to the first training page (see Figure 16-2).

Figure 16-2: The Voice Training Wizard actually trains the speech recognition system, not your voice.

What's going on here? You are going to read various passages of text, and the wizard is going to listen carefully and record information about the way you say the words. When you say *Welcome*, the wizard listens to the way you say it and records the information so it will recognize the word the next time (and to help it recognize other words with some of the same syllables as *welcome*). Each time you say a few words, the wizard listens and highlights the words you've said.

The wizard may get stuck, however. If you notice that it has stopped highlighting words, just wait a few moments and see what it does. It may catch up, but more likely, it will either stay where it is or back up a word or two. Continue reading at the *first unhighlighted word*. If you have a real problem with a particular word that you simply cannot get Word to understand, click the Skip Word button.

Note   There's no need to talk slowly. In fact, it's best if you talk at a fairly normal pace. Remember that you are teaching the system to recognize how you speak. If you speak slowly and carefully now, and then speak normally—and not so slowly and carefully—later, when dictating to the system, it won't be able to recognize you. Of course, if you usually speak very indistinctly, you may *have* to speak more carefully to get the system to recognize the words. Oh, and background sound can cause real problems. You really should use the speech-recognition system with almost no sound in the background.

When the wizard reaches the end of a passage, there will be a short pause, and then it will display the next passage. Continue reading until you have read all the text. When you're finished, the wizard takes a few moments to save all the information it has gathered. As Word works, it creates a speech *profile* for you. This profile describes your speech patterns—nobody else's. No one else can use your speech profile to convert their speech to text—at least, it won't work very well.

Tip   Multiple people can use the speech-recognition system, but each person must create a separate speech profile. To create a new profile, choose Tools ➪ Options from the Language bar. In the Speech Properties dialog box, click the New button and follow instructions. You can then switch between users by choosing Tools ➪ Current User ➪ *profilename*.

On the final screen of the Voice Training Wizard, there's a More Training button. Click this to see a list of other training sessions, including passages from famous writers such as H. G. Wells, Bertrand Russell, and Edith Wharton. We recommend that you *do* read more of these passages; in fact, read them all. The speech-recognition system is going to need all the help it can get. Microsoft claims that the initial training will give you 80–90 percent accuracy, and that range may well be correct. (On the other hand, some of you might find yourself *wishing* you got an accuracy level of 80 percent or more.) But if just one or two words out of every ten are wrong, the system is virtually unusable. Further training of the system can improve this accuracy percentage.

Tip　If you choose not to do further training now, you can return to the session later by choosing Tools ➪ Training from the Language bar.

After you finish training, the wizard closes and the Language bar opens (see Figure 16-3). You can open this bar from now on by choosing Tools ➪ Speech. Note that this is not really a Microsoft Word toolbar—you won't find it in the View ➪ Toolbars menu. It's actually a Microsoft Office toolbar, as the speech tool is available in all Office applications.

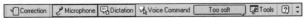

Figure 16-3: The Language bar.

Taking Dictation

Now that you've trained the speech-recognition system, you'll want to see how well it recognizes your voice. Click the Dictation button on the Language bar. (If this button isn't present, click the Microphone button to expand the toolbar.)

Three buttons on the Language bar are related: Microphone, Dictation, and Voice Command. The Microphone button turns on the microphone and displays the Dictation and Voice Command buttons. One of these modes—Dictation or Voice—is on as long as the buttons are displayed. When you first click the Microphone button, Dictation mode is on; clicking Voice Command turns off Dictation and turns on Voice Command mode, which we look at a little later.

Tip　You can press [Windows key]+V to activate the microphone instead of clicking the Microphone button on the Language bar. The Windows key is the one on your keyboard with the little Microsoft Windows flag symbol.

Now speak into the microphone. Instead of entering text, you'll see a highlight bar with dots at the bottom. Word is recording your speech and converting it to text. When you pause, Word converts this highlight bar to actual text. With luck, it's the text you wanted, or at least close to it. To turn off Dictation, click the Microphone button to hide the Dictation and Voice Command buttons.

You can say a number of things into the microphone that carry out special commands, such as entering punctuation or pressing the Enter key. Table 16-1 explains these commands.

Table 16-1: Voice Commands

Say ...	To do this...
colon	Enters a colon into the text.
comma	Enters a comma into the text.
dash	Enters two hyphens into the text.
enter	The equivalent of pressing Enter.
forcenum	Makes the system enter numbers as digits rather than words: *2* rather than *two*. When you're finished saying the digits, pause for a moment to turn off forcenum mode.
hyphen	Enters a hyphen into the text.
microphone	The equivalent of clicking the Microphone button on the Language bar (in theory, but we could only get it to type the word *microphone*).
new line	The equivalent of pressing Shift+Enter to create a line break.
new paragraph	The equivalent of pressing Enter.
period	Enters a period into the text.
semicolon	Enters a semicolon into the text.
spelling mode	Puts the system into a mode in which you can spell out a word letter by letter. When you're finished saying the letters, pause for a moment and the system reverts to normal dictation mode.
spelling mode space	Enters a space into the text.
tab	The equivalent of pressing the Tab key.

Fixing problems

Now, there's a good chance that much of what you dictated did not convert to text properly. Unfortunately the correction tools are weak, and unless you speak very clearly and the system is very well trained, you may find that it takes a great deal of work to clean up your text.

First, let's look at the ideal situation. Word recognized most of your speech but misinterpreted one word. Here's how to fix it. Highlight the word and click the Correction button. A list of alternative words appears, and at the same time your computer plays your voice speaking the word that it converted incorrectly. Click the correct word, and Word replaces the misinterpreted word with the correct one (see Figure 16-4). You can also click the number key corresponding to the number of the item in the list.

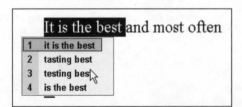

Figure 16-4: Word tries to help you fix its mistakes.

Tip   You can also open the Correction list by pressing [Windows Key]+C.

The problem with the speech-recognition feature is twofold:

✦ Sometimes Word is so far off the correct interpretation that everything is mixed up. It's not just a matter of a word being misinterpreted; it's more a matter of its misinterpreting sounds and syllables. So, for instance, instead of getting 10 words you get 13. Although you can click on one misinterpreted word, you can't replace it with the correct word because the sound was just part of a word. You can, however, select several words at once and click the Correction button. Perhaps you said *let's see*, but Word typed *that's a*. Select *that's a*, click the Correction button, and Word replays your voice saying *let's see* and displays a list of possible corrections (such as *Betsy, bitsy,* and so on). Unfortunately, what you *can't* do here is type the correct word, and the list may not contain it.

✦ And that's the other problem. Even if Word matches one for one—ten words for ten words—the list of alternatives that it displays quite likely doesn't include the correct word.

Continued training

You'll probably want to continue training Word's speech-recognition system. You can choose Tools ➪ Training on the Language bar to go through a full training session, as you saw earlier in this chapter. You can also choose an alternative method. You can actually add particular words to the system. Suppose Word consistently misinterprets a particular word that you say. Choose Tools ➪ Add/Delete Word(s) to display the dialog box in Figure 16-5.

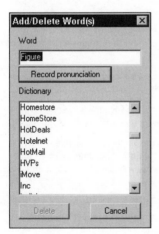

Figure 16-5: The Add/Delete Word(s) dialog box.

Type the word with which Word is having a problem and click the Record Pronunciation button. Speak the word into your microphone, and then keep quiet for a moment so that Word knows you are finished.

Voice commands

You can also use this system to enter voice commands: *File* to open the File menu, and *Save* to save the document, for example. Click the Voice Command button on the Language bar to enter this mode, or press [Windows Key]+T to switch back and forth between these modes.

The system has to be trained to recognize your voice, of course, and most of what you say in this mode won't do anything. The system only takes action when you say a word that matches a particular command.

Personally, we think you're better off sticking to your mouse or keyboard if you can. Speech recognition simply doesn't work all that well, so attempting to use your voice to control your computer can be extremely frustrating. Many thousands of voice-control kits have been sold over the last few years, but how often do you see folks actually using their microphones to control their computers? It's pretty rare. The Windows speech-recognition kit simply isn't much better than most of the others out there, so you may end up wasting your time.

More Voice Settings

A number of settings are related to the Language bar and speech recognition. Table 16-2 explains these settings.

Table 16-2: Language Bar Settings

Command	Action
Right-click on the Language bar for these commands:	
Minimize	Hides the language bar; click the EN button on the Windows taskbar and then click on the Show the Language Bar menu option that appears to reopen the bar.
Transparency	Turns the toolbar into an almost transparent bar that you can see through.
Text Labels	Adds labels to the buttons on the Language bar. Remove the checkmark to reduce the size of the buttons.
Additional Icons in Task Bar	Displays not only the EN button on the taskbar, but also a microphone icon when you minimize the Language bar. You can single-click this button as an alternative to clicking the Microphone button on the Language bar.
Settings	Opens the Language bar's Settings dialog box, where you can see what services are installed (in addition to speech-recognition).
Close the Language Bar	Closes the Language bar.

Command	Action
Click the Tools menu for these commands:	
Learn from document	Lets you read the document that is currently open, to train the system.
Options	Opens the Options dialog box.
Show Speech Messages	Causes a message button to appear to the right of the Voice Command button, displaying what mode you are currently in.
Training	Opens the Voice Training dialog box, where you can continue training the system.
Add/Delete Word(s)	Lets you train the system word by word—type a word and pronounce it.
Save Speech Data	Saves your actual speech, along with the text, when you save the document. When you open the file again, you can highlight text and click the Correction button to play your words.
Current User	Displays a list of user profiles from which you can choose.

Summary

Speech recognition is by no means perfect. Still, with the right training—of the system, not you—you may find this system beneficial, especially if you have trouble typing. Here are some of the highlights of this chapter:

✦ Before you use speech recognition, make sure that your computer's sound input and output are properly configured—you must be able to use a microphone to talk to your computer and be able to listen to sounds played by your computer.

✦ You can choose Tools ➪ Speech and run the wizards to set up your microphone and teach the speech-recognition system your speech patterns.

✦ If you're serious about using speech recognition, read through *all* the training passages provided. It will take some time, but it will be worth it.

✦ You use the Language bar to turn on speech recognition and to correct mistakes. Click the Dictation button and speak into your microphone.

✦ You can correct mistakes by highlighting the words, clicking the Correction button, and selecting the correct word or words.

Inserting Pictures and Other Content

◆ ◆ ◆ ◆

In This Part

Chapter 17
Illustrating Your
Documents with
Graphics

Chapter 18
More Object Types—
Drawings, Text Boxes,
and More

Chapter 19
Advanced Graphics
and Multimedia

Chapter 20
Linking Information from
Other Applications

Chapter 21
Working with Microsoft
Graph Chart and
Microsoft Equation

◆ ◆ ◆ ◆

Illustrating Your Documents with Graphics

In This Chapter

Understanding bitmap graphics and vector drawings

Inserting pictures

Moving, copying, resizing, and cropping pictures

Adding borders and shadows

Adjusting picture characteristics

Positioning objects on the page

Adding graphics to illustrate your documents makes those documents more appealing. The pictures that you insert can come from numerous sources, such as stand-alone graphics programs, scanned art, and clip art. Word allows you to add existing graphics to your document in a variety of ways. You also can create your own graphics from scratch using Word's powerful drawing tools.

This chapter explains how to use Word's graphic tools to add and work with graphics in your documents and how to work with text boxes to lay out text and graphics anywhere you want on a page.

Understanding Bitmap Pictures and Vector Drawings

Before you begin working with pictures in Word, it helps to know that graphic formats fall into two main camps:

✦ **Bitmap graphics:** Composed of small dots called *pixels*. Each pixel is represented by one or more bits in the computer's memory that define both color and intensity. A bitmap graphic is stored at a fixed resolution that is determined by the number and the layout of the pixels. You can edit an image at that fixed resolution, but if you enlarge the graphic, you distort the picture and lose image quality.

Images containing subtle colors or a great deal of detail, such as photographic images, work best as bitmap graphics. Microsoft Image Composer, Adobe PhotoShop, and Paint Shop Pro from Jasc are examples of programs that create and edit bitmapped pictures.

✦ **Vector graphics:** Composed of a set of drawing instructions that describe the dimension and shape of every line, circle, arc, or rectangle. The resolution of a vector image is not fixed. The resolution of your output device—your printer or screen— determines the quality of a vector image's appearance. You can enlarge, reduce, and otherwise edit vector graphics without affecting their resolution or image quality. Vector graphics are best for line art. Word allows you to create simple vector images directly in your documents using Word's drawing toolbar.

Bitmap graphics require more disk space than vector graphics because bitmap graphics must contain information about each pixel displayed on the screen. Vector graphics, in contrast, are stored as commands that create images. Sometimes vector graphics take longer to render (to convert from vector outlines to fully formed graphics), however, because your processor must draw them. Small bitmap images are simply loaded directly into memory.

Graphics File Formats Supported by Word

Word is compatible with most popular graphics programs. You can insert into a Word document any picture or object created using any of the programs or formats listed in Table 17-1.

Table 17-1: Graphics File Formats Supported by Word

Program Format	File Extension	Graphics Type
AutoCAD Format 2-D	dfx	Vector
AutoCAD Plot files	plt	Vector
GIF (Graphics Interchange Format)	gif and gfa	Bitmap
Compressed Windows Enhanced Metafile	wmz	Bitmap/vector
Compressed Windows Enhanced Metafile	emz	Bitmap/vector
Computer Graphics Metafile	cgm	Bitmap/vector
CorelDRAW	cdr	Vector
Encapsulated PostScript	eps	Bitmap/vector
FlashPix	fpx	Bitmap
JPEG File Interchange Format	jpg, jpeg, jfif, and jpe	Bitmap
Kodak Photo CD	pcd	Bitmap
Macintosh PICT	pct, pict	Vector
Macintosh PICT, compressed	pcz	Vector
Micrografx Designer and Micrografx Draw	drw	Vector
Picture It!	mix	Bitmap
PC Paintbrush	pcx	Bitmap
Portable Network Graphics	png	Bitmap
Tagged Image File Format	tif, tiff	Bitmap
Targa	tga	Bitmap
Windows Bitmap/Windows Paint	bmp, dib, rle, and bmz	Bitmap
Windows Metafile	wmf	Bitmap/vector
Windows Enhanced Metafile	emf	Bitmap/vector
Windows Enhanced Metafile, Compressed	emz	Bitmap/vector
WordPerfect Graphics	wpg	Bitmap/vector

Note   As you can see in Table 17-1, many different image formats are available. But you can, quite frankly, forget most of them. Most of these formats are rarely used these days. You may use one or two of the unusual formats, but it's unlikely that you'll use more than that. Which ones are the most common? The JPEG and GIF files are now common, thanks to the World Wide Web. Windows bitmap files—in particular, the .bmp format—are also quite common, as are Windows metafiles. Encapsulated PostScript (EPS) files are frequently used as well. Beyond that, most of these file formats are relatively rare, and you are unlikely to run into them unless you happen to use the specific program that creates them.

Word typically uses import filters to place pictures into a document. Some programs such as CorelDRAW, however, include OLE support, which allows you to insert pictures as objects (see Chapter 20). If you chose the Complete Setup option when you installed Word, all the graphics import filters were added to your system. If you chose a Custom installation, however, you may not have installed all the filters. To see which filters are installed on your computer, choose Insert ➪ Picture ➪ From File and then open the Files of Type list. If you need to install an additional graphics filter, use the Add/Remove Software function in the Control Panel.

If the graphics filter that you need to import a graphic is not shipped with Word, you must open the file in an image-editing program instead. You can then select the graphic, copy it, and paste it into your Word document. The graphic now becomes a Windows metafile (.wmf), which stores both vector and bitmap data. Another alternative is to see if you can open the file in another application and then save it in a format listed in Table 17-1. Most image-editing programs, such as Adobe PhotoShop and Paint Shop Pro, allow you to save files in a different format, and you can also download more filters at the Microsoft Web site: `www.Microsoft.com/office/`.

Where to Get Graphic Images

You may have wondered where people find professional images for desktop publishing. Numerous companies sell royalty-free digital photos and clip-art packages, but beware: many more companies sell cheap, low-quality digital photos and clip art. One source for graphics is the World Wide Web. Many Web sites archive non-royalty images of varying quality, some of which are free for downloading. Be careful when you use an image from a personal Web site, however, because verifying whether that image is royalty-free or being published illegally is difficult. The following discussion lists only companies that sell high-quality clip art and photo software.

Commercial clip art and photographs

Commercial clip art and photographs are widely available on the Web—search at Yahoo! for *stock photography*, for instance, and you'll find a category with literally scores of sites. You'll find sites that focus on a particular category of photography—architecture, people in business situations, photos of Greece, and so on—as well as a few truly massive libraries, such as the Getty Images and Corbis. Many of these sites allow you to pick and choose the image you want online, and download that and only that. Or you can buy and download a collection of images. Or you can buy a CD. Images are available in many different forms these days.

Here are a few great places to check for commercial images:

www.Corbis.com

www.EyeWire.com

www.GettyImages.com

www.ClipArt.com

www.nvtech.com

www.novadevcorp.com

Free clip art

There are also plenty of free images online. Microsoft has a site for downloading and adding clips to the ClipArt gallery that ships with Word. (Downloading and adding clips from Microsoft's site is covered later in this chapter.) But you can find lots of additional sites that offer free graphics; just use any Web search engine. For example, you can find links to commercial clip-art sites, animated GIFs, and Web directories for clip art by searching at Yahoo for *free clip art*. Remember, however, that you use free images off the Web at your own risk. Many sites, unfortunately, post images that break the copyright laws.

Tip

A slick trick for inserting an image from a Web page is to open your browser and then to open Word. This way, you can see both windows and drag the image from the browser window and into the Word document window. (This only works if the image does *not* have hyperlinks placed on it.) You also can download any image off a Web site and store it on your disk for use later in a Word document. To save the image to your disk, load the Web page in your browser, right-click on the image, and choose the Save Image option from the shortcut menu.

Inserting Pictures into Documents

Word is extremely flexible in how you can insert a picture into a document. For example, you can place the picture in-line with existing text or insert it in a text box or table. Different techniques offer different advantages. Inserting a picture in a text box, which you then can position anywhere in your document, enables you to have both text and images stored in easily movable containers. Unfortunately, the way Word handles these containers is a little buggy, and sometimes they won't go where you want them to go! You can also insert a picture in a cell of a table, allowing you to position the picture next to text in an adjacent cell.

When you insert a picture in your Word document, that image appears where the insertion point is located. When you place the image in a text box, the image moves with the text if you add or delete the paragraph mark either preceding or following the picture. (Working with text boxes to position pictures independently of text is covered later in this chapter.)

You can insert a picture in your document in various ways:

✦ Use the Insert ➪ Picture command, and choose either the Clip Art or From File submenu. Another way to insert a picture from a file is to click the Insert Picture button on the Picture toolbar.

✦ Use the Insert ➪ Object command to insert a picture that you can later edit with the program that created it.

Cross-Reference See Chapter 20 to learn more about using the Insert ➪ Object command to embed objects in your Word document.

✦ Open the program used to create pictures, and copy (or cut) a picture to the Windows Clipboard. Then use the Edit ➪ Paste command to paste the picture into your Word document.

✦ Drag an image from a Web browser and drop it into the Word document. (Only works with non-hyperlinked images.)

✦ Drag an image from another Word document and drop it into the current Word document.

Inserting clip art and pictures

Choosing Insert ➪ Picture ➪ Clip Art displays the ClipArt task pane (see Figure 17-1). Note that this task pane helps you find images in two ways: you can search for a keyword related to the image, or you can view the contents of a particular collection. And it's not just clip art, by the way—this task pane can help you find movies, photographs, and sounds also. Table 17-2 describes the functions of the components in this task pane.

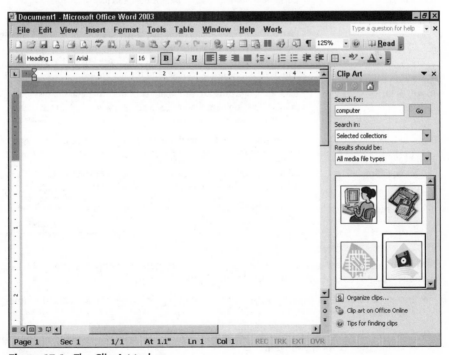

Figure 17-1: The Clip Art task pane.

Table 17-2: Using the Clip Art Task Pane

Component	Purpose
Search For	You can enter a search term in here if you wish—*but you don't have to*. If you leave this blank, when Word searches for clip art it will search all the locations specified in Search In and find everything.
Search In	Click on the triangle on the right side of this box, and a little tree opens showing you where Word is going to search. Click on the + boxes to open the tree branches. You have three primary choices: My Collections, Office Collections (clip art provided by Office), and Web Collections (clip art libraries on the Web). Click on the check boxes to omit areas from the search or to add them back in.
Results Should Be	Open this drop-down list box to see what Word will search for: Clip Art, Photographs, Movies, and Sounds. If you open each tree, you'll see exactly what type of file Word will search for. Note that the categories are not completely precise. You'll find .pcx and .bmp files under Photographs, for instance, though they may not be photos.
Go button	Click the button, and Word begins the search.
Large list box	The large list box is where you'll see the results of the search. It may take a while to complete, especially if you are including Web Collections in your search. Point at an image to see a pop-up box providing information: the keywords associated with the image, the pixel dimensions, the size of the file, and the file format.
Images in list	Click an image once to load it into your document, at the insertion point. Merely point at the image to see a triangle box on which you can click to open a menu.
Organize Clips	Click here to open Microsoft Clip Organizer, an Office program that helps you organize your media files of all kinds.
Clip Art on Office Online	Click here to open a browser and connect to Microsoft's Clip Art and Media page, where you can find thousands of free media files.
Tips for Finding Clips	Opens a Help page providing information about working with the Clip Art task pane.

Opening an image's pop-up menu—by clicking on the triangle that appears when you point at the image—provides a number of tools for managing the image:

✦ **Insert:** The same as clicking once on the image; it places the image in the document at the insertion point.

✦ **Copy:** Copies the image to the Clipboard, so you can paste it into the document when you find the position you want.

✦ **Delete from Clip Organizer:** Removes the image from the folder.

✦ **Copy to Collection:** Opens a box in which you can select a directory in the My Collections folder so you can copy the image. For instance, if you find an image on the Web, you may want to save it to your hard disk.

✦ **Move to Collection:** Allows you to *move* the image to another folder. You can't do this if the image is in the Office or Web Collections.

✦ **Edit Keywords:** Allows you to modify the keywords associated with images stored in the My Collections folder.

✦ **Find Similar Style:** Word searches for similar files.

✦ **Preview/Properties:** Opens the Preview/Properties dialog box (see Figure 17-2). This shows you information about the file, including file name, type, size, file location, the location of the catalog in which this information is stored, and so on. You can also click the Edit Keywords button (if the image is in a My Collections folder) to add, change, or remove search keywords associated with this image. Notice the left- and right-arrow buttons—these let you preview each image in the same folder one by one.

Note

The folders shown in the Search In drop-down and the Copy to and Move to Collection boxes are not real. The files shown in My Collections and Office Collections are actually stored in the Media directory inside the directory in which Microsoft Office was installed. The folders are *virtual* directories. When you move or copy a file, the file stays where it is, but the reference to it is moved or copied into one of these virtual directories.

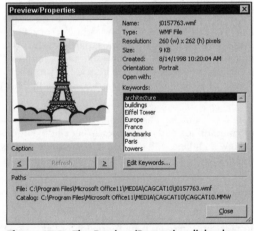

Figure 17-2: The Preview/Properties dialog box.

Working with Microsoft Clip Organizer

Microsoft Clip Organizer is a great little Office tool that helps you organize your media files. Click the Organize Clips link in the Clip Art task pane to open it (see Figure 17-3). The first time you open it you'll see a message box asking if you want to catalog the media files on your system—it's going to search all accessible drives, including network drives.

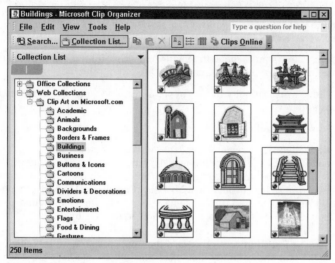

Figure 17-3: Microsoft Clip Organizer.

If you click Later, each time you open the program you'll see the box, so you don't have to worry about doing this search the first time you use the program (it takes quite a while). If you choose to do this search, Clip Organizer creates a folder under My Collections for each folder containing media files, and even adds keywords for each file (though of course it's guessing, so you may not like what it adds—it uses the directory and subdirectory names, and the file extension). You may be surprised what images Word finds, particularly if you have teenage children. Word ignores some folders, such as your browser cache folders. Note, however, that you can click the Options button before running this utility. The program scans your hard drive looking for directories containing media files, displays the list, and lets you choose which ones to include.

The basic purpose of this program is to help you quickly find and organize your images—clip art and photographs—your movies, and your sounds and music files. You can do a number of things here. First, note that when you view an image, you can use it in the same way as in Word's Clip Art task pane—open the pop-up menu and you'll find similar options. In addition, you can carry out these functions:

✦ **Search for files:** Click the Search button on the toolbar, and a task pane similar to the Clip Art pane opens.

✦ **Collection List:** Click the Collection List button to go back to the folder list task pane, after using Search.

✦ **Open Microsoft's Clip Art and Media Home page on the Web:** Choose Tools ➪ Clips Online.

✦ **Fix and Compact your Media Catalog:** Choose Tools ➪ Compact.

✦ **Add clips to the Clip Organizer:** Choose File ➪ Add Clips to Organizer ➪ Automatically to run the disk-search again and catalog everything on your hard disk. Choose File ➪ Add Clips to Organizer ➪ On My Own to open a box in which you can select the files and folders you want to add to the Organizer. Choose File ➪ Add Clips to Organizer ➪ From Scanner or Camera to grab an image directly from a scanner or digital camera.

✦ **E-mail an image to someone:** Click an image and choose File ⇨ Send to Mail Recipient (As Attachment) to open your e-mail program and create a message.

✦ **Create a new Collection folder:** Click on My Collections, or on a subfolder, and choose File ⇨ New Collection.

✦ **Copy and move images between folders:** Use the same commands you saw in the Clip Art task pane. You can also copy by just dragging and dropping images out of one folder and into another.

Microsoft's online clip-art gallery

The Clip Art task pane's Clip Art on Office Online link opens your browser and loads Microsoft's online clip-art archive. This is a great site, allowing you to search for clips by keyword or browse clips by category. This page also includes links to new clip art and seasonal categories, such as Christmas clips in December. When you choose a category, a series of thumbnails (small images) appears for you to choose the image you want to download (see Figure 17-4). Click on a thumbnail to open a preview window, which also displays information about the image (size and format, for instance). To select an image for download, click on the check box next to it. Or use the pop-up menu to place a copy on the Clipboard. When you are ready to download the clips, click the Download *x* Items link in the Selection Basket on the left side of the page. A media package file will be downloaded to your computer (an .mpf file). If Clip Organizer doesn't automatically import this file, double-click this file to load it into your Clip Organizer.

Figure 17-4: Microsoft's Clip Art and Media Web site.

Scanning and digital cameras

Word includes options for scanning pictures directly into a page. To scan a picture into a Word document, choose Insert ⇨ Picture from Scanner or Camera. The Insert Picture from Scanner or Camera dialog box appears (see Figure 17-5). You can choose the device you want to use from the Device drop-down list. You also can choose the TWAIN device driver that supports your scanner or digital camera if one is available. (TWAIN is the industry standard protocol for scanning images into programs.)

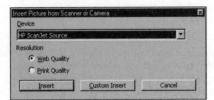

Figure 17-5: The Insert Picture from Scanner or Camera dialog box.

Web pages require a much lower resolution than printed pictures. Most screens display images at a resolution of only 72 or 96 pixels per inch; printers typically print at resolutions from 150 to 1,400 dots per inch. To support both printing and publishing Web pages, Word presents two choices for the resolution setting. With Web Quality, you can insert the scanned image using a low resolution. With Print Quality, you can insert the scanned image at a high resolution.

When you click the Insert button in the Insert Picture from Scanner or Camera dialog box, the Source dialog box appears, varying dependent on the type of scanner or camera that you chose. You can also click the Custom Insert button to open the application that is associated with the device you chose.

Note also the Add Image to Clip Organizer check box—select this if you want to automatically add the image.

Copying pictures into documents

One of the easiest ways to insert a picture that you created with a graphics program into a Word document is to use the Clipboard. You can copy the image in your graphics program, place the insertion point into the Word document, and press Ctrl+V to paste the image into the document; or use Edit ⇨ Paste Special to choose what format to use when pasting. For example, depending on the image type you may be able to paste the picture as an object so that you can edit it later using the program associated with the file, as a Windows Metafile picture, or as a bitmap. By linking a picture to the original file, you can update the picture if you make changes to the original later.

Resizing and Cropping Pictures

After you insert a picture, you can scale or stretch it to a smaller or a larger size by some percentage, either proportionally or non-proportionally. You also can size a picture to the exact desired width and height, or you can crop away parts you do not want displayed. Resizing is useful when you need a picture to be a certain size. Cropping is effective when you want to show only part of a picture. You can resize and crop pictures using either the mouse or a dialog box.

Resizing and cropping using the mouse

As with text, to perform a formatting command you need to select the graphic first. To select a picture, simply click it. When you select a picture, sizing handles appear on the picture's corners and sides—eight in all. You can use the mouse to drag the selection handles and thereby resize or crop the picture. With the corner handles, you can scale or crop from two sides (for example, top and left) at the same time. When you use a corner handle to resize a picture, the picture remains proportional . . . probably.

Note   By default, Lock Aspect Ratio on the Size tab of the Format Picture dialog box, is turned on. However, if this feature is turned off, the picture is not sized proportionally unless you hold down the Shift key while you drag.

The side handles enable scaling and cropping from just one side. When you use a side handle to resize, however, the picture's proportions change. Move a handle on the left side of the image, for instance, and you make the image thinner, but its height won't change.

Cropping a picture is very similar to sizing it. When you click on the image, the Picture toolbar should appear. If it doesn't appear, choose View ➪ Toolbars ➪ Picture. (Figure 17-6 shows the Picture toolbar.) Then click the Crop button, which appears as two overlapping corner angles. You can now drag the handles on the image to remove portions of the image, in the same way you sized it.

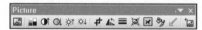

Figure 17-6: The Picture toolbar.

Figure 17-7 shows an image that has been resized and then cropped. Incidentally, Word does not remove portions of the inserted picture when you crop; it's all there, just not displayed, so you can restore the cropped portion of the picture later. However, the Compress Pictures dialog box, which you see later in this chapter, has an option that removes the cropped areas so they cannot be retrieved, saving file space.

Note   Reducing an image's size (resizing, not cropping) doesn't make the file size smaller. The file is the same size, but Word simply displays it as a different size. If you are concerned with file size, you should reduce the size of the image in an image-editing program and then import the image into Word.

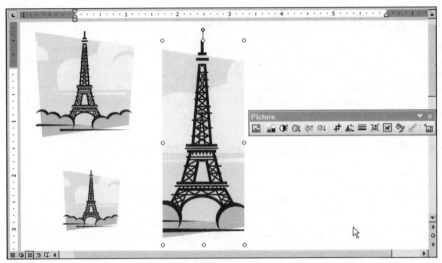

Figure 17-7: A picture that has been reduced as well as cropped and then enlarged.

Resizing and cropping using the Format Picture dialog box

Although it's convenient and has the added advantage of letting you see what you're doing as you work, using the sizing handle to resize or crop a picture is not nearly as precise as using the Format Picture dialog box. Click the Format Picture button on the Picture toolbar (third button from the right) or choose Format ⇨ Picture to display the Picture tab in the Format Picture dialog box (see Figure 17-8).

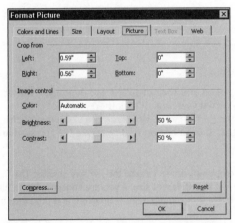

Figure 17-8: The Picture tab in the Format Picture dialog box.

The Size tab (see Figure 17-9) contains controls for adjusting the size of the image, while the Picture tab has cropping controls.

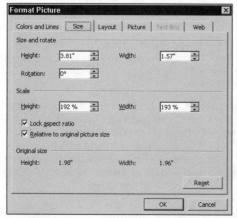

Figure 17-9: The Size tab in the Format Picture dialog box.

These controls allow you to adjust the size and cropping of the image from four sides, in $\frac{1}{100}$-inch increments. There are two important sizing controls:

✦ **Lock Aspect Ratio:** Mentioned earlier in the chapter, this control ensures that when you change size in one dimension, the other dimension changes proportionally. In other words, you are implementing proportional sizing, as if you were moving the corner handles. Clear the check box, and it's as if you are dragging a handle on the side.

✦ **Relative to Original Picture Size:** Tells Word to show sizing adjustments relative to the size of the original image. If you enter 50% in the Height and Width boxes, click OK, and open the dialog box again, you see 50% in the dimension boxes. Clear the Relative to Original Picture Size check box, and those dimensions change to 100%. Word takes the current size as the new starting point for your adjustments.

Tip   You can reset the image to its original size and restore cropped portions—use the Reset buttons in the Size and Picture tabs, or click the Reset button at the end of the Picture toolbar.

Adding Borders to Pictures

You can add a border around a picture or a drawing in several ways. Click the image and choose one of the following methods:

✦ Choose the Format ➪ Borders and Shading command.

Cross-Reference   See Chapter 5 for information on working with borders and shading.

✦ Choose Format ➪ Picture to open the Format Picture dialog box. Click the Layout tab, and select any wrapping style other than In Line With Text. Click OK, reopen the dialog box, click the Colors and Lines tab, and select a line color.

✦ Insert the image in a text box, and use the Lines button in the Drawing or Picture toolbar.

✦ Click the Crop button in the Picture toolbar and drag the corners out to perform a negative crop. Right-click on the image, choose Format Picture, click the Colors and Lines tab, and choose a fill from the Color list box.

✦ Create a rectangle or a shape on top of the image and extending beyond its edges. Then choose Draw ➪ Order ➪ Send Behind Text from the Drawing toolbar (which is probably at the bottom of the window). Choose Format AutoShape from the shortcut menu, click the Colors and Lines tab, and enter a Fill color.

A common misconception held by many Word users is that they can select a picture they have just inserted, choose Format ➪ Picture, and click the Colors and Lines tab to choose a line style border for an image. If you do this, however, probably the only available option is the Color list box in the Fill group (see Figure 17-10). And selecting a fill color may have no effect unless you have a transparent background color specified. (For more on setting a transparent color, see the section "Creating a transparent background for an image," later in this chapter.) In fact, you can add a line around an image only if it's *not* an inline image.

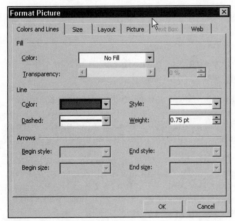

Figure 17-10: The Colors and Lines tab in the Format Picture dialog box.

You look at text wrapping and inline images later in this chapter in the section "Object Layout and Position." For now, just note that when you insert an image into a Word document, it is placed as an inline image by default. And you have limited formatting capabilities for inline images. However, you can change the default behavior. In the Options dialog box (Tools ➪ Options), click the Edit tab, and select one of the Insert/Paste Pictures As options.

To make the Line options available, choose Format ➪ Picture, click the Layout tab, and select any wrapping style other than In Line With Text. The line options in the Colors and Lines tab are now available, as are the line options in the Picture and Drawing toolbars.

At this point, you can select your line color using the Line Color box. The Line Color box includes two additional options: More Line Colors, and Patterned lines. If you choose the More Line Colors option, you can select colors from a standard or a custom palette. The Patterned line styles box includes a variety of line patterns. If you want, you can have a dashed line surround the image by clicking the Dashed Line button and selecting one of the many dashed line patterns.

The fastest way to add a border to a picture is to choose the Format ➪ Borders and Shading command. The Borders and Shading dialog box allows you to apply Box, Shadow, 3-D, or Custom borders. Using the Borders and Shading dialog box with a picture is the same as working with text.

 Cross-Reference For more information on working with the Borders and Shading dialog box options, see Chapter 5.

Adding Shadow Borders

To give your picture more definition, you can use the Shadow button in the Drawing Toolbar to add a shadow to one or two sides of the image. Click the image, and then click the Shadow Style button in the Drawing toolbar to open a little menu of shadow styles. You have a number of options—single shadows on one or two sides, double shadows on one or two sides, and so on.

After you place the shadow, you can adjust it. Click the Shadow Style button and select Shadow Settings to open another toolbar. This device allows you to quickly remove and replace the shadow; nudge the shadow up, down, to the left and right, and change the shadow color.

Figure 17-11 shows a picture with a drop shadow created by clicking the Shadow button and then choosing a shadow style.

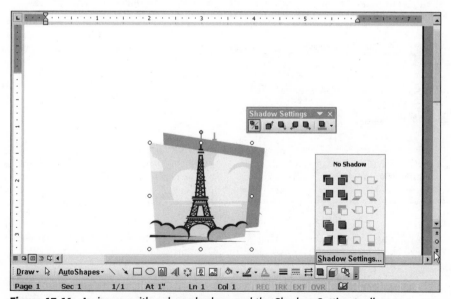

Figure 17-11: An image with a drop shadow, and the Shadow Setting toolbar.

Adjusting Picture Characteristics

You have a few ways to modify picture characteristics. Double-click on the image to open the Format Picture dialog box and then click the Picture tab. You'll see the Image Control area, which is explained in Table 17-3.

Table 17-3: The Image Control Area of the Format Picture Dialog Box

Component	Purpose
Color	If Automatic is selected, the image is displayed using all the available information for that image—a color image will appear in color, for instance. Choose Grayscale to remove colors, leaving black, white, and gray; Black and White to remove all colors and gray; and Washout to create a very light gray image that might be suitable for a watermark—text can sit on it and still be read.
Brightness	You can adjust the brightness of the image using these controls; either drag the slider bar, or enter a value into the text box.
Contrast	Use these controls to adjust contrast.
Compress	Click this button to reduce the document's file size by compressing the images. This component is discussed following this table.
Reset	Click this button to set the image color, brightness, and contrast back to the original settings.

When you click the Compress button, the Compress Pictures dialog box opens (see Figure 17-12). This is described in Table 17-4.

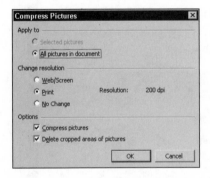

Figure 17-12: The Compress Pictures dialog box.

Table 17-4: Using the Compress Pictures Dialog Box

Component	Purpose
Apply To	Select whether you want to compress or modify Selected Pictures or All the Pictures in Document.
Change Resolution: Web/Screen	This converts the image to a 96-dpi (dots per inch) resolution, an image suitable for the Web or viewing on a screen, but not really good enough for printing.
Change Resolution: Print	This converts the image to a print image, 200 dpi.
Change Resolution: No Change	This tells Word *not* to change the image from its current state.
Compress Pictures	If this is checked, Word will attempt to compress the image to reduce the file size.
Delete Cropped Areas of Pictures	Another way to reduce file space is to remove the areas of images that you have cropped out. You learned that cropping images only changes what is displayed on-screen, that the cropped portions can be retrieved. This check box determines that cropped areas *cannot* be retrieved.

Adjusting the contrast and brightness of an image

You can adjust brightness and contrast of an image in the Format Picture dialog box, or directly from the Picture toolbar. By changing the contrast, you are changing the relative difference between the light and the dark areas of an image. Changing brightness, on the other hand, increases or decreases all colors in the image. The following list describes the contrast and brightness buttons on the Picture toolbar:

✦ **More Brightness:** Adds white to lighten the colors in the selected picture

✦ **Less Brightness:** Adds black to darken the colors in the selected picture

✦ **More Contrast:** Increases the saturation (or intensity) of the colors in the selected picture; the higher the contrast, the less gray the color

✦ **Less Contrast:** Decreases the saturation of the colors in the selected picture; the lower the contrast, the more gray the color

Along with buttons for changing the brightness and contrast of an image, the Picture toolbar includes buttons for adjusting the colors (grayscale, black and white, and washout), and for compressing the image.

Creating a transparent background for an image

One of the great capabilities of the GIF file format is that you can specify a color to appear transparent, so an object can appear to float on the page. When a GIF image contains a transparent background color, the page background shows through it—the image will display the background below, no matter what type of background you use. Figure 17-13 shows images both with and without a transparent background color.

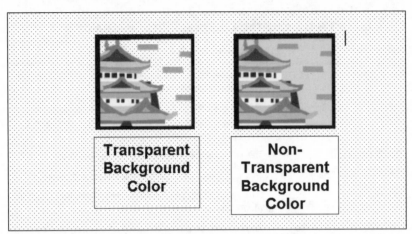

Figure 17-13: A transparent background color specified using the Set Transparent Color button of the Picture toolbar.

To set a transparent color from within Word, follow these steps:

1. Select the picture in Word for which you want to create a transparent area (it must be a .gif image). The Picture toolbar appears.

2. On the Picture toolbar, click Set Transparent Color.

3. Click the color that you want to make transparent. The background of the page then displays wherever the chosen color appears in the image.

If an image already has a transparent color set, you can still use this tool to set a different color as the transparent color; the original transparent color then becomes visible again. If you click on a color and it does not appear transparent, it may be because you clicked on a dithered, rather than solid, color—you clicked on a pixel of one color, but the other pixels in the dithering combination did not change.

Hiding Pictures

Including a large number of in-line pictures in your documents slows down Word's performance. This is more of a problem with large documents with many images, of course, and it was a much more serious problem a few years ago—today's computers, assuming they have sufficient memory, can handle this situation reasonably well. Still, Word allows you hide in-line pictures and to display picture placeholders to speed up working with a document. For example, you can display the pictures while you're inserting and formatting them, and you can hide pictures while you work on the text in your document. A picture placeholder appears as an empty box outlined by thin lines. You can select and work with hidden pictures as though they are displayed.

To speed up scrolling by hiding pictures, open the Options dialog box (Tools ➪ Options), click the View tab, and select the Picture Placeholders check box under the Show group.

Object Layout and Position

In this section, you look at a number of graphic components, including drawings, organization charts, and WordArt. There is a common characteristic among these objects—and pictures—that you should learn about first. Word provides special tools for positioning objects on the page, and these tools work in the same manner for all of these objects.

When you first insert an object, Word uses default position settings and anchors that object to the nearest paragraph. If that paragraph moves, the text box or picture moves with it. This default positioning is known as *in line with text*.

Note   As noted earlier, you can change the default positioning behavior by choosing Tools ➪ Option, clicking the Edit tab, and selecting an Insert/Paste Pictures As option.

Word offers these seven different position types:

✦ **In Line With Text:** The image is placed on a line along with the text; you might even consider it as a single character. You can type in front of and after it. And unless it's a small image the size of a text character, the image increases the line *leading* or spacing to make room for it.

✦ **Square:** The image is not linked to the text. Instead, the text *wraps* around the rectangular canvas area in which the object is placed. (We talk about the canvas later. For now, you just need to understand that regardless of the shape of the actual object, it's sitting on a rectangular area, much as an oil painting is painted on a rectangular canvas.)

✦ **Tight:** In this case, the text wraps around the object, but more tightly. You cannot adjust the space between the top and bottom edges of the object and the text; it will always be close. (Conversely, with the Square position, you can add substantial space if you want.) The text can impinge on the rectangular canvas area, up to the actual object inside the canvas.

✦ **Behind Text:** The object sits behind the text, rather like a watermark.

✦ **In Front of Text:** The object sits on top of the text, obscuring it.

✦ **Through:** The text is wrapped around the object. In most cases, this is exactly like the Tight layout. However, if you choose to edit the wrapping points in an object (which you look at later in this chapter), the Through layout wraps following those points, even if they lead the text over the object.

✦ **Top and Bottom:** This is a combination of the In Line With Text and Square positions. Instead of the image sitting on a line with text or the text wrapping around the sides of the object, however, the text stops, the object appears below that line, and a new line of text begins below the object.

Tip   Disappearing images? If you change the wrapping style of an image from In Line With Text to any other style, the image cannot be displayed in Normal view. Your document automatically changes to Print Layout view, and whenever you change back to Normal view, your images disappear.

These different layouts provide a lot of flexibility. For each layout, of course, there are other settings—the specific position on the page, the distance between the object or canvas and the text, anchor locking, overlap, and so on. Not all settings are available for all layout types, of course. In Line With Text, for example, has almost no settings, because the object is treated as a piece of text.

Choosing a layout

It's important to understand that objects act differently depending on the layout chosen. In particular, there's a big difference between In Line With Text and the other layouts. When an object is In Line With Text, you can't use Format Picture to place a border around it, as we discussed earlier. It's also difficult to position. On the other hand, because it can't be moved around quite as easily as the other layouts, it's harder to lose. With the other layouts, you may notice that objects sometimes jump to positions unexpectedly. Depending on what you are doing with an object, choosing a layout for the object may be the first thing you do after creating or inserting it.

Suppose that you just inserted a picture or created a drawing. Now you want to specify a layout. Open the Format Picture dialog box. In the case of a picture, you can simply double-click the image, and the Format Picture dialog box opens. In other cases, you must double-click the border of the object. If you double-click the border of the drawing canvas, the Format Drawing Canvas dialog box opens. But if you double-click *inside* the canvas, you may end up opening the Format dialog box for an object inside the canvas, which will have different layout characteristics. You can tell Word not to use the drawing canvas by choosing Tools ➪ Options, clicking the General tab, and clearing the Automatically Create Drawing Canvas When Inserting AutoShapes check box.

Tip   If you're not very good at double-clicking on border lines, select the object and then select Format ➪ *Object* (Format ➪ Drawing Canvas or Format ➪ Picture, for example).

After you open the Format Picture dialog box, click the Layout tab (see Figure 17-14). You can see that only five of the seven basic layouts are shown here. Click the Advanced button to open the Advanced Layout box (see Figure 17-15), and click the Text Wrapping tab to see all the layouts. Table 17-5 shows the settings available to you on both of these tabs.

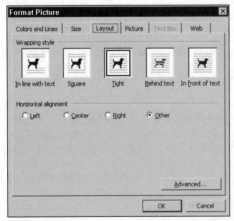

Figure 17-14: The Layout tab of the Format Picture dialog box.

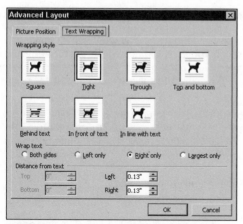

Figure 17-15: The Text Wrapping tab in the Advanced Layout dialog box.

Table 17-5: Text Wrapping Options

Option	Effect
Wrapping Style	Select one of the layout or wrapping styles discussed earlier.
Horizontal Alignment	These settings define where the object sits on the page; on the Left, in the Center, or on the Right. The Other setting has no effect; once you have selected a Wrapping Style other than In Line With Text you'll be able to use the mouse to drag the object around on the page, or use the position settings in the Advanced Layout dialog box. If you move an object and then return to the Format dialog box, the Other option button is selected. Note that the Horizontal Alignment settings affect all Wrapping Styles with the exception of In Line With Text.
Wrap Text	These settings define where Word should wrap the text (these settings are not available for all Wrapping Styles, of course). You can wrap text on Both Sides of the object; Left Only (text appears only to the left of the object); Right Only (text appears only to the right); or Largest Only (text is placed on the side of the object with most room between the object and the margins).
Distance From Text	These controls allow you to define the distance between the four sides of the object and the text around it. Not all settings are available for all Wrapping Styles, of course.

Tip

You can also select the seven different wrapping styles from the Picture and Drawing Canvas toolbars. Click the Text Wrapping button and a drop-down list appears. Click the one you want, and it is applied to the object. Note that at the bottom of the list is the Edit Wrap Points option, which we look at next.

High-resolution wrapping

It's possible to get very fancy with text wrapping, defining exactly where on an object the wrapping should occur. (This affects just the Through wrapping style; it's ignored by all others.) You can lead text into an object, overlaying parts of it, or you can extend the wrapping area way beyond the object, creating extensive white space around it. You can create wrapping lines of any shape—irregular, straight, or curved.

Click the object, click the Text Wrapping button on the Picture toolbar, and select Edit Wrap Points. (Alternatively, you can choose Draw ⇨ Text Wrapping on the Drawing toolbar and select Edit Wrap Points.) A dotted line sprinkled with little black squares appears around your object. The more complicated the shape of the object, the more squares are displayed.

Tip   Zooming in on the page will make the object easier to work with.

This line is the line that the text follows when it wraps around the object. The text doesn't necessarily touch this line—the Distance From Text settings are the distance between the text and this line. So moving this line adjusts the manner in which text wraps around the object.

Here's how to work with this line:

✦ Point to a black square, click and hold the mouse button—the mouse pointer changes to a cross-hairs symbol—and drag the square. Move the line until the square is where you want it; then release the mouse button.

✦ Point to any area on the line and do the same—you will create a new square, and move the square and the line to the new position.

The squares are nodes, of course, joined by straight lines. If you want to create a curved line, you need to add squares and create a series of straight lines that together make up the curve. (See Figure 17-16.)

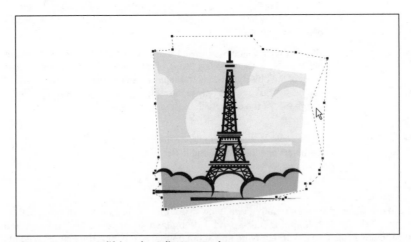

Figure 17-16: Modifying the Edit Wrap points.

Positioning the object

After you define the wrapping style and distance from text, you can define the position of the object on the page. You can simply drag the object around the page using the mouse. For more precise settings, however, use the Format Picture dialog box. You can also use this box to *anchor* the object in relation to a particular piece of text; if the text moves, the object moves with it.

Open the Format dialog box (select the object and then choose Format ➪ *Object*, such as Format ➪ Picture) or double-click on the object or its border. Click the Layout tab, click the Advanced button, and then click the Picture Position tab (see Figure 17-17). Table 17-6 describes the Picture Position tab options.

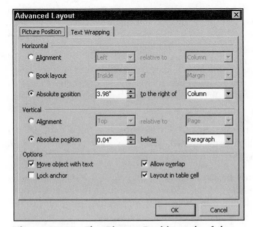

Figure 17-17: The Picture Position tab of the Advanced Layout dialog box.

Table 17-6: The Picture Position Tab Options

Option	Effect
Horizontal settings	You have three horizontal settings, to define the horizontal position of the object.
Alignment	Places the object Left, Centered, or Right, relative to the Margin, the Page edge, Column, or Character (which refers to the left edge of the paragraph). For instance, Right Margin aligns the right edge of the object with the right margin; Left Margin aligns the left edge with the left margin; Centered Character aligns the middle of the object with the left edge of the text.
Book Layout	Positions the object Inside or Outside the Margin or Page. The position will flip between odd and even pages.
Absolute Position	Specifies the absolute position of the object; you define the distance, in $\frac{1}{100}$ths of an inch, between the object and the Margin, Page, Column, or Character (left edge of the paragraph).

Continued

Table 17-6 *(continued)*

Option	Effect
Vertical settings	These two settings allow you to define the object's vertical position.
Alignment	Positions the object at the Top, Center, Bottom, Inside, or Outside positions, relative to the Margin, Page, or Line.
Absolute Position	Specifies the absolute position of the object; you define the distance, in ¹⁄₁₀₀ths of an inch, between the object and the Margin, Page, Paragraph, and Line.
Move Object With Text	Determines if the text box or picture moves with the paragraph to which it is anchored. This setting has no bearing on the horizontal positioning option settings, but it does set the Vertical group Absolute Position to link to the Paragraph. Also, if you choose a Vertical Alignment, Move Object With Text will be cleared when you close the dialog box.
Lock Anchor	This locks the anchor to the paragraph it's currently placed in. If you later move the object, even a page or two away, it remains anchored to that paragraph, and, if Move Object With Text has been selected, it moves when that paragraph moves.
Allow Overlap	Specifies if an object can overlap, or be overlapped by, another object. If one or both objects do not allow overlap, when you try to place one object over another, the other object moves out of the way.
Layout in Table Cell	You can use tables to position objects on the page. However, you need to have Layout in Table Cell selected if you want to do that. With this *not* selected you can place an anchor in a cell, yet have the image outside the cell, ensuring that the object moves with the table cell.

Tip If you want an object to appear in the left margin, enter a negative number in the Absolute Position box and choose Margin. To place the object in the right margin, enter a number that equals or exceeds the value on the horizontal ruler that marks the right margin, such as 7.25". Entering a negative number in the Absolute Position box and then choosing Margin places the text box in the top margin of the page. A text box will not fit entirely in the margin unless the margin is wider than the text box. If the text box is wider than the margin, that text box either extends into the text itself or falls off the page.

Using anchors

We just mentioned them a few paragraphs earlier, so we'd better discuss *anchors*. Word anchors every object to a paragraph, the paragraph in which the insertion point was placed when the object was inserted. There are two kinds of anchors. If an object is an In Line With Text object, it's anchored to the paragraph by default. It's *part* of the paragraph. But other kinds of objects can move around, can lie across two or more paragraphs. These objects are anchored to a particular paragraph, even if the object is not in or on that paragraph.

Word uses an actual anchor icon to display the anchor position (see Figure 17-18). You can't see the anchor, though, unless you turn on hidden characters; click the Show/Hide button on the Standard toolbar, and you'll see the anchor of a selected object. (The anchor disappears when you click somewhere out of the object.) You can, if you wish, make Word display anchors even when you are *not* displaying other hidden characters. In the Options dialog box, under the View tab, in the Print and Web Layout Options group, select the Object Anchors check box.

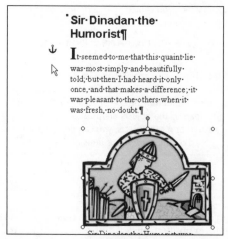

Figure 17-18: A text box anchored and locked to the preceding paragraph.

Tip Did your object disappear when you deleted some text? You probably deleted the paragraph to which the object was anchored. Choose Edit ➪ Undo, turn on hidden characters so that you can see the anchor, and move the anchor to another paragraph before deleting the text.

Also, when you insert an object Word automatically enables the Move Object With Text option in the Picture Position tab of the Advanced Layout dialog box. So, if you move the paragraph to which an object is attached, that object moves along with the paragraph. If, however, you drag the object to a different location on the page, Word breaks the connection and anchors that object to the nearest paragraph when you drop it.

In addition to dragging the object away from its anchoring paragraph, you also can drag the *anchor* icon itself to a different paragraph, thus linking the object to the new paragraph. But you can also lock the anchor to a specific paragraph. This way, the text box or picture moves in relation to the paragraph, no matter how far from the paragraph the anchor is placed. When you lock the anchor, a small padlock icon appears with it. To lock an anchor to a paragraph, select Lock Anchor in the object's Advanced Layout dialog box.

Tip You can keep an object on a specific page by clearing both the Lock Anchor and the Move With Text check boxes. As text moves down, the anchor jumps from paragraph to paragraph to remain in the same position.

Positioning with the Drawing toolbar

You can also use the Drawing toolbar to position objects in general positions—the Draw menu on this toolbar contains several menus and commands to help you position objects in a variety of ways. Table 17-7 explains these commands.

Table 17-7: The Drawing Toolbar Positioning Commands

Option	Effect
Grid	Opens the Grid dialog box, in which you can set up the manner in which objects are moved when you nudge or drag.
Nudge	Select one of the Nudge commands—Up, Down, Left, or Right—to shift the object a little bit.
Align or Distribute	This menu lets you place the object horizontally—Left, Centered, Right—or vertically—Top, Middle, Bottom. It also allows you to distribute several objects across the page, equally spaced, either horizontally or vertically. By default Relative to Page is selected, meaning the objects are positioned relative to the page edges. But if you select two or more objects, you can de-select Relative to Page, so the positioning is based on the current positions of the objects.

Selecting objects

You can select objects in several ways before you act on them. Click on an object, and it is selected. If an object such as a square or a circle is unfilled, click its edge to select it. (You cannot select an unfilled object by clicking its center.) Click on another, and that object is now selected, while the previous one is no longer selected. Press Ctrl or Shift while you click to select multiple objects, adding one each time you click.

You can also use the Select Multiple Objects button on the Drawing toolbar. This opens the dialog box shown in Figure 17-19, where you can click Select All to select all the objects in the document, or click on an individual object's check box to select just that one. Note that the Select Multiple Objects button does not appear on the toolbar by default—you have to add it using the Add or Remove Buttons menu that opens when you click the Toolbar Options button at the end of the bar. And even if you add the button, it's disabled until you have at least one object in your document that is *not* an In Line With Text object.

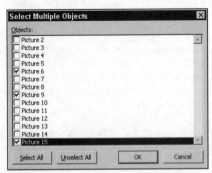

Figure 17-19: The Select Multiple Objects dialog box.

Here's another way to select a group of objects: click the Select Objects button and then drag the mouse to completely enclose all the objects that you want to select. Make sure that no part of any object you want to select is outside the area you are selecting.

Once you have selected a group of text boxes, you can use the mouse to drag them as a group to a new position on the page, or use one of the various positioning commands. You can even select Format ➪ *Object* to use the Format dialog box to apply settings to all the objects at once.

Aligning objects using the Drawing Grid dialog box

Word contains a built-in, invisible grid that aligns objects to the nearest ¹⁄₁₀ inch and allows you to line up objects. You can change the horizontal or vertical spacing of the grid or even turn the grid off altogether by choosing Draw ➪ Grid (from the Drawing toolbar), which opens the Drawing Grid dialog box (see Figure 17-20). The Drawing Grid dialog box includes the Snap Objects To Grid and the Snap Objects To Other Objects check boxes that allow you to choose whether to align objects automatically according to the grid or in relation to other objects.

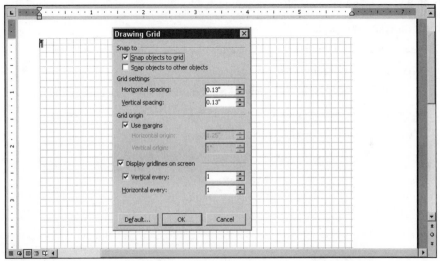

Figure 17-20: The Drawing Grid dialog box, shown on top of visible gridlines.

The Grid Origin group allows you to determine the grid's beginning point. The Use Margins check box tells Word to create a grid bounded by the page margins, but if you clear this check box you can set the distance from the page edges at which the grid should start.

Word allows you to display gridlines in your document. To show gridlines, select the Display Gridlines on Screen check box. You can then choose whether you want to view vertical grid lines, and define how often vertical and gridlines should be shown on the page. (1 means show a line every single horizontal-spacing unit.)

The grid constrains the movement of your mouse pointer as you draw and drag. You may find that your drawings snap to the gridlines. As a result, you can use the drawing grid to help you draw straight lines and the sides of objects in certain increments. For example, to draw squares with ½-inch sides, set your drawing grid to 0.5".

Tip   The Alt key tells Word to ignore the gridlines—you can move and draw without being constrained. Or, if Snap Objects to Grid is not selected—so the gridlines are not active—pressing and holding down the Alt key makes Word use the grid.

Note that these grid settings apply in two places: in your pages and inside a drawing canvas.

Aligning objects

You can align objects across a page. Select the objects, click the Draw drop-down arrow on the Drawing toolbar, and point to the Align or Distribute option. A pop-up menu appears that includes alignment options allowing you to align the group by their left or right edges or vertical centers, align the group by their top or bottom edges or horizontal middle, or distribute the group horizontally or vertically. If you select the Relative to Page option, the alignment relates to the whole page rather than to the current positions of the group.

Summary

Word allows you to bridge the chasm of diverse graphic formats to work with almost any type of graphic. In addition, Word provides a tremendous number of options for creating and adding drawings as well as special effects to work with them once you've inserted them. Using this chapter as a guide, you can do the following:

✦ Import graphics from other applications into your Word documents.

✦ Position a graphic anywhere on the page.

✦ Add borders and shadows, change image color schemes, brightness, and contrast.

✦ Work with the seven different Wrapping Styles.

✦ Position objects using the mouse, the Drawing toolbar, and anchors.

✦ Work with gridlines to help you position objects on the page.

✦   ✦   ✦

More Object Types— Drawings, Text Boxes, and More

In This Chapter

Using Word's drawing tools

Working with text boxes

Using WordArt

Creating organization charts

Adding callouts to objects

Adding captions to objects

In Chapter 17, we discussed how to insert images into documents and manipulate them in various ways. You may recall that an image is just one kind of a number of different kinds of *objects* that you can place in a document. In this chapter, we talk more about objects.

Much of what we discussed in Chapter 17 will serve you well in this chapter because the various kinds of objects share many of the same characteristics and tools. You move and size them in the same way, for example, and you apply border colors and fills in the same manner. We begin this chapter by looking at Word's sophisticated drawing tools.

Drawing in Word

Word has a number of built-in drawing tools. These tools allow you to create vector images called *objects*. A Word drawing can consist of many objects, such as lines and circles. These objects appear directly on the page as you draw them. You then can move them anywhere on the page—even above or beneath the text.

When you use Word's drawing tools, you work directly on a page in your document in Word's Print Layout view. The objects that you create are location-independent, so you can move a drawing simply by dragging it. This section explains how to work with Word's Drawing toolbar to create graphics directly on the page.

Beginning a drawing

There are several ways to begin a drawing:

✦ **Choose Insert ➪ Picture ➪ New Drawing:** Word places a *drawing canvas* (a gray-bordered box) in your document and opens the Drawing toolbar if it isn't already open. You can now use the toolbar to create objects inside this canvas.

✦ **Choose Insert ➪ Picture ➪ AutoShapes:** The AutoShapes toolbar opens. When you select a shape, Word creates a canvas on which you can draw the shape.

✦ **Choose Insert ➪ Picture ➪ Organization Chart:** Word places a drawing canvas in the document and inserts a basic organization chart that you can work with.

✦ **Choose Insert ➪ Picture ➪ WordArt:** The WordArt tool opens. You can create art with this tool that is then placed into your document (although not on a drawing canvas).

✦ **Open the Drawing toolbar and click on a drawing tool:** Word places a canvas in the document where you can use the tool.

A little later in this chapter, you take a look at the AutoShape, Organization Chart, and WordArt specialized drawing tools. The next section, however, shows you the drawing canvas and discusses the basic drawing tools provided on the Drawing toolbar.

Working with the drawing canvas

The *drawing canvas* is a rectangular area in which you can create your drawing. As you may have noticed from the preceding bullet list, the drawing canvas is created automatically under certain conditions and comes with a Canvas toolbar. The canvas itself is quite obvious—it has a thick cross-hatched line, with large handles on the corners and sides. You can do several things with this canvas, either directly or using the Canvas toolbar (see Figure 18-1):

✦ **Change the size of the canvas without adjusting the size of the objects within:** Drag the handles.

✦ **Change the size of the canvas *and* the objects within:** Click the Scale Drawing button; then drag the circular handles that appear on the corners and edges of the canvas.

✦ **Move the canvas:** Drag the border.

✦ **Set the Wrapping Style:** Choose a style from the Text Wrapping button.

✦ **Reduce the canvas to the smallest size that encloses the objects within:** Click the Fit button.

✦ **Increase the size of the canvas:** Click the Expand button.

Tip   Remove the Canvas toolbar by right-clicking on the canvas border and selecting Hide Drawing Canvas Toolbar.

Note that the canvas itself is an object—you can configure its wrapping style for example. Within the canvas are other objects, however, as we talk about soon.

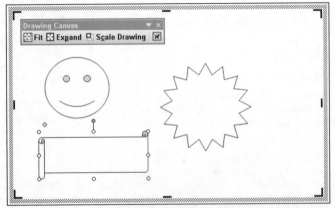

Figure 18-1: A drawing canvas, with objects inside, and the Canvas toolbar.

Tip If you hate the drawing canvas, you can disable it. Choose Tools ➪ Options, click the General tab, and clear the Automatically Create Drawing Canvas When Inserting AutoShapes check box.

Using the Drawing Toolbar

You can open the Drawing toolbar in a number of ways:

- ✦ Choose Insert ➪ Picture ➪ New Drawing. Word opens the toolbar and places the drawing canvas in the document, ready for you to begin drawing.
- ✦ Click the Drawing button on the Standard toolbar.
- ✦ Right-click anywhere on the background of a toolbar and choose Drawing.
- ✦ Choose View ➪ Toolbars and select Drawing from the Toolbars list.

If you open the Drawing toolbar by using the first method in the preceding list, your drawing canvas is ready to go. If you use any of the other methods, Word creates the drawing canvas as soon as you click a drawing tool in the Drawing toolbar.

Figure 18-2 shows the Drawing toolbar. If you move the mouse pointer over a button, Word displays a ToolTip that shows the name of the button. Table 18-1 describes each of the buttons on the Drawing toolbar.

Figure 18-2: The Drawing toolbar.

Table 18-1: Word's Drawing Toolbar

Button	*Name*	*Function*
	Draw	Opens a drop-down menu that enables you to Group, Ungroup and/or Regroup objects or pictures. You can choose to Order your selected objects or pictures by choosing from Bring to Front, Send to Back, Bring Forward, Send Backward, Bring in Front of Text, or Send Behind Text. You can also choose to set your Grid parameters, Nudge, Align or Distribute, and Rotate or Flip your pictures and objects in every direction. Additionally, you can set Text Wrapping options; Edit Points of a line drawn in a curve, freeform, or a scribble; change the shapes of AutoShape objects with the Change Autoshape option; and/or Set AutoShape Defaults.
	Select Objects	Click this button then click an object in your drawing to select that object.
	AutoShapes	Opens a drop-down menu of drawing options: Lines, Connectors, Basic Shapes, Block Arrows, Flowchart, Stars and Banners, and Callouts.

Continued

Table 18-1 *(continued)*

Button	Name	Function
	Line	Draws straight lines. When you hold down Shift, draws straight lines snapping to positions in 15-degree increments. Hold down Ctrl to make the starting point the center of the line.
	Arrow	Draws a basic arrow. When you hold down Shift, draws straight arrows snapping into positions at 15-degree increments. Hold down Ctrl to make the starting point the center of the line.
	Rectangle	Draws rectangles. When you hold down Shift, draws squares. In both cases the point at which you click and begin dragging is a corner; press Ctrl, though, and the starting point is the center.
	Oval	Draws ovals. When you hold down Shift, draws circles. Again, the starting point may be on the edge of the circle or oval, or, if you press Ctrl, may be the center.
	Text Box	Draws a rectangular text box. Press Ctrl to make the starting point the center rather than a corner of the box.
	Insert WordArt	Opens the WordArt Gallery dialog box, allowing you to insert WordArt.
	Insert Diagram or Organization Chart	Opens the Diagram Gallery, from which you can select a diagram or organization chart.
	Insert Clip Art	Displays the Clip Art task pane.
	Insert Picture	Displays the Insert Picture dialog box, allowing you to select a file to insert.
	Fill Color	Fills a selected shape with color. If no shape is selected, sets the default fill color. Also enables you to select Fill Effects.
	Line Color	Colors a selected line (or the line around a selected shape). If no shape is selected, sets the default line color. Also enables you to create Patterned Lines.
	Font Color	Changes the color of the selected text. If no text is selected, sets the default text color.
	Line Style	Changes the width and style of a selected line. More Lines opens the Format AutoShape dialog box, where you have additional line style options.
	Dash Style	Allows you to select a line style from a number of choices.

Button	Name	Function
⬌	Arrow Style	Changes the style of a selected line to one of several preset arrow options. More Arrows opens the Format AutoShape dialog box, where you have additional arrow and line options.
◨	Shadow Style	Adds or changes the shadow of a selected object or picture. Shadow Settings allows you to turn Shadow On/Off, Nudge Shadow Up, Down, Left, or Right, and select a shadow color.
◰	3-D	Adds or changes a 3-D effect of a selected object or picture. 3-D displays the 3-D Settings toolbar that allows you to turn 3-D On/Off. Tilt Up, Down, Left and/or Right, gives you control over the Depth, Direction, Lighting, Surface, and 3-D Color.
◳	Select Multiple Objects	Displays a list box showing all the objects in the current drawing, allowing you to select them all or several. (This option is not on the toolbar by default; you must use the Add or Remove Buttons menu at the end of the toolbar to add it.)

Drawing lines and shapes

To create a line or shape, click the drawing button that you want (your mouse pointer becomes a crosshair), click the page on which you want the shape to begin (or within an existing canvas), in the position in which you want the shape to begin, and drag the pointer to where you want the shape to end. When you release the mouse button, the shape appears with small, square handles at the ends or corners of the shape. The handles indicate that the shape is active. You can delete an active shape by pressing Delete or Backspace (unless Typing Replaces Selection is turned off in the Options dialog box; if it is, click the Insert button). The object that you draw appears in the layer above the text and on top of any other objects that you've drawn. You also can change the layer position of an object (as explained in the "Layering drawing objects" section later in this chapter).

Tip You can press the Esc key to cancel a line or a shape before it is completed.

Choosing line styles, line colors, and fill colors

An object that you draw appears on the screen in the default line style, line color, and fill color. You can choose a different width for a line by choosing a line from the Line Style palette (see Figure 18-3). With your line selected, you can specify a different fill or line color using the Fill Color palette or Line Color palette. For example, if you want all your lines to be drawn in red, choose the Line Color button and select Red from the color palette. You can select an object and change its color, fill, or line style at any time. Your most recent choices then become the defaults used for the next drawing.

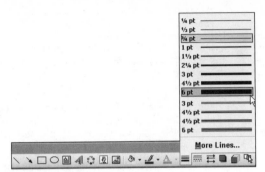

Figure 18-3: The Line Style palette.

 Tip   When you click on a shape button and draw the shape, the button is then deselected and the Select Object button is selected. This often confuses new users, because when they try to draw *another* shape, they end up selecting and moving objects instead. If you plan to draw multiple objects of the selected type, *double-click* the button.

Saving time with AutoShapes

The AutoShapes menu on the Drawing toolbar, and the AutoShapes toolbar itself (which opens when you choose Insert ➪ Picture ➪ AutoShapes), contain a variety of submenus providing predefined shapes, including Lines, Connectors, Basic Shapes, Block Arrows, Flowchart images, Stars & Banners, and Callouts. Figure 18-4 shows each available AutoShapes submenu.

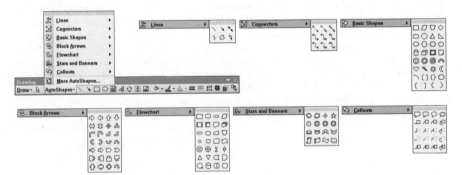

Figure 18-4: The AutoShape submenus.

If you click More Autoshapes, the Clip Art task pane appears, displaying clip art from All Collections (see Figure 18-5).

These shapes are clip-art images that you insert just as you would any other clip art. To add a shape, make sure that the line and fill colors you want to use are selected and then choose the shape that you want from the AutoShapes submenu and draw the image in the drawing canvas by dragging the mouse. Once inserted, these shapes can be resized, rotated, flipped, colored, and combined with other shapes to create more complex shapes.

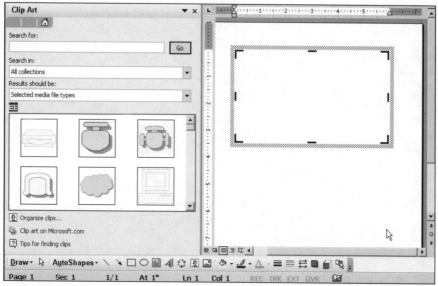

Figure 18-5: The Clip Art task pane is displayed when you select More AutoShapes.

Drawing lines

The Line button allows you to draw straight lines. Pressing Shift as you draw constrains the line; you can create straight horizontal, vertical, or diagonal lines—you'll find that the line "snaps" into positions at 15-degree increments. Hold down Ctrl to draw a line from the center outward instead of drawing from one end to the other (in other words, the line extends in two directions).

Tip   The Shift and Ctrl keys have effects that are common with most of the drawing tools. Shift is the *constraining* tool: it limits lines and arrows to particular angles, limits the rectangle and text box tools to drawing squares, limits the oval tool to drawing circles, ensures that when you size AutoShapes the shapes increase or decrease in all directions proportionally. The Ctrl key changes the starting position, making the starting position the *center* of the object rather than a corner or end. You can also use the Alt key to suppress or apply Snap Objects to Grid (see Chapter 17 to find out more about Snap Objects to Grid).

Drawing lines with arrowheads

Word provides several options for adding arrows to your document. The fastest way to add an arrow is to click the Arrows button and draw a line. You also can choose AutoShapes ➪ Lines for some simple lines with arrowheads. The Arrow Style button opens a menu that allows you to add arrowheads at either end (or both ends) of both straight lines and arrow lines. Simply select a line and then select the arrow style you want to use. Alternatively, you can click More Arrows on the Arrow Styles menu to display the Format AutoShape dialog box and then click the Colors and Lines tab (see Figure 18-6). With this tab, you get more control over your lines and arrowhead styles.

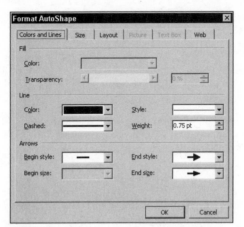

Figure 18-6: The Colors and Lines tab in the Format AutoShape dialog box allows you to control the size and style of an arrowhead.

Drawing curves and freeform shapes

The AutoShapes submenus provide a wide assortment of predefined shapes. Choosing AutoShapes ➪ Lines allows you to draw a curve, a freeform line, a scribble, a straight line, or a polygon. A completed freeform or polygon comprises any combination of line segments connected by nodes (see Figure 18-7). When you select a line or shape, that line or shape appears in the selected line color or style. To fill a closed polygon, click the Fill button. To keep your straight-line segments perfectly vertical, horizontal, or at a set angle, hold down the Shift key as you draw.

Figure 18-7: A freeform shape or polygon comprises line segments connected by nodes.

Drawing is really quite easy. After selecting a tool, click on the canvas area and drag the mouse. Click again and drag again—each time you click you are fixing the previous segment of the line. To finish drawing, either click the starting point (you can create an enclosed area by joining the start and finish), double-click anywhere, or press Esc.

Each tool works differently, as the following list explains:

✦ **The Curve tool:** Click once, move the mouse, click again; as you move the mouse again, Word creates a curve, using the second click point at a sort of pivot.

✦ **The Freeform tool:** Hold the mouse button down while you move the mouse to draw a line wherever the mouse pointer moves; don't hold the mouse down to draw a straight line from click to click.

✦ **The Scribble tool:** You can click to start, but as soon as you release the mouse button the object is finished. Wherever you drag the mouse with the button held down, the tool draws a line.

Drawing basic shapes

Choosing AutoShapes ➪ Basic Shapes allows you to quickly add rectangles, squares, ellipses (ovals), or circles. But there's more. You'll find a Smiley Face, a Donut, a "No" symbol, and other weird stuff. The shapes that you draw with these tools can be empty or filled, bordered or not, and in color or in blacks and grays. Figure 18-8 shows a few sample shapes created with using the Basic Shapes option.

You can create your own circles and rectangles using the Rectangle and Circle buttons on the Drawing toolbar. If you hold down the Shift key as you draw after choosing the Rectangle button, you can draw a perfect square. If you hold down the Shift key as you draw after choosing the Ellipse button, you can draw a perfect circle. Hold down the Ctrl key to draw a rectangle, square, ellipse, or circle from the center outward, and use the Shift and Ctrl keys together to draw a perfect square or circle from the center outward. To draw from the center outward, hold down the Ctrl key as you draw. Press the Alt key while drawing and you have more control over positioning. Snap Object to Grid is turned off, so you can draw smoothly.

Figure 18-8: A few sample shapes created using the Basic Shapes submenu.

Drawing shadowed lines and shapes

You can choose from several different shadow options for any line or shape. The Shadow Settings and 3-D buttons allow you to add drop shadows and to provide interesting 3-D effects to lines, rectangles, and ovals. To display the 3-D toolbar, click on the 3-D button and select 3-D Settings. Figure 18-9 shows the 3-D Settings available by clicking on the 3-D button and the 3-D Setting toolbar.

Figure 18-9: The 3-D menu on the Drawing toolbar.

Drop shadows can be applied to arcs just as they are applied to lines and other shapes. Select Shadow Settings to use the Shadow Settings toolbar, from which you can turn shadows on and off, nudge them in all directions, and create a custom shadow color. Figure 18-10 shows the Shadow Settings toolbar and a drop shadow added to an image. The 3-D Settings toolbar allows you to quickly turn 3-D settings on or off and tilt 3-D objects up, down, and to the left or right. You can also change the depth, direction, lighting, surface type, and color using buttons on the 3-D Settings toolbar.

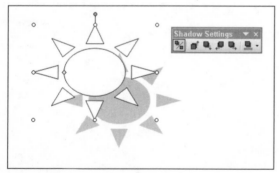

Figure 18-10: Drop shadows added to images using the Shadow Settings toolbar.

Editing drawing objects

Changing an object is a process similar to drawing an object. For example, you follow the same steps to change the color of a line as you do when you first select the color of a line. Just select the object and change the line color using the Drawing toolbar.

Tip To display the Format AutoShapes dialog box to edit a line or an AutoShape quickly, double-click on the line or AutoShape.

Using Change AutoShape

Here's a very quick way to change one object into a completely new one. You can do this with almost *any* object you've drawn, not just objects you created using the AutoShape tool. (The exception is that you cannot convert objects drawn with one of the line tools.)

Simply select the object you want to convert, choose Draw ⇨ Change AutoShape, pick an AutoShape menu and an AutoShape . . . and voilà, the object is converted.

Grouping and ungrouping objects

You can group individual drawing objects into a single object to make editing those objects easier. By grouping multiple objects together, you can work with the drawing as a whole, such as moving or resizing it as a single object. If you later need to separate objects, you can ungroup them.

You can even group object groups as well as individual objects. For example, you may want to separate the components of a complex drawing into several smaller groups for easier handling, but group all the subgroups together at some point to work on it as a whole—you can group and ungroup, so any decision you make is not irreversible. Figure 18-11 shows several objects both before and after being grouped.

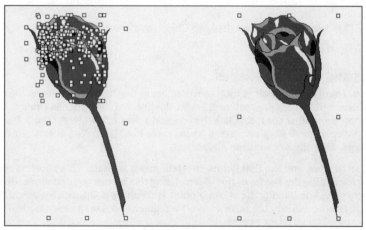

Figure 18-11: Objects before and after being grouped.

When you click a group to select it, selection handles appear, just as they do when you select a single object. In effect, the items have now become a single object.

To group objects, select the objects you want in the group and then choose Draw ⇨ Group from the Drawing toolbar. Or right-click on the group and choose Grouping ⇨ Group.

When you want to work on any individual part of a group, select the group and then choose Draw ⇨ Ungroup from the Drawing toolbar or Grouping ⇨ Ungroup from the pop-up menu. After making your changes you don't have to select the entire group again. Just click on one of the objects that was in the group that you just ungrouped, and choose Draw ⇨ Regroup or Grouping ⇨ Regroup to re-create the group.

Resizing lines and shapes

You can resize an object by dragging its selection handles. (When a line is selected, selection handles appear at each end. When a shape is selected, square selection handles appear at the corners and sides.) To set precise measurements for a line or a shape, use the Format dialog box. To display the Format dialog box, choose the Format ⇨ Object command or double-click the selected line or shape.

The following rules apply to resizing a line or shape:

✦ If you drag a side handle, you resize only from that side.

✦ If you drag a corner handle, you can resize from two directions at once.

✦ If you hold the Shift key as you drag a corner handle, the object retains its proportions (a square stays square, with the same ratio of line lengths, a circle stays round, and a freeform retains the same shape).

✦ Hold the Shift key as you resize a straight line to keep it in the same orientation—you'll adjust the length, but not the direction in which it points.

✦ If you hold the Ctrl key as you resize, you can resize from the center outward.

✦ If you hold the Alt key as you resize, you will turn off Snap Object to Grid.

Cross-Reference

See Chapter 17 to find out more about the Snap Object to Grid feature.

Editing curves and freeform shapes

Lines can be edited using the Edit Points tool—any line, including lines drawn using the Line, Arrow, Freeform, or Scribble tools, for instance. Select the line and then choose Draw ⇨ Edit Points from the Drawing toolbar (or right-click the line and select Edit Points). You'll see that the shape is composed of small lines connected by movable handles, called points or nodes. To change the shape, drag any one of these nodes.

Right-click again on the line, and the Edit Points shortcut menu appears. This shortcut menu lists your options for editing the points of the object. Using this menu, you can move, delete, and add nodes, close the line (linking the starting point and ending point with a straight line), break the line at any node, join any break, or convert a segment—a line between nodes—from a curved line to a straight line, or vice versa.

Adding a node between existing nodes provides you another node with which to smooth a curve. Deleting a node joins the line segments on both sides of that node.

Rotating and flipping objects

You can rotate and flip objects, using a couple of methods. When you select an object inside a drawing—or another object, such as a picture you've inserted into your document—you'll notice a little green handle, attached to a small bar. Point at this, and the mouse pointer changes to an incomplete circle with an arrow on it. Simply drag the green handle to rotate. Figure 18-12 shows rotated and flipped objects.

There's also a Draw ⇨ Rotate or Flip command. Select an object and then choose Draw ⇨ Rotate or Flip ⇨ Rotate Left 90 or ⇨ Rotate Right 90.

Tip

You cannot rotate text boxes. However, you can rotate WordArt objects. And you can change text direction inside the text box. We'll look at text boxes later in this chapter.

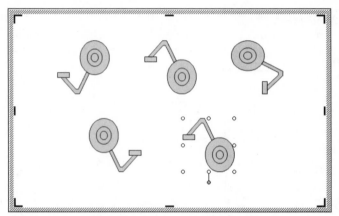

Figure 18-12: Sample rotated and flipped objects.

Removing lines and shapes

You can easily remove a shape or group of shapes from your drawing. Just select the objects that you want to delete, and then press Delete. If you delete an object accidentally, choose the Edit ➪ Undo command before doing anything else. You also can remove an object by selecting it and then cutting it (choose Edit ➪ Cut or press Ctrl+X).

Moving and copying lines and shapes

You can move any line, shape, or group of lines and shapes from one part of your drawing to another or from one part of your document to another. The quickest way to move an object is to drag it to a new position on the page. When you drag to the edge of the screen, the page automatically scrolls, and in this way, you can move objects beyond the area of the page being displayed. To move longer distances or to move objects between documents, use Word's Cut, Copy, and Paste commands.

Tip   Hold the Shift key while dragging an object, and the movement is constrained to vertical or horizontal directions—you can't move the object diagonally.

Here's another quick way to copy an object to a position a short distance away. Start dragging the original object, and then, before you release the mouse button, press the Ctrl key. A small + sign appears next to the mouse pointer. When you release the mouse pointer, a copy of the object is inserted into the document or canvas.

Positioning drawing objects

We've discussed how to position an object on the page, but what about positioning objects within a canvas? You can drag the object, as you've seen, but if you double-click an object, the Format dialog box opens. Click the Layout tab and you'll see very simple positioning controls, allowing you to position the object in relation to the Top Left Corner or Center of the canvas (see Figure 18-13).

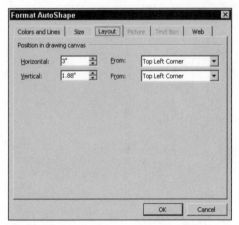

Figure 18-13: The Layout controls in the Format dialog box for an object in a canvas.

Layering drawing objects

Word provides various *layers* in which you can work:

✦ **The text layer:** The layer you are accustomed to working in when using a word-processing program—this is where your text is placed. You can place both text and objects on this layer, but it has no sublayers.

✦ **The layer above the text:** The layer above the text. Within this layer you can have sublayers—objects can be placed on top of each other.

✦ **The layer below the text:** Again, within this layer, you can have sublayers—objects can be placed on top of each other.

These are, of course, invisible layers. You can't see them, but if you use objects much, you'll soon get the feel for the layers. You can move objects between layers. Pictures can be placed in front of or behind text. Objects behind text can be layered one upon another. And within a drawing object you can layer objects, putting some on top of others.

The Draw ➪ Order command on the Drawing toolbar allows you to move any object between layers. Selecting objects that are behind the text layer is handled the same way as selecting objects in a drawing layer. (When you first draw objects, they appear in the layer, on top of the text.) If an object is hidden behind another object, select the topmost object and drag it out of the way, or move it behind the hidden object.

Figure 18-14 shows an example of Word's layering. Objects or pictures in the top layer obscure text, and objects in the text layer force the text to wrap. This feature is apparent when you choose the Print Layout view or Print Preview. Objects behind the text show through the text. The Drawing toolbar has four separate tools for rearranging layers: two for moving objects in front of and behind other objects in the drawing layer, and two for moving objects behind or in front of the text layer.

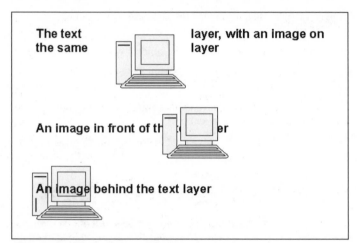

Figure 18-14: An example of Word's three layers.

When you draw an object, that object is automatically placed on the top of the drawing layer, above other objects in the drawing layer. You can select any object and move it to the top or bottom of those objects. How you layer objects determines how much of an object is visible. For example, you can layer multiple objects by selecting the top object and moving it to the back, selecting the next object and moving it to the back, and so on, until only those portions of the objects that you want to show are displayed. Figure 18-15 shows an object layered behind text.

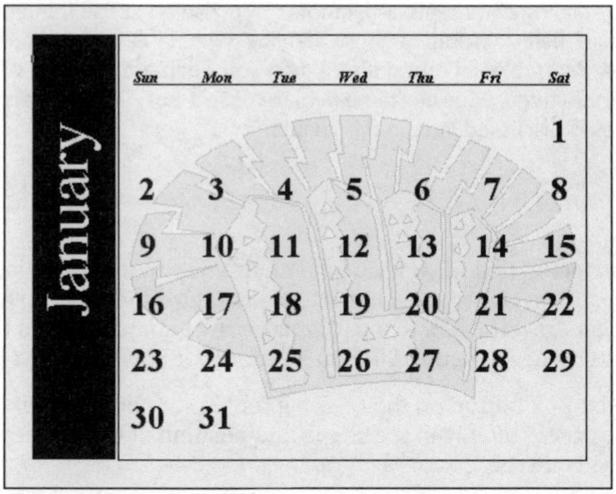

Figure 18-15: You can see through the text to an object layered behind the text.

To layer drawing objects and text, follow these steps:

   1. Select the object or objects that you want to move.

2. Choose Draw ➪ Order, or right-click to display the shortcut menu and choose Order. Then do one of the following:

- Choose the Send Behind Text option to move objects behind the text layer.

- Choose the Bring in Front of Text option to move objects in front of the text layer.

- Choose the Bring to Front option to move objects to the front of all the other objects in the same layer (the object remains behind the text if that's where it was; it isn't shifted to the drawing layer).

- Choose the Send to Back option to move objects behind all the other objects in the current layer (the object remains above the text if it was in the drawing layer).

Laying Out Text and Graphics with Text Boxes

A text box is, well, a box that can hold text. But unlike a normal page full of text, you can work with a text box in the same way you can work with the other objects we've looked at, pictures and drawing canvases. You can position it anywhere on the page, add fill colors, borders, and so on.

But a text box doesn't have to contain just text. You can also place images in a text box. So, you can create a sort of hybrid object, both images and text together in a single object. You can move it around in the document, or you can anchor it to a particular paragraph. You can wrap text around a text box and even add some sophisticated formatting with the Drawing toolbar, such as 3-D effects, shadows, colors, and background fills and textures.

Note Some time ago, earlier versions of Word used *frames* instead of text boxes. Text boxes are a more advanced replacement for frames, but frames are still used for a few purposes, such as positioning text or graphics containing comments or footnotes. You also must use frames to position text containing certain fields, including those dealing with tables of contents, indexes, document references, and tables of authorities. When you open a document with frames and then open the Format menu, you see Frame in place of Text Box. (The process of converting frames to text boxes is discussed later in this chapter.)

Inserting a Text Box

You can insert a text box around selected text in your document, or you can insert an empty text box as a placeholder, into which you can later paste text or a graphic object. If you are inserting an empty text box, you can draw the box to a particular size or simply click in the document and size the text box later. These are the different methods for creating a text box:

- ✦ Select text; then click the Text Box button on the Drawing toolbar or choose Insert ➪ Text Box. Word creates a text box, roughly in the shape and position of the selected text, and places that text inside the box.

- ✦ Choose Insert ➪ Text Box, or click the Text Box button on the Drawing toolbar. Word creates a drawing canvas. Draw your text box, inside the canvas or outside, at the size you want. (If you don't draw inside the canvas, Word deletes the canvas box.)

- ✦ Choose Insert ➪ Text Box, or click the Text Box button on the Drawing toolbar. Word creates a drawing canvas. Click inside the canvas or outside, and Word places a text box at that point. (If you don't draw inside the canvas, Word deletes the canvas box.)

Note When you insert a text box, the Text Box toolbar opens. This is used for linking text boxes and changing text orientation, which we'll look at later in this chapter.

If you insert a text box around a selection while in Normal view, Word automatically switches to Print Layout view. After inserting a text box, that box is automatically selected, so you can work with it immediately. You can tell when a text box is selected by the cross-hatch border and the eight square handles around the text box. What can you do with the box? Well, in a moment we'll look at some specific actions, but many of the things we've looked at in this chapter and the previous chapter also apply to text boxes. You can define how text wraps around the box; position it on the page; align it with other objects; add a fill color and border color or style, and so on.

Note To remove a text box and its contents, select the text box in Print Layout view and then press Delete or Backspace. To take the text or graphic out of a text box and remove only the box itself, you must first use the Copy or Cut function to remove the contents from the text box. Then paste the contents to another position in your document, select the text box, and press Delete or Backspace.

Adding text and drawing objects to the text box

To enter text in the new text box, simply place the insertion point in that box and begin typing. The text automatically wraps within the box. If you type more text than is visible on the screen, however, the box does not automatically expand to show the text. You must resize the text box to show all the text.

When you insert or paste a picture or other drawing object in a text box, that picture resizes to fit the box. Add another picture, though, and the box may have to resize to get both pictures in, so the second picture may not have to resize to fit. (Just a little idiosyncrasy; you can always size the images once they're in the box.)

To add a picture or other drawing object to your text box, you can choose an option from the Insert menu or use the Cut, Copy, and Paste buttons on the Standard toolbar or the shortcut menu. Figure 18-16 shows a text box with both text and a picture.

Tip Some AutoShapes can accept text. For instance, you can place text inside the Stars and Banners shapes. Right-click on an AutoShape, select Add Text, and begin typing.

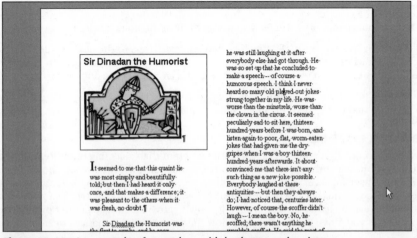

Figure 18-16: An example of a text box with both text and a picture.

Tip

To place an existing graphic object in a text box, insert an empty text box first and then paste the graphic in it. If you try to draw a text box around the graphic object, that text box will not contain the object.

Setting internal margins in a text box

The Format Text Box dialog box allows you to choose a variety of settings, most of which you have seen already (such as the Colors and Lines, Size, and Layout tabs described earlier in this chapter and in the preceding chapter). However, some settings specific to text boxes are available under the Text Box tab (see Figure 18-17).

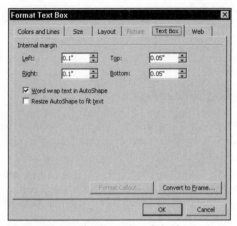

Figure 18-17: The Text Box tab in the Format Text Box dialog box.

This tab allows you to set the internal margins of the box, the distance between the edge of the box and the text within it. You can enter measurements in the Left, Right, Top, and Bottom boxes, or you can use the up and down arrows. The measurements are in the default unit of measure as set in the General tab of the Options dialog box (Tools ➪ Options). If you enter the measurements in inches (in), centimeters (cm), points (pt), or picas (pi), Word converts them to the default unit of measure.

This tab contains two more settings with wonderfully ambiguous labels:

✦ **Word Wrap Text in AutoShape:** If turned on, text wraps to the next line, leaving the text box width unchanged. If turned off, the width of the box increases to make room for a line of text—it won't wrap until the box is as wide as the document.

✦ **Resize AutoShape to Fit Text:** If this is checked, the text box changes height, if necessary, so that all the text remains visible. The box gets taller to fit the text.

Selecting a text box

Selecting a text box that contains text is a little different than selecting other items in Word, because you can select the text in the text box without selecting the text box itself. To see this, start by inserting a text box around some selected text. Then select something outside the text box so that neither the box nor the text inside the box is selected. The framed paragraph will have a single-line border around it. Slowly move the mouse pointer over the text box border. As you move the pointer, note how the pointer briefly changes to an outline arrow pointing to the upper-left with a four-headed arrow as you cross the border. This is known as the positioning pointer. After you pass the pointer over the border and move into the text, the pointer changes back to the I-beam shape.

If you click when the pointer becomes the positioning pointer, you select the text box itself—the border changes into a thicker, cross-hatch border with handles. If you click inside the box when the pointer has returned to the I-beam shape, you position the insertion point in the text. The border remains the same thick border, but any actions you carry out will be on the text, not the box.

Selecting a text box containing a graphic object is a little more complicated. When you drag the mouse pointer over the border, the pointer becomes the positioning pointer and stays that way as you move over the graphic itself. If you click the mouse button as the positioning pointer passes over the border, you select the text box, but if you click on the graphic, you select the graphic.

Copying and moving a text box

To copy a text box and its contents, right-click the text box border and then choose Copy from the shortcut menu. This creates a Clipboard copy of the current text box and its contents that you can paste to another location. To paste the text box, simply right-click in the document and choose Paste from the shortcut menu, or press Ctrl+V.

To move a text box and its contents from its present position to a new location, click and drag the border of the box to a new location. Alternatively, you can choose Cut from the shortcut menu and then Paste the box somewhere else.

By the way, when you copy or move a text box to a part of the page that already has text, that text box either obscures or displaces the existing text depending on your wrapping setting. In the Layout tab of the Format Text Box or Format Picture dialog box, you can choose whether the existing text should wrap around the text box or stop above the text box and then resume beneath it.

Cross-Reference   Chapter 17 looks at text wrapping in more detail.

Resizing a text box

The easiest way to resize a text box is to select the text box so that its sizing handles show and then to click and drag one of those handles. To change the size of a text box from the center out, hold down Ctrl while you drag the handle—the box will expand on all edges. You also can resize a text box by specifying measurements in the Format Text Box dialog box.

To change the size of a text box proportionally, select the text box and then position the pointer on one of the corner handles. The pointer then changes to a two-headed, diagonal arrow. Hold down Shift while you drag the pointer in the direction that you want; this constrains the sizing so that it expands proportionally in the vertical and horizontal directions. As with images, you can press and hold the Alt key to turn off Snap Object to Grid.

Note   When you insert a picture into a document, the Lock Aspect Ratio check box in the Size tab of the Format Picture dialog box is turned *on*. But this isn't the case with text boxes. By default, text boxes have the Lock Aspect Ratio feature turned *off*. This means that when you drag the corner handle on a picture, the picture resizes proportionally. When you drag the corner of a text box, however, it doesn't resize proportionally unless you press and hold down Shift as you drag.

To set the dimensions of a text box more precisely, use the Size tab of the Format Text Box dialog box, which we discuss in Chapter 17.

Formatting text in a text box

You format text in a text box the same that you format regular text. There is, however, one added feature: You can change the text direction so that it reads vertically. As mentioned, when you type in a text box, that text wraps inside the text box. If you type more text than the box will hold, the additional text is accepted but is hidden from view until you resize the box. The text box does not expand vertically to accommodate new text. (However, this behavior can be changed, as you read about earlier, using the Word Wrap Text in AutoShape and Resize AutoShape to Fit Text check boxes in the Format Text Box dialog box.)

To format the contents of a text box quickly, just select the text and then apply the formatting. You can apply styles to text before or after you place the text in a text box (though of course adjusting the style, as with any formatting really, can change the appearance or position of the text box on the page).

Tip
You can actually create special styles for text that will be placed in *frames* (which are similar to text boxes, as you'll see a little later in the chapter). Adding frame formatting to a style allows you to quickly format and position text in your document. For example, if you commonly position a side head in the left margin for a certain type of document, you can create a style that includes both the text and the frame formatting. Then, when you apply the style, the text has the correct position as well as the correct formatting.

You can use paragraph formatting in a text box for even more precise alignment. In Word, text boxes treat the contained text as a block that you can drag to different locations on the page. With paragraph formatting, you can align the text in the text box, but this alignment has no bearing on the position of the text box itself. For example, centering text within a text box is different from centering the text box itself. If you drag a text box with centered text to a different location on the page, the text within the box remains centered. This also is true of indentation applied to text within a text box.

Flowing text from one box to another

Word has a great little feature that allows you to flow text from one text box to another. If you fill the first box with text but continue typing, the new text appears in the next, linked, text box. Fill that, and that typing continues in the next linked one. Why? For example, a rather long article in a newsletter may begin on page one, continue on page two, skip a page, and end on page four. When you edit the text in any segment, the text in the linked box accommodates the changes seamlessly.

When you lay out this type of newsletter, you insert empty text boxes in the size and position where you want the continuing story to appear. These boxes may appear on different pages. As you enter text into the first text box, it overflows into the second, and then into the third linked text box. You can enter text in the first text box before linking the boxes, but the others must be empty. Figure 18-18 shows how linked text boxes can flow from one linked text box to another, whether or not the boxes appear on contiguous pages. Initially you can enter text only in the first of the linked text boxes; once the boxes are filled, though, you can enter and edit text in any of them. As the first text box fills up, the text continues in the next text box in the story. Note also that if you press Ctrl+A while the insertion point is in any of the boxes, the text in all boxes is selected.

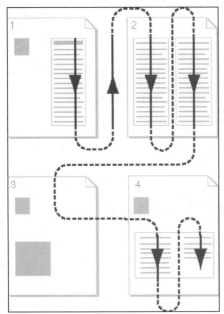

Figure 18-18: An illustration of three linked text boxes.

Each text box has only one forward link and one backward link, and you can break the link between any two text boxes in the chain and create two stories. All the other links remain intact, but the text boxes after the break remain empty, ready for the new story.

You can link boxes using the right-click pop-up menu (right-click on the text-box border), or the Text Box toolbar, which is shown in Figure 18-19. Simply select the text box you want to start from, and select Create Text Box Link on the menu or the toolbar. You'll see the icon change to a pitcher shape. Then click the text box you want to link to (which must be *empty*, by the way). When you point at a text box that you can link to, the pitcher tips forward as if to pour the text in. You can then repeat the process, linking *that* text box to another. That's all there is to it. Just type normally, and the text flows between the boxes. How can you tell later which boxes are linked together? Click in a text box that is part of a link *chain*, and one or both of the Previous Text Box and Next Text Box buttons on the Text Box toolbar are enabled. Click on these buttons to jump between linked text boxes. And if you ever need to break a link between boxes, select the first text box and click the Break Forward Link button.

Tip   If the pitcher icon gets stuck on-screen, press Esc to remove it and get out of linking mode.

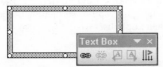

Figure 18-19: The Text Box toolbar.

Changing the direction of text

Most text in a Word document runs in one direction only. In text boxes and frames, however, you can orient the text or images either horizontally or vertically. You can choose Format ➪ Text Direction to open the Text Direction - Text Box dialog box (see Figure 18-20), which shows three text direction options: horizontal, vertical reading up, and vertical reading down. The Preview pane shows how the text appears in the selected orientation. The Text Box toolbar also includes the Change Text Direction button that cycles through the three orientations.

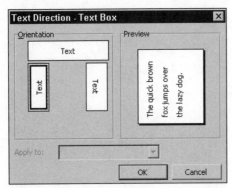

Figure 18-20: The Text Direction - Text Box dialog box.

After you set the text orientation, you can use the alignment buttons on the Formatting toolbar to further align the text. If you select the horizontal orientation, you have a choice of Align Left, Align Right, Center, or Justify. If the text is oriented vertically, the toolbar buttons change to Align Top, Center, Align Bottom, and Justify.

Changing between text boxes and frames

As mentioned earlier, Word has both frames and text boxes. Frames can be used to place text containing comments, footnotes, or fields, such as tables of contents, indexes, document references, and tables of authorities, which cannot be placed in text boxes. So now and then you may want to convert text boxes to frames. You can do this in the Format Text Box dialog box.

Click the Text Box tab, and then click the Convert to Frame button (the button is disabled if the text box is part of a link chain). Click OK in the message box that appears, and the job is done. Your text box may disappear, though Word may have to shift it to a different position, so look around and you should be able to find it close by. Unfortunately, there's no way to go *back*; no way to convert frames to text boxes.

Tip   How can you tell the difference between a text box and a frame? The borders actually look the same; they are thick cross-hatched lines. But the frame's handles are black squares, while the text box's handles are white circles. Also, double-click on the border and you'll soon see—either the Format Frame or Format Text Box dialog box opens. Formatting frames is very similar to working with text boxes, but with far fewer options.

Text boxes and publishing techniques

You can use text boxes to lay out and add special effects in your documents. You can use text boxes to create side headings, for example, instead of the usual headings positioned above a paragraph. A common layout for newsletters and reports is a centered graphic to break up the page, and another nice effect is a graphic in the header or margin of every page. The margin display of graphics can include text formatted in WordArt, which is treated as a graphic. The following sections explain each of these layout techniques. (Note, by the way, that you can create similar effects using tables.)

Creating a side heading with a text box

A side heading is a heading placed to the left rather than above the text. Figure 18-21 illustrates a side heading. Side headings are common in textbooks and manuals, but they provide a nice visual emphasis for any type of document. The key to using side headings is to create a margin large enough for the heading. The example in Figure 18-21 has a 2.25" margin. Assuming that the margin is wide enough, you can create the side heading in a text box and then drag it into position.

If you use side headings, be sure to set the width of the text box to an exact figure. This way, the heading wraps around rather than extending into the text. The width of the text box must be less than the margin. If the text box extends into the text, use the mouse to resize the width. You also should lock the anchor to the paragraph next to the heading and enable the Move Object With Text setting. This way, the heading stays with its text regardless of any future editing. You can also use paragraph formatting to further define the side heading. In Figure 18-21, for example, the side heading is right justified.

Centering a text box between columns

A common task for those who produce newsletters is to center a graphic using a two-column layout. (A two-column layout refers to snaking columns, or newspaper-style columns. It does not refer to two columns in a table.) The following discussion explains how to center a text box as shown in Figure 18-22. You can use these steps as a guideline for this type of task, but you may need to adjust some settings for your own specific layout. (You can drag the text box to the position that you want, but using the Draw ➪ Align and Distribute menu in the Drawing toolbar is more precise.)

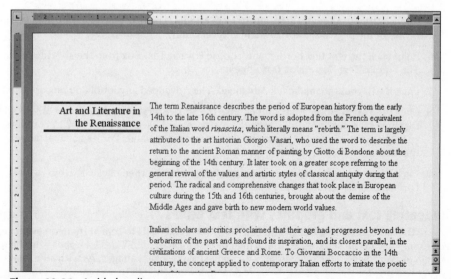

Figure 18-21: A side heading.

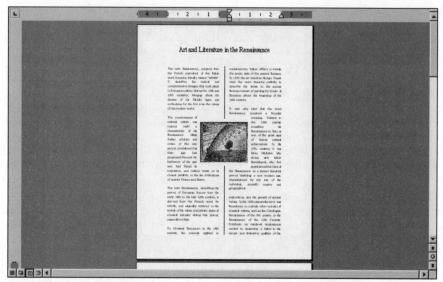

Figure 18-22: A centered text box.

To center a text box over a two-column layout, follow these steps:

1. Make sure you are in Print Layout view.

2. Select the text box in the document.

3. Choose Draw ➪ Align or Distribute ➪ Relative to Page on the Drawing toolbar.

4. Choose Draw ➪ Align or Distribute ➪ Align Center. The text box then is aligned horizontally.

5. Choose Draw ➪ Align or Distribute ➪ Align Middle. The text box now is aligned in the center of the page both horizontally and vertically.

6. Right-click the text box border, and choose Format Text Box from the shortcut menu. The Format Text Box dialog box appears.

7. Click the Layout tab, and click Advanced. The Advanced Layout dialog box appears.

8. Click the Text Wrapping tab, and choose the Square wrapping style. Enter **.15"** in all the Distance From text boxes. (This is the measurement used in Figure 18-22.) For more space between the text box and the text, increase the value. For less space, decrease the value.

9. Click OK to close the Advanced Layout dialog box, and then click OK again to close the Format Text Box dialog box.

Repeating text and graphics with text boxes

One of the more intriguing things you can do with text boxes is to repeat them on every page. For example, you can set it up so that a logo or text formatted in WordArt appears in the left margin of every page. This technique can create striking visual images. As with side headings (described previously), the key is to have a margin wide enough to accommodate the object.

To repeat a graphic on every page, follow these steps:

1. Choose File ⇨ Page Setup to specify a top margin wide enough to accommodate the text box.

2. Choose View ⇨ Header and Footer. This action switches you to Header/Footer view and automatically displays the Header and Footer toolbar.

Cross-Reference For information about creating headers and footers, see Chapter 10.

3. Type the text, if any, that you want for the header. If you do type text, press Enter after you finish to create a separate paragraph for your graphic insertion.

4. Draw an empty text box in the header, and size the box to the desired dimensions.

5. Insert the graphic or picture.

6. Crop and size the graphic as necessary.

7. Select the text box, and then drag the graphic to the position that you want. Alternatively, you can use the Drawing toolbar Align or Distribute options.

8. If you do not want the graphic to appear on the first page of the document or you want to specify odd or even pages, click the Page Setup button on the Header and Footer toolbar to open the Page Setup dialog box. Click the Layout tab, make your selections under the Headers and Footers section, and then click OK.

9. Click Close on the Header and Footer toolbar to return to your document. You can see the new header both in Print Layout view and in Print Preview. Figure 18-23 shows some sample pages with a header graphic repeated on every page.

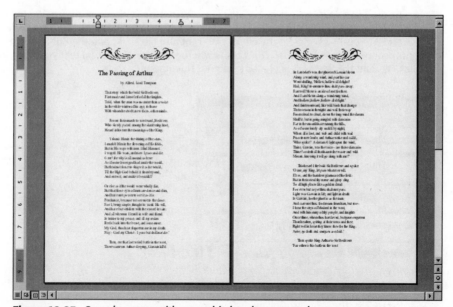

Figure 18-23: Sample pages with a graphic header repeated on every page.

Adding Special Effects to Graphics with WordArt

With WordArt, you can turn ordinary words into graphic objects. Among other things, you can sculpt text into a variety of shapes, flip or stretch letters, rotate or angle words, or add shading, colors, borders, or shadows to text. By mixing WordArt effects, you can create hundreds of interesting designs. Figure 18-24 shows a few sample WordArt images.

Note   Remember, WordArt objects are objects like any other. You can resize, move, copy, adjust layout, and so on, using many of the techniques you have learned in this and the previous chapter.

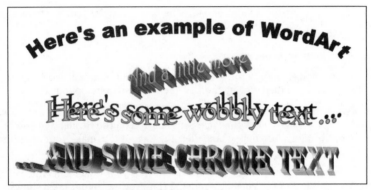

Figure 18-24: Samples of WordArt images.

You insert a WordArt image by choosing Insert ➪ Picture ➪ WordArt. Alternatively, you can click the Insert WordArt button on the Drawing toolbar. You'll see the WordArt Gallery dialog box (see Figure 18-25). Select the effect you want and click OK, and the Edit WordArt Text dialog box appears (see Figure 18-26). This is where you type the actual text you want to use. Click OK, and the WordArt is placed into your document.

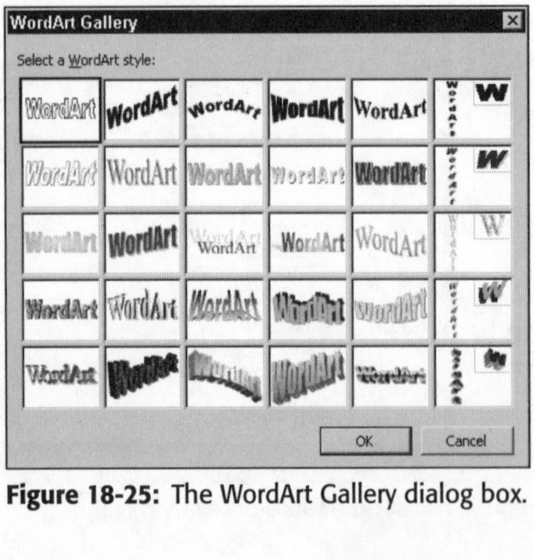

Figure 18-25: The WordArt Gallery dialog box.

Note that all special effects apply to all the text in the Edit WordArt Text dialog box. You cannot apply an effect to just a few letters, although you can easily create separate WordArt images and position them next to each other.

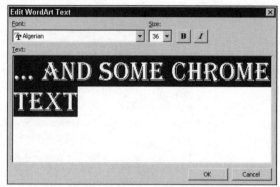

Figure 18-26: The Edit WordArt Text dialog box.

Editing WordArt graphics

You can redisplay the WordArt screen or display a WordArt dialog box at any time to edit an existing WordArt image. All the techniques for editing a WordArt image share one rule: select, and then do. In other words, you must select your WordArt image before you can change it. Here are three ways you can edit an image:

✦ Double-click your WordArt image, or click once and select Edit Text from the WordArt toolbar (see Figure 18-27). The Edit WordArt Text dialog box appears so you can change your text, change the font, and change the size and format (bold and italic).

✦ Click your WordArt image and choose Format ⇨ WordArt, or right-click on the WordArt image and choose the Format WordArt option from the shortcut menu. The Format WordArt dialog box appears, where you can change the color and transparency.

✦ Use the WordArt toolbar buttons to carry out actions.

Figure 18-27: The WordArt toolbar.

Table 18-2 describes the buttons available on the WordArt toolbar.

Table 18-2: The WordArt Toolbar

Button	Name	Purpose
![Insert WordArt icon]	Insert WordArt	This does not affect an existing WordArt object; rather, it opens the WordArt Gallery so that you can create *another* WordArt object.

Continued

Table 18-2 *(continued)*

Button	Name	Purpose
Edit Te_x_t...	Edit Text	Opens the Edit WordArt Text dialog box so that you can modify the text in the object.
	WordArt Gallery	Opens the WordArt Gallery so that you can select another format for the selected WordArt object.
	Format WordArt	Opens the Format WordArt dialog box so that you can change the color, wrapping, and so on.
	WordArt Shape	Displays a drop-down menu from which you can select another shape for the WordArt object.
	Text Wrapping	Allows you to specify the text-wrapping style (see Chapter 17).
	WordArt Same Letter Heights	Adjusts the text in the WordArt object so that all letters are the same height, assuming they are in simple rectangular shape (in fact letter heights still vary dependent on the overall shape used for the WordArt).
	WordArt Vertical Text	Changes the text between left-right orientation and top-bottom.
	WordArt Alignment	Adjusts the alignment of the text in the object—you can select Left, Center, Right, or Word Justify (the same as Justify in a normal paragraph).
	WordArt Character Spacing	Adjusts the spacing of the letters in the WordArt.

Shaping text

The Shape button on the WordArt toolbar displays a grid of different shapes (see Figure 18-28). When you select one of these options, the text in the Edit WordArt Text dialog box changes into that shape. Some shapes produce different results depending on how many lines of text you are shaping. For example, the circle shape turns a single line of text into a circle, but multiple lines of text are changed into a vertical half-circles. Experiment to get the result that you want.

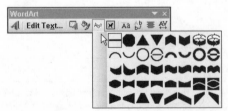

Figure 18-28: WordArt Shape options.

Lengthening text and stretching letters

The WordArt Vertical text button allows you to flip your text so that it appears vertically on the page. Stretching letters pulls them out to fit the WordArt frame. Although you can change the size of letters in a WordArt image by dragging the handles around the WordArt object, stretching is the only way to lengthen such text vertically. To stretch letters, drag a handle. Figure 18-29 shows vertical and horizontal text as well as text both before and after stretching.

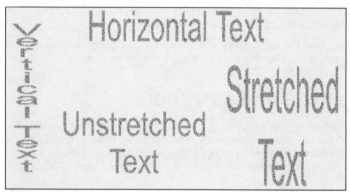

Figure 18-29: Samples of text before and after being flipped vertical and stretched.

Tip   You can rotate and flip your WordArt image using the Draw ➪ Rotate or Flip commands on the Drawing toolbar.

Aligning WordArt text

WordArt text is centered by default, but you can align WordArt text either flush left or flush right. You also can Stretch Justify text to widen the letters to fit the WordArt frame, Letter Justify text to space the letters out to fit the frame, or Word Justify text to space the words to fit the frame.

With your text entered in the Edit WordArt Text dialog box, click the WordArt Alignment button on the WordArt toolbar to change the text's alignment. A list of alignment options appears. Simply select the one that you want.

Kerning and adjusting spacing between characters

WordArt also allows you control the spacing between letter pairs or between all the letters in an image. For example, you can turn on kerning, which is the adjustment of spacing between character pairs, to improve the image's look. In general, kerning tightens the spacing between letter pairs such as *To* and *Wa*. If your type is larger than normal reading size, kerning can make your text more readable.

Tracking, meanwhile, is the adjustment of spacing between all letters. In WordArt, you can loosen or tighten tracking, and you can even set tracking to an exact percentage of normal spacing.

To adjust the spacing between letters and words, follow these steps:

1. Select the WordArt image in your document that you want to adjust.

2. Click the WordArt Character Spacing button on the WordArt toolbar. The WordArt Character Spacing menu appears.

3. Do one of the following:

   • Choose a tracking option: Very Tight (60 percent of normal), Tight (80 percent), Normal (100 percent), Loose (120 percent), or Very Loose (150 percent). You also can choose Custom and select a percent of normal.

   • Choose the Kern Character Pairs option if you want WordArt to kern character pairs automatically. Clearing the check box turns off kerning.

Using the Organization Chart Tool

Word is to a great degree a corporate tool. So it shouldn't be a surprise that you'll find an Organization Chart tool in the program. Choose Insert ➪ Picture ➪ Organization Chart and Word inserts a drawing canvas in your document with a very simple 2-level organization chart inside it. Word also opens the Organization Chart toolbar (see Figure 18-30).

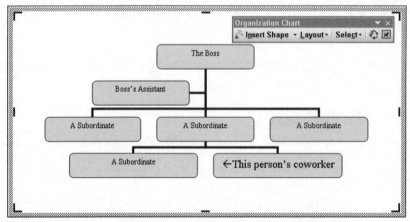

Figure 18-30: An Organization Chart inside a drawing canvas, with the Organization Chart toolbar next to it.

Here's how to use this tool:

✦ **To add text to a box:** Click in the box and type.

✦ **To edit text in a box:** Click inside the box and edit as normal.

✦ **To add a subordinate:** Click on a box and click the Insert Shape button once; a box is added on the lower level.

✦ **To add an assistant:** Click on a box and then click the Insert Shape button's triangle to open the menu, and select Assistant. A box is added at an intermediate level between the selected box and the subordinate level.

✦ **To add a coworker:** Click on a box and then click the Insert Shape button's triangle to open the menu, and select Coworker. A box is added at the same level.

✦ **To delete a box:** Click the box and press Del.

✦ **To change the chart layout:** Select a layout from the Layout button.

✦ **To change the format (the colors, line styles, and so on):** Click the AutoFormat button and select from the AutoFormat dialog box.

✦ **To change the object's wrapping style:** Click the Text Wrapping button and select from the menu.

✦ **To change connecting-line colors:** Choose Select ➪ All Connecting Lines from the toolbar; then choose Format ➪ AutoShape from Word's menu bar and pick a color.

✦ **To change fill colors:** Select the boxes you want to modify; then choose Format ➪ AutoShape.

✦ **To select multiple lines and boxes:** Use the Select menu on the toolbar; you may have to click on a box first.

Tip   Before you change a layout, save your document. You may find that Undo does not work properly here; so if you don't like the results of your changes, you can close the file and reopen to get back to the previous layout.

Changing layouts

You have a variety of different chart layouts available to you, which you can apply by selecting from the Layout menu on the toolbar. Select a box representing a manager with subordinates and then apply the layout to modify just that portion of the chart. You can use the Standard layout (subordinates on a horizontal line below the manager), Both Hanging (subordinates connected both sides of a vertical line below), or Right or Left Hanging (subordinates connected on one side of a vertical line below).

You can also Fit Organization Chart to Contents (the drawing canvas contracts to closely enclose the chart), Expand Organization Chart (the chart increases in size each time you select this command), or Scale Organization Chart (the drawing canvas is selected so that you can drag a handle).

Notice the AutoLayout option at the bottom of this menu. Turning off this option stops Word from automatically moving things around. If you select a Layout option, Word tells you it must turn on AutoLayout.

Changing formats

Formats are not the same as layouts, of course. While layouts define where boxes are placed, formats define what the boxes and connecting lines look like. Click the Autoformat button to open the rather inconsistently named Organization Chart Style Gallery dialog box (see Figure 18-31). Click on the different formats (styles?), and you'll see how they appear in the Preview box. You've got a wide range of different color and shading styles, and even different box styles, to choose from. Click Apply when you find one that you like.

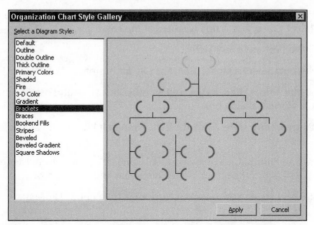

Figure 18-31: The Organization Chart Style Gallery dialog box.

Adding Callouts to Objects

A callout is a type of text box that also includes a line for pointing to any location on the document. A callout is helpful when you need to identify and to explain parts of a picture (see Figure 18-32). You can include text and even insert pictures in a callout. As with text boxes, you can define a fill color, line style, and color. If you want a callout to appear as text only, select None as your fill and then choose your line colors. You can change, move, and layer callouts as well.

When you insert a callout, you draw a line from where you want the callout to point to where you want the callout text to be inserted. To insert a callout, follow these steps:

1. Choose the AutoShapes ⇨ Callouts command on the Drawing toolbar, and then select the style of callout that you want to use.

2. Move the crosshair to where you want the callout to point.

3. Click and hold the mouse button, and then drag to where you want to place the callout text.

4. Release the mouse button.

5. Type the callout text.

Once you've created a callout, you can format it in the same way you format a text box. In fact it *is* a text box; you can even link a callout to a text box in the manner we described earlier in this chapter, so text can flow from a callout to a text box to a callout.

You apply colors and line styles to a callout just as you do for any other object that you draw. There are, however, additional options available for callouts. Open the Format AutoShape dialog box, click the Text Box tab, and click the Format Callout button to open the Format Callout dialog box, shown in Figure 18-33. Using this dialog box, you can determine the style and angle of the callout line, how the callout line is attached to the callout text, and whether a border appears around the callout text. You can choose one of four callout styles for the pointer and text box using the Type box. The selections that you make in the Format Callout dialog box apply to the current callout as well as to the following callouts you create. Table 18-3 describes the options available. (Not all options are available for all callout types.)

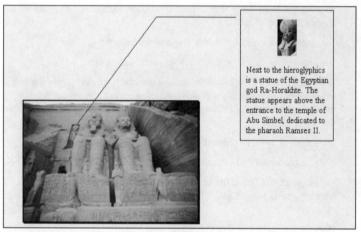
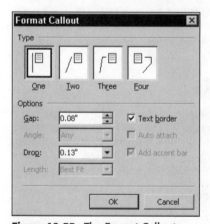

Figure 18-32: Callouts help to explain illustrations in your document.

Figure 18-33: The Format Callout dialog box.

Note   The Format Callout dialog box is not available for all types of callout boxes. The cartoonish-looking boxes at the top of the AutoShapes ⇨ Callouts menu, for example, cannot be formatted.

Table 18-3: Format Callout Dialog Box Options

Option	Description
Type	Defines the type of callout line and the relationship to the callout box. The actual effect depends on the type of callout. (And changing the selection can actually change the type of callout.)
Gap	The distance between the callout line and the callout text.
Angle	The angle of the line from the item that you're calling out.
Drop	The space between the top of the callout text and the beginning of the first part of the callout line. This is the position where you want the callout line attached to the callout text, attached at an exact distance from the top or attached at the Top, Center, or Bottom.
Length	The length of the callout line: Best Fit or a measurement that you specify.
Text Border	Places a border around the callout text.
Auto Attach	Places the callout line at the bottom of the callout text when that text is to the left of the callout line. This action ensures the callout line does not overlap the callout text.
Add Accent Bar	Places a vertical line next to the callout text.

Tip   You can change one type of callout to a different type. Select the callout, choose Draw ⇨ Change AutoShape ⇨ Callouts on the Drawing toolbar, and select another callout type.

Attaching Captions to Objects

Have you noticed the captions that accompany each figure in this book? Word lets you add captions to figures, tables, selected text, and other items. The caption numbers increase automatically as you add more captions. If you move or delete a caption, the related caption numbers adjust automatically. In addition, you can use the Cross-reference command to refer to specific captions in the text or other areas of your document.

Cross-Reference   See Chapter 11 to find out more about cross-references.

You can type captions manually, or you can let Word create the caption for you. If you want to add captions automatically to all items of a particular type (for example, pictures, charts, or equations), Word's AutoCaption feature does most of the work for you.

Entering captions directly

You can also add captions to specific items manually. If you've already inserted objects that require captions into your document, use this feature as follows:

1. Select the object that you want to caption.

2. Choose Insert ⇨ Reference ⇨ Caption. The Caption dialog box appears (see Figure 18-34).

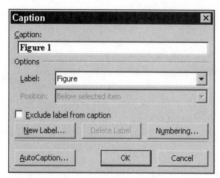

Figure 18-34: The Caption dialog box using default numbering.

The Caption text box initially contains a default label name and item number. The label identifies the object and appears in front of your caption text. Captions for each label name are numbered sequentially.

3. To add text after the label, type it in the Caption text box. To change or remove the label, follow the instructions in step 4. Figure 18-35 provides an example of a caption with a label and additional text. The label identifies the object as the first figure in this section, and the text describes the particular figure.

4. To edit or change the label, do one of the following:

   • To choose an existing label, select from the Label drop-down list.

   • To add a custom label name, click New Label, type a name in the Label text box, and then click OK. After you create a new label, its name appears in the Label drop-down list and can be selected like any other label.

   • To remove the label entirely, check the Exclude Label from Caption check box.

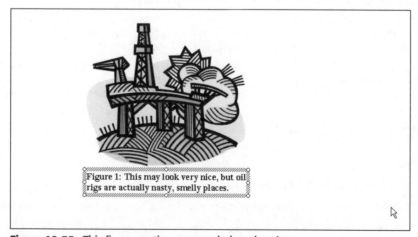

Figure 1: This may look very nice, but oil rigs are actually nasty, smelly places.

Figure 18-35: This figure caption appears below the picture.

Tip   Note that you can modify the label later, in the caption itself.

5. To change the numbering option, click Numbering, modify the selection in the Caption Numbering dialog box, and click OK. (Caption numbering options are covered later in this section.)

6. To change the caption's position relative to the object, select Below Selected Item or Above Selected Item from the Position drop-down list. Sometimes, depending on the object type, you'll also be able to choose Left of Selected Item or Right of Selected Item.

7. Click OK to insert the caption.

What have you just created? That depends as follows:

✦ If you are attaching a caption to an In Line With Text object, Word created a new paragraph, above or below the object, and then placed the label and an SEQ field code (for numbering), followed by the text you entered.

✦ If you are attaching a caption to an object with another wrapping style, Word placed a text box in the document above or below the object. This text box included the label, SEQ field code, and text.

Note that Word does a very bad job of linking captions to the object, so be careful when you move the object. If you move a figure or other object with a caption, that caption doesn't move with the object automatically. To be sure that your captions stay with their associated objects, there are a couple of things you can do:

✦ Place the object in a text box and add the caption. The caption will be placed in the text box, too, and both will move together.

✦ If you've added a caption to an object that has any wrapping style other than In Line With Text, select both the object and the text box containing the caption, and choose Draw ➪ Group to create a combined object.

Adding captions with AutoCaption

Use the AutoCaption feature if you want to add captions to all items of a particular type automatically. After you turn on AutoCaption for a given object type, each object matching that criteria is captioned automatically using the label and any other options that you specify.

Word uses caption labels to determine the numbering sequence. All captions with the same label are numbered sequentially. If you want to number a particular set of captions separately from the rest, make sure that you use a unique label name—create one if necessary.

It's a good idea to plan ahead if you want to use automatic captioning. If you decide to use AutoCaption for all figures after you've inserted several into your document, note that only those figures that you insert after turning on AutoCaption are captioned.

To add captions automatically, follow these steps:

1. Choose Insert ➪ Reference ➪ Caption.

2. Click AutoCaption. The AutoCaption dialog box, shown in Figure 18-36, appears.

3. Select the type of object that you want to caption from the Add Caption When Inserting list box. If you want several object types to use the same label and numbering scheme, select those types. Each type of object will be numbered sequentially within its own group.

Figure 18-36: The AutoCaption
dialog box.

4. Select a label from the Use Label drop-down list, or click New Label and type a new label name.

5. Select Above Item or Below Item from the Position drop-down list.

6. Click Numbering if you want to change any of the numbering options.

7. Repeat steps 3–6 for each type of object you want to label automatically.

8. Click OK.

You can add descriptive text to an automatic caption by placing your insertion point directly after the caption number in your document and then typing the additional information.

Updating your captions

Caption numbers are inserted as fields, which means that they can be displayed, edited, updated, and used in macros just like any other field (the actual label is inserted as text). Press Alt+F9 to turn on the mode in which you can see the actual field codes. You'll notice that the number in your captions changes to something like this:

```
{SEQ Figure \* ARABIC}
```

Cross-Reference For more information about fields and field codes, see Chapter 23.

In most cases, Word updates and renumbers your captions for you, so you can move, copy, add, or delete captions to your heart's content without worrying about the numbers—Word automatically updates numbers when you print, for instance. Alternatively, you can select a field and press F9 to update it, or you can press Ctrl+A to select everything in your document and then press F9 to update all your fields.

Note that deleting a caption does *not* automatically update the other fields. And remember to delete a caption if you delete an object. (Adding captions, though, *does* update the other fields, so if you insert a figure, for instance, before other figures, the subsequent caption numbers will update.)

Editing caption labels

Word comes with three built-in caption labels: Equation, Figure, and Table. When creating a caption, you can choose one of these labels or create a new one. After you have created captions, you can easily change the label for all captions of the same type as well.

> **Tip**   Because captions of a particular type are linked for numbering purposes, you cannot simply change a label name for an individual caption. If you want to relabel only one caption, select that caption, press Backspace or Delete, and then create a new caption using the techniques covered earlier in this chapter.

To change caption labels, follow these steps:

1. Select a caption with the label that you want to change.

2. Choose Insert ➪ Reference ➪ Caption.

3. Do one of the following:

   • Select a label name from the Label drop-down list.

   • Click New Label, and type a new label name.

4. Click OK.

   All captions of the same type are relabeled. For example, if the label of your selected caption is Figure and you change that label to Drawing, all of the captions that use the label Figure are then relabeled Drawing.

Deleting labels and captions

You cannot delete any of the built-in label names (Equation, Figure, or Table), but you can delete any of the labels that you create. To do so, open the Caption dialog box, select the label that you want to delete, and click Delete Label.

Because caption numbers are inserted as fields, you delete a caption number just like you delete any other field or text. Select the entire field, including the brackets, and then press Delete or Backspace. It's easier to select a field to delete when the field codes are displayed. To display the field codes, press Alt+F9 or choose Field Codes in the View tab of the Options dialog box.

Changing the caption style

Word assigns a built-in style called Caption to all captions. This style is basically the Normal style, but with bold type and a line space above and below the paragraph added. You can modify this style just as you can any other style. If you make changes to the Caption style, all of the captions in your document reflect those changes.

Cross-Reference   For more information on working with styles, see Chapter 13.

To change the formatting for a particular caption, select that caption and then use any standard Word formatting technique to make your changes. You can edit a caption's text just as you edit any other document text.

Changing the caption numbering style

By default, Figure and Table captions are numbered using Arabic numerals (1,2,3) and Equation captions use lowercase letters (a,b,c). You can change the numbering style to uppercase or lowercase letters or to Roman numerals as well.

To change the appearance of caption numbers, follow these steps:

1. Select an item with the label type that you want to renumber. For example, if you select an item with the Figure label, all figure captions in your document will reflect any changes that you make.

2. Choose Insert ➪ Reference ➪ Caption.

3. Click Numbering. Figure 18-37 shows the Caption Numbering dialog box.

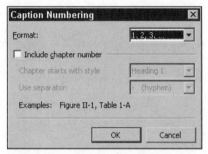

Figure 18-37: The Caption Numbering dialog box provides several options to format captions.

4. Select a numbering style from the Format drop-down list.

5. Click OK twice.

Using chapter numbers in a caption

If your document consists of chapters, you can instruct Word to include chapter numbers in your captions. Look at the figures in this book. Each figure caption begins with the word Figure, which is followed by the chapter number and a hyphen. After that, the figures are numbered sequentially within each chapter. If you use one of Word's built-in heading styles for your chapter titles, you can also include the chapter number in your captions. Note, however, that this technique can be used for any headings that use the standard heading styles. It's not limited simply to chapter titles.

Make sure that your chapter headings use one of the nine built-in heading styles, such as Heading 1, and that each chapter heading uses the same style. Also, be certain that the heading style used for the chapter titles isn't used anywhere else in the document.

To choose a style for your chapter titles, do the following:

1. Choose Format ➪ Bullets and Numbering to display the Bullets and Numbering dialog box, and then click the Outline Numbered tab.

2. Select a numbering style, and then click OK.

More Object Types

What is an object anyway? An object might be thought of as something that is not mere text, inserted into your Word documents. It's something that you want to have visible in the document, too, not something such as field codes (see Chapter 23) that Word inserts to get a particular job done.

There are, of course, many types of different objects: pictures (clip art and photographs, for instance), drawings created within Word, organization charts, WordArt, text boxes, and so on.

There's also a class of objects we treat rather differently and discuss in Chapter 20: objects that are linked to other applications. Additionally, in Chapter 21, we describe two more object types, those created by Microsoft Graph Chart and Equation. All objects have similarities, and can be treated in similar ways (moved and sized, for instance). But these other objects are slightly different in some ways, so we've dealt with them separately.

After you select a style for the chapter titles, you can specify that style as the source for the chapter numbers in the captions. To include chapter numbers in captions, follow these steps:

1. Select an item with the label type in which you want to include the chapter numbers.

2. Choose Insert ⇨ Reference ⇨ Caption.

3. Click Numbering.

4. Select Include Chapter Number.

5. Select Chapter Starts with Style, and select the heading style you used for your chapter titles (usually Heading 1).

6. Select Use Separator, and then select a character that will separate the chapter number from the item number (usually a hyphen).

7. Click OK to return to the Caption dialog box, and then click OK again.

Summary

If you learn Word's various object tools, as explained in this chapter and the previous one, you'll find that Word is a far more sophisticated desktop-publishing tool than you might have realized, certainly far more sophisticated than is commonly understood. This chapter has shown you a variety of things that you can do with Word's drawing, text box, caption, and callout tools:

✦ Use Word's drawing tools to create lines, shapes, and callouts to your document.

✦ Insert and position a text box, and use it as a placeholder for laying out complex documents such as a newsletter.

✦ Create a side heading with a text box in the margin.

✦ Add a text box to a heading to print on every page of your document.

✦ Link text boxes to create a continuing story in a document.

✦ Create WordArt and organization charts.

✦ Add callouts to any object you have inserted.

✦ Add captions to objects of all kinds.

✦   ✦   ✦

Advanced Graphics and Multimedia

In This Chapter

Understanding image editors and plug-ins

Optimizing images for the Web

Adding tiled and transparent backgrounds

Adding animations, sound, and video

In Chapters 17 and 18, you learn how to add existing graphics and to work with the drawing tools in Word. In this chapter, you learn how to edit your image files and to use Word's graphics editing tools to ensure that those images load fast and look good both in your documents and on your Web pages. Additionally, you learn how to liven up your pages by using animation, sound, and video clips.

Image Editing Tools

Image editing is essential to creating impressive documents, which is why Word provides direct access to the drawing and picture toolbars. Several tools and utilities can greatly simplify both editing and optimizing images. The following sections describe some of these image editors, tools, and plug-in utilities, a few of which are included on the CD accompanying this book.

Image editors

To work with images, you may want to find a full-featured editor. For example, Jasc Paint Shop Pro is a very effective shareware image editor. Another impressive commercial image editor is ULead's PhotoImpact, which ships with an impressive GIF animation tool and image optimization utilities.

On the CD-ROM   You can find a copy of Paint Shop Pro on the CD-ROM that accompanies this book.

The industry-standard image editor is Adobe Photoshop. Photoshop sells for around $600, so if you're just starting, you may want to stick with Paint Shop Pro or with PhotoImpact, which sell for less than $100. If you plan to work with graphics regularly and can afford Photoshop, however, buy it. It is a power-packed image editor and our personal choice. Go to www.adobe.com/products/tryadobe/main.jhtml#product=39 to download a free try-out version of Photoshop.

In addition to these image editors, some image-editing packages specialize in creating and optimizing Web graphics, such as Macromedia's Fireworks, which sells for close to $300. Any of these third-party image-editing solutions, however, should help you to get the job done. (To download a free trial version of Fireworks, go to `www.macromedia.com`.)

Image editor filters or plug-ins

Most major shareware and commercial image-editing programs support third-party Adobe Photoshop-compatible plug-ins or filters. A plug-in or filter is an add-on utility that extends the capability of an image editor. Most good image editors have special-effect filters built in. Eye Candy and Xenofex from Alien Skin Software are two examples of special-effect filters.

Filters quickly create impressive results. Trying to make an image of large letters appear with a smooth, glass-like finish could take hours of tweaking with a high-end editor such as Photoshop. Using the Eye Candy filter, however, you can create a similar image with the special effect in less than a minute. Plug-ins are available from several companies and range in price from free to several hundred dollars (or more).

Optimizing Images

Knowing a few fundamentals about image editing can make the difference between a crisp, fast-loading document and a difficult-to-read, slow-loading one. You undoubtedly have come across printed documents and Web pages with images that display text with jagged edges or that have edges with halos. When you create Web pages, it helps to know that different monitors can display pages differently. For example, a background appears lighter on a Macintosh. Colors themselves can display differently on different monitors as well. The following sections explain what you can do to ensure that you use the right file format for your printed documents and Web images as well as that the images look the same on different platforms. Most importantly, this section shows how to optimize your images so they retain a high-quality look but still download fast.

Choosing the right file format

If you are creating paper documents alone, graphic-file format isn't particularly important. Word can work with many different formats, as you've already seen. Most formats that you're likely to run into, in fact. However, the Web is a bitmap world. When you save a file as an HTML document, Word converts AutoShapes and other vector-shaped graphics into bitmaps. However, Office has something called the Vector Markup Language (VML), which allows you to display vector art using Internet Explorer 5 or later. Besides VML, Word also supports numerous graphic file formats.

To display an image in most Web browsers, the image must be converted into one of three bitmap file formats: GIF, JPEG, or PNG. Ultimately, you want to save your image in one of these three formats when you are finished editing the image. Until you have made all your changes, save the file in the default format of your image-editing program. The following list describes the three image file formats required by most Web browsers:

✦ **GIF (Graphic Interchange Format):** This file format is appropriate for line art or images using a limited number of colors. The GIF image uses a palette of as many as 256 colors. GIF images also can be used to specify a transparent color so that an image can appear to float on a page. In addition, this format allows you to create animations called animated GIFs. (Creating transparent backgrounds and adding animated GIFs are covered later in this chapter.)

✦ **JPEG (Joint Photographer's Expert Group):** This file format does not have the color limitations of the GIF format JPEG images can display millions of colors and are best for photographs. If you use the JPEG format for line art or include text or geometric shapes in a JPEG image, stray dots (or pixels) appear around the letters or the geometric shapes. JPEGs also do not work well with solid colors, and the format does not support transparency. There are two types of JPEG images: JPEG, and Progressive JPEG. Progressive JPEGs result in a somewhat smaller file size and are *interlaced*, which refers to how the image displays as the image is downloaded. (Interlacing is explained later in this chapter.)

✦ **PNG (Portable Network Graphics):** This file format offers the best of both the GIF and JPEG file formats. You can use PNG images for line art and photographs. The biggest advantage of PNG is that you no longer encounter the problem of stray pixels when combining text and photographs. If you are using an older browser, you may not be able to display PNG images.

Figure 19-1 shows examples of images suited for the GIF, JPEG, and PNG formats.

Figure 19-1: From left to right: examples of GIF, JPEG, and PNG images.

For printed documents, use the native format of your image editor or the Tagged Image File Format (TIFF). TIFF is a non-lossy format that ensures you do not lose any part of your picture. If you use a lossy file format such as the JPG format, your image loses quality each time you save it.

Changing your monitor resolution and color settings

What You See Is What You Get, or WYSIWYG, has long been a battle cry of computer users who want to ensure that a program such as Word prints exactly as it displays on the screen. On the Web, things are a little different; not everyone uses the same resolution and color settings you do. Therefore, using a WYSIWYG word processor, such as Word, does not necessarily mean that others see the same pages in the same way as they display on your monitor. Most monitors can display resolutions of 1024 x 768, 800 x 600, and the classic 640 x 480. You also can set your monitor to display a different number of colors. For example, suppose you create a page on your PC at 800 x 600 resolution with 24-bit color (millions of colors) and then you post it to the Web. You tell your friends to check out your Web page. One friend is using a laptop that displays only 640 x 480 with 16-bit color (thousands of colors), and another friend has just been playing a game that set the monitor to a lower number of colors, such as 256. But these scenarios are not so common these days—most Internet users are now working with monitors that have at least a resolution of 800 x 600 and millions of colors.

To change the resolution setting of your monitor to see how pages display on PCs with low-resolution monitors, follow these steps:

1. Right-click on the desktop, and a desktop shortcut menu appears.

2. Choose Properties. The Display Properties dialog box appears.

3. Click the Settings tab, which should be displayed similar to that in Figure 19-2.

4. Change the Display area slider to 640 by 480 pixels, and load your Web page in a browser. Now you can see how your page and its images appear on a low-resolution monitor. You also can use the Color Palette drop-down menu to see how your images appear on screens set to different numbers of colors (bit-depths). For example, you may want to switch to 256 colors to see how the page appears on such a monitor.

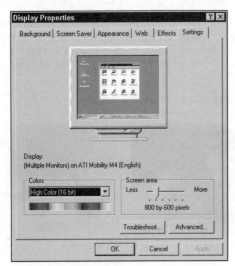

Figure 19-2: The Settings tab of the Display Properties dialog box.

Tip

How important is it, these days, to create Web pages for VGA monitors—640 x 480 with 16 colors? Probably not terribly. Such monitors have not been sold for quite a few years now. However, it depends on your target. If your pages are going to be viewed by people in big companies, it's really not an issue. VGA monitors are extremely rare in such an environment. If your pages will be viewed by an audience in third-world countries, it would be a completely different matter—older computers are going to be far more common.

Changing the resolution of an image

Images that print usually are stored at a much higher resolution than images published on the Web. For example, most printers use an output setting somewhere between 150 to 1,400 dots per inch. Most monitors, however, are set to display at a much lower resolution, such as 72 pixels per inch (ppi). To print an image on your printer, you want to use a high-resolution image. To create an image for the Web, however, you want to keep the file size as small as possible. Therefore, it is a good idea to change the resolution of your image to 72 ppi. Some monitors can display 96 ppi, but saving an image at a resolution higher than 96 ppi is overkill for Web graphics. We once scanned a photograph at 300 dpi, and the image was 1,505K. We then adjusted the resolution to 72 ppi, and the file size decreased to 49K.

All decent image-editing programs provide tools for changing an image's resolution. For example, if you are using Paint Shop Pro (which is on the CD), choose Image ➪ Resize to open the Resize dialog box. Click the Actual/Print Size option, and type **72** in the Resolution text box. Click OK to apply the new resolution setting.

You can also choose the resolution setting for a new image in the dialog box that opens when you choose File ➪ New.

Avoiding the jaggies

One common technique for creating sharp, visually impressive GIF images is to use a drawing program like Adobe Illustrator or CorelDRAW to produce vector art or text and then to export the vector art to a bitmap image editor. The import process converts the vector art into a bitmap, which is called *rasterizing*.

When you convert a vector image to a bitmap graphic, however, the pixels can create stairsteps or jagged edges, particularly if the image contains large text. These jagged edges are sometimes referred to as *aliased* edges or as the *jaggies*. To convert a vector image to a bitmap, make sure that you choose the *anti-aliasing* option. The anti-alias option in image editors helps to eliminate the jaggies by averaging the brightness values of adjacent pixels, thus making the edges appear to be smooth and to blend into the background. Anti-aliased text and images that have been selected and cut from one background and then pasted onto a different color background have halos, however, because the image uses the background color to create the pixels that offset the jagged edges. Figure 19-3 shows an example of aliased (jaggies) and anti-aliased (smooth) text.

Figure 19-3: Anti-aliased text makes the edges of fonts appear smooth.

Compressing images

Keeping the size of an image file small is especially important when creating Web pages (though it can also be important for any document that contains a lot of images—such documents can get very large). The larger the file, the longer it takes to download and to display in the browser window. When you first save a JPEG image, you are presented with a dialog box that includes a slider or similar control to select the amount of compression that you want to apply to your image. It is difficult, however, to see just how much you are changing the quality of the image by adjusting the compression setting. Some image compression plug-ins can compress images to a much smaller file size than most image editors can achieve, and a few image editors, such as Macromedia's Fireworks, include built-in compression features. One benefit of using a compression plug-in or an image editor with compression features is that it allows you to see how changing the compression setting affects the image.

The GIF format keeps track of the number of colors used in an image. It stores information about each color change as well, so the less the colors change in a GIF image, the smaller the file size. For example, a solid blue image is much smaller than an image containing gradients of blue. Because GIF images are based on a palette of 256 colors, you can reduce the size of the GIF file somewhat by reducing the number of colors used in the palette or removing unused colors from the palette.

If you are using Paint Shop Pro and you want reduce the number of colors, choose Colors ➪ Decrease Color Depth. You can choose to store the image with 2 colors (1-bit), 16 colors (4-bit), Grayscale (8-bit), or 256 colors (8-bit). Click OK, and the Decrease Color Depth dialog box appears. Click OK again to accept the default settings. Be aware, however, that reducing the number of colors can reduce the quality of the image. If you reduce the colors and the image quality is too degraded, choose Edit ➪ Undo to return the file to its previous colors. You can now choose File ➪ Save to save your image.

If you are using Photoshop, you can reduce the number of colors stored in the image's palette to the exact number of colors actually used in the image. First, make sure that you're in RGB Color mode by choosing Image ➪ Mode ➪ RGB Color. Then choose Image ➪ Mode ➪ Indexed Color, and the Indexed Color dialog box appears. Choose Web from the Palette list box, and close the dialog box.

Next, choose Image ➪ Mode ➪ RGB Color, and then choose Image ➪ Mode ➪ Indexed Color mode. This time, when the Indexed Color dialog box appears, choose Exact from the Palette list box. The number of colors is then reduced to the number of colors actually in use, and you now can choose File ➪ Save to save your image.

Interlacing images

Another option that you are typically confronted with when saving an image file for the first time is an Interlace check box. Choosing to save an image as *interlaced* creates the illusion that images are downloading faster than they actually are. Skipping rows or distributing the pixels evenly throughout an image when displaying the picture on the screen creates this illusion. This allows the viewer to see the basic outline of the image before the whole image is displayed. GIF images display different rows, making four passes to display the entire image. PNG images display pixels distributed evenly throughout the image. Figure 19-4 shows an example of the different stages of an interlaced GIF image being displayed.

When you save a file in the PNG format, a check box labeled Adam 7 appears. This check box allows you to choose whether to interlace the PNG image. *Adam* comes from the name of its creator, Adam Costello, and *7* refers to the seven passes this option uses to display the image. In most cases, you can make out the basic outline of the image much faster using PNG than using GIF or Progressive JPEG.

One of the main differences between JPEG and Progressive JPEG images is that Progressive JPEG images are interlaced. Progressive JPEGs also show different-quality resolutions of the image. The first is a supecompressed, low-quality version of the image. The successive passes add more detail until the final image is displayed.

Tip   You only want to interlace large images. If the image is small, it likely will download fairly quickly on its own.

Figure 19-4: Interlacing provides the illusion that an image is downloading fast.

Adding tiled and transparent backgrounds

In Chapter 10, we discuss how to add a background to a page, including how to tile an image. Choose Format ➪ Background ➪ Fill Effects, and click the Texture tab. However, when you use an image to create a tiled background, the edges of the image can be seen around each tile. Paint Shop Pro includes an option for quickly creating a seamless background tile, though. To create a seamless background tile image using Paint Shop Pro, follow these steps:

1. Open the image file that you want to use as a tile for your background.

2. Choose Colors ➪ Increase Color Depth ➪ 16 Million Colors (24-bit). If this option is dimmed, the image most likely already is a 24-bit image.

3. Click the Selection button (the rectangle), and drag your mouse to select the center portion of the picture. A fair amount of space outside the selection is required to make the edge appear to be smooth.

4. Choose Selections ➪ Convert to Seamless Pattern. If an error message appears and states that your selection is too close to the edge of the image, click OK and then reselect a smaller portion closer to the center of your image.

5. Choose File ➪ Save, and save the image as a JPEG-JFIF Compliant file if it is a photographic-type image or as a CompuServe Graphics Interchange file if it is line art. If you are sure that everyone viewing your page is using Version 4 or higher of Netscape or Internet Explorer, you can save the image as a PNG file. Save the file in the same directory as your HTML document.

6. Choose File ➪ Exit to close Paint Shop Pro and start Word.

7. Choose Format ➪ Background ➪ Fill Effects. The Fill Effects dialog box appears.

8. Click the Texture tab, and then click the Other Texture button. The Select Texture dialog box now appears.

9. Navigate to the file you saved in step 5, and click OK.

10. Click OK to close the Fill Effects dialog box, and your image is tiled to create a background.

Converting pictures to Word Picture format

In some cases you can convert a picture object from its original format to Microsoft Word Picture format. For example, you can convert a clip-art file from a CorelDRAW (CDR) format to a Microsoft Word picture. Once converted, you can edit the Word picture using Word's drawing tools. Word also allows you to preserve your picture's original format, so you can specify that the picture be activated in but not converted to a different format.

To activate or convert a picture object in a different format, follow these steps:

1. Select the picture object that you want to convert. The picture should have been inserted using the Edit ➪ Paste Special command to be inserted in your page as an object.

2. Choose Edit ➪ Object, and then choose Convert from the submenu. The name of this command varies depending on the type of picture selected and whether the object is linked. The Convert dialog box appears (see Figure 19-5), and the format of your picture is displayed as Current Type.

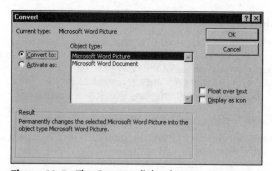

Figure 19-5: The Convert dialog box.

3. Do one of the following:

- To convert the picture object permanently, choose Convert To and then select the picture's target format. Choose Display as Icon if you want to display your converted picture as an icon.

- To activate a picture temporarily without converting it to a different format, choose Activate As and then select the target format.

4. In the Object Type box, select the application whose file format you want to convert the picture object to and then click OK.

Protecting Your Images

You can download any image from a Web page, which begs the question "Is there any way I can protect my own images?" The answer is "Not really, though there are a few games you can play." The fact is that if your image can be displayed, it can be stolen. However, you can make it inconvenient, and remind people that they shouldn't take images.

To add copyright information to an image and notify users that an image is copyright-protected, you need to add a digital watermark. You can do this by using Auto FX's watermark utility included in WebVise Totality or Digimarc's ImageBridge technology. With a utility like either of these, a special watermark, which is imperceptible to the human eye, is added to the image. Copying an image with an embedded watermark also copies the watermark and any information associated with it. The watermark works in both digital and printed forms. You can even edit or change file formats, and in most cases, the watermark remains detectable.

Embedding a digital watermark in an image also allows viewers to obtain contact information about the creator of that image. This provides viewers an avenue to connect with the image's creator. For more detailed information on Digimarc watermarks, check out Digimarc's Web site at www.digimarc.com.

Digimarc embeds a special message inside your images that can be used to track down images published on the Web. This embedded message acts like a homing signal, and it allows Digimarc's MarcSpider service to locate your images. MarcSpider constantly scans the Web and provides online reports of when and where your images are found.

Adding Animation, Sound, and Video

Word provides several ways to make your documents come to life, such as allowing you to add animated images, sound, or videos. Creating such animated images, sound clips, and videos requires programs beyond Word, but this section shows how to add existing ones. In addition, Word ships with animated images, sound, and video clips as well.

Adding animated GIFs

Animated images are stored in the GIF89a format. A single GIF89a file can contain a sequence of images that are played back, one after another, to produce an animation effect. Like cartoon cell animation, each image stored in the file is slightly different, and the images are each displayed in sequence, which simulates motion.

You insert an animated GIF in the same way you insert any other picture file. Word includes a folder in the Clip Art task pane where you can store and quickly access animated GIFs and other sound and video clips. Just choose Insert ➪ Picture ➪ Clip Art. In the Results Should Be drop-down list box, select Animate GIF under the Movies heading. Deselect all other file types, and click Go. Everything that is shown in the results list box will be animated GIFs.

Paint Shop Pro includes Animation Shop for creating and optimizing animated GIF files. Our favorite program for creating animated images, however, is GIF Animator from ULead.

You can find a copy of GIF Animator on the CD-ROM that accompanies this book.

Note   Don't edit the animated GIF in Word, or you'll break it.

Sounding off with audio clips

You can insert sounds into Word, too. Select Insert ⇨ Picture ⇨ Clip Art and then, in the Results Should Be drop-down, deselect all the branches except Sounds. Click Go, and Word will search for sound files. The standard file format for playing sounds using Windows is the waveform (.wav) format, but this format works only on the Windows platform. If you plan on adding sounds to a Web page, use a cross-platform format such as AU, MIDI, MP2, or MPEG audio. You also can insert sound files in AIF, RMI, and SND formats, but be aware that these file formats do not work on all platforms.

You can also embed a sound object in a Word document, allowing you to create and edit the sound file from within Word. To embed a sound object in a Word document, follow these steps:

1. Position the insertion point in the document where you want the sound icon to appear.

2. Choose Insert ⇨ Object, and the Object dialog box appears.

3. Choose Wave Sound to insert a waveform (.wav) file. A speaker icon is inserted in the document, and the Sound Object (Sound Recorder) window appears.

4. Choose Edit ⇨ Insert File from the Sound Object window. The Insert File dialog box appears.

5. Navigate to the waveform sound file that you want to use, and choose Open. The sound is loaded in the Sound Object window.

6. Choose File ⇨ Exit & Return to Document. To play the sound file, double-click the speaker icon. If the person reading your document clicks on the speaker icon, a message appears in the status bar informing the reader to double-click on that icon to play the file.

To insert a background sound file for Internet Explorer using Word's Web Tools toolbar, follow these steps:

1. Choose View ⇨ Toolbars, and select Web Tools. The Web Tools toolbar appears.

2. Click the Sound button, and the Background Sound dialog box appears.

3. Enter the path and name of the file, or click the Browse button to locate the file of the sound that you want in the Sound text box.

4. Select the number of times you want the sound to repeat from the Loop list box. You can repeat a sound from one to five times or continuously. If you want it to loop continuously, choose Infinite, but if you do, be aware that most browsers provide no way for the person to stop the sound from playing when viewing the Web page.

5. Click OK, and the background sound begins playing, just as it will when the Web page is loaded in a browser.

Note Do you really need sounds in Web pages and Word documents? The answer is almost always *No*. Sounds make the pages and documents large and much slower to load.

Inserting video clips

You also can add a video clip to a Word document or an inline video to a Web page. If you are adding the video to a Web page, you can specify whether the video plays when the page is opened or when the user moves the mouse pointer on top of the video itself. The person viewing the document must have a media player installed to play back the video. Most video clips are extremely large, however, so to be safe, you may want to provide alternative text and images or avoid presenting essential information in videos.

To embed a video in a Word document, follow these steps:

1. Position the insertion point in the document where you want the video clip to appear.

2. Choose Insert ➪ Object. The Object dialog box appears.

3. Choose Media Clip to insert the clip and click OK. An icon is placed into the document, and the Media Player toolbar and menu bar appear at the top of the document (see Figure 19-6). Alternatively, you can choose the format that matches the file type you want to insert. For example, you can choose Video Clip to insert an Audio Video Interleaved (.avi) file.

4. Open the Insert Clip menu and choose the menu option for the object type that you want to insert. For example, to include a QuickTime movie, choose 1 Video for Windows. The Open dialog box appears.

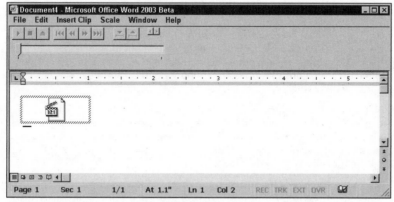

Figure 19-6: When you choose Media Clip to insert the clip, the Media Player toolbar and menu bar are displayed.

5. Navigate to the video file that you want to insert, and click the Open button. The Media Player includes the Edit ⇨ Options command, which displays the Options dialog box. Selecting the Control Bar On Playback check box allows you to specify whether a control bar appears, and the Caption text box allows you to change the caption at the bottom of the video clip. The Edit ⇨ Selection command displays the Set Selection dialog box, which allows you to specify where you want to begin as well as end playing the video clip.

6. Click in the background area of your document, and the Word menus replace the Media Player menus and editing options.

The Windows Media Player works in conjunction with Word to play videos. You can download the latest version of the Windows Media Player from `www.microsoft.com/windows/mediaplayer/download/default.asp`. If you don't want the video to appear on the page when it loads, you can insert a hyperlink to the video. That way, the person can click the hyperlink to download the video and then play it.

Cross-Reference

For more on working with hyperlinks, see Chapter 26.

To insert a video that appears in a Web page, follow these steps:

1. Choose View ⇨ Toolbars ⇨ Web Tools. The Web Tools toolbar appears.

2. Click the Movie button. A media player icon is inserted in the document, and the Movie Clip dialog box appears.

3. In the Movie text box, enter the path to the video file or click Browse to locate the file. Alternatively, you can enter a URL for a video file.

4. In the Alternate Image box, enter the path to a graphics file that you want to designate as a substitute while the video downloads or if the person has set the browser not to display videos.

5. In the Alternate Text box, enter the text that you want to appear in place of the video when the user's browser does not support videos or if the person has set the browser not to display videos.

6. Select how you want the video to begin playing from the Start list box. The Open option causes the video to play when the user downloads the Web page. The Mouse-over option specifies to play the video when the mouse pointer is on top of the video. The Both option specifies that the video play when the user downloads the video or later moves the pointer onto the video.

7. Select the number of times that you want the video to repeat from the Loop list box. You can choose to repeat the video from 1 to 5 times or continuously. If you want it to loop continuously, choose Infinite, but if you do, be aware there is no way for a person to stop the video from playing when viewing the Web page.

The video plays after you insert it. If you have selected the Mouse-over option for video playback, the video also plays in your Web page document when you move your mouse pointer on the video.

Summary

This chapter has given you some powerful ways to create and edit the right graphic for the right type of document. It included several tips to ensure your graphics look great on the Web no matter what type of operating system the viewer is using. You can create impressive special effects and easily bring your pages to life with multimedia using Word. With this chapter as a guide, you now can do the following:

✦ Use the right file format for photographic and line-art images.

✦ Anti-alias text and graphics so that images display with smooth edges.

✦ Avoid dithered color shifts using the Web-safe palette.

✦ Interlace images.

✦ Convert images to Word format.

✦ Include multimedia files such as animated GIFs, sound clips, and video files in a Word document.

✦ ✦ ✦

Linking Information from Other Applications

In This Chapter

Embedding and linking objects in Word

Inserting information from Microsoft Excel into a Word document

Inserting information from Microsoft Access into a Word document

Inserting information from Microsoft PowerPoint into a Word document

By linking information across Office applications, you can create sophisticated documents that include data from Microsoft Access, worksheets and charts from Microsoft Excel, and even slide presentations from Microsoft PowerPoint. This chapter explains the powerful tools in Word for sharing information from other Office applications—or from any other Windows applications that support OLE (Object Linking and Embedding).

Linking and Embedding Objects in Word

Object is the term used to define the information that is exchanged between applications. Objects can include text, documents, images, charts, tables, voice annotations, and even video clips. Thus, when you copy and embed an Excel chart into your Word document, that chart becomes an object. You can use a *linked* or *embedded* object to add all or part of a file created in another Office program (or in any program that supports OLE).

Linked versus embedded objects

The main differences between linked objects and embedded objects are where the data is stored and updated after being placed in the destination file. These two types of objects are described in the following list:

✦ A *linked* object is information created in one file, called the *source* file, that is inserted into another file, called the *destination* file, while maintaining a connection between the two files. The linked object in the destination file is updated automatically when the source file is updated.

✦ An *embedded* object is information that is inserted into a file just as you would for a linked file, but once it's embedded, it has no connection back to the original object. Changing the original information in the source file has no effect whatsoever on the embedded object in the destination file.

When you double-click a *linked* object, the program in which that object was created (the source program) opens. When you save your changes, however, they are saved in the original file, not in the Word document.

When you double-click an *embedded* object, the program in which that object was created (the source program) opens, just as it does with a linked object. When you close the source program, any changes that you made are updated in the Word document. All the information necessary to edit the object is contained by the embedded object inside Word.

Linking and embedding are similar, but as you can see, they also have some substantial differences. One method may be more practical than the other depending on the task that you need to accomplish. The differences between linking and embedding have several ramifications. For one, embedding makes your Word document substantially larger than linking does, because embedding stores the entire object in the Word document. Linking, however, takes up less space in the file because each time you open the file Word retrieves the information it needs from the source object—it only saves enough information to know where to go to get the linked object.

You can place information from another application into a Word file by using any one of these three methods:

✦ **Copying and pasting:** When you copy and paste cells from an Excel spreadsheet to a Word document, for example, the content is converted to Word text in a Word table. There is no longer any relationship between the data in the Word file and the original data or even the original application, Excel.

✦ **Embedding an object:** When you embed data from another application, it's embedded in a special format that is not merely Word data. In the case of Excel spreadsheet cells, for example, they are not converted to a Word table but remain in an Excel-type table. If you try to edit the table, Word opens Excel inside the Word application so that you have access to all the normal Excel commands and features.

✦ **Linking an object:** When you link data, the information is placed into Word in a similar manner to embedding, with the added feature of linking with the original data. If you change the original information, the information inside the Word file also changes. And if you change the information in the Word file, you are, in fact, changing the original information.

In this chapter, we examine linking and embedding (copying and pasting text is covered in Chapter 2). When do you use copying rather than linking and embedding? You use this method when all you want is the raw data. You don't care if the source data changes, and you don't need to edit the copied data using the original application. All you need is the data in some kind of Word format, using tables and text, for instance.

When, then, do you want to use linking or embedding? When the opposite is true, of course. You use linking or embedding when basic Word text and tables are not enough; when you want to work with the data using the features of the original application, or when you want the information in the Word file to be continually updated as the data in the source file changes.

Suppose that you know you need to use linking or embedding. How do you decide which one to use? Table 20-1 provides some guidelines for making this decision.

Table 20-1: Linking versus Embedding

Task	Approach and Comments
Include information in your Word document that becomes part of the document and is always available even if the original source file is not.	Use embedding. Note, however, that if you open the Word file on a computer that doesn't have the original application installed you cannot use the original application to update the embedded object.
Include information from a separate file, such as an Excel spreadsheet, with any changes that are made to original file being included in the Word document.	Use linking. This is especially useful when you want to copy data (such as the Excel spreadsheet) to several different files (such as Word documents or PowerPoint graphs).
Include a very large object, such as a sound or a video clip.	Use linking to keep the size of your Word file manageable; embedding such a large object makes the Word file extremely large.

OLE, COM, and ActiveX

Embedding and linking objects among Windows applications is handled by OLE (Object Linking and Embedding), which provides an easy way to move different types of information across different programs. The idea behind OLE is to give users a *document-centric* view of computing rather than an *application-centric* view.

Component Object Model (COM) provided the foundation for OLE 2. COM defined a common format for interaction among all kinds of software. The term OLE was used for anything built around COM technology. COM defines the standard approach by which one chunk of software supplies its services to another, and it's transforming the way that software is constructed. It is also the underlying force behind the dramatic changes in Word.

In early 1996, Microsoft introduced ActiveX, which is associated with Internet technologies but is also now integrated into Office applications, including Word. Both OLE and ActiveX are built on COM technology, and the diverse group of COM technologies, once grouped under the OLE banner, are now labeled as ActiveX. As a result of ActiveX technology, Word and Office offer an impressive collection of features for linking information.

Embedding Objects in Word Documents

When you embed information from another application (or Word document), you create an object. That object resides entirely in your Word document and not in the originating application. All of the information that Word needs to edit the object is stored with that object. To *edit* an embedded object that was created in another application, however, you must either have that other application installed on your computer or have an application that can read objects of that type. You won't be able to use Word itself to edit the object.

Note   When you install any Windows application that supports OLE, Windows automatically makes that application available to your other applications. This way, any application that supports linking and embedding automatically appears in the Object dialog box. If an application that you install doesn't appear in the Object dialog box, it doesn't support OLE.

Embedding an object

There are two ways to embed an object into Word:

✦ You can create a brand new object in a different application, embed it in your Word document, and save it in the Word document. At this point the only place the information is saved is inside the Word document.

✦ You can also embed an existing file in a Word document. When you do this, Word copies the information from the original file, so now the information is stored in two places, the original file and the Word file.

Note also that there are two ways that your embedded object can appear in your document:

✦ **As data:** You can read the information on your screen, and it appears if you print the data.

✦ **As an icon:** You'll see an application icon in your document—the Excel program icon if it's an Excel object, the Microsoft Paintbrush icon if it's a bitmap image, and so on. You will not see the actual information—if you want to see the information you have to double-click on the icon. We'll look at this a little later in the chapter.

In most cases you'll want to display an embedded object as the actual object, not as an icon. For example, if you embed an Excel chart, you want Word to display the actual chart and not just an icon representing that chart. However, icons are useful for representing embedded sound and video clips. When you embed a sound or a video object, double-clicking the icon representing that object then causes the clip to play.

Embedding a new object

To create a new object and embed it into your Word document, follow these steps:

1. Position the cursor where you want to embed the object.

2. Choose Insert ➪ Object to display the Object dialog box.

3. Click the Create New tab (see Figure 20-1), if it's not already selected. The items displayed in the Object Type list depend on which Windows applications are installed on your computer.

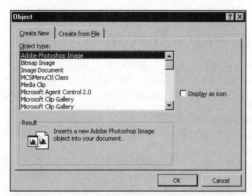

Figure 20-1: The Create New tab in the Object dialog box.

4. To display the embedded object as an icon in your document (rather than the actual data that you can read), choose the Display as Icon option. This causes the Change Icon button to appear (see Figure 20-2). Clicking the Change Icon button to open the Change Icon dialog box (see Figure 20-3) allows you to choose a different icon from the suggested one that appears in the Object dialog box. The selection of available icons depends on the application that you choose. To see more icons, click the Browse button to choose a different file.

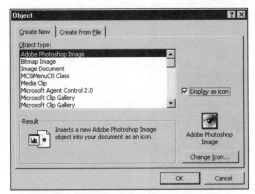

Figure 20-2: The Change Icon button appears when you choose the Display as Icon option.

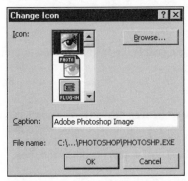

Figure 20-3: The Change Icon dialog box.

5. Select the application that you want to use to create the object, and click OK. That application's window then appears.

6. Create the object in the application.

7. When you finish, return to Word by clicking anywhere outside the application window and then click Close. Alternatively, you can choose File ➪ Exit in the application window.

Embedding an existing file

Now we'll look at how to embed an existing file. There are two ways to do this—we're going to look at how to embed the entire data file. In a moment, you'll also see how to embed just part of the data from that file, using the Copy/Paste Special method.

To embed an existing file, follow these steps:

1. Position the cursor where you want to embed the file.

2. Choose Insert ⇨ Object to display the Object dialog box.

3. Click the Create from File tab (see Figure 20-4).

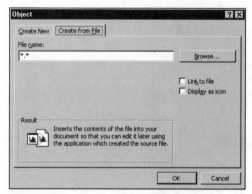

Figure 20-4: The Create from File tab in the Object dialog box.

4. Click the Browse button and then choose the drive and directory of the file that you want to embed.

5. Click on the file you want to use, and click OK.

6. To display the embedded object as an icon, enable the Display as Icon option. The Change Icon button then appears.

7. Click OK to embed the file.

Tip   When you create an embedded or linked object from an existing Excel worksheet, the entire workbook is inserted into your document. However, only the first worksheet is displayed. To display a different worksheet, double-click the Excel object to open it in Excel, and then click a different worksheet and close Excel. Word will now display the other worksheet.

Embedding while working in another application

You can embed an object in a Word document *while* you work in a different application. Use this procedure:

1. While working in the other application, select the information that you want to embed. For example, in Microsoft Excel, select a worksheet or a chart.

2. Choose Edit ⇨ Copy. This copies the selection to the Clipboard.

3. Switch to the Word document in which you want to embed the object.

4. Position the cursor where you want the object to be embedded.

5. Choose Edit ➪ Paste Special to display the Paste Special dialog box (see Figure 20-5). The options available in the Paste Special dialog box depend on the type of information that you selected in step 1. Table 20-2 describes the various options in the Paste Special dialog box.

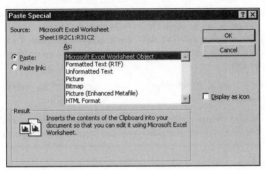

Figure 20-5: The Paste Special dialog box.

6. Select the type of information you want to embed from the list of data types—for instance, if you are copying Excel spreadsheet cells you will probably want to select Microsoft Excel Worksheet Object (though you can embed the information in a variety of different types of data). Select Display as Icon if you want the data to be represented as an icon in the document.

7. After you choose the options that you want, click OK to embed the object.

Tip　You can quickly place a blank, embedded Excel spreadsheet into your Word document by clicking the Insert Excel Spreadsheet button on the Standard toolbar.

Table 20-2: Options in the Paste Special Dialog Box

Option	Action
Source	Displays the name of the source file and its location. If you copied the object from an application that didn't provide the source data, this display shows Unknown. You won't be able to use the originating application to edit the embedded object.
Paste	This really should say *Embed*, not *Paste*. It tells Word to embed the information, copied from the other application, into the document rather than linking to it. This is *not* the same as the ordinary Edit ➪ Paste command.
Paste Link	Also a little ambiguous. Choose this and Word places the object in the document and links to the original source data. If the source application doesn't support linking, this option is not available. If you choose this option, you can have Word update the object automatically if you make changes to the original data, or you can specify manual updating.
As	Lets you specify the type of object to paste. We'll look at these choices later in this section.

Continued

Table 20-2 *(continued)*

Option	Action
Display as Icon	Displays the selection as an icon. This option is available only if you choose the original source format of the data in the As box, or if you choose to Paste Link. For instance, if you copied from Excel and you choose to place the data into the document as an HTML data, the icon is not available. If you select Display as Icon, the As choice is irrelevant (because it's going to appear as an icon, after all!).
Result	Describes the result of your selections — a description of the operation that will be carried out.
Change Icon	Enables you to choose a different icon to represent the linked or embedded object. This button is not available unless the Display as Icon option is chosen.

Note   After pasting with some formats, you may find they don't work as you think they will. Some formats appear to be non-linked: if you double-click on the information, the source program does *not* open. For example, if you paste linked data from an Excel spreadsheet using the Formatted Text (RTF) format, the information is pasted into the document in a format that appears to be normal text in a table. However, right-click anywhere in this text, and you will find the Update Link and Linked Worksheet Object options. Note also that selecting Display as Icon in the Paste Special dialog box overrides the As choice. If an icon is placed in your document, it's an icon, not Formatted Text, not HTML format, not Unformatted Text, and so on.

When you embed an object, Word inserts an EMBED field—{EMBED...}—into the document. If you see this field rather than the object when you embed it, press Alt+F9. This keystroke toggles the view between showing the code and showing the object. Figure 20-6 shows an example of an EMBED field code.

{·EMBED·Excel.Sheet.8··}

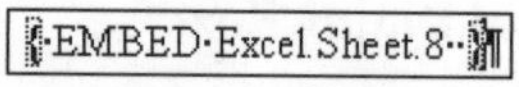

Figure 20-6: An example of an EMBED field code.

By default, the field codes are turned off in Word. In most cases, you probably should keep them this way, because field codes can quickly clutter up a screen. If you want to display field codes, however, choose Tools ➪ Options, click the View tab, and then click Field Codes. Better still, just press Alt+F9. If you work with linked objects a lot, you may want to add this to a button (see Chapter 32).

Cross-Reference   For more information on working with field codes, see Chapter 23.

Next, we talk a little about file formats. You saw in the Paste Special dialog box that the As list allows you to determine how the data will be placed into your document. A variety of formats are available, depending on the type of data you have copied:

✦ **The original file format:** At the top of the list you'll see the original file format. For instance, select Excel cells and you'll see Microsoft Excel Spreadsheet Object. In most cases this is what you'll select.

✦ **Formatted Text (RTF):** RTF means *Rich Text Format*, and it's a special format designed for the sharing of word-processing data between different word processors. Unlike, for instance, ASCII text, RTF keeps much of the text's formatting information. This is actually the same as pasting the information using Ctrl+V or Edit ⇨ Paste. It does *not* create an embedded or linked object!

✦ **Unformatted Text:** This format is raw ASCII text—text without any formatting. It will have tabs, but won't be in a table.

✦ **Picture (Windows Metafile):** A vector graphics format designed for use by Windows programs.

✦ **Picture (Windows Enhanced Metafile):** A more advanced version of the Windows metafile.

✦ **HTML Format:** Web-page format.

✦ **Unformatted Unicode Text:** In most cases this will appear the same as Unformatted text. Unicode is a more advanced character format that has many more characters than ASCII text.

✦ **Bitmap:** A Microsoft Paintbrush type image file.

✦ **Device Independent Bitmap:** Another, larger, bitmap image file type.

✦ **Word Hyperlink:** This appears if you select Paste Link. The data is placed into the document as Formatted Text, and defined as a hyperlink. Clicking on the data opens the original data in the source application.

Using drag-and-drop

You can also embed objects from other programs into Word using *drag-and-drop*. To create an embedded object using drag-and-drop, follow these steps:

1. Arrange the program windows so that both the source file and the destination file are open and visible.

2. Select the information, and then use the right mouse button to drag the selection to the new location in the Word document. A pop-up menu appears.

Note You don't have to have both windows open and visible. Instead, you can drag from the source application and, while still holding down the mouse button, hold the mouse pointer over the taskbar button representing the application to which you want to copy the information. When the target application window opens, you can drag and drop the data into that document.

3. On the shortcut menu, select Copy Here.

Tip How do you drag *from* an application? Each application may work differently. For instance, in Excel you can't just select a box of cells, click and hold the mouse button while pointing in the middle, and drag. It's not going to work. Rather, you can select the cells, point at the *border* of one of the cells at the edge of the selection, and drag *that*. And if Allow Cell Drag and Drop is turned off in Excel, you won't be able to use this feature. (You can find that in Excel's Options dialog box, under the Edit tab.)

You can also drag with the left mouse button, and hold down the Ctrl key at the same time to copy the information (if you don't hold down the Ctrl key you'll actually move—cut and paste—the information from the original application).

Cross-Reference   Be careful with drag and drop. It doesn't always work the same way in all applications. In some cases, you may actually *move* information out of the source application and into the Word document when you intended to copy. If you drag a text block from PowerPoint, for example, it's *removed* from the PowerPoint document! So the first time you work with a particular application, experiment to see what happens when you drag and drop.

Editing embedded objects

One of the major reasons to use embedding is the simplicity of editing objects that it provides. You can edit an embedded object either by double-clicking on it to open it, or by clicking once and choosing Edit ➪ Object. You must use Edit ➪ Object to edit embedded video and sound clips, however, because double-clicking plays these objects.

Note   The Edit ➪ Object Edit command changes to the name of the object to be edited. For example, if you inserted an Excel chart into your document, the Edit ➪ Object command appears as Edit ➪ Chart Object.

To edit an embedded object, follow these steps:

1. Double-click the embedded object. Or click once and choose Edit ➪ Object ➪ Edit. The application window opens inside the Word document, with the object's contents displayed.

2. Edit the object as desired.

3. When you have finished, return to Word by clicking in the Word document anywhere outside the object.

Note   Right-clicking anywhere on the object displays the shortcut menu, from which you can access the editing tools for that object. The specific contents of this menu change depending on the object that is selected.

Converting embedded objects to different file formats

When you embed an object, the entire object, including information about the application that created it, is stored in the Word document. To edit the object, double-click it to use the original application for editing. Sometimes, however, the original application may not be available, such as when you copy the Word file to a computer that doesn't have the original application installed. In this case, you can convert the object—either permanently or temporarily—to a different file format.

For instance, if you have an object in your Word file that was created using Microsoft Works— a chart or spreadsheet—but you do not have Works on your system, you can use Office applications to work on the data; but Word has to know which application to use. In fact you'll be given two choices. You can actually Convert the object to the new format, or you can merely Activate it so you can use it with the other application, but still save it in the original format. (Perhaps it's going back to someone who has Works but not Office.)

To convert or activate an embedded object to a different file format, follow these steps:

1. Select the object that you want to convert.

2. Choose Edit ➪ Object ➪ Convert to open the Convert dialog box (see Figure 20-7).

Figure 20-7: The Convert dialog box.

3. Choose the Convert To option if you want to permanently convert the object. Choose Activate As if you merely want to work on the object but wish to store it in the original format.

   When you choose the Activate As option, the list of options in the Object Type list box may change, and the option to display the object as an icon is not available.

4. To display the embedded object as an icon, enable the Display As Icon option.

5. In the Object Type list box, select the application you want to use to work on the object and click OK.

Converting embedded objects to graphics

When you convert an embedded object to a graphic, you can no longer edit that object in its original application. If you double-click the graphic after such a conversion, Word then opens a separate window and displays the Picture toolbar so that you can edit the graphic as a Word Picture. The significant advantage of converting an embedded object to a graphic is that you reduce the file size of the Word document.

To convert an object to a graphic, select the object to be converted and then press Ctrl+Shift+F9. You cannot convert the graphic back to an embedded object, but you can undo the conversion using the Edit ➪ Undo command (Ctrl+Z) if you change your mind (and if you do so during the current session!).

Linking Objects in Word

Linking is very similar to embedding. The difference is that Word doesn't store the entire linked object. Instead, Word stores a field code indicating the source of the object and a visual representation of that linked object. (Figure 20-8 shows an example of a LINK field code.) In truth, you are linking to another file where the information is actually stored. Why? Two good reasons: you keep the size of your Word document file to a minimum, and you eliminate a problem common in document management—the divergence of different versions. If you have information that is likely to change frequently, or even occasionally, you don't want to end up with multiple documents that you have to change each time. It's much better to have a single document to which other documents link. Make your changes once, and all the linked documents are updated automatically.

{ LINK Excel.Sheet.8 "C:_Data\\Profit and Loss Statement.xls" "" \a \f 0 \p * MERGEFORMAT }

Figure 20-8: A sample LINK field code.

After you establish a link, many options are available in Word for using it. For example, you can specify that Word update the original file automatically, or you can manually update any changes.

Note   The major problem with linked objects is the object getting lost. It's moved, or deleted, or the file is moved to another computer. Linked objects are a great little tool, as long as you know the original data will be available.

Creating links

As with embedding, you can create a link while working in Word or while working in another application. You have already seen several ways to embed objects:

✦ Choose Insert ➪ Object and click the Create New tab

✦ Choose Insert ➪ Object and click the Create From File tab

✦ Choose Edit ➪ Paste Special

✦ Drag-and-Drop

To create a *linked* object, you use the last three methods in the bullet list in almost exactly the same way as you do for embedding. The difference is that you must click the Link to File check box or the Paste Link option button, or you select Link Here from the drag-and-drop pop-up menu. (You can't create a linked object using the Create New tab of the Object dialog box because you are creating a new object—there is no original object to link *to*.)

Updating links

Word can update links in two ways, automatically and manually:

✦ With automatic links, Word updates the links whenever you open the destination file and whenever the source information changes while the Word document is open.

✦ With manual links, Word updates the links only when you decide to update them.

The default setting is to update all links automatically when the information in the source file changes, but you can specify either method for any link.

Controlling link updates

You can use the procedure outlined here not only to specify automatic or manual updating for your links but also to break and lock links. In addition, you can use it to change the source file.

To specify how links are updated, follow these steps:

1. Choose Edit ➪ Links to display the Links dialog box (see Figure 20-9). Table 20-3 describes the options in the Links dialog box. The Links command is not available, however, unless you have at least one link in the Word document.

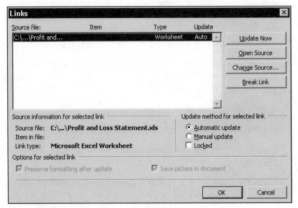

Figure 20-9: The Links dialog box.

2. The Links dialog box lists all of the links in the active Word document. Select one or more. To select multiple links, click once on the first link, press Ctrl, and then click once on each of the other links that you want to edit. If you have several links and want to select them all, click once on the top link, press Shift, and then click once on the last link in the list.

3. Choose Automatic for automatic links, or choose Manual for manual links. You can specify different options for different links.

4. Click OK.

Note If you break a link for an object displaying an icon, that icon remains in your Word document but becomes a Word picture. There is no longer any connection between the icon and the original file. If you break a link for text or an image, it remains in your Word document but is no longer linked with the original.

Table 20-3: Options in the Links Dialog Box

Option	Action
Source File	Displays the name and location of the source file.
Item	Defines the range of data within the file if the object doesn't contain the whole file. If the linked object is a file, this option is blank.
Type	Displays the application that created the linked object.
Update	Defines the type of update, Automatic or Manual.

Continued

Table 20-3 *(continued)*

Option	Action
Source Information for Selected Link	The information below here describes the link object, showing which file it comes from, where in the file the data comes from, and the type of data.
Update Now	Updates all the selected links.
Open Source	Opens the selected file in the source application so that you can edit it.
Change Source	Enables you to specify a different source file for a selected link. Clicking this button opens the Change Source dialog box, which looks and works just like the File Open dialog box.
Break Link	Breaks the link for all of the selected links.
Automatic	Updates the link each time the source data changes.
Manual	Doesn't update the link automatically. You must take an action to update the link.
Locked	Locks the selected link so that it doesn't update until you unlock the link. If you lock a link, the Update Now option is unavailable for that link.
Preserve Formatting After Update	Select this feature to tell Word that if you add any formatting to the object, it should not throw away the formatting each time it updates it from the source file.
Save Picture in Document	Saves a graphic representation of the linked object in the Word document. (This option is available only if you select a link to a graphics file.) If you don't choose this option, Word stores only the link in the document, and the file size doesn't increase appreciably.

Updating links manually

There are two methods to update links manually. The simplest is to position the cursor somewhere in the linked object and then press F9. The other is to choose Edit ➪ Links. Using Edit ➪ Links may be quicker, however, if you have several links in your document because this method enables you to see a list of all links. On the other hand, you can also press Ctrl+A to select everything in your document and then press F9. (Unfortunately, Ctrl+A doesn't select links inside headers, footers, and comments, although it's rare that linked objects are placed in these areas.) This updates *all* fields in your document, not just linked objects.

Updating links each time you print the document

Another option is to update all of the links in your Word document whenever you print that document. If you choose this option, all of the links are updated automatically when you print your document (even the ones set to Manual updates).

To update links automatically whenever you print the document, follow these steps:

1. Choose Tools ➪ Options.

2. Click the Print tab to display the print options.

3. Enable the Update Links check box.

4. Click OK.

Editing linked objects

Editing linked objects is similar to editing embedded objects. Double-click an object to open the source application, or click once and choose Edit ⇨ Linked Object ⇨ Edit Link. Unlike with an embedded option, however, a source application does not open *within* Word. Rather, it opens the entire application and loads the source file into the application.

After you make the changes that you want, save the file and close the application. If the linked object updates automatically, your changes are reflected immediately; otherwise, select the linked object and press F9.

Breaking links

Breaking a link means that the linked information remains in your Word document, but you cannot update that information in the Word document from the source application. The simplest method of breaking a link is to select the linked object and then press Ctrl+Shift+F9. After you break the link, you cannot restore it, but you can undo the action by pressing Ctrl+Z. You can also break a link in the Links dialog box—select the link and click Break Link.

Tip   If you have a lot of links, how do you know which in the Links dialog box is the one you want to act on? Right-click on the object, and select Linked Object ⇨ Links from the pop-up menu. The Links dialog box opens, displaying the selected link highlighted.

After you break the connection to a linked object, you must insert that linked object into your document again if you ever wish to reconnect it.

Locking and unlocking links

Locking a link prevents the object from being updated by the original application file, such as an Excel spreadsheet file. The difference between locking a link and breaking it is that you can later unlock the link. After you break a link, you cannot restore it, you must rebuild it. You can lock and unlock a link in the Links dialog box, as you've already seen. However, you can also lock a link by selecting a link and pressing Ctrl+F11; unlock the link by pressing Ctrl+Shift+F11.

Tip   Rather than locking a link, why not set the link to Manual and then just don't update it—to ensure that you don't accidentally manually update it. If, for instance, you press Ctrl+A to select the entire document and then press F9 to update the table of contents, index, and cross-references, you are also updating unlocked manual links.

Shading Linked and Embedded Objects

You can shade fields in Word documents, including linked and embedded objects, so that you can quickly see where your fields are. In this context, of course, shading fields will allow you to quickly see where all your objects, both linked and embedded, are placed in your document.

To shade fields, choose Tools ⇨ Options, and then click the View tab. In the Field Shading drop-down list, choose Always so that all fields, including linked and embedded objects, are shaded. You will see the shading in all views with the exception of Reading Layout and Print Layout—the shading is intended for use while editing, not in final output.

Tip   Shading fields is a very good idea. It ensures that you will always notice fields and know not to edit the text inside them unnecessarily. Shading reminds you that if you modify text in a linked field, it may be modified again the next time the source document is modified. Shaded fields are especially useful in workgroups that share complicated documents.

You also may want to shade information that serves as a source for links to another file, because any change that you make to such information results in a change being made to the linked data as well. Under the View tab in the Options dialog box you will find the Bookmarks option—make sure this is checked, and all bookmarks are then displayed enclosed in large gray brackets. As data that is linked into another application is treated as bookmarks, your linked data will be enclosed in brackets.

Inserting Data from Access

We've talked a lot about working with Excel, but of course you can embed or link data from all the Office applications. You can insert the contents of an Access table or query, for instance, using a query to filter, sort, and select specific fields. This way, you get exactly the data that you want. To keep the data in your document up to date, you can create a link to the Access data, and whenever the data is changed in Access, Word can update it in your Word document automatically.

Note   Word actually treats the data inserted in the following manner differently from the data we've looked at so far. Although you can link data so that it can be manually updated from the source data, it's not treated like one of the links we've described—the Edit ➪ Links command won't display one of these links in the Links dialog box, for instance.

To transfer Microsoft Access data to a new Word document, you can export an Access table, query, report, or other database object. You can then use Word to format and edit the data, or you can use the data as a mail merge data source.

Cross-Reference   For more information on working with Word's mail merge features, see Chapter 22.

Note   Office includes Microsoft Query, which you can use to construct a query to retrieve data that you want from an external database source, such as Microsoft Access, Microsoft SQL Server, or Microsoft Excel. You can construct a simple query using the Query Wizard, or you can construct a more complex query using the advanced features of Microsoft Query.

To insert Access database information into your Word document, follow these steps:

1. In the Word document, click where you want to insert the contents of the Access table or query.

2. Choose View ➪ Toolbars ➪ Database to display the Database toolbar (see Figure 20-10).

Figure 20-10: The Database toolbar.

3. Click the Insert Database button (fourth from the right) to open the Database dialog box (see Figure 20-11).

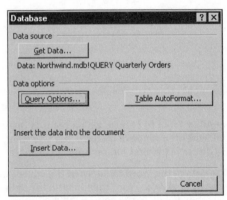

Figure 20-11: The Database dialog box.

4. Click Get Data.

5. Select Access Databases (*.mdb;*.mde) from the Files of Type drop-down list.

6. Select the database file you want to use, and click Open. The Select Table dialog box opens (see Figure 20-12).

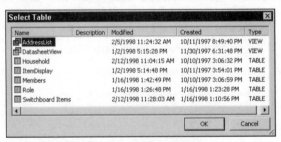

Figure 20-12: The Select Table dialog box.

7. Select the table you want to work with and click OK.

8. To create your own customized query, click Query Options in the Database dialog box. This allows you to tell the system which data entries from the database you want to include in the object you are going to place in Word. Select the options that you want, and then click OK.

9. Word is going to create a table for the data it inserts; to customize the table formatting for your data, click Table AutoFormat, select the options that you want, and then click OK.

10. Click the Insert Data button to open the Insert Data dialog box (see Figure 20-13).

Figure 20-13: The Insert Data dialog box.

11. In the Insert Records group, select All or From to choose which records to include in the Word table. If you choose From, enter the range of records that you want to include. For example, 1 through 10 displays the first ten records of the table.

12. If you want the capability to update data in the Word table when the source data change, select the Insert Data As Field check box. Word then inserts the data in the Word table as a DATABASE field, which is *linked* to the source table or query. To update the field, click in the table and press F9.

13. Click OK, and the data that you specified appears as a table in your Word document (see Figure 20-14).

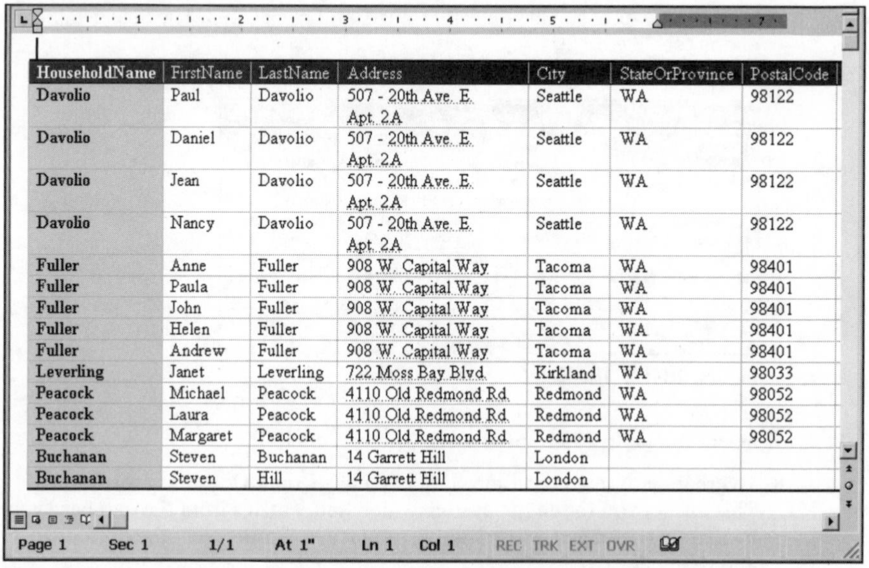

HouseholdName	FirstName	LastName	Address	City	StateOrProvince	PostalCode
Davolio	Paul	Davolio	507 - 20th Ave. E. Apt. 2A	Seattle	WA	98122
Davolio	Daniel	Davolio	507 - 20th Ave. E. Apt. 2A	Seattle	WA	98122
Davolio	Jean	Davolio	507 - 20th Ave. E. Apt. 2A	Seattle	WA	98122
Davolio	Nancy	Davolio	507 - 20th Ave. E. Apt. 2A	Seattle	WA	98122
Fuller	Anne	Fuller	908 W. Capital Way	Tacoma	WA	98401
Fuller	Paula	Fuller	908 W. Capital Way	Tacoma	WA	98401
Fuller	John	Fuller	908 W. Capital Way	Tacoma	WA	98401
Fuller	Helen	Fuller	908 W. Capital Way	Tacoma	WA	98401
Fuller	Andrew	Fuller	908 W. Capital Way	Tacoma	WA	98401
Leverling	Janet	Leverling	722 Moss Bay Blvd.	Kirkland	WA	98033
Peacock	Michael	Peacock	4110 Old Redmond Rd.	Redmond	WA	98052
Peacock	Laura	Peacock	4110 Old Redmond Rd.	Redmond	WA	98052
Peacock	Margaret	Peacock	4110 Old Redmond Rd.	Redmond	WA	98052
Buchanan	Steven	Buchanan	14 Garrett Hill	London		
Buchanan	Steven	Hill	14 Garrett Hill	London		

Page 1   Sec 1   1/1   At 1"   Ln 1   Col 1   REC TRK EXT OVR

Figure 20-14: Data from a Microsoft Access database in a Word document.

Inserting a PowerPoint Slide or Presentation

Microsoft PowerPoint is the standard tool for creating slide presentations to use with speeches or any other activity that involves getting across the key points of your message. You can embed or link a Microsoft PowerPoint add-in, presentation, slide, slide show, template, or wizard into a Word document. Linking is useful when you want to include presentations prepared by a different department and also keep that information up to date in Word. Linking also helps to minimize the file size of your Word document.

Unlike Access, PowerPoint data can be inserted into Word using the same Object commands we've already looked at. When you embed or link a PowerPoint presentation into your Word document, only the first slide appears in the document (see Figure 20-15). You can view the entire presentation as a slide show by double-clicking the slide, which then expands to cover the entire screen. Click to navigate through the slide show. To edit the PowerPoint presentation, select that presentation and then choose Edit ➪ Presentation Object ➪ Edit.

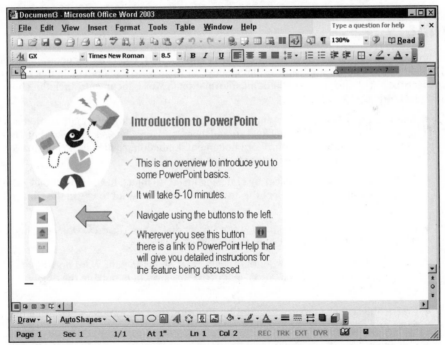

Figure 20-15: A Microsoft PowerPoint presentation inserted in a Word document.

To insert a PowerPoint slide or slides using the copy and paste method, follow these steps:

1. Open both the Word document and the PowerPoint presentation from which you want to create an embedded object.

2. Switch to PowerPoint, and then switch to Slide Sorter View.

3. Select one or more slides or the entire presentation. To select multiple slides, hold down Ctrl and then click each slide that you want.

4. Click the Copy button on the toolbar.

5. Switch to the Word document, and then click where you want to insert the embedded object.

6. Choose Edit ➪ Paste Special.

7. Click Paste.

8. Do one of the following:

   - If the embedded object is a single slide, click Microsoft PowerPoint Slide Object in the As box.

   - If the embedded object contains multiple slides or is an entire presentation, click Microsoft PowerPoint Presentation Object in the As box.

Summary

By linking information across different Windows applications, you can produce sophisticated documents and incorporate features that go beyond what Word itself offers. In this chapter, you learned about linking and embedding information in Word documents, including how to do the following:

✦ Differentiate between linking and embedding objects. Linking information creates a link to a separate file, such as an Excel spreadsheet, and any changes made to that file are reflected in the object in your Word document. Embedding a file places information in your Word document without links to the original file.

✦ Create a new embedded object by choosing Insert ➪ Object. In the Object dialog box, click the Create New tab, select the application that you want to use in the Object Type list and click OK.

✦ Embed an existing file by displaying the Object dialog box (Insert ➪ Object). Then click Browse and find the file you want to use and click OK.

✦ Edit an embedded object by double-clicking that object in your Word document. Edit the object in its native application, and then click anywhere outside the object to return to Word.

✦ Create objects linked to existing files by choosing the Link options when using the same procedures as for embedding.

✦ Embed or link a Microsoft Excel worksheet, Microsoft Access database, or Microsoft PowerPoint presentation into a Word document.

✦   ✦   ✦

Working with Microsoft Graph Chart and Microsoft Equation

✦   ✦   ✦   ✦

In This Chapter

Entering, editing, and formatting data in a Graph datasheet

Creating different types of charts to represent your data graphically

Formatting and customizing charts

Getting data from Word tables and Excel spreadsheets

Importing charts from Excel into Graph

Using Microsoft Equation to add mathematic equations to Word documents

✦   ✦   ✦   ✦

This chapter covers two programs that come with Word: Microsoft Graph Chart (we refer to it as simply Graph in this chapter) and Microsoft Equation. The first program is a charting application with which you can create quick and easy charts to include in Word documents—charts based on numbers you input. Using Graph, you can display numeric data in graphic form, which makes the data clearer, more interesting, and easier to read than it would be if presented in a table.

The other program, Microsoft Equation, is an equation editor with which you can incorporate mathematic symbols to create equations in Word documents.

Using Graph

Charts that you create using Graph are inserted into Word documents as embedded objects. As with other embedded objects, you can copy, delete, and resize the chart using Graph's commands. To edit the data or format any part of the chart, double-click the chart to activate Graph.

Note   To work with charts created in Graph, you must have Microsoft Graph Chart installed on your computer.

Starting and quitting Graph

To start Graph, place the insertion point at the location in your document where you want to create a chart and choose Insert ➪ Object to display the Object dialog box. Choose Microsoft Graph Chart from the Object Type list in the Create New tab and click OK. The default chart is placed into the document, and a Datasheet window appears above it (see Figure 21-1). Notice also that the Word window changes—both the menu bar and the toolbar change. Graph has two toolbars. As in Word, you can drag these toolbars to place them where you want, and you can place your pointer on the button to display the button's label.

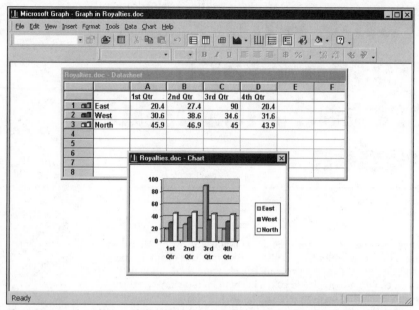

Figure 21-1: The Chart and the Datasheet window appear when you open Graph.

Tip   Graph Charts are objects, so you can create them using the Insert ➪ Object command. But there's a quicker way: choose Insert ➪ Picture ➪ Chart.

The default chart displays the data in three-dimensional (3D) columns with a legend and some other standard formatting. The Datasheet window appears as a spreadsheet with default entries in the columns and rows. Data in the Datasheet window automatically appear in the chart. You can enter your own data to replace the sample data, or you can import data from another document. In either case, the chart is updated to display the new data—each time you enter information in a cell and tab to the next one, the chart is updated. Once you enter or import your data in the Datasheet window, you can choose different types of charts to represent it. For example, you can change the default 3D bar chart to a pie chart. Graph has 14 basic chart types to choose from, and you can customize these charts as well.

When you have finished working on your chart, simply click outside the chart box and the Datasheet window will close.

Note   As with other objects, you can insert graphs into your document as icons if you wish; double-clicking an icon opens the Graph program in its own window. Choose File ➪ Exit & Return in the Graph window to close it. You'll see that you cannot save Graph charts in their own files—they must be saved within a Word document.

Working in the Datasheet window

The Datasheet window is similar to a typical spreadsheet in Microsoft Excel. The top row contains the column titles—in the case of the default datasheet, the 1st, 2nd, 3rd, and 4th quarters. The leftmost column, meanwhile, contains the row titles—in this case, the East, West, and North regions.

How does this relate to the chart? The data in each column of the datasheet creates one set of data on the chart—one group of bars. The data in each cell of the column creates one bar in each group of bars. Thus three rows of data means three bars in each group of bars. Add another column of data to add another group of bars; add another row to add another bar to each group.

Initially, the Datasheet window shows only a few columns and rows, but you can expand the window display by moving the pointer to any window edge and then either dragging outward to expand it or dragging inward to reduce it. Using the scroll bars at the right and the bottom, you can navigate around a datasheet. Figure 21-2 shows an expanded Datasheet window.

		A	B	C	D	E	F	G
		1st Qtr	2nd Qtr	3rd Qtr	4th Qtr			
1	East	20.4	27.4	90	20.4			
2	West	30.6	38.6	34.6	31.6			
3	North	45.9	46.9	45	43.9			
4								
5								
6								
7								
8								
9								
10								
11								
12								
13								
14								
15								

Royalties.doc - Datasheet

Figure 21-2: An expanded Datasheet window.

Entering data in a datasheet

You can enter new data over the existing data, or you can select the text in the Datasheet window and delete it, as explained later in this chapter. To enter more data than the number of rows that appear in the Datasheet window by default, scroll to display new columns and rows. When you enter data in the cell, a new row or column is created automatically, and the chart reflects the additions automatically as well. You can expand the Datasheet window by pointing to a corner or side and then dragging outward.

Enter data into a cell by clicking on the cell and typing. A cell in the Datasheet window can display as many as eight characters. If your data contains more than eight characters, the data in the cell are noted with a shorthand entry representing the actual number. For example, if you enter 123456789 in a cell, the number appears as 1.23E+08. The number that you entered in the cell is there, but that number is too big to display in the default eight-character width of the column. You can enlarge the width of any column, however, by pointing to the vertical line to the right of the column heading (the column headings are the A, B, C, and so on at the top of the Datasheet window). When the pointer changes to a vertical bar with arrows on each side, drag to the right to widen the column. When you reach the width of your data in the column, the actual data replaces the number signs.

Tip Double-click the dividing line between column headings to readjust the column size to fit the data within the cells without leaving excess space while allowing the numbers to fit fully within the cell.

After typing a number in a cell, press Tab to move to the next cell on the row or an arrow key to move to a cell in the direction of the arrow.

Tip   You can close and reopen the Datasheet window. Close the window using any normal Windows Close command—click the X button or press Alt+F4, for instance. You can also open and close this window using the View Datasheet button on the Standard toolbar or choose View ➪ Datasheet.

Note that the datasheet is *not* a spreadsheet. A spreadsheet allows you to carry out calculations. The Graph datasheet merely stores data. For instance, in Excel you can place calculations inside a cell—33 + 22 – 3, for instance—or enter a calculation based on other cells—C3 + B9 – B8. You cannot do this in the datasheet; all you can do is place numbers and text in cells.

Selecting and navigating within a datasheet

The easiest way to move about in a datasheet is to click where you want to go. As you select cells with the mouse, however, remember the following:

✦ One cell—the active cell—is always selected. To make another cell active, click that cell.

✦ To select several cells, drag the mouse over them.

✦ To select an entire row or column, click the shaded area (header) to the left (for a row) or above (for a column) the area that you want.

✦ To select several rows or columns, drag the mouse over their headers.

✦ To select the entire datasheet, click the area where the row and column headers meet or press Ctrl+A.

Sometimes you may want to use the keyboard to navigate within a datasheet and to select a cell. Tables 21-1 and 21-2 list important key combinations.

Table 21-1: Navigating a Datasheet Using the Keyboard

Press This	To Move Here
Arrow keys	One cell in the direction of the arrow
Home	First cell in row
End	Last cell in row
Ctrl+Home	Top-left cell
Ctrl+End	Lower-right cell
Page Up (Page Down)	One screen up (down)
Ctrl+Page Up (Ctrl+Page Down)	One screen left (right)

Table 21-2: Selecting Cells Using the Keyboard

Press This	To Select This
Arrow key	One cell in the direction of the arrow
Shift+arrow key (or F8)	Series of cells
Shift+spacebar	A row

Press This	To Select This
Ctrl+spacebar	A column
Ctrl+Shift+spacebar	Entire datasheet

Moving and copying information in a datasheet

To move or copy cells in a Graph datasheet, use the Cut, Copy, and Paste buttons on the Standard toolbar. Alternatively, use the Edit ➪ Cut (Ctrl+X), Edit ➪ Copy (Ctrl+C), and Edit ➪ Paste (Ctrl+V) commands. Select the cells that you want to copy or move. Then choose the Cut button, Copy button, or the command to place those cells on the Clipboard. Position the cursor where you want the information to move, and then choose the Paste button or command to move or copy that data to its new location. To replace existing cells with the new information, select the cells to be replaced before you paste the copies.

Deleting and inserting information in a datasheet

To delete a row or a column, select a cell in that row or column and then choose Edit ➪ Delete. The Delete dialog box appears, as shown in Figure 21-3. Choose the Entire Row or Entire Column option, and then click OK.

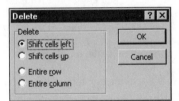

Figure 21-3: The Delete dialog box.

To delete a cell or selection of cells, click the cell or select the group of cells. Choose the Shift Cells Left radio button to delete the cells and shift the remaining cells to the left, or choose the Shift Cells Up radio button to delete the cells and shift the remaining cells upward.

To delete the *contents* of a cell, row, or column without any confirmation, and without shifting the cells anywhere, just select the cell or cells that you want to delete and press the Delete key. The contents of the selected cells are then deleted.

To insert a row or a cell, select a cell in the row or column that you want to insert above in the case of a row or before in the case of a column. Choose Insert ➪ Cells to display the Insert dialog box, as shown in Figure 21-4. Choose the Entire Row or Entire Column option, and then click OK. To insert a cell or selection of cells, click the cell or select the group of cells. Choose the Shift Cells Right radio button to insert the cells and shift the remaining cells to the right, or choose the Shift Cells Down radio button to insert a new cell and move the others down.

Use the following commands to remove particular content from cells:

✦ **Edit ➪ Clear ➪ All:** Removes the content and formatting from a cell

✦ **Edit ➪ Clear ➪ Content:** Removes the content from a cell, but the formatting remains

✦ **Edit ➪ Clear ➪ Format:** Converts the format of the cell back to the default format for the datasheet

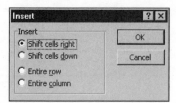

Figure 21-4: The Insert dialog box.

Formatting data in a datasheet

You can format data in your datasheet quickly using the Graph Formatting toolbar. This toolbar includes a subset of standard Word formatting features, which you can apply to the entire datasheet. You can change the font and font size used for data entries, and you can boldface, italicize, or underline the data entries.

Unique to the Graph toolbar are its last five buttons. You can use these buttons to format your data entries as well. You can apply a currency, percent, or comma style to data, or you can increase or decrease the decimal point value. For example, if you want all of the values in your datasheet to represent dollars, press Ctrl+A to select the entire datasheet and then click the dollar sign ($) button.

You can format individual cells to some degree, also. Right-click a cell and select Number to open the Number dialog box, in which you can select a form of formatting: a Number, a Date, a Percentage, a Fraction, and so on. For many of these formats you can specify details. For instance, if you want to format the cell as a Currency cell, you can specify the number of decimal places, the currency symbol to use, and how to display negative numbers.

 Note You cannot format the font in a cell individually. Any changes to the font format affect *all* the numbers and text in your datasheet.

Working with charts

Data entered in your datasheet automatically appears in the default bar chart. The Graph program provides a variety of chart styles to choose from, and it also provides tools for customizing your chart. A typical chart includes items such as a title, axis values, data labels, gridlines, data series, a chart area, a plot area, and a legend. The following items explain the key elements of charts:

✦ **Data series:** One row or column of values (called *data points*) displayed as a set of data markers such as bars, lines, or pie slices on the chart. What you enter in the first row and column of cells and the orientation you choose (series in rows or series in columns) determines how the data are plotted on the chart. The default chart is plotted with groups of bars, each group representing one column.

✦ **Data marker:** A bar, area, dot, slice, or other symbol in a chart that represents a single data point or value originating from a datasheet cell. Related data markers in a chart comprise a data series.

✦ **Tick marks:** The small lines that intersect an axis (like divisions on a ruler). Tick marks are part of and can be formatted with the axis. Tick-mark labels identify the categories, values, and series in a chart. Tick marks come from and are automatically linked to the cells in your datasheet selection.

✦ **Data points:** The individual values plotted in a chart that originate from single cells in the datasheet. Data points are represented by bars, columns, lines, pie slices, and other shapes. These shapes are called data markers.

✦ **Axis:** The lines bordering the plot area that provide the frame of reference for measurement or comparison on a chart. A two-dimensional (2D) chart has two axes; a 3D chart has two or three axes. For most charts, data values are plotted along the value (y) axis, which is usually vertical, and categories are plotted along the category (x) axis, which is usually horizontal. Pie and doughnut charts, however, don't have axes.

✦ **Gridlines:** Lines that you can add to your chart that extend across the plot area from the tick marks on an axis. Gridlines come in various forms to make viewing and evaluating data easier.

✦ **Category:** A grouping of data usually plotted along the category (x) axis on a chart. If you define data series in rows on the datasheet, the categories are in columns; if you define the data series in columns on the datasheet, the categories are in rows.

✦ **Legend:** A box containing entries and keys that identify the data series or categories in a chart. The legend keys, which are to the left of each entry, show the patterns and colors assigned to the data series or categories in the chart.

After you create a chart, you can position it in your document using standard Word paragraph formatting and positioning commands. You can also enlarge a chart by clicking it to display the sizing handles and then dragging those handles.

Changing chart types

After you enter data in a datasheet, you can view that data using various chart types. Table 21-3 lists the styles of charts available in Graph. To display the data in your datasheet using a different chart style, click the down arrow on the Chart Type button on the Graph's Standard toolbar and then choose the type that you want from the drop-down menu. Graph automatically converts the data into the specified chart.

Table 21-3: Chart Types Available in Graph

Chart Type	Use
Area	Shows how values change in proportion to a total. An area chart doesn't handle multiple series well, however, and large values tend to swallow the representation of smaller ones.
Bar	Compares items or shows individual figures at a specific time. A bar chart can handle multiple series well.
Bubble	Groups data as bubbles. Very hard to visualize most types of data.
Column	Shows variations over time. Two options (stacked and 100%) show relationships to a whole.
Cone	Shows data as clustered cone columns.
Cylinder	Shows data as clustered cylinder columns.
Doughnut	Shows parts of a whole (like a pie chart), but can also show more than one data series (unlike the pie chart). Each category of data is a ring in the doughnut.

Continued

Table 21-3 *(continued)*

Chart Type	Use
Line	Shows trends in data or changes in a group of values over time.
Pie	Portrays one series as a relationship to a whole.
Pyramid	Displays data as clustered pyramid columns.
Radar	Shows changes or frequencies of data series relative to a center point and one another.
Stock	Displays stock High-Low-Close data.
Surface	Shows relationships between large amounts of data. (Appears as if a rubber sheet were stretched over a 3D column chart.)
XY (Scatter)	Shows the relationship between two sets of numbers. You can use XY charts to discover patterns.

You can also choose a chart using Chart ➪ Chart Type, which displays the Chart Type dialog box (see Figure 21-5). Select a chart type from the Chart Type list, and the available charts within the selected category appear in the Chart Sub-Type area of the dialog box. Click one of the choices and click the Click and Hold to View Sample button to see what the chart will look like. Then click the OK button to select the type you want.

To use a type of chart other than the bar chart as the default, select the type of chart that you want and then click Set as Default Chart in the Chart Type dialog box.

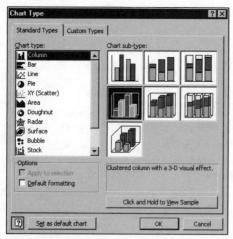

Figure 21-5: The Chart Type dialog box.

Excluding data in a chart

Sometimes you may not want Word to include some rows or columns of data in a chart. For example, you may enter data for several different charts in one datasheet, and as a result, you may want to display only some of the information in a certain chart. By inserting and removing rows and columns, you can see changes in the chart by adding or removing data. This doesn't actually remove the data in the rows and columns, but it does suspend the selected information from appearing in the chart.

Position the cursor where you want to exclude a row or a column, and then choose Data ➪ Exclude Row/Col to exclude the data from the chart. The adjustment to the chart occurs automatically. To restore the excluded data to the chart, choose Data ➪ Include Row/Col. You can also include or exclude rows and columns by double-clicking the column or row header in the datasheet.

Note   Cells that are being excluded appear with gray text to differentiate them.

Customizing and refining charts

Once you create a chart, you can make a variety of changes to it using the Chart Options dialog box (see Figure 21-6). Choose Chart ➪ Chart Options to display this dialog box.

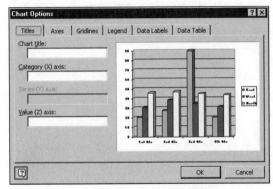

Figure 21-6: The Chart Options dialog box.

The following list describes the functions of the tabs in the dialog box:

✦ **Titles tab:** Lets you add titles for your chart and for the x- and y-axes. An axis consists of the lines bordering the plot area of a chart that provide a frame of reference when comparing data.

✦ **Axes tab:** Lets you turn on or off the display of axis values. By default, the chart appears with axis labels and values displayed.

✦ **Gridlines tab:** Lets you add vertical and horizontal gridlines. When you create a chart, it has some gridlines by default to make reading data values and categories easier, but you can change the kind of gridlines displayed. Major gridlines delineate larger ranges of values or categories along the axis; minor gridlines further break down the ranges.

✦ **Legend tab:** Lets you choose whether to display the legend and decide where to position it if you do. When you create a chart, it has a legend by default to identify the different data series displayed. A chart legend details the name of each series and indicates how each series is represented (for example, by color or shading). If you delete the legend from an existing chart, you can always add it again by clicking the Legend button on the Standard toolbar.

✦ **Data Labels tab:** Lets you add labels to a data series (the columns of data), to a category (a group of data sets), or to each value—each point or bar displays the actual value. You can also place a separator character between the labels, and place a Legend key on the chart.

✦ **Data Table tab:** Lets you add a table showing the data used to create the chart. The table will be placed underneath the chart.

Formatting charts

When Graph is activated, you can format different parts of a chart by double-clicking that particular part in the chart display. For example, double-clicking a chart legend displays the Format Legend dialog box, in which you can format and fine-tune the chart's legend. Depending on the chart type being used, different dialog boxes as well as different options within those dialog boxes may appear. The following items explain the formatting dialog boxes that appear when you double-click particular sections of a 3D bar chart after activating Graph:

✦ **Format Gridlines dialog box:** Displayed when you double-click a chart's gridlines (see Figure 21-7). In the Patterns tab, you can specify the style, color, and weight of the gridlines. In the Scale tab, you can specify the scale to use for those gridlines.

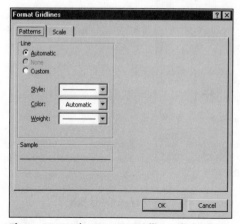

Figure 21-7: The Format Gridlines dialog box.

✦ **Format Data Series dialog box:** Displayed when you double-click a chart's data series. The tabs in this dialog box change depending on the type of chart being used.

✦ **Format Axis dialog box:** Displayed when you double-click a chart's data axis.

✦ **Format Legend dialog box:** Displayed when you double-click the chart's legend.

✦ **Format Chart Area dialog box:** Displayed when you double-click in the white space of the chart area. This dialog box includes Patterns and Font tabs.

✦ **Fomat Walls dialog box:** Displayed when you double-click the wall of a chart.

✦ **Format Plot Area dialog box:** Displayed when you double-click anywhere in the plot-area background.

Tip   Hold the mouse button over an area for a moment and a little box with a title appears: Plot Area, Legend, Category Axis, and so on. Now you know which dialog box will open when you double-click.

Getting data and charts from other sources

Sometimes you may have the data that you want to chart already in a table or a spreadsheet file. You can import any information in another application or in Word tables into Graph's datasheet. The following sections explain how to use data from a Word table or an Excel spreadsheet.

Getting data from Word tables

With Graph, you can easily copy information from a Word table into the datasheet. After the information is in the datasheet, you can create the type of chart that you want in the same way that you do when entering information directly into the datasheet. By converting data from a table to a chart, you can show that data in the table as well as in the chart.

To convert tables into charts, follow these steps:

1. Enter the data and text in a table.

Cross-Reference   For more information about tables, see Chapter 9.

2. Select the table; no need to copy the text.

3. Choose Insert ⇨ Picture ⇨ Chart or Insert ⇨ Object ⇨ Create New and select Microsoft Graph Chart. The standard Datasheet and graph windows then appear, with your table data in use.

You can also select the data in a table using the Copy button or the Edit ⇨ Copy command in Word. After you select the data, activate Graph, display the Datasheet window, select the data that you want to replace or click the cell from which you want the table data to start, and then choose Edit ⇨ Paste or press Ctrl+V. The data from the table is placed into the datasheet.

Getting data from Excel spreadsheets

If you use Excel, you may want bring information already in a spreadsheet into the Datasheet window.

Cross-Reference   Note, however, that you can also link or embed a spreadsheet from Excel using Word's linking and embedding features, which are explained in Chapter 20. By linking an Excel spreadsheet to Word, you can use the full features of Excel.

To import spreadsheet data into a Graph datasheet, follow these steps:

1. Place the insertion point where you want the chart to be. Then choose Insert ⇨ Picture ⇨ Chart.

2. To erase all sample data from the datasheet, click that datasheet. Press Ctrl+A to select all of the data, or click the area where the row and column headers meet. Then press the Delete key.

3. Position the cursor in the top left row of the now-blank datasheet, and then click to make the cell active.

4. Click the Import File button (the button resembling a bar chart) or choose Edit ⇨ Import File, select your data file in the Import File dialog box, click Open, and you'll see the Import Data Options dialog box, as shown in Figure 21-8.

Figure 21-8: The Import Data Options dialog box.

5. Choose the worksheet file that you want to import and do one of the following:

   • To import the entire worksheet, choose the Entire Sheet option button.

   • To instruct Word what range of cells to import from the chosen spreadsheet, choose the Range option button and then enter the range of cells that you want.

   • If you leave the Overwrite Existing Cells check box selected, Word replaces cell content in the datasheet.

6. Click OK. The data is then entered in the Datasheet window automatically.

Importing charts from Excel

With Graph, you can also import a chart generated in Excel. Once you import the chart, you can work with it using Graph.

To import a chart from Excel, follow these steps:

1. Position the cursor where you want the chart to appear in your Word document.

2. Open the Graph program.

3. Click the Import Chart button on the Graph Standard toolbar, or choose Edit ⇨ Import File. The Import File dialog box appears.

4. Navigate to the directory with the Excel chart file that you want.

5. Select the chart file and click OK. A message box then prompts you to confirm overwriting the current chart in Graph. Click OK, and the Excel chart appears in your Word document.

Working with Microsoft Equation

Microsoft Equation helps you add fractions, exponents, integrals, and so on to Word documents. You start building an equation by opening Microsoft Equation. Choose Insert ⇨ Object, choose Microsoft Equation from the Object Type list, and click OK. A little Equation window opens, along with the Equation toolbar (see Figure 21-9).

Note　When you first open the Equation Editor, the Equation Editor Tip dialog box appears and asks if you want to know more about MathType, which is a powerful upgrade for Equation Editor. If you frequently work with equations in your documents, you can purchase MathType from Design Science, Inc.

The Greek-looking items in the top row of the Equation toolbar are symbols and operators that you may want to insert into an equation. The items on the bottom row of the toolbar are called *templates.* In effect, these templates are the subcomponents of the equation you are building. These subcomponents, such as parentheses and lines, hold the symbols.

You build an equation by assembling templates and associated symbols in the *slot*—a box bounded by dotted lines—that appears in the work area. As you build your equation, the slot changes in position and size. In fact, more than one slot can be associated with an equation.

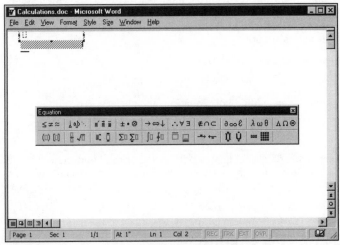

Figure 21-9: The Microsoft Equation window and toolbar.

Positioning the insertion point

You can move the cursor around in an equation by using the keystrokes shown in Table 21-4.

Table 21-4: Keystrokes for Moving the Cursor within an Equation

Press This	To Move Here
Tab	To the end of the current slot or to the next logical slot
Shift+Tab	To the end of the preceding slot
Right-arrow key	Right one unit in the current slot
Left-arrow key	Left one unit in the current slot
Up-arrow key	Up one line

Continued

Table 21-4 *(continued)*

Press This	To Move Here
Down-arrow key	Down one line
Home	To the beginning of the current slot
End	To the end of the current slot

Building a sample equation

You never can tell when you may feel that indescribable need to write your mother about frictionless, incompressible fluids and Torricelli's Equation. (Torricelli's Equation states that velocity equals two times the square root of the acceleration caused by gravity, times the distance between the liquid surface and the center of the nozzle.) Luckily, Equation Editor can ease your discomfort in this situation.

To build Torricelli's Equation, follow these steps:

1. Position the insertion point where you want the equation to be.

2. Choose Insert ➪ Object, select Microsoft Equation, and click OK. The Equation Editor opens.

3. Type **V=**.

4. Click the Fractions and Radicals Templates button (the second button from the left on the bottom row), and then select the square root symbol (the fourth button down in the first column).

5. Type **2gH** in the slot under the square root.

Adjusting spacing and alignment

Only rarely should you need to adjust an equation's formatting. The Equation Editor automatically handles subscripts and superscripts, as well as most other formatting. Nonetheless, you can manually adjust the spacing and alignment of equations in three ways:

✦ Use the Spaces and Ellipses button on the Equation toolbar (second from left, top row). With this button, you can include spaces that act like characters, taking up room from zero length to the equivalent of a quad space.

✦ When Equation Editor is open, you can choose Format ➪ Spacing to display the Spacing dialog box (see Figure 21-10). With this dialog box, you can adjust line, matrix, subscript, and superscript spacing.

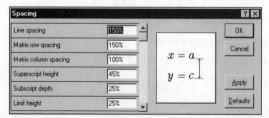

Figure 21-10: The Spacing dialog box.

✦ The final method, called *nudging*, is more precise. Select the item that you want to adjust, hold down the Ctrl key, and then click the arrow pointing in the direction that you want the item to move. The selected item moves one pixel per click. A *pixel* is short for *picture element* and represents the smallest element of your computer screen, which is broken up into hundreds of thousands of pixels (dots).

Summary

You now have the fundamentals for working with Microsoft Graph Chart and Microsoft Equation, which come with Word. In this chapter, you learned how to do the following:

✦ Start Graph by choosing Insert ➪ Object to display the Object dialog box, choosing Microsoft Graph Chart from the Create New tab, and then clicking OK.

✦ Format data in a data sheet as currency or percentages, add commas, and increase or decrease the decimal point placement using the last five buttons on the Formatting toolbar.

✦ Change the chart type by clicking the down arrow on the Chart Type button or choosing Format ➪ Chart Type.

✦ Get data from a Word table by selecting the table, opening Graph from the Object dialog box, and then clicking OK.

✦ Import data from an Excel spreadsheet by choosing Edit ➪ Import Data or clicking the Import Data button on the Standard toolbar.

✦ Open the Equation Editor by choosing Insert ➪ Object to display the Object dialog box and selecting Microsoft Equation. The Equation Editor toolbar appears, and you can add mathematical symbols by choosing the appropriate ones from buttons on the Equation Editor toolbar.

✦   ✦   ✦

Complex Documents: Mail Merge, Forms, Outlines, and Web Pages

◆ ◆ ◆ ◆

In This Part

Chapter 22
Creating Form Letters, Envelopes, Labels, and Catalogs

Chapter 23
Creating Dynamic Documents Using Field Codes

Chapter 24
Creating Forms

Chapter 25
Getting Organized with Outlines and Master Documents

Chapter 26
Creating Basic Web Pages

Chapter 27
Advanced HTML and XML

◆ ◆ ◆ ◆

Creating Form Letters, Envelopes, Labels, and Catalogs

◆ ◆ ◆ ◆

In This Chapter

Creating and printing
form letters

Producing envelopes,
mailing labels, and lists

Screening records
before printing

Changing the order of
printing

Working with merge
fields and fill-in fields

◆ ◆ ◆ ◆

This chapter covers the fundamentals of creating and printing various kinds of merged documents. It also discusses some of the more advanced techniques, such as selecting certain letters or labels to print, sorting documents before printing, and varying the text of a letter based on field value.

Merging Letter and Address Files

Word's capability to automatically insert information from one file into another is a very useful and powerful feature. With this process, which is called *merging*, you can do any of the following:

- ✦ Print personalized letters addressed to tens, even hundreds, of recipients very quickly.

- ✦ Print multiple envelopes for the letters.

- ✦ Print multiple mailing labels.

- ✦ Print lists and catalogs.

Merging involves creating a main document, such as a form letter, that contains some placemarkers embedded within the text. Then, in a simple database, you enter information that is intended to replace the placemarkers, such as names and addresses.

When Word merges these two files, the result is a one document for each set of data in the database—one letter, one envelope, one invoice, or whatever. If you have 50 addresses, you end up with 50 different letters, for instance. Each of these resulting documents contains the text of the original main document with the text from the database document inserted in place of the markers.

The best-known use for *mail merging* is to create form letters, such as those announcing that you, personally, have won millions of dollars in a sweepstakes. A typical main document for a form letter consists of the text of that letter with markers indicating the positions for the addressee's name, street address, city, state, and zip code. The database contains a list of the actual addressees' names and addresses, and Word merges these two documents together to print the personalized letters.

In addition to creating form letters, Word can merge data for envelopes and mailing labels. Word can also merge data between a main document and a database document to produce formatted lists, such as catalogs and directories.

That is just the beginning of what you can do with merging. A main document can also include fields that define conditions. A condition in the main document might define the conditions under which data in the database will be used. You can print letters, envelopes, or labels for people living in a certain city, for example, or for people whose addresses are within a certain range of zip codes. The possibilities are limitless.

Like many of Word's features, you can use merging in a straightforward way to satisfy many of your needs, but you can explore its advanced capabilities as well. Suppose that you work in a billing department and want to automate the process of sending reminder letters to customers more than 30 days delinquent in paying their bills. Just create a suitable letter and save it as the main document. Then create a database that contains your customers' names and addresses and the date on which they were originally billed. You can have Word merge the two documents, selecting only those customers who were billed more than 30 days before the current date. You can even increase the severity of the reminder letter as the account becomes more delinquent.

The first part of this chapter deals with straightforward merging to print form letters, envelopes, mailing labels, and lists. Later sections deal with some of the more sophisticated ways to use Word's versatile merge feature.

What Is Merging?

As was mentioned in the preceding section, *merging* is the process of taking a piece of data from one document and automatically inserting it into another document. In most cases, this is done multiple times, as information from the data file is inserted into many different versions of the main document to create many different versions of the main document.

This section looks at merging from the most common perspective—that of creating a mass mailing, with multiple letters drawing data from a single data file. You need two things for the merging process: the main document, which contains the letter, and the database, which contains the names and addresses of those people you want to send the letter to.

The main document

The main document for a form letter contains the text (and perhaps even graphics) that should be in every letter. It also contains markers, called *merge codes*, where the personalized text should go. Figure 22-1 shows a typical main document.

The words enclosed in chevrons (« and ») in the main document are the merge codes that identify data to be inserted from the database. In effect, these fields say "go get the data matching this name from the database." Other text in the main document (the text not enclosed in chevrons) appears in every letter.

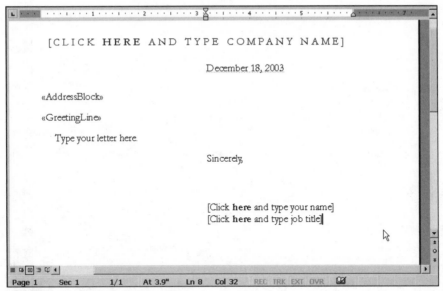

Figure 22-1: A typical main document.

Note You don't type the chevrons and the merge codes that they enclose. As discussed later in this chapter, you use Word tools to place these codes in your document.

The database

The database contains the information that replaces the merge codes in the main document. In earlier versions of Word a database was used—the data was stored in a table in a normal Word document. However, Word is now using a real database file to store information, which is actually far more convenient. We'll see how you can create and manage this file in a moment.

Note, by the way, that the database can be a simple database that you create within Word, or a database created in Microsoft Access.

Putting the two documents together

After creating a main document and a database, you just have to tell Word to merge them. The result is a set of customized letters, such as the one shown in Figure 22-2.

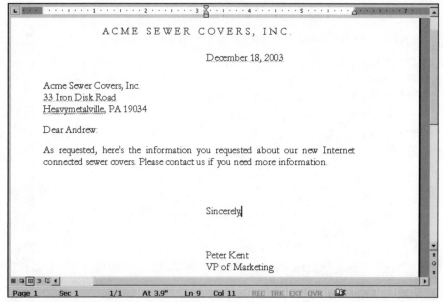

Figure 22-2: A typical customized letter.

Here are some important facts to remember about merging:

✦ Each letter contains data from the database in its proper place.

✦ Some fields (Title, LastName, and City) are used more than once—that's okay, Word doesn't care, it simply follows instructions. If you tell it to grab the LastName a thousand times in a document, it will do it.

✦ In some cases data fields are blank—not all addresses use the Address2 field, for instance. In these cases, Word doesn't leave a blank line in its place, it simply continues as if the field were not there.

✦ Customized letters are created in the same order as the names are listed in the database. You can easily change this order, however.

✦ Fields in the database need not be in any special order.

Writing Form Letters

Word guides you smoothly through the process of creating a form letter. Simply follow the instructions in the dialog boxes as they appear.

If you follow the steps in the next section, you can create several files. Before you start, however, use Windows Explorer to create a folder for these files, so you can save them all together in the same place. (Our example steps assume that you have created a folder named My Mail Merge within your own personalized folder or the main Word folder.)

Using the Mail Merge Wizard

The process described here assumes that your form letters aren't based on an existing letter and that you haven't yet compiled a list of people to whom you want to address these letters. How to adapt an existing letter and use an existing list of names and addresses is discussed later in this chapter. To begin creating a set of form letters using Word's Mail Merge Wizard to create the letter, do the following:

1. Open a blank document.

2. Choose Tools ⇨ Letters and Mailings ⇨ Mail Merge Wizard to open the Mail Merge task pane, as shown in Figure 22-3. Word provides five document types from which you can choose.

3. Click Letters; at the bottom of the task pane, click the Next link.

4. You can now choose whether to create a new document from a template, use the document that is currently open, or select an existing document. For the purposes of this example, select Start From a Template.

   When you select Start From a Template, you see the Select Template link. Click this and select a template to apply to the open document. For example, you might select the Contemporary Merge Letter. Word clears everything from the existing document and applies this template. You then see a generic letter, with some merge fields already inserted (see Figure 22-4).

   After you apply the template, the Use the Current Document option is selected automatically.

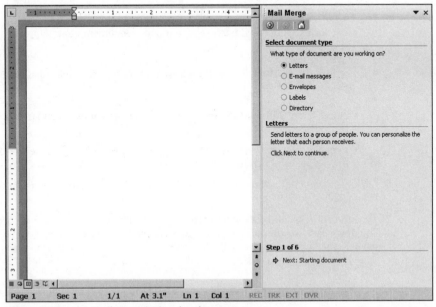

Figure 22-3: The Mail Merge Wizard task pane.

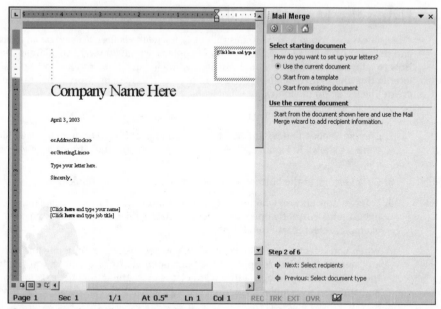

Figure 22-4: The Mail Merge Wizard, with the Contemporary Merge Letter applied to the open document.

5. Click the Next link at the bottom of the task pane. You can now select how you are going to provide the database with the list of letter recipients:

   • **Use an Existing List:** Enables you to open a document containing the list of recipients.

   Note   If you open an Access database, you'll see a list of the tables within that database. Select the specific table and click OK.

   • **Select from Outlook Contacts:** Enables you to select recipients from a Microsoft Outlook address book.

   • **Type a New List:** Tells the task pane to add a Create link. Choose this option for the purposes of this example.

6. Click the Create link. Word displays the New Address List dialog box, as shown in Figure 22-5.

7. Type the address information into the text boxes. Press Tab to jump from box to box. You don't have to enter all the information necessarily. For example, you might not have phone numbers and e-mail addresses.

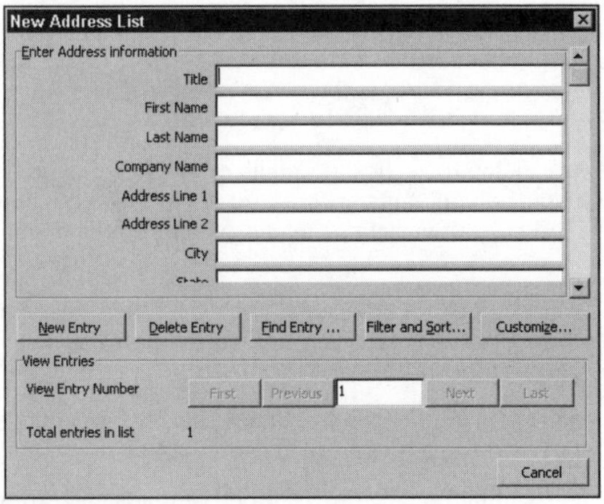

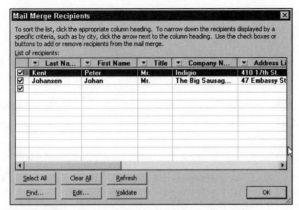

Figure 22-5: The New Address List dialog box.

8. At the end of the list, press Tab and the New Entry button is highlighted; press Enter, and the information you entered is saved, the text boxes are cleared, and the insertion point is placed back in the Title field. Repeat step 7 for every address.

   Note that you can use the buttons in this box to manage the information you are creating. You can delete an entry, of course. But you can also use Find Entry to search for a particular entry; Filter and Sort to determine which entries should be available; Customize to add, remove, rename, and move data fields in the entry list; and the First, Previous, Next, and Last buttons to move through the list of entries that you have created.

9. After you have added the last address, click the Close button. (When you enter data, the Cancel button changes to Close.) Word prompts you to save the information in a file in your My Data Sources folder. Provide a name for the file and click Save. The Mail Merge Recipients dialog box opens (see Figure 22-6).

Figure 22-6: The Mail Merge Recipients dialog box.

Selecting recipients

So far, you have created or selected a document and entered names into the recipient list (or perhaps selected an existing recipient list). Now, follow these steps to select the recipients of the letter:

1. In the Mail Merge Recipients dialog box, click a triangle on the heading line to sort by that particular field. For instance, you might sort addresses by zip code, so you can do a bulk mailing in zip code order (with very large mailings using a bulk-mailing permit saves money).

2. Select the recipients you want to mail to. You can click on the check boxes in the first column to select and deselect; use the Select All and Clear All buttons; or use the Find button go to a particular entry in the list.

3. If you notice any errors in an entry, you can select it and click Edit to change the information.

4. If you have installed address-validation software (a tool that reads an address and matches it against a database of zip codes and street addresses to see if it's correct), you can use the Validate button to check the addresses and ensure that they are good. If you haven't installed such software, clicking the Validate button opens a message box that takes you to a Web site where you can find more information.

5. When you have selected all the recipients and sorted the list the way you want it, click OK to close the dialog box.

6. Click the Next link at the bottom of the task pane.

Writing the letter

Now the wizard is ready for you to write your letter. In fact the letter, if you selected a template, may be half done; the Contemporary Merge Letter, for instance, already has some of the merge fields—the <<AddressBlock>> and <<GreetingLine>>. These fields tell Word to grab the Address fields—the recipient's name and address—and the *Dear* greeting fields.

Assume for a moment, that you have a blank letter and need to insert the fields. Follow these steps:

1. Write your letter, leaving blanks where you want to insert information from the data source. You can even use some kind of marker, such as ?? or *** to remind you to come back to that field.

2. When you want to insert the recipient's address, place the insertion point at that position and click the Address Block link in the task pane. The Insert Address Block dialog box opens (see Figure 22-7).

3. If you want to include the recipient's name in the address block, make sure the Insert Recipient's Name in This Format check box is selected, and click on one of the name formats.

4. If you want to include the company name, check the Insert Company Name check box.

5. Check the Insert Postal Address check box to include the address, of course. You can also choose whether to always include the country, never include the country, or always include the country if it is different from the one specified in the drop-down list box.

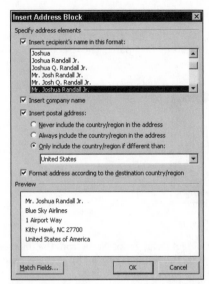

Figure 22-7: The Insert Address Block
dialog box.

6. Different countries use different address formats. Select Format Address According to
the Destination Country/Region check box to make Word enter the addresses correctly.

7. If necessary, click the Match Fields button to open the Match Fields dialog box (see
Figure 22-8) and ensure that your fields match. You won't have to do this if you created
a simple address list from scratch, but if, for instance, you opened an existing database,
or created a new one and added fields, you can use this dialog box to match the field
names in your database with those used by the Mail Merge Wizard.

Figure 22-8: The Match Fields dialog box.

8. Click OK to insert the field into the document.

9. When you want to insert the greeting line in the letter, place the insertion point at that position and click the Greeting Line link in the task pane. The Greeting Line dialog box opens (see Figure 22-9).

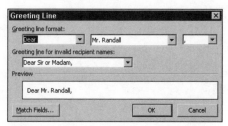

Figure 22-9: The Greeting Line dialog box.

10. In the first Greeting Line Format box, select Dear, To, or None from the drop-down list box, depending on how you want to start the letter. (Look in the Preview pane at the bottom of the dialog box to see the effect of your selections.)

11. In the next two boxes to the right, choose the name format you want to use and the ending character: a comma, colon, or no ending character.

12. Select a Greeting Line for Invalid Recipient Names. This line is used if Word is unable to provide the correct name components from your database. You can choose to enter Dear Sir or Madam, To Whom it May Concern, or to omit the greeting line entirely in such a case.

13. If you want to enter another field at some point, place the insertion point where you want it and click the More Items link to open the Insert Merge Field dialog box (see Figure 22-10). You would use this step if, for example, you wanted to enter the recipient's name in the body of the letter: *We've tried calling you a dozen times about this debt, Fred, but we're getting the idea you are avoiding us!*

The Insert Merge Field dialog box enables you to insert fields in two forms. First, you can select Insert Address Fields, which, unfortunately, is an incorrect and ambiguous term. If you select this form, you see a list of all the Mail Merge fields recognized by the Mail Merge Wizard—the same fields you saw in the Match Fields dialog box. (You can reopen these fields by clicking the Match Fields button at the bottom.). Or, you can select Insert Database Fields, in which case you see the fields in the database you are working with.

14. Select the field you want to insert, and click Insert. Then click OK to close the dialog box.

Note   You'll also see the Electronic Postage and Postage Bar Code links in the task pane. These are, of course, for creating envelopes, which we'll look at later in this chapter.

Save your document! Once you've created a merge document, save it so you can use it again for future mailings.

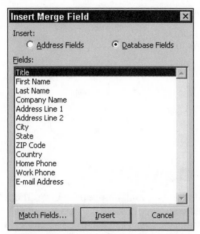

Figure 22-10: The Insert Merge Field dialog box.

Previewing and printing the letter

After you finish composing the letter, follow these steps to check it and print it:

1. Click the Next link at the bottom of the task pane, and the wizard displays a copy of the letter, pulling data from the first record in your database.

2. You can now see how other records will appear in the letter, using the << and >> arrows at the top of the task pane. You can even click the Find a Recipient link to view a particular entry from the database.

3. If you preview an entry and realize it should be excluded, click the Exclude This Recipient button. (If you accidentally click this button, click the Edit Recipient List link to rectify the problem.)

4. If you notice an error in the data for a recipient, you can open the Mail Merge Recipients list by clicking the Edit Recipient List link and make your changes.

5. If you find problems in the letter text, click the Previous button to return to the previous wizard page and make your changes.

6. When you have finished on this page, click the Next link at the bottom of the task pane.

7. If you want to immediately print your documents, click the Print link. The Merge to Printer dialog box opens, as shown in Figure 22-11.

8. Simply click the OK button to print letters for all records you selected in the Mail Merge Recipients dialog box. Or click Current Record and then click OK if you want to click a single letter for the last previewed record. Finally, you can enter a range of recipients and click OK.

9. If you prefer to see the document files so that you can modify them by hand, click the Edit Individual Letters link in the wizard task pane. When the Merge to New Document dialog box opens, click OK.

That's it—you're finished! You created a mail-merge letter. Actually pretty simple, isn't it?

Figure 22-11: The Merge to Printer dialog box.

Working with existing documents directly

You don't have to use the Mail Merge Wizard to create mail-merge projects, although it certainly provides a very convenient way to create such documents. If you frequently create mail-merge documents, however, you may want to bypass the wizard. You can also take existing documents and add mail-merge fields. Perhaps, for example, you have many letters that you've created in the past, and you want to use them in mail-merge campaigns. You can take these old letters and update them with the merge fields. Follow these steps:

1. Open a document—an existing one perhaps, or use one of the mail-merge templates.

2. Open the Mail Merge toolbar by choosing Tools ➪ Letters and Mailings ➪ Show Mail Merge Toolbar.

3. Click the first button, the Main Document Setup button, to see the Main Document Type dialog box (see Figure 22-12).

Figure 22-12: The Main Document Type dialog box.

4. Select a document type and click OK.

5. Click the next button on the toolbar, the Open Data Source button, to open a database file.

6. Type the letter and use the Mail Merge toolbar (explained in Table 22-1) to create your merge project.

Table 22-1: Mail Merge Toolbar Buttons and Their Functions

Button	Name	Function
	Main Document Setup	Sets the document type.
	Open Data Source	Selects the database from which merge fields are taken.
	Mail Merge Recipients	Opens the Mail Merge Recipients dialog box, where you can edit, sort, and select recipients for the mailing.
	Insert Address Block	Opens the Insert Address Block dialog box, in which you can configure how the address block should look, and insert it into the document.
	Insert Greeting Line	Opens the Greeting Line dialog box, in which you can configure how the greeting line should look, and insert it into the document.
	Insert Merge Fields	Opens the Insert Merge Field dialog box so you can insert a field into the document.
Insert Word Field ▾	Insert Word Field	Inserts a Word field into the main document. These are *not* fields defining data to be taken from the data source. Rather, they are the sorts of informational fields you'll learn about in Chapters 23 and 24.
	View Merged Data	Toggles between viewing merge fields and merged data. Click to replace the fields with actual data taken from your database.
	Highlight Merged Data	Highlights all the merge-data fields in your document, to make them easier to see.
	Match Fields	Opens the Match Fields dialog box, so you can match the field name in your database with the field names that the Mail Merge system recognizes.
	Propagate Labels	Loads data into the labels on the screen, so you can preview them.
	First Record	When you have the merged data, rather than the data fields, displayed, this button moves to the first record in a database.

Continued

Table 22-1 *(continued)*

Button	Name	Function
	Previous Record	Goes to the previous record in a database.
1	Go to Record	Goes to a specific record in the database.
	Next Record	Goes to the next record in a database.
	Last Record	Goes to the last record in a database.
	Find Entry	Lets you search for a particular entry in your database.
	Check for Errors	Checks for errors in merged documents.
	Merge to New Document	Displays merged documents on-screen so you can view or edit them.
	Merge to Printer	Merges the documents and sends them to the printer.
	Merge to E-mail	Merges the documents and sends them to your e-mail program.
	Merge to Fax	Merges the documents and sends them to your fax program.
Insert Merge Field ▾	Insert Merge Field	This button probably isn't visible unless you add it. It provides a convenient drop-down menu full of merge fields that can quickly be dropped into your document.

Using an Address Book

Word allows you to use your Outlook address book as your data source. You have to use the Mail Merge task pane to do this. While working your way through the wizard, you should see the option to select an Outlook address book in step 3. (Alternatively, while you are working in a merge document using the toolbar, choose Tools ➪ Letters and Mailings ➪ Mail Merge Wizard and click the Next link twice to get to step 3.)

On step 3 of the wizard, click the Select From Outlook Contacts option button and the information below changes. Click the Choose Contacts Folder link that appears. When the Select Contact List Folder dialog box opens, click the Contacts entry and click OK to open the Outlook address book.

You should see the Mail Merge recipients dialog box, as you saw earlier; but this time the data in the box has been pulled from the Outlook address book you selected.

Creating Envelopes, Mailing Labels, and Lists

In addition to creating form letters, you can use Mail Merge to print envelopes or labels for those letters. You can also print a list of names and addresses using the database that you already have.

Using Mail Merge to print envelopes

Printing envelopes using an already-existing database is similar to creating form letters. The difference is that in this case the envelope is the main document.

Word helps you to create the envelope layout as a main document. To do so, Word needs to know what type of printer you plan to use for the envelopes. Before you begin these steps, select that printer so that Word configures the envelopes correctly. Selecting the correct printer before proceeding is very important. Choose File ➪ Print to open the Print dialog box, select the printer from the Name drop-down list box, and click the Close button.

Word uses the text in the Mailing Address section of the User Information tab of the Options dialog box (Tools ➪ Options) as the default return address on envelopes. Make sure that this information is filled in and correct before you prepare to print your envelopes.

As mentioned previously in the chapter, when you start a merge document, you have to define what type it is. In step 1 of the wizard, select Envelope as the document type and click Next. In step 2, click the Envelope Options link to see the Envelope Options dialog box (see Figure 22-13) or simply click the Next link. Word opens the dialog box automatically when you click the Next link, anyway. Table 22-2 explains the options in this dialog box.

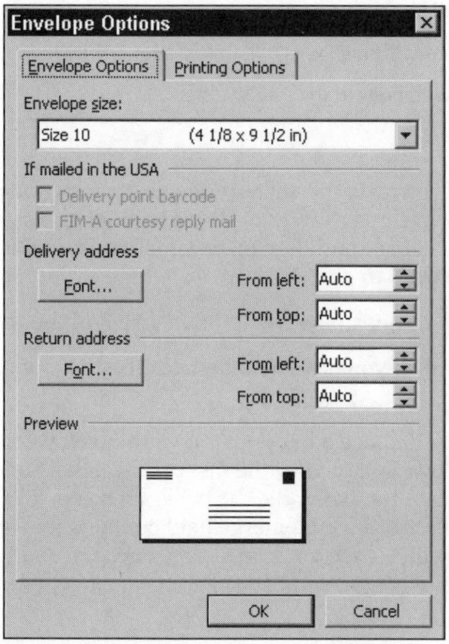

Figure 22-13: The Envelope Options dialog box.

Table 22-2: The Envelope Options Dialog Box

Option	Purpose
Envelope Size	Select the size of the envelope you are going to use.
Delivery Point Barcode	If the envelope is being mailed from the USA, you can choose to include the address barcode—this can speed up delivery.
FIM-A Courtesy Reply Mail	These are bar codes that appear in the top-right of a pre-addressed envelope—companies often provide these to customers to return payments, for instance. (These are *not* prepaid envelopes; the sender still has to stamp the envelopes.)
Delivery Address	Use this area to set the font and position used for the delivery address.
Return Address	Use this area to set the font and position used for the return address.
Printing Options tab	*The options under this tab relate to how the envelopes are printed*
Printer	Shows the name of the selected printer. Make sure you have selected the correct one.
Feed Method	Select the manner in which your envelopes will be fed into the printer.
Face Up/Face Down	Select whether the envelopes are inserted into the printer face up or face down.
Clockwise Rotation	If envelopes are not printed correctly, you may have to experiment with orientation. This check box changes the position of the envelopes shown in the last three Feed Methods shown above.
Feed From	Select the tray or feeder through which the envelopes will be fed.
Reset	Click this to reset the options to the printer defaults.

After you have set the envelope options, Word converts the current document to an envelope format and puts your return address onto the envelope. Now everything is much the same as when you created letters. You have to select a database and then place your <<AddressBlock>> field onto the envelope where you want the address to go.

The following list describes two more envelope options offered to you in step 4 of the wizard:

✦ **Electronic Postage:** This option works only if you have installed an electronic postage system (discussed in Chapter 6).

✦ **Postal Bar Code:** This option enables you to place a bar code on your envelope to speed up delivery. Click the Postal Bar Code link to view the Insert Postal Bar Code dialog box (see Figure 22-14). In order to create the bar code, the program has to know the zip code and street address. This box tells Word which merge field contains this information. It's probably already correct, in which case you can simply click OK and Word installs the bar code on the envelope.

Figure 22-14: The Insert Postal Bar Code dialog box.

If you want to display the FIM-A code (the large black bars in the top-right area of the envelope), click the FIM-A Courtesy Reply Mail check box. Note, however, that this option may not be enabled until you have selected the Merge Field With Zip Code setting. Even if the dialog box already shows the correct field name, you may have to re-select it before the FIM-A check box is enabled.

After everything is set, preview the job, and look closely at the preview to ensure that everything looks good. If you're satisfied with the appearance, print one or two samples to make sure that the envelope stock is feeding properly. Envelopes are often a little tricky to print, so don't assume everything's okay and go for lunch while you print a thousand. Look over the first couple carefully before printing the rest.

Note Ideally your printer's feeder contains blank envelopes. If your envelope feeder holds a stack of envelopes, printing should start soon after you begin printing. If you're using a manual feeder that holds only one envelope, however, you must insert an envelope into the feeder and press a button on the printer to print each envelope. The printer button is labeled Continue on many printers, but it may have a different name on yours. Some printers automatically print the next envelope when they sense an envelope is in the feeder. You may have to check your printer's documentation.

You can also use one of the Word wizards to create and print your envelopes. Choose File ➪ New, click the On My Computer link, and then choose the Envelope Wizard from the Letters & Faxes tab of the Templates dialog box.

Cross-Reference See Chapter 6 to find out more about printing envelopes.

Merging labels

Using Mail Merge to print mailing labels is not much different from using it to print envelopes. In the wizard, select Labels. Then, in step 2 of the wizard, click the Next link to see the Label Options dialog box shown in Figure 22-15.

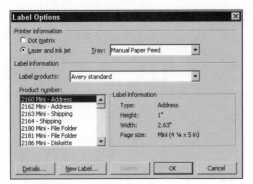

Figure 22-15: The Label Options dialog box.

To create mailing labels, follow these steps

1. In the Printer information box at the top of the Label Options dialog box, choose Dot
   Matrix if you plan to print labels on a dot-matrix printer with pin feed, or choose Laser
   and Ink Jet if you plan to print labels on a laser, ink jet, or similar sheet-feed printer.
   (Is anyone still using a dot matrix?!)

2. If you chose Laser and Ink Jet, select the paper tray in the Tray list box containing the
   sheets of labels (normally the default tray). If you chose Dot Matrix in step 1, this
   choice is not available.

3. In the Label Products list box, select the general type of labels, which in most cases is
   the name of the label manufacturer.

4. In the Product Number list box, select the specific product number of the label that you
   plan to use. (The product number is printed on the label package.) The Label
   Information box then displays the label type and dimensions.

5. To display information about the size and layout of the labels on the sheet, click
   Details. An information dialog box with all of the margin and spacing dimensions for the
   selected label type then appears.

6. Click OK to return to the Label Options dialog box.

7. Click OK again to accept your choice of labels. Word tells you that it has to clear the
   current document. When you click OK, Word sets up the document with the appropriate layout for the selected labels.

To use labels not defined in Word, choose a type of label with similar dimensions. Then, in
step 5 of the preceding list, change the dimensions in the label information dialog box to suit
your needs or design a new label from scratch.

**Cross-
Reference**   For more details about creating custom label designs, see Chapter 6.

Merging catalogs and directories

You can use Mail Merge to create a list based on the data in a database. For example, you can
create a list of the names and addresses in the database that you created when you were
preparing the form letters.

The procedure for creating a list (which Word calls a catalog or directory) is similar to that for printing envelopes or mailing labels. In step 1 of the wizard, select the Directory option and click Next. Now continue through the same steps you used when printing letters or envelopes to create a new main document and to select a database. Then enter the merge fields and preview your document. The final step allows you to save the document in a new file, not print it; although, of course, once it's saved, you can do what you want with it. The document that you produce in this way is a normal Word file. You can edit, save, and print this file in the usual manner. You can see, in Figure 22-16, what a main document for a directory or catalog may look like. Figure 22-17 shows the results of the merging.

Figure 22-16: A typical main document for a catalog.

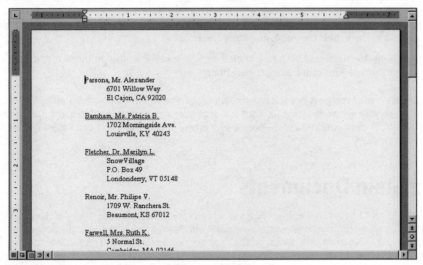

Figure 22-17: A typical list created from a database.

Merging E-mails and Faxes

You can also merge e-mails by using Word, or you can send merged faxes. (You won't see the fax option available to you, however, unless you have installed fax software). The process is similar to creating letters. You begin by selecting E-mail Messages from step 1 of the wizard. Then right at the end, in step 6 of the wizard, you click the Electronic Mail link to complete the process. When you click this link, the Merge to E-mail dialog box opens (see Figure 22-18). This is all pretty simple, really. In most cases, all you have to do is type a Subject Line for the messages and click OK. Word then launches your e-mail program and sends the messages.

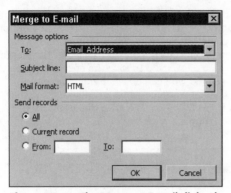

Figure 22-18: The Merge to E-mail dialog box.

The Merge to E-mail dialog box offers these options:

✦ The To field shows which data field in the database includes the recipients' e-mail addresses. It's probably in the Email_Address field, but if you are using a custom database it may be a different field—select the correct one.

✦ The Mail Format field lets you choose whether to send the message as an Attachment (Word sends a plain text e-mail, with the Word document attached to it), as Plain Text (the document is converted to text, and the images thrown out), or HTML (a Web page is sent in the e-mail message, including the images).

✦ The Send Records section lets you choose which records should be included in the merge, as with the other merge operations.

Note   Word's e-mail merge is not suitable for large lists! You will end up with an individual message in your e-mail program for each message you are sending. So if you are mailing out dozens, or even hundreds, of messages, your e-mail program will end up clogged and could even crash.

Editing Main Documents

You can edit and format text and graphics in a main document the same way as you can in any other Word document. However, you cannot edit merge fields in the main document without displaying them as merge codes, as the next section explains. You can delete merge codes, however, and you can apply formats to them. You can also use the Clipboard to copy or move complete fields.

Deleting, inserting, and formatting merge fields

If you have placed a field in the wrong position in a main document or placed the wrong merge field entirely, delete that field and insert the correct merge field in the proper position.

To delete a merge field, follow these steps:

1. Click and drag the insertion point over the entire field, including the chevrons. When the merge code is selected, the characters in that field appear in reverse video (white on dark gray if that option is selected in the View tab of the Options dialog box).

2. With the entire field and the chevrons that enclose it highlighted, press Delete to remove that field completely.

3. To delete all of the merge fields in one line, select them all by dragging the insertion point over them or by triple-clicking in one field. Then press Delete.

Note

You may notice that you can edit the characters within a field name, but even though you can see these changes on the screen, Word ignores them. You cannot change from one merge field to another by editing its name in this way. For more information about replacing fields, see the "Editing merge codes" section that follows. For detailed information on working with field codes, see Chapter 23.

After you delete an incorrect field, you can insert the correct field. Click the Insert Merge Field button in the Mail Merge toolbar, and then choose the correct one from the list of available fields.

When Word merges the database and the main document, those data are displayed in the font and font size of the merge field and are formatted according to the format of the field. The font, font size, and formatting of data in the database do not affect the appearance of text in merged documents. If you want the text that replaces the merge fields to appear in a specific font, font size, or formatting, format that merge field in the main document accordingly.

Editing merge codes

So far, you've seen merged data in main documents indicated by a field name enclosed within chevrons, which is Word's default way of showing merge codes. Note, though, that these merge codes are actually Word field codes, which are widely used throughout the program for many purposes (and explained in detail in Chapter 23). Press Alt+F9 to toggle the viewing of field codes, and you will notice your merge codes changing to field codes. For example, <<Last_Name> would appear as {MERGEFIELD Last_Name }.

You can directly edit a merge field by modifying the underlying field code. Suppose that you incorrectly place the First_Name field where the Last_Name field should be. If you simply change <<First_Name>> to <<Last_Name>>, you break the merge code; it just won't work. Or Word may simply throw away your changes and return the field to the original so that the field remains a First_Name field. However, if you view the underlying field code and change { MERGEFIELD First_Name } to { MERGEFIELD Last_Name }, you have just converted the field. When you press Alt+F9, you'll see the field is still called <<First_Name>>. But if you do a Preview and then return to the non-preview document, Word will have converted the field to <<Last_Name>>.

Figure 22-19 shows field names in a main document displayed as full field codes. Compare this with the way that Mail Merge normally displays fields, as you saw in earlier figures.

{MERGEFIELD LastName }, {MERGEFIELD Title } {MERGEFIELD FirstName } {
MERGEFIELD MiddleName }
        {MERGEFIELD Address1 }
        {MERGEFIELD Address2 }
        {MERGEFIELD City }, {MERGEFIELD State } {MERGEFIELD PostalCode }

Figure 22-19: Field names displayed as full field codes.

When full field codes are displayed, you can (with caution) edit the field names to replace one field with another. To replace a field name, carefully backspace over the characters only, leaving the space after the first curly bracket and before the last bracket untouched. Then type the new name exactly as it appears in the database. However, you may find it easier simply to delete the incorrect field and replace it using the buttons on the Mail Merge toolbar.

Merging Specific Records

The simple situation that you've been working with in this chapter produces one letter, envelope, or label, or item in a catalog list for each record in the database. Often, however, you want to be selective. If your database contains a record for each of your customers but you want to send letters only to those who live in a particular state, what do you do? The answer is simple: use a query.

With a query, you can specify conditions under which a record in the database is included when you merge. A query can be quite simple, such as asking for the records of people living in one state, or it can be more complex, such as asking for all of the Smiths who owe more than $500.

Selecting records for one state

Take a look at this example of how to select records for people living in a particular state. In the main document, open the Mail Merge Recipients dialog box—either click the Mail Merge Recipients button on the Mail Merge toolbar, or click the Edit Recipient List link in step 3 of the wizard. Then click the Edit button to open the Edit Address List dialog box, and click the Filter and Sort button to open the Query Options dialog box.

This dialog box offers two tabs. With the Filter Records tab selected, select the name of the field that you want to use on the first line. In this case, select State. The phrase *Equal to* appears in the Comparison box to the right. In this case, you want to look for the content of the State field to be equal to something, so make no change here.

In the Compare To box, type the state abbreviation: CO, NY, VT, or whatever state you are looking for. At this time, the dialog box looks like the one shown in Figure 22-20. Word automatically prepares for an additional query condition by adding And to the second line, which you can use or ignore. Click OK, and Word closes the Query Options dialog box. It uses this filter to print your merged letters, envelopes, labels, or whatever else you are working on.

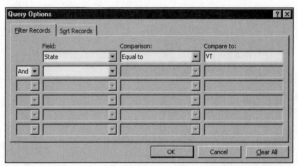

Figure 22-20: A query specified in the Filter Records tab of the Query Options dialog box.

Using other comparison operators

By default, Word offers `Equal to` as the type of comparison between the content of a field and what you place in the Compare To box. If you open the Comparison list box, however, you have a choice of other methods of comparison, as listed in Table 22-3. One of the comparisons, `is blank`, is handy for finding records lacking data in a critical field, such as the zip code field.

Table 22-3: Comparison Types

Comparison	Explanation
Equal to	Contents of the field exactly match the comparison text.
Not equal to	Contents of the field do not match the comparison text.
Less than	Contents of the field are less than the comparison text.
Greater than	Contents of the field are greater than the comparison text.
Less than or equal	Contents of the field are less than or equal to the comparison text.
Greater than or equal	Contents of the field are greater than or equal to the comparison text.
Is blank	The field is empty (the Compare To box is ignored).
Is not blank	The field is not empty (the Compare To box is ignored).
Contains	The field contains the specified text.
Does not contain	The field does not contain the specified text.

Selecting with two rules

Each comparison is called a rule. In the example, the content of the State field is compared with some text using a single rule. However, you can specify multiple rules—as you add a line, a new line opens up below.

Using two rules, you can specify that a record is to be selected only if both rules are satisfied (select And) or if either or both rules are satisfied (select Or). Suppose that you want to select the records of people with VT or CA in the State field. Now, if you merge, you get all records in which the State field contains VT, plus all records in which the State field contains CA.

Note

Be careful how you use the And comparison. If you have two lines, connected with And, but analyzing the same data field, you're asking for two comparisons that cannot be true at the same time. For instance, no State field can be both VT and CA at the same time. If you try this comparison and then try to merge, Word displays a message saying that no data records match your query options.

You don't need to have the same field in both rules. One rule can select records in which the State field is CA, for example, and the other rule can select records in which the FirstName field is George. If the second rule starts with Or, merging gives you the records for all residents of California and for all people with the first name George, regardless of the state in which they live. On the other hand, if the second rule starts with And, merging gives you only those records for people living in California who also have the first name of George.

Selecting with more than two rules

When you define more than two rules in the Query Options dialog box, three possibilities exist:

✦ Each rule is related to the previous one by Or. In this case, a record is included in the merge if one or more of the rules are satisfied.

✦ Each rule is related to the previous one by And. In this case, a record is included in the merge only if all of the rules are satisfied.

✦ Some rules are related to the previous one by Or and others by And. This possibility requires further explanation.

You must understand two principles about how Word selects records when both Or and And occur in rules:

✦ Or and And define the relationship between a rule and the rule that immediately precedes it.

✦ And takes precedence over Or.

To understand these principles, look at the four rules shown in Figure 22-21.

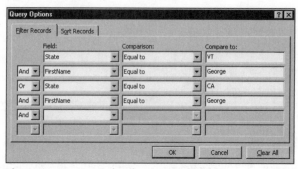

Figure 22-21: Four rules that use And and Or.

Because And rules have precedence, think about them first. The second rule in Figure 22-21 starts with And, so for a record to be used in the merge both the first and the second rules must be satisfied. The fourth rule also starts with And, so both the third and the fourth rules must be satisfied as well. The third rule, however, starts with Or. Therefore, a record is used if the first and second rules are satisfied or if the third and fourth rules are satisfied. A record is also used if both pairs of rules are satisfied. To summarize, this set of rules selects records for people with the first name of George if they live in either California or Vermont.

Adding ranges to rules

With some comparison conditions, you can specify a range of values for which merge uses a record. In this case, you can use one rule as the lower limit of the range and another as the upper limit. For example, to print letters for people with a zip code in the range of 40000 to 49999, use two rules. To ask for records in that range, select the zip code field. The first rule should contain a Greater than or equal comparison of 40000, the lower limit. The second rule, starting with And, should contain a Less than or equal comparison of 49999, the upper limit.

Sometimes, you need to use only one rule to specify a range. For example, suppose that you want to print letters for only those people living in the western states. To do so, ask for records in which the zip code is in the range of 90000 to 99999. Select the appropriate field, and then select Greater Than or equal for the Comparison and 90000 for the Compare To text. No five-character zip code is larger than 99999, so you don't have to be concerned about an upper limit.

Removing rules

After you set rules, those rules apply to all merges until you either cancel them or terminate your Word session. To clear rules without terminating your Word session, click Clear All in the Query Options dialog box and then click OK.

Setting the Record Order

By default, Word prints merge documents in the same order as the records occur in the database. You can change this order, however, and base it on the values in any field. You might want to print records (and envelopes or labels) in order by zip, for example, or you might want to print a catalog in alphabetical order by last names.

To sort records in zip-code order, display the Query Options dialog box as described previously. Then display the Sort Records tab, as shown in Figure 22-22.

Figure 22-22: The Sort Records tab of the Query Options dialog box.

To sort records by zip code, follow these steps:

1. In the Sort By list box, select the field that contains zip codes (or PostalCode).

2. Choose the Ascending or Descending option, according to your preference.

3. Click OK to return to the Merge dialog box.

When you proceed to merge, the form letters are arranged in zip-code order. You are not limited to sorting in one field, however. You might want to sort primarily by order of last names, for example, and if two or more people have the same last name, to sort them by order of first names. If two or more people have the same first and last names, you can sort them by order of middle names. Just select the first sort field in the Sort By box, the second sort field in the first Then By box, and then the third sort field in the second Then By box.

As with comparisons, sort specifications remain in effect until you clear them or terminate your Word session. To clear sort specifications, click Clear All at the bottom of the Query Options dialog box.

Adding Special Word Fields to a Main Document

You've already seen how you place merge fields into a main document. These fields are then replaced with text from the database when you merge the two documents. In addition to merge fields, however, you can also place Word fields in a main document. Word fields are instructions that tell Word to perform an action when the merge occurs.

For example, the main document used earlier in this chapter offered a certain book to people. Suppose that you want to offer that book to most of the people on your list but also want to offer a different book to people living in California. Using a Word field in the main document, Merge can do just that.

Word fields also might be useful when you want to add a personal message to some of the letters that you're sending. For example, you may be preparing a holiday greeting letter to send to your clients. In many cases, you might want to end the letter with a traditional greeting, but in some, you might want to replace that greeting with a more personal message.

Specifying text to appear in merged documents

This example creates merged letters that contain the book name *Tales from America's Great Authors* for those records in which the State field is not CA and that prints the book name *Tales from California's Great Authors* for those records in which the State field is CA.

Here's how you would create such a field:

1. Place the insertion point where you want to insert this *variable* field.

2. Click the Insert Word Field button on the Mail Merge toolbar to display a list of available Word fields.

3. Choose If...Then...Else... to display the Insert Word Field: IF dialog box, in which you specify the text to include when the State field is CA and the alternate text to include when the State field is not.

4. In the Field Name list box, select the field to use as the basis for this decision. In this case, you want to base the decision on the content of the State field, so select that field.

5. In the Comparison list box, select the basis for the decision. In this case, select Equal To.

6. In the Compare To text box, type the comparison text. In this case, type **CA.**

7. Place the insertion point in the Insert This Text box, and then type what should appear in the letter if the comparison is satisfied. In this case, type **Tales from California's Great Authors.**

8. Place the insertion point in the Otherwise Insert This Text box, and then type what should appear in the letter if the comparison is not satisfied. In this case, type **Tales from America's Great Authors**, for instance. The completed dialog box should look similar to the one shown in Figure 22-23.

9. Click OK to return to the main document.

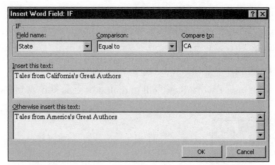

Figure 22-23: The completed Insert Word Field: IF dialog box.

When you return to the main document, all that you see of the selected Word field is the text that appears if the condition is satisfied. Select the text in the merge field and then format it as you would any other text (or in italics in this case). To see the field in more detail, press Alt+F9 to reveal the field codes. After you press this key combination, all of the field codes in the main document are shown, as explained earlier in this chapter. The Word field, as shown in Figure 22-24, displays the instruction in detail. To return to the normal display in which field codes are not shown, press Alt+F9 again.

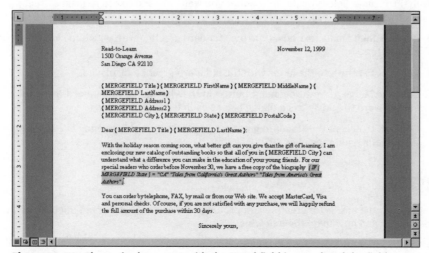

Figure 22-24: The main document with the Word field inserted and the field codes revealed.

To verify that the Word field acts as you intend, display some form letters on your screen by previewing the documents.

Using Fill-in fields in merged documents

Suppose that you've written a holiday greeting letter as a main document. You're content to end most letters with a traditional phrase, such as "Wishing you and your staff a happy holiday and a prosperous New Year." For some clients, however, you want to replace that message with a more personal greeting. You can use the Fill-in Word field for this purpose as follows:

1. At the end of your letter, go to a new paragraph.

2. Click the Insert Word Field button in the Mail Merge toolbar.

3. Choose Fill-in to display the Insert Word Field: Fill-in dialog box, as shown in Figure 22-25.

Figure 22-25: The Insert Word Field: Fill-in dialog box.

4. In the Prompt box, type the words that you want Word to use to request a greeting, such as **Type greeting here.**

5. In the Default Fill-in Text box, type the standard greeting with which to close most of your letters.

6. Click OK to return to the letter with the standard greeting displayed.

7. Click the Merge to New Document button in the Mail Merge task pane. During the merge, Word then displays a dialog box as each letter is merged.

8. Click OK to accept the standard greeting. To insert a special greeting in a letter, type that greeting and then click OK.

Summary

You now know the basics for creating and printing several types of merged documents with Word. You learned how to do the following:

✦ Print form letters that are personalized for each recipient.

✦ Print envelopes using the letters' files of names and addresses.

✦ Use Word's merge feature to print mailing labels for larger packages.

✦ Print a list of your addresses by creating a catalog.

✦ Print only selected merge documents.

✦ Change the order of printing for merge documents.

✦ Vary the text of a letter based on a field value.

✦   ✦   ✦

Creating Dynamic Documents Using Field Codes

In This Chapter

Displaying field codes

Understanding fields

Dissecting field codes

Using switches to format field results

Protecting fields

Working with Smart Tags

In earlier chapters, you worked with fields: when you inserted names and addresses in form letters and mailing labels, when you created cross-references, tables of contents, and indexes, when you inserted linked and embedded objects, and so on. In most of those cases, however, you really didn't need to understand much about the fields you were creating—or even that you *were* creating fields—because Word did the work for you.

Fields, however, provide a very powerful advanced tool that you can use for a variety of other purposes, such as creating fill-in forms. This chapter looks at fields in more detail so that you have a good background on the subject. A good solid foundation in fields is important as you move on to creating forms that actively request information from the reader, as discussed in Chapter 24.

What Are Field Codes?

Field codes are flexible and powerful behind-the-scenes tools that help you automate many of the repetitive chores associated with word processing. At its simplest, a field code is a set of instructions that tells Word what information to insert in the document and how that information should look. A field code may tell Word to insert the date in the header or the author's name in the footer. It may also tell Word to do something complex, such as "take whatever it was that you put in over here, copy it to over there, add it together with this other stuff, and then place the result in this table with bold and italic formatting."

The most comforting thing about field codes is that they are extremely logical, consistent, and not that difficult to master. You don't need to remember the names of every field code, either. Word gives you the tools to select and then modify them to obtain just the result that you want.

Working with Field Codes

You seldom see field codes themselves on the screen. Instead, they lurk in the background, and what you do see is the result of the field code's actions. If, for example, you insert an author's name in a document (Insert ➪ Field, select the Document Information category, select Author), Word inserts the name of the document's author into the document at that point.

You'll see the author name, but what Word actually sees is this field: { AUTHOR * MERGEFORMAT }, which loosely translates as "Go to the User Information Tab in the Options menu, pull out the information stored in the Name field, plop it in here, and keep the same character format as the rest of the paragraph." (The * MERGEFORMAT part of the field code is discussed later in this chapter.) You can see the field code in two forms in Figure 23-1: the first is what readers see in the document, the second is the code itself.

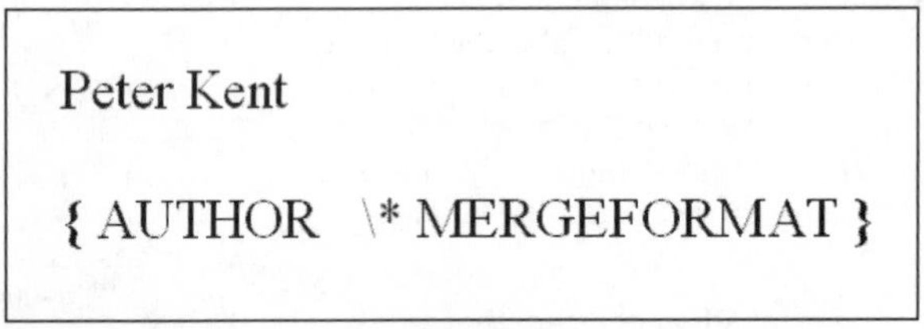

Peter Kent

{ AUTHOR   * MERGEFORMAT }

Figure 23-1: The result of the field code, *Peter Kent*, followed by the actual AUTHOR field code.

Finding fields

As you work on a document, you normally see the results of the field codes that you've inserted instead of the actual codes themselves. Because of this, these field results may be difficult to distinguish from normal text, so Word has added a feature called *shading* that helps you to locate such results. When this feature is turned on, the information that represents the results of a field code is placed over a gray background shading.

To change the shading setting, choose Options from the Tools menu and then click the View tab. The Field Shading drop-down list box provides three different options:

✦ **Never:** Turns off the shading feature altogether.

✦ **Always:** Shades all field codes all the time.

✦ **When Selected:** Shades field codes or their results whenever the cursor is placed on them.

Note   Field shading lets you know where the fields are located in a document. This shading doesn't show in Print Preview, however, and it doesn't print with the document.

As you work on your document, you may want to skip from one field to the next to verify that you've inserted the ones that you want. You can use shortcut key combinations to move to the next or the previous field code. Press F11 to move to the next field code, or press Shift+F11 to move to the previous field.

The Word Select Browse Object button on the vertical scroll bar provides another way to move quickly from field to field in your document. Click the button, and choose Browse by Field from the palette (see Figure 23-2). Then just click the navigation buttons by the Select Browse Object button to move to the previous or the next field.

Figure 23-2: Use the Select Browse Object button to move among fields.

Tip

To experiment with some of these simple commands, insert a Date and Time code into a document so that you can play with it. Choose Insert ➪ Date and Time, ensure that Update Automatically is selected (it should be by default), and press Enter.

Displaying field codes

The shading feature is handy if you just want to see where the field codes are located in a document, but it doesn't show you the field code itself. To see the code in a particular field, click inside the field and press Shift+F9, or right-click inside and select Toggle Field Codes from the pop-up menu.

To toggle *all* the field codes in a document at once, press Alt+F9. The insertion point need not be in any field to use Alt+F9.

Another option allows you to view all of the field codes as the default setting. Select Options from the Tools menu, click the View tab, and then check the Field Codes check box in the Show area. This changes the default setting for all of your documents, not just for the current document.

Caution

Be aware that the field codes and their results are of differing lengths, so formatting and page length may not display correctly. Your best bet is to leave this option off and use Shift+F9, Alt+F9, or the shortcut menu to toggle between viewing field codes and their results.

Updating fields

After modifying information in a field, you need to update the field results. For instance, if you change the Author name in the document properties, Word will not necessarily update the field automatically. Place the cursor in the field and press F9 to update it and show the new author's name (or right-click in the field and select Update Field). To update all of the fields in the document at once, choose Edit ➪ Select All (or press Ctrl+A) and then press F9.

There are cases in which Word will automatically update your fields. You can tell Word to automatically update all the fields in the document before it prints the document. Choose Tools ➪ Options, click the Print tab, and check the Update Fields check box.

Tip

Don't rely on this feature to ensure that your field codes are properly printed. The problem is that when you update field codes, they can change document pagination. For example, if you update a table of contents—which is created using a field code—it may push down onto the next page if it adds enough entries. And cross-references can expand, pushing a paragraph onto the next page. (Plus you may sometimes run into a problem in which a cross-reference pulls in literally pages of information accidentally, as is described in Chapter 11.) Unless you are working with only a few very simple fields, such as date and author, you should always update fields manually before printing and then check them. You should also check for fields in headers and footers, footnotes and endnotes, and comments.

Also note that it is possible to print the field codes in your document instead of their results—something you rarely want to do. In the Print dialog box, click Options, click the Field Codes check box, and click OK.

Unlinking fields

Sometimes you may want to disassociate the current field results from the source information so that they *cannot* be updated. Perhaps you've finalized a project or a report, or perhaps you're sending something off to the printer, and you want to fix a date in place, for instance, so it can't change.

Word provides the option of *unlinking* your fields—it converts the field to raw text. For instance, if you convert the { DATE \@ "M/d/yyyy" } field, Word removes the field and instead places the date shown by the field in the document in plain text. Note that we didn't say it places the *current* date. It doesn't update the field before unlinking, so if you haven't updated the field in three days you get the date from three days ago, not today's date.

To unlink a field, simply select the field, or place the cursor inside it, and press Ctrl+Shift+F9. Unlink with caution, however, because the unlink is permanent and the only way to restore the link is to reinsert the field.

Inserting Field Codes

You already know several ways to enter fields into your document—create a table of contents, a cross-reference, linked object, and so on. This section discusses ways to insert field codes directly rather than using Word's various feature tools: selecting fields from the Field dialog box, and adding them manually from the keyboard.

Tip Three fields are used so often that Word provides shortcut-key combinations to do the job: To insert the date, press Alt+Shift+D; to insert the time, press Alt+Shift+T; to insert the page number, press Alt+Shift+P.

Using the Field dialog box

Inserting a field using the Field dialog box (opened with Insert ➪ Field) is the easiest and most straightforward way to place a field code directly into a document. This method also provides quick access to all of Word's more than 70 field types. To make things even easier, the field types are grouped into categories such as Date and Time, Index and Tables, and User Information.

To insert a field containing the name of the current file, for instance, follow these steps:

1. Place the cursor where you want to enter the field.

2. Choose Insert ➪ Field. The Field dialog box opens (see Figure 23-3).

3. Leave the Preserve Formatting During Updates check box selected; this is the default, and tells Word to include the MERGEFORMAT switch with the field code. (MERGEFORMAT and other switches are discussed in more detail later in this chapter.)

4. Select Document Information in the Categories list. You can also select (All), but that option shows all of the field codes in the Field Names list, which makes finding a specific field harder.

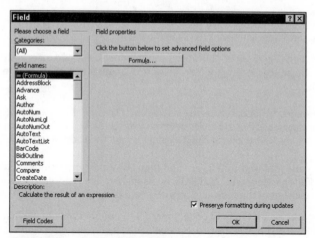

Figure 23-3: The Field dialog box.

5. Select FileName from the Field Names list. The Field Properties area of the dialog box changes to show choices related to the FileName field.

6. To tell Word how to display the text of the file name—all uppercase or all lowercase, for example—select an option from the Format list box. (Formatting and switches are discussed in more detail later in this chapter.)

7. To include the path name with the file name—the names of the folder and subfolders in which the file is stored—check the Add Path to Filename check box.

8. Click OK.

The field that you entered in the previous exercise displays the file name, and perhaps the path if you chose that option. If you haven't saved this file yet, you'll see *Documentx*. To see the actual code, place the cursor in the field and then press Shift+F9 to toggle on the code, which looks something like { FILENAME * FirstCap \p * MERGEFORMAT }. Each part of this field is discussed later in this chapter. For now, though, note that there are always spaces just inside the bracket characters separating them from the field code, and that the code begins with a command—in this case FILENAME—and is followed by "switches," information that modifies the command in some way.

Inserting field codes directly

If you're an advanced user and know just what you want or you're using a code that you've customized in some manner, you may want to type the codes directly from the keyboard instead of using the Field dialog box. Quite frankly, this is something that fewer than one Word user in a hundred will ever do; but if you happen to be that one in a hundred who uses a lot of field codes, you can save substantial time with this method.

Manually entering field codes is not an exercise for the faint-of-heart. With this method, no friendly dialog boxes guide your fingers to the successful completion of the task, and you can make some simple—yet highly frustrating—errors.

To add a field manually, follow these steps:

1. Position the cursor where you want to place the field.

2. Press Ctrl+F9, which places a set of braces { } in the document and inserts the cursor between them. These braces are special characters that instruct Word where a field begins and ends.

Note   Field codes are enclosed by special characters that look a lot like braces { }. Unfortunately, these characters are *not* braces, and if you try to insert them by merely typing from the keyboard in the usual manner (using the keys to the right of the letter P), your field codes won't work.

3. Enter the field name followed by a space and then any field instructions or switches that you want. For example, type **AUTHOR** by itself. (See the section "Looking at Fields" for a discussion of the various parts of a field code.)

4. With the cursor still inside the field code, press F9 to update the field. (When Word inserts field codes for you, it does this automatically; when you type codes, the code does not work, in most—although not all—cases until you manually update it.)

It's easy to make two errors when inserting fields from the keyboard:

✦ If you put in the first character of the field code name and receive only beeps, or if the characters you type simply don't appear, you probably turned on Overtype mode. To fix this problem, press the Insert key on the keyboard (the letters OVR should disappear from Word's status bar).

✦ If your field code disappears after you have toggled field codes off (Shift+F9 or Alt+F9), you probably forgot to update the field. To solve this problem, press Alt+F9 to toggle all of the fields in the document and to show the field codes. Next, position the cursor anywhere within the offending field and press F9 to update it. You can then toggle the field codes off again using Alt+F9 and you'll see the field results.

If you see Error! Bookmark not defined in your document, the field is "broken"; it won't work. You have mistyped something, or perhaps information elsewhere that the field refers to is not available

Looking at Fields

Different fields act in different ways in Word. Some fields insert information. Some instruct Word to take some kind of action. Some just provide location markers. This section discusses each kind of field:

✦ Fields that insert information are called *result* fields. Examples include the { DATE } field, most of the fields used in a mail merge, the { FILLIN } field, the { AUTHOR } field, and any other field that directs Word to retrieve some information and to put it in the document.

✦ Fields that do something to the document but don't insert text are called *action* fields. One example is the { HYPERLINK } field. Clicking { HYPERLINK } in a Word document jumps the user to another location on the hard drive, local area network, Internet, or within the document itself, such as a bookmark or a slide. This function is useful in documentation and instructional works.

✦ Location markers are called *marker* fields. These fields don't take any action, and they don't insert any text. They do, however, act as signposts and guides. Examples include the fields marking table of contents entries { TC } and index entries { XE }.

Cross-Reference See Chapter 11 to find out more about bookmark fields; see Chapter 12 for more on table of contents and index fields.

Taking a field apart

Fields are divided into three parts: field *characters*, field *type*, and field *instructions*. The following field inserts the current time into the document in the format 12:34 AM:

```
{ TIME \@ "h:mm AM/PM" }
```

The two characters that look like braces (but aren't) are field characters. TIME is the field type, and \@ "h:mm AM/PM" is the field instruction.

Field types

The field type defines what the field is supposed to do—it's the "command." It immediately follows the space after the first field character ({).

Note that field types aren't case-sensitive. This means that { fillin } and { FILLIN } both work.

Field instructions

Field instructions provide a great deal of flexibility to the field. They define and refine the actions to be performed, and you can modify them to do some pretty amazing stuff. If your word-processing demands are rather simple and you choose most of your field codes directly from a menu, you probably know enough about the anatomy of a field code already to skip to the "Changing the Appearance of Field Results" section of this chapter. If you have a burning desire to master field codes, however, continue on with the next section.

Dissecting field instructions

If you really want to get into the nitty-gritty of field codes, you need to delve into the world of field instructions. Like field codes, field instructions can have several different parts.

The possible parts of a field instruction include:

✦ Arguments

✦ Bookmarks

✦ Expressions

✦ Identifiers

✦ Text

✦ Switches

Arguments

An argument is information that is placed in a field instruction to help a field decide what to do. For example, the field { AUTHOR } by itself would insert the name of the author as shown in the document's summary field. If, however, you include the argument *Fred Farkle* in the field—changing the field to { AUTHOR "Fred Farkle" }—the code first changes the name of the author in the document summary to Fred Farkle and then inserts that text into the document.

Text arguments that include spaces usually must be enclosed in quotation marks. In other words, `Fred Farkle`, if used as an argument in the previous example, doesn't work, but `"Fred Farkle"` does. But that doesn't matter to you unless you are typing field codes directly—if you use the Fields dialog box, Word should enter the quotation marks when needed.

You can also use arguments to provide directions to users of a document. For example, using the Field code `FILLIN` along with the argument `"Please enter the customer's name here"`—`{ FILLIN "Please enter the customer's name" }` opens a dialog box that prompts the user for the customer's name (see Figure 23-4).

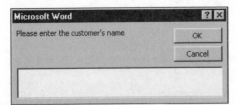

Figure 23-4: { FILLIN "Please enter the customer's name" } opens this dialog box.

Note When you first create the `FILLIN` field and update the field by pressing F9, a dialog box prompting for information appears. But how do you get this dialog box to appear automatically when you open a fill-in form document? We cover that subject in Chapter 24.

Bookmarks

The second part of a field instruction is called a bookmark. At first glance, this description may be confusing because bookmarks are also used in the text of a document. Suppose, however, that you have a chart, table, or several paragraphs of text that you want to refer to several times. Using a field code with a bookmark inserts that text or graphic represented by the bookmark anywhere in the text.

To set and use a bookmark in a field, follow these steps:

1. Type some text and then select it, or select some text that you have already written.

2. Create a bookmark by pressing Ctrl+Shift+F5, and then give that bookmark a name. The name *George*, for example, will do nicely.

3. Move to another place in your document, and then choose Insert ➪ Field to open the Field dialog box.

4. Choose Links and References in the Categories box, and then choose Ref in the Field Names list. The Field Properties and Field Options areas change (see Figure 23-5). You'll see a list of all the bookmarks in the current document.

5. Select the bookmark that you created in step 2, choose any other options you need, and click OK to insert the field.

6. If field codes are being displayed (press Alt+F9 if they are not), you will see { REF George * MERGEFORMAT } in the document (* MERGEFORMAT is included if you selected Preserve Formatting During Update).

7. Place the insertion point in the field code and press Shift+F9 to toggle to the field results. The text you named *George* now appears.

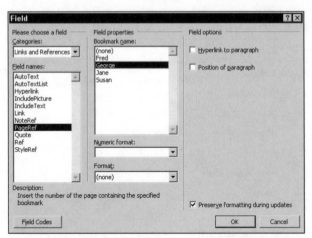

Figure 23-5: Field dialog box set up to insert a cross-reference to the bookmark called George.

This is a pretty simple field. Instead of selecting the bookmark from the Options dialog box, you could simply press Ctrl+F9 and type REF George * MERGEFORMAT directly into the field.

Inserting stuff that is already in the document may seem to be unnecessary. After all, why not just copy and paste? Consider the case when the bookmark represents a chart depicting a corporation's share of the market by region, however. If this chart is inserted in several places in the document by pasting from one original chart, updating every copy of it can be quite a nuisance. It's much easier to update the chart once and then press F9 to update all of the other instances of it throughout the document.

Expressions

If you're familiar with a spreadsheet, you should feel right at home dealing with expressions. You can include expressions (or formulas) right in a field instruction. For example, insert { =24-10 } in a field, and you see the display 14.

This is far from exciting, certainly, but couple this feature with some other information that you already know and you can make numbers into bookmarks and then add, subtract, multiply, divide, raise to powers, average, and compare them. Consider the use of the IF field in the following example (be sure to put spaces around the > and < operators):

```
{ IF midwest > northeast, "Great job midwest region!" < "Let's show a
better effort next quarter!" }
```

Translated, this field code says "If the value of the *midwest* bookmark is greater than that of the *northeast* bookmark, return the result 'Great job midwest region!' If, however, the value of the *midwest* bookmark is less than that of the *northeast* bookmark, return the result 'Let's show a better effort next quarter!'"

Expressions can include one or more of the operators listed in Table 23-1.

Table 23-1: Operators Used in Expressions

Operator	Description
+	Addition
-	Subtraction
*	Multiplication
/	Division
%	Percent
^	Powers and roots
=	Equal to
<	Less than
<=	Less than or equal to
>	Greater than
>=	Greater than or equal to
<>	Not equal to

If the results referred to by the expression are found in a Word table, you can use many mathematical formulas. Word recognizes the cell-naming conventions of most spreadsheets, and it applies these conventions to tables.

When working with tables, rows are numbered and columns are lettered. Therefore, the cell in the second column and the third row has the unique name of B3. Ranges of cells are indicated by naming the first cell, inserting a colon, and then naming the last cell. Thus, you would name the block of cells between the very first cell in the upper-left corner and the cell in the eighth row and the eighth column as A1:H8.

Cell naming can be a little confusing, but if you learn the proper methods, you can use any of the Word functions in formulas. Only a few functions accept cell references as arguments, however. Table 23-2 lists those functions that you can use with cell references.

Table 23-2: Functions and Their Descriptions

Function	Description
SUM (B2:C3)	Adds the contents of all cells between B2 and C3.
PRODUCT (B2:C3)	Multiplies the contents of all cells between B2 and C3.
MAX (B2:C3)	Shows the largest value in the cells between B2 and C3.
MIN (B2:C3)	Shows the smallest value in the cells between B2 and C3.
AVERAGE (B2:C3)	Shows the average of the values in the cells between B2 and C3.
COUNT (B2:C3)	Shows how many cells are in the range between B2 and C3.

Tip   Word is not a full-blown spreadsheet. If your needs are extensive, why not use a real spreadsheet in Excel to do the work? You can then embed or link an Excel object in your document, as is explained in Chapter 20.

The mathematically inclined can easily use the information in Table 23-2 to put together the formula for a standard deviation or whatever else you might need to calculate meaningful field results.

Identifiers

Identifiers distinguish between different parts of a document or name a series of items, such as figures or tables, to number sequentially. Perhaps the best example of an identifier is the sequence (SEQ) field. If you're writing a book about college football, you may want to start each game description with a title like "Game Plays from Game { SEQ Game }." Word keeps track of the number of times that the { SEQ Game } field is in the document. Therefore, when you assemble the book, the first game description reads "Game Plays from Game 1," the second reads "Game Plays from Game 2," and so on.

If you're keeping track of Charts, the SEQ field can be { SEQ Chart }. If tables are the object, the SEQ field can be { SEQ Table }. If you are tracking the Golden Oldies of the '60s, you can construct the SEQ field as { SEQ Oldies } or some such identifier. Thus you can have as many sequential numbering lists as you want, each identified by a different list name: Chart, Table, Oldies, Game, and so on.

An identifier may contain as many as 40 characters, including letters, numbers, and the underline character, but it may not include spaces.

Tip   The Insert ⇨ Caption command provides another way to construct sequence identifiers. You can select New Label to use labels such as Oldies or Yogurt.

Text

Text is just what you would expect: words that you want to appear in the document or on the screen, such as a prompt, a comment, or a document name. The ASK and FILLIN fields are good examples of asking for text to be used in a field. If you're constructing an order form and want to find out who sold the product, you can include the { ASK salesperson "Who received this order?" } field, bookmark, and text field instruction combination to get a text response. The text response is then assigned to the salesperson bookmark and is inserted wherever that bookmark appears in the document. We look at fill-in forms in detail in Chapter 24.

Switches

Switches come in two broad categories: general and field specific:

✦ **General switches:** Optional instructions that work on most fields and either change the way that field results look or lock fields to prevent change

✦ **Field-specific switches:** Also optional, but vary depending on the type of field that you insert

All Word field-code switches start with a backslash, and the switches appear after all of the other instructions. You can add more than one switch to a field code. An example of a switch in use is { ASK salesperson "Who received this order?" * Caps }, in which * is the formatting switch and Caps instructs Word to capitalize the first letter of every word in the result.

The four general switches (described in Table 23-3), can be used with most fields, with the exception of these:

AUTONUM	GOTOBUTTON
AUTONUMLGL	LISTNUM
AUTONUMOUT	MACROBUTTON
EMBED	RD (Referenced Document)
EQ (Equation)	TA (Table of Authorities)
FORMTEXT	TC (Table of Contents Entry)
FORMCHECKBOX	XE (Index Entry)
FORMDROPDOWN	

Table 23-3: General Switches and Their Uses

Switch	Name	Usage
*	Format	Use this switch to specify the character and number format of the field result or to specify Arabic or roman numerals. You can also use this switch to prevent changes to the existing format of the field results.
\#	Numeric Picture	Use this switch to specify how numbers should appear. With this switch, you can specify the number of decimal places, whether to use commas, and any leading character such as $. You can also change numbers to their text equivalents.
\@	Date-Time Picture	Use this general switch to format date and time field results. You can also use this switch to indicate the form of date or time to be reported, such as 10/2/98 or Thursday, 1:42 p.m.
\!	Lock Result	Use this switch to prevent updating the results of BOOKMARK, INCLUDETEXT, and REF fields.

You can format field-specific switches in the Field dialog box; when you select the type of field you want to insert, the dialog box changes to display the options available. In fact, the best way to learn how to use fields is to play with the Fields dialog box—select different fields and options and see what the field looks like once you've inserted it.

Changing the Appearance of Field Results

Except for the lock result switch (\!), each of the general switches discussed in the previous section (*, \#, and \@) has a host of options that instruct Word exactly how you want the results to look.

You may, for example, have the identical field in several places. In one location, you may want the results to be bold, underlined, and in a format that looks like *1,560*. Elsewhere, you may want the sum to be spelled out with initial caps, such as *One Thousand Five Hundred Sixty*.

You can accomplish basic character formatting (bold, italic, underline, font, and so on) in two ways:

✦ You can simply select the field code result and then apply the formatting that you want.

✦ You can include a switch within the field.

Fixing the field in this manner ensures that the formatting won't change as fields are updated—in fact, it ensures that when you *do* update, the formatting will revert to the defined format, even if you have modified the formatting in the paragraph in which the field appears.

Using the format field switch (*)

The format field switch has three categories of format names: character formatting, case conversion, and number conversion.

Character formatting

Some types of fields adopt the same format as the source of the results. Two character formatting options offer a way to control the result in an independent field:

✦ The first character formatting switch preserves the format you applied to the field when you update the field.

✦ The second character formatting switch specifies the format of all of the characters in the result by doctoring the first character of the field name.

The following sections describe these two very useful switches.

* MERGEFORMAT

Word automatically includes the * MERGEFORMAT switch if the Preserve Formatting During Updates option is checked in the Field dialog box. Use this option when you want to format a field result and keep it the same even with new field results. However, the way this works is a little more complex than one might imagine.

Let's say that you used the REF field to insert text from a bookmark (we'll call the bookmark *freddie*), and then underlined one word in the resulting text: **The flock of fowl Fred found <u>finally</u> finished flapping**.

Now say that the bookmark is updated, with an additional word inserted: **The frightful flock of fowl Fred found finally finished fishing**.

When the field is updated, the MERGEFORMAT switch ensures that Word tries to format the resulting text in the same way. As the seventh word was originally underlined, the seventh word in the updated field will be underlined. Now the results say: **The frightful flock of fowl Fred <u>found</u> finally finished flapping**.

* Charformat

The * Charformat option takes its instructions from the appearance of the first character in the field type (the first character after the opening bracket).

Referring back to the freddie bookmark used previously, if you change the REF field code to { ʀEF freddie * Charformat }, in which the *R* in REF has been formatted to be bold, underlined, and a small cap, the freddie bookmark is inserted into your text as <u>THE FLOCK OF FOWL FRED FOUND FINALLY FINISHED FLAPPING</u>.

Note When using Charformat, you need to understand that it's an all-or-nothing deal. In other words, all of your field results take on the formatting of the first letter of the field type—no matter how long the result is.

Of course, you don't have to use either of these switches. If you don't, the field takes on the formatting of the paragraph into which it's placed.

Case conversion

You can use the text-formatting switch (*) to display the first letter or all letters in the field results as uppercase or lowercase.

* Caps

The Caps option changes the first letter of every word in the field results to uppercase.

* FirstCap

The First Cap option changes only the first letter of the first word in the field results to uppercase.

* Lower

The Lower option changes all of the letters in the field results to lowercase.

* Upper

The Upper option changes all of the letters in the field results to uppercase.

Number conversion

You can also use the text formatting switch * to change the way that numbers are displayed in the field results. Use the following options to see the described results. In the switches that convert numbers to their text equivalents, you can also add a second switch to control the capitalization (as described previously).

* alphabetic

The alphabetic option instructs Word to convert numbers to their letter equivalents. For example, 1 becomes *a*, 2 becomes *b*, 3 becomes *c*, and so on. Type the option as * ALPHABETIC to display the field results in uppercase letter (A, B, C, and so on).

* Arabic

The Arabic option instructs Word to convert the field results to Arabic cardinal numbers.

* CardText

The CardText option instructs Word to convert the field results to cardinal text numbers, such as *one hundred fifty-six*. Lowercase is the default, but you can add another switch (* Caps) to change the capitalization to show *One Hundred Fifty-Six*.

* DollarText

The DollarText option instructs Word to convert the field results to cardinal text numbers, but it also includes the wording *and 00/100 dollars* (for example, one hundred three and 59/100 dollars). Adding the switch * Upper results in ONE HUNDRED THREE AND 59/100.

* Hex

The Hex option instructs Word to convert the field results to hexadecimal numbers, such as A, B, and C to represent 10, 11, and 12. For example, the number 715 displays as 2CB in hexa-decimal format.

* Ordinal

The Ordinal option instructs Word to convert the field results to ordinal numbers, such as 1st, 2nd, and 3rd.

* OrdText

The OrdText option instructs Word to convert the field results to ordinal text numbers, such as first, second, and third. You can add another switch to change the capitalization.

* roman

The roman option instructs Word to convert the field results to roman numerals, such as i, ii, and iii. Type the option as * ROMAN to get I, II, and III.

Using the number picture field switch (\#)

The *number* picture field switch is used to define how you want numeric results to be printed or displayed in field results. If, for example, you want the results to be listed in dollars and cents, "draw" a picture that looks like *$#,###,###.00* and then place it in a field code by using the number switch. The switch with the picture looks like this:

    \# $#,###,###.00.

The number switch is almost always used in expression fields, such as { =bookmarka*bookmarkb \# $#,###,##0.00. } or { =22/7 \# #.####### }.

The number switch involves three types of picture items, which are called *placeholders* (0, #, and x), and several instructions. Use them to build a picture that represents numbers just the way that you want them to look. If the field results are not numeric, however, this switch is ignored.

0 (zero) placeholder

A zero in a numeric picture indicates that you want some kind of digit to appear in that place—no matter what. If some digit is in the place occupied by a zero placeholder, it is displayed; if some digit is not, a zero is displayed. For example, if you're formatting dollars and cents and you want every entry to include cent values, you would end the numeric picture with .00.

If a field result ends as a number with no decimals, two zeros are added. For example, 4 is displayed as 4.00 and 4.1 as 4.10. In addition, if a result is longer than the number of digits specified by the instruction, it will be rounded off to conform to the number picture. For example, { =4.666+3.21 \# #.00 }—which is 7.876—shows the result 7.88. Note, by the way, that if you use zeros throughout the picture, without # signs (which we'll look at in a moment), you'll get zeros to the left of your number. For instance, { =4.666+3.21 \# 0,000,000.00 } results in 0,000,007.88.

(number sign) placeholder

A number sign in the numeric picture indicates that you want a digit to appear here only if the field result includes one. If a digit is not included in the result, a space is inserted in its place.

For example, { =4.666+3.21 \# #,###,###.## } still displays the result 7.88; spaces are substituted for the first six number signs. Like the 0 placeholder, extra digits are rounded off to conform to the number picture.

x (truncate) placeholder

When the truncate placeholder is on the left of the decimal character, it drops any digits to its left. When the truncate placeholder is on the right of the decimal, it rounds the value to that place and drops any subsequent digits.

For example, { =966.466 \# x.x } displays 6.5. The 9 and the 6 are truncated (dropped) from the front of the number. The 4 is rounded up to a 5, and the two 6s are dropped from the end.

decimal point symbol (period or comma)

The character used as a decimal point is set in the Regional Settings Properties dialog box in the Windows Control Panel (known as the Regional and Language Options box in Windows XP). In the United States, this character is a period, but a comma is used in many other countries.

Inserting the decimal point character in the number picture inserts it in the field result. For example, { =5x3 \# ###.00 } displays 15.00.

digit grouping symbol (comma or period)

The digit grouping symbol separates groups of three digits in large numbers and, like the decimal point, varies between a comma and a period depending on where you live. Select the proper option in the Regional Settings Properties/Regional and Language Options dialog box of the Windows Control Panel.

Inserting the digit grouping symbol in the number picture inserts it in the field result. For example, { =GrossSales \# $#,###,### } may display $5,426,705.

– (minus sign)

This instruction adds a minus sign if the result is a negative number. If the field result is a positive number, a space is inserted instead. For example, { = 6-9 \# -## } displays the result –3 and { =9-6 \# ## } displays 3.

+ (plus sign)

This instruction is a little more demanding than the simple minus sign. It adds a plus sign if the result is positive, a minus sign if the result is negative, and a space if the result is zero. For example, { = 6-9 \# +## } displays the result –3, { = 6+9 \# +## } displays the result +15, and { = 6-6 \# +## } displays a space (it will not display 0).

; (semicolon)

The semicolon separates number-formatting sections. If you want one format to apply to positive numbers, another to negative numbers, and a third to zero sum results, use the semicolon to separate the arguments and then enclose all of them in quotation marks. Note that the third argument, formatting zero sum results, is optional. For example, the field { =taxesdue \# "$#,##0.00;-$#,##0.00; 'None, congratulations!'" } returns a normally formatted number if the value of the bookmark *taxesdue* is a positive number. It returns a bold and italic number with a leading minus sign if the value is negative, and it returns the words *None, congratulations!* if the value of taxes due is zero.

' (single quotation marks) literal text

Single quotation marks are used to include text in a field result. The text to be included must be surrounded by single quotation marks.

A field switch that contains any spaces should be enclosed in double quotation marks. For example, { =3-1 \# "# 'is the value of this field.'" } returns the following phrase: *2 is the value of this field.*

` (grave accent) sequence value

This instruction includes the value of a sequence, such as the current value of the { SEQ Game } field or the current caption number. Use the value of a sequence by enclosing the sequence name in grave accents (backward apostrophes—the key to the left of the 1 key at the top of your keyboard). The result is displayed in Arabic format.

For example, examine the following field: { =bookmarka+bookmarkb \# "### 'is the total number of first downs in game' `Game`" }. This displays the following phrase: *12 is the total number of first downs in game 4.*

character

Simply typing a desired character includes it in the field result. If you want to include the Yen or pound sterling sign, or a character such as the percent sign, in a result, just include it where you want it to be, as in the following two examples:

{ =17+39 \# ¥## } displays ¥56

{ =2500/100 \# ##% } displays 25%

Using the date-time picture field switch \@

Using the date and time field switch is similar to using the number field switch. You include characters to paint a picture of how you want the results to appear. For example, the field { DATE \@ "MMMM d, yyyy', at 'h:mm AM/PM" } displays the field results in the following form: *January 6, 1999, at 12:50 PM.*

M (month) placeholder

The M placeholder is used to control the appearance of the month. The *M* must be in upper-case to distinguish it from *m*, which is the placeholder for minutes. The month can display in one of four possible formats depending on how many placeholders you include:

M	Displays the month number without a leading zero. December is displayed as 12 and January as 1.
MM	Displays the month number with a leading zero. December is displayed as 12 and January as 01.
MMM	Displays the month as a three-letter abbreviation. December is displayed as Dec and January as Jan.
MMMM	Displays the full name of the month. December is displayed as December and January as January.

d (day) placeholder

The d placeholder is used to control the appearance the day of the month. You can use uppercase or lowercase placeholders. The day can display in one of four possible formats depending on how many placeholders you include:

d or D	Displays the day number without a leading zero. The sixth day of the month is displayed as a 6.
dd or DD	Displays the day number with a leading zero. The sixth day of the month is displayed as a 06.
ddd or DDD	Displays the day as a three-letter abbreviation. Monday is displayed as Mon and Tuesday as Tue.
dddd or DDDD	Displays the full name of the day. Monday is displayed as Monday and Tuesday as Tuesday.

y (year) placeholder

The y placeholder is used to control the appearance of the year. You can use uppercase or lowercase placeholders. The year can display as two or four digits depending on how many placeholders you include:

yy or YY	Displays the year as a two-digit number, with a leading zero as necessary. For example, 1999 is displayed as 99 and 2006 as 06.
yyyy or YYYY	Displays the full number of the year. For example, 1999 is displayed as 1999 and 2006 as 2006.

h (hour) placeholder

The h placeholder is used to control the appearance of the hour. The hour can display in one of four possible formats depending on the number and case of the placeholders included:

h	Displays the hour on a 12-hour clock without a leading zero. For example, 9 p.m. is displayed as 9.
hh	Displays the hour on a 12-hour clock with a leading zero. For example, 9 p.m. is displayed as 09.
H	Displays the hour on a 24-hour clock without a leading zero. For example, 9 p.m. is displayed as 21 and 9 a.m. as 9.
HH	Displays the hour on a 24-hour clock with a leading zero. For example, 9 p.m. is displayed as 21 and 9 a.m. as 09.

m (minutes) placeholder

The m placeholder, which is a lowercase *m* to distinguish it from the month placeholder M, is used to display minutes. The minutes can display in one of two possible formats:

m	Displays the minutes without a leading zero. For example, five minutes after the hour is displayed as 5.
mm	Displays the minutes with a leading zero. For example, five minutes after the hour is displayed as 05.

am/pm placeholder

This placeholder displays a.m. or p.m. in one of four formats:

AM/PM	Displays the morning or afternoon indicator in uppercase. For example, 9 in the evening is displayed as 9 PM.
am/pm	Displays the morning or afternoon indicator in lowercase. For example, 9 in the evening is displayed as 9 pm.
A/P	Displays the morning or afternoon indicator in uppercase as an abbreviation. For example, 9 in the evening is displayed as 9 P.
a/p	Displays the morning or afternoon indicator in lowercase as an abbreviation. For example, 9 in the evening is displayed as 9 p.

' (single quotation marks) literal text

Single quotation marks are used to include text in a date/time field result just as they are in a number field. You must enclose the text to be included in single quotation marks.

You should surround a field switch that contains spaces with quotation marks. For example, `{ DATE \@ " 'Date Read: 'dddd, MMMM dd, yyyy" }` displays as *Date Read: Tuesday, January 27, 2004*.

Again, if your text includes any spaces, the whole expression must be contained in double quotations marks.

character

Simply typing a desired character includes it in the field result. To add a colon or a hyphen to a date, include it where you want it to be just as you would for a number field. (Be sure to enclose the field switch in quotation marks.) For example:

`{ DATE \@ "HH:mm MMM-d" }` displays *21:09 Apr-2*.

Editing Field Codes

When you want to change the format or content of any field result, you can edit its field code. For example, you can change the formula field `{ =bonus/4 }` to calculate one-third of the bonus rather than one-fourth. Press Alt+F9 to see the field, change the 4 to a 3, and press F9 to update the field. When you press Alt+F9 again, the new field results are displayed.

Protecting Fields

Sometimes, you just don't want anybody meddling with your fields, so you can lock your fields to retain the current values. This requires the process of locking, unlocking, and unlinking fields. Locking a field prevents it from being updated whenever its BOOKMARK, INCLUDE-TEXT, or REF field is updated. When a field is linked to a document, the field result is subject to change whenever there is a change in the referenced text.

You can lock fields temporarily in one of two ways: you can use the `\!` switch in the field, or you can lock fields on the fly from the keyboard.

To lock a field result with a field switch, add `\!` as the last switch in the field code. For example, `{ INCLUDETEXT C:\Sales\gross sales.doc \# $#,###,### \! }` displays the value found in the gross sales document at the time the field was first evaluated. Subsequent changes in the document don't affect the field results.

To lock a field on the fly, do the following:

1. Position the cursor in the field that you want to lock. (If you want to lock several fields, select them all.)

2. Press Ctrl+F11.

After a field is locked, nothing happens if you try to update it. The Update Field command on the shortcut menu is also disabled. Unlocking a field so that you can update it is just about as hard as locking it:

1. Position the cursor in the field that you want to unlock. (If you want to unlock several fields, select them all.)

2. Press Ctrl+Shift+F11.

Note   Remember also that you can use Ctrl+Shift+F9 to unlink a field. But locking a field allows you to come back and unlock it later. Unlinking it breaks it totally, actually removes the link from the document and replaces it with the result text.

Working with Smart Tags

A more recent type of field available to Word users is the Smart Tag. These are very powerful automated fields. You can tell Word to look for text that appears to be an address, date, financial symbol, a person's name, a place, a telephone number, or a time. If the Smart Tags check box is selected (under the View tab of the Options dialog box), when Word finds this kind of text, it *smart tags* it. It places a purple dotted line under the tagged text. When you click on smart-tagged text, a little button with an *I* symbol on it appears close to the text. In most cases, you just have to point at the text to see the tag button. In some cases, however, Word needs a little nudge, so try clicking the text if the tag button doesn't appear. Clicking this button opens a menu from which you can select a variety of actions.

Suppose that you've turned on Smart Tags for people's names. If Word recognizes a name and tags it, you can open a menu that provides the options listed in Table 23-4. (Figure 23-6 shows the Smart Tag menu.) Word can recognize names in two ways: the names of people to whom you have sent e-mail using Outlook or common names. More options are available for the former type of Smart Tag than for the latter.

Table 23-4: The Person Name Smart Tag Menu

Menu Option	Purpose
Send Mail	Opens an Outlook Compose window, with, if available, the person's e-mail address already entered.
Schedule a Meeting	Opens Outlook's Meeting window so that you can schedule a meeting with the person.
Open Contact	Opens the person's contact information.
Add to Contacts	Opens the Outlook Contact window so that you can add the person to your Outlook address book.
Insert Address	Grabs the person's address from Outlook and pastes it into the document on the line after the name.

Menu Option	Purpose
Remove this Smart Tag	Removes the tag from the text but doesn't stop Word tagging the text if it sees it elsewhere in the document.
Stop Recognizing "*name*"	Enables you to tell Word to stop recognizing the name As a Person (Word removes the tags from every incidence of the name, and stops tagging the same text again as a person—in the unusual case that the text could be tagged as some other item, Word can do so); or as a Smart Tag. Word will never tag this text again as any kind of Smart Tag.
Smart Tag Options	Opens the Smart Tags tab of the AutoCorrect dialog box.

Note Did you accidentally tell Word to stop recognizing some text? Open Windows Explorer and go to this folder: \Documents and Settings\<*username*>\Application Data\Microsoft\Smart Tags\Exceptions. Find a file called ignore.xml, open the file in Notepad, and search the file for the text you want to start recognizing again. Delete the text beginning with (and including) the first <ST:item> and ending with the next </ST:item>.

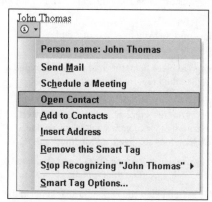

Figure 23-6: A name with a Smart Tag button and menu.

Tip Sometimes it takes a few moments for Smart Tags to work. You type a name, type a space afterwards, and wait, but nothing seems to happen. Try clicking somewhere else, a line or two above or below, and the text may be tagged. (Assuming, that is, that the text is recognizable.)

You can define how Smart Tags will work in the AutoCorrect dialog box by choosing Tools ⇨ AutoCorrect Options and clicking the Smart Tags tab. Table 23-5 describes the components you'll find there (see Figure 23-7).

Table 23-5: The Smart Tag Components of the AutoCorrect Dialog Box

Component	Purpose
Label Text with Smart Tags	Enables you to turn Smart Tag operations off and on.
Address (English)	Tells Word to tag text that it believes is an address. The address has to be on a single line. For example, Word recognizes *1 Main St.*, and *1 Main St., Denver, CO 80202.*
Date (Smart Tag Lists)	Tells Word to tag text that it believes is a date. You need a year to make this happen. That is, it won't recognize *June 15*, but it will recognize *June 15, 2003*. And the system doesn't like superscripted text after the number. So it won't recognize *June 15th, 2003*, for example. For the science-fiction writers among you, it won't recognize all years. It can't do anything with June 15, 2929, for example.
Financial Symbol (Smart Tag Lists)	Tells Word to tag financial symbols that it finds in the text. For example, it will tag *MSFT* or *IBM*, considering them stock symbols.
Person Name (English)	Tells Word to tag words that it believes are full English names. For example, it will tag *Ann Smith* and *Wendy Ann Smith* but not *Ann* or *Wendy.*
Person Name (Recent Outlook E-mail Recipients)	Tells Word to tag names that you have recently sent e-mail to using Microsoft Outlook.
Place (English)	Tells Word to recognize place names if you have downloaded a Smart Tag library. (See the Properties button.)
Telephone Number (Smart Tag Lists)	Tells Word to tag telephone numbers. It can recognize *(720) 555-3246*, but it may not recognize all your numbers. It won't recognize numbers from other countries unless you've downloaded a Smart Tag library that does so. (See the Properties button.)
Time (Smart Tag Lists)	Tells Word to recognize when you type times if you download a time-related Smart Tag library. (See the Properties button.)
Properties	Word enables this button when you click particular items in the list. Click this button to open a Web page from which you can download Smart Tags of the selected type.
Recheck Document	Checks the document looking for text that can be smart tagged. Note that it's linked to the grammar checker, so you will be rechecking grammar as well.
More Smart Tags	Click this button to go to an area on the Microsoft Web site from which you can download more Smart Tags from a variety of vendors.
Remove Smart Tags	Removes all Smart Tags from the document.

Component	Purpose
Save Options	Opens the Save tab of the Options dialog box where you'll find two more Smart Tag options. You can tell Word to Embed Smart Tags. Clear this check box, and Word won't save the tags in your document; when you close the document, the tags are lost, although you can recheck them the next time you open. (Why bother? Files are larger if a lot of Smart Tags are saved.) You can also tell Word to Save Smart Tags as XML Properties in Web Pages. If you save the document as a Web page, the Smart Tags are saved in the page.
Show Smart Tag Actions Buttons	Stops the *i* button from appearing when you click on smart-tagged text. The text remains tagged, but you won't be able to use it until you turn the button back on.

What sort of additional Smart Tags are available? Here are a few examples:

✦ **FedEx:** Smart Tags to help you create shipping labels from addresses, ship a package, track shipments, check an address, and so on.

✦ **MSNBC:** Type a city name; then use the Smart Tag to find the city's latest news, sports, and weather.

✦ **LexisNexis:** Type a person's name or address, or a legal case name, and use the Smart Tag menu to look up related information.

✦ **ESPN:** Use the Smart Tag menu to search for sports information.

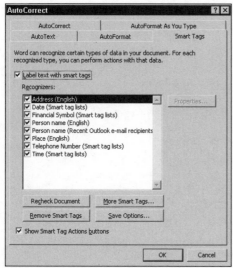

Figure 23-7: The Smart Tags tab of the AutoCorrect dialog box.

Summary

This chapter discussed how to build field codes that instruct Word to insert fields and to display them in just the way that you want. You learned how to do the following:

✦ Display field codes and field results.

✦ Insert field codes in a document.

✦ Add formatting switches.

✦   ✦   ✦

Creating Forms

From the local library or supermarket to the Internal Revenue Service, forms have become a way of life. Simply put, a form is a way to collect all the essential pieces of information about a subject, whether it's a job application or a list of itemized deductions. In this chapter, we discuss how to create new data-entry forms with text and form fields.

Understanding Word Forms

The application that you use to create your form depends on the purpose of that form and the type of data you intend to collect with it. Word, Access, and Excel all provide form-creation capabilities. If your form contains complex text and data formatting, pictures, check boxes, drop-down lists, or linked objects, use Word or Access to design it. If you're collecting a large amount of information or need relational-database capabilities, use Access. If you're collecting information for use in calculations, statistical analyses, or financial reports, use Excel.

In Word, a form is a special kind of template, and each time you use the form to collect data, you're actually creating a new document based on the form template. To keep a user from changing the form, you can protect it before you save it. This way, the user can move from one data entry field to another and enter the desired information, but not change the structure or format of the form.

Word provides several predesigned document templates that you can use to create common types of forms, such as invoices, purchase orders, fax cover sheets, and weekly time sheets. You can use these templates as they are or customize one to suit your needs. You can create a form for almost any use: for contracts, invoices, job applications, or other repetitive data-gathering purposes.

Creating a New Form in Word

If you already have a printed form that you want to duplicate in Word, you can go ahead and create a new form template using the printed form as a pattern. Otherwise, you should sketch the form design first and make sure that it includes spaces for all of the desired information as well as sufficient explanatory text for the user. You should

In This Chapter

Adding text and form fields

Changing form field properties

Adding Help messages

Protecting forms

Using and printing forms

also decide what kind of data to enter in each field and how you want it to look. Then, after carefully reviewing the design, you are ready to create the form. Creating a new form is a four-step process:

1. First, start a new template.

2. Second, enter the desired text, interspersed with properly identified form fields where the data is entered.

3. Third, protect the form template with a password so that a user has access only to the data entry fields.

4. Finally, save the form in the template folder.

Figure 24-1 shows a typical Word form, which in this case can be used to gather information about new customers of an educational book mail-order business. The shaded areas represent the data entry fields; the rest of the form is inaccessible to the user.

The first step in creating a new form is to start a new template using an existing template as a pattern. Open a new document from a template—either the Blank Document template or an actual form template—and save the document with a new name.

Tip   Microsoft's Templates library has literally dozens of form templates, from the Pledge form to the Resignation Due to Merger form. Click Templates Home Page in the New Document task pane.

At this point, adjust the margins and put the basic information in place. Treat your form template exactly as you would any other Word document. Make the document appear the way you want—then you'll add the form fields and labels.

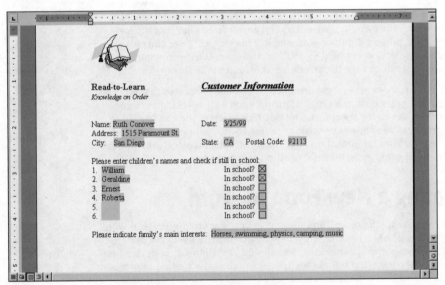

Figure 24-1: A typical information collection form in Word.

Adding Text and Inserting Form Fields

After you type the form title and introductory text, move to the beginning of the data entry area where you insert one or more form fields. You can choose from three types of form fields: text, check box, and drop-down list. The type that you insert depends on what kind of information you expect from the user, how that information is entered, and how you want it to be displayed.

You insert a form field using the Forms toolbar by choosing View ➪ Toolbar ➪ Forms (see Figure 24-2). This toolbar includes buttons for inserting each type of form field, a table, or a field. Other buttons toggle the field shading and the form protection on and off, and reset the fields. Table 24-1 describes these buttons. Emphasizing the data entry fields with shading is a handy way to find the fields quickly, especially in a large and complicated form.

Figure 24-2: The Forms toolbar.

Table 24-1: The Forms Toolbar Buttons

Button	Name	Purpose
ab|	Text Form Field	Inserts a text field into document.
☑	Check Box Form Field	Inserts a check box into the document.
	Drop-Down Form Field	Inserts a drop-down list box.
	Form Field Options	Opens the Options dialog box for the select field, or the field that the insertion point is sitting next to.
	Draw Table	Enables you to draw a table, into which you can place form fields.
	Insert Table/Insert Cells/Insert Columns/Insert Rows	Button name changes depending on where the insertion point is placed. Use it to insert cells, rows, or columns into a table or to create a new table.
	Insert Frame	Inserts a frame into the document, into which you can place form fields.
@	Form Field Shading	Turns field shading on and off.
	Reset Form Fields	Changes form fields back to their default settings and content.
	Protect Form	Activates your form so that you can use it; while active, you can't modify or edit the form fields.

To insert a form field, place the insertion point where you want the field, and click one of the form-field buttons in the toolbar. The field is dropped into the document, and shaded. (If it isn't shaded, click the Form Field Shading button to turn on shading.)

After inserting a form field, you can select it, and then move it by dragging it to a new position in the same way you can drag text. You can also add or delete spaces or text before it in the template, or you can press Tab to push it to the right. To delete a field, select the field and press Delete. To copy it into the Clipboard, place the cursor to the left of the field and press Shift+right arrow, and then press Ctrl+C.

Tip   To design a form with the fields in exactly the positions you want, use tables and frames to position them.

Understanding Form Fields

As mentioned, form fields come in three basic types: text fields, check boxes, and drop-down list boxes. You can customize each of these field types through its Options dialog box. You can open the Options dialog box in these ways:

✦ Double-click the form field.

✦ Right-click the form field, and then choose Properties from the shortcut menu.

✦ Select the form field, and then click the Form Field Options button on the Forms toolbar.

Note   Were going to look at how to define each of the form field types in turn now. We won't examine a number of issues for the moment, though: how to define Help text, add macros to the fields, work with bookmarks set on fields, set Fill-In Enabled, or Calculate on Exit. These procedures can be used for all of the field types, so we'll look at them a little later in this chapter.

Defining text fields

A text field can be modified in a variety of ways. You can define the type of data it contains, enter text that appears in the box until the user types something over it, change the field size, and so on. The Text Form Field Options dialog box is shown in Figure 24-3.

These are the text field types that you can define:

✦ **Regular Text:** A plain text field that enables the user to type any kind of text, such as the answer to a question, a city name, a street address, and so on.

✦ **Number:** A field containing a number, such as a telephone number or zip code.

✦ **Date:** A field that lets the user enter a date, such as a date of birth.

✦ **Current Date:** A field that the user cannot manipulate; instead, the computer enters the date at the point at which the form is saved.

✦ **Current Time:** A field that the user cannot manipulate; instead, the computer enters the time at the point at which the form is saved.

✦ **Calculation:** A field in which the user can place a formula; the field carries out a calculation based on the information entered.

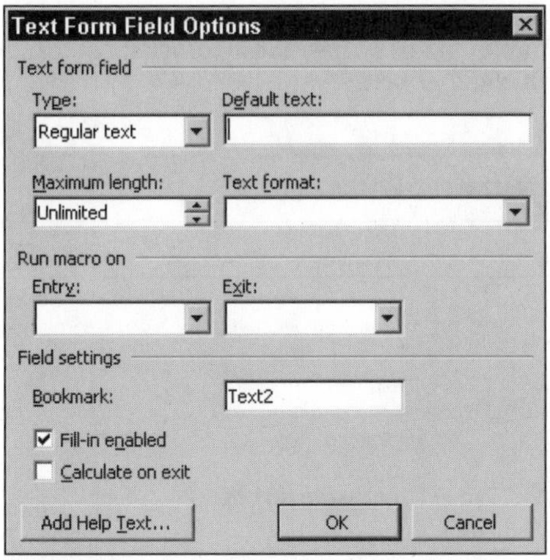

Figure 24-3: The Text Form Field Options dialog box.

Regular text

A regular text field allows the user to enter text, numbers, symbols, or spaces. One example is a field following the question "In what city do you live?" that holds the user's response. You can enter default text if you wish, something as simple as *Type Your Answer Here*, for instance, or perhaps a default value—you might enter, for example, Indianapolis if your form is primarily used there. The field then displays Indianapolis so that users don't have to type an entry unless they want to change the answer.

You can select one of four formats for the text the user enters from the Text Format drop-down list. Leave the Text Format box blank if you want to leave the user's entry as entered and with no special formatting. Table 24-2 shows examples using these options.

Table 24-2: Text Format Options

Option	Result
Uppercase	EVERYTHING IS IN CAPITAL LETTERS.
Lowercase	everything is in lowercase letters.
First capital	The first letter of the first word is capitalized.
Title case	The First Letter Of Each Word Is Capitalized.

Number

Use this data type when your form requires a numeric entry. The user's response may be used in a calculation, or it may be an answer to a question such as "How old are you?" or perhaps hold a zip code. Unlike a text field, which can accept text as well as numbers, number fields can accept only numeric entries. If someone answers the preceding question by typing **eighteen**, for example, an error message appears and the insertion point remains in the field until the user changes the answer to **18** or some other number.

Selecting an option from the Number Format drop-down list defines the number formats that can be applied to a number form field, and Table 24-3 describes these formats. You can also specify a default numeric value in the Default Number box.

Table 24-3: Number Formats

Option	Result
0	123
0.00	123.45
#,##0	1,234
#,##0.00	1,234.56
$#,##0.00;($#,##0.00)	$1,234.56 or ($1,234.56) if a negative number
0%	1%
0.00%	1.00%

Chapter 23 describes all of the possible number placeholders and formatting codes. You can choose from the list provided, or you can construct a custom number format for any display that you desire. The following sections briefly explain what the symbols used mean.

0 (zero) placeholder

A zero in a number format indicates that a digit should appear in that place, no matter what. If a digit is in the place occupied by a zero placeholder, that digit is displayed, but if not, a zero appears in its place. For example, if you're formatting dollars and cents and want every entry to include two decimal places, you end the numeric picture with .00. This way, 4 will appear as $4.00 and 4.1 as $4.10. In addition, if a result is longer than the number of digits specified by the instruction, that result is rounded to conform to the specified number format.

(number sign) placeholder

A number sign in the number format indicates that a digit should appear if one exists. If the result doesn't have a digit to display, however, a space (instead of a zero) is inserted in its place.

; (semicolon)

The semicolon acts as a formatting separator in several types of format specifications. When you want different formats to apply to positive and negative numbers, you can specify two number formats that are separated by a semicolon. For example, a form field with the predefined number format $#,##0.00;($#,##0.00) displays positive numbers as usual but negative numbers enclosed in parentheses.

Date

Use a date form field if the form requires that the user enter a date. Date fields don't accept entries other than date entries, however. Therefore, if someone types an invalid date, an error message appears and the insertion point remains in the field until the user makes a proper response.

The Date Format list contains date formats that can be applied to a date form field. Table 24-4 describes these formats.

Table 24-4: Date Formats

Option	Result
M/d/yy	1/15/03
dddd, MMMM dd, yyyy	Friday, January 15, 2003
MMMM d,yyyy	January 15, 2003
M/d/yyyy	1/15/2003
yyyy-MM-dd	2003-Jan-15
d-MMM-yy	15-Jan-03
M.d.yy	1.15.03
MMM. d, yy	Jan. 15, 03
d MMMM yyyy	15 January 2003
MMMM yy	January 03
MMM-yy	Jan-03
M/d/yy h:mm am/pm	1/15/03 6:25 pm
M/d/yy h:mm:ss am/pm	1/15/03 6:25:15 pm
h:mm am/pm	6:25 pm
h:mm:ss am/pm	6:25:15 pm
HH:mm	18:25
HH:mm:ss	18:25:15

Chapter 23 describes all the available time and date placeholders. You are not limited to the predefined formats found in the drop-down lists: you can construct a custom date or time picture in any format that you desire.

Current date and current time

The current date and current time fields are used to insert the current date and time as shown by the computer's clock. You can use all of the date and time placeholders described in the previous section (and in Chapter 23) in any combination that you desire.

Note   Because the current date and time are taken directly from your computer system, you cannot specify a default setting. Also note that the value in the filled-in form will be wrong if the computer on which the form is filled in has the wrong date and time defined, which is not uncommon.

Word can update the current date or current time form field when the document is printed. For this to occur, open the Options dialog box (Tools ➪ Options) and select the Update Fields check box in the Printing Options area of the Print tab.

Calculation

Use a calculation form field to insert an expression that derives a value from other fields in the form. An expression is constructed with a leading = sign and then a formula. An example would be *=Amount*Percent*, which multiplies the value in the field named *Amount* by the value in the field named *Percent*. You can enter an expression to do almost anything that you want. Table 24-5 lists the operators that are supported in expressions.

Note Not sure what we mean when we say a field is *named*? We'll get to that later in the chapter, when we describe bookmarking fields.

Table 24-5: Operators Supported in Expressions

Operator	Description
+	Addition
-	Subtraction
*	Multiplication
/	Division
%	Percent
^	Powers and roots
=	Equal to
<	Less than
<=	Less than or equal to
>	Greater than
>=	Greater than or equal to
<>	Not equal to

Expressions are not confined to the usual numeric operators listed in this table, however. Because Word can recognize the cell-naming conventions of most spreadsheets and apply these conventions to tables, you can construct some pretty sophisticated equations.

For example, to sum all of the information in a column on an invoice, you can enter a calculation field that looks like =SUM(D4:D9). SUM() is a Word function that adds the values specified in the argument (enclosed in the parentheses). To figure the amount of sales tax due on total sales, you can insert an expression that looks like =PRODUCT(totsale,.05), where *totsale* is the bookmark assigned to the field named Total Sale.

Cross-Reference For more information on expressions and functions, see Chapter 23.

The calculation field can use the same formatting specifications as those discussed for the number field mentioned earlier. You can set the maximum allowable length of the calculation field by filling in the Maximum Length box; this feature is particularly helpful if you make a calculation that returns a value such as pi.

Setting field length

Whichever field type you select, you can set the field length. Either set it to Unlimited, in which case users can enter as much text into the field as they wish, or specify the number of characters that can be placed there. For instance, if you create a zip-code field, you might set the field to 5, so the user can only enter a 5-character zip code or set the field to ten, so a user might enter a 9-character zip code and a hyphen. Not limiting the data entry makes it easier for users to make mistakes.

Defining check boxes

If you want to work with a check box in your form, you need to open the Check Box Form Field Options dialog box (see Figure 24-4). In this dialog box, you can define the size of a check box, in points. For instance, a 12-point check box is as high as 12-point text (as wide, too, of course, because a check box is a square). Select either Auto—in which case Word will set the size automatically, dependent on the text in which the check box is placed—or Exactly and define a size.

Figure 24-4: The Check Box Form Field Options dialog box.

You can also define whether the check box should be selected or not when the form is first opened. For instance, if you want the person filling in the form to opt-in for something—to allow you to send a newsletter periodically, for instance, or send special offers—then you may want to leave the check box turned on to begin with. Select Not Checked or Checked, as appropriate, in the Default Value area.

Tip Set the field default to what is most likely to be entered; or, as in the newsletter example above, to what you *want* the user to enter.

Creating drop-down fields

Drop-down list boxes contain, yes, lists. A form user can select one of the items from the field. For instance, a form might allow the user to select a country name or state code from a list. This ensures that the user does not mistype a value. For instance, to ensure that you get as little bad information as possible when collecting addresses, don't let a user enter a state in the address—some users may type a full state name, others may type the two-character code, and some will mistype. Rather, use a drop-down and they can select the information. You can see an example of such a field in Figure 24-5.

Figure 24-5: A sample drop-down field list.

After inserting the drop-down field, enter the items that you want to appear in the list from which the user selects. To enter the items, open the Drop-Down Form Field Options dialog box (see Figure 24-6). In the Drop-Down Item box, type the entry you want to appear at the top of the list and press Enter; type the one you want second, and press Enter; type the third, and so on.

Figure 24-6: The Drop-Down Form Field Options dialog box.

Note   Fields don't become real fields until you have protected the form. So the drop-down arrow in a drop-down list box doesn't appear with the field when you first create it.

After the items have been added to the list, you can remove them or rearrange their order in the Items in Drop-Down List box:

✦ To move an entry, select it and then press the up or down arrow to the right of the list.

✦ To remove an entry, select it and then click Remove.

Attaching macros to fields

All fields can have macros attached to them. These macros can run when the insertion point enters or leaves the field. For instance, you may want to build a macro that updates the fields and performs calculations while the form is being completed by the user. You can also have macros that run when a user enters data in a particular field within the form, such as to get additional information about the data just entered.

As you've seen in the illustrations of the various field Options dialog boxes, you can assign macros to field Entry and Exit by selecting a macro from the associated drop-down list box. That is, the macro runs when the insertion point enters or leaves the field, when you Tab into or out of the field, or when you click in the field or in another field.

It's important to remember, however, that the macros you want to use in your form must be saved in the form template. If they are not, you won't be able to see them in the drop-down list boxes, and they won't be in the form when you send it out to the users.

Cross-Reference   For a complete discussion of macros, see Chapter 33.

Assigning bookmarks to fields

Word automatically assigns a bookmark to every form field. You can change the name of this default bookmark to something more meaningful than `Dropdown1` by entering a new name in the Bookmark box in the field's Options dialog box. As the field is bookmarked, you can refer to the contents of the field using the bookmark name. Bookmarks can be used in calculations and in macros to represent the results of the field, such as `=SUM(Sales97,Sales98)`.

Calculate on Exit

All three form field types discussed have the Calculate On Exit setting available to them. If Calculate On Exit is selected in the field's Options dialog box, Word will update any calculations that involve the field when the user moves to another. By default, this setting is not checked, however, because if your form contains many calculations, it can slow the data entry process.

Enabling fields

Each of the three field types has an Enabled option in its respective Options dialog box:

- ✦ **Fill-In Enabled:** This option for text form fields toggles the read-only status of that field. When the option is cleared, the user may not enter data in that field.

- ✦ **Drop-Down Enabled:** This option for drop-down fields enables the user to select a value from the drop-down list. When the option is cleared, however, the list doesn't appear, and the first item in the list is the default value (which cannot be edited).

- ✦ **Check Box Enabled:** If this option for a check box form field is cleared, the user cannot change the preset default value.

Adding help text

Each type of form fill-in field allows you to include helpful text to guide the users of your form. This message can be displayed in the status bar, in a Help dialog box in response to pressing the F1 key, or both. Click the Add Help Text button to open the Form Field Help Text dialog box, shown in Figure 24-7.

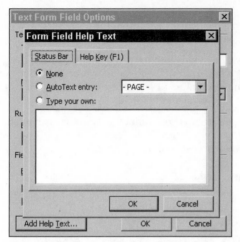

Figure 24-7: The Form Field Help Text dialog box.

The Form Field Help Text dialog box contains two identical tabs:

✦ **Status Bar:** Use this tab to specify the help text that you want to display on the status bar when the insertion point is in the field.

✦ **Help Key (F1):** Use this tab to specify the help text to display in a Help box that opens if F1 is pressed while the cursor is in the associated form field.

Table 24-6 lists the options available in both tabs.

Note   Word limits the amount of help text that you can display. If you want the help text to display in a dialog box, you can enter up to 255 characters. In the status bar, however, you are limited to 138 characters. This is because the entire message must be displayed on one line across the bottom of the screen.

Table 24-6: Options in the Form Field Help Text Dialog Box

Selection	Action
None	Displays no help text for the form field.
AutoText Entry	Allows you to retrieve text that you've previously defined as AutoText and to place that text either on the status bar or in a Help Text dialog box. This list includes items from the User Information tab of the Options dialog box and any AutoText entries you have defined.
Type Your Own	Allows you to type in the information that you want the user to see on the status bar or in a Help Text dialog box.

Drawing and inserting tables

The Draw Table and Insert Table buttons on the Forms toolbar work the same way as their equivalents on the Standard toolbar. With Draw Table, you first draw the outside boundaries of the table and then the lines to configure the rows and columns. If you make a mistake, click the Eraser on the Tables and Borders toolbar and then drag to remove the line that you don't want.

With Insert Table, you drag the mouse pointer over the table grid to define the number of rows and columns that you want.

 Cross-Reference For information on working with tables, see Chapter 9.

Adding frames

Frames add emphasis and visual appeal to forms, just as they do to documents. You can add a frame to hold special text or to enclose one or more form fields, and then you can drag the frame into the exact position where you want to place the fields. Add a frame to your form design by clicking the Insert Frame button on the Forms toolbar. After the frame is in your form, you can resize it and change the format of the borders and shading, just as you can with any other document.

 Cross-Reference For more information on frames, see Chapter 18.

Even though in recent versions of Word text boxes have almost totally taken the place of the frames used in earlier versions of Word, form fields are an exception. You cannot place fields into text boxes.

Adding ActiveX controls

In addition to the form fields that you can add from the Forms toolbar, you can open the Control Toolbox (View ➪ Toolbars ➪ Control Toolbox) and add any of those controls to the form. You can choose from spin buttons, scroll bars, command buttons, list boxes, toggle buttons, images, and the More Controls button that opens a long list of additional ActiveX controls from which to choose.

When you click a control in the Toolbox, Word automatically switches to design mode and inserts that control in the form. It first appears as a floating control, however, so that you can place it anywhere in the form. If you want the new control to fit directly in the text at the insertion point, hold down the Shift key as you click the Toolbox button.

Locking and Protecting the Form

After the form's structure is created and the fields are inserted, you need to do three things:

✦ **Protect the form:** This turns on the fields and stops them from being edited. Once protected, the form is, in effect, "live" and can be used. But protecting the form does a little more. In effect, you are telling Word that the document is a fill-in form—Word will disable many menu commands, limiting the user's ability to make formatting changes to the document.

✦ **Protect the document:** This stops anyone else from unprotecting the fields. Protecting and unprotecting the form is as simple as clicking a button, but once the *document* is protected, the form contained by the document cannot be unprotected without a password.

✦ **Save the document as a template:** This creates the final form template that others can open and use.

You can protect the form at any time by clicking the Protect Form button on the toolbar. This is really a quick way to turn form fields on and off while you're working to test the form. But once you're ready to protect both the form and the document, forget the Protect Form button and use this procedure:

1. Choose Tools ⇨ Protect Document to open the Document Protection task pane.

2. Select the check box labeled Allow Only This Type of Editing in the Document, under Editing Restrictions.

3. Select Filling in Forms from the drop-down list box.

4. Click the Yes, Start Enforcement Protection button. The Start Enforcing Protection dialog box opens.

5. Type a password in the Enter New Password box, and press Tab.

6. Type the password again.

7. Press Enter.

Note   The Enter New Password box is labeled as *Optional*. If you don't enter a password, though, anyone can unprotect the document, using Tools ⇨ Unprotect Document. Also, if you are going to protect documents, you'd better remember the password. And if the documents are for use by other people, in a company for instance, you should have some kind of password repository system so that the company doesn't have to throw all the documents away if you get hit by a bus.

8. Choose File ⇨ Save As. The Save As dialog box opens.

9. In the Save As Type drop-down select Document Template (*.dot). The dialog box changes to show the User Templates directory.

10. Type a file name and press Enter.

The file has now been saved as a template. You can open it from the Templates dialog box (File ⇨ New ⇨ On My Computer) to create a new document.

Note   See Chapter 34 for more information on protecting documents.

Once protected, a form cannot be edited without unlocking it using the password, which keeps busy fingers away from your work. To unprotect a form, choose Tools ⇨ Unprotect Document from the Tools menu or click the Protect Form button in the Forms toolbar again. You are then asked to enter your password (if you provided one when you protected the form).

Tip   You don't necessarily have to protect the entire document. If you divide the body of the form into parts using section breaks (see Chapter 10 for information on sections) while constructing it, you can protect any combination of sections that you want. You can see how to do this in Chapter 34.

Filling Out a Form

After your new form template is completed, protected, and saved in the template folder, anyone can use it to enter information. You use the form just as you do any other template in creating a new document. As you enter the information in the fields, you are actually creating a new document using the form as a template. This new document contains all of the text in the form, as well as the field values entered by the user. If you protected the form, the user can enter text or make selections in form fields, but cannot enter text anywhere else.

Printing a Form

Printing a form is not much different from printing any other document. However, there is one unusual situation: printing information from a Word form onto preprinted forms. That is, you can create a Word form that exactly matches a preprinted form, use the Word document to gather the data, and then print onto the preprinted paper forms.

If you do this, you want to print nothing but the information in the forms—no background images or colors, no shading, no explanatory text. To limit printing in this way, click Options in the Print dialog box to open the Print tab of the Options dialog box. Then, under the Options for Current Document Only, choose Print Data Only for Forms and click OK twice to send your form data to the printer. The text prints in exactly the positions in which it appears in the form.

Summary

In this chapter, you learned the basics of creating forms to use as templates for data collection. You saw that Word provides the tools to build any kind of form that you need. Armed with these versatile Word tools, you can now create a form for any purpose. Here are several fundamentals worth remembering:

✦ Forms are composed of text and data entry fields.

✦ The form can control the values entered and offer help to the user.

✦ Protecting the form limits users to entering and selecting within fields only—they can't enter text anywhere else.

✦ It's possible to protect a form, while leaving the rest of the document unprotected.

✦　　✦　　✦

Getting Organized with Outlines and Master Documents

In This Chapter

Creating, editing, and arranging outlines

Adding numbers to outline headings

Formatting and printing outlines

Building and formatting master documents

Creating and editing subdocuments

In this chapter, you learn how to use outlines to organize your thoughts and give focus to your ideas. In addition, you learn how the master document feature, which builds on Word's outlining techniques, makes it easy to apply consistent formatting to long documents by combining small documents into a large framework.

Using Outlines

The outline feature in Word is intertwined with the heading styles. When you create an outline, Word automatically assigns the appropriate heading style to each level of the outline. For example, a level one heading uses the Heading 1 style, and if you change the heading to level two, that heading automatically takes on the Heading 2 style. Conversely, assigning a standard heading style to text in Normal or Page Layout view automatically prepares the document for an outline. Therefore, if you use the standard heading styles as you create the document, you can also make an outline of the document simply by switching to Outline view (View ⇨ Outline).

Cross-Reference You can format heading styles just as you do any style in Word. For more on working with styles, see Chapter 13.

This marriage of outlines and styles provides considerable flexibility in approaching the outlining process. You can create an outline from scratch by turning on Outline view and then assigning levels to your headings and body text as you type. Alternatively, you can write your document in Normal or Page Layout view and then switch to Outline view to make it easier to arrange sections and to assign or reassign heading levels. Some people use Outline view only now and then, as a way to help them rearrange things in large documents—because you can control the amount of text that is visible on the screen in Outline view, you can move large chunks of text with minimal effort. Others write virtually everything in Outline view.

You can use outlines as a brainstorming aid: just type your thoughts without worrying where they fit into the overall picture. Then, after you have a basic outline in place, you can change the heading levels and rearrange entire sections of data. Creating an outline has other benefits as well. For example, you can use an outline to create a table of contents, to number headings, and even to build a master document.

Understanding Outline View

Whether you want to create an outline from scratch or work with an existing document in outline format, you must first turn on Outline view. Choose View ➪ Outline, or click the Outline View button on the left side of the horizontal scroll bar. (Alternatively, you can press Alt+Ctrl+O to change to Outline view. To return to Normal view, press Alt+Ctrl+N; to return to Print Layout view, press Alt+Ctrl+P.) Figure 25-1 shows a document in Normal view. Figure 25-2 shows the same document in Outline view.

When you activate Outline view, the Outlining toolbar replaces the horizontal ruler—Outline view is not a page-layout view, so you don't need the ruler. In other words, you can't define exactly where on the page the text appears in this view. Rather, Outline view uses the page to show you different hierarchical levels, but indenting sub-levels to the right. The outline display has nothing to do with the document's formatting, so don't try to do any document formatting you can do in Normal or Print Layout view. In fact, the paragraph formatting features of Word aren't even accessible in Outline view.

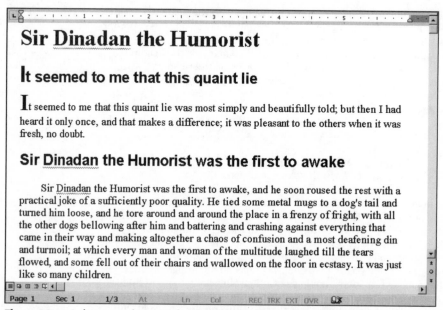

Figure 25-1: A document in Normal view. All headings are formatted using Word's built-in heading styles.

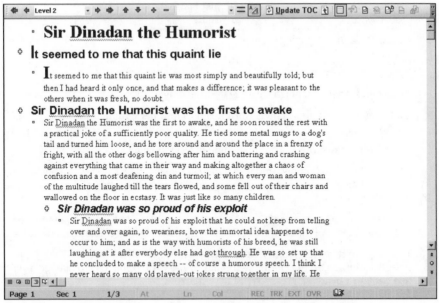

Figure 25-2: The same document shown in Figure 25-1 in Outline view.

Note In some ways, Outline view is similar to the Document Map (see Chapter 1). There are two major differences, however. Document Map doesn't require that you use the Heading styles. It does its best to build an outline based on what it thinks are probably headings. And, of course, Document Map is a simple feature—it doesn't have all the tools associated with Outline view.

Each heading or text paragraph is indented to its respective level and preceded by a plus sign, a minus sign, or a box. The plus sign indicates that body text, headings, or both are below the heading. The minus sign indicates that body text or headings are not below the heading. The small box indicates a body text paragraph.

Creating outlines

To create an outline from scratch or to outline an existing document, switch to Outline view and then assign outline levels to your headings and paragraphs.

To create a new outline, follow these steps:

1. Switch to Outline view. Figure 25-3 shows the Outlining toolbar and identifies its buttons; Table 25-1 describes the buttons on the Outlining toolbar. Note, however, that the Outlining toolbar also displays Word's Master Document buttons, which are explained later in this chapter.

   Word assigns the Heading 1 style to the first paragraph where you have positioned the cursor. If you don't want the entry to be at the first level, promote or demote the heading using the techniques described in step 4 before proceeding to step 2.

Figure 25-3: The Outlining toolbar.

2. Type your first heading.

3. Press Enter when you finish with the first heading.

   Each time that you press Enter, Word begins a new paragraph at the same level as the previous heading.

4. To promote or demote a heading, do one of the following:

   • To demote a heading (move it to a lower level), click the Demote button on the Outlining toolbar or press Alt+Shift+right arrow until the heading is at the level that you want.

   • To promote a heading (move it to a higher level), click the Promote button on the Outlining toolbar or press Alt+Shift+left arrow as many times as necessary.

5. To change to body text, rather than merely a lower-level heading, click the Demote to Body Text button on the Outlining toolbar or press Ctrl+Shift+N. To change from body text back to a heading, press Ctrl+Shift+left arrow.

> **Note**
>
> The term *Body Text* is a little confusing here. The button should really be called *Normal Text.* Selecting Demote to Body Text converts the text to the Normal style, *not* the Body Text style present in the default Word template.

6. Continue entering text, promoting and demoting it through the levels as desired.

Table 25-1: Buttons on the Outlining Toolbar

Button	Name	Action
	Promote to Heading 1	Promotes a heading or body text to the Heading 1 level.
	Promote	Promotes a heading to the next higher level or body text to the level of the preceding heading.
Body text ▾	Outline Level drop-down list box	Displays the outline level of the selected text. Select a level from the drop-down to change the text to that level.
	Demote	Demotes a heading to the next lower level or body text to a heading at a level below that of the preceding heading.
	Demote to Body Text	Demotes a heading to Normal text.
	Move Up	Moves the selected heading or body text up the page to above the previous heading or body text paragraph. Only visible paragraphs are taken into account, and moved headings and body text retain their current levels.

Button	Name	Action
⬇	Move Down	Moves the selected heading or body text down the page to below the next outline item. Only visible items are taken into account, and moved headings and body text retain their current levels.
➕	Expand	Expands the heading in which the insertion point is placed to show the level below it, showing the hidden text.
➖	Collapse	Collapses all of the headings and body text subordinate to the selected heading, hiding them.
Show All Levels ▾	Show Level	Selects a level to view; all levels, starting from Level 1 down to the selected level will be shown. Lower levels will be hidden.
═	Show First Line Only	Toggles between displaying the full text of each body text paragraph and displaying only the first line of each paragraph. (Multi-line headings are not affected; all lines of a heading are shown even if you turn on Show First Line Only.)
ᴬ𝐀	Show Formatting	Toggles between displaying and hiding character formatting.
⟳ Update TOC	Update TOC	Updates the Table of Contents, if you have one in the document.
🗎	Go to TOC	Moves the display to the Table of Contents and selects it.
🗎	Master Document View	This button, and all those to the right (when displayed), are related to master documents, which we look at a little later in this chapter.

To create an outline from existing text, switch to Outline view and promote or demote levels as desired using the toolbar. If you haven't used any of Word's nine built-in Heading styles, everything in the document will be shown as body text. As you promote text to a heading level, Word applies the appropriate style.

Note Don't select text while promoting or demoting, simply place the insertion point in the paragraph. In some cases, if text is selected and you promote, Word will apply the Heading style to the selected text, not change the outline level or change the paragraph style.

As you promote and demote headings, you can see the current level by looking at the Style box on the Formatting toolbar. In addition, if you want to view all of your styles at once, you can display the style area. Choose Tools ➪ Options, click the View tab, and then enter a measurement in the Style Area Width box. When the style area is displayed, you can adjust its width by dragging the vertical line that divides the style area from your document text. You can also close the style area display by dragging the vertical line to the left until the style area disappears.

Rearranging your outline

As you create an outline, don't worry about getting the arrangement and levels exactly the way that you want them. The beauty of working with outlines is that you can enter your thoughts as they occur and later rearrange the text in a flash by moving sections up and down.

Selecting in Outline view

Before you rearrange an outline, you need to understand how selection works in Outline view. The following list describes selection techniques that apply specifically to outlines:

✦ When you click a plus icon, the heading and all of its subordinate levels are selected.

✦ When you click a box symbol, or a minus sign, only that paragraph of body text is selected.

✦ When you click in the selection bar to the left of a paragraph, only that paragraph is selected. Therefore, if you click in the selection bar next to a heading with a plus sign, only that heading (and not any of its subordinate levels) is selected.

✦ You can select multiple headings or paragraphs by dragging up or down the selection bar.

✦ You can use any standard Word technique for selecting text in an outline paragraph, but once a selection crosses to a new paragraph, both paragraphs are selected in their entirety. In other words, you cannot select only a portion of more than one paragraph in Outline view.

Tip   If your text moves when you try to select it, you may have accidentally dragged a plus or minus symbol instead of clicking it. In this situation, choose Edit ➪ Undo and try again.

Promoting and demoting outline levels

To promote or demote a heading, place your insertion point anywhere in the heading and then use one of the following methods:

✦ **The Outlining toolbar.** Choose the Promote or Demote button to change the heading level. Choose the Demote to Body Text button to change any heading to body text.

✦ **Keystroke shortcuts.** Press Alt+Shift+left arrow to promote a heading to the next level, or press Alt+Shift+right arrow to demote a heading to the next level. For the first three heading levels, you can also press Alt+Ctrl+#, with # standing for the outline level to which you want the text assigned. For example, to change a heading to level two, press Alt+Ctrl+2.

✦ **The mouse.** Drag the plus symbol to the left or the right. When you place the mouse pointer over an outline icon, the pointer changes to a four-headed arrow, and as you drag, a vertical line appears at each heading level. Release the mouse button when you reach the desired level.

You can promote or demote multiple headings or body text paragraphs at the same time.

Tip   Here's a great trick for globally promoting or demoting outline headings. Suppose that you want to change all level two headings to level three headings. Simply use Word's Find and Replace feature. Choose Edit ➪ Replace. Then, with your insertion point in the Find What text box, click More, click Format, choose Style, and select the Heading 2 style from the Find What Style list box. In the Replace With text box, select the Heading 3 style from the Replace With Style list box. Finally, click Replace All. You can also use the Styles and Formatting task pane, using the Select All button. (You learn more about styles and formatting in Chapter 13.)

When you use the Outlining toolbar buttons to promote or demote a heading, only the actual paragraph where your insertion point is located is moved. Unless you select an entire section by clicking the plus icon or by using any other selection method, subordinate levels aren't affected—with the following exceptions:

✦ Body text is always promoted or demoted along with its heading.

✦ Any outline elements that are collapsed under the heading are always moved along with that heading.

If a heading is collapsed, any structural changes that you make to that heading affect any subordinate headings or body text paragraphs. This makes it easy to move sections of a document. Simply collapse your outline to its highest level, and then promote, demote, and move the headings.

Moving outline headings

Before you move headings, decide whether you want to move only one particular heading or all of the subheadings and body text associated with that heading. If a heading is collapsed when you move it, any subordinate text moves with that heading. If the heading is expanded to show its subordinate levels, however, some movement techniques move only the specified heading. You can take advantage of this to move whole sections without going through the process of selecting text. With the outline collapsed, dragging any plus icon will move all of its associated text.

To move a heading without moving any of its associated subheadings or body text, use the Move Up or Move Down button on the Outlining toolbar or press the Alt+Shift keys in combination with an up- or a down-arrow key. Whenever you drag a plus icon, all of the text associated with that heading is moved.

When you place your mouse pointer on a plus icon, the pointer changes to a four-headed arrow. Then, as you drag up or down, a horizontal line with a right arrow is displayed. Release the mouse button when the line is positioned where you want the text to be located.

To move multiple headings, select the headings that you want to move. Then hold down the Shift key as you drag the last heading icon in your selection. Make sure that you don't drag any heading except the last one. Once you click any heading in a selection other than the last one, your selection is cleared and only the heading where your mouse pointer is at is selected.

Tip   Outline view is a handy way to rearrange table rows. When working in a table, you can move a row or selected rows to a new location by switching to Outline view and then dragging them.

Using keyboard shortcuts

When your fingers are already on the keyboard, pressing a keystroke combination is often easier than lifting your fingers off the keyboard to use the mouse. For example, if you're all set to type a body text entry, press Ctrl+ Shift+N rather than choosing the Demote to Body Text button. Table 25-2 lists some of the most useful keystroke shortcuts for working with outlines.

Note   Tab and Shift+Tab are two handy keystroke shortcuts in Outline view. With your insertion point in a heading, pressing the Tab key demotes that heading to the next level, and pressing Shift+Tab promotes that heading to the next level (or promotes body text to a heading). These keystrokes have this effect only in Outline view, however. To promote or demote a heading in Normal view, use the Alt+Shift+arrow key combinations. To insert an actual tab character in Outline view, press Ctrl+Tab.

Table 25-2: Keystroke Shortcuts in Outlines

To Do This	Use These Keys
Switch to Outline view	Alt+Ctrl+O
Switch to Normal view	Alt+Ctrl+N
Promote a heading or body text to the next level	Alt+Shift+left arrow (or press Tab)
Demote a heading to the next level	Alt+Shift+right arrow (or press Shift+Tab)
Promote or demote a heading to a specific level	Alt+Ctrl+1 through Alt+Ctrl+3. Note that keystrokes are assigned only for the first three levels.
Demote a heading to body text	Ctrl+Shift+N
Move a paragraph up	Alt+Shift+up arrow
Move a paragraph down	Alt+Shift+down arrow
Show all headings and body text, or show all headings without body text	Alt+Shift+A
Show only the first line of body text, or show all body text	Alt+Shift+L
Show or hide character formatting	/ on the numeric keypad
Expand selected headings	Alt+Shift++ (plus sign) on numeric keypad
Collapse selected headings	Alt+Shift+- (minus sign) on numeric keypad

Viewing both Outline and Normal view at once

One way to work effectively with outlines is to split the document screen into two panes. In one pane, you can display your document in Outline view, and in the other pane, you can display your document in Normal view. This way, you can take advantage of Outline view to rearrange your text while simultaneously viewing the result of your actions in the full document.

To split your document into two equal panes, double-click the split bar (at the top of the vertical scroll bar) or choose Window ➪ Split. You can also simply drag the split bar to tailor the size of the panes. To restore the split window to its original condition, double-click the split bar or choose Window ➪ Remove Split. Figure 25-4 shows an outline in split view.

Printing an outline

When you print from Outline view, only the visible portion of your document is printed. For example, if your outline is collapsed to level one, only the Level 1 headings are printed. The Outline symbols don't appear on a document printout, though.

Before you print from Outline view, expand or collapse your outline to display what you want to print. To print your document as it should appear in its final form, switch to Normal or Print Layout view before you print.

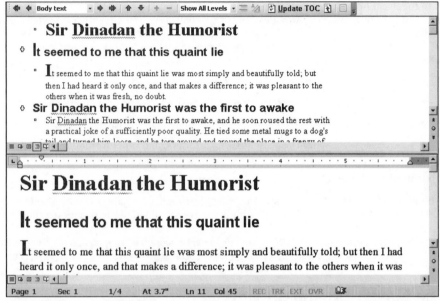

Figure 25-4: An outline split into two panes.

Copying an outline

In Outline view, if you select and copy headings that include collapsed subordinate text, the collapsed text is also copied. Unfortunately, you cannot copy just the visible headings with Word. You can, however, quickly list those headings in a table of contents and then omit the page numbers. For more information about creating a table of contents using the Index and Tables command (on the Insert menu), see Chapter 12.

After you create a table of contents, click in it and press Ctrl+Shift+F9 to convert the table of contents to regular text. You can then copy the headings from the table of contents.

Understanding Master Documents

Suppose that you want to add all your data into one colossal document or take several existing documents and turn them into one larger document. If you do this, you may find yourself running into a couple problems:

✦ Word begins to function less efficiently when a document is too large. (What's too large? There's no hard-and-fast rule, it all depends on the speed of the computer you have, the amount of memory, the number of images in the document, the number of links to external content, and so on.) Certain tasks such as scrolling and searching can take longer to accomplish, and the possibility of a system error increases.

✦ Only one person can work on any given file at a time. Therefore, if everything is crammed into the same file, you lose the capability to have different people working on a project.

With the master-document feature in Word, however, you can consolidate several documents into a large framework. This provides the consistency and other advantages of working with one large document and also keeps the convenience of working with individual subdocuments. In addition to these advantages, the master document feature enables you to do the following:

✦ Cross-reference items among several documents.

✦ Use the Outline view tools to rearrange items spread among several documents.

✦ Create indexes, tables of contents, and lists that span several documents.

✦ Easily assign consistent page numbering, headers, and other formatting across multiple documents.

✦ Print multiple documents with one command.

A book is ideally suited to the master document feature. Each chapter can be a subdocument, and the elements common to the entire book can be contained in the master document itself.

Note   In earlier versions of Word, the master-document feature has a reputation for being a little unstable. With today's faster computers, master documents may not be as necessary as before.

The Master Document view

Imagine an outline view that combines multiple documents. That's Master Document view. In effect it's an extension of Outline view, and uses the Outlining toolbar—the buttons on the right side of the bar that we haven't looked at yet.

What's the point? Imagine you have a very large document, perhaps hundreds of pages long, with lots of pictures. Such a document can get unwieldy—moving around can take a long time, Word can slow down, and so on. On the other hand, having everything in one document is rather nice—you can use Outline view to move things around, search the entire document to find things, create tables of contents and indexes spanning all the documents, and so on. The answer, the compromise, is the master document. Bring all the text into one document when you need it there, but work on small portions, in individual files, when you don't.

You can create a master document from scratch or combine existing documents into a master document. Turn on Master Document view by choosing View ➪ Outline. The last eight buttons on the bar are master-document buttons, but the last seven are not always displayed. Click the Master Document View button to expand or contract the toolbar; the button also changes the document display, though until you've actually created a master document you won't notice any difference.

Note   You might think of the master document as a sort of interactive index inside a normal document. A master document contains two things: normal document stuff—text and graphics, tables and text boxes, and so on—and links to other documents. Those links can be used to pull in the information from the documents to which the master documented is linked.

Figure 25-5 shows the Master Document buttons on the Outlining toolbar, and Table 25-3 identifies and describes those buttons.

Figure 25-5: The Master Document buttons.

Table 25-3: Master Document Buttons on the Outlining Toolbar

Button	Name	Action
	Master Document View	Switches between Master Document and Outline views, and expands and contracts the toolbar.
	Expand/Collapse Subdocument	Expands the master document, by pulling in data from the subdocuments, or collapses the document, by removing the information and displaying the links to the subdocuments.
	Create Subdocument	Turns selected headings and text into subdocuments, automatically saving a new document and creating a link from the master document to the subdocument.
	Remove Subdocument	Pulls the data from the subdocument into the master document and breaks the link to the subdocument—but it doesn't actually delete the subdocument file.
	Insert Subdocument	Enables you to create a link to use an existing file as a subdocument.
	Merge Subdocument	Combines multiple subdocuments into one subdocument.
	Split Subdocument	Divides one subdocument into two subdocuments.
	Lock Document	Toggles the entire document or selected subdocuments to a locked or an unlocked state. Note that this provides only cursory protection, however. Any user can unlock the subdocument simply by choosing the Lock Document button again. (See Chapter 34 for more information about document protection.)

Building a master document

There are three main methods of building a master document:

✦ Begin a new document in Master Document view. Create an outline for your master document, and then use those headings to break the outline into separate subdocuments.

✦ Break an existing document into subdocuments.

✦ Combine existing documents into a master document by inserting them as subdocuments. Any existing Word document can be treated as a subdocument.

Master documents, like outlines, use Word's built-in heading styles (Heading 1 through Heading 9).

Cross-Reference   You can create a table of contents or an index from an outline or a master document. For more information on this, see Chapter 12. For more information on how to use master documents to create cross-references that span several documents, see Chapter 11.

Starting from scratch

To build a master document from scratch in Master Document view, follow these steps:

1. Open a new document.

2. Switch to Master Document view by choosing View ➪ Outline; then click the Master Document View button on the Outlining toolbar.

3. Create an outline for your master document using any of the techniques covered previously in this chapter, typing headings to begin each subdocument. Before you create the outline, however, decide which heading level you want to use to begin each subdocument.

4. When you're ready to break portions of the document into subdocuments, select all of the headings and text that you want to convert. You can expedite this process by collapsing the outline to the heading level at which you want to begin your subdocuments before you make your selection.

Note   You cannot convert body text without a heading into a subdocument. The selected text must have at least one heading.

Word uses the level of the first heading in your selection to determine where each subdocument begins. For example, if your selection begins with a level two heading, Word begins a new subdocument at each level two heading in your selected text area.

5. Click the Create Subdocument button.

Each subdocument is enclosed in a box, and a subdocument icon is displayed in the upper-left corner of each box, as shown in Figure 25-6.

6. Save the master document.

When you save a master document, Word creates a new file, in the same directory as the master document, using a file name based on the first line of text in the file. Note also that Word adds a body text paragraph between each subdocument. This makes it easy to add additional text or subdocuments outside the existing subdocument boundaries.

Caution   Because Word automatically assigns subdocument file names, you can end up with strange results if your headings have similar names or if the file names assigned by Word would conflict with files already in the destination directory. As a simple demonstration, suppose that your directory contains a document called *Chapter 1.doc*. Now suppose that you create a subdocument in which the first heading is titled *Chapter 1*. When you save the master document, Word assigns the name *Chapter 2.doc* to your subdocument because *Chapter 1.doc* is already taken. When a naming conflict occurs, Word uses numbers to differentiate the file names. Therefore, your neatly numbered headings may not correspond with their subdocument file names. For this reason, you should check and, if necessary, rename subdocument file names before you close the master document. For instructions, see the "Renaming or moving a subdocument" section later in this chapter.

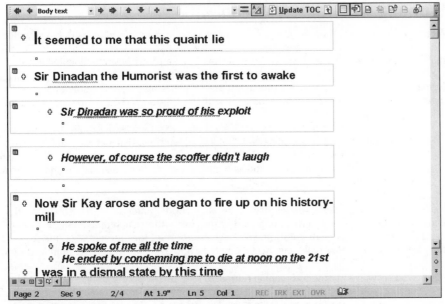

Figure 25-6: A master document divided into subdocuments.

Converting an existing document

To convert an existing document to a master document, open the file and switch to Outline view. Set up all the headings and levels the way you want them.

Next, select the section that you want to split into subdocuments. Make sure, however, that the first selected heading is the level at which you want each subdocument to start. Click the Create Subdocument button, and save the master document. At that point Word creates the subdocuments, saving them in the same directory.

Inserting existing documents into a master document

You can create a master document from a number of existing files. Open the document you want to become the master document—it could be a new blank document, or an existing document to which you want to add subdocuments.

Place the insertion point where you want to add a subdocument, and click the Insert Subdocument button. Find the file you want to insert in the Insert Subdocument dialog box, and click Open. That's it; the document link is dropped into the master document.

Note   When you open a subdocument from within its master document, the template and formatting assigned to the master document take precedence over any formatting originally assigned to the subdocument. If you open the subdocument separately, however, the subdocument reverts to its original formatting.

Working with master documents

After you build a master document, you have several options for working with it. In Outline view, you can treat the entire document as one large outline, and you can expand, collapse, promote, and demote sections at will. In Normal view, you can work with the document just as you would with any other document. You can cut and paste text or graphics between sections, add formatting, and perform any other document task. You can also open an individual subdocument and work on it separately by double-clicking the subdocument icon in the left margin.

Note   When you switch from Outline/Master view to any other view, even Reading view, you'll see the document in the condition it was in before you switched. That is, if you had collapsed the document, you'll see the links to the subdocuments. If you had expanded the document, you'll see all the text from the subdocuments, with a section break before and after each subdocument.

Be aware that Word inserts section breaks for each subdocument, because this may affect your formatting decisions. You can apply different formatting (including headers, footers, margins, paper size, page orientation, and page numbering) for different sections. You can see the section breaks in Normal view by clicking the Show/Hide button on the Standard toolbar.

Note   Working with a master document in Normal or Print Layout view is just like working with any other document. You can apply formatting to the entire document or any part of it. In addition, because each subdocument is a section, you can apply or modify any section-level formatting, such as page numbering or margins. You can also insert new sections within the subdocuments for formatting purposes.

If you follow the next two rules, you won't have any problems formatting master documents:

✦ If you want the formatting (for example, page numbering) to apply to the entire document, apply that formatting in the master document rather than in a subdocument.

✦ If you want the formatting to apply only to one subdocument, place your insertion point inside the subdocument in which you want to apply the formatting (or open the subdocument) before you proceed.

Also, remember that if you insert an existing document as a subdocument, that subdocument retains its original section formatting—except where that formatting would be overridden by the master document's template or styles. If you want one header or footer to continue throughout the entire master document, make sure that your individual subdocuments don't contain their own headers or footers. To create different headers or footers for each subdocument, however, set them up in the individual subdocuments.

Working with the entire master document in Normal or Print Layout view makes it easy to move text and graphics among the subdocuments using Word's standard cut-and-paste techniques, including drag-and-drop. You can also navigate through a large document and use Word's Find and Replace feature to make global changes across several documents.

Working with subdocuments

In Master Document view, you can open any subdocument to work on it separately. This is especially useful if several people are working on a project, because different people can then open and edit several subdocuments simultaneously. You can also change the order of the subdocuments, combine subdocuments, nest subdocuments within other subdocuments, and even break a portion of a subdocument into a new subdocument.

Opening a subdocument

You can open an individual subdocument from within a master document by double-clicking its subdocument icon in Master Document view. If you make changes to the subdocument, however, save both the edited subdocument and the master document before closing the master document. In case someone else may need to work on another part of the master document while you're editing the subdocument, close the master document once you open the subdocument in which you want to work. As long as your subdocument has been previously saved with the master document, that subdocument retains its link to the master document even after you close the master document file.

You can also open a subdocument using the File ➪ Open command, but with this method, certain changes may not be properly updated in the master document. To ensure that a subdocument's links are accurately updated in the master document, open subdocuments from the master document.

If you opened the subdocument from the master document, closing that subdocument returns you to the master document. If you opened the subdocument as a normal document or you opened it from the master document but then closed the master document with the subdocument still open, closing the subdocument is the same as closing any regular document.

Renaming or moving a subdocument

In order to rename a subdocument or move it to a different directory or drive, open the subdocument from the master document and use the File ➪ Save As command. Then resave the master document.

Caution   If you move or rename a subdocument through Windows Explorer or use any method other than the one just described, the master document loses its link with the subdocument.

Removing subdocuments

To merge a subdocument into a master document, click the subdocument icon to select the subdocument and then choose the Remove Subdocument button. When you do this, the text remains in the master document but is no longer attached to the subdocument.

To remove the subdocument text entirely from the master document, click the subdocument icon and press Delete. The subdocument text—and the link to it—is then deleted from the master document.

Neither of these actions deletes the subdocument file from the disk. They only break the subdocument's attachment to the master document. To delete the subdocument file from the disk, you must do so from outside, using Windows Explorer or another standard file-deletion method.

Caution   Don't delete a subdocument from the disk without first deleting it from the master document. If you delete the subdocument file first, you get an error message the next time you open the master document. Be very careful when working with master documents that are entirely on, or have components on, removable disks. Don't remove the disk until you've closed Word completely. Simply closing the master document may not be enough in some cases, and removing the disk can damage the files.

Rearranging the order of subdocuments

Master Document view makes reorganizing your subdocuments a snap. You can also reorganize subdocuments by selecting and moving text in Normal view, but reorganizing subdocuments in Master Document view is a simple matter of dragging the subdocument icon.

You can also move a subdocument by positioning your insertion point anywhere in the subdocument. Then hold down the Alt+Shift keys as you press an up- or a down-arrow key.

If you move a subdocument inside the boundaries of another subdocument, the subdocument that you move becomes part of the destination subdocument. If you want a subdocument to retain its integrity as a separate subdocument, move it to a location outside any other subdocument's boundaries.

Splitting subdocuments

A subdocument may become too large to work with effectively. Alternatively, you may want more than one person to work on different portions of the subdocument simultaneously.

To split a subdocument into two separate subdocuments, follow these steps:

1. Open the master document, and switch to Master Document view.

2. Select the entire heading or body text paragraph that will begin the new subdocument.

3. Click the Split Subdocument button on the Outlining toolbar. The subdocument then splits just above the selected paragraph.

Merging subdocuments

You can also combine several small files into one subdocument. You may want to do some editing afterward, however.

To merge multiple subdocuments into one subdocument, make sure that the subdocuments you're going to merge are adjacent; then select them and click the Merge Subdocument button on the Outlining toolbar. When you save the master document, Word assigns the file name of the first document in your selection to the merged subdocument.

Sharing subdocuments

Word uses the Author information in Summary Info to determine the owner of each subdocument. If you're the owner, you have full rights to open and edit the document. If you didn't create the document, however, the document is locked, and a small padlock icon appears just under the subdocument icon. Figure 25-7 shows a master document in Master Document view with one subdocument locked.

Figure 25-7: The first subdocument on this screen has been locked using the Lock Document button. Note the padlock under the subdocument icon.

To lock or unlock a subdocument, select the subdocument and click the Lock Document button on the Outlining toolbar. Remember, though, that Document option doesn't provide real protection. Anyone can unlock the document simply by clicking the Lock Document button. If you need a higher level of protection, add a password.

 Cross-Reference See Chapter 34 for more information about adding passwords.

Summary

With the outline feature in Word, you can organize your thoughts into headers and then rearrange them as needed. With the Master Document feature, you can create large documents by combining subdocuments, which provides you the best of both worlds: the capability to work with all the files at once without forcing you to deal with one huge file. In this chapter, you learned how to do the following:

✦ Create and work with outlines using the Outlining toolbar, which appears when you choose View ➪ Outline or click the Outline View button on the horizontal scroll bar. The outline feature is essential for helping you to organize your thoughts in a document using headings.

✦ Create and work with master documents by clicking the Master Document View button on the Outlining toolbar. With the Master Document feature, you can work efficiently with large documents by organizing them into subdocuments.

✦　　✦　　✦

Creating Basic Web Pages

In This Chapter

Creating Web pages using Web page templates

Saving existing Word documents as HTML documents

Working with frames

Using HTML styles

Inserting hyperlinks into Web documents

Adding visual and multimedia elements to Web pages

Working with Web Folders

Publishing your pages on the Web

Microsoft Word has extensive Web-document authoring capabilities. You can save your paper documents directly as Web pages, or even create pages that are only intended for Web use. Word simplifies the creation of Web pages by acting as a WYSIWYG ("What You See Is What You Get") Web-authoring tool, and the facilities within Word are based on many of the same commands used to create Word documents, thus making Web documents very easy to create. This chapter takes you through creating Web pages using Word's Web authoring tools.

However, before we move on we should explain one thing. Although Word can create Web pages, that doesn't mean you should use Word to do so. We'll be looking at how Word works with these Web tools, but you should be aware that Word creates very "heavy" HTML code. HTML—HyperText Markup Language—is the coding that creates Web pages. Word creates extremely complex HTML code that can cause problems in a number of ways:

+ It may not work well in many Web browsers, in particular in the second-most popular browser, Netscape Navigator, and even in old versions of Internet Explorer.

+ Because the code is so complex, it's very hard to work with in a text editor, as is often necessary with Web pages—so if the page is to become part of a Web site and probably require later edits and modification, it may be hard to deal with.

+ It almost certainly won't work well in most HTML-authoring programs, thanks to the complexity of the code.

+ Many Word documents, with a wide variety of formatting, tables, images, and so on, won't even work well in advanced HTML-authoring programs, even in Microsoft's own program, FrontPage.

We're not saying you should never use Word to create Web pages. What we're saying is that there are many times, most perhaps, when Word should not be used. For instance:

+ Do not use Word as a primary tool for creating Web sites. There are far better tools available. In fact professional Web designers or coders using Word to create Web sites are as rare as wheels on snowboards.

✦ Do not use Word to create Web pages that you plan to pass on to a Web designer or coder for inclusion in a site. At the very least, they'll be displeased; they may even send it back to you.

✦ Do not use Word to create pages that you want to post on a site visited by a wide range of users—the pages may not display well in the browsers of some visitors.

✦ Do not use Word to create pages that will have to be edited in the future in other HTML programs.

You may now be thinking, "Wow, that doesn't leave a lot of times you can use Word to create Web pages!" And you'd be right. Here are some occasions in which you can use Word to create Web pages:

✦ You plan to use the pages for you alone, or a small number of people who know you are using Word and are okay with it. You could, for example, post reference information on an intranet or private Web site for use by your company's department.

✦ You are creating pages to be viewed by a limited range of people, you know for sure that these folks all use a recent version of Internet Explorer, and you check carefully that the pages you create can be viewed properly. (The last criteria is really a rule that you should follow however you create pages.)

✦ You are using Word to create paper documents or perhaps PDF (Adobe Acrobat) documents, you also want to put the documents on the Web, and you don't care too much about browser-compatibility issues.

So, having said all that, some of you may not bother reading on. For the others who still want to know how to create Web pages using Word, read on.

Creating Web Pages

You can create Web pages with Word in several ways:

✦ Start a new Web page using the Web Page template from the New Document task pane

✦ Use one of the templates in Microsoft's online template library

✦ Convert an existing document to a Web page

After you create your Web pages using the templates, those pages appear just like any other document in Word. In effect, Word is a word processor for Web pages. Most of the menus, toolbars, and features work for both Word and Web documents. If a feature doesn't work in a Web document because it's not supported by Web browsers, Word alerts you that this feature isn't available.

Tip
Microsoft Internet Explorer includes the Edit With button on the toolbar (located in between the Print and Discuss buttons). Click the little triangle on this button, and a variety of options appear: Edit with Microsoft Excel, Edit with Notepad, Edit with Microsoft FrontPage, Edit with Microsoft Word, and perhaps others. Select Edit with Microsoft Word to open the current document in Word.

Using a Web Page template

You create a document using a Web Page template the same way that you create any new document in Word. Choose File ➪ New to display the New Document task pane; then click the

Web Page link in the pane. You can also find the Web Page template in the Templates dialog box under the General tab.

Note that earlier versions of Word had more than half a dozen Web-page templates and a Web Page Wizard. These, with the exception of the basic Web Page template, are now gone. Perhaps Microsoft intends for people to use FrontPage if they really want to create anything more than simple Web pages.

Microsoft's template library

Another place to find Web page templates is Microsoft's online template library. Choose File ➪ New to open the New Document task pane; then click the Templates Home Page link to open the Templates Home page in your browser. We've looked at this site before—it contains a wide range of templates for Word and Excel, but, at the time of writing at least, few if any Web page templates. However, no doubt, as this library grows (it's a work in progress), Web page templates will be added, so take a look now and then.

Saving Word documents in HTML

You can also open an existing Word document, and save it in the HTML Web page format. When any Word document is saved as a Web page, almost all of that document's information, including content, formatting, and document properties, are retained in the HTML (HyperText Markup Language) document. Some aspects of the Word document, however, may not convert to HTML. Fortunately, Word helps you with the conversion of Word documents to Web documents by automatically detecting any incompatibilities and telling you what actions Word can take to convert those offending items.

Note You can view any Word document as a Web document before converting it to one by choosing View ➪ Web Layout (Word displays the document in a simulated browser layout inside the Word program itself) or using File ➪ Web Page Preview (Word creates a temporary file and loads it into your Web browser).

Saving a Word document as a Web page is easy. Choose File ➪ Save as Web Page, which displays the Save As dialog box. By default the Single File Web Page (*.mht; *.mhtml) format is selected, but you actually have three different formats available:

✦ **Single File Web Page (*.mht; *.mhtml):** This is a special non-standard Microsoft format for a Web page. It will not work in many browsers! Word takes everything in the Word document and puts it into a single document. This includes images, which is not the way standard Web pages are created. When you see a Web page on the Internet that contains images, those images are not in the Web page itself; they are stored elsewhere, and *linked* to the document. With the .mht/.mhtml format, though, the images are converted to a special text coding, so they can be saved in the Web-page documents (which are just text documents). When loaded into Internet Explorer, the browser reads the code and converts it back to an image.

✦ **Web Page (*.htm; *.html):** When you use this format, Word saves the .htm file in the directory you specify. It then creates a subdirectory with the same name, in which it saves two copies of each image—one in the .gif format and one in the .png format. (The Web page can display the most appropriate format, depending on the browser in which it is being displayed.) Word also creates filelist.xml, an XML Schema file.

Cross-Reference You learn more about XML in Chapter 27.

✦ **Web Page, Filtered (*.htm; *.html):** This is closer to the standard Web page format. In fact, when you use this format, Word removes some features in the document. It then creates a folder of the same name and inside places a single copy of each image in the document, in .jpg format. Still, it's by no means a "clean" HTML document; it can be several times larger then an equivalent file created in FrontPage, for instance.

> **Note** Only use the first two formats if you are absolutely sure only people using a recent version of Internet Explorer will be viewing the files. The final format is the most widely compatible. Use it under most circumstances to ensure that the files are most likely to be usable, taking into consideration the caveats from the beginning of this chapter.

The Change Title button in the Save As dialog box allows you to change the page title for the document you are saving, which appears on the title bar of the Web browser window. When you save a Word document as a Web page, Word closes that document and then reopens it in the HTML format.

However, if you selected the last format—Web Page, Filtered—formatting and other items that aren't supported by HTML are removed or converted to something else. You'll see a warning message, and when you continue, if the document includes formatting that isn't supported by Web browsers, a dialog box appears and lists the formatting features in question (see Figure 26-1). Clicking the Tell Me More button displays Word Help information describing which features can and cannot be carried over to the Web document.

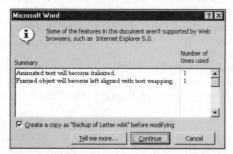

Figure 26-1: An information dialog box telling you that some of the features in a document aren't supported by Web browsers.

> **Tip** To create Web pages that use only formatting supported by Web browsers, create a new document based on a Web template or the Web Page Wizard. Don't begin with a Word document and convert to HTML.

Word and FrontPage

As we discussed earlier in this chapter, Word is by no means the perfect Web-page tool. But suppose that you have few options: you have Word documents that somehow you have to get into Web pages. What do you do? How, for instance, do you use Word documents within FrontPage, Microsoft Office's true HTML program.

The challenge is to get rid of all the superfluous HTML tags that Word uses. A Web page created by Word can be several times the size of a page created with a more traditional HTML program, such as FrontPage. You want to be able to get your work out of Word and into FrontPage—or another HTML-editing program—still maintaining formatting such as italics and bold, and with cleaner HTML tags. Figure 26-2 show you a comparison. On the left, the text was copied from Word and dropped into FrontPage. On the right, you can see pretty much the same text, but the HTML code was created directly inside FrontPage. In the top frame of each window is the HTML code used to create the text. As you can see, the text copied from Word is several times the size of the text generated by FrontPage.

Here are a few tips for taking your Word text and using it in FrontPage or another HTML Web-page editor:

✦ You can simply copy and paste text from a Word document and drop it into many HTML editors, such as FrontPage. As you can see in Figure 26-2, however, the HTML created is still a little messy.

✦ If you don't have too much text to put into a Web page, and you really want to make sure that the text is clean, copy the text into a text editor, such as Notepad. Then select it again in the text editor, and copy and paste it into the HTML editor.

✦ When you save Web pages from Word, use the Web Page, Filtered format. This provides the cleanest HTML that Word can manage.

✦ Choose Tools ➪ Options, click the General tab, and then click the Web Options button. In the dialog box that appears, clear the Rely on CSS for Font Formatting check box. Make sure that Disable Features Not Supported By These Browsers is selected, and select the browser option at the top of the People Who View This Web Page Will Be Using drop-down list box. These settings will give you the smallest pages.

✦ Microsoft publishes a special HTML filter designed for reducing the size of HTML files created by Word. Then strangely, they hide the filter. It's on the Microsoft Web site, but it's not easy to find if you don't know what to look for. In any case, there's a catch. At the time of writing, the latest filter, designed for Office 2000, doesn't work with Office 2003! To check to see if Microsoft has updated the filter, go to www.microsoft.com/office/ and search for *office html filter*.

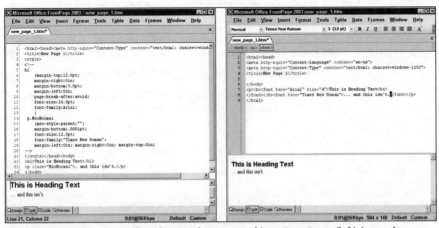

Figure 26-2: You can see that the Word text pasted into FrontPage (left) is much more complicated than the HTML code created by FrontPage (right).

Tip   When you save an HTML file from Word, notice that it has a special icon. It looks like the normal icon used for HTML files, but it has a small Word icon in the top-left corner. In other words, Word recognizes the HTML file as its own. If you try to open this file by double-clicking it, it loads in Word. In fact, if you try to open it using FrontPage, FrontPage *won't* open it. It passes it on to Word to open! How do you fix this so that you can open it in another HTML editor? First, be sure that the file is not open in Word; then open the file in a text editor, such as Notepad. Look for this tag: `<meta name=Generator content="Microsoft Word (filtered)">`. This is the tag that Windows, Word, and FrontPage recognize. Delete the tag and save the file. The icon changes, and now Word recognizes the file as a normal HTML file that you can open in FrontPage.

Working with Frames

Word lets you create frames in either Word or Web documents. Frames help make your Web documents better organized, more easily navigated, and more impressive in appearance. Both Microsoft Internet Explorer and Netscape Navigator support the use of frames.

Frames are sub-windows within a Web browser, each containing a different document. Clicking a link in one frame can change the document in that frame or change the document in *another* frame. Figure 26-3 shows a Web document with frames.

Note   The term *frame* here refers to something very different from the frame "boxes" used in Word (and explained in Chapter 18). Frames, in the context of Web pages, refer to the partitioning of a Web browser window, with a different document being loaded into each frame (each partition).

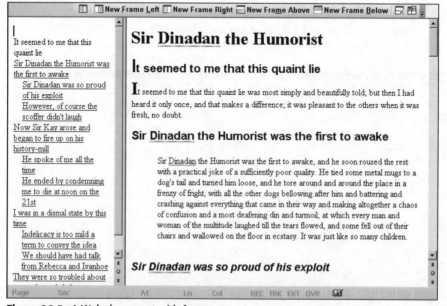

Figure 26-3: A Web document with frames.

Creating frames

Creating a Web document with frames is easy. Choose Format ➪ Frames ➪ New Frames Page. A new document and the Frames toolbar appear (see Figure 26-4). Table 26-1 explains the buttons on the Frames toolbar; you can also access the same commands from the Frames command submenu in the Format menu.

Figure 26-4: The Frames toolbar.

Table 26-1: Frames Toolbar Buttons

Button	Description
Table of Contents in Frame	Creates a vertical frame with a Table of Contents field code inside it, to the left of the frame in which the insertion point is placed.
New Frame Left	Creates a vertical frame to the left of the frame in which the insertion point is placed.
New Frame Right	Creates a vertical frame to the right of the frame in which the insertion point is placed.
New Frame Above	Creates a horizontal frame above the frame in which the insertion point is placed.
New Frame Below	Creates a horizontal frame below the frame in which the insertion point is placed.
Delete Frame	Deletes the selected frame in which the insertion point is placed.
Frame Properties	Displays the Frame Properties dialog box, for the frame in which the insertion point is placed.

Click the appropriate button to add a frame. A frame border also appears along with a scroll bar. You can adjust the frame by dragging the border. We had better explain what's going on here, because it's a little confusing, in particular for people who are used to working with frames using HTML-authoring tools. The way in which Word displays file names in the title bar exacerbates this confusion—it's hard to tell sometimes exactly which file you're working on.

Before you can choose Format ➪ Frames ➪ New Frames Page you must have a document open. When you select this command, a new document is created and becomes what is sometimes known as a *frame-definition document*. This is a file that describes a *frameset*—a collection of frames and the documents inside them. Someone viewing the frames and documents never actually sees the frame-definition document; rather, the Web browser reads the document to find out how to build the frames.

When you select the command, Word creates a new frame-definition document and then takes the original document and places it in a single frame in the new frameset. Click the Save button on the toolbar and Word asks you to provide a new name for that frame-definition document.

Now what do you have? You have a frame-definition document that tells Word—and a Web browser in which it may be loaded—to create a frameset that contains a single frame, and in that single frame to place the original document. Now you can create more frames, and place more documents inside them.

Adding documents to frames

Each time you add another frame, a blank document is opened inside the frame; you can use this document, or replace it with another:

✦ Add text and images to the document, and then right-click inside the frame and select Save Current Frame As.

✦ With the insertion point in the frame, click the Frame Properties button, or right-click in the frame and select Frame Properties. Under the Frame tab of the Frame Properties dialog box click the Browse button to find the file you want. Leave the Link to File check box selected.

✦ Do the same as above, but clear the Link to File check box.

Here's another weird little idiosyncrasy you should understand. If you leave the Link to File check box checked, Word uses the selected document as the one to place in the frame. If you *clear* this check box, Word creates a copy of the file and saves it somewhere—not anywhere logical, not necessarily in the same directory as the frame-definition document, unfortunately. Look in the directory *above* the directory in which you placed the frame-definition document, and you'll probably find it there.

Note, of course, that after you have created this new copy, closed and saved your document, and then you reopen it, there is a link to this new document. If you open this document separately and then modify it, those changes appear in the document once displayed in the frame. If you open the Frame Properties dialog box, you can see that the Initial Page text box has the correct path to the new, copied document, but the Link to File box is still cleared. This doesn't make sense. In fact, the way in which frames are managed is rather confusing. So you may want to play around with this feature to figure out how to use it before you employ it for real.

Note   So what are you left with after creating all these frames? Suppose you have three frames. What you actually have are four documents: the invisible frame-definition document, plus the three documents inside the three frames. Close the frameset document, find one of the three document files in Windows Explorer, or using File ➪ Open, and what happens? That document alone opens in Word. What if you open the frame-definition document? Word reads the document, creates the frames, and opens all three frame documents.

Configuring frames

Using the Frame Properties dialog box you can configure frames in a variety of ways, specifying what the frame borders look like, the frame sizes, whether they can be resized, and so on. Table 26-2 describes all these settings. Figures 26-5 and 26-6 show the dialog box tabs.

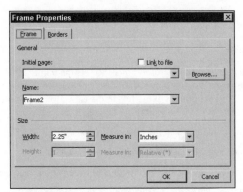

Figure 26-5: The Frame tab in the Frame Properties dialog box.

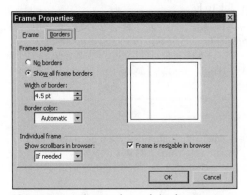

Figure 26-6: The Borders tab in the Frame Properties dialog box.

Table 26-2: Frame Properties

Option	Description
Initial Page	The page that loads into the frame when it first opens (it can change when the viewer clicks a link, as we'll explain later in this chapter).
Link to File	Click this to tell Word to use the file you select with the Browse button, rather than creating a copy of the file.
Name	Every frame is assigned a name, and you can type or select one. (If you don't assign a name, Word will.) You can use the frame name to point to the frame when linking from one document to another, as discussed in the "Linking between frames" section later in this chapter.
Width	The width of the frame, in the Measure In units.

Continued

Table 26-2 *(continued)*

Option	Description
Measure In	Select Inches, Percentage (for instance, 50 sets the frame to half the width of the Word or browser window), or Relative (if one frame is 2 and the other is 1, the first frame is two-thirds and the second is one-third of the width).
Height	The height of the frame, in the Measure In units.
No Borders	Click this to create frames with no borders between them.
Show All Frame Borders	This, the default setting, displays borders between the frames.
Width of Border	Use this to enlarge or narrow the width of the borders between frames.
Border Color	The default is gray, but you can pick another color.
Show Scrollbars in Browser	Select If Needed (scroll bars display only when part of the document is hidden from view), Always (scroll bars display at all times, whether needed or not), Never (scroll bars won't display even if some of the content is hidden).
Frame is Resizable in Browser	Clear this, and the user won't be able to resize frames in the browser.

Tip   When linking to a frameset, remember to link to the frame-definition document. Link to an individual document displayed in a frame, and you'll load that document, not the frameset.

Using HTML Styles

As with Word documents, you can use styles to add the most common HTML tags as you create Web documents. With a Web document in Word, the Style box on the Formatting toolbar contains a collection of common HTML formats and some basic Word document styles that work within the Web authoring environment. If you're an HTML coder at heart, however, you can always bypass the styles and enter HTML tags directly using the source code view of the Web page.

Note   You can add HTML directly to the source code in two ways. You can close the document and then open it in a text editor (assuming you have already saved the document as an HTML file). Then, in the text editor, you can add, remove, and modify HTML tags. You can also choose View ⇨ HTML Source to open the document inside Microsoft Script Editor, a text editor designed for use with script languages such as JavaScript, but that can also be used for HTML files. Note that you won't see the View ⇨ HTML Source command until you have saved the document in HTML format.

Word provides a number of special HTML styles, although they're initially hidden. To see them, open the Styles and Formatting task pane (Format ⇨ Styles and Formatting) and select All Styles from the Show list box at the bottom. Scroll down the list, and you'll notice a number of styles that start with HTML—HTML Address, HTML Cite, HTML Keyboard. These are styles that correspond directly with HTML tags recognized by Web browsers.

Note If these styles are not visible, open the Styles and Formatting task pane (choose Format ➪ Styles and Formatting), select Custom from the Show drop-down list box at the bottom, and select the styles you want in the Format Settings dialog box.

Other styles are converted by Word directly into an HTML tag. For instance, text that you set as Heading 1 will be saved in a Web page using the `<H1></H1>` tags. In other cases Word uses CSS—Cascading Style Sheets—to define text formatting. For instance, text may be formatted in this manner:

```
<p class=MsoBodyTextIndent>This is the link text</p>
```

This is not a standard HTML text-formatting tag, Rather, the tag tells the browser to look earlier in the document, for a class called `MsoBodyTextIndent`. This class defines what the text looks like.

Of course, most of this is transparent. The average user doesn't know or need to know exactly how Word is coding text to make it viewable in a browser.

Inserting Hyperlinks

Hyperlinks are what make connections to information possible via the World Wide Web. A hyperlink can jump to a location in the current document, to another of your documents, or to someone else's document anywhere on the Web. You can even use hyperlinks to jump to multimedia objects such as sound files or video clips. The hyperlink can be placed on text or images.

To insert a hyperlink on existing text, follow these steps:

1. Select the text you want to link from, and choose Insert ➪ Hyperlink, press Ctrl+K, or click the Insert Hyperlink button. The Insert Hyperlink dialog box appears (see Figure 26-7). Make sure the Existing File or Web Page button is selected.

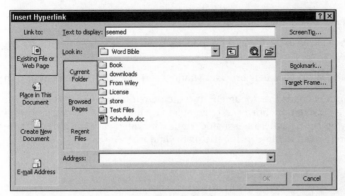

Figure 26-7: The Insert Hyperlink dialog box.

2. Type a URL to which you want to link in the Address box, or use the folder tree to navigate to a file. You can use the Current Folder, Browsed Pages, and Recent Files buttons to change the view—Browsed Pages, for instance, shows a list of pages recently viewed in your browser.

   To link to something in the same document, click the Place in This Document button or the Bookmark button—you'll be able to link to a bookmark, to the top of the document, or to a heading.

To create an e-mail hyperlink—one that opens the user's e-mail program—click the E-mail Address button and enter an e-mail address and a subject line.

To create a link to a new document, click Create New Document.

3. To change the text that appears for your hyperlink, you can modify it in the Text to Display box.

4. To add a ScreenTip, click the ScreenTip button. The Set Hyperlink Screen Tip dialog box appears in which you can type the text that you want to appear when a user moves a mouse pointer over the object. Note that most people using Internet Explorer will see this, but those using other browsers will not.

5. Click OK.

Linking between frames

If you are working with frames, you can create two types of hyperlinks. The standard link loads the referenced document—the one to which you are linking—into the same frame that holds the document with the link. When the user clicks the link the first document is removed and replaced by the second.

But you can also create links that load the referenced document into another frame. For instance, if you have a Table of Contents frame on the left of a 2-frame frameset, clicking a link in the Table of Contents document can load the referenced document into the right frame.

Click the Target Frame button to open the Set Target Frame dialog box (see Figure 26-8). Click on the frame into which you want to load the document, or select from the list box. In fact, several other options are available in the drop-down list box, beyond just the names of the frames:

✦ **Page Default:** The default setting; uses whatever you have set as the page default (note the Set As Default for All HyperLinks check box); if you haven't set a default, uses Same Frame.

✦ **Same Frame:** Loads the referenced document into the same frame.

✦ **Whole Page:** Breaks the frameset and loads the referenced document, by itself, in the browser window.

✦ **New Window:** Opens a new browser window and loads the document into that window.

✦ **Parent Frame:** Loads the document into the parent frame, which is usually the same as the Whole Page option; however, in complex frame systems (which you should never create!) you could have frames inside frames, in which case the parent frame is not the entire window but a frame inside the main window.

Figure 26-8: The Set Target Frame dialog box.

Creating hyperlinks using AutoFormatting

Using the automatic formatting features in Word, you can create a hyperlink just by typing the address of the file to which you want to jump. Network paths and Internet addresses can automatically become hyperlink display text that a reader clicks to jump to the hyperlink destination.

To create hyperlinks using AutoFormatting, follow these steps:

1. Choose Tools ➪ AutoCorrect Options.

2. Click the AutoFormat As You Type tab.

3. Under the Replace As You Type setting, click the Internet and Network Paths With Hyperlinks check box.

4. Click OK.

When you type the address of the file located on a network or the Internet, Word changes that address to a hyperlink. The address of the file then becomes the display text on which the reader clicks.

Adding Tables to Web Pages

Working with tables in Web pages is just like working with tables in Word documents. You can create a new table structure and enter text, or you can convert existing text to a table grid layout. You can format a table in a wide variety of ways. You can merge and split cells, format some or all of the gridlines, add borders and shading, adjust column width and spacing, adjust row height, and delete rows and columns. You can even create forms based on Word tables that act as front ends for databases and worksheets. Use the commands in the Table menu or the Tables and Borders toolbar to create and modify tables in your Web documents.

Cross-Reference   For more information on working with tables, see Chapter 9.

Adding Visual Elements to Web Pages

Web pages are a visual medium that allows the use of visual elements to enhance the presentation of your material and provide structure to your documents. These basic visual elements include themes, background and text colors, horizontal lines, borders, shading, bullets, and numbered lists. Because Word has seamlessly integrated the creation of Word documents and Web documents, the commands used to create these same elements in Word documents also create them in Web documents.

A theme is a set of unified design elements and color schemes for background images, bullets, fonts, horizontal lines, and other document elements. A theme provides a consistent look for your document using color, fonts, and graphics. When you apply a theme to a document, Word customizes the following elements for that document: background color or graphic, body and heading styles, bullets, horizontal lines, hyperlink colors, and table border colors. You can apply a new theme, change to a different theme, or even remove a theme by choosing Format ➪ Theme, which displays the Theme dialog box (see Figure 26-9).

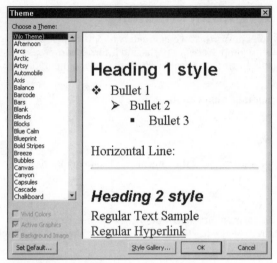

Figure 26-9: The Theme dialog box.

Many of these themes are horrible and should never be used. Others are not quite so ugly. A few are reasonably attractive. However, you can modify the appearance of each theme by using the Vivid Colors, Active Graphics, and Background Image check boxes.

✦ The Vivid Colors feature modifies some of the themes colors.

✦ Active Graphics turns the use of animated graphics on and off.

✦ The Background Image check box allows you to remove or add the background image.

Not only are these themes often ugly, they can also make the Web pages much larger and slower to load.

Cross-Reference   See Chapter 14 for more information about themes.

Adding Multimedia Elements to Web Pages

Images, sounds, and video clips make your Web pages come alive, and Word's Web authoring environment provides tools for adding and working with these multimedia elements. Remember that sound and video files can be large, however, which can be a problem for Web users with slower modems.

Note   Word Text Effects in the Font dialog box (Format ➪ Font) don't work in Web pages, and animated text becomes italicized text when converted to a Web document.

Adding images and drawing objects

Pictures are a big part of Web documents, and Word makes adding them to a Web document easy. Once the picture is inserted in your Web document, you can work with it just as you would work with a picture in a Word document. If you insert an image that is not a GIF or

JPEG format file, that image is automatically converted to GIF. Word saves the images as Image.gif, Image1.gif, Image2.gif, and so on. If you insert a JPEG image, the JPEG format and file name extension (.jpg) are retained. Drawing objects such as AutoShapes, text boxes, and WordArt effects can also be inserted into Web pages as GIF files.

In addition, you can insert animated GIF images that display movements. For example, an animated GIF file of a pair of scissors may show them cutting, and another animated GIF image might show a bouncing ball. You can use these to create activity for your bullets or buttons. You insert an animated GIF file just as you would insert any other graphic file, and they are supported by most Web browsers.

Cross-Reference   For more information on working with images and drawing objects in Word, see Chapters 17 and 18.

Adding sound and video objects

Word's Web authoring environment provides several tools for integrating sounds into your Web documents. For Web users to hear these sounds, however, they must have a sound system installed on their computer, and their Web browser must support the format of the sound file that you inserted. You can insert sound files in WAV, MID, AU, AIF, RMI, SND, and MP2 (MPEG audio) formats. To add a sound file to a Web document, choose Insert ➪ Picture ➪ Clip Art and select Sounds from the Results Should Be drop-down list box.

Once the file is inserted into your Web page, it appears with a speaker icon. Double-clicking the icon plays the sound. You can also insert a hyperlink on which the user can click to download the sound file instead of playing it. (See the "Inserting Hyperlinks" section earlier in this chapter.)

In addition, you can add inline video clips to your Web page, which means that the video is downloaded when the user opens the page. You can determine whether the video plays when the page is opened or when the user points to the video. You can also insert a hyperlink to a video, which means that the user can click on the hyperlink to download the video and play it. Microsoft videos are in the AVI format, but AVI is not the standard format for video clips on the Internet. Use the .MPG or .MPEG formats or the QuickTime .MOV format for your video files instead. To insert a video clip into a Web document, choose Insert ➪ Picture ➪ Clip Art and select Movies from the Results Should Be drop-down. Video clips are typically large files, however, so use them sparingly.

Note   For more information on working with multimedia in Word, see Chapter 19.

Previewing Web Pages

In Word's Web authoring environment, your Web page looks a lot like the finished product a Web user would view, but it's not an exact version. Choose File ➪ Web Page Preview to display your Web document in the Internet Explorer Web browser. If you've made any changes that you didn't save before choosing Web Page Preview, Word prompts you to save your changes before executing the preview.

Of course Word also has the Web Layout view. Choosing View ➪ Web Layout displays any document as a Web document. Unlike the Web Page Preview command, however, this view shows you how a document would appear as a Web page without invoking Internet Explorer. You can use the Web Layout command to check out a Word document before saving it as a Web document to see how the converted document would appear—before you actually convert it.

Using the Web Toolbar

The Web toolbar is another example of the tight integration of Word with Internet Explorer. Whether you're authoring a Web document or not, you can take advantage of this integration by displaying the Web toolbar. Choose View ➪ Toolbars ➪ Web to display the Web toolbar (see Figure 26-10), with which you can access the Web and move back and forth among Web pages that you create. (There's also a Web Tools toolbar, which we look at in Chapter 27.)

Figure 26-10: The Web toolbar.

The Web toolbar adds several Internet Explorer toolbar buttons to Word. When you use them to browse to a Web page, that page opens in an Internet Explorer window. The Favorites button stores the same Web page bookmarks that you may have stored in Internet Explorer; the Start Page button takes you to whatever page you've established as your home page in Internet Explorer.

After your Internet connection is established, you can use the Web toolbar to switch quickly between local documents and documents on the Web. The Address drop-down list box stores the last 25 documents that you've viewed in either Word or Internet Explorer—whether those documents are stored on your hard disk, your network, your intranet, or the Web. To view any of these documents from within Word, select it from the Address drop-down list box on the Web toolbar.

It's convenient to use the browsing buttons on the Web toolbar. You can click the Back and Forward buttons to move among documents that you've opened, and you can click Stop to halt the loading of a file or Refresh to reload a fresh copy of it. You can even hide other toolbars that may be in your way by clicking Show Only Web Toolbar.

Working with Web Folders

A *Web Folder* is a shortcut to a Web server where you can publish documents to be viewed in Web browsers. Before you can create, copy, save, or manage Web folders and files, however, you must have access to a Web server. The Web server must also support Web Folders to use this feature. You can use the Microsoft Personal Web Server (PWS) or Microsoft Internet Information Server as your Web server, or you can use any Web server that supports Web Folders. The Web server can be on your local network, or it can be on a server run by a Web hosting service or Internet service provider.

You can view and manage the contents of Web Folders from within Word using the File ➪ Open or File ➪ Save As commands. In either the Open or Save As dialog box, click the Web Folders icon on the Places list (the wide shaded bar that runs down the left side of the dialog box). Figure 26-11 shows the Save As dialog box with Web Folders created. You can create new Web Folders by clicking the Create New Folder button in the Save As (or the Open) dialog box.

Figure 26-11: The Save As dialog box with Web Folders displayed.

Note

To create a Web folder for any existing Web server location, type the Web address in the File Name box of the Save As dialog box. For example, type **http://www.bookware.com/ folder** to create a Web folder to that destination. If the Web server requires a username and password to gain access, the Enter Network Password dialog box appears.

You can also create and manage your Web Folders by clicking the Web Folders icon in My Computer, which displays the Web Folders window (see Figure 26-12).

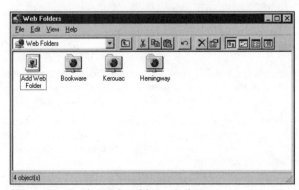

Figure 26-12: The Web Folders window.

Publishing Your Web Documents

After you've created your HTML documents using Word, you may want to find an ISP or Web-hosting company that allows you to make your pages available to the world.

Note An ISP (Internet Service Provider) is a company that provides access to the Internet, such as America Online, EarthLink, Juno, and so on. ISPs usually provide some space for Web pages, too, so you can post a Web site on their servers. A Web-hosting company is a firm that provides hosting for Web sites, but probably doesn't provide Internet access. That's fine, you don't have to post your pages with the same company that provides you with Internet access, and true Web-hosting companies provide many more hosting features than do ISPs. Check out the hosting-directory sites, such as www.TopHosts.com and http://webhost.thelist.com/.

To publish your pages to a Web server hosted by an ISP or hosting company, you need to transfer the HTML documents and image files to your HTML document directory provided by the company. You can use a number of methods to do this:

✦ **FTP:** The most common method is FTP (File Transfer Protocol). A number of FTP tools are available, but our favorite is CuteFTP (www.CuteFTP.com/).

✦ **A Custom Tool:** Your ISP or hosting company may provide a special tool for transferring files.

✦ **Microsoft's Web Publishing Wizard:** This is a tool that you may be able to download from Microsoft's Download Center, although it's well hidden: www.microsoft.com/downloads/.

✦ **Save directly from Word:** You can type a Web-site URL, and any appropriate directory path, in front of a file name in the File Save dialog box and, in many cases, when you click Save you'll see a Login dialog box. Provide the right User ID and password, and the file will be saved directly to the Web site.

Which method should you use? That depends on the firm you are working with. Check your ISP or hosting company for directions on uploading files to their servers.

Summary

As we explained at the start of this chapter, you may not want to use Word's Web-creation tools very often. Still, the tools are there for the occasions on which it does make sense. This chapter explained some of the ways in which you can use Word to create Web pages:

✦ Create Web pages using templates from the Web Page Wizard. Choosing File ➪ New displays the New dialog box. Clicking the Web Pages tab displays Web page templates and the Web Page Wizard. You can also use the Web Page template in the General tab to create a new Web page without any formatting.

✦ Save a Word document as an HTML document by choosing File ➪ Save as Web Page.

✦ Create documents with frames using the Format ➪ Frames command.

✦ Insert hyperlinks by choosing Insert ➪ Hyperlink, pressing Ctrl+K, or clicking the Insert Hyperlink button. In the Insert Hyperlink dialog box, you can specify a path to or URL for the object that you want.

✦ Apply basic visual elements to your Web pages, including adding background colors or textures, changing text colors, adding horizontal lines, adding borders and shading, and creating bulleted and numbered lists.

✦ Insert images and multimedia elements into your Web pages by clicking the Insert Picture button on the Standard toolbar or by choosing Insert ➪ Picture.

✦ View your Web pages in a Web browser by choosing File ➪ Web Page Preview, or view your document in the Word window as a Web page using View ➪ Web Layout.

✦ Use the Web toolbar (View ➪ Toolbars ➪ Web) to navigate your Web pages from within Word.

✦ Work with Web Folders in Word using the File ➪ Open or File ➪ Save As command; then click the Web Folders icon on the Places list.

✦ To publish to a Web server, check with your ISP or hosting company for instructions.

✦   ✦   ✦

Advanced HTML and XML

✦ ✦ ✦ ✦

In This Chapter

Word and HTML, styles, and XML

Creating HTML forms

Adding a script to your Web page

Adding video, sounds, and scrolling text

Working with XML

✦ ✦ ✦ ✦

This chapter covers the more advanced Web-authoring tools provided by Word, such as how to add form components and insert multimedia in Web pages. We also look at XML (eXtensible Markup Language), a misunderstood coding language that few Word users are likely to work with, despite the fact that Microsoft has put a lot of time into adding XML support to the program. If you really need XML, there's a good chance you'll use a dedicated XML tool. If you don't need it . . . well, obviously you won't need to use Word for XML either.

Let's be honest here: Word is not the best Web-authoring or XML tool available. In addition, there's another issue. Although we look at how these tools work, in most cases they won't do you much good unless you understand what they are for. Unfortunately, there isn't room in this book to provide much *detail* on XML and advanced HTML. These are complicated subjects on which hundreds of complete (and fat) books have been written. Fully teaching those subjects is way out of the scope of this book.

Understanding HTML, XML, Styles, and Word

HTML stands for *HyperText Markup Language* and is used to specify the structure and formatting of text for Web pages. HTML uses codes within angle brackets to specify the formatting instructions. For example, to specify that text appear in boldface, you would surround the text with `<B> </B>` tags. The opening `<B>` tag instructs the browser to begin displaying the text in boldface, and the closing `</B>` tag instructs the browser to end displaying the text in boldface.

Tags also can include additional elements, called *attributes*, which are used only in the opening tag to help define specific properties for the element. For example, to add a paragraph, you would use the `<P> </P>` tags. To center the paragraph, you would add the `ALIGN=center` attribute, so the tags would appear as `<P ALIGN=center></P>`.

All HTML documents should consist of the following basic tags:

```
<HTML>
<HEAD>
 <TITLE>Page Title</TITLE>
```

```
<HEAD>
<BODY>
Page contents are inserted here...
</BODY>
</HTML>
```

Text that appears between the opening `<TITLE>` and the closing `</TITLE>` tags is what appears in the title bar of the browser window. The text and images between the opening `<BODY>` and the closing `</BODY>` tags is what appears in the browser window. HTML is not case sensitive, so you can enter tags in either upper- or lowercase. Word creates HTML tags in lowercase. If you are familiar with HTML and use the View ➪ HTML Source command, however, you're in for a surprise. HTML documents saved in Word include the standard HTML tags, but these tags are surrounded with styles and XML tags. (View ➪ HTML Source opens the Script Editor, as shown in Figure 27-1.)

Note The View ➪ HTML Source command is not available for all Web documents. If you save as an .MHT file, or as a non-filtered .HTM/.HTML file, the command is there; if you save as a "filtered" .HTM/.HTML page, the most standard Web-page format, the command is not available. You can still open the file in another HTML-authoring program, though, or in a text editor.

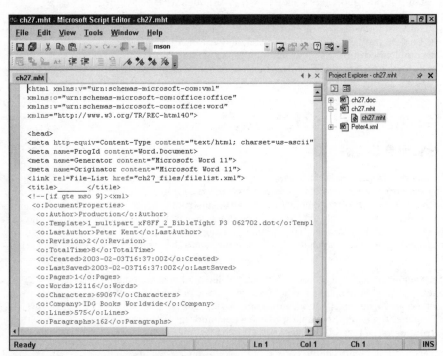

Figure 27-1: The Microsoft Script Editor.

Styles are an addition to the HTML standard that allow you to go far beyond the early HTML tags by providing a way to specify fonts and layout, such as margins and indents. Styles can be set in three ways: as a style sheet to format multiple Web pages, as a group of styles for a specific page, or as in-line styles to specify formatting for part of a Web page. Look at the top of a Web page saved using Word, and you see a `<style>` tag followed by the styles that specify the margins, typeface, and font size, headers and footers, and so on.

Understanding styles is fairly straightforward. The selector can be any tag for which you want to specify formatting instructions. For example, a style might appear as follows:

```
H1 {font-size: 24}
```

The H1 is a selector that refers to the HTML Heading 1 tag, or `<H1>`. The style also consists of a property and a value surrounded by curly braces. In this example, the property is the font size and the value is 24. Note that a colon separates the property and the value. You can specify multiple properties and values by separating each with a semicolon.

One powerful feature of styles is the ability to apply different styles to an HTML tag by creating different classes. When you add a tag, you can add the class attribute to apply all of the styles set for that class. For example, Word uses the `MsoNormal` class to define the paragraph `<P>` and the list item `<LI>` tags. At the top of the styles listed in the Word HTML source is the following code:

```
p.MsoNormal, li.MsoNormal {
   mso-style-parent: "";
   margin:0in;
   margin-bottom:.0001pt;
   mso-pagination:widow-orphan;
   font-size:12.0pt;
   mso-bidi-font-size:10.0pt;
   font-family:"Times New Roman";
}
```

If you look at a default paragraph in Word using the View ⇨ HTML Source command, it appears with the class attribute set to `MsoNormal`:

```
<p class=MsoNormal>Paragraph text.</p>
```

The properties and values set in the `MsoNormal` class control the formatting of your paragraph text. If you change any of the properties and values in the `p.MsoNormal` style, all the standard paragraphs reflect that change. Different sections of text are formatted using `<span>` and `<div>` tags. The `<span>` tag is used extensively in Word to specify where to begin and where to end adding the styles. The `<div>` tag is used to specify formatting for an entire section of a document, just as sections do in Word.

XML stands for *eXtensible Markup Language,* and it allows you to define your own markup elements. *Markup* simply refers to codes or tags used to mark components of a page, to add formatting and layout to a document. If a tag does not exist in HTML, you can create your own using XML. Specifying what elements and attributes are allowed in an XML document is accomplished by creating a Document Type Definition (DTD)—a document that defines the tags you want to use in your document. Microsoft was quick to embrace XML, because it allows you to create a DTD including tags that could be used to format Word and other Office documents so they could be displayed as Web pages. Microsoft has made a major commitment to XML to simplify the sharing of Office documents on the Web.

Note   Working with HTML styles and XML are complex subjects that we won't go into great detail with in this book. We'll look at how to use Word's tools to work with these things, but you should be aware that they are subjects requiring books-worth of knowledge, not a few pages.

The Web Tools Toolbar

Word has a special toolbar for working with advanced Web functions, the Web Tools toolbar (see Figure 27-2). Open this by right-clicking any toolbar and selecting Web Tools. Table 27-1 describes the buttons available in this toolbar.

Figure 27-2: The Web Tools toolbar.

Table 27-1: The Web Tools Toolbar

	Button	Function
	Design Mode	Turns on Design mode. In Design mode you can view component properties and see form boundaries.
	Properties	Opens the selected component's Properties dialog box.
	Microsoft Script Editor	Opens the Microsoft Script Editor, in which you can view the document's source HTML code.
	Checkbox	Inserts a check box into the document.
	Option Button	Inserts an option button.
	Drop-Down Box	Inserts a drop-down list box.
	List Box	Inserts an open list box.
	Text Box	Inserts a single-line text box.
	Text Area	Inserts a text-area component, a multi-line text box.
	Submit	Inserts a Submit button.

Button	Function
Submit With Image	Inserts a Submit button using an image.
Reset	Inserts a Reset button.
Hidden	Inserts a hidden form component (used to pass information to the script handling the form input).
Password	Inserts a password field.
Movie	Inserts a movie file.
Sound	Inserts a sound file.
Scrolling Text	Inserts a scrolling text banner.

Creating Forms

Forms allow you to interact with your readers and to provide dynamic data. For example, you might want to add a form that allows readers to provide feedback about your site, conduct a survey, or order a product. With the Web Tools toolbar, you can add form elements and set the properties for those form elements.

Information entered in a form is stored as `name=value` pairs. For example, if a form had a text box to allow the reader to enter his or her first name, you might specify that the name you want to use for the `name=value` pair would be called `fname`. The text the person enters in the text box would be the value of the `name=value` pair. If a person entered the name Herman, the `name=value` pair would be stored as the following:

```
fname=Herman
```

When all the contents of the form are submitted, the data are sent in a special format known as URL encoded data, which joins each `name=value` pair entered in the form with an ampersand (&). Spaces are converted to plus signs, and some characters, such as quotes, appear as numbers preceded by a percentage sign. The following shows an example of three `name=value` pairs (fname, lname, and book) sent as URL encoded data:

```
fname=Herman&lname=Melville&book=Moby+Dick
```

But what happens to this data? Word can help you create forms, but it doesn't create the scripts that use the data when it's transmitted back to the server. Such scripts can be Perl scripts, or full-blown programs written in C or Visual Basic. That's a very different subject. Although we won't leave you hanging with a form that doesn't work—we provide an example of a working form—remember that this is only a cursory introduction.

Understanding form elements and properties

Form elements in Word are not standard HTML tags; rather, they are ActiveX controls based on standard HTML form elements used on the World Wide Web. When you save the file, these controls are converted into their HTML equivalents. When you first insert a form element, Top of Form and Bottom of Form boundaries are inserted. These boundaries appear only in Design mode, however. They do not appear when the page is viewed in a Web browser. You insert additional elements you want in the form between those boundaries. It is possible to have more than one form on the same Web page. Figure 27-3 shows a sample form created using Word.

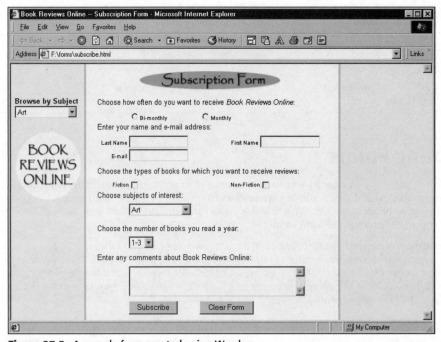

Figure 27-3: A sample form created using Word.

Adding form elements to a Web page

Forms such as feedback and survey forms are easy to create using Word. The following explains how to create a form as well as how to add form elements to a Web page:

1. Choose View ➪ Toolbars and click Web Tools, or right-click on a toolbar and choose Web Tools. The Web Tools toolbar appears.

2. Position the insertion point where you want the form element to appear, and then click the form element button in the Web Tools toolbar to insert that element. For example, choose the Text Box button, and Word automatically changes to Design mode and inserts a text box in the document. The first time that you enter a form element, Word inserts the top of form and the bottom of form boundaries around that element.

3. Double-click the Text Box form element in your document. The Properties dialog box opens (see Figure 27-4).

Figure 27-4: The Properties dialog box for the Text Box form element.

4. Enter the properties for the form element.

5. Repeat steps 2 through 4 until you have added all the form controls that you want. Make sure to keep the form elements between the Top of Form and the Bottom of Form boundaries. The last form control that you need to add is a Submit or an Image Submit control element so the reader can submit the form.

6. Add or modify any content that you want to introduce your form elements.

7. Click the Exit Design Mode button when you finish adding and editing your form elements, and then choose File ⇨ Save as Web Page to save your HTML document.

Adding check boxes

Check boxes allow a reader select one or more items. If you want the check box to be selected by default, double-click the check box to display the Properties window and click the Checked field. A drop-down arrow then appears. Choose the True setting from the drop-down list. In the example shown in Figure 27-3, the HTMLName fields are set to **fiction** for the first check box and to **nonfiction** for the second. Set the Value to the name that you want to identify the check box. Check boxes that are not checked are ignored when a form is submitted. When you receive the name=value pair, the setting for the check box is set to **on** for all the check boxes that are checked.

Adding option buttons

Option buttons, which also are called radio buttons, are used for a group of items that are mutually exclusive. In other words, the reader can select only one option button from a group. An option button is either on or off, so that when you receive the name=value pair, only one option button from a group is set to on. As with check boxes, you can set the Checked property to True to have the option button be selected by default. Use the same HTMLName for each option button element in the same group—that's how a group is defined, in fact: all the option buttons with the same HTMLName. The Value property setting is the value to return if the button is selected. Multiple groups of option buttons are permitted within the same form, but be sure to use unique HTMLNames for each group.

Adding a drop-down box

The Drop-Down Box button inserts a list box that displays available choices in a drop-down list format. If the list exceeds the size of the box, the user can scroll through that list to view the additional choices. You enter the items to appear in the list in the DisplayValues property box. Each list item needs to be separated by a semicolon in this box. In addition, do not type spaces between the items. In the example shown in Figure 27-3, the person is asked to select from the drop-down box the number of books he or she reads each year. The DisplayValues properties are set to the following:

```
1-3;4-6;7-9;10+
```

The HTMLName is the name that is assigned to the `name=value` pair. The Value property is the value returned for each item in the list. The names of the values can differ from the display values, but the number of values must be equal to or greater than the number of display values. By default, the values are set to match the DisplayValues. If you change any of the values, be sure to separate each with a semicolon, and do not type spaces between them.

The Selected property determines whether the first item appears in the box and is selected by default—sets the property to True or False. You can allow a person to select more than one item from a list by setting the MultiSelect property to True. The default MultiSelect setting is False. If you change MultiSelect to True, the control becomes a list box. If you change the MultiSelect settings, the settings for Selected are cleared. The Size property refers to the number of items to display in the drop-down list, the default size of which is 1.

Adding a list box

A list box displays the values of a list of items. If the number of items is larger than the displayed list box, a scroll bar appears. To add items to a list box, select the DisplayValues and then enter the items for the list, each separated by a semicolon (do not type spaces between them). The HTMLName is the name portion of the name=value pair that is assigned to the form element.

The Value property is the value returned for each item in the list. Word creates this list for you, by duplicating the DisplayValues that you entered, but you can change them—the names of the values can differ from the display values, but the number of values must be equal to the number of display values.

You can determine whether readers can select more than one item from a list box by setting the MultiSelect property to True (which it is by default). If you change MultiSelect settings, the settings for Selected are cleared. The Selected property determines whether the first item appears in the box and is selected by default (set it to True). The default size of the list box is set to three items. You can change the size, however, by entering the number of list items in the Size property box.

Adding a text box

Clicking the Text Box button in the Control Toolbox inserts a text box that allows the reader to enter a single line of text. In the example shown in Figure 27-3, a text box is provided for the reader to enter his or her e-mail address. The HTMLName is set to e-mail. Because we do not want to have a default address appear, we have left the text box Value property blank. You can specify the maximum numbers of characters that a person can enter by filling in the MaxLength property. The default setting is 0, which does not restrict the length of the entry.

Adding a text area

One of the simplest and most functional form elements is the text area box. You can easily create a feedback form with a text area box and a Submit and Reset button. The Text Area button on the Web Tools toolbar inserts a control in which the user can enter multiple lines of text. When you create a text area box, you can specify the number of columns and rows to display. In Design mode, when you double-click the text area box, the Properties box is displayed. Click Columns to change the width of the text area, and click Rows to change the height of the text area. You can have default text appear in the text area box by entering that text in the Value field.

Because the text area allows the reader to type in whatever he or she wants, you probably want to control how text is handled in this area, using the WordWrap property. You can choose from Virtual, Physical, or Off, the default setting. Words automatically wrap in the text area box if WordWrap is set to Virtual or Physical. Virtual causes new line characters to be added, so text appears in the text area. The new line characters are not included, however, when you receive the submitted form data. If the setting is Off, words do not wrap. Note that not all Web browsers support WordWrap.

Adding a hidden field

The Hidden field hides information from the reader, but passes it along with the data submitted by the person filling out the form. Hidden fields often carry information telling the processing script how to handle the data, such as providing an e-mail address of someone to notify when the form is submitted. The Hidden field is not visible unless you are in the form's Design mode or unless hidden text is set to show in your document. The HTMLName is the name portion of the `name=value` pair, and the Value property is the default text that is sent.

Adding a password

The password is similar to the text field, but instead of displaying the characters a person types, asterisks appear in the text box. The HTMLName is the name portion of the `name=value` pair. You can add a default value to the password field, but doing so would defeat its purpose. You can restrict the number of characters that can be entered in a Password text box by changing the MaxLength property. The MaxLength setting defaults to 0, which does not restrict the length of the entry.

Adding the Submit button or Image Submit button

To process the contents of a form, you must add a Submit button to the page. You can change the text that appears on a Submit button by entering a new button name in the Caption property box. By default, the Caption is set to Submit.

Note   There are two methods for submitting form data: POST and GET. GET is the default method, and it adds the URL-encoded data to the end of the URL. POST is used to store the data as standard input. Unless a program instructs you to use GET, you should change the method being used from GET to POST.

Another way to present a Submit button to the reader is to use the Image Submit button. This allows you choose an image to use as a button. When you click the Image Submit button control, the Picture dialog box appears for you to select the image that you want to use. When you copy the Web page to the server, be sure to copy the button image as well. Other than the Source property, which is the name of the image source file, the Image Submit properties are the same as those for the Submit button.

If you are familiar with HTML FORM tags, you may find the method Word uses to add attributes to the FORM tag a bit confusing. In HTML, you add the ACTION attribute to the FORM tag to specify the location of the file to run when the user clicks the Submit button. Word, however, wants you to enter this information using the Action property of the Submit button. If you look at the source after setting the Action property, you note that the Action property is added as the URL of the FORM tag's ACTION attribute.

Including a Reset button

The Reset button allows a reader to quickly remove his or her form entry data so that the form displays only the default settings. The value setting specifies the text that appears on the button, and the default setting is Reset.

Caution   Don't put Web-form components into a normal Word form (you learn about forms in Chapter 24). Web-form components are designed for use in Web pages only. The form components discussed in Chapter 24 are for use in normal Word documents. If you *add* Web-form components to a Word document, they won't work anyway . . . and even worse, they stop the Word-document form components from functioning. You won't be able to use the Protect command to turn on the form components. If you accidentally add a Web-form component, delete it, and then save and close the document. When you re-open the document, the form will work again.

Processing a Form

To process a form, you need a special program running on the server to accept and process the information submitted from the form. CGI (Common Gateway Interface) scripts are often used for this process. You can use any language to write a CGI script, but because most ISPs run Unix, you probably need to create a CGI script using a programming language such as Perl. Using Perl, you can store data in a file or use a Sendmail program to forward the form data to your e-mail address. The name of the CGI script file is added to the URL following your Web site's domain name or IP address as the Submit action property setting.

Note   Explaining how to process forms is well beyond the scope of this book. Either you need to write a script to handle the form, or you must send the information submitted by the form to a script provided by someone else. In either case, the complexities are many. Word is merely set up to create forms, but the far more complicated part of forms processing is creating the script.

Adding a Script to a Web Page Using Word

The Web Tools toolbar includes the Microsoft Script Editor button to display the Microsoft Script Editor window. The default setting for adding scripts using the Script Editor is VBScript, which is rather limiting, however, because these scripts run only using Microsoft Internet Explorer. The standard for cross-platform Web scripts is JavaScript.

Note   Microsoft calls its version of JavaScript JScript. Actually, a standard version of JavaScript was created by a European standards committee and is called ECMAScript. Netscape created JavaScript, however, so most people generally refer to all three of these versions simply as JavaScript.

The following example uses JavaScript to preload images, and it also adds the `onmouseover` and `onmouseout` JavaScript events to an image to demonstrate how to add a script for creating a mouse rollover using Word and the Microsoft Script Editor. This example works in both Microsoft Internet Explorer and Netscape Navigator. When a person moves the mouse pointer over the image, the script replaces the first image with a different one. To achieve this effect, you need to create two sets of images. (This example uses only a single image, however.) You can easily modify this script to add additional buttons. Figure 27-5 shows a Web page that has multiple rollover buttons; when the person moves the mouse pointer over a blue button, that button is replaced by the red version of the button.

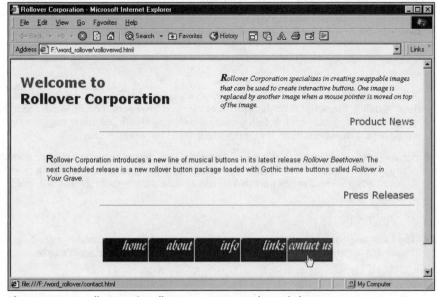

Figure 27-5: A rollover script allows you to create dynamic buttons.

The following steps show you how to insert a script into a Web page. In this example, you create a *rollover* image from two image buttons: home_red.gif and home_blue.gif. For many readers, this may all seem a bit confusing. We don't have the space to teach you how to write scripts, only how to use the tools. Consequently, if you don't understand scripting, this procedure may seem difficult. Nonetheless, follow these steps to use Word's scripting tools:

1. Choose Tools ⇨ Options to open the Options dialog box, and click the General tab.

2. Click the Web Options button near the bottom of the dialog box. The Web Options dialog box appears.

3. Click the Files tab, and clear the Organize Supporting Files in a Folder option. Click OK to close the Web Options dialog box, and then click OK to close the Options dialog box.

4. Create and save a Web page that includes an image linked to the page or file that you want to load when a person clicks on the image.

5. Choose View ⇨ Toolbars ⇨ Web Tools. The Web Tools toolbar appears.

6. Click the Microsoft Script Editor button, and the Microsoft Script Editor window opens.

7. Click the box that shows VBScript, to the right of the default ClientScript property in the Properties window in the lower-right corner of the main window. A drop-down arrow appears.

8. Click the drop-arrow and select JavaScript from the list.

9. In the main window, find the `</head>` tag, place the cursor immediately before it, and press Enter. A blank line now appears above the closing `</head>` tag. Place the cursor on the blank line.

10. Right-click in the Script Editor on that line, and choose Insert Script Block ➪ Client; the following lines are added to your Web page:

```
<script language=JavaScript>
<!--

//-->
</script>
```

This begins the JavaScript code. The `<!--` is an opening HTML comment tag that begins hiding the script from JavaScript-challenged browsers. The `//` is a JavaScript single line comment, which is followed by the closing HTML comment tag (`-->`) that stops hiding the script from JavaScript-challenged browsers.

11. Type the following line to begin an *if statement* that makes sure the browser understands image objects. Note that the JavaScript appears in blue, and a pop-up box appears when you enter document. You can choose images from the list box and finish entering the line.

```
if (document.images) {
```

12. The following code creates two image objects, named `homeBlue` and `homeRed`. JavaScript is case-sensitive, so make sure that you match the example's case.

```
homeBlue = new Image( );
homeRed = new Image( );
```

13. Add the following two lines to use the `.src` property to associate the `homeBlue` object with the blue button (`home_blue.gif`) and the `homeRed` object with the red button (`home_red.gif`) GIF images. Don't forget the end curly brace, which ends the first part of the `if` statement.

```
homeBlue.src = "home_blue.gif";
homeRed.src = "home_red.gif";
}
```

14. Enter the `else` portion of the script for browsers that do not support JavaScript image objects. To complete the `else` statement, create the following variables: `homeRed`, `homeBlue`, and `document.home`. Then set them to an empty setting as shown. To create an empty setting, use double-quotation marks with nothing in between. When you type the period after the word *document*, a pop-up list box of options appears, but you must type `home` manually because it does not appear in the box. These empty variables keep older browsers from displaying error messages.

```
else {
     homeBlue =" ";
     homeRed = "   ";
     document.home = " ";
     }
```

15. Create a function for when the mouse pointer moves over the image.

```
function imgOn(imgName) {
        if (document.images) {
        document[imgName].src = eval(imgName + "Red.src");
}
}
```

16. Create a function for when the mouse pointer moves off the image.

```
function imgOff(imgName) {
        if (document.images) {
        document[imgName].src = eval(imgName + "Blue.src");
}
}
```

17. Add the `onmouseover` event to call the `ImgOn` function to the opening anchor tag. When you add the `mouseover` event, the image appears in red. In other words, this replaces the default image, `home_blue.gif`, with the `home_red.gif` (`document.home.src=homeRed.src`).

```
<a href="home.html" onmouseover="imgOn('home') ">
```

18. Add the `onmouseout` event to call the `ImgOff` function to the opening anchor tag. This replaces the "hot" image that is displayed when the person moves the mouse pointer over the button, `home_red.gif`, with `home_blue.gif` (`document.home.src=homeBlue.src`) when the person moves the pointer off the image.

```
<a href="home.html" onmouseover="imgOn('home')"
onmouseout="imgOff('home')">
```

19. Choose File ➪ Save to save your HTML document, and then choose File ➪ Exit to exit the Microsoft Script Editor window. A tilted J icon then appears in your document, indicating that it contains JavaScript code.

20. Open the file in Notepad. (Click the Windows Start button, and then choose Programs ➪ Accessories ➪ Notepad.) Locate the `img` tag, add the `NAME` attribute, and set it to `"home"`. For some reason, the Word Script Editor strips out the `NAME` attribute, which is essential for the rollover to work. If you add the `NAME` attribute after saving the file in Word using an ASCII text editor, however, the script will work.

```
<img NAME="home" border="0" width="85" height="85" SRC="image001.gif"
shapes=_x0000_i1026" alt="Home Button" >
```

21. Choose File ➪ Exit to exit Notepad.

22. Navigate to the folder containing the file, and double-click the file's icon to open the Web page in your browser. Move the mouse pointer over the button to display the rollover image.

Adding Multimedia

As you've seen, the Web Tools toolbar provides three buttons that provide multimedia tools. The last three buttons on the bar let you insert movies, sounds, and scrolling text banners.

Inserting movies

Click the Movie button on the Web Tools toolbar to insert a movie into your Web page. The Movie Clip dialog box opens (see Figure 27-6). Table 27-2 describes the options in this box.

Figure 27-6: The Movie Clip dialog box.

Table 27-2: The Movie Clip Dialog box

Button	Function
Movie	This is the name of the movie clip. Use the Browse button to find the movie file you want to use.
Alternate Image	This is the name of an alternate, static image that you can place in the movie position—it will load while the movie is still being transferred.
Alternate Text	This is a short description that is seen if the user points at the movie.
Start	Defines when the movie starts—when the movie loads in the page, or when the user points at it.
Loop	Defines how many times the movie plays. You can select 5 from the drop-down list box, or you can type any number you want, or select Indefinite to continue looping indefinitely.

Inserting sounds

Click the Sound button to insert a sound into your Web page. The Background Sound dialog box opens (see Figure 27-7). Simply select the sound file you want to use, and the number of times the sound should loop. But be prepared for frustration. Getting background sounds to work consistently in Web pages is difficult, thanks to the different manner in which various browsers handle different types of sound files! In most cases, background sounds are little more than a nuisance. They're often annoying, and they can sometimes be embarrassing for users in offices where other users get to listen, too.

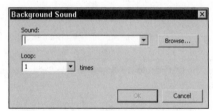

Figure 27-7: The Background Sound dialog box.

Inserting scrolling text banners

Word allows you to create scrolling text banners in your Web pages. Click the Scrolling Text button to open the Scrolling Text dialog box (see Figure 27-8). Table 27-3 describes the options in this box.

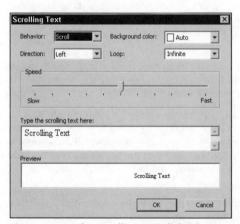

Figure 27-8: The Scrolling Text dialog box.

Table 27-3: The Scrolling Text Dialog box

Button	Function
Behavior	You can make the text Scroll across the page continually, or Slide into position and then stop. Or you can make it Alternate, which means it slides across the page, bounces off the side, and goes back the direction it just came.
Background Color	Leave this set to Auto to use the document background color, or specify a background color for the scroll area.
Direction	Select the direction in which the text slides or scrolls (unless you've selected Alternate for behavior, in which case Direction is disabled because it's going to alternate).

Continued

Table 27-3 (continued)

Button	Function
Loop	Define how often the text should scroll (select Slide Behavior and this is disabled).
Speed	Use this control to define how quickly the text moves.
Type the Scrolling Text Here	Type whatever message you want to appear in the scroll box.
Preview	Adjust the controls above, and view the changes here.

Working with XML

Now we're going to return to XML because Word provides a number of tools for working with this system. As indicated earlier in the chapter, XML means eXtensible Markup Language, and it's a way to encode information. There's a lot of confusion about XML among non-programmers. Many people seem to think that XML is the next HTML, or an extension of HTML, but the truth is more complicated.

HTML is really quite simple, and anyone can quickly learn how to use HTML to create pages that can be opened by Web browsers and thus viewed by people using the World Wide Web. For this reason millions of people have learned and employed HTML.

XML is very different from HTML. In fact, XML is close to useless for most people who have learned HTML. HTML provides a way to format information so that a browser knows how to present the information—how to make it appear in the browser window. All browsers know that text between <TITLE></TITLE> tags should be placed in the browser's title bar, and that text between <B></B> tags is bold. It doesn't know what the information is, just what to do with it in a very simple way.

XML, on the other hand, *labels* the information to explain what the information actually represents. The <PatientName></PatientName> tags could, for instance, enclose the name of a patient, <Rx></Rx> tags could enclose a prescription name, and so on. We say *could* because it all depends. A program must be written to accept data in this form. Someone, somewhere, may already have produced a program that recognizes these tags, or maybe not.

Thus XML is of no use to a single person creating Web pages, because browsers won't recognize the tags. XML is intended for use by software development teams, and in fact is already in wide use. Suppose your company sells a mapping system designed to produce maps for use in Web pages, and that my company owns 5,000 fast-food restaurants around the United States. My company wants to use your mapping system to show people how to get to our restaurants on our Web site. Somehow, our two systems have to talk to each other. My database contains the street addresses of all my restaurants, and your database has a huge mapping archive of every street in the United States. We can use XML to pass information back and forth between our two systems.

Note   XML is simply a system for storing and transferring information. It allows programmers to define what each piece of information represents. It's not a programming language—you can't write programs using XML—and it's not a browser language. Web browsers won't understand what the information is, despite the fact that they support XML.

Here's another example. You could create a resume in Word that uses XML to encode each piece of information. Your name, the various components of your address, the names of previous employers, description fields—all could be labeled using XML so that a program designed to read resumes could do so.

Note This last example, in fact, is one that XML proponents sometimes give to explain why you might use XML; but the example is flawed. By the time resume-reading XML programs are in wide use, resume-creating XML programs will also be in wide use. The average user won't even know the programs are labeling fields using XML, any more than the vast majority of word-processor users understand how text is labeled inside a word-processing file.

Thus, XML is a specialized system that few Word users will ever touch. You don't need it for creating memos or letters, for doing mail-merge, or creating books and newsletters. You don't even need it for creating Web pages (and few enough people use Word to create Web pages!). Although Word contains XML tools, it's unlikely that you will use them very often. Consequently, we don't go into great detail about XML in this chapter. If you want to use Word's XML tools, you need to learn XML, and that's a very different subject that's beyond the scope of this book.

Tip Want to learn more about XML? A number of Web sites provide free XML tutorials. One great place to start is www.w3schools.com/xml/.

Creating an XML document

To create a basic XML document, choose File ➪ New, and click the On My Computer link in the New Document task pane. In the Templates dialog box, under the General tab, double-click the XML Document icon.

The XML task pane opens. Now you need to add an XML schema. Click the Templates and Add-Ins link to view the XML Schema tab of the Templates and Add-Ins dialog box (see Figure 27-9).

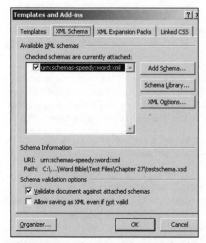

Figure 27-9: The XML Schema tab of the Templates and Add-Ins dialog box.

A *schema* is a data description. The schema file defines the XML tags that are used in your document. You can't create an XML document without attaching a schema first, because Word won't recognize all the tags. However, note that Word is very fussy about its schemas. If the schema is quite properly formed, Word won't open it.

Click the Add Schema button to display a typical File Open dialog box. You can also open a schema from the Schema Library dialog box (see Figure 27-10), opened by clicking the Schema Library button. The Schema Library is just what it sounds like; a library of schemas you can use for various purposes.

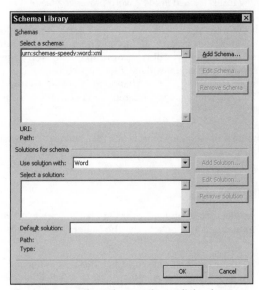

Figure 27-10: The Schema Library dialog box.

After you add the schema, you see the XML Schema task pane (see Figure 27-11), and you can begin creating your XML data document. You can place tags around existing text, or place tags, and then enter text.

XML is a hierarchical system of tags. In the example shown, the addresslist category contains a subcategory called address; within the address subcategory are a variety of data components—first name, last name, street, state, and so on. You cannot, for instance, enclose text with subcategory tags until you have enclosed it in the main category's tags.

So, for instance, in this example, you could select a full address and then click the addresslist element from the lower list box. Word automatically encloses the text in the appropriate tags.

Then you would click the address element, now visible in the lower box (the lower box displays all the element tags available to you for your selection in the document), again enclosing the address with those tags. You can now select the various elements. Select the first name and click firstname in the lower list box; select the last name and click lastname, and so on, until you have completely coded all the data.

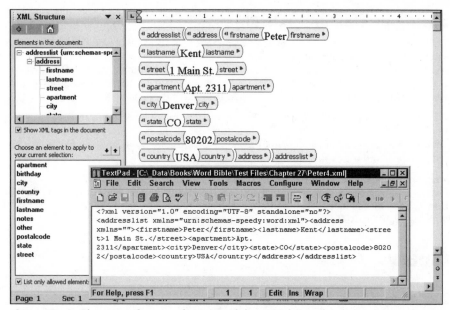

Figure 27-11: The XML Schema task pane and the XML document showing tags, along with a text editor showing the underlying document.

Note the two check boxes in the task pane:

   ✦ **Show XML Tags in the Document:** Places and removes the tags

   ✦ **List Only Allowed Elements:** Tells Word whether to show all the available elements or only those allowed for the current text selection

The Elements in the Document list at the top of the XML Structure task pane shows you the structure as you build it. You can see the data elements you've added to your document, and in fact if you click on an entry in the list Word will highlight the corresponding data element in the document.

A number of XML-related commands sit on the right-click menu:

   ✦ **Remove Tag:** Removes the tag you've selected, and the corresponding opening or closing tag

   ✦ **Attributes:** Opens a dialog box showing the tag's attributes

   ✦ **View XML Structure:** Opens the XML Structure task pane

   ✦ **Apply XML Elements:** Displays a list of elements that are appropriate for the selection or insertion position

Saving in XML and WordML

Word has two ways to save XML files: as plain XML files and as WordML files. A WordML file can save anything you can place inside a Word document. You could place images in a document along with XML elements, for instance, and save the document as WordML. If you save that document as a plain XML document, Word has to strip out the formatting, images, and whatever other Word-related objects are inside it, and save just the XML tags.

When you save an XML file, Word first checks the document against the schema to ensure that it's valid. For instance, if the schema states that all datasets must include a particular data element, and that element is not present, Word won't let you save the file as an XML file until you've fixed the problem.

Word then asks if you want to save the file as a plain XML file or a WordML (unless the Save Data Only check box in the Save As dialog box has been cleared). If you save as XML, Word throws away all the font and paragraph formatting, the images, and everything else that is not directly related to XML.

Summary

This chapter has covered a number of advanced Web subjects, including working with scripts and XML. In this chapter, you learned the following:

✦ How to add Web-form elements to your pages.

✦ How to create dynamic mouse rollover buttons.

✦ How to add movies, sounds, and scrolling text.

✦ How to add XML schemas to documents.

✦ How to code data elements in XML documents.

✦   ✦   ✦

Distribution and Collaboration

P A R T

VI

✦   ✦   ✦   ✦

In This Part

Chapter 28
Faxing and E-mailing
with Word

Chapter 29
Comments and
Reviewing

Chapter 30
Online Collaboration

✦   ✦   ✦   ✦

Faxing and E-mailing with Word

◆ ◆ ◆ ◆

In This Chapter

Faxing documents

E-mailing documents

Writing e-mail messages

Routing documents

Using Word in Outlook

◆ ◆ ◆ ◆

What good is creating a document if you can't get it to anyone? While some documents are very private things, intended for use by the author alone, most are created by one person for use by another, or by many others. This chapter looks at a couple of ways to get your documents from your computer into the hands of someone else, by fax and by e-mail. It also looks at how you can use Word as an e-mail editor, so you can actually create your e-mails in your familiar word-processing interface.

Faxing from Word

For some time now, Windows has shipped with fax software, variously named Microsoft Fax, Fax Service Management, or Fax Console. In addition, a number of sophisticated fax programs are available as add-ons, such as WinFax. And some online fax services (often referred to as *e-mail fax*) provide software that allows you to send faxes from Word across the Internet.

You can send faxes from Word by choosing File ➪ New and clicking the On My Computer link. Then, in the Templates dialog box, click the Letters and Faxes tab and double-click the Fax Wizard. Alternatively, you can choose File ➪ Send To ➪ Recipient Using a Fax Modem. Either way, Word uses the Fax Wizard to walk you through both creating and sending a fax. Before you can send a fax from Word, however, you need to install and configure Microsoft Fax, and you also must have a fax modem installed.

Tip To set up faxing in Windows XP, right-click inside the Printers and Faxes folder and choose Set Up Faxing. A Fax object appears in the folder, and Word will work through that device.

Sending a fax from Word

Sending a fax from Word is both quick and easy. If you are beginning from scratch, you can choose the Fax Wizard from the Letters and Faxes tab in the Templates dialog box (File ➪ New and click the On My Computer link). If you want to send an existing document as a file, start Word and then open the document you want to fax.

To send a fax from Word using the Fax Wizard, follow these steps:

1. Open the file you want to fax.

2. Choose File ➪ Send To ➪ Recipient Using a Fax Modem. The Fax Wizard window appears.

3. Click Next. Make sure the document you want to fax is selected in The Following Document drop-down box. Select With a Cover Sheet. You also have the option to send the document without a cover sheet or to send only a cover sheet with a note.

4. Click Next. Then choose to send your fax with Microsoft Fax (or simply Fax in XP). Alternatively, you can choose to use a different fax program or to print the document so that you can send it from a separate fax machine.

5. Click Finish. The fax document then appears in Word with the Fax Wizard toolbar, which includes the Send Fax Now button. You can make any changes to your fax document before sending it.

6. Click Send Fax Now, and the document is sent to your fax modem.

Now, here's the weird thing. There should be several more steps, and indeed these steps are available if you select *another* fax program. For some reason, though, when you use the Windows fax program, those steps don't appear. Maybe this is a bug that will be fixed at some point with a service-pack upgrade. Anyway, after step 4 you *may* find these additional steps:

5. Click Next, and the Recipients window appears. Enter the name of the person you want to send the fax to in the Name box. If you have entered names and phone numbers in the Outlook Address Book, just click the Address Book button and select the recipient.

6. Click Next, and the cover sheet window appears. You can choose from three types of cover sheets: Professional, Contemporary, or Elegant. Just choose the style you want to use.

7. Click Next. The Sender window appears and provides the information you entered when you set up the Fax program. Fill in any missing information that you want to add to your cover sheet.

8. Click Finish; then click Send Fax Now.

Using online fax services

Fax modems can be a nuisance. In order for a fax modem to work, your computer has to be connected to a phone line. That's often a problem for businesspeople, because connecting a modem through the sort of telephone switch used to route calls in most offices these days is not easy. And even if you can solve that technical problem, getting modems to dial properly—setting up the right area codes and so on—is often a hassle.

These days far more computers are connected directly to the Internet than are connected to phone lines in a manner that they can send faxes. So why not fax through the Internet? Even business travelers may find it easier to fax via the Internet than through a phone line. Although many hotels now provide fast Internet access—sometimes even for free—getting your modem to work in a hotel room is often a hassle.

Fax through the Internet—how is that possible? Easy. After you sign up with a fax service, you transmit your fax documents to the service across the Internet—along with information about where to send the fax—and the service sends the documents out through its own fax machines. You don't have to worry about setting up your fax modem or waiting for the receiving modem to be free to accept the fax. Just send it and let the service handle it all.

Word has a File ➪ Send To ➪ Fax Service command that is not functioning when you first try to use it. You'll see a message box. Click OK, and Word loads a Web page into your browser in which you can find more information about this service. Microsoft currently has a relationship with Venali Inc., to provide this service, and you can try it free for 30 days. After that, you pay $4.95 to $19.95 a month, depending on the service you choose.

Note that this service provides both in-bound and out-bound faxing—you can sign up for a service providing one or the other, or both. Not only can you fax from Word—or any other application—you can also receive faxes in your e-mail program. Having used online (e-mail) faxing for several years now, we're fans. No longer do you have to worry about your fax machine running out of paper or ink or being offline. No longer do you have to be in your office to receive faxes. As long as you can get to your e-mail, you can receive faxes.

Note You don't have to use Microsoft's service. Other fax services, such as JFax (www.JFax.com) provide the same sort of service using print drivers. When you print to JFax, an e-mail is created with the printed document attached. You send the e-mail, and JFax handles the rest.

Sharing Documents via E-mail

Word provides a way for you to quickly attach a document to an e-mail message and send it on. In fact, Word provides several ways to do this.

✦ **File ➪ Send To ➪ Mail Recipient:** This option appears only if you have Microsoft Outlook installed. It allows you to send a file directly from within Word; you'll see the To:, Cc:, Bcc:, and Subject: lines inside Word, along with an Introduction box in which you can type a short message. The information from the document is inserted inside the message, not as an attached file but with the content visible inside the message itself.

✦ **File ➪ Send To ➪ Mail Recipient (for Review):** Word makes a copy of the file you want to send, turns on Reviewing, creates an e-mail message in the default mail program, and attaches the file to that message. When the recipient sends the file back to you, its changes can be merged back into the original document.

Cross-Reference See Chapter 29 for more about Word's Reviewing feature and merging changes.

✦ **File ➪ Send To ➪ Mail Recipient (as Attachment):** Word attaches a copy of the file you want to send to an e-mail message so you can send it to someone. The term *as Attachment* is a little ambiguous because all but the first of these methods of sending documents send the file as an e-mail attachment. This method is the simplest method, though—Word simply sends a copy of the file, without turning on reviewing features.

✦ **File ➪ Send To ➪ Routing Recipient:** You may see several different Routing Recipient commands. If you haven't yet routed the current document, you will see Routing Recipient. But if the document has already been routed, you'll see Next Routing Recipient and Other Routing Recipient. These allow you to send a file to several people in sequence, as we discuss later in the chapter.

Note When you try to send mail, Word sends the document to your default e-mail program. That may nor may not be Microsoft Outlook—although for most people it will be. Still, it could be just about any other e-mail program, depending on what has been installed and configured on your computer. Also, note that when routing files, Word attempts to simply send the document without any further input from you, but some e-mail programs will catch the outgoing message and ask you if you want to see it before it is sent.

To change the default mail program, open Internet Explorer and choose Tools ➪ Internet Options. Click the Programs tab, and select the mail program you want to use in the E-Mail drop-down list box.

Sending mail from within Word

If you have Microsoft Outlook installed on your system, you can use Word as an e-mail program, and send messages directly from within the program:

✦ Choose File ➪ New, and click the E-mail Message link in the New Document task pane—this opens a blank message document.

✦ Double-click E-mail Message in the General tab of the Templates dialog box; this also opens a blank message document.

✦ Open the document you want to send to someone; then choose File ➪ Send To ➪ Mail Recipient to place a copy of your document inside a message.

✦ Open the document you want to send to someone and click the E-mail button on the Standard toolbar.

Note   These features do not work if your computer cannot connect to the mail server for some reason, such as a network problem or if you are traveling and your laptop is not connected.

When you use one of these methods, your Word window will add the messaging bars that you can see in Figure 28-1, and you can click the To, Cc, and Bcc buttons to open Outlook's address book and find the addresses of the people you want to mail to. Also, type a Subject line, and you may also type an Introduction message (when sending a document to someone, rather than starting a new, blank message, you'll see an Introduction box in which you can type some extra introductory text to explain what you are sending).

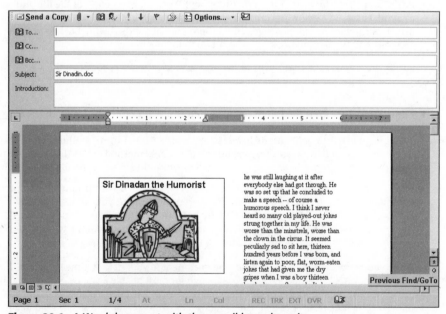

Figure 28-1: A Word document with the e-mail bars above it.

This is a full-featured e-mail composition window. The WordMail toolbar, shown in Figure 28-2, provides a number of features, as described in Table 28-1. If you know how to use Outlook, you already know how to use these features, as they are simply a subset of the Outlook tools.

Figure 28-2: The WordMail toolbar.

Table 28-1: WordMail Toolbar

Button/Field	Name	Description
 **Send a Copy**	Send a Copy	Sends the e-mail message to your e-mail program for delivery.
 **Accounts ▾**	Accounts	Enables you to choose the account you want to use to send your message if you have multiple e-mail accounts set up.
 📎 ▾	Insert File	Displays the Insert File dialog box for selecting files to add as attachments to your e-mail message.
 📖	Address Book	Displays the Outlook Address Book that contains e-mail addresses for recipients.
 ✓	Check Names	Enables you to check names from your Outlook Contacts list.
	Permission	Appears if you have installed the Information Rights Management Service (see Chapter 34) and allows you to restrict the use of the message. Recipients can read it, but they can't forward or print it or copy the contents.
 ❗	Importance: High	Ranks the priority of the e-mail message— if the recipient's e-mail program can display the rank. It provides a way to catch the recipient's attention.
 ⬇	Importance: Low	Ranks the priority of the e-mail message as low.
 ⚑	Message Flag	Adds a flag to the message in your Outlook Sent box, to remind you to follow up later. You can even specify a date by which you should follow up.
	Create Rule	Opens Outlook's Rules dialog box so that you can create a message filter.

Continued

Table 28-1 *(continued)*

Button/Field	Name	Description
Options... ▾	Options drop-down list	Displays the Message Options dialog box, which allows you to customize delivery options for your e-mail message.
	Options|Bcc	Click the triangle on the Options button and select Bcc to add or remove the Bcc field from the message heading. Bcc means *blind carbon copy*. This field allows you to specify e-mail addresses of people who should receive copies of a message without the original recipient—or other Bcc recipients—seeing the e-mail addresses. Clicking the Bcc button adds a Bcc field under the Cc field.
	Options|From	Adds the From field to the message heading, allowing you to specify a Sender name. You can select from the address book, but you won't be able to send in another person's name if you don't have permission to do so.
	Digitally Sign|Sign This Message*	Allows you to sign the message using Outlook's digital-signature features (see Chapter 34 for more information).
	Digitally Sign|Encrypt This Message*	Allows you to encrypt the message using Outlook's encryption features.

* You will see the Digitally Sign buttons only if you have checked the Add Digital Signature to Outgoing Messages option in Outlook's Options dialog box (under the Security tab).

> **Tip**   How do you remove the E-mail bar if you decide *not* to send the message? Just select File ➪ Send To ➪ Mail Recipient again.

Routing a document

Routing provides a way for you to send documents to people one by one, in a particular sequence. You want Joe to read it first, followed by Susan. After Susan has finished with it, Ann needs to take a look, and so on. The document can go in a circle like this, being reviewed by any number of people and finally ending up back with you. Each person can see the changes made by the previous recipients.

Alternatively, you can send it to everyone at once. You are informed automatically as each recipient forwards the document to the next person. You also can remind the recipient to forward the document to the next person. After all the recipients have finished reviewing the document, it automatically returns to you. The edited document will contain revision marks, which you look at in detail in Chapter 29. For now, all you need to know is that revision marks enable you to see who changed what, and also let you merge all the changes into a single document.

Before you can route a document, you must prepare a routing slip for it with the names and addresses, presented in the desired order, of all the recipients. To create a routing slip, follow these steps:

1. Open the document that you want to route, and choose File ⇨ Send To ⇨ Routing Recipient. The Routing Slip dialog box appears (see Figure 28-3).

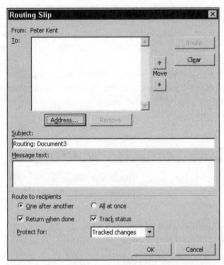

Figure 28-3: The Routing Slip dialog box.

2. Click the Address button to open the Outlook address book. You want to enter the names or addresses in the To box. Either select from the list, or type an address directly into that box. When you have all the names and addresses you want to use, click OK. (If typing multiple names in this list box, separate each with a semicolon and a space.)

3. Type a Subject Line and an introductory Message Text.

4. Select either One After Another or All At Once. The first sends a single message to the first person on the list; that person can then forward the message to the next person on the list. The latter option sends a copy to everyone at once.

5. Check Return When Done if you want *you* to be the last person on the routing list, so you get the document back for comparison.

6. Check Track Status if you want to know where the message is on its journey; you'll get a message when the document is forwarded to the next person on the list.

7. Select a Protect For option; you can limit recipients to making tracked changes or adding comments (see Chapter 29) or making changes to form fields only (see Chapter 24).

Note   Word will turn on the selected form of protection, but not password-protect the file, so it's really working on the honor system. If you want to lock the file so the recipient cannot turn off the protection method you chose, see Chapter 34.

8. If you are ready to send the file, click Route. If you want to add the routing slip now but send the file later, click the Add Slip button. (When you first add an address, the OK button changes to Add Slip.) Later, when you want to send the file, you use the File ➪ Send To ➪ Next Routing Recipient command.

When you send the file you will probably see two warning messages, one telling you that a program is trying to access your Outlook address book, and one telling you that a program is trying to send a message automatically. Just tell each box to continue. (In some cases you will see four of these messages; if someone sent you a routed message which you have to forward, and the sender selected Track Status, two messages are sent, one to the next person on the list, and the status message to the original sender.)

Tip

If the document has a routing slip associated with it but you do not want to send it to all the recipients on that list, or maybe you want it to route in a different sequence, you can send the document without using the routing slip. When you use File ➪ Send To ➪ Next Routing Recipient a small dialog box provides this option.

Using Word as your Outlook Compose window

Word lets you to use its editing and formatting features when you compose e-mail messages from within Outlook. This enables you to create more sophisticated messages with the tools you use regularly.

To use Word as your e-mail editor, open Microsoft Outlook and choose Tools ➪ Options. Then click the Mail Format tab (see Figure 28-4). You'll find two options here. Check the Use Microsoft Word to Edit E-Mail Messages check box to use Word as your editing tool. You can also select Use Microsoft Word to Read Rich Text E-mail Messages if you wish, to automatically open incoming rich-text messages in Word.

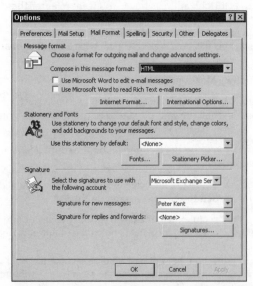

Figure 28-4: The Mail Format tab in Outlook's Options dialog box allows you to choose Word as your default e-mail editor.

Note   When you use Word to create or view Outlook messages, it's not immediately apparent. Outlook actually uses a little bit of the Word software *inside* Outlook. You won't see an actual Word window open, but you will notice that many of the toolbar buttons and menu options come from Word.

Setting Up E-mail Options

Word has a number of e-mail options that you can configure. You can create signatures from within Word, for instance. A signature is a block of information automatically dropped into the end of an outgoing e-mail message. Signatures typically include contact information that you routinely want to add.

Word allows you to create personalized stationery for your e-mail messages as well. You can set background images and colors, as well as font colors and styles to enhance the appearance of your messages. You can even apply Themes to customize e-mail messages.

Cross-Reference   To find out more about using themes, see Chapter 26.

Choose Tools ➪ Options, click the General tab, and click the E-mail Options button to see the E-mail Options dialog box (see Figure 28-5). Table 28-2 describes the options available.

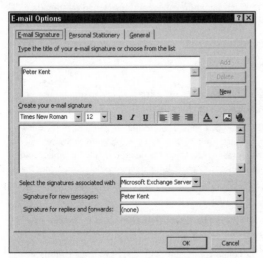

Figure 28-5: The E-mail Options dialog box.

Table 28-2: The E-mail Options Dialog Box

Option	Description
Signature Tab	
Type the Title of Your E-mail Signature or Choose from the List	To create a new e-mail signature, type a name in the top list box. Alternatively, you can select an existing signature to edit from the list.
Add	After typing the name of a signature and creating the signature in the Create Your E-mail Signature area, click this button.
Replace	The Add button changes to Replace if you make a change to an existing signature. Click the button to save changes.
Delete	Removes the selected signature.
New	Clears the edit area and places the cursor in the top text box so you can type a new name.
Create Your E-mail Signature	This area provides simple editing tools for creating and editing the signature.
Select the Signatures Associated With	The mail server you are set up to work with.
Signature for New Messages	Select which signature you want to use when creating new messages.
Signature for Replies and Forwards	Select which one to use when replying to or forwarding messages.
Personal Stationery Tab	
Theme	Clicking this button allows you to select a theme for use in every e-mail message you send from Word.
Font	The Font text box allows you to define, if you have chosen a theme, which fonts to use. You can tell Word to always use the themes fonts; to use the fonts defined below for replies and forwards; and to use the fonts defined below for *all* messages.
New Mail Messages: Font	Click this button to define what font to use for new messages you write.
Replying or Forwarding Messages: Font	Click this button to define what font to use for replies and forwards.
Mark my comments with	You can define some kind of marker to precede comments inserted into replies and forwarded messages.
Pick a New Color when Replying or Forwarding	Tells Word to use a different color for the comments you make in replies and forwarded messages.
Composing and Reading Plain Text Messages: Font	Click this button to define what font should be used when working with plain-text—as opposed to HTML or Rich Text—messages.

Option	Description
General Tab	
HTML Filtering Options	When creating HTML messages, Word can remove some of the HTML coding. None means it makes no changes, and sends the messages with everything in them. High removes a lot of the information to greatly reduce file size.
Rely on CSS for Font Formatting	You probably shouldn't use this feature. It tells Word to use Cascading Style Sheets to define font formatting, but most e-mail programs don't support this, and so they won't be able to display messages properly.
Save Smart Tags in E-mail	This tells Word to keep any Smart Tags in the documents you send as e-mail. Of course, this has no effect on documents sent as attachments, only for documents sent *within* an e-mail message. (See Chapter 23 for more information about Smart Tags.)

Summary

This chapter has covered many Word tools that allow you to make Word a part of your faxing or e-mailing strategy. In this chapter, you have learned how to do the following:

✦ Send a document via fax, or via an online fax service.

✦ Drop documents into e-mail messages.

✦ Create new e-mail messages within Word.

✦ Send files as attachments.

✦ Route a document across the network.

✦ Use Word as the Outlook editor.

✦   ✦   ✦

Comments and Reviewing

CHAPTER

29

✦ ✦ ✦ ✦

In This Chapter

Adding comments to documents

Marking documents with revision marks

Comparing and merging documents

Comparing documents side by side

Using Reading Layout view

✦ ✦ ✦ ✦

In Chapter 28, you saw how to send e-mails to colleagues to get their input on your documents. During that discussion, we mentioned Word's magical *reviewing* tool. This useful feature enables your colleagues to make changes to the document, lets you merge those changes into the original, and makes the changes stand out so that you can see all suggestions.

For many of us—especially those of us in the publishing business—Word's reviewing tools have become an essential part of our word-processing arsenal. We remember a few years ago when word-processed documents were still being marked up by hand. FedEx made a lot of money from the publishing business in those days, as editors would make changes to printed copies of pages and ship them to authors, who would make their changes and ship them back.

These days, FedEx isn't doing quite so well off publishers, and the publishing business has sped up. Everyone working on a file can now make changes to an electronic version and e-mail it to the next person. It's much easier, much quicker, and far less hassle. This chapter looks at the tools that Word provides to you for comments and reviews, tools that enable people to add information to your documents, yet still provide you with the power to approve or disapprove the changes.

There are two ways for people to make comments or changes to a document in a collaborative setting. You can place *comments* in the document, or you can *track changes* with the *reviewing* tools.

✦ Comments are great for when you don't want to change the text itself, you simply want to add your own thoughts to it.

✦ The track changes/reviewing feature is a more advanced feature that enables two or more people to actually modify the document, with Word tracking who made each change.

Placing Comments in Documents

Word's *comments* feature is a quick and easy way to add ancillary information to a document. You can use comments to leave reminders for yourself or notes to other people. Comments do not affect a document's formatting, and they do not print with the document (unless you specifically tell them to). Therefore, you can insert comments anywhere without worrying about them ending up in your final printout by mistake.

To insert a comment, choose Insert ➪ Comment. Word places brackets around the word you just typed, inserts a tag showing your initials, and either opens the Reviewing pane—if you are in Normal or Outline view (see Figure 29-1)—or displays a comment balloon in the right margin if you are in any other view. It also opens the Reviewing toolbar. You can now type your comment.

Note   Word assigns reviewer initials based on the information in the User Information tab of the Options dialog box (Tools ➪ Options). The Reviewing pane also shows your name, in the center of the comment's title bar. If you want to be identified differently, simply edit the User Information tab.

You can switch between the Reviewing pane—which contains both comments and information about reviewing changes, which we look at later in this chapter—and your document-editing area by clicking in either area or by pressing F6. You can adjust the size of the Reviewing pane by dragging the split bar that separates the two panes on your screen, and you can close it by double-clicking the split bar.

You can also use the Reviewing toolbar (View ➪ Toolbars ➪ Reviewing) to work with Comments. This toolbar is intended mainly for use with the Reviewing features, which you learn about later in the chapter, but it also has a few comment-related features. The toolbar includes the Insert Comment button and the Delete Comment button. You click the Insert Button at the point where you want to place a comment; you click inside a comment and then click the Delete Comment button to remove a comment. The Reviewing Pane button opens and closes the Reviewing pane. In Figure 29-2, the toolbar has been expanded. Not all the buttons appear by default. You can add several other comment buttons, including Previous Comment and Next Comment (used to move between comments) and Edit Comment.

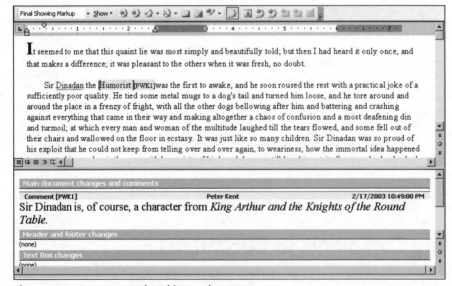

Figure 29-1: A comment placed into a document.

Tip   To turn the display of comments on and off, you need to click the Show drop-down arrow on the Reviewing toolbar and select Comments from the list.

Figure 29-2: The Reviewing toolbar.

Working with comments

Comments can be identified in a number of ways, even while the Reviewing pane is closed. Assuming that you have turned on the display of comments in the Reviewing toolbar (Show ➪ Comments), comments can be seen in all views. A light pink background is placed behind the word to which the comment is attached and behind the reviewer's initials. In addition, the word being commented on is enclosed in red brackets, and the initials are enclosed in black brackets. When you click on comment text inside the Reviewing pane, the corresponding comment tag within the document is shown with a deeper pink and darker, thicker red brackets.

In some views (Print Layout, Web Layout, Reading Layout, and Print Preview), you see a comment balloon instead of the pink background and brackets within the text (see Figure 29-3). The balloon appears in the margin to the right of the comment and has a pink background. Comment balloons are visible in the views just mentioned unless the display of balloons has been turned off. Click the Show button on the Reviewing toolbar and select Balloons to see if Word is set to Always Show Balloons or Never Show Balloons. (Note that you can choose View ➪ Markup to turn off the color behind the comment but leave the initials in place.)

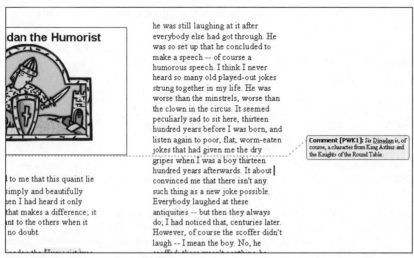

Figure 29-3: The comment balloon.

To reopen the Reviewing pane—in which you can read comments—double-click a comment mark in the document or click Reviewing Pane on the Reviewing toolbar. If you plan to insert or edit multiple comments, you can leave the Reviewing pane open while you work on your document.

When you select a comment in the Reviewing pane, Word automatically highlights the corresponding document text. If you want the comment to refer to more than one word in the document, select the text before inserting the comment.

Tip   Deleting comments is generally quite easy. Place the cursor immediately after a comment and press the Backspace key twice. Alternatively, you can right-click inside the comment, or in the comment text inside the Reviewing pane, and select Delete Comment.

Inserting voice comments

If your computer has sound capabilities—and most do these days—you can use voice comments to add some personality to your comments. You can even combine text and voice comments for the same reference area. Just create a standard text comment using the techniques described earlier. Then, with your insertion point directly after the comment mark in the document window, add the voice comment.

To insert a voice comment, follow these steps:

1. Position your insertion point where you want the voice comment to appear. If you want the comment to refer to a specific section, select the text before you proceed.

2. Click the Insert Voice button on the Reviewing toolbar. The Reviewing pane opens, the normal Comment brackets and shading are placed in the document, a loudspeaker icon is placed inside the Reviewing pane, and Windows Sound Recorder opens (see Figure 29-4).

3. Click the red Record button in Sound Recorder—the last button at the bottom right—and begin speaking.

4. Record your words and then click the black-rectangle Stop button in Sound Recorder when you have finished. You can record up to 60 seconds.

5. Close Sound Recorder.

Tip   Before you create sound comments, be sure you know whether the other people looking at the document also have sound capabilities on their computers. If they don't, they won't be able to listen to your comments.

To listen to a sound comment, simply double-click the loudspeaker icon in the Reviewing pane. You also can right-click the icon, point to Sound Recorder Document Object in the shortcut menu, and then choose Play.

Don't think, however, that you can use voice comments all over the place—whenever and wherever you want. Voice comments take up a lot of room. A single short comment may make the file too large to fit on a floppy disk for instance, or too large to place in an e-mail message.

Note   If your computer system is pen-equipped, you can also add handwritten pen comments. Pen comments are treated like drawing objects.

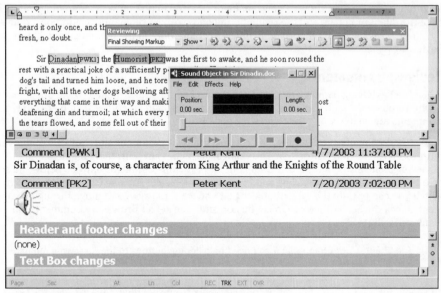

Figure 29-4: Use Sound Recorder to add a voice comment.

Changing and manipulating comments

Working in the Reviewing pane, you can edit and format comments just like any other text. Use any of the techniques in the next section to find the comment that you want to edit or format, and then fire away. You can include most Word elements in a comment; graphics, frames, and even tables are all fair game. The TC (table of contents entry) and XE (index entry) fields cannot be inserted in comments, but most things that you can use in a regular document can also be used in a comment.

You can move, copy, or delete comments just like any other element. Just remember that you first must select the comment mark before you can move, copy, or delete it. When you move, copy, or delete comments, Word automatically renumbers the comment marks both in the document window and in the Reviewing pane.

To move or copy a selected comment to different locations in the same document, or even to different documents, use any standard cut, copy, or paste technique, including dragging and dropping with the mouse.

The Replace feature can globally delete all comments in your document. Just choose Edit ⇨ Replace and type **^a** in the Find What text box. Leave the Replace With text box blank, and choose the Replace All button.

If you plan to pass the document back to the original reviewer or to someone else for further edits, you can answer a comment inserted by someone else. After you view a particular comment in the ScreenTip to which you want to respond, place the insertion point to the right of the mark and then click the Insert Comment button on the Reviewing toolbar. Word then inserts a new comment directly following the current one, and Word also moves the insertion point to the Reviewing pane, in which you enter your comment. The new comment with your initials appears right after the original reviewer's comment, and all comments are renumbered accordingly. Figure 29-5 shows a new comment inserted in response to an existing comment. Note the different initials and the renumbering of the other comments. In addition, comments by different reviewers are displayed in different colors both in the document and in the Reviewing pane.

Reviewing comments

When the Reviewing pane is open, you can view all comments attached to the document simply by scrolling through the pane, just as you scroll through any other text. By default, all comments are visible when the Reviewing pane is open.

To review comments sequentially, you can use the Next Comment and Previous Comment buttons on the Reviewing toolbar. The vertical scroll bars in both the document and Reviewing pane also contain Next Comment and Previous Comment buttons below the scroll arrows. The button between Next and Previous is the Select Browse Object button, with which you can specify the type of object that you want to review. To move through comments, click the Select Browse Object button and then select Browse by Comment from the displayed palette.

Cross-Reference   See Chapter 1 or Chapter 32 if you need help adding buttons to the Reviewing toolbar.

To search for a specific comment or for comments from specific reviewers, use the Go To feature, which you can access by choosing Edit ➪ Go To, pressing Ctrl+G, or pressing F5. Word numbers comments sequentially for all reviewers throughout a document, but comments by individual reviewers are not numbered separately. As comments are inserted or deleted, the existing comments are renumbered accordingly.

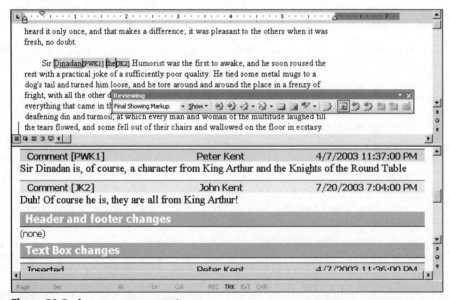

Figure 29-5: A response comment.

To search for a specific comment, follow these steps:

1. Choose Edit ➪ Go To, press Ctrl+G, or press F5. The Find and Replace dialog box appears with the Go To tab displayed.

2. Select Comment in the Go to What list. Figure 29-6 shows the Go To tab with Comment selected.

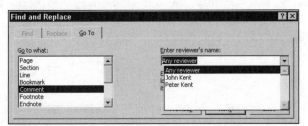

Figure 29-6: The Go To tab of the Find and Replace dialog box with Comment selected.

3. Do one of the following:

   • To find a specific reviewer's comment, select that reviewer's name from the Enter Reviewer's Name drop-down list. The names of all reviewers who have added comments to the document appear on this list.

   • To find a specific comment, enter the number of that comment (without the reviewer's initials) in the Enter Reviewer's Name text box. Note that when you enter a number, the Next button in the Go To dialog box is replaced by a Go To button.

   • To find a comment that is positioned relative to your current location, enter a number preceded by a plus or a minus sign. For example, to find the third comment following your current position, enter +3 in the text box.

4. If you specified a comment number or a relative position, click the Go To button. If you specified a reviewer, click the Next or Previous button to jump to the next or the previous comment for that reviewer.

   The insertion point jumps to the specified comment mark in your document window. You then can view, edit, or delete that comment.

Tip   You also can use Word's Find feature to search for comment marks without specifying a particular comment or reviewer. Just choose Edit ➪ Find to open the Find and Replace dialog box. Type ^a into the Find What box. When you use this feature to find a comment, Word opens the Reviewing pane and then moves the insertion point to the next or previous comment (depending on your Search rule) inside the Reviewing pane.

Note   If you want to prevent reviewers from changing a document, you can protect the document for comments. That way, the only elements that anyone can add to that document are comments. See Chapter 34 for information on protecting your documents.

Printing comments

Comments print depending on the manner in which you display them.

✦ Hide the balloons, hide the Reviewing pane, and print. Your document prints without comments.

✦ Show the balloons and print, and your document prints with the balloons in the right margin. Note, however, that Word may have to adjust the margins to provide room for the balloons.

✦ Open the Reviewing pane, click inside the pane, and print. The Reviewing pane itself is printed, without the rest of the document.

Highlighting text

The Highlight button on the Reviewing or the Formatting toolbar is another tool for online document revision. The button, and the ScreenTip text that appears when you point at it, indicates the current color selection.

You can use the Highlight button in several different ways:

✦ Select the text and click the button to color the text background.

✦ Select the text and click the Highlight down-arrow; then choose a color from the drop-down palette of colors.

✦ Don't select any text. Click the button or select a color, and the mouse pointer changes into a pen. Drag the pen across the text you want to color or, if you want to highlight only a single word, double-click that word. To discontinue highlighting, click the Highlight button again or press Esc. The highlight gives the effect of having marked the text with a colored felt pen.

Tip   If you plan to print the document, be sure to use a light color. This way, the text shows through the highlight.

After you have added your highlighted comments or revisions, you can use the Edit ➪ Find command to locate each occurrence. Select Highlight in the Format list and then click Find Next.

To change the color of all the highlighted text in the document, use the Replace option on the Edit menu. Start by selecting a new highlight color; then choose Edit ➪ Replace, place the insertion point in the Find What text box, and select Highlight from the Format button menu. Place the insertion point in the Replace With text box, and again select Highlight from the Format button menu. Click Replace All, and the old color is replaced with the new.

Tip   The View tab of the Options dialog box (Tools ➪ Options) includes an option for showing or hiding the highlight both on-screen and when the document prints.

Using Reviewing Tools

You can use the Track Changes/Reviewing feature to keep track of the changes made to a document, no matter how many people work on it. Instead of each person actually changing the original document as he or she edits it, changes are marked as revisions that can later be accepted and incorporated into the document or rejected and discarded. The Reviewing toolbar has all of the tools you need for tracking as well as processing changes to your documents.

Note   You can protect your document to stop reviewers making changes to the document without tracking changes. See Chapter 34 for more information.

Adding revision marks

To have Word mark additions, deletions, and format changes automatically, turn on the Track Changes option. After you turn on change tracking, any changes that you make are marked. For example, if you move text, the text in the original location does not disappear, but it is marked for deletion. Likewise, the text in the new location is marked for insertion. If you delete text that was added while editing, however, that text actually is deleted. Word also provides change tracking for changes in formatting as well as in text.

Tip   Before you begin marking a document, save a copy of it under a different name. That way, you can always go back to the original if any problems arise or you need to double-check something.

To turn on change tracking, choose Tools ➪ Track Changes, press Ctrl+Shift+E, or double-click the TRK box in the middle of the status bar. The Reviewing toolbar opens automatically. By default, Final Showing Markup appears in the drop-down list box. But if you don't want revision marks to be displayed while you work (they can be very distracting), select Final. Word will continue marking the changes; you just won't be able to see them until you change this setting.

Personally, we prefer the Final setting. Working in a document that displays all changes can be very confusing. With Final selected, you can go ahead and make whatever changes you want and forget about tracking . . . with one caveat. If you turn off the tracking of changes for some reason, you may forget to turn it back on because you are used to working without seeing the changes marked.

Note   To turn off tracking, double-click the TRK box on the status bar, right-click the TRK box and select Track Changes, or click the Track Changes button on the toolbar.

Viewing changes

Now that you've made a few changes, how can you see them? Select one of the Display for Review settings from the drop-down list box on the Reviewing toolbar:

✦ **Final Showing Markup:** Shows the final document—containing all changes made—and marks all the changes so you can quickly see them.

✦ **Final:** Shows the way the final document would appear if you accepted all the changes. The changes are not marked in any way.

✦ **Original Showing Markup:** This is very similar to Final Showing Markup, with the exception that formatting changes are not included. For instance, if you changed a paragraph from one format to another, the paragraph will be shown with the original, not the final, formatting.

✦ **Original:** This shows the document as it appeared before changes were made.

To see the changes you need to select either Final Showing Markup or Original Showing Markup, which are very similar. In most cases, you'll probably want to use the former. The latter is the same with the exception that you will see the paragraph and font formatting that was in the original document rather than the final.

And what exactly will you see? Something like that shown in Figure 29-7:

✦ Text that has been added is shown underlined.

✦ Deleted text has a strikethrough line through it (although you don't see it in Page Layout view; it's simply removed).

✦ A vertical line is placed in the document margin next to changes.

✦ Changes from various reviewers are shown in different colors (up to eight reviewers).

✦ Point at a change and pause for a moment, and a box opens describing the change and telling you who made it and when (choose Tools ➪ Options, click the View tab, and then click to enable the ScreenTips option in the Show section for this to work).

✦ In Print Layout, Reading Layout, Web Layout, and Print Preview, you'll see balloons in the right margin with lines pointing to the changes. The balloon text explains the change made. For this to work, Show ➪ Balloons ➪ Always Use Balloons must be selected on the toolbar. You can also choose Show ➪ Balloons ➪ No Insertion/Deletion Balloons to limit the number of balloons that appear. With this option selected, you see only balloons describing formatting changes.

✦ Choose Show ➪ Insertions and Deletions to turn off the display of underlining, strikethrough, and color for insertions and deletions. Show ➪ Formatting turns off the display of Formatting changes.

✦ Click the Reviewing Pane button to open the pane. Then scroll through to see a list of all the changes made in the document, with the name of the reviewer in the middle of each item's title bar. The title bar also shows the time and date of the change.

Reviewing, accepting, and rejecting changes

As you can see, you can view all the changes that have been made, and even tell who made them. You can read through, figure out which changes you want to keep, and accept or deny changes. When you accept a change, the revision marking for that item is removed. In other words, text marked for deletion is cut from the document, text marked as inserted text is incorporated into the document, and text marked for reformatting is reformatted.

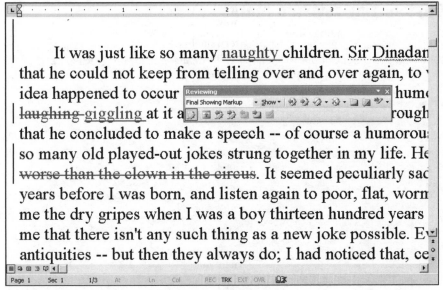

Figure 29-7: A document with revisions marked.

Use the Reviewing toolbar buttons to quickly review changes:

✦ Jump between changes using the Previous and Next buttons.

✦ Accept a selected change by clicking the Accept Change button.

✦ Click the triangle on the Accept Change button to open a menu, and select Accept Change, Accept All Changes Shown, or Accept All Changes in Document (to accept all changes in the document in one fell swoop).

✦ Click the Reject Change button to reject the selected change.

✦ Click the triangle on the Reject Change button to open a menu, and then select Reject Change, Reject All Changes Shown, or Reject All Changes in Document (to reject all changes in the document in one fell swoop).

Note
Good news! When you click on Accept Change or Delete Change, the change is accepted or rejected . . . and Word doesn't move. You can now see the change you've just made, and then click the Next button to move on. That may not sound important, but some versions of Word automatically jumped to the next change when you accepted or rejected a change so that you couldn't see the change being incorporated. (You need to see the incorporation because it's hard to anticipate what the final text will look like.) This jumping to the next change was a huge mistake, and we're happy to say that Word has finally returned to this way of working after several years of experimenting with the other method.

Note also that you can use the right-click pop-up menu to accept or reject revisions.

Customizing revision marks

You can change the options that control how revision marks appear in the document. Choose Tools ⇨ Options and click the Track Changes tab. Alternatively, right-click the TRK box in the status bar and select Options to open the Track Changes dialog box (see Figure 29-8). Table 29-1 describes the available options in this box.

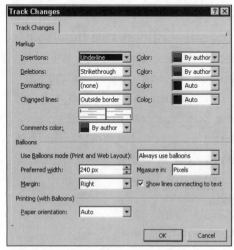

Figure 29-8: The Track Changes dialog box.

Table 29-1: The Track Changes Dialog Box

Option	*Function*
Insertions	Lets you choose how inserted text should be marked: underlined, shown only with a color, bold, italic, double-underlined, or shown with a strikethrough. You can also select the color to be used for the insertion. By default it's set to By Author, meaning Word selects a different color for each reviewer.
Deletions	Lets you choose how deleted text should be marked. In addition to the methods explained earlier, you can also have Word hide the text or replace the text with a # or ^ symbol.
Formatting	Lets you choose how Formatting changes should be indicated.
Changed Lines	Enables you to tell Word where to place the vertical line indicating a change—on the left border, the right border, or the outside border . . . or to omit them altogether.
Comments Color	Enables you to define how Word should color comments—different colors for each person entering comments or a specific color for all of them.

Option	Function
Use Balloons Mode	Enables you to define the manner in which balloons are handled—whether or not to use them at all and whether to display them for insertions and deletions.
Preferred Width	Lets you define the width of the balloons. Remember that balloons take up room in the margin, and Word has to "squeeze" the document to make room.
Measure In	Lets you choose the units used for measuring the balloon width.
Margin	Lets you choose which margin Word should place the balloons in.
Show Lines Connecting to Text	Lets you choose to have lines drawn from the balloons to the point in the text that they relate to.
Paper Orientation	Affects how the document prints with balloons displayed. You can force Word to print the document in landscape orientation, to print in the mode for which the document is set up, or to automatically select the most appropriate. (Note that this doesn't affect how the document appears in Print Preview, only how it prints.)

Comparing and merging documents

Here's a neat trick. Suppose you received a document that has been revised, but without tracking turned on. Or perhaps you didn't protect the document, and a reviewer turned off tracking.

Well, you can add revision marks to a revised version of a document that was edited with the change tracking feature not enabled. When you use this feature, the original document is not changed. The revised document is marked for your review instead. Text that appears in the original document but not in the revised version is marked for deletion, and text that appears for the first time in the revised document is marked for insertion.

You can use this comparison feature a couple of different ways:

✦ You can use it to compare two documents, and see a new document showing the differences between the two.

✦ You can use it to merge documents together, adding changes made to a copy—or multiple copies—back into the original.

Comparing documents

First take a look at how to compare documents. You open a document, select another document to compare to it, and then Word creates a third document that shows you the changes. This can be a little confusing at times because it's hard to figure out where all the changes came from. Think of it this way: You are creating a new document that shows you the revisions you would have to make to the *second* document in order to turn it into the *first* document you opened. Here is what you see in the third document that Word creates:

✦ Text that is in the first document but not the second is marked with revision marks and shown as an addition.

✦ Text that is in the second document but not in the first is marked as a deletion.

The system, it seems, is designed for comparing a revised document with the original. That is, you open the revision and then select the original to compare with the revision. However, you can open in any order you prefer.

To compare two versions of a document, follow these steps:

1. Open a document.

2. Choose Tools ⇨ Compare and Merge Documents. Select the document to compare with.

3. Make sure the Legal Blackline check box is selected—when it is, the button to the right will show the label Compare.

4. Click the Compare button.

5. If either of the documents has content that is already marked with revision marks, Word tells you that if you continue it's going to carry out the process under the assumption that revision marks should be accepted. Click the Yes button to continue.

6. Word now creates a new document, a copy of the first one you opened, and marks the differences between the two. Depending on the size of the document, this could take some time.

7. After you have marked a document using this technique, you can follow the procedures described earlier for accepting or rejecting the changes.

What is Legal Blackline? The wrong label! The way this is set up really doesn't make sense. If you want to compare documents, you have to select Legal Blackline. If you want to merge documents, you have to clear the Legal Blackline check box. Legal Blackline is simply the term given by Microsoft to the compare process, breaking two basic rules of software development: don't use multiple terms for the same function or component, and don't use ambiguous terms. Why are they using this term? Perhaps because WordPerfect was, for a long time, the word processor of choice for law firms, and Microsoft has had a long-term strategy of competing with WordPerfect. In the legal business, *blacklining* (not *blackline*) is the process of marking one document to show how it differs from another.

Notice also the Find Formatting check box. This check box tells Word to look for not only content additions and deletions, but changes in formatting. If selected, Word will place a bar indicating a change next to lines that contain formatting changes. For instance, if a word is normal text in one version, and bold in another, Word marks it with the revision bar in the margin.

Merging comments and revisions from multiple reviewers

In Chapter 28, we discussed how you can route documents to multiple reviewers—you can send a single document, passing from one to another—but you can also send a copy of the document to *all* the reviewers at once. Word provides a way for you to merge multiple documents into one, so you can see all the revisions in a single document. To merge comments and tracked changes, do the following:

1. Open a copy of the original document to which you want to merge the changes.

Note Make sure that all the revised documents that you want to merge have been marked for revisions. If changes were not tracked for any document, open that document and *compare* it to the original. Save the document with the revision marks included, and then merge it into the original.

2. Choose Tools ⇨ Compare and Merge Documents.

3. Select one of the shared documents that has changes you want to merge with the original file.

4. Clear the Legal Blackline check box. In effect, you are telling Word that you want to Merge documents, not compare. The button to the right now says Merge.

5. Click the triangle on the right side of the button, and a little menu opens.

6. Select one of the following:

   • **Merge:** Word marks up the *second* document, showing additions and deletions as if they had been made directly in the second document; you might think of this as merging the original document into the new document.

   • **Merge into Current Document:** Word adds the revisions to the original.

   • **Merge into New Document:** Word creates a new document showing the revisions. Why would you do this? After all, if you compare the original with a single modified document, the new document will exactly match the modified document. But you could merge one revised document into the original, compare the modified original with another revised document, and end up with a new document showing the changes between the modified original and the second revision.

7. Repeat steps 2 through 6 for each revised version of the original document.

   Any comments or revisions that were already in the original document remain. Word uses different colors to distinguish the merged comments and revisions for each of as many as eight reviewers.

After merging the reviewed copies of the document, you can examine all the comments and proposed changes and either accept or reject them as discussed before.

Comparing side by side

Word provides another way to compare documents, a tool that helps you visually compare. Open the two documents you want to compare, and then select Window ➪ Compare Side by Side With. You should see a list of the documents you have open. Select the one you want to compare with, and click OK.

Word opens a small toolbar with these three buttons:

   ✦ **Synchronous Scrolling:** Click this button to turn synchronous-scrolling mode on and off.

   ✦ **Reset Window Position:** Click this button to place the two documents side by side on your screen, if they are not in such a position already.

   ✦ **Break Side by Side:** Click this button when you're finished to turn off the Compare Side by Side mode.

The two documents will probably be placed on your screen side by side—but maybe not. If not, click the Reset Window Position button. You can switch between different modes as often as you like. Click one document's Maximize button (on the window's title bar) to open it up; then click Reset Window Position to bring it back to the side-by-side position.

With Synchronous Scrolling mode turned on, you can scroll in one document and the other document scrolls down, too. So if you have two versions of the same document—an original and a revised version—you can scroll through the two documents at once, and view the changes.

Reading Layout View

Word 2003 has a variety of features intended to help users *read* documents. Microsoft has been gradually developing a variety of e-book tools and features—such as Microsoft Reader— over the last few years, and some of these have found their way into Word.

These changes are in recognition of the fact that people spend a lot of time using Word to *read* documents, not just create them. Corporate users often e-mail each other documents, which recipients may read on-screen. In many cases, however, recipients print the documents before reading them because reading on-screen is not very comfortable. The e-book tools Microsoft has created are intended to make reading on-screen easier and more pleasant, making the wasteful practice of printing before reading unnecessary in many cases.

This is all part of a larger strategy of introducing the concept of e-books to the world. For example, in November 2002 Microsoft released *Windows XP Tablet PC Edition*, an operating system designed for use with the new Tablet PCs released by most major PC manufacturers at the same time.

Note   What's a Tablet PC? It's a laptop-sized computer with a touch screen that works with a pen (*stylus*) to give you the flexibility of pen and paper for note taking and similar tasks. Some Tablet PCs look just like laptops . . . until you spin the screen and close it so that the screen is on the *outside*. Others don't even include a keyboard. You can't open them, they're simply rectangular blocks with a screen on one side.

You'll find the new Reading Layout view a much easier way to read documents than any of the other views, even the Print Layout view. It's a great way for someone revising a document to read through the document on-screen. And the good news is that the reviewer can still make revisions to the document in Reading Layout view.

The Reading Layout view isn't intended to match Print Layout view. The purpose isn't to show you what the page would look like on paper, so page breaks will be different in Reading Layout view than what you see if you print the document.

To get to Reading Layout view, click the Read button (on the Standard toolbar), or choose View ⇨ Reading Layout. The Word window changes to display your document in two pages. Most of the tools around the window are removed—the status bar, the Document Map and task pane, if they're open, most of the toolbars, and so on. You are left with a special Reading Mode toolbar, and a Reading Mode Markup toolbar (which is the same as the Reviewing toolbar we looked at earlier). You can replace components if you wish. For example, click the Document Map button to display the Map again (see Figure 29-9). And if you prefer, you can view two pages at a time. Simply click the Allow Multiple Pages button button near the right end of the toolbar.

Note   When you switch a multi-column document to Reading Layout view, you lose the columns— Word displays it in a single-column layout.

Moving around in Reading Layout view

You have a variety of ways to move around in Reading Layout view. Table 29-2 describes these methods.

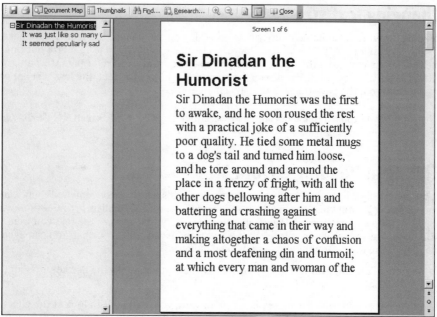

Figure 29-9: Viewing a document in Reading Layout view.

Table 29-2: Moving Around in Reading Layout View

Button or Key Name	Action
Up and Down Arrow keys Page Up and Page Dn keys	Moves you through the document a screen at a time.
Start of Document button	The last button on the Reading Layout toolbar; this displays the document's first page.
The scroll bar	Use as normal to move around—of course, in Reading view you'll move page by page, not line by line.
Thumbnails button	Click this to display thumbnail images of your pages. Use the scroll bar to move through these images, and click on an image to go to that page.
Document Map button	Click to display the document map; use as usual (see Chapter 1). Note that you can use the Document Map or the Thumbnails, but not both at the same time.
Find button	Use as usual (explained in Chapter 3); you can search for text, go to a specific page number, and so on.

Changing text size

Reading layout is all about legibility, so if you wish, you can change the text size to make the document easier to read. Simply click Increase Text Size and Decrease Text Size buttons on the toolbar. As you do so the text gets bigger or smaller, and Word reformats the paragraphs on the pages (or *screens*, as Word refers to them). The bigger the text, the less text appears on the page, but the page doesn't actually change size.

Note   You *cannot* zoom into the document in this layout; the View ⇨ Full Screen and View ⇨ Zoom commands are disabled.

Editing in Reading Layout view

You can actually edit in the Reading Layout view, but it's a little inconvenient. When you first open Reading Layout view, the cursor is nowhere in the document. The arrow keys move pages, not the cursor, after all. If you want to edit text, double-click in the text you want to work with. The cursor is now placed in the text, so you can edit as normal. You can even use the View menu to add the toolbars you'll need, if you wish.

To get out of Edit mode and back into normal Reading mode, press the Esc key, or simply go to another page.

If you do make changes while in Reading Layout view, you may want to look at the effect; click the Actual Page button near the end of the toolbar to temporarily take you out of Reading Layout view. While the window controls remain unchanged—you don't actually go back to the previous window settings, with all your toolbars, status bar, and so on—the page is displayed as it would appear on paper. Click the button again to return to full Reading Layout view.

Note   If you have Wrap to Window turned on while working in Normal view, switch to Reading Layout, and then switch back to Normal. Wrap to Window is automatically turned off. You can find Wrap to Window under the View tab of the Options dialog box. The Wrap to Window option tells Word to make the text use the entire width of the screen in Normal view.

Summary

Many Word users work in conjunction with others, and Word's collaboration tools—comments, reviewing tools, comparison and merge tools, and Reading Layout view—are truly useful. In this chapter, you learned a number of things:

✦ Place comments into documents using the Insert ⇨ Comment command.

✦ Record and place comments into documents using the Insert Voice button on the Reviewing toolbar.

✦ Text can also be highlighted. Select the text and then click the Highlight button.

✦ Choose Tools ⇨ Track Changes to turn on reviewing mode.

✦ The Reviewing toolbar allows you to quickly review the changes made to the document, and accept or reject those changes.

✦ Use the Tools ➪ Compare and Merge Documents command to see how documents differ and to merge changes from copies into an original.

✦ Choose View ➪ Reading Layout to open Reading mode.

✦　　✦　　✦

Online Collaboration

In This Chapter

Using SharePoint Team Services

Sharing files through SharePoint

Working with file versions

Using Web discussions

Using NetMeeting

Working with Exchange folders

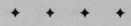

In most offices, documents are shared with others to disseminate information or to solicit comments and track revisions. Word includes several collaboration features that allow you to share, review, and revise documents in a workgroup environment.

In Chapter 29, we look at how more than one person can edit the same document simultaneously and how revisions made by others reviewing your documents can be tracked. But what tools are available to help you communicate with others on your team? This chapter looks at the tools Word provides to help you link to and communicate with your colleagues.

SharePoint Team Services

SharePoint is a wonderful tool for bringing together teams to help them share information and files and collaborate in a number of different ways. SharePoint is a Web-based system, allowing teams to work together not just through a corporate intranet, but across the world. Employees or team members throughout the world in any city or nation can connect to the Internet, log into a SharePoint account, and work together. First, though, your system administrator needs to install a SharePoint server and provide you with an account—an ID and a password. Actually there are two ways to access SharePoint services:

+ You can install the software on your own servers.

+ You can rent SharePoint services. A number of companies, such as some Web-hosting organizations, can provide you with as many SharePoint services as you want for a monthly fee for each account.

Tip   SharePoint services are in the reach of companies of all sizes, not just the corporate giants with sophisticated intranets. Go to a search site such as Yahoo! and search for **SharePoint hosting**. You'll find companies that rent SharePoint service for just a dollar or two per account each month.

Assume that you have a SharePoint account. Enter the URL for accessing the server in your Web browser, and you'll be prompted for your account name and password. Enter the appropriate information to log on to the SharePoint server. From there, you should have access to a variety of services:

✦ **Document repository:** Place files in this area so other team members can access them.

✦ **Pictures:** A picture library to hold images of your products or your Christmas party.

✦ **Contact lists:** A team address book.

✦ **Meeting area:** An area in which you can plan for meetings.

✦ **Task lists:** An area in which you can store task lists.

✦ **Discussion groups:** Exchange messages in group discussions.

✦ **Surveys:** Poll team members about any subjects on which you need feedback.

✦ **Announcements:** Announce news, events, or useful information you've run across.

✦ **Link directory:** Provide useful links to other Web sites or intranet folders; you can give each link a name and a description.

✦ **Calendar/Event directory:** Set up sales meetings, parties, planning meetings, and whatever else you need to schedule.

We're not going to look at all these services because they are beyond the scope of this book, useful though they may be. Rather, we take a quick look at the document-related features—the features of the *document-management workspaces*.

Note   What's a *workspace*? It's a SharePoint area. A *document-management workspace* is an area of the site in which team members can store and share files. A *meeting workspace* is an area used to plan and record information related to a meeting, such as the agenda, document libraries, attendee list, a picture library, a list of "things to bring." An *index workspace* contains information such as links to Internet sites and so on.

Sharing files

Workgroups in most medium- to large-size companies these days use network servers to share files. These servers are fast and convenient, but SharePoint document-management libraries and workspaces have a number of advantages over simply storing files on servers:

✦ Because SharePoint is Web-based, employees can access the system whether they're in Los Angeles, London, or Lusaka. SharePoint provides a very cheap way to network employees in multinational companies.

✦ You can provide document folders with descriptions to help team members identify the information they are seeking (a significant problem in teams that generate large numbers of files).

✦ You can ask SharePoint to tell you what's going on in a document library; it can send you e-mails immediately when someone works in the library or send a daily or weekly summary.

✦ You can add related resources to files, such as links to related resources online or on other services, task lists to track tasks related to working with the documents, and additional documents related to a document.

Admittedly, companies can provide access to intranets through VPNs (virtual private networks), but VPNs are generally more complicated to configure, manage, and access than SharePoint, and they don't provide all the features of SharePoint.

Files can be stored for use by you alone—perhaps you want to access documents while traveling—or can be placed in a shared-access area so that other team members can get to them. You can create additional document libraries, provide a name and description for each one, and determine how they handle the files.

On the main SharePoint page you'll see a Documents heading with a list of the document libraries below. Click one of the libraries to enter and add or manage files, or click Documents to create new libraries. Click the Create Document Library link to see the page in which you can create a new library (see Figure 30-1).

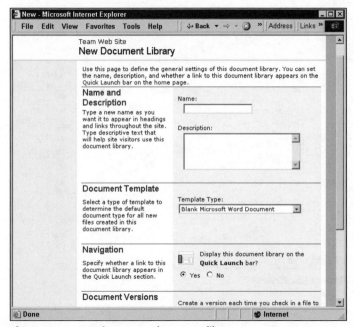

Figure 30-1: Creating a new document library.

When creating a new library, provide the following information:

✦ **Name:** The name of the library, as it appears in the list of libraries.

✦ **Description:** A description of the library; this text appears in the Description column of the list of libraries, inside the Documents and Lists page.

✦ **Document Template:** When you create a new file directly in the document library, rather than uploading a file, you can have SharePoint open a particular type of document. For example, you can tell SharePoint that when you click the New Document button it should create a new Word document.

✦ **Navigation:** You can place a link to the library in the main page navigation bar if you wish, or just access it from within the main Document Library page.

✦ **Document Versions:** You can tell SharePoint how you want to handle updates to files. If you choose to create a version each time you check a file in, SharePoint keeps a copy of the previous version, so you can always go back to a copy in any prior condition.

The Document Library page

The Document Library page (see Figure 30-2) lists the documents stored, of course, but also provides a number of features. Table 30-1 explains these features.

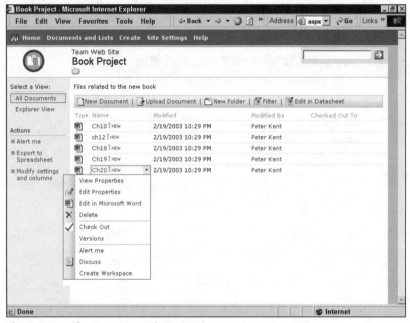

Figure 30-2: The Document Library page.

Table 30-1: The Document Library Features

Feature	Description
Select a View: All Documents	Displays the documents in the standard list view (refer to Figure 30-2).
Select a View: Explorer	Displays the documents in more of a Windows Explorer-type view, with folders and files displayed as large icons; double-clicking on an icon opens the folder or file.
New Document	Downloads a new document template and opens it in Microsoft Word. When you save this file, it's saved in the document workspace.
Upload Document	Uploads one or more documents to the library from your hard disk or any other disk—such as on a server, for example—to which your computer has access.

Feature	Description
New Folder	Creates a subfolder in the library, so you can group files.
Filter	Adds a drop-down list box at the top of each column; you can use these drop-downs to select the files you want to include in the list—files created by a particular person, on a particular date, and so on.
Edit in Datasheet	Displays the files and folders in a spreadsheet-type layout.
Alert Me	Tells SharePoint when you want to receive notification e-mails related to actions carried out in the library—when items are added, changed, removed, or discussed. You can choose to receive immediate notifications, or daily or weekly summaries.
Export to Spreadsheet	Enables you to save an .iqy file that can be opened in Microsoft Excel. This file lists the files in the libraries.
Modify Settings and Columns	Takes you to a page where you can modify background information, such as the library name and description, pick a new template, change column positions, and so on.
Type	Opens the file when you click an icon. The icon also identifies the type of file.
Name	Opens the file when you click the file name. Or click to the right of the name to open a menu of commands related to file operations.
Modified	Shows when the file was last saved.
Modified By	Enables you to view information about the author, including the person's e-mail address. The person indicated here is the last person to modify the file.
Checked Out To	Tells you who has checked out the file (which we look at later in the chapter). You can also click the name to find out more information about that person.

You've just seen that clicking on a file name opens a menu of options (see Figure 30-2). These options are explained in Table 30-2.

Table 30-2: The File Name Drop-Down Menu

Feature	Description
View Properties	Displays a page showing the document's name and title. From there you can choose to edit or delete the document, upload an updated version, or receive an alert telling you when the document is modified.
Edit Properties	Displays a page in which you can change the document name and title, edit in Microsoft Word, delete it or check it in or out, view a list showing you the version history, or post a message related to the document.

Continued

Table 30-2 *(continued)*

Feature	Description
Edit in Microsoft Word	Downloads the document to your computer and opens it in Microsoft Word so that you can edit it. When you close the document, you have the chance to save the changes to the SharePoint server.
Delete	Removes the document from the library.
Check Out/Check In	Checks a document out or, if you checked it out earlier, checks it back in.
Versions	Displays the Versions page, in which you can see a history of modifications to the document.
Alert Me	Shows the Alert Me page in which you can specify under what conditions SharePoint should send you an alert regarding the file.
Discuss	Downloads the file to your system so that you can add discussion notes to the file. We look at document discussions later in this chapter.
Create Workspace	Allows you to create a document workspace related to the selected document, in which you can add related files, a list of links to related resources, and a task list.

Uploading files

Uploading files to a library is pretty simple. Click the Upload Document button, and you see a page in which you can click a Browse button to select a file off your hard drive, or click Upload Multiple if you want to upload multiple files. If you click Upload Multiple, SharePoint reads your hard drive and displays a Windows-Explorer–type layout showing your folders and files (see Figure 30-3). Click the check boxes next to the files you want to upload, and click the Save and Close button. Be careful with the Overwrite if File(s) Already Exist(s)? check box. This option is selected by default, so you will overwrite files of the same name as those you are uploading.

Checking out files

A major problem for teams that share files is that of ensuring that two people don't work on the same file at the same time. SharePoint certainly lets you download a file after someone else has done so, but there's also a check-out system that helps you keep these things straight.

You can check the documents out. Click on a file name in the library, and select Check Out from the pop-up menu. After a file is checked out, your name appears in the Checked Out To column, and other people, although they can download a copy, can't upload a copy. You have dibs on the file.

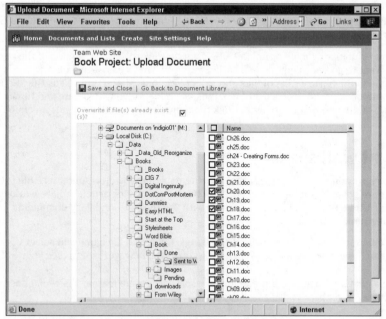

Figure 30-3: Uploading multiple files into a document library.

Checking a file out doesn't download it to your system. It simply reserves the file for you. *So remember to check files back in when you're finished with them!* When you want to work on the file, click the file icon, or click to the right of the file name and select Edit in Microsoft Word from the pop-up menu. You can work on the file, and when you close it, you see several options:

✦ **Save changes and check in:** Word uploads the file to the library, saves your changes, and checks the file back in.

✦ **Save changes only:** Word saves your work in the library but doesn't check the file back in. It's still reserved for you.

✦ **Discard changes and undo check out:** Word checks the file back in, but it doesn't save your changes.

✦ **Discard changes only:** Word discards the file, but it remains checked out.

Working with versions

The versions feature is extremely useful. If you've ever worked with a file for a few days and then realized that the version you were working on three days ago contained some important information *that has now disappeared*, you'll understand. The version feature allows you to go back and grab a prior version of the file.

You have to set up the library to create versions. When you create a new library, one of the options is Document Versions: Create a Version Each Time You Check in a File to this Web Site? Select the Yes option.

Now, each time you modify a file or upload a new version, Word saves a version of the previous edition. Want to go back and open an earlier version? That's easy—just click to the right of the file name in the library's list of files and select Versions. SharePoint opens the Versions Saved for *file name* page. You see a list of versions, each identified with a date and time, along with the name of the person modifying it. Click the name, and SharePoint sends a version to Word.

Document workspaces

Suppose you're working on a document that represents a major project, perhaps a big proposal that you're going to submit to a client, or a book or magazine article. You're working on this document with a team, and a lot is involved with the project—ancillary documents, task lists, online resources, and so on.

Create a document workspace to manage these things. Click on a file name and select Create Workspace. You'll see a message page—click OK to open the new workspace (see Figure 30-4).

Tip   Bookmark the page after you arrive at the workspace. For some reason, SharePoint doesn't make it easy to get back to these workspaces!

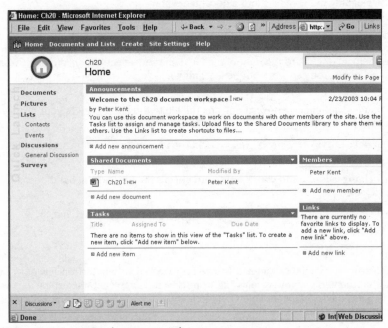

Figure 30-4: A new document workspace.

A document workspace is almost a SharePoint site just for that document. Here you can add supporting documents in document libraries, post announcements, create task lists, create link lists (links to other online resources), upload images, hold online discussions, create contact lists, and hold online surveys.

Web discussions

The Office Web Discussion feature is a system that allows users to discuss documents using a network news-type of messaging system. To use the Web discussion feature in Word (or any Office application), you must have a discussion server set up on a Windows Server of some kind. Or you can use SharePoint, which includes a discussion server.

Web discussion participants can discuss the document from anywhere on the Internet or a local area network. In this case, discussions are messages that are stored separately from the document in a database and then are merged transparently into the document when you view it. These Web discussions are threaded, meaning that replies to a particular discussion remark are nested directly under that remark.

Using Web discussions, you and your colleagues can insert remarks into the same documents. You can start a discussion either about a specific portion of the document or about the document in general. Multiple discussions also can occur within the same document at the same time. You and your colleagues can even insert discussion remarks into the same document without anyone routing the document or reconciling comments in multiple copies of the document.

As a document is passed around, you can hold a "conversation" with the other reviewers. In effect, this feature is a form of linked comments.

Cross-Reference   See Chapter 29 to find out more about Word's Comments feature.

Click to the right of the file name in the SharePoint document library, and a pop-up menu opens. Select Discuss, and you can choose whether to Open or Save the file. If you open the file—or save the file now but open it later—you'll see the Web Discussions toolbar at the bottom of the window, above the status bar (see Figure 30-5). Table 30-3 offers a description of each button.

Figure 30-5: The Web Discussions toolbar.

Note   When you first use one of the Web Discussion commands, you have to provide a server address. Ask your server administrator for the right information. If you use a discussion command from within SharePoint, however, Word will probably figure out the server address for itself because the server is hosted within SharePoint.

Table 30-3: The Web Discussions Toolbar

Name	Button	Description
Discussions ▾	Discussions	A button that opens a menu with the following commands.
	Insert in the Document	Allows you to insert a discussion message in the document, in an icon in the document body.
	Insert About the Document	Allows you to insert a general-discussion message in the Discussion pane.
	Refresh Discussions	Updates the discussion to add messages that may have been posted since you opened the pane.
	Filter Discussions	Allows you to filter the discussions shown in the pane; you can choose to see messages from a particular participant and select a duration.
	Print Discussions	Prints the discussion messages.
	Discussion Options	Opens the Discussions dialog box, in which you can select a Discussion server, select the fields you want to display in the Discussion pane, and decide whether or not you want to display closed discussions.
	Insert Discussion in the Document	The same as Insert in the Document on the Discussions menu.
	Insert Discussion About the Document	The same as Insert About the Document on the Discussions menu.
	Previous	Jumps to the previous discussion item.
	Next	Jumps to the next discussion item.
	Show General Discussion	General discussions are those related to the document in general, rather than a specific portion of the document. This button opens the discussion pane and displays the messages inserted using Discussions ➪ Insert About the Document.
Subscribe...	Subscribe	Opens the Get Notified When Changes Occur dialog box; you can request alerts when the document is modified or deleted, or when a discussion item is added or removed. You can ask for an immediate, daily, or weekly notification.

Name	Button	Description
🖧	Stop Communication With Discussion Server	Stops sending messages to, and receiving messages from, the discussion server.
⬆	Show/Hide Discussion Pane	Opens and closes the Discussion pane, which appears at the bottom of the window.
<u>Close</u>	Close	Closes the Web Discussions toolbar.

You can reply to discussions by clicking on the yellow message icon next to a message; a menu pops up, from which you can select Reply—when you add a message it's placed below the first message and indented, so it's clearly a reply. You can also select a number of other options from the menu: Edit, Delete, Close (which removes the message from the pane), Close Item and Replies, and Activate.

Accessing file libraries directly from Word

You can access SharePoint document-management workspaces—the document libraries—directly from within Word, by setting up the workspace as a Network Place. You can save and open files in SharePoint, in your own personal folders and shared folders. Here's how:

1. Double-click the My Network Places icon on your desktop; the My Network Places window opens.

2. Double-click the Add Network Place icon to open the Add Network Place Wizard.

3. Type the URL of the workspace. Ask your system administrator for the URL. It's likely that the URL you need is the URL you use to access SharePoint on the Web, followed by /share. For instance, it might be something like the following:

   http://pkent.sharepointservices.com/share

4. Click the Next button. The Enter Network Password dialog box opens.

5. Type your User Name and password, and click OK.

6. You are prompted for a name for this network connection; type any name you want, such as My SharePoint Files, and click Finish.

7. A folder window opens, showing you several folders in your document workspace at the SharePoint server.

After you've set up the SharePoint document workspace, you can access it directly from within Word. In the Open or Save As dialog boxes, click the My Network Places button and then double-click on the name you entered for the document workspace (My SharePoint Files, for example). You have to log on using your account name and password, and once connected you see a list of folders (see Figure 30-6). Click on a folder to access it and then use it as if it were a folder on your hard disk.

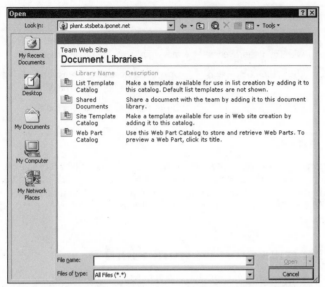

Figure 30-6: The Open dialog box, showing the SharePoint document workspace.

Online meetings

Office used to include Microsoft NetMeeting, which has for years been the main online collaboration tool from Microsoft. But Microsoft has now incorporated NetMeeting into MSN Messenger, Microsoft's Instant Messenger tool. Now, when you select Tools ➪ Online Collaboration ➪ Meet Now, you see a message prompting you to download and install MSN Messenger. You also have to sign up for a Microsoft .NET Passport account. Passport is intended to provide universal account access. Many Web sites use Passport for user access, enabling people to use a single password for many different accounts. You'll use your Passport account to sign on to MSN Messenger.

The Online Meeting toolbar (see Figure 30-7), from earlier versions of Word, is still there, but it won't do you much good until you've installed Messenger (which comes with NetMeeting). Clicking any of the buttons simply displays a message telling you to use MSN Messenger. Just click the last button on the toolbar—the End Meeting button—to get rid of the toolbar, and then use MSN Messenger externally. Quite frankly, it's easier to use NetMeeting through Messenger than through Word.

Figure 30-7: The Online Meeting toolbar.

Here are some of the things that MSN Messenger can help you do:

✦ Send files to colleagues, friends, and family—as easy as drag and drop

✦ Chat via text messages

✦ Send instant messages

✦ Send e-mails

✦ Send messages to mobile devices

✦ Browse the Web with others

✦ Hold group discussions

✦ Use a whiteboard to pass sketches over the Internet

✦ Use a Webcam and microphone to see and hear each other

✦ Use MSN Phone to dial any phone number in the world and talk through your computer's microphone

✦ And yes, play games

So, you still have great online-collaboration tools available, they are just disconnected from Word.

If you've never used collaboration tools like these, you may not realize just how useful they can be. Originally intended for use *between* offices, they are also frequently used for *intra-office* communications. Someone in one office can send messages and files to a colleague just a few doors down.

Sending files, for instance, is a breeze. From the Online list in MSN Messenger, simply right-click the name of the person you want to send the file to and select Send a File or Photo. An Open box appears, in which you can select the file you want to send—the file is placed into the Conversation box (see Figure 30-8). Click Send, and away it goes.

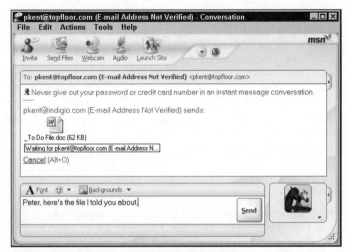

Figure 30-8: Sending a file through Messenger.

The Conversation box is not only where you send files but, not surprisingly, where you hold conversations. It's actually a chat window in which you can send real-time messages. In fact, you can use it as the command center—all your tools are available from here, and many operate through the window. If you want to hold a Webcam conversation, for example, you can click the Webcam button to get started. Or you can click the Audio button to begin talking with someone else, whether in another office or on another continent (assuming, of course, that you both have sound cards, speakers, and microphones).

As mentioned before, NetMeeting is still available, although you may not use it much. To use it you simply choose Actions ➪ Start NetMeeting in the Conversation window. Although NetMeeting lets you chat, Messenger's Chat window is easier to use. NetMeeting also lets you share files, but the process is quicker and easier through Messenger. A few tools in NetMeeting don't have equivalents in Messenger, however, such as the Whiteboard (see Figure 30-9). NetMeeting also provides a tool that enables you to share programs running on your desktop, along with another tool that lets you set up your desktop so that you can automatically run programs on it from another machine, through NetMeeting, at any time. You can also use NetMeeting's video-conferencing tools, although you may find that you prefer the Webcam tools found in Messenger.

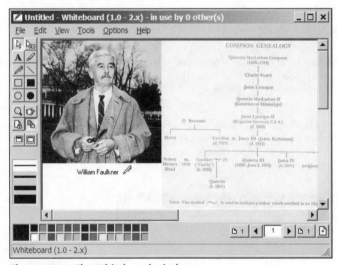

Figure 30-9: The Whiteboard window.

NetMeeting was never widely used, at least not to the degree that popular chat tools are used. You will likely find that Messenger provides all the tools you need, and that you never access NetMeeting.

Exchange Folders

Most corporate offices these days have networks with file servers on which workgroups can save files that they work on together. However, Microsoft Exchange server—which provides services to Microsoft Outlook—comes with a simple, built-in file-sharing tool, Exchange Folders. You and your colleagues can place documents you need to share into these Exchange folders.

To place a copy of the document you have open into a folder in Exchange, select File ⇨ Send To ⇨ Exchange Folder, and the Send To Exchange Folder dialog box opens (see Figure 30-10). Open one of the Favorite folders or create a new one by clicking on a folder and clicking New Folder. When you've found the folder into which you want to place the document, click OK.

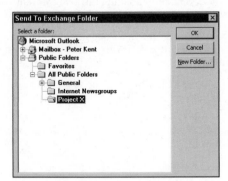

Figure 30-10: The Send To Exchange Folder dialog box.

Now any team member can get to a copy of the document you've saved by opening Microsoft Outlook on their computer and opening the folder in which the document is saved. The document can be moved to a computer by dragging and dropping out of Outlook and onto the desktop or into a Windows Explorer folder; or simply double-click on the document in the folder. (See Figure 30-11.)

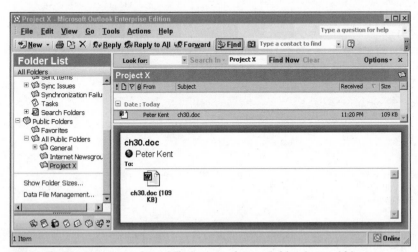

Figure 30-11: Opening a shared file in an Exchange Folder, from within Microsoft Outlook.

Summary

This chapter covered a number of Word tools that allow you to share documents within your workgroup. The following points were discussed:

✦ In order to use SharePoint, you need a SharePoint server set up. But you can rent space on one for a dollar or two per employee per month.

✦ SharePoint has many features; documents can be stored in a document library. You can also create document workspaces related to specific documents and add supporting documents, task lists, reference lists, and more.

✦ SharePoint can save a copy of a prior version of a file when you modify it; when you create a new library, select the Yes option button under Create a Version Each Time You Check in a File to this Web Site?

✦ Web discussions allow you to hold "discussions" inside a document—different reviewers can enter, and reply to, comments.

✦ To share files through Exchange Folders, choose File ➪ Send To ➪ Exchange Folder.

✦ You can open a file stored in an Exchange Folder from within Microsoft Outlook.

✦   ✦   ✦

Customizing and Troubleshooting Word

◆ ◆ ◆ ◆

In This Part

Chapter 31
Troubleshooting and
Overcoming Word's
Idiosyncrasies

Chapter 32
Customizing Menus,
Options, Toolbars, and
Keys

Chapter 33
Making the Most of
Word Macros and VBA

Chapter 34
Securing Your Data

◆ ◆ ◆ ◆

Troubleshooting and Overcoming Word's Idiosyncrasies

✦ ✦ ✦ ✦

In This Chapter

Resolving Word's installation and interface quirks

Controlling how Word automatically replaces and formats text

Optimizing Word and reducing the size of Word files

Recovering from a system crash and repairing Word application files

Preventing macro virus attacks

✦ ✦ ✦ ✦

Word is full of little idiosyncrasies that can be quite annoying—and some that are downright infuriating. This chapter shares some solutions and workarounds to control Word's most frustrating automatic interface, text correction, and formatting options. It also includes helpful information about optimizing Word, reducing the size of Word documents, as well as Web page files, and troubleshooting Word.

Installation and Interface Quirks

With each new release, Microsoft adjusts how the Word program works and modifies the user interface. Word includes a feature called *install on demand* and several interface modifications, such as personalized menus and toolbars that display the most recently used commands and buttons. The following sections explain why these features can be frustrating. These sections also list some ways to work around the quirks arising from these installation and interface features.

Install on Word's demand

It's going to happen. You're going to click on an option, and Word is going to display a message informing you that the option is not installed. The idea behind *install on demand* is to prevent Word from bloating your system with features you may never use. This idea seems to make sense, but Microsoft still has to decide what features to install by default. If you are an avid Word user, keep your Word CD next to your computer. Otherwise, you may spend a lot of time hunting it down to perform operations.

If you have plenty of disk space, you can run the installation again and load all the features you're likely to need onto the hard disk. Open the Windows Control panel (Start ⇨ Settings ⇨ Control Panel), and double-click the Add/Remove Programs icon. Find Microsoft Office in the list of applications, click it, and then click the Change button. In the Setup dialog box select the Add or Remove Features option, and click Next. You can then select which Office applications—and which components of each application—are available. In fact, when you click a button's triangle, you open a little menu that provides these options:

✦ **Run from My Computer:** Installs the component on your computer's hard drive so that it's always available quickly.

✦ **Run all from My Computer:** Installs the component, and all the subcomponents, on your hard drive.

✦ **Installed on First Use:** Office doesn't install the component on your hard drive; when you need it, Office prompts you to install it.

✦ **Not Available:** Office doesn't allow you access to the component.

Tip

The Install on Demand feature is quite possibly Microsoft's way of ensuring that users have a CD, thus discouraging users from running illegal copies of Word. The Word Install program requires the 25-character CD-ROM key number provided with Word. It is located on the sticker on the back of the jewel case. If you have installed Word already and have misplaced the case, you can choose Help ⇨ About to display the About Microsoft Word window that includes the CD-ROM key. It's a good idea to copy the CD key to a text file on your PC as well. We also write the number on the CD with an indelible pen. Don't rely on getting the info from Word itself; if Word crashes and must be reinstalled, and you can't locate the CD-ROM key, you're out of luck.

Missing menu options

By default, Word now displays full menus. In earlier versions, Word automatically personalized menus and toolbars for you as you worked. When you opened a menu, only the commands that were most significant or most recently used would be immediately visible. To display the full set of menu commands, you had to click the down-pointing arrows at the bottom of the menu. These personalized menus can be a little disconcerting if you expect a command to always appear in a particular place. Seeing all the menu options displayed can be more comfortable for some people, especially for new users, which is why Microsoft has changed the behavior. However, if you like the abbreviated menus, it's still possible to turn that behavior back on.

Note, also, that Word now displays the Standard and Formatting toolbars on a single row by default. That means a number of buttons are not available unless you move the toolbars. To have Word display the Standard and Formatting toolbars on separate rows, so that more buttons are visible, and to turn on the abbreviated menu items feature, follow these steps:

1. Choose Tools ⇨ Customize, and click the Options tab. The Customize dialog box appears (see Figure 31-1).

2. Select the Show Standard and Formatting Toolbars on Two Rows check box.

3. Clear the Always Show Full Menus check box.

4. Click Close.

Figure 31-1: The Customize dialog box includes options for disabling Word's personalized menus.

Uncluttering the taskbar

When you open or create several documents, each has its own window. You'll notice, for instance, that if you have five Word documents open, you'll have five Word icons on the Window taskbar, and when you switch between applications using Alt+Tab, you'll see five icons in the selection box that appears.

Back in the old days, Microsoft's programs worked differently. You'd have a single Word window, a single taskbar icon, and a single Word icon in the Alt+Tab selection box. To switch between documents you would use the Window menu or press Alt+F6 (both of these methods still work for switching between documents).

Some of us prefer the old way because when you have a number of programs open, and quite a few documents inside each program, the taskbar quickly fills up. Microsoft has added the capability to work in the old way—you can tell Word to display a single button in the taskbar, rather than a button for each document (this affects the Alt+Tab selection box). Simply choose Tools ➪ Options, click the View tab, and clear the Windows in Taskbar check box.

You might like to try a compromise, though. You can keep the normal Windows functioning—one button for every document—but resize your taskbar to display more documents, and reposition it, too.

To resize the taskbar, move your mouse pointer onto the edge of the taskbar; the mouse pointer turns into a two-headed arrow. Then just drag the taskbar to resize it. You can hide the taskbar automatically by choosing the Start menu, choosing Settings ➪ Taskbar and Start menu, and then selecting the Auto Hide check box. The taskbar now slides out of view while you work. To display the taskbar, move your mouse onto the screen edge containing the taskbar. To find a particular document, move your mouse pointer on a Microsoft Word icon in the taskbar, and a ToolTip appears that lists the name of the document.

You can also reposition the toolbar. Some users like to place the toolbar on the left side of the screen, for instance, and make it fairly wide. This way you see a horizontal button for each open document, and if you make the taskbar wide enough you can see each document title. To move the taskbar, point at a blank area, press and hold the mouse button, and drag the toolbar up and to the left or right. You'll see the bar jump to another side of the screen; simply release the mouse button when you have the taskbar where you want it.

Persistent toolbars

You may find unwanted toolbars appearing in the Word window. Word allows you to remove toolbars, but some keep coming back every time you reopen Word. Other programs may install Word toolbars—Adobe Acrobat, for instance, installs a small toolbar with two buttons. Some label printers place toolbars into Word, too, and many other programs load toolbars.

Cross-Reference See Chapter 32 to learn more about customizing and removing toolbars.

How do you get rid of these toolbars? Simple. Choose Tools ➪ Templates and Add-ins, click the Templates tab, and look for an appropriate global template in the large list box. For example, if you are trying to get rid of the Adobe Acrobat toolbar, you are likely to find a template called PDFMaker.dot (if you use Acrobat, you probably know that the files it creates are PDF files).

Click the file name and look down at the bottom of the dialog box. You should see the path to the folder holding this document. In fact, it is in the folder designated as the Startup folder. You need to remove this template from that folder because every time Word opens a file, it loads the templates in that folder as global templates. Remove the file, and you won't get those toolbars anymore.

Editing Quirks and Problems

Much of the frustration experienced by Word users relates to how the program anticipates the type of text and formatting you want to display. Word's AutoCorrect and AutoFormat features can work for as well as against you, however. The following sections explain how to solve formatting problems manually and to control what automatic text and formatting is applied as you type.

Deleting paragraph marks does strange things

The problems that plague beginning Word users the most are rooted in how Word stores formatting instructions and is set to work by default. The first thing you should do when you encounter a formatting problem is click on the Show/Hide button to reveal the hidden characters. Paragraph marks (also called *pilcrows*) are fundamental to how Word works. As explained in Chapter 1, Word stores formatting for each paragraph in the paragraph mark. If you delete a paragraph mark, strange things start to happen. Things, in fact, don't seem to do what you might expect.

First, how can you demonstrate that paragraph formatting is attached to the paragraph mark at the end of a paragraph? Try this. Turn on nonprinting characters so that you can see the paragraph marks, and select one. Place the cursor at the end of the paragraph and press Shift+right arrow to highlight it. Then press Ctrl+C to copy the paragraph mark into the Clipboard. Now place the cursor at the end of a paragraph with a completely different style. If you selected a Heading 1 paragraph mark, for instance, place the cursor at the end of a paragraph of Normal text. Press Ctrl+V to paste the paragraph mark into the document. What happens? All of a sudden, the paragraph of Normal text changes to Heading 1 text.

Here's where it gets strange. Delete a paragraph mark and what happens? You probably think that the text from the paragraph now takes on the formatting from the *next* paragraph. After all, you've just removed the paragraph mark, so the text has to merge into the next paragraph.

But that's not what happens, which makes it so confusing. In fact, the *second* paragraph—which still has its paragraph mark—now takes on the style of the *first* paragraph, the one for which you deleted the paragraph mark. Understand this, and working with Word will seem much easier.

This idiosyncrasy explains, at least partially, how headings at the top of pages sometimes get accidentally converted to Normal text. Here's the scenario. You have a paragraph of Normal text, followed by a paragraph mark, followed by a hard page break, followed by a Heading paragraph on the top of the next page.

Suppose that while cleaning up text at the bottom of the first page, you accidentally delete the paragraph mark immediately before the page break. Here's what happens. The page break mark (make sure you've turned on hidden text) moves up and sits in the place of the deleted paragraph mark. The following paragraph, the Heading text, now takes on the formatting of the Normal paragraph. But because there's a page break, it still appears on the next page . . . but it's no longer a Heading. This is a little odd, because generally you can't put a page break inside a paragraph. Place the insertion point in a paragraph and press Ctrl+Enter to insert a page break, and Word first inserts a paragraph mark.

Now, here's where it gets stranger still. Suppose that you select the paragraph mark *and* the first character in the next paragraph, or perhaps a few words or lines. What happens when you delete this content? In this case, the remaining text takes on the style of the *second* paragraph. So, here's a quick guideline:

✦ **Delete the paragraph mark:** The second paragraph takes on the style of the first.

✦ **Delete the paragraph mark and at least the first character in the second paragraph:** The first paragraph takes on the formatting of the second paragraph.

AutoCorrect and AutoFormat hell

Word's IntelliSense technology—the technology used by AutoCorrect and AutoFormat—can sometimes seem like IntelliNonsense because Word is carrying out operations that are not clearly defined. For example, if you enter three consecutive pound signs (###) in your document and then press Enter, Word automatically places three horizontal border lines across the page (a heavy line between two thin lines).

The three number signs do not exist in the AutoCorrect Replace As You Type list. Instead, they are included in the Borders option under the AutoFormat As You Type tab, in the AutoCorrect dialog box (Tools ➪ AutoCorrect). Word also expects that every hyperlink you enter should be a live link that a user can click to display the Web page or file. For example, when you type a URL, it is automatically turned into a blue, underlined hyperlink. That the hyperlinks appear as live links with special formatting can be quite frustrating when you are preparing a document for printed publication. And sometimes you find that when you press Tab you end up changing paragraph indents—also very irritating.

If you really want to display the text without applying automatic formatting, you can choose Undo AutoCorrect each time Word applies the formatting. It is much more convenient, however, just to turn off the AutoFormat option that you don't want applied to your text. The most troublesome AutoFormat options are related to headings, bulleted and numbered lists, hyperlinks, and indents.

To change these settings, follow these steps:

1. Choose Tools ➪ AutoCorrect. The AutoCorrect dialog box appears.

2. Click the AutoFormat As You Type tab (see Figure 31-2).

3. Clear one or more of the following check boxes:

- Built-in Heading Styles in the Apply As You Type group.

- Automatic Bulleted Lists and Automatic Numbered Lists in the Apply As You Type group.

- Internet And Network Paths With Hyperlinks in the Replace As You Type group.

- Set Left- and First-Indent With Tabs and Backspaces in the Automatically As You Type group.

4. Click OK.

Note If Word continues to add headings after you clear the Headings check box on the AutoFormat As You Type tab, clear the Define Styles Based on Your Formatting check box.

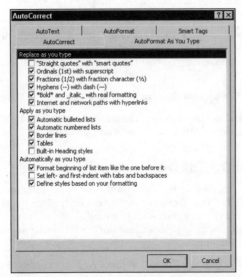

Figure 31-2: You can resolve many formatting problems using the AutoFormat As You Type tab.

Recurring and disappearing text

One quirk continues to appear in Word. When displaying your document in Print Layout View, some text at the end or the beginning of a page can appear twice—or even disappear altogether. It may, for instance, appear at both the bottom of one page and the top of the next.

If you are editing a section of text and encounter this problem of ghost text, you can sometimes resolve this problem by simply minimizing and then maximizing the Word window. If this does not resolve the problem, change the View mode to Normal (View ➪ Normal) to edit the problematic text. You then can switch back to Print Layout (View ➪ Print Layout) and continue editing the rest of your document.

For a long-term fix, consider updating your video drivers. It may be that your computer does not have the latest video drivers for its display adapter. You may find that visiting your computer manufacturer or display adapter manufacturer's Web site, and downloading the latest drivers, will provide you with the fix you need.

Having pictures appear where you want them

Positioning pictures is often tricky. You may sometimes find that pictures suddenly jump away when you move them to a new position, and you have to go looking through the document to find where they end up. We're talking, of course, about pictures that are not In Line With Text. Those that are In Line With Text are easy to deal with because they always sit in the correct position. Rather, we're talking about pictures that you are trying to position using one of the six other text-wrapping styles.

 If you work much with pictures, spend some time in Chapters 17 and 18. It's helpful to have a good understanding of all the positioning and text-wrapping features.

Here are a few things that may make working with pictures easier. First, if you are having trouble placing an image, see if anchor locking is the problem. To unlock the anchor, double-click the picture to open the Format Picture dialog box, or click once and choose Format ➪ Picture. Then click the Layout tab, and click the Advanced button. On the Picture Position tab, clear the Move Object With Text and Lock Anchor check boxes. You might also try clearing Allow Overlap.

Sometimes, a picture gets stuck in a position on a page—often at the top edge. No matter how much you drag the picture down onto the page, it won't stick. It keeps popping back up to the top of the page. Try going into the Picture Position tab of the Advanced Layout dialog box (double-click the image, click the Layout Tab, and then click the Advanced button) and changing the Absolute Position settings to an inch or two below and to the right of the Page setting. Then you'll be able to drag the picture into a different position.

After you make these changes, you should find that the picture behaves much better and is more willing to follow your instructions.

Resolving font problems

If fonts do not display properly, try formatting the text with another font to see if it corrects the problem. For example, you can select the text in question and then change the font to Times New Roman. If the text now appears correctly, the font you are using may be either corrupted or not be available on your system.

The introduction of fonts that support Unicode encoding bring solutions to creating multilingual documents, but they also can introduce font problems. In some cases, you may find when using a Unicode font that characters do not appear as you expected—or in older versions of Word or other applications are replaced with empty block characters. If you plan to share a document with readers who do not require the Unicode font—and few readers of this book will run into a situation in which they have to use Unicode fonts—use a standard font instead.

You can check to see if a TrueType font is installed and working correctly by double-clicking My Computer and then double-clicking the Control Panel icon. Next, double-click the Fonts icon and try to locate the font you are using in your Word document. If you double-click the TrueType font and a window does not open displaying sample text, or if the sample text displays incorrectly, you need to reinstall the font. Some font problems are related to print drivers. (For more on resolving font problems, see the section "Peripheral devices and problems with files" later in this chapter.)

Optimizing Word and Reducing the Size of Files

Various factors affect how well Word performs. If you note the program is taking a long time to perform tasks, this problem may not relate directly to Word itself. After all, Word is running in conjunction with Windows, so optimizing Windows may solve your problem.

However, in some cases, a particular document can make Word perform slowly. This is especially true of long documents and of those with many pictures. Sometimes you may be shocked at the size of a Word document or a Web page as well. The following sections explain what you can do to speed up Windows and Word and to reduce the size of your Word document and Web page files.

Speeding up Word

As you copy, move, and install programs on your disk, files can become fragmented on your drive. You see, what is shown in Windows Explorer is just a simple representation of files stored on your disks. The reality is too complicated to work with, so you are shown just enough information for you to get along. In reality, computer files are stored in segments, little pieces, which may or may not be together. A Word document, for instance, may be stored in several pieces in different areas of your disk drive; one piece here, another there, another in yet a third location, and so on. The longer you use your computer, and the less free space you have on your hard drive, the more fragmented the drive becomes. This slows the computer down, because instead of going to one place to open a file, or save to the file, or to do anything else to the file, it may have to go to, say, five different places.

Note Fragmentation is particularly a problem if you have very little free disk space on your hard drive.

By defragmenting your hard disk, however, you can make all the files for the programs on your hard disk contiguous, which can speed up accessing files. To speed up Windows in general, run the Window's defragmentation program: Click Start, choose Programs ➪ Accessories ➪ System Tools ➪ Disk Defragmenter, select the disk where the Word program resides, and click Analyze. The tool analyzes your disk and tells you if you should defragment.

Working with multiple programs also can slow down Word. For example, you may have another application open that is eating up memory. You can see other running programs by looking at the icons in the taskbar; the more icons, the more memory is being used, and the slower your system is likely to move.

In Word itself, more than a few things can slow the program to a crawl. If you are working with a large document, one with numerous pictures, or are experiencing sluggish performance, use the following list to make editing in Word faster:

✦ Work in Normal view most of the time, and only switch to Print Layout view (View ➪ Print Layout) when you need to check formatting. This especially helps when you are working in a document with many images.

✦ Hide pictures while you are editing your document. To do this, choose Tools ➪ Options, click the View tab, and check the Picture Placeholders check box.

✦ Disable Word from checking your grammar and spelling as you type. If you see the red squiggly lines under words as you type, choose Tools ➪ Options and then click the Spelling & Grammar tab. Clear the Check Spelling as You Type and Check Grammar as You Type check boxes.

Reducing the size of Word documents and Web page files

The Allow Fast Saves option under the Save tab in the Options dialog box sounds like a good idea. Unfortunately, it may also cause your files to become bloated and, reportedly, corrupted (you may not be able to open the document). Instead of saving your complete file, Word keeps track of your edits and then appends those changes to the end of the file. This means that old text you really don't need still exists in the file. Someone who knows the tricks may be able to look at the contents of the file and see text you thought you had deleted. And in most cases enabling Allow Fast Saves does not speed up Word much anyway! To keep the size of your files to a minimum, turn off Allow Fast Saves.

Word also can create huge files when you insert pictures. To keep the file size down, you may want to link to the picture file rather than actually insert that picture into the document. Remember, however, that if you remove or move the picture file from its location, it no longer displays in your Word document. You may also want to compress the images; open the Format Picture dialog box, click the Picture tab, and then click the Compress button.

For details on linking pictures, see Chapter 20. See Chapter 17 for more information on using the Format Picture dialog box.

Web pages are especially prone to size problems. Web pages typically use the .JPG and .GIF image formats, which are bitmap images. If you add a *vector* image to your page, Word adds special code that enables Internet Explorer to display the images, and this can really bloat the size of your Web page files. You may want to think twice before using an unneeded graphic. Even adding a small AutoShape can increase the size of your Web page file dramatically.

Choosing Tools ➪ Options, clicking the General tab, and then clicking Web Options displays the options for creating Web pages. The General tab contains the option Rely on CSS for Font Formatting. Do not be misled, however. You may think that turning off this CSS option reduces the file size of your Web pages, but it does not. Word still stores the style definitions in the file, but it replaces the in-line styles with font-tag information. Clicking the Pictures tab and then clearing the Rely on VML for Displaying Graphics In Browsers also is misleading. This does not reduce the size of your files because the VML data remain stored in the Web Page file.

Saving Word Documents

Word automatically appends a .doc extension to your Word documents and an .htm extension to your Web page files and stores them in a folder named My Documents. By default, Windows does not show you these file extensions. Most experienced computer users find this very frustrating, if not downright misleading at times. The following sections explain how to store your document files in another directory and how to view the file name extensions in Windows.

Changing the default folder

My Documents is the default folder for saving Word documents. To change the default folder from My Documents to some other folder, follow these steps:

1. Create the directory in which you wish to store your Word files.

2. Choose Tools ➪ Options. The Options dialog box appears.

3. Click the File Locations tab.

4. Select Documents in the File Types group, and click the Modify button. The Modify Location dialog box appears.

5. Navigate to the folder, and click OK twice to close the open dialog boxes. The new folder is now the default folder for all your Word documents and Web page files.

File name extensions for Windows and Word

By default, Windows hides the .doc, .htm, and other file name extensions for Word files. For example, if you save a file in the Rich Text Format (.rtf) and another file with the same name as a Word document file (.doc), the same Word icon and file name appears for both files. This can make recognizing different types of document files difficult—you have to go by the appearance of the icon, which is not always easy.

To show the file name extensions, double-click the My Computer icon on your desktop and choose Tools ➪ Folder Options; the Folder Options dialog box appears. Click the View tab, and clear the Hide File Extensions for Known Type check box. You can make working with Windows a little easier still if you also select Display the Full Path in Title Bar check box.

Because Word recognizes files by the file name extension, working with standard HTML files can be a little more difficult. If you do not want to use the HTML format that Word produces but still want to use Word as an HTML editor and enter the HTML tags directly in Word, save the file as ASCII text only. You then can use Windows Explorer to change the file name extension from .txt to .htm or .html. If you want to load the file in Word, be sure to change the file extension back to .txt or Word converts your HTML into Word's HTML format.

Note   Using spaces in file names is sometimes a problem—not when you work locally with Word, but if you share files or copy folders, you may encounter problems. For example, suppose you publish a folder using a space in the file name. Word adds %20 for the space in the HTML source. Thus, it is safer to use an underscore rather than a space for folder names and file names, especially for folders and files you plan to publish on the Web.

Recovering and Backing Up Files

Inevitably, one day you're going to lose a file. The power could go out, a sector on your hard disk could go bad and corrupt a file, or you may overwrite a file accidentally. You cannot recover all files that you lose, but luckily Word is fairly adept at recovering most.

An ounce of prevention is worth a pound of cure, though. By taking the necessary precautions, you can ensure that if you do have a power outage or overwrite a file, all is not lost. You may want to use, for instance, the Always Create Backup Copy check box on the Save tab of the Options dialog box. Word will save a backup copy each time that you save the file. Consider also the Allow Background Saves option, to have Word automatically save your work periodically.

Tip   Most of us who have been using computers for 15 or 20 years have had so many problems with our many systems that we've learned The Golden Rule: Save, Save, Save. Get into the habit of manually saving files every few minutes. After a while you'll do it unconsciously, and rarely lose much data when disaster strikes.

If you use the Backup option, each time Word saves a file it copies the previously saved version to another file called *Backup of* filename.*wbk*. Word will recognize this file as a Word format, so if a problem such as a power failure occurs, and Word is unable to recover your work, just open the file to restore the last version. You won't have any changes made since the last save operation, but at least you will have most of your file.

Finally, don't forget AutoRecovery, a good system that will surprise you with its effectiveness. Word has saved us hours of work by automatically recovering work that could have been lost in a system or program crash. Turn on AutoRecovery under the Save tab of the Options dialog box, and set the Save AutoRecovery Info Every x Minutes to a time as low as you can. In most cases, you won't even notice this feature at work.

Note　　Remember, the biggest drawback to saving files using the backup method is that backup versions take up space on your hard disk.

What to do when a file will not open

If you try to open a corrupted file, you'll see a message informing you that the file cannot be opened. It prompts you to make sure that the file ends with a .doc extension. In some cases, Word may lock up when you try to open a corrupted file, or your entire computer may hang (stop responding).

This is maddening, but it does happen now and then. Having a backup file can save you much grief. If you have no other option, though, Word provides a special file converter for recovering text from a damaged document file. If a file is corrupted, Word automatically displays the Convert File list box. You can use this file converter to recover manually text stored in the file by doing the following:

1. Choose File ➪ Open. The Open dialog box appears.

2. Click the Files of Type down arrow, and select the Recover Text from Any File *.* item. (If you do not see Recover Text from Any File *.* in the Files of Type box, you need to install the file converter.)

3. Click Open, or double-click the file.

If this process fails, try opening the file in Notepad (Start ➪ Programs ➪ Accessories ➪ Notepad) or WordPad. Then cut and paste the text into a Word document. If the file format is not recognized, try opening the file in a different format. For example, try opening the file as a text file (.txt), and then save the document in Word format.

If a file opens but is corrupted and contains control or other characters you do not want in the final document, use the Edit ➪ Paste Special command and then choose the Unformatted Text option to copy text from that file into a new Word document. This eliminates any control characters that Word may have difficulty displaying. Another way to remove control characters is to cut and paste text to the Notepad text editor and then to paste that text back into Word. The Notepad editor is a true text editor, so it automatically strips any control characters from the file.

Automatically repairing Word application files

Word comes with an option on the Help menu to detect and repair missing or corrupt files. Choosing Help ➪ Detect and Repair displays the Detect and Repair dialog box (see Figure 31-3). When you click the Start button, Word runs the self-repair program that automatically detects and fixes errors. If necessary, the program also automatically verifies and reinstalls the files and registry entries needed to run Word successfully. Detect and Repair scans Word files for discrepancies between the original installation state and the current state of a user's computer, and it then fixes any problems wherever possible.

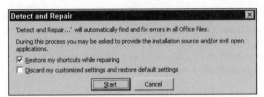

Figure 31-3: The Detect and Repair dialog box allows you to fix Word application files automatically.

Troubleshooting Problems from Outside Word

As mentioned, Word does not work in a vacuum. For example, problems you experience in Word may result from an incorrect or corrupt print driver, an external program clashing with Word, or a directory to which you cannot write. Among the most common and threatening problems you may encounter are Word macro viruses. Word macro viruses can occur when you share files with other users or when you download files off the Web and blindly choose to enable macros contained in those files. The following sections explain how to resolve problems you encounter from outside Word.

Peripheral devices and problems with files

If you open a document and it does not appear as it should, you can troubleshoot the problem in several ways. For one thing, you can trace some problems back to how Windows was set up. For example, if fonts do not appear, you simply may have installed or selected the wrong printer. Make sure the printer to which you are printing is the same as that selected in the Print dialog box. To display and change the printer, choose File ➪ Print and then choose the printer you want to use from the Printer Name drop-down list. In cases where fonts or document files do not appear correctly, you may want to reinstall your printer by opening the Printer folder in My Computer and then double-clicking the Add Printer icon. If problems persist, check with the manufacturer of your printer to see if a new print driver is available.

An incorrect or old version of a display driver can cause the screen to become distorted or to display stray characters. It also is possible that your display driver can cause Word to display a `General Protection Fault` error message. If you try to start Word and either of these problems occurs, try changing to a standard VGA driver and then reinstall your display driver software. If the problem persists, you may want to check with the manufacturer of your video card to see if a new version of the Windows driver is available.

Tip   In some cases, printer and scanner drivers can become corrupted or clash with Word. If you are having a problem with printing or scanning from Word, you may need to reinstall your printer or scanner driver. Be careful doing this, however. Windows is known to replace printer and scanner drivers with other drivers that appear to be newer versions but actually are older. If the driver that comes with Windows does not work, try using the original driver or, if possible, download an updated driver from the manufacturer's Web site.

What to do when Word will not save your file

One of the most frustrating problems is when Word displays a message informing you that it cannot save a file on which you have been working. This message also may state that your drive is full. This is especially aggravating when you know—for a fact—that your disk drives have lots of space. The most common reason for this message is that the Temp folder has hit the limit of the number of files that can be contained in a folder. The solution here is easy: double-click the My Computer icon (in Windows XP, choose Start ➪ My Computer) and then right-click on the drive containing Windows. The shortcut menu appears. Click on Properties, and the Properties window appears.

Click the Disk Cleanup button, and Disk Cleanup begins analyzing your hard disk to find out what can be removed to free up space. Eventually the Disk Cleanup dialog box appears. Click the Temporary files option, and click OK. Windows then removes the temporary files. To remove the temporary files manually, go to the temp directory, delete any old temporary files, return to Word, and try to save the file again. A dialog box then appears and informs you that it cannot delete any files that are currently in use. Temporary files begin with a tilde (~) and end with the .tmp extension. If you are removing temporary files manually, try deleting just a few files at first, double-click the Recycle Bin on your Desktop, and choose File ➪ Empty Recycle Bin. Otherwise, you may not be able to delete all the files you have selected.

In some cases, Word may display an `Unrecoverable Disk Error` message, which appears when Word cannot open a temporary file that it needs in order to save the file in the current folder. If you are saving the file on a floppy disk, make sure the original file from which you loaded the document is still in the drive. You cannot change floppy disks in the middle of a session to save a file to a different disk. Instead, save the file, change the floppy disk, and then choose the File ➪ Save As command. It is a much safer practice to exit Word first, however, and then to copy the file from Windows.

If Word continues to display the error message, the disk may have limited space or be damaged. You may want to try another floppy disk. Finally, if the file is located on a network drive, you may not have permission to the folder on that network drive in which it is stored.

Macro viruses: What to do if Word starts acting strange

If Word does not work as it should, your Word document may have contracted a *macro* virus. A macro virus distributes itself through Word documents containing macros. The Prank macro virus (also known as the Concept virus) was one of the first that received a considerable amount of media coverage. The Prank virus made it so that you could save documents only as templates. After you open a document containing a macro virus, the virus can be passed to other documents; thereafter, any document you save in Word can contain a copy of the macro virus. The Prank macro virus was soon followed by the Nuclear and DMV macro viruses, and more recently by the Klez virus, which can corrupt every Office document on your system. Microsoft released a macro virus protection tool to combat these existing macro viruses. Word automatically checks for these macro viruses, but other macro viruses are bound to raise their ugly heads in the future. A document infected with a macro virus can infect any version of Word that supports macros.

On its own, Word cannot determine whether the instructions in the macro are desired or not. It really is close to impossible to determine if a macro is actually a macro virus. Each new macro virus must be evaluated and treated on a case-by-case basis. Most virus-protection software companies now include macro virus killers in their latest releases, and we recommend that you work with one of these programs, such as Norton AntiVirus (`www.symantec.com/avcenter/`) or McAfee VirusScan (`www.mcafee.com`).

Summary

This chapter pointed out some problems that you may encounter and provided solutions so that you can control Word rather than have Word control you. It also covered how to optimize Word and reduce the size of files created with it and what to do to help counter the danger of macro viruses. Some of the more significant points covered in this chapter include how to do the following:

✦ Turn off Word's personalized custom menus so that commands and toolbar buttons appear in the same place all the time.

✦ Avoid Word automatically replacing and formatting your text by changing the settings on the AutoFormat As You Type tab (Format ⇨ AutoCorrect).

✦ Optimize Word and reduce the size of your files by turning off features that can slow Word down and bloat the size of your documents.

✦ Protect yourself from losing work caused by a power failure or a system crash by creating backup files and using AutoRecover.

✦ Detect and repair Word application files automatically using the HelpDetect and Repair command.

✦ Locate problems by checking your printer and video drivers when Word does not display your document correctly. If you cannot open a Word document file, use Word's converter to recover the text from a corrupted file. You also can save a file even if Word erroneously reports you are out of disk space.

✦ Check to see if Word has contracted a macro virus if the program starts acting strange, and squash the bug with a virus-protection program.

✦ ✦ ✦

Customizing Menus, Options, Toolbars, and Keys

✦ ✦ ✦ ✦

In This Chapter

Choosing options

Customizing toolbars

Customizing menus

Customizing keyboard shortcuts

✦ ✦ ✦ ✦

For the most part, the previous chapters of this book deal with Word as it appears before you make any changes to it. This chapter, however, deals with customizing Word to better suit your needs. Bear in mind, however, that no description of customizing Word can be complete. Although Word is a word processor, it also contains a versatile programming language (as you discover when you read about macros in Chapter 33), so you can always choose to do additional customization by using macros.

Customizing Word

After installation, Word has certain default settings for its commands and options. Some of these settings include:

- ✦ The menu bar, with nine named menus; the Standard and Formatting toolbars, each with certain buttons; the status bar at the bottom of the window; and the horizontal and vertical scroll bars all appear on your screen.

- ✦ When you type nonprinting characters, such as a space or a tab, only a white space appears on-screen.

- ✦ The keystrokes you use to edit a document cause Word to respond in the default way.

- ✦ Word looks for certain types of information, such as templates and documents, in specific directories.

- ✦ Keyboard shortcuts are assigned to certain commands.

These are just a few of the Word defaults that you can accept and use. Alternatively, you can change most aspects of Word to suit your own needs. You've probably already used many of these options as you've worked with Word's features.

Changing Word's Options

Options control the way you interact with Word. Certain options, for example, affect what you see on-screen, whereas others affect what Word does when you press certain keys. To change the optional Word settings, display the Options dialog box and choose the options that you want. All of the options you choose remain in effect throughout the current Word session. When you terminate your Word session, all the options that were in effect are then saved, so the next time you open Word, those same options apply.

Note   Some options apply only to the current document, but in such cases the Options dialog box clearly labels the options as document related. For instance, there are Options for Current Document Only components under the Print tab.

View tab

Choices in the View tab of the Options dialog box modify the appearance of the application and document windows as well as the appearance of documents. Table 32-1 lists the options that are available on the View tab (see Figure 32-1). Some View options function in all the different views; others are available only in particular views. To check what View options are available in a particular view, switch to that view before opening the Options dialog box. For example, switching to Normal or Outline view before opening the Options dialog box displays the options that apply to these views. Likewise, switching to Print Layout or Web Layout view before opening the Options dialog box displays the options that apply to those views.

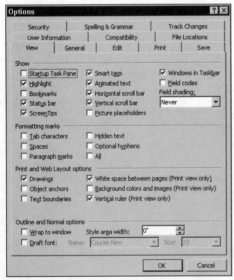

Figure 32-1: The Options dialog box with the View tab displayed and the default options selected.

Table 32-1: Options in the View Tab

Show Group	Default	Effect
Animated Text	Checked	Displays text animation on the screen. Clear the Animated Text check box to see how the text looks when printed.
Bookmarks	Not checked	Displays bookmarks and links.
Field Codes	Not checked	Displays field codes instead of field values.
Field Shading	When selected	Identifies fields by shading them When Selected, Always, or Never.
Highlight	Checked	Displays and prints highlighted text in a document.
Horizontal Scroll Bar	Checked	Displays the horizontal scroll bar.
Picture Placeholders	Not checked	Displays graphics as empty boxes.
ScreenTips	Checked	Displays reviewers' comments in yellow pop-up boxes on the screen when you hover with the mouse pointer above the comment reference mark.
Smart Tags	Checked	Displays Smart Tags in documents (see Chapter 23).
Startup Task Pane	Checked	Displays the Home task pane when you open Word directly (if you open a document first, the task pane is not displayed).
Status Bar	Checked	Displays the status bar.
Vertical Scroll Bar	Checked	Displays the vertical scroll bar.
Windows in Taskbar	Checked	Tells Word to function in the normal Windows manner, placing a button in the taskbar for every open document. Clear the check box if you want so see a single button. To switch between documents, use the Window menu, or press Ctrl+F6 or Alt+F6.

Formatting Marks Group	Default	Effect
All	Checked	Displays all formatting marks. This works in conjunction with the Show/Hide button on the Standard toolbar. Clicking that button turns this option on and off.
Hidden Text	Not checked	Displays hidden text.
Optional Hyphens	Not checked	Displays optional hyphens.
Paragraph Marks	Not checked	Displays paragraph marks.
Spaces	Not checked	Displays spaces as dots.
Tab Characters	Not checked	Displays tab characters.

Print and Web Layout Options	Default	Effect
Background Colors and Images (Print view only)	Not checked	Displays, you guessed it, background colors and images in print view. If this isn't checked, background colors and images are not shown, in any view, as they are really intended for Web pages, not Word documents.
Drawings	Checked	Displays objects created using the Word drawing tools in Print, Web, and Reading Layout views.
Object Anchors	Not checked	Displays object anchors, which indicate that an object is attached to a specific paragraph.
Text Boundaries	Not checked	Displays dotted lines around page margins, text columns, and objects in Print Layout view.
Vertical Ruler (Print view only)	Not Checked	Displays the vertical ruler on the left side of the document window in the Print Layout view. (The Ruler must be selected in the View menu.)
White Space Between Pages (Print view only)	Checked	Clear this check box to "squeeze" pages together in Print Layout view to save screen space—Word will remove the gray area around the pages, along with the headers and footers, and any blank space in the margins. This check box may be disabled; if so, close the Options dialog box, change to Print Layout view, and return.

Outline and Normal Options Group	Default	Effect
Draft Font	Not checked	Displays most character formatting as underlined and bold, and displays graphics as empty boxes. Uses the typeface and size selected in the components to the right. Select the Draft Font check box to speed the screen display in documents with extensive formatting.
Wrap to Window	Not checked	This tells Word to use the entire window width for text lines in Outline and Normal views—Word extends the lines of text all the way to the right margin before wrapping, without regard to the page margins and indents.
Style Area Width	0"	Provides space at the left of document window for the style name.

Note   To reiterate, the Formatting Marks group of the View tab works in conjunction with the Show/Hide button on the Standard toolbar. For example, select Tab Characters in this area, and tab characters are always displayed. Clicking the Show/Hide button makes the *other* items visible or invisible, but the tab characters will always be there.

General tab

Choices in the General tab of the Options dialog box modify various Word settings that don't fit in any of the other Options dialog box tabs. Table 32-2 lists the options available in the General tab (see Figure 32-2).

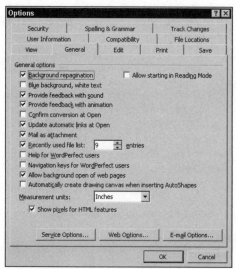

Figure 32-2: The General tab in the Options dialog box.

Table 32-2: Options in the General Tab

Option	Default	Effect
Allow Starting in Reading Mode	Checked	When someone opens a document you sent to them using the Mail Recipient (For Review) command, the document will open in Reading mode.
Background Repagination	Checked	Repagination occurs while you work.
Blue Background, White text	Not checked	Displays white text on blue background (designed for people switching from WordPerfect).
Confirm Conversion at Open	Not checked	If you open a file created in another application, Word asks you to confirm first.
E-mail Options		Displays the E-mail Options dialog box, which includes options for working with WordMail.

Continued

Table 32-2 *(continued)*

Option	Default	Effect
Help for WordPerfect Users	Not checked	Shows the Word equivalent when you press a WordPerfect for DOS key combination. When this check box is selected, WPH appears in the status bar, and certain keystrokes will work differently from the norm.
Mail as Attachment	Checked	Attaches the current document to an e-mail message when you choose File ➪ Send To Mail Recipient. Clear this check box if you want Word to insert the contents of the current document into an e-mail message instead of attaching it. This check box is available only if an e-mail application is installed on your computer.
Measurement Units	Inches	Sets the measurement units to inches, centimeters, millimeters, points, or picas for measurements in dialog boxes and on the horizontal ruler.
Show Pixels for HTML Features	Not checked	Word will use pixels as the measurement unit for Web-related features.
Navigation Keys for WordPerfect Users	Not checked	Changes the functions of various keys, such as the PgUp, PgDn, Home, End, and Esc keys, to their equivalent WordPerfect actions.
Provide Feedback with Animation	Checked	Animates the movement of your mouse in Word, and uses special animated cursors in place of standard static cursors for a variety of actions.
Provide Feedback with Sound	Checked	A beep occurs when you make certain actions. To change the sound that is associated with an event, open the Sounds folder in the Windows Control Panel.
Recently Used File List	4	Determines number of file names displayed at the bottom of the File menu. You can choose as many as nine entries in the Entries box.
Service Options		Displays a dialog box in which you can set options related to privacy, Microsoft.com connections, and Shared Workspaces.
Update Automatic Links at Open	Checked	Updates the information linked to other files at Open when you open documents.
Web Options		Displays the Web Options dialog box, which includes options for controlling the features involved in creating Web documents.

Edit tab

Choices in the Edit tab of the Options dialog box modify certain editing actions that are performed by Word. Table 32-3 lists the options available in the Edit tab (see Figure 32-3).

Cross-Reference For more information on working with Word's editing features, see Chapter 2.

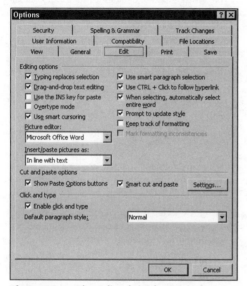

Figure 32-3: The Edit tab in the Options dialog box.

Table 32-3: Options in the Edit Tab

Editing Options Group	Default	Effect
Drag-and-Drop Text Editing	Checked	Moves or copies selected text without the need for cutting and pasting.
Insert/Paste Pictures As	In line with text	Select one of the seven text-wrapping modes as the default for inserting images and other objects.
Keep Track of Formatting	Checked	When checked, Word adds information to the styles listed in the Style drop-down list box on the Formatting toolbar when you directly format characters and paragraphs (such as +*bold* added to the style name). You may find this option frustrating when sharing documents in workgroups, so you may want to turn it off.

Continued

Table 32-3 *(continued)*

Editing Options Group	Default	Effect
Mark Formatting Inconsistencies	Not checked	When checked, Word marks formatting that it thinks may be inconsistent. If you apply bullets to text formatted with the Heading style, for example, as well as to nonheading text, Word considers that inconsistent and underlines it with a wavy blue line. Note that Word analyzes the inconsistencies slowly, so it sometimes takes a few minutes for the wavy lines to show up.
Overtype Mode	Not checked	Replaces existing text as you type rather than inserting characters. This is disabled if the document is in Track Changes mode. Note also that using this option is the same as pressing the Ins key on your keyboard.
Picture Editor	Microsoft Word	Selects the application used for editing pictures.
Prompt to Update Style	Checked	This should probably remain checked at all times; Word asks for your permission before modifying a style based on changes you made to a paragraph.
Typing Replaces Selection	Checked	Deletes selected text when you begin typing. If you clear this, when you start typing Word unselects the text and places the insertion point at the beginning of the selection, which is where your typing will be placed. Also, if this is turned off, the Backspace key won't delete selected text.
Use CTRL+Click to Follow Hyperlinks	Not checked	By default when you click on a link—such as in a table of contents or index, or a URL—Word jumps to the appropriate position or page. Check this to stop this rather irritating action; you'll have to press and hold Ctrl and then click to jump.
Use Smart Cursoring	Checked	When this is checked, scrolling through the document using the vertical scroll bar moves the insertion point, so the insertion point is always in the same position on the screen regardless of the page you've scrolled to. When unchecked, the insertion point remains on the page where it was before you began scrolling.
Use Smart Paragraph Selection	Checked	When checked, selecting the last character at the end of a paragraph also selects the paragraph mark.
Use the INS Key for Paste	Not checked	Pastes Clipboard contents when you press Insert.
When Selecting, Automatically Select Entire Word	Checked	Selects the entire word when part of it is selected. If this feature is turned on, you can format entire words without selecting them. Place the insertion point in a word—without selecting it—press Ctrl+B, for instance, and the entire word is formatted as bold text.

Cut and Paste Group	Default	Effect
Show Paste Options Buttons	Checked	When you paste something into a document, Word displays the little Clipboard button that allows you to select how the item should be pasted.
Smart Cut and Paste	Checked	Removes unneeded spaces when you cut, and adds necessary spaces when you paste.

Click and Type Group	Default	Effect
Enable Click and Type	Checked	Turns on Click and Type mode (described in Chapter 5).
Default Paragraph Style	Normal	Enables you to change the default paragraph style used when working with Click and Type.

Print tab

Choices in the Print tab of the Options dialog box modify the way that documents print and control what is printed. Table 32-4 lists the options available in the Print tab (see Figure 32-4).

Cross-Reference

For more information on printing documents in Word, see Chapter 6.

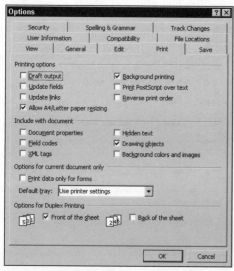

Figure 32-4: The Print tab in the Options dialog box.

Table 32-4: Options in the Print Tab

Printing Options Group	Default	Effect
Allow A4/Letter Paper Resizing	Checked	In some countries, the standard paper size is Letter; in others, the standard is A4. Select this check box if you want Word to automatically adjust documents formatted for another country's standard paper size so they can print correctly on your own country's standard paper size.
Background Printing	Checked	Allows you to continue working in a document while it prints.
Draft Output	Not checked	Prints a document with minimum formatting (the effect depends on the printer being used).
Print PostScript Over Text	Not checked	Prints PostScript code in a converted Word for the Macintosh document on top of the document text instead of underneath it.
Reverse Print Order	Not checked	Prints pages beginning with the last one.
Update Fields	Not checked	Updates all fields in a document before printing.
Update Links	Not checked	Updates all linked information in a document before printing.

Include with Document Group	Default	Effect
Background Colors and Images	Not checked	By default, Word won't print background colors, patterns, and images, under the assumption that you are using them for Web pages, not printed documents. Select this option to include them in printouts.
Document Properties	Not checked	Prints summary information on a separate page at the end of document.
Drawing Objects	Checked	Prints Drawing objects.
Field codes	Not checked	Prints field codes instead of field results.
Hidden Text	Not checked	Prints all hidden text.
XML Tags	Not checked	Prints XML tags along with the document text.

Options for Current Document Only Group	Default	Effect
Print Data Only for Forms	Not checked	Prints form input only.
Default Tray	Use printer settings	Chooses the paper tray in the printer.

Options for Duplex Printing Group	Default	Effect
Front of the Sheet	Checked	The front of the sheet will be printed first when printing in Duplex mode.

Options for Duplex Printing Group	Default	Effect
Back of the Sheet	Not checked	The back of the sheet will be printed first when printing in Duplex mode.

Track Changes tab

Choices in the Track Changes tab of the Options dialog box modify the way that Word displays changes to a document, and preview boxes in this tab show you the effects of your choices. Table 32-5 lists the options available in the Track Changes tab (see Figure 32-5).

 Cross-Reference   To find out more about working with Word's revision features, see Chapter 29.

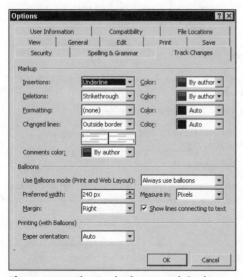

Figure 32-5: The Track Changes tab in the Options dialog box.

Table 32-5: Options in the Track Changes Tab

Markup Group	Default	Effect
Changed Lines	Outside Border	Choose None to omit revision bars, Left Border to place revision bars in the left margin, Right Border to place revision bars in the right margin, and Outside Border to place revision bars in the outside margins of facing pages.

Continued

Table 32-5 (continued)

Markup Group	Default	Effect
Color	Auto	Choose the color for revision bars.
Comments Color	By Author	The default setting tells Word to select a different color for each person entering comments, but you can select a specific color for everyone.
Deletions	Strikethrough	Choose from a variety of methods for marking deleted text.
Color	By Author	Choose the color for deleted text.
Formatting	None	Choose the options for marking text with formatting changes in your document.
Color	Auto	Choose the color for revision bars.
Insertions	Underline	Choose from a variety of methods for marking inserted text.
Color	By Author	Chooses the color for inserted text.

Balloons Group	Default	Effect
Margin	Right	Defines in which margin revision and comment balloons should be placed.
Preferred Width	2.5"	Defines the width of the balloon margin.
Measure In	Inches	The units used for describing the balloon margin.
Show Lines Connecting to Text	Checked	Word displays a line from the balloon to the revision or comment position.
Use Balloons Mode (Print and Web Layout)	No insertion/ deletion balloon mode, despite the label.	Enables you to define the conditions under which balloons are used. Note that balloons are also used in Reading Layout

Printing (with Balloons) Group	Default	Effect
Paper Orientation	Auto	Defines if Word should always display documents that contain balloons in landscape, if it should always keep the formatting, or if it should decide for itself.

Note   The default Color selection for Inserted text and Deleted text is By Author. This selection instructs Word to use unique colors for the first eight authors who revise the text. Alternatively, you can choose Auto, in which Word uses the default text color set in the Windows Control Panel, or you can choose a specific color.

User Information tab

Choices in the User Information tab of the Options dialog box allow you to specify the name, initials, and address of the primary user. This is information that Word uses in certain kinds of documents. Word initially places information about the registered user in this tab, but you can change this information. Table 32-6 lists the options available in the User Information tab (see Figure 32-6).

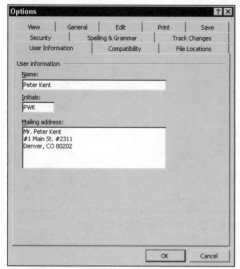

Figure 32-6: The User Information tab in the Options dialog box.

Table 32-6: Options in the User Information Tab

Option	Default	Effect
Name	Name of the registered user	Word uses this text as the author's name in document summary information.
Initials	Initials of the registered user	Word uses these initials with annotations to identify your comments.
Mailing Address	Address of the registered user	Word uses this text as the return address on envelopes.

Compatibility tab

Choices in the Compatibility tab of the Options dialog box control how Word displays documents that were created in older versions of Word and in other word processors. You can use these options to display such a document so that it more closely matches the original. The options that you choose in this tab affect only the way that Word displays the document; they do not affect the actual document itself. Table 32-7 lists the options available in the Compatibility tab (see Figure 32-7).

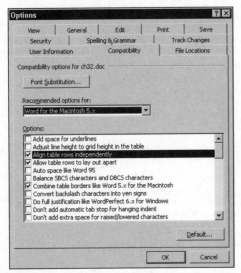

Figure 32-7: The Compatibility tab in the Options dialog box.

Table 32-7: Options in the Compatibility Tab

Option	Effect
Font Substitution	Selects the fonts available on your system to substitute for those unavailable in the current document.
Recommended Options For	Selects the word processing application for which you want to set options, including Word 2003, 2002, 2000, 97, 6.0/95, Word for Windows 1.0 and 2.0, Word for the Macintosh 5.x, Word for MS-DOS, WordPerfect 5.x, WordPerfect 6.x for Windows, WordPerfect 6.0 for DOS, and Custom. Selecting from this list adjusts the settings in the Options list.
Options	Lists the options that affect how a document from a non-Word 2003 source displays in Word 2003. Selected options affect how the document is displayed only while you're working with it in Word.
Default	Enables you to change default settings for all documents created from the current template.

After you've chosen the appropriate options, you can click the Default button to save those options in the active template. If you open a document, open the Options dialog box, and then click the Compatibility tab, you can also click the Font Substitution button to determine whether fonts in the document are available on your computer. If all of the required fonts are available, Word displays an information box that tells you this. If one or more fonts are not available, however, Word displays a Font Substitution dialog box, in which you can specify the fonts that you wish to use as substitutions.

Note Word can automatically choose appropriate options for displaying and printing a document created in certain other applications. To choose these options, select the appropriate application in the Recommended Options For list box. When you do this, Word automatically checks the appropriate options for you. If a suitable combination of options is not available, you can choose the options that you want manually.

File Locations tab

Choices in the File Locations tab of the Options dialog box allow you to specify the directories in which Word looks for certain kinds of files. If you wish, you can move specific types of files to different directories, but if you do, you must also define the new location of these files by making changes in the File Locations tab. Table 32-8 lists the options available in the File Locations tab (see Figure 32-8). (The specific default locations of files may vary according to various installation choices.) To modify any location, select that location and then click Modify.

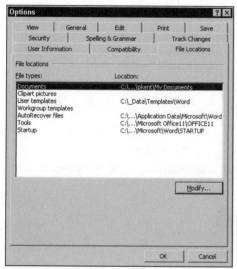

Figure 32-8: The File Locations tab in the Options dialog box.

Table 32-8: Options in the File Locations Tab

File Types	Default Location	Notes
Documents	My Documents folder	This is the folder Word opens when you first save a new document.
Clipart Pictures	No default location	You can create a clipart repository somewhere if you wish (See Chapter 17 for information about working with the Clip Organizer and Clip Art task pane.)

Continued

Table 32-8 *(continued)*

File Types	Default Location	Notes
User Templates	C:\Program Files\ Microsoft Office\ Templates	This is where the templates that appear in the General tab of the Templates dialog box are stored.
Workgroup Templates	No default location	If you install Word on a network, you can share templates among the workgroup, and individual users can have their own templates. In this case, the Workgroup Templates row in the dialog box indicates the location of the shared templates.
AutoRecover Files	C:\Documents and Settings*username*\ Application Data\ Microsoft\Word	Defines where Word stores the AutoRecover files (described in Chapter 7).
Tools	C:\Program Files\ Microsoft Office\Office	Defines where Word saves application tools.
Startup	C:\Documents and Settings*username*\ Application Data\ Microsoft\Word\STARTUP	This is where you save global templates that Word automatically loads on startup (see Chapter 14).

Save tab

Choices in the Save tab of the Options dialog box modify how Word saves documents. Table 32-9 lists the options available in the Save tab (shown in Figure 32-9).

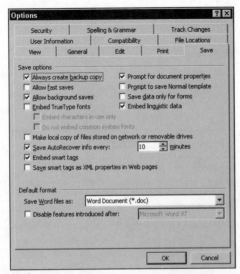

Figure 32-9: The Save tab in the Options dialog box.

Cross-Reference For more information on saving your documents in Word, see Chapters 1 and 7.

Table 32-9: Options in the Save Tab

Save Options Group	Default	Effect
Allow Background Saves	Checked	Saves documents in the background so that you may continue working in Word as you save a document. A pulsing disk icon appears in the status bar when Word is saving in the background.
Allow Fast Saves	Not checked	Speeds the saving of your work by recording only the changes to a document.
Always Create Backup Copy	Not checked	Creates a backup copy in the same folder as the original when you save a document. When you select this, Word clears the Allow Fast Saves check box, because Word can create backup copies only when it performs a full save.
Embed Linguistic Data	Checked	When Word saves a document it also includes information about the document language.
Embed Smart Tags	Checked	Word includes smart tags in saved documents.
Embed TrueType Fonts	Not checked	Saves any TrueType fonts used in a document when you save that document.
Embed Characters in Use Only	Not checked	Check box becomes active when Embed TrueType Fonts is checked. This allows you to specify saving only the characters of a font used in the document rather than the entire character set (if you used 32 or fewer characters). When you check this option, the document's fonts become part of the saved file—as long as the fonts in question permit this kind of save to be performed. This option is advantageous because it allows you to open, view, and print a file using the original fonts even when you're working on a computer without the required fonts installed.
Do Not Embed Common System Fonts	Not checked	Check box becomes active when Embed TrueType Fonts is checked. Tells Word not to include system fonts when embedding fonts.
Make Local Copy of Files Stored on Network or Removable Drives	Not checked	Word creates a local, synchronized copy of a file on a network or removable drive when you work on it.
Prompt for Document Properties	Not checked	Displays the Summary Information dialog box when you save a new document.

Continued

Table 32-9 *(continued)*

Save Options Group	Default	Effect
Prompt to Save Normal Template	Not checked	Displays a message asking whether you want to save changes to Normal.dot when you close Word. Useful when modifying toolbars and menus, for instance, so that they're available the next time you open the program.
Save AutoRecover Info Every	Checked	Automatically saves AutoRecover files at a defined interval.
Save Data Only for Forms	Not checked	Saves the data entered in an online form as a single, tab-delimited record so that you can also use that record in a database. Word saves this file in a text-only format.
Save Smart Tags as XML Properties in Web Pages	Not checked	If you have Smart Tags in a page (see Chapter 23), when you save the document as a Web page, Word saves the tags as XML tags.

Default Format Group	Default	Effect
Save Word Files	Word Document	Selects the file format that you want Word to use by default whenever you save a document.
Disable Features Introduced After	Not checked	Removes any features in the document that are not supported by the selected version of Word.

Spelling & Grammar tab

Choices in the Spelling & Grammar tab of the Options dialog box control how Word checks spelling and allow you create custom dictionaries. Table 32-10 lists the options available in the Spelling & Grammar tab (see Figure 32-10).

Cross-Reference   For detailed information about spell checking, see Chapter 8.

Table 32-10: Options in the Spelling & Grammar Tab

Spelling Group	Default	Effect
Always Suggest Corrections	Checked	Always suggests spellings for misspelled words.
Check Spelling As You Type	Not checked	Checks spelling automatically and marks any errors as you type. When unchecked, the Hide Spelling Errors in This Document check box is not available.
Custom Dictionaries		Displays the Custom Dictionaries dialog box for creating, editing, and deleting custom dictionaries.
Hide Spelling Errors in This Document	Not checked	Hides the wavy red lines that denote possible spelling errors.

Spelling Group	Default	Effect
Ignore Internet and File Addresses	Checked	Ignores Internet addresses, file names, and e-mail addresses during spell checks.
Ignore Words in Uppercase	Checked	Ignores words that contain only UPPERCASE letters.
Ignore Words with Numbers	Checked	Ignores words that contain numbers.
Suggest from Main Dictionary Only	Checked	Suggests correct spellings from the main dictionary but not from the custom dictionaries.

Grammar Group	Default	Effect
Check Grammar As You Type	Not checked	Checks grammar automatically and marks any errors as you type.
Check Grammar With Spelling	Not checked	Checks grammar at the same time that spell checking is performed.
Hide Grammatical Errors in This Document	Not checked	Hides the wavy green line under possible grammatical errors.
Settings		Displays the Grammar Settings dialog box in which you can customize the writing style and grammar rules that Word uses for the selected style in the Writing Style list.
Show Readability Statistics	Not checked	Displays readability statistics at the end of the grammar check. This is disabled if Check Grammar With Spelling is not checked.
Writing Style	Grammar Only	Selects the writing style that Word uses to check grammar in this document.

Proofing Tools Group	Default	Effect
Check Document/ Recheck Document		This button name appears as Check Document if you haven't yet run the spelling and grammar checker during the current Word session. After you change the spelling or grammar options or open a custom dictionary, however, this button changes to Recheck Document so that you can recheck your document.

Security tab

Choices in the Security tab allow you to password protect your document, protect your privacy, and limit the manner in which macros can run. See Chapter 34 for information on these features. Table 32-11 lists the options available in the Security tab (see Figure 32-11).

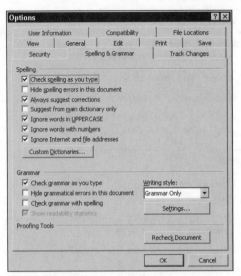

Figure 32-10: The Spelling & Grammar tab in the Options dialog box.

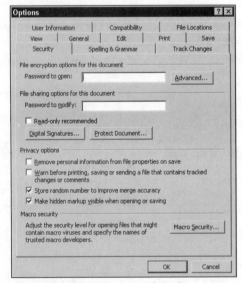

Figure 32-11: The Security tab in the Options dialog box.

Table 32-11: Options in the Security Tab

File Encryption Options For This Document Group	Default	Effect
Password to Open	None	The document cannot be opened without the password entered here.
Advanced		Select this to define which encryption method is used.

File Sharing Options For This Document Group	Default	Effect
Password to Modify	None	The document cannot be modified without the password entered here.
Read-only Recommended	Not checked	Word displays a message box when someone opens this document, recommending (but not enforcing) that the document be opened in Read-only mode.
Digital Signatures		Allows you to attach a digital signature to the document, or review the attached signature.
Protect Document		Opens the Document Protection task pane.

Privacy Options Group	Default	Effect
Make Hidden Markup Visible on Opening or Saving	Checked	Every time you open or save a document, hidden markup is displayed. (See Chapter 29 for information on the Show menu on the Reviewing toolbar.)
Remove Personal Information from This File on Save	Not checked	Word removes your name from the file Properties Author and Saved By fields, and removes your name from any revisions you have made to the document, when you save the file.
Warn Before Printing, Saving, or Sending a File That Contains Tracked Changes or Comments	Not checked	Does exactly what it states.
Store Random Number to Improve Merge Accuracy	Checked	This is used when merging comments and changes from multiple reviewers (see Chapter 29). It helps Word identify related documents.

Macro Security Group	Default	Effect
Macro Security		Allows you to set macro security options (see Chapter 34).

Working with Toolbars

The more that you work with Word, the more you may come to rely on the buttons in the toolbars for quick access to certain functions. Word comes with two toolbars—the Standard and Formatting toolbars—that contain the most frequently used buttons. Other toolbars, such as the Drawing toolbar and the Tables and Borders toolbar, contain occasionally used, special-purpose buttons. You may want additional toolbars, however, with buttons that suit your personal needs. You can customize the toolbars in several ways:

✦ Add buttons to existing toolbars.

✦ Delete buttons from existing toolbars.

✦ Move buttons between toolbars.

✦ Change the icons in existing buttons.

✦ Modify the action of existing buttons.

✦ Create new toolbars with existing or new buttons.

Before continuing with this subject, you should understand how Word saves changes made to the toolbars and the buttons they include. All of the changes that you make are saved in a template, either the one on which your current document is based or the Normal template. If you save toolbar changes in any template other than a global template (see Chapter 14), those changes are available only when you're working with documents based on that particular template. If you save toolbar changes in the Normal template, however, those changes apply to all documents. If the toolbar changes that you want to make are useful only in certain kinds of documents, you should save those changes in the templates on which those documents are based.

Tip   You can move toolbars from templates or documents into other templates or documents using the Organizer dialog box (Format ➪ Style ➪ Organizer). You can move toolbars the same way that you move styles (see Chapter 14).

Using the Customize dialog box

A toolbar button represents a Word action. Therefore, before you add a button to a toolbar, the action that button represents must be defined. Word comes with many predefined buttons, some of which are already in toolbars. Other buttons are defined but not initially available in toolbars. You can add any predefined button to any toolbar, and you can even add a button that appears in one toolbar to another.

To access buttons defined in Word, choose Tools ➪ Customize or View ➪ Toolbars ➪ Customize to display the Customize dialog box (see Figure 32-12).

Cross-Reference   See Chapter 33 to find out how to define your own buttons and add them to toolbars. This chapter discusses only buttons that are already defined in Word.

The Toolbars tab of the Customize dialog box lists all of the toolbars that you can customize. The Categories list box in the Commands tab (see Figure 32-13) lists the categories of commands organized by menu name or by type. If you scroll down the list, you see various categories of tools. Click a category to change the list of commands in the Commands box. For example, choose File in the Categories list, and the list of file-related commands and buttons appears in the Commands list. Choose Edit, and you'll see commands related to editing.

Figure 32-12: The Customize dialog box, showing the Toolbars tab.

Figure 32-13: The Commands tab in the Customize dialog box.

Adding buttons to a toolbar

You can add buttons to any Word toolbar that is listed in the Toolbars list of the Toolbars tab. Any toolbar or menu bar that is already displayed is checked in this list. To add buttons to any toolbar, follow these steps:

1. Open a new document based on the template that you want to use.

2. Choose Tools ⇨ Customize to open the Customize dialog box. Click the Toolbars tab in the dialog box.

3. Click the check box for the toolbar to which you want to add the button, if it's not already open. The toolbar appears in the Word window.

4. Click the Commands tab.

5. Open the Save In drop-down list box at the bottom of the dialog box, and then choose the template or document in which you want to save toolbar changes. Note that the toolbars shown in the Word window may change. You will only see toolbars associated with the selected template.

6. Choose a category in the Categories list box.

7. Find the button you want to add to the toolbar in the Commands list.

8. Drag the button out of the dialog box and onto the toolbar. You can place the button anywhere you like within a toolbar or even the menu bar. Notice the icon next to the mouse pointer—if the button is over a place in which it can be positioned, you'll see a + sign. If not, you'll see an X sign.

9. Click Close to close the dialog box.

Moving and copying toolbar buttons

When you added buttons to the Standard and Formatting toolbars in the last section, you probably weren't entirely satisfied with their positions. Luckily, you can adjust the spacing between buttons and move a button from one place to another in a toolbar, and you can even move buttons or copy a button from one toolbar to another.

Buttons in Word's toolbars are grouped by function. For example, the first four buttons in the Standard toolbar relate to file operations. When you add a button to an existing toolbar, you can place it with a group of related buttons. If you want to move buttons or adjust their spacing, you have to open the Customize dialog box as before—in effect, whenever this box is open the toolbars (and menus) are in edit mode.

 Tip   You don't have to open the Customize dialog box to carry out all these toolbar and menu procedures. Press and hold the Alt key, and you'll find you can drag toolbar buttons around. Press Alt+Ctrl and drag, and you'll copy rather than move.

With the dialog box open, you'll find that you can drag buttons around. Drag them to different positions on the toolbar, to another toolbar, or onto the menu bar. Notice also that if you hold the Ctrl key while you drag, you will make a copy of the button and place that copy in the new position. (You'll see a + sign by the mouse pointer as you drag.)

Deleting toolbar buttons

You may never use some toolbar buttons, or your needs may change from project to project. In many cases, you may want to delete buttons to simplify your toolbars. You can delete any toolbar button by dragging it out of the toolbar and into the document area. When you release, the button is removed. (You'll see an X sign by the mouse pointer as you drag.)

Note a couple of things about deleting buttons. First, if the button is part of the toolbar's default set, you can quickly return it by clicking on the triangle on the right side of the toolbar, clicking Add or Remove Buttons, and clicking the name of the toolbar; you'll see a list of all the toolbar buttons, and the one you removed should be there. Just click on it to add it back in. (If it's not there, it wasn't one of the default set for that toolbar.)

Also, if you delete a predefined or a default button, you can always choose it in the Customize dialog box and add it back into a toolbar. If you delete a button that you created from a macro, however, you cannot retrieve that button.

Cross-Reference   See Chapter 33 to find out more about macro buttons.

Restoring a toolbar to its original state

You can restore any toolbar supplied with Word to its original state using a couple of methods. In the Customize dialog box, under the Toolbars tab, highlight the toolbar that you want to reset from the Toolbars list and then click the Reset button. A dialog box opens in which you can choose the template for which you want to reset the toolbar, and click OK.

There's another, quicker way to do this. Click the triangle on the right side of the toolbar, click Add or Remove Buttons, and click the name of the toolbar; at the bottom of the list of all the toolbar buttons you'll see a Reset Toolbar option.

Note   You cannot restore changes that you've made to custom toolbars and then deleted.

Editing buttons

You can edit toolbar buttons in a number of ways, from changing the button image to changing the text that appears when you point at the button. Simply open the Customize dialog box and right-click on a button to see a pop-up menu. The commands on this menu are described in Table 32-12. Figure 32-14 shows what results when you choose the Edit Button Image command from this pop-up menu, and Figure 32-15 shows the result of choosing the Change Button Image command.

Tip   Remember that a button and a menu option are essentially the same thing. As you saw earlier, in the section "Adding buttons to a toolbar," you can drag a command from the Customize dialog box and drop it onto a toolbar *or* onto a menu. You can edit both toolbar buttons and menu options in the way described in Table 32-12, so some of the descriptions in the table refer to menu-related tasks. (To edit a menu option, click on the menu, and then right-click on the option while the Customize dialog box is open.)

Table 32-12: The Toolbar Button's Edit Menu

Button	Purpose
Reset	Returns the button to its default condition.
Delete	Removes the button from the toolbar.
Name	The text that appears when you place the mouse pointer over the button for a few moments, or that appears as the menu text. Type a new name and press Enter to modify it. Note that the & symbol indicates that the following letter is the *accelerator* letter, the one that activates a menu option. For instance, the v in Print Preview is that menu command's accelerator. Open the File menu and press v to activate the command.
Copy Button Image	Copies the button image to the Clipboard. You can now paste it into a document or an image program, or onto another button.

Continued

Table 32-12 *(continued)*

Button	Purpose
Paste Button Image	Pastes whatever is on the Clipboard onto the button as its new image. If there's text in the Clipboard, the button is blank.
Reset Button Image	Returns the button image to its original.
Edit Button Image	Opens a small editing program in which you can edit the button image, pixel by pixel.
Change Button Image	Displays a submenu of generic button images from which you can select.
Default Style	Uses Word's default style for displaying the button or menu option.
Text Only (Always)	Whether in a menu or toolbar, the icon is not displayed—only the name of the command is displayed.
Text Only (in Menus)	If this command is on a menu, the text is displayed and the icon omitted. But move the command onto a toolbar and the icon is displayed with no text.
Image and Text	Displays both the icon and the text name.
Begin a Group	Places the selected icon in a new group on the toolbar or menu, placing gray dividing lines each side of it.
Assign Hyperlink	Opens a submenu: Open allows you to define a file that will be opened when you click the toolbar button or menu option; Insert Picture lets you define an image that will be inserted into the document; and Remove Link removes a hyperlink if you have defined one.

Note   You must use the mouse to edit toolbar buttons. Word provides no keyboard commands for this action.

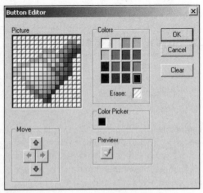

Figure 32-14: The Button Editor dialog box.

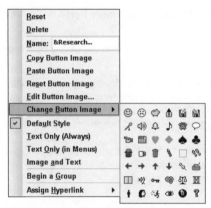

Figure 32-15: The shortcut menu with ready-made button images.

As mentioned in Table 32-12, you can edit an image in the Button Editor dialog box by clicking individual pixels. To change the color of a pixel, click the color you want in the Colors box and then click the pixel in the enlarged image. To change a pixel to the background color, click Erase in the Colors box and then click the pixel. To clear all of the pixels to the background color so that you can design your own icon, click Clear. In addition to picking a color from the Colors box, you can also point to a pixel with the color that you want for the enlarged button image and then click the right mouse button.

To move all image pixels one pixel to the left, right, up, or down, click the appropriate arrow in the Move box. While you are editing a button, you can see the effect on that button as it appears on the toolbar in the Preview box.

When you finish editing, click OK to close the dialog box and replace the old version of the button in the toolbar with the edited version. Alternatively, if you want to abandon your changes, click Cancel.

Working with custom toolbars

You've already seen how you can modify existing toolbars by adding, deleting, moving, and changing buttons. You can also create custom toolbars. For example, you may want to consolidate all your frequently used commands from several toolbars into a single toolbar named Handy Tools. You can create a custom toolbar containing any of the buttons available in the Customize dialog box as well as any that you define as macros. To create a custom toolbar, follow these steps:

1. Open a document based on the template in which you want to save the new toolbar.

2. Choose Tools ➪ Customize to open the Customize dialog box; click the Toolbars tab.

3. Click the New button to display the New Toolbar dialog box.

4. In the Toolbar Name box, type a name, such as Handy Tools, for the new toolbar.

5. In the Make Toolbar Available To list box, choose the template to which you want the toolbar attached.

6. Click OK to close the New Toolbar dialog box. Word automatically opens a new toolbar—floating in the Word window—which also appears in the Toolbars list. The new toolbar initially appears with room for only two buttons.

7. Add buttons to the toolbar, as explained earlier. As you add more buttons, the toolbar automatically widens.

8. After you finish adding buttons, click Close to close the Customize dialog box, leaving the new toolbar displayed.

To move the new toolbar into an area above the horizontal ruler, double-click the toolbar's title bar or drag the bar into position. You can now work with this toolbar just as you can with those toolbars originally available in Word. Remember, however, to save the template so that the new toolbar is available whenever you open a document based on that template.

Note   You cannot rename or delete the toolbars provided by Word, but you can easily change the name of any custom toolbar you have created, or delete it. Simply select the toolbar in the Customize dialog box, and click the Rename or Delete button.

Customizing Menus

You can customize menus on the menu bar, or even add your own menus. And there's a useful, but hidden, tool for editing the shortcut pop-up menus that appear when you right-click on things in Word. There are several reasons to customize menus:

✦ To provide extra facilities by adding commands to menus.

✦ To simplify the Word interface by deleting commands from menus.

✦ To address certain tasks by adding menus.

✦ To place all your most commonly used commands on one menu.

Just as it does when saving changes to toolbars, Word saves changes to menus in templates or documents.

Creating a new menu

To create a new menu for the menu bar, follow these steps:

1. Choose Tools ⇨ Customize to open the Customize dialog box.

2. Click the Commands tab and scroll down the Categories list to find New Menu.

3. Click New Menu in the Categories list.

4. Drag New Menu from the Commands list to where you want the menu to appear on the menu bar. A new menu labeled New Menu then appears on the menu bar.

5. Click Close.

6. Right-click New Menu, type the name for the new menu in the Name box of the pop-up menu, and press Enter.

7. Click Close in the Customize dialog box.

Adding a command to a menu

You add commands to menus in the same way you added toolbar buttons to the toolbars. Open the Customize dialog box, and drag the command onto the menu name. The menu opens, and you can now drag the command onto the menu and drop it into place.

Editing shortcut menus

Editing the menus on the menu bar is simple enough, but how do you edit the shortcut menus, the menus that appear when you right-click on something in Word? For instance, if you right-click on text in a document, a menu pops up providing commands that allow you to cut, copy, and paste, modify the font format, and so on.

For some reason Microsoft hid this away. Open the Customize dialog box, click the Toolbars tab, and find the Shortcut Menus toolbar. Click on this option, and Word displays a small toolbar with three words, Text, Table, and Draw, each representing a menu. Click on one of these menus, and the menu opens, displaying a large list of shortcut menus.

You can use these menus to modify the shortcut menus. For instance, if you'd like to add Insert Picture to the pop-up menu that appears when you right-click on text, click the Commands tab, click on the Insert category, and find From File in the Commands list.

Now drag this onto the Text menu on the Shortcut Menus toolbar, and then onto the Text submenu; when the Text submenu opens, drag it into the position in which you want to drop it and release the mouse button. You can now right-click on it and change its name.

Changing accelerator keys

Every command in a menu has an *accelerator* key underlined in the command name. You can press this key to activate the command, instead of clicking on it. For most commands, the accelerator key is the first character in the command name. Ideally, each command in a menu, however, must have a different accelerator key. If two or more commands in a menu have the same first character, characters other than the first are used as the accelerator keys. For example, the File menu contains Save and Save As, and both cannot use the same accelerator key.

Word automatically assigns accelerator keys for any existing commands that you add to a menu, but you can assign a different accelerator key. Before starting the process of adding a command to a menu, make a note of the accelerator keys used by commands already in that menu so that you can pick a new accelerator key.

With the Customize dialog box open, open the menu and right-click the command for which you want to change the accelerator key; a shortcut menu appears. In the Name text field, the name of the command appears with an ampersand character (&) immediately in front of the assigned accelerator key. For example, the two Save commands in the File menu are written as &Save and Save &As, which means that the commands appear with the underlined accelerator keys as Save and Save As.

To change an accelerator key for the selected command, reposition the ampersand character (&) to immediately in front of the desired accelerator key. You should, of course, designate an accelerator key that is not already assigned to another command in the menu. (You aren't required to use a different key. If two commands are assigned the same accelerator key, pressing the key moves the highlight to the first command using that accelerator key, but does not activate it. Pressing the key again moves to the next command. You can activate the command by pressing Enter when the key is highlighted.)

Organizing commands into groups

In addition to the names of commands, Word menus contain separators that divide these commands into related groups. To organize commands into groups, follow these steps:

1. Open a document based on the template containing the menu with the command that you want to remove.

2. Choose Tools ⇨ Customize to open the Customize dialog box.

3. Open the menu to which you want to add a separator.

4. Right-click the command in a menu that you want to be first in the new command group. A shortcut menu then appears.

5. Choose Begin a Group. The separator then appears above the selected command, and a check mark appears at the left of the Begin a Group command.

6. Go to the command that appears immediately *after* the last item in the group, and repeat steps 4 and 5.

Customization options

Word uses a technology called IntelliSense to create custom menus based on your most frequently used commands. These Personalized Menus can be easily expanded to reveal all of the commands, and they can also expand automatically based on IntelliSense rules. When users first start Word, the application menus contain those commands that are used 95 percent of the time; this way, infrequently used commands don't immediately clutter the menus. At the bottom of each menu is a down-arrow button that expands the menu to the full selection of choices, so you can still easily find all of the menu commands.

As mentioned, the menu also automatically expands based on IntelliSense rules. As you access individual menu commands, those commands are "promoted" and displayed higher on the list. Over a period of usage, menus display those commands that are used most often and visually suppress the ones that are never or only rarely used. You can tailor personalized menus or shut them off by using the Options tab (see Figure 32-16) in the Customize dialog box (Tools ⇨ Customize). In addition, you can set several other options related to toolbars and menus. Table 32-13 describes the options for configuring menus in the Options tab.

Figure 32-16: The Options tab of the Customize dialog box.

Table 32-13: Options for Configuring Menus in the Options Tab

Personalized Menus and Toolbars Group		Default Effect
Always Show Full Menus	Not checked	Word will show the full menu as soon as you open it, not just most frequently used commands.
Show Standard and Formatting Toolbars on Two Rows	Checked	Word gives each toolbar its own row, providing more room for buttons. Uncheck this to squeeze them onto one row.
Show Full Menus After a Short Delay	Not checked	Displays the full menu from the abbreviated personalized menu after the menu has been open several seconds. This option is disabled if Always Show Full Menus is selected.
Reset Menu and Toolbar Usage		Click this button to tell Word to throw out all the prior information and start tracking menu and toolbar usage afresh.

Other Group	Default	Effect
Large Icons	Not checked	Displays large—*very* large—icons on the toolbars; great if you have vision problems.
List Font Names in Their Font	Checked	Displays font names in the Format toolbar's Font drop-down list box in the actual typeface the name represents. Also displays style names in the appropriate typeface in the Style drop-down list box.
Show ScreenTips on Toolbars	Checked	When you point at a toolbar button, the name of the button pops up.
Show Shortcut Keys in ScreenTips	Not checked	Included with the name of the button is, if applicable, the command's keyboard shortcut.
Menu Animations	None	Sets the way that menus are opened. The default (None) instantly drops down the menu. Random rotates the menu animations randomly between None, Unfold, Slide, and Fade menu animations. Unfold makes the menu unfold before your eyes instead of instantly dropping-down; Slide means the menu slides down like a window blind; and Fade displays the menu by going from very light to full contrast over a second or so.

Customizing Keyboard Shortcuts

If you use Word for anything more than writing simple letters, you probably spend a great deal of time opening menus, choosing commands, and picking options in dialog boxes. Wouldn't you be more productive if you could use simple key combinations instead? That's what keyboard shortcuts do.

Keyboard shortcuts are key combinations that provide fast access to commands, fonts, symbols, AutoText entries, styles, and macros. Many keyboard shortcuts are built into Word. You can change the meaning of the built-in keyboard shortcuts, however, and you can also define other keyboard shortcuts.

Tip   For a complete list of Word's built-in keyboard shortcuts, type **keyboard shortcuts** into the Type a Question For Help box (the top-right of the Word window) and press Enter. When Word finds a list of topics, click on the one called Keyboard Shortcuts. The window that appears provides shortcuts in many different categories. You can, if you wish, click the Show All link at the top to open up all the categories and then click the Print button.

You can see the format of various built-in shortcut key combinations in Table 32-14.

Table 32-14: Examples of Word's Built-In Shortcut Key Combinations

Shortcut Key Combination	Action
Ctrl+]	Increases the font size by one point
Ctrl+[	Decreases the font size by one point
Ctrl+B	Makes text bold
Ctrl+I	Makes text italic
Ctrl+Shift+*	Displays nonprinting characters
Ctrl+E	Centers a paragraph
Ctrl+L	Left-aligns a paragraph
Ctrl+K	Starts AutoFormat
Alt+Ctrl+1	Applies the Heading 1 style
Alt+Ctrl+2	Applies the Heading 2 style
Ctrl+F3	Cuts to the Spike
F1	Accesses Help
F2	Moves text or graphics
Alt+Shift+D	Inserts a Date field
Shift+F9	Switches between field code and result
Alt+F9	Switches between all field codes and all results

As you can see from Table 32-14, some built-in keyboard shortcuts consist of a single function key. Most, however, entail pressing Shift, Ctrl, Alt, or some combination of these keys while pressing another character. The custom keyboard shortcuts that you can create consist of similar key combinations. As discussed in the next section, you can also create two-part keyboard shortcuts that contain a key combination followed by another key. Like changes to toolbars and menus, the custom keyboard shortcuts that you create are saved in the active template.

Creating a shortcut key for a style

You can create shortcut key combinations to make your life with Word more enjoyable and productive. Suppose, for example, that you frequently use certain styles in your work. Therefore, instead of dropping down the Style list box in the Formatting toolbar and scrolling up or down to find the style that you want, you can create shortcut key combinations that give you fast access to specific styles.

Suppose that you frequently use the Normal, Heading 1, Heading 2, Heading 3, and Heading 4 styles. You can work faster if keyboard shortcuts give you instant access to these styles.

Before creating keyboard shortcuts for these styles, however, you should determine whether they already exist in Word. The easiest way to do so is to look in the Keyboard Shortcuts Help, as explained previously. If you do, you find the following:

✦ Ctrl+Shift+N applies the Normal style.

✦ Alt+Ctrl+1 applies the Heading 1 style.

✦ Alt+Ctrl+2 applies the Heading 2 style.

✦ Alt+Ctrl+3 applies the Heading 3 style.

Word doesn't have a shortcut key to apply the Heading 4 style. To assign a shortcut key to the Heading 4 style, follow these steps:

1. Open a document based on the template in which you want to save the new shortcut key.

2. Choose Tools ➪ Customize to open the Customize dialog box.

3. Click the Keyboard button. The Customize Keyboard dialog box appears (see Figure 32-17).

4. In the Categories list, choose Styles.

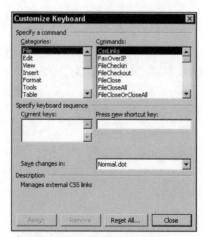

Figure 32-17: The Customize Keyboard dialog box.

5. In the Styles list, choose Heading 4. Note that the Description box at the bottom of the dialog box contains a description of the style that you choose. Also, if someone has already assigned a shortcut key to the Heading 4 style, that shortcut key appears in the Current Keys list box.

6. Place the insertion point in the Press New Shortcut Key text box, and then press Alt+Ctrl+4 (the shortcut key that you want to assign to the Heading 4 style). Notice that [unassigned] appears under Currently Assigned To, indicating that the keyboard shortcut key you've chosen is not currently assigned—if it is in use for some other command, that command name will appear here.

7. In the Save Changes In drop-down, select the template you want to modify.

8. Click Assign to assign the keyboard shortcut to the style. Word then confirms the assignment by displaying the shortcut in the Current Keys list box.

9. Click Close to close the dialog box.

In the previous example, you assigned a one-part shortcut key combination (Alt+Ctrl+4) to perform a specific task. However, you can also assign two-part keyboard shortcuts. You can, for example, assign the following:

✦ Alt+Ctrl+H,1 to the Heading 1 style.

✦ Alt+Ctrl+H,2 to the Heading 2 style.

✦ Alt+Ctrl+H,3 to the Heading 3 style.

✦ Alt+Ctrl+H,4 to the Heading 4 style.

To assign Alt+Ctrl+H,4 to the Heading 4 style, place the insertion point in the Press New Shortcut Key text box, press Alt+Ctrl+H, and then press 4. Word automatically places a comma between Alt+Ctrl+H and 4. After you assign a two-part shortcut key, you can use it by pressing the first part (in this case, Alt+Ctrl+H), releasing all the keys, and then pressing the second part (in this case, 4). Don't type the comma.

Note   Word is a little sensitive here; when typing into the Press New Shortcut Key text box, do so quickly or Word may repeat a key you hold down too long.

Assigning keyboard shortcuts for other purposes

Using shortcut key combinations to provide quick access to styles is only one of the many productive ways to use keyboard shortcuts. The Categories list box in the Customize Keyboard dialog box contains many categories for which you can assign keyboard shortcuts. These are as following:

✦ All commands (those in the menus as well as others)

✦ Macros

✦ Fonts

✦ AutoText entries

✦ Styles

✦ Common symbols

Before you get too enthusiastic about styles, however, a word of caution is appropriate. Keyboard shortcuts are easy to create, but they are also difficult to remember. You can create many keyboard shortcuts and have different keyboard shortcuts in separate templates, and unless you have a supercomputer for a brain, you won't be able to remember all of them. You can easily become counterproductive by creating too many keyboard shortcuts. Try to avoid a situation in which you spend more time trying to find the right shortcut key than you would spend selecting what you need from a menu or dialog box.

Be systematic. Decide which keyboard shortcuts you need on a regular basis, and assign only those combinations. As much as possible, save your keyboard shortcuts in the Normal template so that the same shortcuts are available in all of your documents. If you're a member of a workgroup, make it a high priority that every member of the group uses the same keyboard shortcuts. You can follow this procedure by making one person responsible for updating the template.

Restoring shortcut key assignments

Just a few steps can restore all of the original shortcut key assignments in a template:

1. Open a document based on the template for which you want to restore keyboard shortcuts.

2. Choose Tools ➪ Customize to open the Customize dialog box, and then click the Keyboard button.

3. Click Reset All to open a dialog box in which Word asks you to confirm that you want to restore the shortcut key assignments.

4. Click Yes to restore these assignments and return to the Customize dialog box.

5. Click Close to close the dialog box.

6. Choose File ➪ Save All to save these changes to the template.

Summary

Few Word users customize the program, yet Word allows dramatic modifications to be made. You can tap into Word's power by mastering its customizing features, including changing its default settings, changing its toolbars and menus, and even defining shortcut key combinations. In this chapter, you learned how to do the following:

✦ Work with the tabs in the Options dialog box (Tools ➪ Options), which include View, General, Edit, Print, Track Changes, User Information, Compatibility, File Locations, Save, Security, and Spelling & Grammar.

✦ Create your own custom toolbars using the Customize dialog box (Tools ➪ Customize).

✦ Add and delete buttons on existing toolbars using the Customize dialog box.

✦ Customize menus by adding your own menu items or deleting existing menu items using the Menus tab in the Customize dialog box.

✦ Customize keyboard shortcuts using the Keyboard button in the Customize dialog box.

✦　　✦　　✦

Making the Most of Word Macros and VBA

✦　　✦　　✦　　✦

In This Chapter

Understanding macros

Recording and saving macros

Editing and managing macros

Introducing Visual Basic

Writing a macro using the Visual Basic Editor

✦　　✦　　✦　　✦

Word contains a galaxy of pre-made commands created using Visual Basic, which is the programming language behind Word and many other applications. You can also create custom commands using Word's macro features to record keystrokes and mouse actions, and you can construct more complex macros from scratch using the Visual Basic Editor.

This chapter explains how to create, edit, manage, and use macros in Word, and it also introduces you to Visual Basic.

Understanding Macros

Macros enable you to automate a set of procedures and then run them with a single command. Macros can be simple recordings of keystrokes, commands, and mouse button clicks, or they can be sophisticated programs that you create. Using macros can improve your efficiency significantly, so if you find yourself performing particular tasks repeatedly, create a macro to do the job and then assign the macro to a menu, toolbar, or shortcut keys. Even simple recorded macros can improve your work efficiency noticeably. Some simple tasks and procedures that you can automate with a macro include:

✦ Opening and arranging a group of files that are used together.

✦ Speeding up routine text formatting and editing.

✦ Opening a document and immediately moving to the last location edited.

✦ Simplifying dialog box selections.

✦ Automating a series of related tasks.

✦ Switching automatically to Outline view.

The easiest way to create a macro is to record your keystrokes and command selections with Word's macro recorder. This process is much like using a VCR to record a television program. When you turn on the macro recorder, Word stores all your keystrokes and command choices as Visual Basic macro commands until you turn off the recorder. In fact, this is the only method for creating macros that most users are likely to attempt; writing macros is far more complicated and better left to those with some programming skills.

Storing Global and Template Macros

You can store a macro in a single document template or in a global template. By default, Word stores macros in the Normal template (Normal.dot). This way, you can use them with any document. When you store a macro in a document template, however, that macro is available only to documents based on that template. If you later change your mind about the location of the stored macro, you can use the Organizer to copy macros from one template to another (as explained later in this chapter). Save macros as global macros only when many documents need to share them. Macros designed for a specific type of document or a specialized purpose should be saved with the template for that document type.

Recording and Saving Macros

Before you record a macro, you need to understand what Word actually records. This information helps you to set up Word properly before starting the macro recorder, and it also prevents you from recording unwanted steps. You can always remove these steps later, but it is easier to record only those steps you actually want.

With the macro recorder on, Word records mouse clicks that select menu commands or dialog box options, but Word does not record mouse movements in the document window. You must use the keyboard if you want to record selecting, copying, or clicking and dragging document text. You can pause recording any time and then resume where you paused.

Cross-Reference   If you are unfamiliar with using the keyboard to select or move text and graphics, see Chapter 2.

Selections made in dialog boxes are recorded within macros only if you click OK to close the box. This action then records the current settings for all options in that dialog box. In the case of dialog boxes containing tabs, such as that opened by choosing Tools ⇨ Options, you can record only the settings of one tab at a time, by clicking OK in that tab. If, for example, you want to record Save, View, and Edit options, you must choose Tools ⇨ Options for each set, select the tab, select the options, and then click OK rather than switching to another tab. If you are in a dialog box, clicking Cancel or pressing Esc prevents that dialog box from being recorded. If you backspace over text that you just typed, the deleted text is not recorded, either.

Some items (such as the ruler) toggle between conditions, in which case the macro recorder records a single statement: DisplayRulers. If the ruler is already on, DisplayRulers turns off the ruler; if the Ruler is off, DisplayRulers turns on the ruler. As a result, running a recorded macro actually could turn off the ruler when you want it to stay on.

Tip   If you intend to use the new macro in another document, make sure none of its commands depend on the contents of the original document.

Recording macros

Before you create a macro, you need to decide whether the macro affects a specific portion of the document, a selected portion of the document, or the entire document. If the macro always affects a specific part of a document, insert bookmarks in the document that name the specific text or graphic so the macro can move to these locations. If you want a macro to work on whatever you may have selected when you run it, make your selection before you begin recording the macro. To record a macro that affects the whole document, make sure that nothing is selected when you begin recording.

Cross-Reference   For more information on working with bookmarks, see Chapter 11.

Open the template in which you want to store your macro, and prepare the document so it is in the condition that warrants running the macro. If you want the macro to be available to all documents, base the document on the Normal template. Alternatively, if you want to use the macro only with documents from a specific template, open a document based on that template. You can see on which template a document is based by choosing the File ➪ Properties command and then reading the template name in the Summary tab.

To record a macro, follow these steps:

1. If you plan to save the macro in a template other than Normal or another global template, open a document based on the template to which you want to apply the macro.

2. Do one of the following to open the Record Macro dialog box (see Figure 33-1):

    • Choose Tools ➪ Macro ➪ Record New Macro.

    • Double-click the REC indicator in the status bar.

Figure 33-1: The Record Macro dialog box.

3. Type a name for the macro in the Macro Name text box. Macro names must begin with a letter, but after that, you can include numbers. Macro names can be as many as 80 characters long, and they cannot contain spaces or symbols. Use a combination of uppercase and lowercase letters to identify the macro more easily.

4. If you want to store the macro as a global macro, make sure to choose All Documents (Normal.dot) from the Store Macro In list. This list includes the global Normal.dot template and templates for all documents that are currently open.

5. Enter a description in the Description text box to help you remember what the macro does. This description then displays in the status bar of the Macros dialog box whenever the macro name is selected. The current date and author are automatically

entered as part of the description, but you may find it useful to include more information when working with and managing your macros.

6. Click OK. The REC indicator in the status bar then changes to bold, and the Stop Recording toolbar displays in the document window. This toolbar contains only two buttons: Stop Recording (the square button) and Pause Recording (two vertical bars and a circle). The mouse pointer also changes to an icon of a cassette tape.

7. Perform the actions that you want to record. To pause the macro, click the Pause Recording button on the Stop Recording toolbar. Click this button (now called Resume Recorder) again to restart macro recording.

8. When you finish entering the macro actions, do one of the following:

   • Click the Stop Recording button on the Stop Recording toolbar. When the recording stops, the REC indicator in the status bar dims, and the toolbar and cassette-tape icon disappear. You also can double-click the REC indicator to stop recording.

   • Choose Tools ⇨ Macro ⇨ Stop Recording to turn off the macro recorder.

Be careful not to give your new macro the same name as an existing Word command. If you do, the new macro command replaces the existing Word command, and Word may not work as it should. Word allows you to overwrite a command without any kind of warning. To make sure that you don't use a Word command name, choose Tools ⇨ Macro ⇨ Macros and then choose Word Commands from the Macros In list. Scroll down the names in the alphabetical list of the built-in Word commands to see if the name is already used.

Note   You must use one of the procedures in step 8 to stop recording. Closing the Stop Recording toolbar does not stop recording. If your mouse and keyboard are running much slower than usual, you may have left the macro recorder running.

Assigning a macro to a toolbar or shortcut keys

To make a macro even easier to use, you can create a button on any toolbar and then you can click that button to run the macro or can assign the macro to a specific key combination. You can even assign the same macro to both methods for flexibility. You might have noticed the Toolbars and Keyboard buttons in the Record Macro dialog box. Before you begin recording, click these buttons to assign the macro.

In the case of a toolbar assignment, you bring up the Customize dialog box; drag the macro named Normal.NewMacros.Macro*x* onto the toolbar in which you want to position it. You can then right-click on the button and edit it, using the techniques described in Chapter 32.

To assign a macro to a shortcut key combination, click the Keyboard button to open the Customize Keyboard dialog box. With the insertion point in the Press New Shortcut Key text box, press the key combination to which you want to assign the macro. If that key combination is already assigned to something else, Word lists the current assignments below the Press New Shortcut Key box. Change the key combination to one that is not already assigned and click Assign.

Note   To assign an existing macro to a toolbar or a shortcut key—one you already have recorded or one provided by Word—use the Customize dialog box available through the Tools menu, as explained in Chapter 32. Later in this chapter, you learn how to assign macros to menu options.

Saving macros

A new macro is stored only in memory. It is not saved to disk automatically. Template macros must be saved before you close the template to which they are attached, and global macros must be saved before you exit Word. When you save a document whose template you have changed by adding a macro, Word asks if you want to save the changes to that template. If you attempt to exit Word and have not saved the macros you added to the template, Word asks if you want to save those changes.

Running Macros

How you run a macro depends on how you assigned it. For example, if you assigned your macro to a shortcut key or a toolbar, you run the macro by pressing that shortcut key combination or by clicking the toolbar button. If you did not assign the macro to one of these, you run it using the Macros dialog box. You can run a global macro at any time, because global templates are always available. To run a macro stored in a specific template, however, you either must open the template itself or a document based on that template. If the macro is designed to work with selected items, you must select those items first and then press the macro shortcut key or choose the toolbar button.

To run a macro using the Macros dialog box, follow these steps:

1. Open a document on which the macro is designed to work. If the macro is designed to work with selected text, select that text before running the macro.

2. Choose the Tools ⇨ Macro ⇨ Macros command. The Macros dialog box appears (see Figure 33-2).

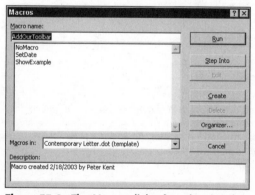

Figure 33-2: The Macros dialog box showing the macros available in the Contemporary Letter template.

3. Select or type the macro name in the Macro Name list box.

4. Click Run.

If the macro that you want does not appear in the Macro Name list, make sure you have opened a document based on the template containing your macro. If you want the macro to be available at all times, use the Organizer to transfer a copy of that macro from its current template and into the Normal template (as explained later in the "Managing Macros" section of this chapter).

Word commands can be displayed and executed directly from the Macro dialog box. Choosing the Word Commands option in the Macros In list displays nearly 1,000 macros corresponding to Word's built-in commands (see Figure 33-3). Many commands are listed that do not appear in Word's menus. For example, FileCloseAll is a file-related command that does not appear on the File menu but that you can run from the Macros dialog box as though it were a menu selection. Or you can add it to the menu if you wish. The Description box shows a short explanation of the selected macro. Note that the Edit, Create, and Delete buttons are dimmed, however, thus indicating that you cannot change the Word command list or any command macro.

Note   Although FileCloseAll doesn't normally appear on the File menu, you can display it very quickly. Simply press the Shift key and then click File. Both Close All and Save All appear on the menu.

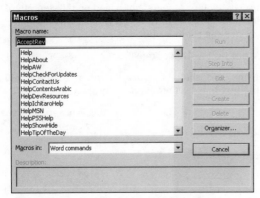

Figure 33-3: Word includes nearly 1,000 built-in commands.

Note   A macro virus can be activated by opening a document or a template that contains a macro infected with that virus. The macro virus then invades your system and may infect every document that you save. For information on setting the security level for your computer to screen out all macros from other sources, which gives you the choice of enabling each macro as you access it, see Chapter 34.

Running macros from previous versions

Word will run macros from some earlier versions of Word (97, 2000, and 2002) without any special conversion. Word automatically converts macros created in Word 6.x and Word 95. The first time that you open the template containing those macros, however, create a new document based on that template, or attach the template to a document with the Templates and Add-Ins command from the Tools menu. That way, the WordBasic commands are converted to Visual Basic. (WordBasic is the macro programming language used in these earlier versions of Word.) The status bar displays a message during conversion. After the conversion is complete, you must save the template to save the conversion; otherwise, Word must convert the macros again the next time you want to use this template.

Note Always save the converted template to a new name. If you save the template over the original template, you lose the WordBasic macros, and as a result, previous versions of Word cannot run them any longer.

Running automatic macros

Word allows you to create automatic macros that run when you open or close a document or you start or exit Word. When creating a macro that runs automatically, you must name it using one of the five unique macro names listed in Table 33-1. The name that you choose depends on when you want the macro to run. For example, you can create a macro to do any of the following:

✦ Automatically open the last document on which you were working.

✦ Prompt users for information when they create a new document with a particular template.

✦ Revert your settings on quitting Word to how they were when you first started the session, thus eliminating any temporary, special settings.

✦ Perform operations that format a document when it opens.

Table 33-1: Word's Automatic Macros

Macro name	Runs
AutoExec	When you start Word
AutoExit	When you quit Word
AutoNew	When you create a new document based on a template containing the macro
AutoOpen	When you open an existing document based on a template containing the macro
AutoClose	When you close a document based on a template containing the macro

You can create only one macro using the AutoExec and AutoExit macro names because these are global macros—only one macro can run when starting or closing. You can create AutoNew, AutoOpen, and AutoClose macros for different templates or as global macros. All of these macros are contained in the Word macro library.

Tip The AutoNew macro combined with the UpdateFields macro is useful for updating all fields in a given document when you open a template for that document. These macros are especially useful in form or document templates containing date and time fields as well as { FILLIN } field codes. When a new document opens from a template with these macros, each field code is updated. For example, all of the { FILLIN } input boxes are displayed in turn.

You can store automatic macros in the Normal template, in another template, or in a document. The exception is the AutoExec macro, which must be stored in the Normal template or another global template in the Startup folder to run automatically when you start Word.

Preventing automatic macros from running

To prevent an automacro from running, hold down the Shift key while you perform the action that starts the macro. For example, to prevent AutoOpen from running when you open a document, hold down the Shift key while you click the Open button in the Open dialog box.

Running macros from a field code

If you want to get really fancy, insert a Word field into a document that runs a macro. The field—{ MACROBUTTON }—can be displayed as text or a graphic in your document. When you double-click this field, Word runs the macro assigned to it.

Cross-Reference   For more information on using field codes, see Chapter 23.

Editing Macros

The macro recorder both records and stores each action that you perform as one or more Visual Basic statements in a macro document. Issuing a Visual Basic statement is the same as choosing the corresponding command. An advanced version of the popular BASIC programming language, Visual Basic is used in all Microsoft Office applications, and you can use it to edit macro statements much like text in a normal document.

With the Visual Basic Editor, you can correct typos, delete unwanted commands, copy parts of a macro from one document or template to another, and reorganize macros by cutting and pasting. You edit macro text just as you do document text.

To edit a macro, follow these steps:

1. Open the template containing the macro you want to edit, or open a document based on that template.

2. Choose the Tools ➪ Macro ➪ Macros command.

3. Select the name of the macro from the Macro Name list box in the Macros dialog box. (Many of these macros cannot be edited—the Word Command macros, for instance, are locked, as are macros in templates that are protected—in which case the Edit button is disabled.)

4. Click Edit. The Visual Basic Editor opens and shows the text of the macro in the editing window. Figure 33-4 shows most of a recorded macro.

5. Make the desired changes just as you would in a normal document. For example, you could change the caption text shown in the macro illustrated in Figure 33-4.

6. When all your changes have been made, choose File ➪ Close and Return to Microsoft Word. The macro is now saved to memory, but you still need to save it with the document to save it to your disk.

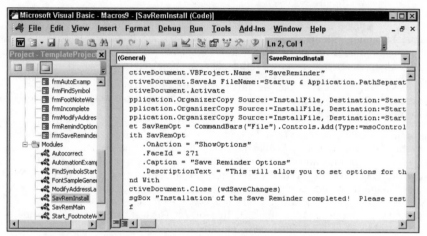

Figure 33-4: The Visual Basic Editor window, showing a macro.

Dissecting a macro

Before moving on, take a look at a sample macro:

```
Sub CodeStyle()
' CodeStyle Macro
' Macro recorded 9/16/03 by Virginia Andersen
    With Selection.Font
        .Name = "Courier New"
        .Size = 12
        .Bold = False
        .Italic = False
        .Underline = wdUnderlineNone
        .UnderlineColor = wdColorAutomatic
        .StrikeThrough = False
        .DoubleStrikeThrough = False
        .Outline = False
        .Emboss = False
        .Shadow = False
        .Hidden = False
        .SmallCaps = True
        .AllCaps = False
        .Color = wdColorAutomatic
        .Engrave = False
        .Superscript = False
        .Subscript = False
        .Spacing = 0
        .Scaling = 100
        .Position = 0
        .Kerning = 0
        .Animation = wdAnimationNone
    End With
End Sub
```

The first few lines of the macro show the macro name and some comments. `Sub CodeStyle()` means a subroutine—a programming term for a small piece of a program—called CodeStyle. The lines beginning with apostrophes are comment lines; any line that begins with an apostrophe is ignored by Word, so you can include comments that contain descriptive information that might help you to remember what the macro is supposed to do.

The lines `With` and `End With` enclose the macro instructions that refer to the same object, in this case the selected text. The line `With Selection.Font` indicates that text is selected and that the Font dialog box is opened.

Most of the remaining statements in the CodeStyle macro represent choices made in the three tabs of the Font dialog box while recording the macro. Each property name is preceded by a period (.), thus indicating that it represents a property of the currently selected text. Each setting is called a property. Any text selection, such as the font name (Courier New), is contained in quotation marks. Numeric settings appear as regular numbers (`.Size = 12`). `False` means that the option was not selected, and `True` means that the option was. All of the Font dialog box options are represented in this macro. The last two lines close the macro and return control to Word. (`End Sub` means "end the subroutine.")

Deleting unnecessary commands

As you can see in the CodeStyle macro, most of the Font dialog box selections were left in the default setting. Only the font name, size, and `SmallCaps` properties were changed. You can delete all Visual Basic statements relating to the unchanged properties without disturbing the macro's performance. You delete commands from a macro the same way you do from any other text: select the line, and press Delete. The condensed macro runs slightly faster than the original, because it sets only three properties instead of all 21.

Adding remarks and comments to a macro

Remarks and comments are helpful for reminding you what is going on in a macro. In Visual Basic, you can add information to a macro in two ways that Word ignores. The `REM` statement is a holdover from early BASIC, in which it was used to identify the line as a remark. The apostrophe (`'`) now is generally used to indicate remarks and comments that you want to see in the macro but that Word should ignore. Also, tabs can be used to indent text, which helps you to understand the hierarchical structure of the macro. Using tabs, remarks, and comments makes your macros easier to decipher.

The following is an example of using comments and tabs to explain the beep command in a macro:

```
Sub BeepMacro()
'
'      The Beep Command
'
'The Beep statement emits a beeping sound.
'
Beep
End Sub
```

Managing Macros

Eventually, you may accumulate macros that have outlived their usefulness. Keeping your macros up-to-date and well organized is a good idea. Word allows you manage your macros in several ways. You can rename and delete macros, and you can copy macros between templates. Using the Organizer dialog box (see Figure 33-5), you can manage your macros by copying them into different templates or by renaming them. By default, Word stores macros in the Normal template, thus making them available for use with every Word document. If you create macros for a specific document, however, save those macros to a template for that document. This technique helps you to keep your Normal template less cluttered.

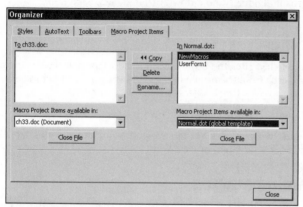

Figure 33-5: The Macro Project Items tab of the Organizer dialog box.

The Word Organizer is a flexible tool for managing macro project items, as well as toolbars, styles, and AutoText entries. The Macro Project Items tab is divided into two major areas that contain lists of macros in selected templates. When you select a macro name from either list, that template then becomes the focus of the operation and, if you want to copy a macro, the source of that macro. The headings above the lists alternate between In and To depending on which list contains the selected macro. The Copy arrows also change direction accordingly.

If you have recorded several new macros in the current template or document, they are lumped together in a macro project named NewMacros rather than being listed separately.

Note   If a template is protected, you must unprotect it before you can delete or rename a macro. To unprotect a template, choose the Tools ➪ Unprotect Document command. You may be prompted to enter the password if one was assigned when the document was protected.

Copying or moving macros between templates

At times, you may want to copy or move a macro from one template to another. To copy or move macros between open templates, follow these steps:

1. Choose the Tools ➪ Macro ➪ Macros command.

2. Click the Organizer button in the Macros dialog box. The Macro Project Items tab of the Organizer dialog box appears.

3. In the Macro Project Items Available In box (on the left side by default), select the template with the macro you want to copy or move. To copy a macro in an unopened template, click the left Close File button to close the open template (the button then changes to Open File), and next, click the Open File button to find and open the template that you want. The Open dialog box appears. Select the template, and click Open.

4. Select the template into which you want to copy or move macros from the Macro Project Items Available In list box (on the right side). To move or copy a macro to an unopened template, click the right Close File button and then the right Open File button. Select the desired template, and then click OK to open that template.

5. Select the macros in the In list that you want to move or copy. To select a series of macros, hold down the Shift key and then click the first and last items in the series. To select multiple macros individually, hold down Ctrl and click each item.

6. Do one of the following:

   • To copy the macros, click Copy.

   • To move the macros, first click the Copy button to copy the selected macros. Then delete the macros from the original template (as described in the next section).

7. To copy or move additional macros from other templates, repeat steps 3 through 6.

8. Click Close, and make sure that you click Yes to save your template and macros when you close the documents (or templates) or exit Word.

Deleting and renaming macros

If a macro is stored either globally or in the active template, you can delete it with the Delete button in the Macros dialog box. To delete a macro stored in an unopened template, use the Organizer dialog box. You can rename a macro using the Organizer dialog box as well.

Renaming a macro is handy when you want to base a new macro on one that comes with Word. Because you are not permitted to edit a Word-supplied macro, you first must copy that macro and then rename it. Then you can edit the new version.

To delete or rename macros using the Organizer dialog box, select the macro and use the Delete and Rename buttons.

Introducing Visual Basic

Visual Basic is a sophisticated descendent of the original Beginner's All-Purpose Symbolic Instruction Code (BASIC) that was developed at Dartmouth College during the 1960s and that still is taught in schools today. Since Word 97, Word has used Visual Basic as the underlying programming language to create its commands and macros. Word 6.x and Word 95 used the earlier version, WordBasic.

The main difference between WordBasic and Visual Basic is a matter of dimension. WordBasic is built around a two-dimensional, flat list of commands, whereas Visual Basic consists of a three-dimensional hierarchy of objects. Each object in turn has access to a specific set of methods (actions) and properties similar to the statements and functions found in WordBasic.

For example, if you want to apply italic formatting to selected text, the WordBasic statement would be as follows:

```
Italic 1
```

The more definitive Visual Basic statement would be as follows:

```
Selection.Font.Italic = True
```

The object is the selected text (`Selection`). `Font` is a property of `Selection`, and `Italic` is a property of `Font`. The equal sign sets the property to the value `True` (or in other words, turns it on). Note that the object, `Selection`, may have many other properties as well, such as borders, columns, footnotes, comments, and dozens more. In turn, each of these properties has another set of related properties.

That's as far as we go in this short discussion of Visual Basic programming. If you have no idea what all this means, it's a good indication that you should stick to recording macros. To be frank, this is pretty complicated stuff. It's programming, and therefore it's not something you can learn in a couple of pages.

Using Visual Basic code for common Word tasks

You've already seen an example of using Visual Basic to apply formatting to selected text in the CodeStyle macro. You can apply formatting to a range object, however, such as the first four paragraphs of the active document. Visual Basic also can change the page margins and the line spacing before or after a paragraph.

Other typical uses for Visual Basic macros include the following:

✦ Finding and replacing text or formatting.

✦ Editing and inserting text.

✦ Changing the view of the active window.

✦ Placing text in headers and footers.

✦ Customizing menus and toolbars.

✦ Creating tables, inserting text, and applying formats.

✦ Creating new as well as opening, saving, and closing documents.

✦ Displaying custom dialog boxes for user input.

Examining the ANSIValue macro code

The following example is the code for a macro named ANSIValue, which examines the selected characters in the current document, converts them to their corresponding ANSI values, and then displays the results in a message box:

```
Sub ANSIValue()
' ANSIValue Macro which displays the ANSI equivalent
' of text characters.
Dim strSel As String, strNums As String
Dim LastFourChar As String
Dim iPos As Integer
Str1 = "Because the selected text contains characters,"
Str2 = " not all of the ANSI values will be displayed."
Str3 = "ANSI Value ("
Str4 = " characters in selection)"
Str5 = " character in selection)"
Str6 = "Text must be selected before this macro is run."
Str7 = "ANSI Value"
strSel = Selection.Text
If Len(strSel) > 0 Then
    For i = 1 To Len(strSel)
```

```
            strNums = strNums + Str(Asc(Mid(strSel, i)))
        Next i
        strNums = LTrim(strNums)
        If Len(strNums) > 255 Then
            LastFourChar = Mid(strNums, 252, 4)
            strNums = Left(strNums, 251) + Left(LastFourChar, 4 - InStr("
    ", LastFourChar))
            MsgBox Str1 + Str(Len(strSel)) + Str2
        End If
        If Len(strSel) = 1 Then Str4 = Str5
        MsgBox strNums, 0, Str3 + LTrim(Str(Len(strSel))) + Str4
    Else
        MsgBox Str6, 0, Str7
    End If
End Sub
```

The first line contains the macro name, and the lines beginning with apostrophes are comments that Word ignores. Variables are named objects that contain information to be used in the macro. The three lines beginning with `Dim` declare three variables as string- (character) type variables and one variable as an integer-type variable. The next seven lines (after the title line and a comment) specify the text to be displayed in the message box as a set of string variables.

The command `strSel = Selection.Text` sets the value of the `strSel` variable to the characters you have selected in the text.

The remainder of the macro is an `If...Then...Else` structure, which first tests the length of the string to see of any characters at all were selected. If the length of the string is 0 (no characters were selected), the macro branches to the `Else` alternative, which includes this statement:

```
MsgBox Str6, 0, Str7
```

This in turn displays a message box with the text contained in the variables `Str6` and `Str7` (`ANSI Value (Text must be selected before this macro is run`)) in the title bar. Actually, if you run the macro with no character selected, the macro returns the ANSI value of the character to the right of the insertion point instead of this message.

Next, the macro processes a loop that steps through the selected characters one by one, converting each to its equivalent ANSI value as it goes. Each number is concatenated to the previous group with the following statement:

```
strNums = strNums + Str(Asc(Mid(strSel, i)))
```

The next `If` statement checks whether the concatenated string of ANSI numbers exceeds the capacity of the message box (255 characters). If so, it then constructs a message using the text in variables `Str1` and `Str2` to explain that not all ANSI values will be displayed.

The last `If` statement substitutes the singular text of `Str5` for the plural text of `Str4` if only one character was selected. Finally, the message box is displayed with `ANSI Values (number of characters selected characters in selection`) in the title bar and the resulting ANSI values in the box.

Figure 33-6 shows the result of running the ANSIValue macro with the Word *document* having been selected.

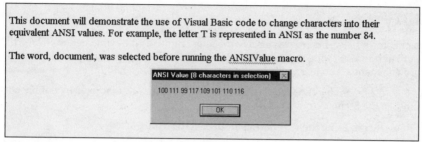

This document will demonstrate the use of Visual Basic code to change characters into their equivalent ANSI values. For example, the letter T is represented in ANSI as the number 84.

The word, document, was selected before running the ANSIValue macro.

ANSI Value (8 characters in selection)

100 111 99 117 109 101 110 116

OK

Figure 33-6: The results of running the ANSIValue macro.

Starting a new macro with Visual Basic

You probably will begin most of your new macros with a few recorded keystrokes or with an existing macro. Some macros, however, are not built on recorded keystrokes and must be started from scratch. To start a new macro, follow these steps:

1. Open the template to which you want to attach the macro, and, if prompted about macro security, choose Enable Macros.

2. Choose Tools ➪ Macro ➪ Macros.

3. Enter the macro name and a description in the Macros dialog box.

4. Choose the name of the template or document in which you want to store the macro (from the Macros In drop-down list box), and choose Create. The Visual Basic Editor window opens with the beginnings of the new macro (see Figure 33-7), including the name and description you entered.

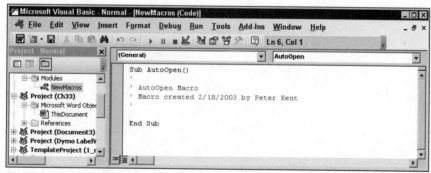

Figure 33-7: The beginnings of a new macro in the Visual Basic Editor window.

5. Type your commands.

6. Choose File ➪ Close and Return to Microsoft Word.

Once you finish entering your macro commands, you can use the Visual Basic Editor to help you debug it. You also can print the macro from the Editor window.

Note

The Visual Basic Editor toolbar contains many handy tools for working with macros and troubleshooting problems with them. Visual Basic is far too complex to cover with any real depth in this book.

Summary

In this chapter, you learned to master macros to get more of what you need from Word. You also were introduced to the powerful Visual Basic programming language that is the basis for all Word commands. You learned how to do the following:

✦ Record a macro by choosing Tools ➪ Macro ➪ Record New Macro or by double-clicking REC in the Status bar.

✦ Run a macro using the Run button in the Macros dialog box.

✦ Copy and move macros among templates using the Organizer dialog box.

✦ Use the sample macros that come with Word, which can be installed in the Macros subfolder in the Program Files\Microsoft Office\Office folder.

✦ Create new macros in the Visual Basic Editor window.

✦   ✦   ✦

Securing Your Data

There are two main reasons to secure your data:

✦ To limit what your coworkers can do with your documents when you share them.

✦ To avoid intentional attacks.

Although the latter, in the form of virus assaults on computer systems, gets the most attention, the former is equally important. In this chapter, we look at how to secure your Word data to ensure that you are not hit with any unexpected surprises, and to make sure that you can collaborate with others on your own terms.

Collaboration Protection

First, let's take a look at how to protect your documents from various forms of modification when you share them with coworkers. For example, suppose you create a document that you want others to review. All you want is to allow them to make notes, to tell you if you've made any mistakes, or to add information. You *don't* want them to actually modify the document itself, especially not in a way that you cannot quickly see. You don't want them to be able to modify formatting, for instance, or change your words in a manner that you cannot review and fix if necessary.

Word allows you to lock the document in a variety of ways to limit exactly what the recipient may do with the document. You can completely lock a document so that only people with your permission can open it. Or you can selectively block actions within the document and even limit restrictions to particular sections within the document.

Open protection

You can completely protect a document by designating that the document can be opened only if the person trying to open it can provide the correct password. When protected in this manner, a small dialog box appears when the user tries to open the file, prompting the user for the password. If the user is unable to provide the password, Word won't open the file. This password protection is a great way to keep the world away from your private thoughts or to circulate sensitive documents containing information about pay raises or layoffs.

In This Chapter

Password-protecting documents

Using advanced encryption

Applying levels of editing protection

Excepting areas of a document from editing restrictions

Using digital signatures for documents

Restricting macros

To provide this sort of password protection, choose Tools ➪ Options, and click the Security tab in the Options dialog box (see Figure 34-1). Then type a password into the Password to Open text box. Click OK; you are prompted to enter the password again to ensure that you typed what you think you typed. Passwords can contain as many as 15 characters, including letters, numbers, symbols, and spaces. As you enter the password, Word displays an asterisk for each character that you type; it doesn't reveal the characters you're entering. Passwords are case-sensitive, so you must type the password exactly as you created it using the correct uppercase and lowercase letters.

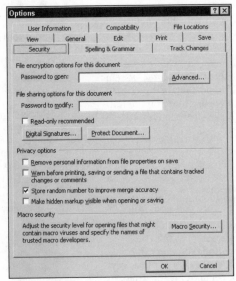

Figure 34-1: The Security tab in the Options dialog box.

Tip   What makes a good password? One you can remember, yet one that others can't guess. The name of your dog, or your date of birth, is not a good idea. Something like 340987$rdf2! would work well, but can you remember it? If you have to write it down, you've already compromised your security to some degree. On the other hand, if you have a password you use to protect business documents, writing the password down at home may be a very reasonable plan (unless you work for a national security agency, in which case the level of security required is obviously a few notches higher). Still, most of us don't require our security systems to allow for any possible scenario, only likely scenarios. Remember, though, if you forget the password, you will not be able to open the file!

More advanced encryption

Initially, when you password-protect your file using Word's default method, you are using a relatively weak form of *encryption*. That is, the mathematical algorithm used to encrypt the file is relatively weak. In fact, you can buy programs that can crack basic Word encryption. However, there are more advanced algorithms available, and Word allows you to select the type of encryption you want to use to lock the file. Notice the Advanced button in the Options dialog box, next to the Password to Open text box. Click this and the Encryption Type dialog box opens (see Figure 34-2).

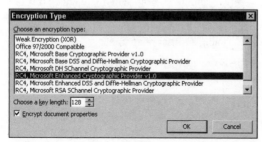

Figure 34-2: The Encryption Type dialog box.

You can choose from a variety of encryption methods. Just remember that if you select one of the RC4 methods, the file can only be opened in Word 2002 or Word 2003. You can't open it if you're using an earlier version. If you want to use the file in Word 97 or 2000, you have to use the default, the Office 97/2000 Compatible method. The RC4 methods use very secure forms of encryption. If you choose, for example, RC4, Microsoft RSA SChannel Cryptographic Provider with the default key length of 128, you can be sure that there is no possible way that the file can be cracked—that is, there is no computer program that can break the code used to encrypt the file. (That doesn't help if you picked an easy-to-guess password, though! Some password-cracking programs use brute force attacks. This method tests simple passwords, often selected from a dictionary, one after another for as long as it takes. If your password can be found in a dictionary, your file can be opened!)

You can select a key length. All you really need to know here is that the longer the key length, the harder the file is to break. But we recommend you don't worry about key length; merely use the default length provided. These are very secure encryption methods already.

Finally, note that if you select one of the RC4 methods, you can also choose whether or not to encrypt the file properties. (The two weakest methods at the top of the list automatically encrypt properties.) In other words, you can encrypt a file, yet not encrypt the properties so that users can still read the properties in the File Open dialog box, for example. If the file is going to sit on a server, accessible to anyone in a workgroup, you might want to make the properties accessible so people can still tell what the file is. You might even put a note in the properties explaining who can open the file. If you hide the properties, one day you may not be able to figure out what the file is and who has the password.

Note   If a file is password-protected, the Preview feature of the Open dialog box cannot display the file properties without the password; when you click on the file with the Preview option turned on, Word prompts for the file password.

Modification protection

You can also protect a document from being modified. In the Security tab of the Options dialog box, enter a password into the Password to Modify text box. This password can be combined with the Password to Open; one password can be required to open the file, and another to modify the file. Or you can allow anyone to open the file, but demand a Password to Modify so only those with the password can make changes.

Notice also the Read-Only Recommended check box in the Security tab of the Options dialog box. This option is not *protection*, but merely recommendation. When you check this box, users who open the file see a message recommending that they open it in read-only mode. That is, if they make changes to the file, they won't be able to save the changes in the file. They'll have to use Save As and save the file using another file name.

Finally in the Options dialog box, notice the Protect Document button. This opens the Document Protection task pane, which allows you to specify the forms of modification protection you want to use. We look at that next.

Specifying levels of protection

You've just seen how to force users to provide a password if they want to open or modify a document. But Word allows you to go further, to specify what sorts of changes users may make to the document. Begin by choosing Tools ➪ Protect Document, or clicking the Protect Document button in the Options dialog box, to open the Document Protection task pane (see Figure 34-3).

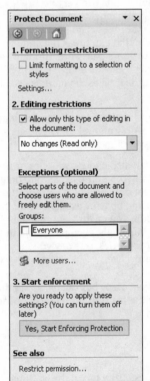

Figure 34-3: The Document Protection task pane.

The task pane enables you to do several things:

✦ Limit formatting changes.

✦ Limit the types of content changes.

✦ Provide exceptions, allowing certain people to edit specific parts of the document.

Tip What's to stop someone from opening a file, copying the contents, saving to a new file, modifying the new version, and then reapplying protection so that the document appears to be unchanged? Well, the person trying to commit fraud won't know your password. (Will he? You did pick a good password, didn't you?) However, there are other ways to further protect a document. See "Restricting Permission" later in this chapter for information on stopping people from copying information from a document, printing it, or forwarding it.

Limiting formatting changes

You can tell Word to allow users to use only specific formatting by clicking the Limit Formatting to a Selection of Styles check box. This feature provides you with a way to limit the available styles, a great method for stopping *style creep*, in which documents' style collections seem to grow as large teams work on them.

Click the Settings link, and the Formatting Restrictions dialog box opens (see Figure 34-4).

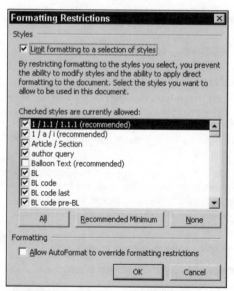

Figure 34-4: The Formatting Restrictions dialog box.

Leave the Limit Formatting to a Selection of Styles check box in this dialog box selected; clearing it simply turns off this feature. Use the Recommended Minimum and None buttons to remove many styles—None really means Bare Minimum. You cannot remove several styles, including Default Paragraph Font and normal. We recommend that you click the None button and then add in the styles that you want to allow.

When you turn on protection—by clicking the Yes, Start Enforcing Protection button and entering a password—Word quickly checks the document to see if it contains any formatting that is not allowed. If so, Word asks if it should remove that formatting.

When a user now opens your document, it's not apparent that the document has been protected. However, the only styles available are those you have specified as valid.

Editing restrictions

You can specify several forms of editing restrictions. Check the Allow Only This Type of Editing in the Document check box and choose from the following options on the drop-down list box:

✦ **No Changes (Read Only):** Users won't be able to make any changes at all; they can only read the document.

✦ **Tracked Changes:** Users can make changes, but all changes are made with reviewing marks on (see Chapter 29).

✦ **Comments:** Users can enter comments, but no other changes, into the document (see Chapter 29).

✦ **Filling in Forms:** Users can fill in forms, but they can't make any changes outside form fields (see Chapter 24).

These restrictions go into effect when you click the Yes, Start Enforcing Protection button.

Exceptions by person and by section

You can allow certain exceptions, dependent on the person viewing the file and the area of the document. For instance, you can allow anyone to make changes to a particular section in the document—or the opposite, allow everyone to make changes to all but a specific section. Or you can allow specific people to make changes to the entire document, or to specific sections. Here's how this feature works.

When you select an Editing Restriction, the Exceptions area of the task pane opens. You can now select the part of the document that you want to allow to be modified and then specify *who* can make changes. By default Everyone is shown in the Groups list, but you can use the More Users link to open the Add Users dialog box and add other network identification names to specify specific people.

Here, for instance, is how to make all but one area of the document read-only:

1. Select the Allow Only This Type of Editing in the Document check box.

2. In the drop-down list box, select No Changes (Read Only).

3. In the document itself, select the area of the document in which you want to allow changes to be made. This could be an entire section, a page, part of a page, a paragraph, even a single word.

4. Select the Everyone check box. Word places bookmark markers at either end of the selected area.

5. Click the Yes, Start Enforcing Protection button. Word displays a dialog box.

6. Enter your password twice, and click OK.

Tip   You can unprotect multiple areas within a document using the multi-area selection techniques described in Chapter 2. For instance, select a paragraph, hold Alt, and then select another paragraph. When you select the Everyone check box, both areas are set as exempt from editing restrictions.

Additional Privacy Features

Word provides several other privacy options, as you can see at the bottom of the Security tab in the Options dialog box:

✦ **Remove personal information from this file on save:** Check this, and when Word saves the file it removes your name from the file Properties Author and Saved By fields, and removes your name from any revisions you have made to the document.

✦ **Warn before printing, saving or sending a file that contains tracked changes or comments:** When this is checked, if you try to print, save, or send a file in which changes or comments have been made, you'll see a warning message.

✦ **Store random number to improve merge accuracy:** You use this option when you are merging comments and changes from multiple reviewers, and it is turned on by default. Word inserts a unique number into each document so that it will recognize it later. Word opens the document to see if it has been modified elsewhere, and it can tell if it has been. It then asks you if you want to merge it into the original.

✦ **Make hidden markup visible when opening or saving:** Check this, and every time you open a document or save a document, hidden markup is displayed.

Cross-Reference   You learn about markup in Chapter 29. The Show menu on the Reviewing toolbar allows you to hide various kinds of markup, such as Comments, Insertions, and Deletions.

Restricting Permission

Word gives you the capability to stop people from forwarding, editing, or even copying files by restricting their file permissions. You'll find a link at the bottom of the Protect Document task pane—the Restrict Permission link. And there's also the File ➪ Permission menu option. When you click the link or select the menu option the first time, you'll see a message box telling you that in order to use the feature you must download Microsoft Rights Management. Click Yes, and the Windows Rights Management Client Web page opens in your browser (assuming that you are connected to the Internet, of course). Follow the instructions to download and install the software.

The next time you click the link or use the menu option, you'll be able to set up the Windows Rights Management service. This service requires a rights-management server that can be accessed across the Internet or through an internal network. When someone tries to open a document that has restricted permissions, the document contacts the server to check the user's rights. Without the server's authorization, the document can't be used.

This is a powerful and very advanced system that can help organizations restrict the use of sensitive information. Authorized users cannot copy the information or share it with others by sending it to them, nor can they print the document and give it to them.

Digital Signatures

Digital signatures provide a way to "sign" documents using a password. Word can read a digital signature and be sure that the only person who could have signed the document was the one with the password that allows him or her to use the corresponding digital certificate. (Again, such security is only as secure as the password—if someone guesses or steals your password, your digital signature can be forged.) We're going to look at how to sign documents and how to check a signature.

Signing a document

In order to sign a document, you need a personal certificate from a certification authority such as VeriSign (www.VeriSign.com/) or Thawte (www.thawte.com/). Visit the Web site and look for instructions for obtaining a personal or e-mail certificate. VeriSign will sell you one for $14.95 a year, and it will give you one that lasts for two weeks for free. Thawte (which is owned by VeriSign) will provide one for free.

Follow the instructions for creating and installing the certificate. Once installed, you can use it to sign documents. Open the document you want to sign and open the Options dialog box. Click the Security tab, and then click the Digital Signature button to open the Digital Signature dialog box (see Figure 34-5). Click the Add button. In the Select Certificate dialog box (see Figure 34-6), select your certificate. If you installed it properly, it should be listed in this box.

Figure 34-5: The Digital Signature dialog box.

Figure 34-6: The Select Certificate dialog box.

Viewing a certificate

If a document has been "signed," you'll see the little red certificate icon in the toolbar. You can check to see who has signed the document by opening the Digital Signature dialog box from the Options dialog box and clicking the View Certificate button. The Certificate dialog box shown in Figure 34-7 opens. This shows you the certificate details, including the owner's name and the certification authority that issued the certificate.

Figure 34-7: The Certificate dialog box.

Tip

Signing a document should be combined with locking it with a password. If a recipient makes changes to the document and then saves it, the signature is removed.

Macro Security

As we discuss in Chapter 33, Word's macros provide mini programs that run within Word, allowing you to automate many tasks. Unfortunately, many virus programmers have figured out how to create malicious Word viruses. Word allows you to define how macros should be managed to ensure only safe macros work on your computer.

Click the Macro Security button in the Options dialog box, to open the Security dialog box (see Figure 34-8).

You have four choices for macro security: Very High, High, Medium, and Low:

✦ **Very High:** Disables all macros except those installed in trusted locations.

✦ **High:** Tells Word to use only macros that are digitally signed by trusted authorities.

✦ **Medium:** Allows you to choose which macros to accept—if a document contains macros when you open it, you'll see a dialog box asking if you want to accept them.

✦ **Low:** Accepts all macros, not a good idea if you don't use a virus checker on your computer.

Click the Trusted Sources tab to see a list of macro sources—companies or individuals that have digitally signed macros. It's this list that Word uses if you select Very High or High; only macros from these authorities are accepted.

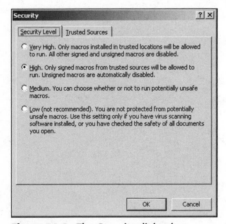

Figure 34-8: The Security dialog box.

Tip   It's a simple thing to remember: Word documents can contain viruses in the form of mali-cious macros. So *you need a virus checker!* Whether you use McAfee, Norton AntiVirus, Panda, or one of several other virus checkers, you need to run a program constantly to check all files downloaded from the Internet, sent to you in e-mail, provided to you on a floppy disk or CD, pulled off the corporate network, or transferred in some other way to your computer from another computer. If you don't have such a program, sooner or later you *will* be hit by a virus!

Summary

Word's security features are both useful and underutilized. Spend a few minutes learning how to use them, and you'll probably think of ways in which they can help you. In this chapter, you learned the following:

✦ You can stop people opening your files by providing a password. Choose Tools ➪ Options, click the Security tab, and then enter a password in the Password to Open text box.

✦ Let people open the file but read it only (not modify it) by providing a Password to Modify.

✦ You can specify specific forms of protection in the Document Protection task pane— choose Tools ➪ Protect Document, check the Allow Only This Type of Editing in the Document check box, and then select from the drop-down list box.

✦ You can exempt certain areas of the document from restrictions by selecting those areas and then checking the Everyone check box under Exceptions.

✦ Digital signatures allow you to legally sign a document by attaching a certificate. You can get a certificate from VeriSign or Thawte.

✦   ✦   ✦

What's New in Word 2003

♦ ♦ ♦ ♦

In This Appendix

Using Word's
task panes

Improvements to
document protection

Improvements to
editing tools

Improvements to
collaboration tools

Miscellaneous changes

♦ ♦ ♦ ♦

With each new version of Word, Microsoft adds new features and refines old ones, all in the quest to make the software easier to use and, at the same time, more encompassing in what it can accomplish. This appendix focuses on the latest and greatest changes in Word—those features that have been added to the software. We've provided these newer features all in one place so that users migrating from an older version of Word can quickly see what's different in this latest version.

Many people upgrading to Word 2003 are, in reality, "jumping" versions. In other words, you may be upgrading to Word 2003 from Word 2000, without ever having used Word 2002. For you, the number of changes evident in Word 2003 will be even greater. Why? Because you are seeing the cumulative changes brought about by two distinct versions of Word (2002 and 2003). If you are jumping versions, don't worry. This appendix touches on the changes that affect you, as well.

Working with Task Panes

Word 2002 introduced a new *look and feel* to Word. Central to this was the introduction of task panes. The use of task panes is continued in Word 2003. If you jumped from an older version of Word directly to Word 2003, bypassing Word 2002, the sudden appearance of task panes can be jolting.

By default, task panes appear at the right side of your program screen, as shown in Figure A-1. The task pane is used to display various options available for accomplishing a specific task or to display information that you request.

Cross-Reference   To find out more about task panes, turn to Chapter 1.

A variety of task panes are available. The content of the task pane can change depending on the actions you take when using Word. For instance, if you choose File ➪ New, the New Document task pane appears (as shown in Figure A-1). You can see the range of available task panes by clicking the drop-down list at the top of the task pane. (The drop-down symbol is the downward-pointing arrow just to the right of the task pane name, and just to the left of the Close button.)

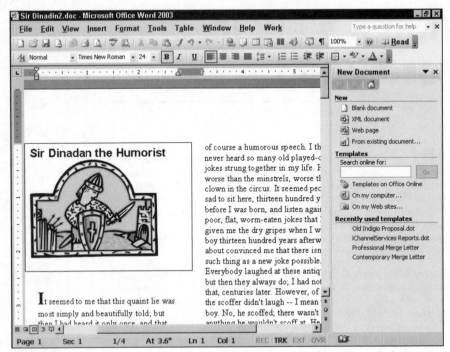

Figure A-1: The task pane appears at the right side of the Word program window.

If you find that the addition of the task pane makes editing your document more difficult, you can minimize the intrusion it represents by any taking any one of the following actions:

✦ Increase the resolution used by Windows to display information on your monitor. The higher the resolution, the more information Windows can display on your monitor at a given time. (Choose Start ➪ Settings ➪ Control Panel ➪ Display, choose the Settings tab, and then adjust the setting in the Screen Area section to a higher number of pixels.)

✦ Maximize your Word program window so that it covers the entire available screen area.

✦ Choose View ➪ Zoom and select a zoom factor that allows you to see more of your document on the screen.

If you still find the task pane intrusive, or if you just want to get rid of it for a while, you can hide it by clicking the Close button in the upper-right corner of the task pane. Rest assured, however, that when Word thinks you need the information or features offered in a task pane, it will appear again.

Document Protection Improvements

Word 2003 has made some giant improvements in how you can protect your documents. Historically, Word has allowed you to protect either an entire document so that users could only add tracked changes or comments, or to protect one or more sections of a document as a form. You could also protect the entire document by requiring that a password be used to open the document.

These approaches to protection are still available in Word 2003, but you now have even more options. You can now lock down styles in Word, and you can specify user-level permissions for changing different portions of a document.

Locking Styles

Styles have been available in Word since the earliest days of the program. Effective use of styles makes it easy to maintain a consistent appearance for documents. This is particularly important in a business environment where documents *should* provide a certain appearance that reflects the image desired for the business.

Cross-Reference   The technique for limiting formatting changes, or *locking* styles, is discussed in Chapter 34.

If a user doesn't know how to use styles, a well-designed document can be easily messed up by the application of direct formatting. Direct formatting overrides styles; so when underlying styles are later changed, those changes may not be apparent because of misapplied direct formatting.

Cross-Reference   To find out more about direct character formatting, see Chapter 4. For more about direct paragraph formatting, see Chapter 5. And to learn about using styles, see Chapter 13.

Word 2003 allows you to lock a document so that only style-based formatting can be applied. More specifically, you can lock the document so that users can only apply a set of styles that you specify. Figure A-2 shows the Formatting Restrictions dialog box, where you indicate which styles can be applied in your document.

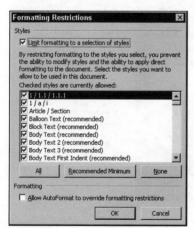

Figure A-2: The Formatting Restrictions dialog box.

If you are familiar with styles, the benefit of this new feature should be immediately obvious. You can now create complex documents in which the formatting remains structured, even when there are multiple people involved in the development of the document.

User Permissions to Make Changes

Word 2003 now includes a long-requested feature: the capability to control who can change specific portions of a document. You do this by protecting the document so it is read-only, and then indicating exceptions to that protection. You can specify the sections of the document that everyone can change, or you can specify a particular person and which sections that person can change. This gives you enormous flexibility in protecting your document.

Cross-Reference Chapter 34 talks about many of the security features provided in Word 2003, including using the Protect Document task pane to control what changes are made to the document,

Using the Protect Document task pane, you can first protect the entire document against any edits, or optionally allow only comments. Then you assign permissions to individual portions of the document by selecting those portions and then choosing which users should be able to edit that selected area. Figure A-3 shows an example of applying this type of protection. Notice that in item 2 of the Protect Document task pane, No Changes is the setting. Then, in the Exceptions area, you specify who can change what portions of the document. In this case, we selected a paragraph of the document and then clicked More Users to display the Add Users dialog box. The user names specified in the dialog box will be able to modify only the selected paragraph.

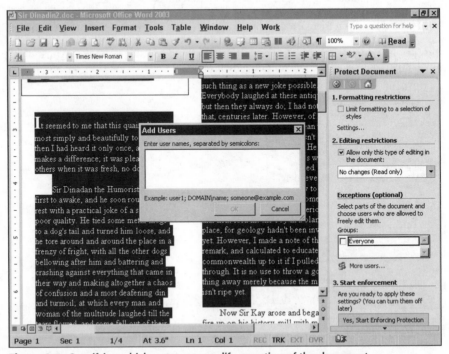

Figure A-3: Specifying which users can modify a portion of the document.

The benefit to this feature, of course, is that you can make sure that a particular user can make changes only to a limited portion of the document, rather than the entire document. This makes later reconciliation of various edits easier.

Rights Management

Word 2003 also takes advantage of the new Windows Rights Management system (available for networks using Windows 2003 Server) to help you protect sensitive documents. If you choose File ➪ Permission, you can utilize the Rights Management system to limit the ways in which documents can be forwarded (via e-mail), edited, or copied.

Cross-Reference You can find more information on the Windows Rights Management system by visiting the Microsoft Web site (www.microsoft.com) and searching for the term *Windows Rights Management*. You can also turn to Chapter 34 to learn more about this system.

Editing and Collaboration Improvements

Word 2003 includes several new features that are designed to help you edit documents easier and to collaborate with others who may be responsible for the same document. The following sections examine these improvements.

Word Count Toolbar

The Word Count feature has been available in Word for some time. You can find out a word count for either a selection or the entire document by choosing Tools ➪ Word Count.

Beginning in Word 2002, Microsoft introduced the Word Count toolbar. This toolbar allows you to easily obtain word counts without the need to access the menus. You can also see other document statistics (such as characters, lines, pages, and paragraphs) by using the drop-down list on the toolbar. Figure A-4 shows the statistics available through the Word Count toolbar.

Cross-Reference Turn to Chapter 7 to find out more about the Word Count toolbar.

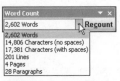

Figure A-4: The Word Count toolbar.

Improved Editing and Comments

It is not unusual for multiple people to work on a single document. Different people bring different responsibilities and areas of expertise to bear on a document, all with the hope of producing a final product that reflects the collective experience of the group.

Word has long provided tools designed to be used in creating such "team" documents. Perhaps the most prominent tools in this area are Track Changes and Comments. Word 2002 introduced some extensive changes to these tools. Most notably, changes and comments appeared as "balloons" at the side of the document, with markings showing the text to which the changes applied. Some people loved this new approach, whereas others hated it.

Cross-Reference Turn to Chapter 29 to learn much more about using comments and track changes.

Despite the mixed reception these changes received in Word 2002, the same approach is carried forward in Word 2003, but with some improvements. Word can now track more types of document changes, and the display of change/comment balloons can be limited or completely turned off, if desired. To reflect the greater flexibility available in these tools, the Reviewing toolbar has been modified to allow complete access to configuration settings for all types of document markup.

In addition to these improvements, the Reviewing toolbar includes a new tool that allows you to insert voice comments, as desired.

The Research Task Pane

If your writing demands that you do a lot of online research, you already know that it can be bothersome to switch back and forth between Word and your Web browser. Recognizing this, Word 2003 includes a new Research task pane that allows you to search information on the Web without leaving the familiar Word interface. Simply choose Tools ⇨ Research to display the Research task pane.

Note The Research task pane doesn't search the Web in the traditional sense of the word. Instead, it connects with online resources specifically designed for use with the Microsoft Office 2003 products through the Research task pane. As more and more such resources become available, they are made available through this one convenient location.

In addition to enabling a user to search the Web, the Research task pane provides access to other tools, such as a thesaurus, translation services, and financial information. Because the resources available through the task pane can change over time, you will periodically want to reacquaint yourself with what the Research task pane has to offer.

Cross-Reference See Chapter 8 to learn more about working with the new Research task pane.

Using Shared Workspaces

If your office is taking advantage of the Microsoft SharePoint services, you can create shared workspaces in Word. These workspaces enable you to collaboratively work on documents with other users, in real time. In such an environment, Word interfaces seamlessly with Windows instant messaging so that you can communicate with others working on the document.

Cross-Reference Chapter 30 provides more details about using SharePoint Team Services and other collaboration tools.

Shared workspaces are created and managed by choosing Tools ⇨ Shared Workspaces. Word then displays the Shared Workspaces task pane, where you can start exchanging information with others on your development team.

Other Changes

A number of other changes have been made in Word 2003. Some of these changes affect the way that Word behaves behind the scenes, and typically won't concern users—these changes are largely transparent to users. (If you are a developer or programmer, however, these changes will be of interest, and you should at least be aware of them.)

XML and Smart Documents

Perhaps the biggest change in Word 2003 is in the area of XML support. Word 2003 supports XML as a native file format and can be used to directly edit XML files.

Cross-Reference   Chapter 27 provides greater detail on the XML features new to Word.

Closely related to Word's XML support is the concept of *Smart Documents*. Developers can create special Word documents that rely on XML content to automatically take action based on what you, as a user, do within the document. For example, a Smart Document could prompt you for a customer name and then automatically pull the customer's information from a database and fill in the document based on the characteristics of that customer.

As you navigate through a Smart Document, the document itself detects the location of your cursor and displays relevant information in the task pane. It might display some context-sensitive action you can perform, a word or two of help, suggested content, or links to data or related information.

A Smart Document is not really an end-user feature. Programmers can create Smart Documents for use within a company, for example, and distribute them in templates via e-mail, on a company intranet, or on a Web site. A discussion of how to create a Smart Document is beyond the scope of this book. However, you'll probably be seeing Smart Documents appearing on the scene soon, as developers discover various ways to use them. In the meantime, you can get a taste of what they are all about by reading about Smart Tags, a feature that is part of the Smart Document suite of tools.

Cross-Reference   Turn to Chapter 23 to find out more about using Smart Tags.

Electronic Postage Support

If you use Word to create envelopes, you can utilize one or more of the online electronic postage services, such as Stamps.com. These services allow you to print valid postage right on the envelopes, making it much easier to mail your items.

Cross-Reference   See Chapter 6 to find out more about using electronic postage.

To take advantage of electronic postage services, examine the Envelopes and Labels dialog box (Tools ➪ Letters and Mailings ➪ Envelopes and Labels). A new Add Electronic Postage check box enables you to specify whether postage should be added to your envelopes. In addition, you can click the E-Postage Properties button to modify how postage is applied.

Note   The first time you click E-Postage Properties, Word will let you know that you need to download and install electronic postage software before you can use the feature. You can then visit the Microsoft Web site to discover what services are compatible with Word and to sign up for the services.

Summary

Word is never a static program, but is constantly improving. Each new version offers changes to old features and entirely new tools. Trying to keep tabs on all the new improvements can be quite a chore. This appendix was designed to help you become familiar with what's new in Word. Not every new feature or improvement is listed here, but the major ones are. (And now you have a "starting point" of where to look for the newest features.)

This appendix covered the following items:

- ✦ The task pane is an integral part of Word that allows you to easily access resources related to what you are doing.

- ✦ Word 2003 allows you to lock documents so that people cannot use any formatting except the styles you allow.

- ✦ You can protect a document so that only certain people can change certain areas of the document.

- ✦ Word 2003 will work directly with Windows 2003 Server's WRM (Windows Rights Management) technology.

- ✦ Word 2003 provides new ways to mark up your document and different ways to configure what you see on-screen.

- ✦ The Research task pane allows you to access, in a single location, a wide range of tools—including searching the Web.

- ✦ Shared workspaces allow multiple people to work on the same document at the same time.

- ✦ Word now treats XML as a native file format and allows developers to create Smart Documents that provide context-sensitive development tools.

- ✦ When creating envelopes, Word works with electronic postage programs to print postage on your envelopes.

✦   ✦   ✦

What's on the CD-ROM

This appendix provides you with information on the contents of the CD that accompanies this book. For the latest and greatest information, please refer to the ReadMe file located at the root of the CD.

This appendix provides information on the following topics:

✦ System Requirements

✦ Using the CD

✦ Files and software on the CD

✦ Troubleshooting

System Requirements

Make sure that your computer meets the minimum system requirements listed in this section. If your computer doesn't match up to most of these requirements, you may have a problem using the contents of the CD.

For Windows 9*x*, Me, XP, Windows 2000, Windows NT4 (with SP 4 or later):

✦ PC with a Pentium processor running at 120 Mhz or faster

✦ At least 32MB of total RAM installed on your computer; for best performance, we recommend at least 64MB

✦ Ethernet network interface card (NIC) or modem with a speed of at least 28,800 bps

✦ A CD-ROM drive

Office 2003 Specific Requirements:

✦ PC with Pentium 133 MHz or higher processor; Pentium III recommended

✦ Microsoft Windows 2000 with Service Pack 3 or Windows XP or later operating system.

✦ Minimum 245MB hard drive space.

✦ Minimum 64MB RAM (128MB recommended)

Using the CD

To install the items from the CD to your hard drive, follow these steps:

1. Insert the CD into your computer's CD-ROM drive.

2. A window appears displaying the License Agreement. Press Accept to continue. Another window appears with the following buttons (which are explained in greater detail in the next section):

Word 2003 Bible: Click this button to view an eBook version of the book as well as any author-created content specific to the book, such as templates and sample files.

Super Bible: Click this button to view an electronic version of the *Office 2003 Super Bible*, along with any author-created materials from the Super Bible, such as templates and sample files.

Bonus Software: Click this button to view the list and install the supplied third-party software.

Related Links: Click this button to open a hyperlinked page of Web sites.

Other Resources: Click this button to access other Office-related products that you might find useful.

Files and Software on the CD

The following sections provide more details about the software and other materials available on the CD.

eBook version of *Word 2003 Bible*

The complete text of the book you hold in your hands is provided on the CD in Adobe's Portable Document Format (PDF). You can read and quickly search the content of this PDF file by using Adobe's Acrobat Reader, also included on the CD.

eBook version of the *Office 2003 Super Bible*

The *Super Bible* is an eBook PDF file made up of select chapters pulled from the individual Office 2003 *Bible* titles. This eBook also includes some original and exclusive content found only in this *Super Bible*. The products that make up the Microsoft Office 2003 suite have been created to work hand-in-hand. Consequently, Wiley has created this *Super Bible* to help you master some of the most common features of each of the component products and to learn about some of their interoperability features as well. This *Super Bible* consists of more than 500 pages of content to showcase how Microsoft Office 2003 components work together.

Bonus software

The CD contains software distributed in various forms: shareware, freeware, GNU software, trials, demos, and evaluation versions. The following list explains how these software versions differ:

✦ **Shareware programs:** Fully functional, trial versions of copyrighted programs. If you like particular programs, you can register with their authors for a nominal fee and receive licenses, enhanced versions, and technical support.

✦ **Freeware programs:** Copyrighted games, applications, and utilities that are free for personal use. Unlike shareware, these programs do not require a fee or provide technical support.

✦ **GNU software:** Software governed by its own license, which is included inside the folder of the GNU product. See the GNU license for more details.

✦ **Trial, demo, or evaluation versions:** Software usually limited either by time or functionality, such as not permitting you to save projects. Some trial versions are very sensitive to system date changes. If you alter your computer's date, the programs may "time out" and will no longer be functional.

Software highlights

Here are descriptions of just a few of the programs available on the CD:

✦ ***Business Card Creator:*** *From AMF. Shareware.* Lets you save time and money by making your own full-color, one- or two-sided business or appointment cards—in the style you like and in just the quantity you need.

✦ ***CD Case & Label Creator:*** *From AMF. Shareware.* Enables you to create professional-looking CD and DVD jewel cases and labels in just minutes. Lets you add your own logos and graphics.

✦ ***SuperFax:*** *From AMF. Shareware.* A Word add-on that provides an easy-to-use interface that lets you simply and quickly fax documents with just the click of a button.

✦ ***PerformX Designer:*** *From Systemik Solutions. Trial version.* Software that lets your organization establish corporate documentation standards. Enables you to designate particular fonts, headers, footers, and other formatting and to generate a template that you can provide to your authors to help enforce your documentation standards.

Comprehensive list of software

Here is a list of all the products available on the CD. For more information and a description of each product, see the Bonus Software section of the CD.

"The Wonderful World of Excel"	3D Charts for Excel	A1 "Bible Sounds"
Acc Compact	Access Form Resizer	Access Image Albums
Access Property Editor	Access to VB Object Converter	AccessBooks
AccessBooks Updater	AccessViewer	AccVerify
ACDSee	Acrobat Reader	AcroWizard
Action Process Automator	ActiveConverter Component	ActiveDocs 2002
Advanced Disk Catalog	Advanced Office Password Recovery	All-in-1 Personal Organizer

Analyse-It

appBuilder

Application Builder/
Application Generator

appWatcher

Attach for Outlook

Attachment Options

AutoSpell for Microsoft Office

B2BDataBus

BadBlue Prsnl Ed

Barcode ActiveX Control & DLL

BlackICE PC Protection

Business Card Creator

Business Forms Library Sampler

c:JAM

CaBook

Camtasia Studio

Capture Express

CD Case & Label Creator

CD Player

Change Management System

Charset Decoding

Check Writer

Classify for Outlook

ClipMate

Code 128 Fonts demo with VBA

Code Critter

Collage Complete

Colored Toolbar Icons

COM Explorer

CompareDataWiz 2002

CompareWiz 2002

CONTACT Sage

Convert Cell Reference
Utility

Cool Combo Box Techniques

Crossword Compiler

CS School Themes

CSE HTML Validator

CSE HTML Validator Pro

Data Analysis

Data Flow Manager, Adv Ed

Data Flow Manager, Stnd Ed

Data Loader

Data Wiz

Database

Database Browser Plus

Database Password Sniffer

DataDict

Datahouse

DataMoxie

DataWiz 2002

DB Companion

DBSync

Debt Anaylzer

DeskTop.VBA

Dialgo Personal Call Center App

Dictation 2002

Digital Juice

DinkIT Listbar AX

Directory Lister

DoctoHtml

Document Management

Drag and View

Drag and Zip

Drag-N-Dropper

Dubit

DynaZIP MAX

EasyT 2000

eForms Word Templates &
Forms

El Scripto

Eliminate Spam!

eNavigator Suite

Excel Import Assistant

Excel Link

Excel Tetris

Executive Accounting

ExLife

ExSign

EZ Access Developer's
Tool Suite

Fax4Outlook

FileBox eXtender

Filter Builder

Fontlister

Fort Knox

Fundraising Mentor

Gantt Chart Builder (Access)	Gantt Chart Builder (Excel)	Gif Movie Gear
GraphicsButton	GuruNet	HiddenFileDetector_addin
HtmlIndex	HyperCam	HyperSnap-DX
IdiomaX Office Translator	IT Commander	JustAddCommerce
Keyboard Express	Lark	Macro Express
Macro Magic	MailWasher Pro	Math Easy for Excel
Mathematical Summary Utility	MathEQ Expression Editor	Mdb2txt
Mouse Over Effects	MultiNetwork Manager	Office Report Builder
OfficeBalloonX	OfficeRecovery Enterprise	OfficeSpy
Outcome XP	OutlookSpy	Paint Shop Pro
PDF Plain Text Extractor	PerformX Designer with Author	PhotoSpin Image Sampler
PlanMagic Business	PlanMagic Finance Pro	PlanMagic Marketing
PlanMagic WebQuest	PocketKnife	Polar Draw Component
Polar Spellchecker Component	Power File Gold	Power Utility Pak
PowerPoint Backgrounds	PrettyCode.Print	PrintDirect Anywhere
PrintDirect Utility	PROMODAG StoreLog	QDocs
Recover My Files	Registry Crawler	ReplaceWiz 2002
Responsive Time Logger	RFFlow	RnR PPTools Starter Set
Scan to Outlook	Schedule XP	Screen Capture
Secrets Keeper	SetClock	SetFileDate
ShortKeys	ShrinkerStretcher	Signature995
SimpleRegistry Control	Smart Login	Smart Online templates
SmartBoardXP	SmartDraw	SnagIt
Soft Graphics Buttons	Splitter for Access	StoreBot 2002 Stnd Ed
Style Builder	Summary Wizard	SuperFax
TelePort Pro	The <WebSite> Promotion SuiteT 2003	Toolbar Doubler
TPH Office Batch Printer	Turbo Browser	TX Text Control
Ulead Gif Animator	UltraPdf	VBAcodePrint
Virtual Check Solutions for Word	Wave To Text	WebCompiler

WebMerge	WebSpice Animation sampler	WebSpice Objects
WinACE	WinFax Pro Automator	WinRAR
WinZIP	Word Link	Wordware 2002
Wordware PIM	WordWeb	WS_FTP Pro
WS_Ping Propack	XLSTAT-Pro	Zip Code Companion
ZIP Disk Jewel Case and Label Creator	Zip Express	Zip Repair

Related Links

Check out this page for links to all the third-party software vendors included on the CD, plus links to other vendors and resources that can help you work more productively with Office 2003.

Other Resources

This page provides you with some additional handy Office-related products.

ReadMe file

The ReadMe contains the complete descriptions of every piece of bonus software on the CD, as well as other important information about the CD.

Troubleshooting

If you have difficulty installing or using any of the materials on the companion CD, try the following solutions:

+ **Turn off any anti-virus software that you may have running.** Installers sometimes mimic virus activity and can make your computer incorrectly believe that it is being infected by a virus. (Be sure to turn the anti-virus software back on later.)

+ **Close all running programs.** The more programs you're running, the less memory is available to other programs. Installers also typically update files and programs; if you keep other programs running, installation may not work properly.

+ **Reference the ReadMe.** Please refer to the ReadMe file located at the root of the CD-ROM for the latest product information at the time of publication.

If you still have trouble with the CD, please call the Wiley Product Technical Support phone number: (800) 762-2974. Outside the United States, call 1 (317) 572-3994. You can also contact www.wiley.com/techsupport. Wiley Publishing, Inc. will provide technical support only for installation and other general quality control items; for technical support on the applications themselves, consult the program's vendor or author. To place additional orders or to request information about other Wiley products, please call (800)225-5945 or visit www.wiley.com.

✦   ✦   ✦

Index

Symbols

& (ampersand character), accelerator key editing, 777
\# (number sign) placeholder, number format, 614
; (semicolon) placeholder, number format, 614
0 (zero) placeholder, number format, 614
3-D toolbar, shadowed lines/shapes, 473–474

A

About Microsoft Word Help, program information, 34
accelerator keys, menu commands, 777
action fields, 590
actions
    duplicating, 123
    File Search task pane, 216
    redoing last undone (Ctrl+Y), 54
    repeating character formatting, 104
    undoing/repeating, 23, 54, 105
active shapes, deleting, 469
ActiveX controls
    COM (Component Object Model) foundation, 521
    form addition, 621
Add Help Text button, form field help text, 619–620
Add Network Place Wizard, 727
Add or Remove Buttons, Standard command, 79
Add/Delete Word(s) dialog box, 431
address book, merges, 570
address files, merge element, 557–558
addresses
    EnvelopeAddress bookmark, 323
    EnvelopeReturn bookmark, 323
adjacent files, selection methods, 195
Adobe Acrobat Reader, versus printing to a file, 174–175
Adobe Acrobat toolbar, hiding/displaying, 738
Adobe Illustrator, vector art, 509
Adobe Photoshop
    bitmap graphics, 437
    decreasing colors, 510
    image editor, 505
Adobe Type Manager, PostScript Type 1 font management, 109–110, 117–118
Advanced File Search task pane, 217–218
Advanced Layout dialog box
    picture position options, 459–460
    text wrapping options, 457
AGFA Compugraphic, ATT fonts, 110
algorithms, encryption, 802–803

aliased edges, avoiding when converting vector to bitmap graphic, 509
Alien Skin Software
    Eye Candy, 506
    Xenofex, 506
Align or Distribute menu, text boxes, 487–488
alignments
    justified, 414–415
    Microsoft Equation, 552–553
    page formatting, 298–299
    paragraph formatting, 125–126, 414–415
    table positioning, 259, 271
    table text, 270
    WordArt text, 493
All Caps (Ctrl+Shift+A), character formatting 98–99
All Programs menu, Word startup, 3
Allow Fast Saves, disabling to enhance performance, 743
Alt key
    column width adjustments, 265
    keyboard/command selections, 22
    menu access method, 8
ampersand character (&), accelerator key editing, 777
anchors
    hiding/displaying, 461
    objects, 460–461
animated GIFs (GIF89a) file format
    uses, 513
    Web pages, 656–657
animated text, document design guidelines, 422
Animation Shop, animated GIFs, 513
animations
    character formatting, 101–102
    Office Assistant, 35
annotation marks, hidden text, 114
announcements, SharePoint service, 718
ANSI character code, finding/replacing special characters, 85–87
ANSI character set
    character code insertion, 64–65
    symbols, 63–64
ANSIValue macro, code display, 797–799
anti-aliasing, fonts, 117
antonyms, thesaurus uses, 242–243
appearance
    bold text, 421
    colored text, 421
    document design, 412–413

Continued

appearance *(continued)*
    image considerations, 421–422
    italic text, 421
    serif versus sans serif typefaces, 417–418
    typesetting characters, 419–420
    underline text, 421
    white space enhancement, 416
applications
    CD-ROM, 822–827
    compatibility options, 761–763
arguments, field instruction element, 591–592
Arial, sans serif typeface, 417–418
arrow cursor, mouse pointer shape, 21
Arrow Style button, drawing arrowheads, 471–472
Arrow Styles menu, drawing arrowheads, 471–472
arrowheads, drawing, 471–472
ASCII text file format, 527
asd (AutoRecovery) file extension, 207
aspect ratio, picture sizing, 449
attachments
    e-mail, 687–683
    macro to form field, 618–619
    template, 397
attributes, HTML tags, 663–664
audio clips, uses, 514
Auto FX, digital watermark utility, 513
AutoCaption, caption addition, 500–501
AutoCaption dialog box, 500–501
AutoCorrect
    adding entries, 237
    versus AutoText, 67
    changing/deleting entries, 70
    disabling, 71
    editing/deleting entries, 238–239
    entry length limitations, 68
    entry naming conventions, 68
    exceptions, 238
    predefined entries, 68
    Smart Tags, 605–607
    text entry conventions, 41, 67–68
    troubleshooting, 739–740
    typesetting characters, 420
    uses, 236–237
AutoCorrect Exceptions dialog box, 238–239
AutoCorrect Options button, 70–71
AutoCorrect pop-up menu, 239
AutoFit, column width adjustments, 266–267
AutoFormat
    hyperlinks, 655
    text entry conventions, 41
    troubleshooting, 739–740
    uses, 383

AutoFormat As You Type
    hyperlinks, 655
    indent settings, 138
    typesetting characters, 419
AutoFormat dialog box
    option settings, 386–388
    reviewing changes, 385–386
    revision marks, 386
    style application, 384–385
automatic date/time, document insertion, 45
automatic hyphenation, uses, 159–160
automatic links, link update method, 530–532
automatic macros, 791–792
automatic pagination, Print Preview mode, 171–172
automatic word selection, enabling/disabling, 51
AutoNew macro, uses, 791
AutoRecover, 207–210, 745
AutoShapes
    adding to a text box, 481
    callouts, 496–498
    drawing curves/freeform shapes, 472–473
    object drawing, 470–471
    object editing, 475
AutoShapes, Basic Shapes command, 473
AutoShapes, Callouts command, 496
AutoShapes, Lines command, 471
AutoShapes toolbar, 470
AutoSummarize dialog box, uses, 212–214
AutoText
    versus AutoCorrect, 67
    duplicating section formatting, 285
    editing/deleting entries, 73–74
    header/footer text entry, 307–308
    inserting, 72–73
    keyboard shortcut support, 782
    printing entries, 74, 166
    renaming entries, 74
    template component, 391
    template entries, 400–401
    text entry conventions, 41, 71
AutoText toolbar, AutoText entry insertion, 73
axes, chart elements, 545, 547

B

background colors, 145, 699
background repagination, page formatting, 297–298
Background Sound dialog box, 514, 676–677
background sounds, inserting, 514
backgrounds
    colors, 312
    document design guidelines, 422
    images, 312–314

patterns, 312–314
textures, 313–314
transparent, 453–454, 511–512
watermarks, 315–316
Web page enhancements, 655–656
backslash (\) character, index entry conventions, 341
Backspace key, 469, 481
backups, files, 210
balanced columns, column formatting, 291–292
balloons, comment, 699
banners, scrolling text, 677
bar tabs, 131–132
barcodes, envelope printing, 180, 572
BASIC (Beginner's All-Purpose Symbolic Instruction Code), 796
Basic Shapes submenu, drawing basic shapes, 473
Batch Conversion Wizard, 203
bitmap graphics
    file format, 527
    pixels, 437
    versus vector graphics, 437–438
Bitstream, BT fonts, 110
blacklining, 710
blank (new) document, creating, 29
Blank Document template, described, 391
body text
    defined, 369
    font sizing guidelines, 420
    serif typeface advantages, 417–418
boilerplate text, template component, 390
Bold button (Ctrl+B), character formatting, 95
bold text, document design guidelines, 421
boldface text (Ctrl+B), character formatting, 95
Bookmark dialog box, 318–319
bookmarks
    broken link concerns, 322
    calculation uses, 323
    content placement, 322
    cross-reference problems, 323–324
    cross-reference support, 325, 326
    displaying/hiding, 319, 320
    EnvelopeAddress, 323
    EnvelopeReturn, 323
    field instruction element, 592–593
    form field assignment, 619
    index page range conventions, 342
    insertion methods, 318–319
    macro uses, 787
    moving/copying/deleting, 321–322
    naming conventions, 319
    navigating between, 320–321
    printing non-support, 319

problem issues, 323–324
SharePoint documents, 724
sorting, 320
supported views, 319
table, 280
uses, 318
viewing, 319–320
Border and Shading Options dialog box, 143, 302
borders
    Borders and Shading dialog box, 141–143
    described, 139–140
    document design guidelines, 422
    document formatting, 301–302
    fitting within a margin, 144
    individual lines, 143
    pictures, 449–451
    removing/changing, 144–145
    shadow, 451
    tables, 273
    Tables and Borders toolbar, 140–141
    text spacing, 143
    Web page enhancements, 655–656
Borders and Shading dialog box, 141–143, 146, 301–302
bracket characters, fields, 306–307
Break dialog box, 284–285
Break Side by Side button, document comparison, 711
brightness, image adjustments, 453
broken links, deleted bookmark concerns, 322
Browse Object button, document navigation method, 16
bulleted lists
    fonts, 149
    picture insertion, 150
    reordering list positions, 150
    special characters, 150
    style editing, 149
    uses, 148
bullets
    document design guidelines, 422
    Web page enhancements, 655–656
Bullets and Numbering dialog box, 148
Button Editor dialog box, 774–775
buttons
    adding to toolbars, 12, 79, 771–772
    deleting from toolbars, 772
    Drawing toolbar, 467–469
    editing, 773–775
    form options, 669–670
    Formatting toolbar, 12–13
    Forms toolbar, 611–612
    Frames toolbar, 649
    macro assignment, 788
    Mail Merge toolbar, 569–570

Continued

buttons *(continued)*
  Master Document, 634–635
  moving/copying to toolbars, 772
  Online Meeting toolbar, 728–729
  Outlining, 628–629
  restoring toolbars to default state, 12, 773
  Standard toolbar, 9–12
  Web Discussions toolbar, 725–727
  Web toolbar, 658
  Web Tools toolbar, 666–667
  WordArt toolbar, 491–492
  WordMail toolbar, 689–690
By Author, default color selections, 760

C

calculation field, forms, 612, 616
calculations
  bookmark uses, 323
  column needs, 288
  tables, 278
Calendar Wizard, 403–404
calendars, SharePoint service, 718
callouts, objects, 496–498
Cancel button, versus Close button, 21
Canvas toolbar, 466–467
capital letters, drop caps, 99
Caption dialog box, 281, 498–499
Caption Numbering dialog box, 503
captions
  AutoCaption, 500–501
  chapter numbers, 503–504
  cross-references support, 325
  deleting, 502
  direct entry, 498–500
  Equation label, 502
  Figure label, 502
  labels, 499–500, 502
  numbering styles, 503
  objects, 498–504
  style selections, 502
  Table label, 502
  table of figures, 358–360
  tables, 280–281
  updating, 501
case conversion, format field switch (*) , 598
catalogs, mail merges, 574–575
category, chart element, 545
CD key, installation information display, 736
CD-ROM
  accessing, 822
  GIF Animator, 513
  Paint Shop Pro, 505

  ReadMe file, 827
  software components, 822–827
  system requirements, 821
  technical support, 827
  troubleshooting, 827
Cell Options dialog box, 268
cells
  copying/moving, 264–265
  Datasheet window entry conventions, 541–542
  deleting Datasheet data, 543
  functions, 594
  inserting in Datasheet window, 543
  inserting/deleting, 263–264
  margin settings, 267–268
  merging/splitting, 271–272
  numbering, 277
  spacing adjustments, 267–268
  text alignments, 270
  text orientation, 270–271
center alignment
  paragraph formatting, 125–126
  table positioning, 259
center-aligned tabs, 131
Certificate dialog box, digital signatures, 809
certification authorities, digital signatures, 808–809
CGI (Common Gateway Interface), form processing
    script, 672
Change Button Image command, 773–774
Change Case dialog box, 108
Change Icon dialog box, displaying embedded object
    as an icon, 523
Change Text Direction button, Tables and Borders
    toolbar, 270
chapter numbers, captions, 503–504
chapters, help system, 36
character codes
  inserting, 64–65
  versus shortcut keys, 65
character formatting
  All Caps (Ctrl+Shift+A), 98–99
  application methods, 93–102
  applied at cursor position, 95
  boldface text (Ctrl+B), 95
  case changes, 108
  character pair spacing, 107
  character spacing, 106–107
  colors, 99–100
  copying with Format Painter (Ctrl+Shift+C), 104
  default font adjustments, 113
  display methods, 102–104
  displaying/hiding text, 113–114
  double underline (Ctrl+Shift+D), 96

drop caps, 99
embossed text, 100
engraved text, 100
finding/replacing, 87–90
font size/styles, 108–113
format field switch (*), 597–598
highlighting text, 105–106
index entries, 344
italicized text (Ctrl+I), 96
outlined text, 101
repeating, 104
Reveal Formatting task pane, 102–104
shadowed text, 101
shortcut keys, 89
Small Caps (Ctrl+Shift+K), 99
strikethrough text, 100
style application methods, 372–373
subscripts (Ctrl+=), 97–98
superscripts (Ctrl+Shift+=), 97–98
text animations, 101–102
underlined text (Ctrl+U), 96–97
undoing, 105
character pairs, spacing adjustments, 107
character spacing, character formatting, 106–107
Character styles
copying styles between documents, 380
described, 368
characters
ANSI character set, 63–64
document naming restrictions, 32
field element, 591
nonprinting display, 39, 42–43
text markers, 78
Chart, Chart Options command, 547
Chart, Chart Type command, 546
chart formatting, methods, 548
Chart Options dialog box, 547–548
Chart Type button, chart type selection, 545–546
Chart Type dialog box, 546
charts
axes, 547
data exclusion, 546–547
data labels, 548
elements, 544–545
formatting methods, 548
gridlines, 547
importing data from Excel, 549–550
legends, 547
organization, 494–496
table conversion, 549
titles, 547
types, 545–546

Check Box Form Field Options dialog box, 617
check boxes
dialog box element, 20
form element, 617, 669
citations, tables of authorities, 360–361
classes, HTML styles, 665
Clear Formatting command, 369
click and type, paragraph insertion, 127
clip art, 422. See also graphics; images; pictures
ClipArt task pane, 441–445, 470–471
document design guidelines, 422
sources, 439–440
ClipArt Gallery, free clip art sources, 440
ClipArt task pane
accessing from AutoShapes menu, 470–471
Clip Art on Microsoft.com link, 445
inserting pictures/clipart, 441–443
Microsoft Clip Organizer, 443–445
Clipboard
copying styles between documents, 380
copying/moving text boxes, 483
copying/pasting pictures into documents, 446
copying/pasting table data into Datasheet window, 549
cutting/copying/pasting text, 55
cutting/pasting pictures, 441
moving/copying Datasheet data, 543
moving/copying lines or shapes, 477
moving/copying selections, 57–59
saving contents when exiting Word, 55
Clipboard Contents, finding/replacing graphics and text, 87
clocks, automatic date/time insertion, 45
Close button
versus Cancel button, 21
exiting Word properly, 39
CodeStyle macro, uses, 794
collaboration
document protection methods, 801–807
Word Count toolbar, 817
collated copies, printing, 165
Collection folder, Microsoft Clip Organizer, 444–445
colon (:) character
index entry conventions, 341
multilevel index entries, 343
colors
background, 312
By Author preference settings, 760
character formatting, 99–100
comments, 105, 699
document design guidelines, 421
heading appearance enhancement, 421

Continued

colors *(continued)*
- highlighting text, 105–106, 704
- line drawings, 469–470
- monitor display settings, 507–508
- picture borders, 450
- print suggestions, 167–168
- shading, 145–146
- transparent backgrounds, 453–454
- Web page enhancements, 655–656

column breaks, column formatting, 291

column formatting
- application methods, 287–288
- breaking a column, 291
- column creation methods, 286–287
- column needs calculations, 288
- length adjustments, 291–292
- navigation methods, 288
- newspaper-style columns, 286–291
- removing columns, 290
- spacing adjustments, 289–290
- text editing, 288–289
- text entry conventions, 288–289
- vertical lines, 289
- width adjustments, 289–290

column titles, Datasheet window element, 540–541

columns
- chart data exclusion, 546–547
- copying/moving, 264–265
- Datasheet window element, 540–541
- font sizing guidelines, 420
- inserting in Datasheet window, 543
- inserting/deleting, 263–264
- justified text issues, 414
- status bar information element, 17
- table headings, 272
- table limitations, 253
- text box placement, 487–488
- width adjustments, 265–267

Columns button, Standard toolbar, 286

Columns dialog box, 287–288

COM (Component Object Model), OLE development history, 521

command button, dialog box element, 20–21

commas, serial, 234

comments
- background colors, 699
- balloon display, 699
- comparing/merging, 710–711
- deleting, 700, 701
- editing, 701–704
- editing enhancements, 817–818
- globally deleting, 701
- handwritten pen, 700
- hidden text, 114
- highlighted text, 105–106
- highlighting, 704
- macro application, 794
- moving/copying, 701
- navigation techniques, 702
- printing, 166, 704
- responding to, 701–702
- reviewer initials, 698
- reviewing, 702–703
- Reviewing toolbar, 698–699
- searches, 702–703
- showing/hiding, 699–700
- switching to Reviewing pane, 698
- text formatting, 701–702
- uses, 697
- voice, 700–701

commercial clip art, sources, 439–440

Common Gateway Interface (CGI), 672

comparison operators, merge query, 579

Compatibility tab, Options dialog box, 761–763

compiling
- indexes, 345–346
- table of contents, 352
- table of figures, 358–360
- tables of authorities, 360–363

Component Object Model (COM), OLE, 521

Compress Pictures dialog box, 452–453

compression, image, 509–510

concordance file
- automatic index entry marking, 338–340
- copying/pasting text, 339
- index entry conventions, 337–340
- multilevel index entries, 343

condensed text, character spacing, 106–107

contact lists, SharePoint service, 718

contents, removing from Datasheet cells, 543

contiguous items, selection methods, 51–52

continuation separator lines, footnotes/endnotes, 333–334

contrast, image adjustments, 453

Control Toolbox, adding ActiveX control to a form, 621

Convert dialog box, 512, 529

Convert File dialog box, 191

Convert Notes dialog box, 333

Convert Table to Text dialog box, 276

Convert Text to Table dialog box, 275

Copy button, 55

copyright, image protection methods, 513

Corbis, stock photography source, 440–441
CorelDRAW
    converting picture to Word picture format, 512
    OLE support, 439
    vector art, 509
corrupted files, troubleshooting, 745
crashes, AutoRecover, 207–210
Create New Folder button, 196
Cross-reference dialog box, 325–326
cross-references
    bookmarks, 323–324, 326
    index conventions, 342–343
    in-document, 325–326
    information types, 326–328
    supported items, 324–325
    updating, 326
Ctrl key
    column width adjustments, 265
    keyboard/command selections, 22
    line drawing uses, 471
    nonadjacent file selections, 196
    noncontiguous selections, 52
current date field, forms, 612, 615
current time field, forms, 612, 615
cursors
    Equation positioning, 551–552
    I-beam, 7
    insertion point, 7
    mouse pointer shapes, 21
    table navigation, 260
Curve tool, drawing curved lines, 473
curves, 472–473, 476
Custom Dictionaries dialog box, 229–231
custom dictionary, uses, 229–231
custom styles, table of contents assembly, 354–355
custom toolbars, creating/editing, 775–776
Customer Service Improvement Program, privacy, 34
Customize Bulleted List dialog box, 149–150
Customize dialog box
    Options tab, 778–779
    toolbar display settings, 736–737
    toolbar options, 770–771
Customize Keyboard dialog box, 66, 781–782
Customize Numbered List dialog box, 152–153
Customize Outline Numbered List dialog box, 155–156
Cut button, 55
CuteFTP, FTP tool, 660

D
data, embedded object display, 522
Data, Exclude Row/Col command, 547

Data, Include Row/Col command, 547
data formatting, Datasheet window, 544
data labels, charts, 548
data marker, chart element, 544
data points, chart element, 544–545
data series, chart element, 544
data tables, charts, 548
Database dialog box, inserting Access data, 535–536
Database toolbar, inserting Access data, 534–536
databases, 557–559
Datasheet window
    closing/reopening, 542
    copying/pasting table data, 549
    data entry conventions, 541–542
    data formatting, 544
    deleting data, 543
    expanding/collapsing, 541
    inserting data, 543–544
    keyboard navigation, 542
    moving/copying data, 543
    resizing columns/rows, 541
    screen elements, 540–541
    selection methods, 542–543
    versus spreadsheet, 542
Date and Time dialog box, 44–45
date field, 317, 612, 614–615
dates, document insertion, 44–45
date-time picture field switch (\@), uses, 601–603
decimal tabs, 131
Decrease Indent button, 136
Delete Cells dialog box, 263–264
Delete dialog box, deleting Datasheet data, 543
Delete key
    active shapes, 469
    removing a text box, 481
    selected text/graphics, 53–54
deleted text, By Author color preferences, 760
Design Science, Inc., MathType, 551
desktop
    adding a document to, 192–193
    document scraps, 61
    document shortcuts, 6
    shortcut placement, 4
Desktop button, Open dialog box, 190
desktop publishing, versus word processors, 411–412
destination file, linked objects, 519–520
Details view, file display, 5
Detect and Repair dialog box, 745–746
Detect and Repair utility, 34
device independent bitmap file format, 527
dialog boxes, 18–21

dictation
    adding/deleting words, 431
    problem solving, 430–431
    speech recognition, 429–432
    voice commands, 430
Dictation button, Language bar, 429
dictionary
    checking spelling/grammar as you type, 223–224
    custom, 229–231
    exclude, 231
    Research task pane, 242–243
    supported spell check languages, 227
Digimarc
    ImageBridge, 513
    MarcSpider service, 513
digital cameras, picture insertion method, 446
Digital Signature dialog box, 808
digital signatures, passwords, 808–809
digital watermarks, image protection method, 513
dimmed (unavailable) command display, 21
directories
    folder path options, 763–764
    mail merges, 574–575
discussion groups, SharePoint service, 718
Disk Cleanup, hard disk free space recovery, 747
Disk Defragmenter, Word performance
            enhancement, 742
display drivers, troubleshooting, 746
Display Properties dialog box, 507–508
Distribute Rows Evenly button, 269
doc (Word document) file extension, 32
document design
    bold text, 421
    clip art, 422
    colors, 421
    image considerations, 421–422
    italic text, 421
    layout guidelines, 412–414
    paragraph formatting, 414–416
    proofreading your work, 422–424
    readability versus appearance, 412–413
    template considerations, 413
    typefaces (fonts), 417–421
    typesetting characters, 419–420
    underline text, 421
    word processor versus desktop publishing, 411–412
Document Image Writer files, printing, 175
document information, printing, 166
document layout information, template component, 390
Document Library page, SharePoint, 720–724
Document Map view, 27

Document Protection task pane
    locking form fields, 622
    protection level assignments, 804–807
Document Recovery task pane, 208–209
document repository, SharePoint service, 718
document scraps, desktop selections, 61
Document Type Definition (DTD), XML, 665
document window
    drag-and-drop editing techniques, 60–61
    splitting, 45–46
document workspaces, SharePoint, 724–725
document-centric view, OLE, 521
document-management workspaces, SharePoint, 718
documents. See also files
    adding to the desktop, 192–193
    adding to Web page frames, 650
    automatically opening last accessed, 6
    autosummary, 212–214
    background sounds, 514
    backgrounds, 311–314
    batch conversions, 203
    body text, 369
    bookmark content placement, 322
    change tracking, 705–711
    character code insertion, 64–65
    closing properly, 39
    color printing guidelines, 167–168
    column formatting, 286–292
    comments, 697–704, 710–711
    comparing/merging, 709–711
    copying styles between, 378–382
    creating a shortcut to, 6
    cutting/copying/pasting text between, 62–63
    date/time insertion, 44–45
    default side margins, 414
    default top/bottom margins, 414
    different first-page header/footer, 309–310
    digital signatures, 808–809
    displaying hidden markups, 807
    displaying/hiding text, 113–114
    doc (Word document) file extension, 32
    dragging an image from a Web page, 440, 441
    DTD (Document Type Definition), 665
    e-mail routing, 690–692
    embedded fonts, 114–117
    embedding a sound object, 514
    Fast Save file corruption concerns, 198, 207
    folder navigation techniques, 196–197
    footers, 303–311
    format converters, 201–202
    frame-definition, 649–650

headers, 303–311
indexes, 337–351
in-document cross-references, 325–326
Letter Wizard, 30–32
line breaks, 43–44
link placement, 334–335
macro security issues, 810
main, 558–559
merge reasons, 557–558
modification protection, 803–804
most recently used list display, 5
moving insertion point when scrolling, 47–49
moving toolbars between, 770
naming conventions, 32
navigating with Reading Layout view, 25
navigation techniques, 46–50
new (blank), 29
new paragraph, 43
nonprinting character display, 39, 42–43
Normal template, 29–30
open protection methods, 801–802
opening methods, 4–6, 189–196
page borders, 301–302
page formatting, 292–301
performance enhancements, 742–743
permission restrictions, 807–808
picture insertion methods, 440–441
previewing before printing, 168–172
printing a list of styles, 382
printing multiple, 165
properties, 210–212
property display, 193–194
protection enhancements, 814–817
protection exceptions, 806–807
protection levels, 804–807
readability statistics, 235
rechecking spelling/grammar, 235–236
renaming when saving, 200–201
save methods, 32–34, 198–207
saving as a template, 395–396
saving as HTML format, 645–646
searches, 214–219
section breaks, 284–286
section formatting, 283–286
sections, 17
sharing with previous Word versions, 206
side-by-side comparison, 711
special characters, 63–67
splitting windows, 45–46
starting from a template, 30
status bar information display, 17
switching between open, 737

symbol insertion, 63–67
table addition, 252–259
table of contents, 351–358
table of figures, 358–360
table positioning, 258–259
text editing, 41–46
thumbnail display, 29
thumbnail views, 193–194
unprotecting multiple areas, 807
video clip insertion, 515–516
viewing as a Web document, 645
viewing multiple versions, 205
watermarks, 315–316
Webviews, 193–194
white space adjustments, 127–130
wizards, 403–408
word counts, 212
XML, 679–681
zoom magnifications, 28
dot (template) file extension, 392
double underline (Ctrl+Shift+D), character
        formatting, 96
drag bar
    moving toolbars, 9
    sizing task panes, 15
drag-and-drop
    embedded objects, 527–528
    linked objects, 530
    printing, 166
    text/graphic editing, 60–61
Draw, Align and Distribute command, 487
Draw, Change AutoShape command, 475
Draw, Edit Points command, 476
Draw, Grid command, 463
Draw, Group command, 475
Draw, Order command, 478
Draw, Order, Send Behind Text command, 450
Draw, Regroup command, 475
Draw, Rotate or Flip command, 476
Draw, Text Wrapping command, 458
Draw, Ungroup command, 475
Draw Table button
    drawing from tables, 621
    drawing non-uniform tables, 255–258
drawing canvas, 465–467
Drawing Canvas toolbar, wrapping styles, 457
Drawing Grid dialog box, object alignments, 463
drawing layer, layering drawing objects, 478–480
drawing objects
    handwritten pen comments, 700
    Web page insertion, 655–657

Drawing toolbar
   3-D lines/shapes, 473–474
   Align or Distribute menu, 487–488
   Arrow Style button, 471
   AutoShapes menu, 470–471
   buttons, 467–469
   callouts, 496–498
   displaying, 8
   drawing lines/shapes, 469–474
   editing curves/freeform shapes, 476
   Fill Color palette, 469–470
   grouping/ungrouping objects, 475
   Insert WordArt button, 490
   layering drawing objects, 478–480
   Line button, 471
   Line Color palette, 469–470
   Line Style palette, 469–470
   object positioning, 461–462
   Text button, 480
drawings
   adding to a text box, 481–482
   arrowheads, 471–472
   AutoShapes menu, 470–471
   curves, 472–473
   drawing canvas, 456, 466–467
   drop shadows, 474
   editing curves/freeform shapes, 476
   fill colors, 469–470
   form tables, 621
   freeform shapes, 472–473
   grouping/ungrouping objects, 475
   layering objects, 478–480
   line colors, 469–470
   line styles, 469–470
   lines, 471
   lines/shapes, 469–474
   methods, 465–466
   moving/copying lines or shapes, 477
   non-uniform tables, 255–258
   object editing, 474–477
   object positioning, 477–478
   organization charts, 494–496
   removing lines/shapes, 477
   resizing lines/shapes, 476
   rotating/flipping objects, 476–477
   shadowed lines/shapes, 473–474
   WordArt, 490–494
drivers, printer, 423
Drop Cap dialog box, 99
drop caps, character formatting, 99

drop shadows
   drawing, 474
   pictures, 451
drop-down boxes, form element, 670
drop-down fields, forms, 617–618
Drop-Down Form Field Options dialog box, 618
drop-down list box, dialog box element, 20
DTD (Document Type Definition), XML, 665
dynamic buttons, rollover scripts, 673–675
dynamic fonts, shared documents, 116

E

ECMAScript. *See* JavaScript
Edit, Clear, All command, 543
Edit, Clear, Contents command, 53, 543
Edit, Clear, Format command, 543
Edit, Copy (Ctrl+C) command, 56–57, 524
Edit, Cut (Ctrl+X) command, 56–57
Edit, Delete command, 543
Edit, Find (Ctrl+F) command, 77, 332
Edit, Go To (Ctrl+G/F5) command, 50, 332
Edit, Import File command, 550
Edit, Insert File command, 514
Edit, Links command, 532
Edit, Object, Convert command, 529
Edit, Object, Edit command, 528
Edit, Object command, 512, 528
Edit, Office Clipboard (Ctrl+C+Ctrl+C) command, 58
Edit, Paste (Ctrl+V) command, 56–57, 441
Edit, Paste Special command, 55–56, 446, 512, 524
Edit, Presentation Object, Edit command, 537
Edit, Repeat (Ctrl+Y/F4) command, 104, 252
Edit, Replace (Ctrl+H) command, 83, 286
Edit, Undo (Ctrl+Z) command, 105, 252
Edit Button Image command, 773–774
Edit Category dialog box, 363
Edit menu, undoing/repeating actions, 23
Edit Points tool, line editing, 476
Edit tab, Options dialog box, 755–757
Edit With button, Internet Explorer, 644
Edit WordArt Text dialog box, 490–491
Edit Wrap Points, text wrapping, 458
editable font embedding, 115
editors, automatically saving new file versions, 206
electronic postage, envelopes, 572
electronic postage services, accessing, 819–820
ellipsis (...) character, dialog box element, 18
em dash character, versus hyphen/en dash, 420
e-mail
   attachments, 687–683
   composing messages in Word, 692–693

digital signatures, 808–809
document routing, 690–692
document sharing method, 687–693
hyperlinks, 654
mail merges, 575–576
Microsoft Clip Organizer media, 445
sending from within Word, 688–690
signatures, 693
stationery, 693
WordMail toolbar, 689–690
E-mail Options dialog box, 693–695
EMBED field, embedded objects, 526
embedded fonts, shared documents, 114–117
embedded objects
    Access data, 534–536
    data display, 522
    defined, 519
    drag-and-drop method, 527–528
    editing, 528
    EMBED field display, 526
    embedding existing file, 523–524
    file format conversions, 528–529
    file formats, 526–527
    graphics conversion, 529
    icon display, 522, 523
    methods, 522–528
    new object embedding, 522–523
    PowerPoint data, 537–538
    switching between embedded Excel worksheets, 524
embossed text, character formatting, 100
en dash character, versus hyphen/em dash, 420
encryption, 803
Encryption Type dialog box, 803
encyclopedia, searches, 245
endnotes
    cross-references, support, 325
    deleting, 332
    displaying, 329, 331
    document insertion, 329–331
    footnote conversion, 333
    moving/copying, 332, 333
    navigating between, 331–332
    reference marks, 331
    searches, 332
    separators, 333–334
    text formatting, 332
    uses, 328
engraved text, character formatting, 100
Enter key
    beginning a new paragraph, 43
    new paragraph, 121
    text entry conventions, 41

Envelope Options dialog box, 178–179, 571–572
Envelope Size dialog box, 179
Envelope Wizard, envelope printing, 573
EnvelopeAddress bookmark, 323
EnvelopeReturn bookmark, 323
envelopes
    electronic postage, 572, 819–820
    EnvelopeAddress bookmark, 323
    EnvelopeReturn bookmark, 323
    FIMs (Facing Identification Marks), 180
    graphics, 180–182
    logos, 180–182
    mail merges, 571–573
    merge reason, 558
    postage addition, 182
    postal barcodes, 180, 572
    POSTNET codes, 180
    printing, 176–182
    printing mailing labels, 182–185
Envelopes and Labels dialog box, 177–179
e-postage, envelope printing, 182
Equation. See Microsoft Equation
Equation Editor, starting, 550–551
Equation Editor Tip dialog box, 551
Equation label, captions, 502
Equation toolbar, 550–551
Eraser tool, merging/splitting cells, 272
Esc key, canceling lines/shapes, 469
ESPN Smart Tag, 607
event directory, SharePoint service, 718
exc (exclude) file extension, exclude dictionary, 231
Excel. See Microsoft Excel
exceptions
    AutoCorrect entries, 238
    document protections, 806–807
Exchange folders, uses, 731–732
exclude dictionary, uses, 231
expanded text, character spacing, 106–107
expressions
    defined, 81
    field instruction element, 593–594
    form calculations, 616
    operators supported in, 616
EXT (extend) mode, status bar display, 17
Extend Mode (F8), extending table selections, 262
Extend Selection mode (F8), 52–53
Extensible Markup Language (XML)
    commands, 681
    described, 665, 678–679
    document creation, 679–681
    DTD (Document Type Definition), 665

Continued

Extensible Markup Language (XML) *(continued)*
    versus HTML, 678
    labels, 678
    saving as WordML file, 682
    schemas, 679–681
    tags, 680–681
    Word 2003 support, 819
Eye Candy, special-effect filter, 506

F

Facing Identification Marks (FIMs), printing, 180
facing pages, page formatting, 295
Fast Save, file corruption concerns, 198, 207
fax modems
    printing to, 176
    sending a fax from Word, 685–686
Fax Wizard, sending a fax from Word, 685–686
faxes
    font sizing guidelines, 420
    mail merges, 575–576
    online fax services, 686–687
    sending from Word, 685–686
FedEx Smart Tag, 607
field codes
    deleting fields, 318
    described, 585
    editing methods, 603
    EMBED field display, 526
    insertion methods, 588–590
    LINK field display, 529–530
    navigation methods, 586–587
    printing, 587–588
    running macro from, 792
    searches, 586–587
    shading, 586–587
    special characters, 590
    switching to results display, 317–318
    template component, 390
    viewing table of contents, 354
Field dialog box
    bookmark calculations, 323
    field code insertion method, 588–589
field instructions, elements, 591–596
field results
    editing methods, 318
    switching to code display, 317–318
fields
    action, 590
    automatic updating, 587–588
    bookmark assignment, 619
    calculation, 612, 616
    characters element, 591
    code versus results display, 317–318

current date, 612, 615
current time, 612, 615
date, 317, 612, 614–615
deleting, 318
described, 317–318
display conventions, 317–318
drop-down, 617–618
EMBED, 526
enabling, 619
fill-in, 583–584
form insertion methods, 611–612
form text, 612–617
header/footer, 307
help text addition, 619–620
hidden, 671
INDEX, 337, 348–350
insertion point navigation, 318
instruction elements, 591–596
length settings, 617
LINK, 529–530
locking/unlocking, 603–604
macro attachment, 618–619
manual insertion method, 589–590
marker, 590
merge documents, 559–560
merge query rules, 579–581
number, 612–614
page numbers, 306–307
regular text, 612, 613
result, 590
results appearance editing, 596–603
searches, 586–587
shading/unshading, 317, 534
Smart Tags, 604–607
templates, 395
TOC (table of contents), 351, 355–357
type element, 591
unlinking, 588, 604
updating, 318, 587–588
XE (index entry), 337, 340, 344–345
Figure label, captions, 502
File, Add Clips to Organizer, Automatically command, 444
File, Add Clips to Organizer, From Scanner or Camera command, 444
File, Add Clips to Organizer, On My Own command, 444
File, Close (Ctrl+F4) command, 39
File, Delete command, 118
File, Empty Recycle Bin command, 747
File, Exit (Alt+F4) command, 22, 39
File, Exit & Return to Document command, 514
File, File Search command, 214
File, Install New Font command, 118

File, New Collection command, 445
File, New command, 30, 392
File, Open (Ctrl+O) command, 4, 189
File, Page Setup command, 292
File, Permission command, 807
File, Print (Ctrl+P) command, 163
File, Print Preview command, 28, 170
File, Properties command, 210
File, Recover command, 196
File, Save As command, 200
File, Save As Web Page command, 33, 203, 645
File, Save (Ctrl+S) command, 32
File, Send To, Exchange Folder command, 731
File, Send To, Fax Service command, 686
File, Send To, Mail Recipient command, 687
File, Send To, Mail Recipient (as Attachment)
        command, 445, 687
File, Send To, Mail Recipient (for Review) command,
        687
File, Send To, Online Meeting Participant command,
        731
File, Send To, Recipient command, 685
File, Send To, Routing Recipient command, 687, 691
File, Versions command, 204
File, Web Page Preview command, 204, 645, 657
file extensions
        asd (AutoRecovery), 207
        doc (Word document), 32
        dot (template), 392
        exc (exclude), 231
        hiding/displaying in My Computer, 744
        htm/html (hypertext markup language),
                32, 203–204, 645–646
        lnk (link), 3
        mht/mhtml (Web page), 645
        Open dialog box display, 191
        wbk (backup), 210, 745
        wiz (Wizard), 392
file formats
        ASCII text, 527
        audio supported types, 514
        bitmap, 527
        device independent bitmap, 527
        embedded object conversions, 528–529
        embedded objects, 526–527
        filtered Web page, 646
        GIF (Graphic Interchange Format), 506
        GIF89a (animated GIFs), 513
        graphics types, 438
        htm/html (Web page), 645–646
        HTML (Hypertext Markup Language), 527, 645–646
        image selection guidelines, 506–507

        JPEG (Joint Photographer's Expert Group), 507
        mht/mhtml (single file Web page), 645
        PNG (Portable Network Graphics), 507
        Progressive JPEG, 510
        RTF (Rich Text Format), 527
        sharing documents with previous Word
                versions, 206
        supported types, 201–202
        Unicode text, 527
        Web browser supported types, 506–507
        Windows Metafile, 527
        Word hyperlink, 527
        WordML, 682
        XML, 682, 819
file indexes, file searches, 217
File Locations tab, Options dialog box, 763–764
File menu, most recently used file list display, 5
File Open dialog box, file searches, 218–219
File Search task pane, file search, 214–218
file sharing, SharePoint, 718–724
File Transfer Protocol (FTP), Web page publishing, 660
FileCloseAll command, 790
files. *See also* documents
        AutoRecover, 207–210
        backup/recovery, 207–210, 744–746
        batch conversions, 203
        concordance, 337–338
        corrupted, 745
        destination, 519–520
        directory path options, 763–764
        displaying, 5
        Document Image Writer, 175
        embedding existing, 523–524
        Fast Save corruption concerns, 198, 207
        folder navigation techniques, 196–197
        format converters, 201–202
        group operations, 195
        most recently used list display, 5
        opening, 4–6
        opening documents, 189–196
        opening recently used, 191–192
        password-protection issues, 803
        performance enhancements, 743
        permission restrictions, 807–808
        printing multiple documents, 165
        printing to, 174–175
        properties, 210–212
        property display, 193–194
        recovering from the Recycle Bin, 196
        removing personal information, 807

                                                Continued

files *(continued)*
   renaming when saving, 200–201
   save methods, 32–34, 198–207
   saving as a separate version, 205–206
   searches, 214–219
   selection methods, 195
   sending to NetMeeting participant, 731
   source, 519–520
   text encoding, 191
   uploading to Document Library page, 722
   viewing multiple versions, 205
   warn before printing protections, 807
   WordML, 682
Fill Color palette, 469–470
fill colors, drawings, 469–470
Fill Effects dialog box, 312–314
fill shading, paragraph formatting, 145
fill-in fields, main document, 583–584
filtered Web page, saving a document as, 646
filters
   graphics, 438–439
   HTML, 647
   image editors, 506
   merge record queries, 578–581
FIMs (Facing Identification Marks), printing, 180
Find and Replace dialog box
   accessing, 77
   adding text to replacement text, 87
   character formatting, 87–90
   comment searches, 702–703
   finding versus highlighting, 79
   finding/replacing special characters, 85–87
   finding/replacing word forms, 85
   match case criteria, 80
   replacing found text, 83–90
   search criteria conventions, 78
   search direction selection, 79–80
   search process, 80–81
   sounds like search, 82–83
   whole word search, 80
   wildcard characters/operators, 81–82
Find Font dialog box, 88
Fireworks, image editor, 506, 509
First Line Indent marker, 137
first-page headers/footers, 309–310
Flesch-Kincaid Grade Level, readability statistics, 235
Flesh Reading Ease, readability statistics, 235
Folder Options dialog box, 744
folders
   changing default path, 743–744
   Collection, 444–445
   directory path options, 763–764

Exchange, 731–732
Fonts, 118
My Mail Merge, 560
navigation techniques, 196–197
new, 196–198
Startup, 4
Temp, 747
Template, 392
User Templates, 392
Web Folder, 658–659
Font dialog box, 18–19, 94
font family, 110
font smoothing, 117
font styles, 110
Font Substitution dialog box, 116–117
fonts
   adding/removing, 118
   anti-aliases, 117
   bulleted lists, 149
   character pair spacing, 107
   colors, 99–100
   default character formatting adjustments, 113
   device-independent, 118
   display troubleshooting, 741
   displaying/hiding text, 113–114
   dynamic, 116
   finding/replacing, 87–90
   footnotes/endnotes, 332
   hiding/displaying font name, 110
   index entries, 341
   index entry formatting, 344
   kerning, 106–107
   keyboard shortcut support, 782
   licensers, 110
   naming conventions, 110
   OpenType, 117
   outline, 109
   plotter, 110
   point adjustments, 112–113
   PostScript Type 1, 109, 117
   proportional versus monospaced, 44
   scalable, 109
   shared documents, 114–117
   size adjustments, 112–113
   sizing guidelines, 420
   stroke, 110
   style editing methods, 111
   style selection guidelines, 111
   substituting unavailable, 116–117
   Symbol, 109
   TrueType, 109, 117
   TrueType Symbol (Ctrl+Shift+Q), 111

versus typefaces, 417
vector, 110
view options, 118–119
Windows management tools, 117–119
Fonts Control Panel, font management, 117–119
Fonts folder, font storage, 118
footers
    different first-page, 309–310
    hiding/displaying text, 308
    odd/even pages, 310
    page numbers, 303–305
    positioning, 310–311
    section formatting, 309
    text entry, 307–307
Footnote and Endnote dialog box, 329–330
footnotes
    cross-references support, 325
    deleting, 332
    displaying, 329, 331
    document insertion, 329–331
    endnote conversion, 333
    moving/copying, 332, 333
    navigating between, 331–332
    reference marks, 331
    searches, 332
    separators, 333–334
    text formatting, 332
    uses, 328
foreground colors, pattern shading, 145
Form Field Help Text dialog box, 619–620
form letters
    mail merge reason, 557–558
    Mail Merge Wizard, 561–568
    My Mail Merge folder, 560
Format, AutoFormat command, 384
Format, Background command, 311, 312
Format, Background, Fill Effects command, 312, 511
Format, Background, Printed Watermark command, 315
Format, Borders and Shading command, 301, 449
Format, Bullets and Numbering command, 277
Format, Change Case command, 108
Format, Columns command, 252, 286
Format, Drawing Canvas command, 456
Format, Drop Cap command, 88
Format, Font (Ctrl+D) command, 18, 88, 94
Format, Frames, New Frames Page command, 649
Format, Object command, 456
Format, Picture command, 448, 456
Format, Reveal Formatting (Shift+F1) command, 102, 122
Format, Style command, 332

Format, Style, Organizer command, 770
Format, Styles and Formatting command, 372
Format, Tab command, 130
Format, Text Direction command, 270, 486
Format, Theme command, 380, 396, 409, 655
Format AutoShape dialog box, 471–472
Format Axis dialog box, chart formatting, 548
Format Callout dialog box, 497–498
Format Chart Area dialog box, chart formatting, 548
format converters, documents, 201–202
Format Data Series dialog box, chart formatting, 548
Format dialog box, positioning drawing objects, 477–478
format field switch (*), uses, 597–599
Format Gridlines dialog box, chart formatting, 548
Format Painter button (Ctrl+Shift+C)
    copying character formatting, 104
    duplicating paragraph formatting, 123–124
Format Picture dialog box
    brightness/contrast adjustments, 453
    Image Control area, 452
    layouts, 456–457
    picture borders, 449–451
    resizing/cropping pictures, 448–449
Format Plot Area dialog box, chart formatting, 548
Format Settings dialog box, custom style views, 371–372
Format Text Box dialog box, text box margins, 482
Format Walls dialog box, chart formatting, 548
formats
    finding/replacing, 87–90
    index, 345–346
    organization charts, 495
    table numbers, 279–280
formatting, direct versus style, 367
formatting marks, showing/hiding, 752
Formatting Restrictions dialog box, 805–806, 815
Formatting toolbar
    character formatting uses, 93–94
    combing/separating, 8
    display settings, 736–737
    displaying/hiding, 93
    indents, 136
    screen elements, 122
    Style drop-down list box, 369
forms
    ActiveX control addition, 621
    bookmark assignment, 619
    calculate on exit, 619
    calculation field, 612, 616
    CGI script processing, 672
    check boxes, 617, 669

Continued

forms *(continued)*
    current data field, 612, 615
    current time field, 612, 615
    data entry conventions, 623
    data printing, 185
    data submission methods, 671
    date field, 612, 614–615
    drawing/inserting tables, 621
    drop-down boxes, 670
    drop-down fields, 617–618
    elements, 668–672
    enabling fields, 619
    field insertion, 611–612
    field lengths, 617
    font sizing guidelines, 420
    four-step process, 610
    frame addition, 621
    help text addition, 619–620
    hidden fields, 671
    HTML, 667–672
    Image Submit button, 671–672
    list boxes, 670
    locking/unlocking, 621–622
    macro attachment, 618–619
    number field, 612, 613–614
    option buttons, 669–670
    password protections, 622
    passwords, 671
    printing, 623
    radio buttons, 669–670
    regular text field, 612, 613
    Reset button, 672
    saving as a template, 622
    scripts, 667
    Submit button, 671–672
    templates, 610
    text area, 671
    text boxes, 670
    text entry conventions, 611–612
    text fields, 612–617
    URL encoded data, 667
    uses, 609
    Web-form component cautions, 672
Forms toolbar, buttons, 611–612
Formula dialog box, 278–279
formulas
    bookmarks, 280, 323
    table calculations, 278–279
fractions, typesetting characters, 420
fragmentation, described, 742
Frame button, adding frames to a form, 621
Frame Properties dialog box, 650–652

frame-definition document, Web pages, 649–650
frames. *See also* text boxes
    adding documents to, 650
    configuration properties, 650–652
    defined, 648
    form addition, 621
    frame-definition document, 649–650
    Frames toolbar buttons, 649
    framesets, 649
    hyperlinks, 654
    switching to a text box, 486
    table of contents, 351
    Web page uses, 648
Frames toolbar, 649
framesets, Web pages, 649
freeform shapes
    drawing, 472–473
    editing, 476
Freeform tool, drawing freeform shapes, 473
FrontPage, theme support, 409
FTP (File Transfer Protocol), Web page publishing, 660
Full Screen view, 27–28
functions
    cell references, 594
    Clipboard Task pane, 58–59
    mouse actions, 22
    table formulas, 278–279

G
General tab, Options dialog box, 753–754
GET method, form data submission, 671
Getty Images, stock photography source, 440–441
ghost text, troubleshooting, 740–741
GIF (Graphic Interchange Format)
    image compression, 509–510
    interlacing, 510–511
    transparent backgrounds, 453–454
    Web pages, 506, 656–657
GIF Animator, animated GIFs, 513
GIF89a (animated GIFs) file format, uses, 513
global macros, storage, 786
global templates
    local template conversion, 399
    versus local templates, 391
    Normal template, 391
    opening automatically, 400
Go To dialog box (Ctrl+G/F5), document navigation, 50
grammar checker
    disabling, 225, 742
    document readability statistics, 235
    rerunning after editing text, 423
    shortcomings, 422–423

uses, 232–235
    writing styles, 234
Grammar dialog box, 232–234
grammar errors
    correcting after working, 224–229
    correcting as you type, 223–224
    rechecking documents, 235–236
Grammar Settings dialog box, 234
Graph Formatting toolbar, datasheet formatting, 544
Graphic Interchange Format (GIF), browser support, 506
graphics. *See also* clip art; images; objects; pictures
    adjustment methods, 452–454
    bitmap versus vector, 437–438
    bulleted lists, 150
    commercial clip art, 439–440
    deleting, 53–54
    displaying as placeholders, 24
    drag-and-drop editing, 60–61
    embedded object conversion, 529
    envelopes, 180–182
    filters, 438–439
    moving/copying, 54–63
    pixels, 437
    placeholders, 454
    repeating with text boxes, 488–489
    selection methods, 51–53
    supported file formats, 438
    white space uses, 416
graphs. *See* Microsoft Graph Chart
Greeting Line dialog box, mail merges, 566
gridlines
    chart element, 545
    charts, 547
    object alignments, 463
    showing/hiding, 273
    tables, 273
Grouping, Group command, 475
Grouping, Regroup command, 475
Grouping, Ungroup command, 475
groups, menu commands, 777–778
gutters, page formatting, 295

H

handwriting-recognition, text service, 426
handwritten pen comments, uses, 700
hanging indents, 135
hard breaks, page formatting, 297
hard drives
    defragmenting, 742
    free space recovery, 747
hardware requirements, speech recognition, 426
Header and Footer toolbar, 307–308

headers
    avoiding automatic numbering, 324
    different first-page, 309–310
    hiding/displaying text, 308
    odd/even pages, 310
    page numbers, 303–305
    positioning, 310–311
    section formatting, 309
    text entry, 307–308
Heading 1 style (Ctrl+Alt+1), 377
Heading 2 style (Ctrl+Alt+2), 377
heading styles
    custom shortcut keys, 781–782
    described, 369
    outline integration, 625
    table of contents use, 351, 352–354
headings
    color enhancement, 421
    cross-reference support, 324
    font sizing guidelines, 420
    promoting/demoting outline levels, 630
    sans serif typeface advantages, 417–418
    tables, 272
    white space uses, 416
height adjustments
    document rows, 269
    table rows, 265
Help, Detect and Repair command, 745
Help, Microsoft Word Help (F1) command, 22, 35
Help, WordPerfect Help command, 38
Help button, dialog box element, 20–21
Help for WordPerfect Users dialog box, 38
Help menu
    About Microsoft Word, 34
    Customer Service Improvement Program privacy
        settings, 34
    Detect and Repair utility, 34
    displaying/hiding the Office Assistant, 34, 35
    interface elements, 34–39
    Office on Microsoft.com Web site access, 34
    product registration, 34
    WordPerfect Help, 34, 38–39
Help system
    About Microsoft Word, 34
    access methods, 34
    CD key information display, 736
    chapters, 36
    Customer Service Improvement Program privacy
        settings, 34
    Detect and Repair utility, 34
    keyboard shortcut display, 780
    Microsoft on the Web, 36

Continued

Help system *(continued)*
    Microsoft Word Help, 34–36
    Office Assistant, 18, 34, 35
    Office on Microsoft.com Web site access, 34
    product registration, 34
    ScreenTip help, 8
    search techniques, 36
    shortcut keys, 22
    WordPerfect Help, 34, 38–39
help text, adding to form field, 619–620
hidden bookmarks, displaying, 320
hidden fields, form element, 671
hidden text (Ctrl+Shift+H), 113–114
Highlight button
    character formatting, 105–106
    highlighting text, 704
highlighted text, character formatting, 105–106
Home task pane, displaying, 15
Horizontal Line dialog box, 147
horizontal lines
    document design guidelines, 422
    Web page enhancements, 655–656
horizontal ruler
    changing left/right margins in Print Layout view, 25
    column width adjustments, 265–266
    displaying/hiding, 16
    indent markers, 137
    margin settings, 294–295
    tab settings, 130, 132–133
    table tab stops, 273–274
horizontal rules, paragraph formatting, 147
horizontal scroll bar
    document navigation, 16
    moving insertion point when scrolling, 48
hourglass, mouse pointer shape, 21
htm/html file extension, 32, 33, 203–204, 645–646
HTML. *See* HyperText Markup Language
HTML styles
    classes, 665
    described, 665
    Web pages, 652–654
hyperlinks. *See also* links
    AutoFormatting, 655
    between frames, 654
    table of contents use, 351, 353
    Web pages, 653–655
Hypertext Markup Language (HTML)
    classes, 665
    described, 527, 663–665
    filters, 647
    forms, 667–672
    icon display, 648

    saving a document as a Web page, 33, 527, 645–646
    source code viewing, 652–653, 664–665
    styles, 665
    tag attributes, 663–664
    tag conventions, 663–665
    Web page coding problems, 643
    versus XML, 678
hyphen (-) character, versus em/en dash, 420
hyphenation
    checking your work, 423
    document appearance uses, 414
    paragraph formatting, 159–161
Hyphenation dialog box, 159–160

I

I-beam cursor, 7, 21
Icon view, file list display, 5
icons
    embedded object display, 522, 523
    HTML file, 648
    inserting Graph Charts as, 540
identifiers, field instruction element, 595
IIS (Microsoft Internet Information Server),
    Web Folders, 658–659
Image Control area, image adjustments, 452
image editors
    filters/plug-ins, 506
    jaggies (aliased edges) avoidance, 509
    third-party solutions, 505–506
Image Submit button, form element, 671–672
ImageBridge, digital watermark utility, 513
images. *See also* clip art; graphics; pictures
    background, 312–314
    brightness adjustments, 453
    bulleted lists, 150
    compression methods, 509–510
    contrast adjustments, 453
    copyright issues, 513
    digital watermarks, 513
    disappearing when changing wrapping style, 455
    document design considerations, 421–422
    file format selection guidelines, 506–507, 438
    finding/replacing with Clipboard, 87
    inline, 450
    interlacing, 510–511
    jaggies (aliased edges), 509
    monitor resolution/color settings, 507–508
    placement troubleshooting, 741
    rasterizing, 509
    resolution adjustments, 508–509
    rollover scripts, 673–675
    stock photography sources, 439–440

thumbnail display, 29
tiled, 511–512
transparent backgrounds, 453–454, 511–512
VML (Vector Markup Language), 506
Web page enhancement, 656–657
white space uses, 416
IME (Input Method Editor), text service, 426
Import Data Options dialog box, 549–550
Increase Indent button, 136
indent markers, 137
indentation, white space uses, 416
indents
    Formatting toolbar, 136
    hanging, 135
    versus margins, 135
    nested, 135
    paragraph formatting, 135–139, 415
Index and Tables dialog box, 339–340
index entry (XE) field, 337, 340, 344–345
INDEX field, 337, 348–350
index workspace, SharePoint, 718
indexes
    automatic entry marking, 338–340
    automatic style application, 378
    backslash (\) character conventions, 341
    character formatting, 344
    colon (:) character conventions, 341
    compiling, 345–346
    concordance file, 337–340
    cross-references, 342–343
    deleting, 351
    entry conventions, 337–338
    field modifying, 344–345
    file search, 217
    hidden text, 114
    INDEX field editing, 348–350
    manually marking entries, 340–342
    master document advantages, 337
    multilevel, 343
    page range references, 342
    planning importance, 338
    styles, 346–347
    subentries, 341, 343
    text formatting, 341
    updating, 347–348
in-document cross-references, uses, 325–326
inline images, default picture placement, 450
inline video clips, adding to a Web page, 657
Input Method Editor (IME), text service, 426
Insert, AutoText, AutoText command, 71
Insert, AutoText (F3) command, 72

Insert, Bookmark (Ctrl+Shift+F5) command, 280, 318
Insert, Break command, 284
Insert, Cells command, 543
Insert, Comment command, 105, 698
Insert, Date and Time command, 44, 587
Insert, Field command, 306, 588
Insert, Hyperlink (Ctrl+K) command, 334, 653
Insert, Object command, 440–441, 514, 522,
        530, 540, 550
Insert, Page Numbers command, 303
Insert, Picture, AutoShapes command, 465, 470
Insert, Picture, Chart command, 540, 549
Insert, Picture, Clip Art command, 441, 513, 657
Insert, Picture, New Drawing command, 465
Insert, Picture, Organization Chart command, 494
Insert, Picture, WordArt command, 466, 490
Insert, Picture command, 440
Insert, Picture from Scanner or Camera command, 446
Insert, Picture Organization Chart command, 465
Insert, Reference, Caption command, 281, 358, 498
Insert, Reference, Cross-reference command, 325
Insert, Reference, Footnote command, 329
Insert, Reference, Index and Tables command, 339
Insert, Symbol command, 63
Insert, Text Box command, 480
Insert Address Block dialog box, mail merges, 565
Insert Cells dialog box, 263
Insert Data button, inserting Access data, 535
Insert Data dialog box, inserting Access data, 535–536
Insert Database button, inserting Access data, 535
Insert dialog box, inserting Datasheet cells, 543–544
Insert Excel Spreadsheet button, 525
Insert File dialog box, sound object insertion, 514
Insert Hyperlink button, 653
Insert Hyperlink dialog box, 334–335, 653–654
Insert key, OVR (overtype) mode, 17, 43
Insert Merge Field dialog box, mail merges, 567
Insert Picture from Scanner or Camera dialog box, 446
Insert Postal Bar Code dialog box, 572–573
Insert Table button, 252, 253, 263, 621
Insert Table dialog box, 252–254
Insert Voice button, voice comments, 700–701
Insert Word Field: Fill-in dialog box, 584
Insert Word Field: IF dialog box, 583
Insert WordArt button, Drawing toolbar, 490
inserted text, By Author color preferences, 760
insertion point
    beginning a new paragraph, 43
    bookmark insertion, 318–319
    document navigation techniques, 46–50
    Equation positioning, 551–552

Continued

insertion point *(continued)*
   field editing, 318
   field navigation, 318
   Go To dialog box navigation, 50
   last editing location return (Shift+F5), 49–50
   manually marking index entries, 340–342
   moving when scrolling, 47–49
   status bar location information, 17
   table navigation, 260
   text area element, 7
   text/graphic selections, 51–52
install on demand, troubleshooting, 735–736
installable font embedding, 115–116
instructions, field element, 591–596
IntelliSense rules, menu command organization, 778–779
IntelliSense technology, Office Assistant, 34
interlaced images, when to use, 510–511
internal margins, text boxes, 482
International Typeface Corporation (ITC), font name licenser, 110
Internet
   online fax services, 686–687
   searches, 244–245
   SharePoint hosting services, 717
Internet Explorer
   Edit With button, 644
   HTML coding issues, 643
   previewing Web pages, 657–658
   viewing a Web page, 204
   Web toolbar integration, 658
Internet Service Provider (ISP), Web page hosting service, 659–660
Italic button (Ctrl+I), character formatting, 96
italic text (Ctrl+I)
   character formatting, 96
   document design guidelines, 421

J

jaggies, avoiding, 509
Jasc, PaintShop Pro, 437, 505
JavaScript
   adding scripts to a Web page, 672–675
   rollover scripts, 673–675
JFax, online fax service, 687
Joint Photographer's Expert Group (JPEG)
   Web pages, 507, 656–657
   versus Progressive JPEG, 510
JScript. *See* JavaScript
jumps, hyperlinks, 653–654
justified alignment, paragraphs, 125–126, 414–415
Justify button, justified text, 414–415

K

kerning
   character pairs, 107
   defined, 106
   WordArt, 493–494
keyboard shortcuts. *See also* shortcut keys
   AutoText entry, 73
   copying/moving selections, 57
   customizing, 779–783
   displaying built-in, 780
   indents, 138
   outlines, 631–632
   printing, 166
   restoring to default, 783
   styles, 781–782
   supported categories, 782
keyboards
   button editing non-support, 774
   command selection techniques, 22
   Datasheet data selections, 542–543
   Datasheet window navigation, 542
   Equation insertion point positioning, 551–552
   field code insertion methods, 589–590
   moving insertion point when scrolling, 48–49
   shortcut-menu key, 57
   table navigation, 260
   table text selections, 262
   text/graphic selections, 52
keystroke shortcuts, promoting/demoting outline levels, 630

L

Label Options dialog box, 183, 573–574
labels
   captions, 498–500, 502
   customizing, 184–185
   dialog box elements, 19
   mail merges, 573–574
   mailing, 182–185
   printing, 182–185
   XML element, 678
landscape orientation, page formatting, 295–296
Language bar
   microphone adjustments, 426–427
   preference settings, 432–433
   speech recognition, 426–433
   text services, 426
   use profiles, 428
   voice training, 427–429
Language dialog box, skipping selected text when spell checking, 226–227

languages
    finding/replacing, 87–90
    Microsoft MultiLanguage Pack for Office, 227
    Microsoft Proofing Tools Kit, 227
    spell-checking support, 227
    thesaurus, 242–243
    translations, 243–244
laptops, character code entry conventions, 64
Large Icons view, file display, 5
layers, drawing objects, 478–480
layouts
    defined, 412
    document design guidelines, 412–414
    object positions, 455–457
    organization charts, 495
    positioning drawing objects, 477–478
    table modifications, 262–270
    text/graphics with text boxes, 480–490
leader tabs, uses, 134
leading, 127
left alignment
    paragraph formatting, 125–126
    table positioning, 259
Left Indent marker, 137
left margin, object positioning, 460
left-aligned tabs, 131
Legal Blackline, comparing/merging documents, 710
legend, chart element, 545, 547
length adjustments, column formatting, 291–292
Letter Wizard, 30–32, 404–407
letters
    Letter Wizard, 31–32, 404–407
    Mail Merge Wizard, 561–568
    merge element, 557–558
    WordArt editing, 493
levels, protection, 804–807
LexisNexis Smart Tag, 607
libraries, SharePoint, 720–724
license number, program information display, 34
line art, vector graphic advantages, 437
line breaks (Shift+Enter)
    described, 43–44
    paragraph formatting, 124–125
Line button, drawing lines, 471
Line Color palette, 469–470
line colors, drawings, 469–470
line numbers, page formatting, 299–301
Line Numbers dialog box, 300–301
line spacing, paragraph formatting, 127–130
Line Style palette, drawing line styles, 469–470
line styles, drawings, 469–470

lines
    arrowheads, 471–472
    borders, 143
    column formatting, 289
    drawing methods, 469–474
    footnote/endnote separators, 333–334
    picture borders, 450
    removing, 477
    resizing, 476
    shadowed, 473–474
link directory, SharePoint service, 718
LINK field, linked objects, 529–530
link (lnk) file extension, shortcuts, 3
Linked Object, Links command, 533
linked objects
    Access data, 534–536
    automatic updates, 530–532
    breaking links, 533
    defined, 519
    destination file, 519–520
    editing, 533
    LINK field display, 529–530
    locking versus manually updating, 533
    locking/unlocking, 533
    manual updates, 532
    methods, 530
    PowerPoint data, 537–538
    source file, 519–520
    updating, 530–532
    updating when printing, 532
links. *See also* hyperlinks
    bookmark concerns, 322
    Clip Art on Microsoft.com, 445
    document placement, 334–335
    document templates, 397–399
    frame-definition document, 652
    On My Computer, 30
    postal bar code, 572
    Table of Contents, 36
    text box text, 485
Links dialog box, updating links, 531–532
list boxes, 670
list styles, described, 368
List view, file display, 5
lists
    bulleted, 148–151
    mail merges, 574–575
    numbered, 151–156
    outline numbered, 154–156
    styles, 157
    unbulleted/unnumbered list addition, 154

lnk (link) file extension, shortcuts, 3
local templates
  converting to global template, 399
  versus global templates, 391
logos, envelopes, 180–182

M

Macro Project Items tab, Organizer dialog box, 795–796
macro viruses, troubleshooting, 746–747
Macromedia, Fireworks, 506, 509
macros
  ANSIValue, 797–799
  automatic running, 791–792
  AutoNew, 791
  bookmark uses, 787
  CodeStyle, 794
  comments, 794
  copying/moving between templates, 795–796
  deleting, 795–796
  deleting unnecessary commands, 794
  description conventions, 787–788
  editing techniques, 792–794
  form field attachment, 618–619
  global storage, 786
  keyboard shortcut support, 782
  naming conventions, 787, 788
  preventing automatic macro from running, 792
  recording, 786–788
  remarks, 794
  renaming, 795–796
  running, 789–792
  saving, 789
  security methods, 810
  shortcut key assignment, 788
  stop recording methods, 788
  template component, 391, 400
  template storage, 786
  toolbar assignment, 402, 788
  UpdateFields, 791
  uses, 785–786
  virus concerns, 790
  writing guidelines, 786
Macros dialog box, running macros, 789–792
Mail Merge Recipients dialog box, 563, 578–581
Mail Merge toolbar, 568–570
Mail Merge Wizard, 561–568
mail merges, reasons for, 557–558
mailing labels
  merge reason, 558
  printing, 182–185, 573–574
main document
  deleting merge fields, 576–577
  fill-in fields, 583–584

inserting merge fields, 576–577
  merge code editing, 577–578
  merge element, 558–559
  merge field formatting, 576–577
  special fields, 582–584
Main Document Type dialog box, mail merges, 568
manual hyphenation, uses, 160–161
Manual Hyphenation dialog box, 160
manual line breaks, described, 43
MarcSpider service, Web image tracking, 513
margins
  adjustments, 415
  border sizing, 144
  changing in Print Layout view, 25
  default side, 414
  default top/bottom, 414
  indenting, 415
  mirror, 295
  page formatting, 292–295
  versus paragraph indents, 135
  paragraph formatting, 415
  Print Preview mode adjustment, 171
  table cell adjustments, 267–268
  text boxes, 482
  white space uses, 416
Mark Citation dialog box, 361
Mark Index Entry dialog box (Alt+Shift+X), 340
Mark Table of Contents Entry dialog
      (Alt+Shift+O), 356
marker fields, 590
markup, 665
master document
  build methods, 635–637
  building from scratch, 636–637
  editing conventions, 638
  existing document conversion, 637
  existing document insertion, 637
  index advantages, 337
  Master Document view, 634–635
  naming conflict avoidance, 636
  saving, 636
  subdocuments, 638–641
  uses, 633–634
Master Document view
  accessing, 634–635
  building a master document from scratch, 636–637
  locking/unlocking subdocument, 641
  merging subdocuments, 640
  moving subdocuments, 639
  opening a subdocument, 639
  removing subdocuments, 639
  renaming subdocuments, 639
  reordering subdocuments, 639–640

sharing subdocuments, 640
splitting subdocuments, 640
match case search, 80
Match Fields dialog box, mail merges, 565
MathType, Equation Editor upgrade, 551
McAfee ViruScan, 747
measurement units
    page formatting, 292
    points, 112–113
    rulers, 16
Media Clip, video clip insertion, 515–516
media files, Microsoft Clip Organizer, 443–445
Media Player toolbar, 515–516
meeting areas, SharePoint service, 718
meeting workspace, SharePoint, 718
menu bar
    described, 8
    template component, 391
menu options, display settings, 8
menus
    adding commands to, 776
    command accelerator keys, 777
    creating, 776
    grouping commands, 777–778
    opening methods, 8
    option display, 8
    option editing, 773–774
    Personalized Menus, 778–779
    shortcut, 22–23
    shortcut editing, 777
    template component, 400
    troubleshooting missing components, 736–737
merge codes, editing in main document, 577–578
merge codes, main document element, 558–559
Merge to E-mail dialog box, mail merges, 576
Merge to Printer dialog box, mail merges, 568
merges
    catalogs, 574–575
    comparing/merging documents, 709–711
    comparison operators, 579
    databases, 559
    directories, 574–575
    e-mail, 575–576
    envelope printing, 571–573
    faxes, 575–576
    fill-in fields, 583–584
    form letters, 560–570
    labels, 573–574
    main document, 558–559
    main document editing, 576–578
    merge codes, 558–559
    My Mail Merge folder, 560
    Outlook address book, 570

random number storage, 807
reasons for, 557–558
record order, 581–582
record queries, 578–581
rules, 579–581
table cells, 271–272
using existing documents, 568–570
mht/mhtl (Web page) file extension, 645
Microphone button, Language bar, 429
Microphone Wizard, speech recognition uses, 427
microphones
    speech recognition, 426–427
    volume settings, 426–427
Microsoft Access, data insertion, 534–536
Microsoft Clip Organizer, media files, 443–445
Microsoft Encarta, encyclopedia search, 245
Microsoft Equation
    alignments, 552–553
    assembly operation, 551–552
    Equation Editor, 551–553
    insertion point positioning, 551–552
    MathType, 551
    operators, 551
    spacing adjustments, 552–553
    starting, 550
    symbols, 551
    templates, 551
    Torricelli's Equation, 552
    uses, 550
Microsoft Excel
    embedding an object in Word, 524–527
    importing data to a Graph datasheet, 549–550
    OLE support, 519
    switching between embedded worksheets, 524
Microsoft Exchange server, Exchange folders, 731–732
Microsoft Fax, sending a fax from Word, 685–686
Microsoft FrontPage, Web page authoring tool, 646–648
Microsoft Graph Chart
    chart data exclusion, 546–547
    chart elements, 544–549
    chart formatting methods, 548
    chart types, 545–546
    Datasheet window, 540–544
    importing data from Excel, 549–550
    inserting as an icon, 540
    inserting as an object, 540
    table conversion, 549
    starting/quitting, 539–540
Microsoft Image Composer, bitmap graphics, 437
Microsoft Internet Information Server (IIS),
        Web Folders, 658–659
Microsoft MultiLanguage Pack for Office, 227
Microsoft NetMeeting, online meetings, 728–731

Microsoft on the Web, online help, 36
Microsoft Outlook
    composing messages in Word, 692–693
    Exchange folders, 731–732
    font embedding non-support, 114
    sending e-mail from within Word, 688–690
Microsoft Personal Web Server (PWS), Web Folders,
    658–659
Microsoft PowerPoint
    data insertion, 537–538
    OLE support, 519
Microsoft Proofing Tool Kits, 227
Microsoft Query, data retrieval uses, 534
Microsoft Rights Management, permission restrictions,
    807–808
Microsoft Script Editor
    adding script to a Web page, 672–675
    rollover scripts, 673–675
    viewing HTML source code, 652–653, 664–665
Microsoft Word 2003
    automatically opening last accessed document, 6
    CD key information display, 736
    default folder path, 743–744
    detecting/repairing missing or corrupt files, 745–746
    exiting properly, 39
    opening documents on startup, 6
    performance enhancements, 742–743
    product registration, 34
    program information display, 34
    screen elements, 7–13
    sharing documents with previous versions, 206
    starting from Windows document list, 192
    startup methods, 3–6
    startup switches, 6
Microsoft Word Help, 34–36
mirror margins, page formatting, 295
mistakes
    dictation taking, 430–431
    undoing (Ctrl+Z), 23, 54, 105
mode indicators, status bar information display, 17
modems
    printing to a fax modem, 176
    sending a fax from Word, 685–686
Modify Location dialog box, 197
Modify Style dialog box, 373, 376–377
monitors, resolution/color settings, 507–508
monospaced fonts, 44
Monotype, MT fonts, 110
mouse
    column width adjustments, 265–266
    command selection techniques, 21–22
    Datasheet data selections, 542
    Datasheet window navigation, 542

    drag-and-drop embedded objects, 527–528
    drag-and-drop text editing, 60–61
    drawing lines/shapes, 469
    I-beam cursor, 7
    moving insertion point when scrolling, 47–48
    pointer shapes, 21
    promoting/demoting outline levels, 630
    resizing/cropping pictures, 447
    right-click shortcut menus, 22–23
    rollover scripts, 673–675
    scroll box document navigation, 16
    table navigation, 260
    table text selections, 261
    text/graphic selections, 51–52
Move Table Column markers, column width, 265–266
Movie button, adding movie clips to a Web page, 676
Movie Clip dialog box, adding movie clips to a
    Web page, 676
MSNBC Smart Tag, 607
multilevel indexes, creating, 343
multiple documents, printing, 165
My Collections, Microsoft Clip Organizer, 443–445
My Computer
    dragging a document shortcut to the desktop, 193
    hiding/displaying file extensions, 744
    opening documents from, 6
    Web Folders, 659
My Computer button, Open dialog box, 190
My Documents button, Open dialog box, 190
My Documents folder, default document storage,
    196, 743–744
My Mail Merge folder, merge data storage, 560
My Network Places, accessing file libraries
    from Word, 727–728
My Network Places button, Open dialog box, 190
My Recent Documents button, Open dialog box,
    190, 192

N

nested indents, 135
nested tables, 255–256, 258
Netscape Communicator, dynamic font non-support, 116
Netscape Navigator, HTML coding issues, 643
networks, document printing, 186–187
networks, print servers, 186–187
New, Shortcut command, 6
New Address List dialog box, mail merges, 563
New Custom Laser dialog box
    template access methods, 392–393
    uses, 30–31
    Web page creation method, 644–645
new (blank) document, creating, 29
New Style dialog box, 157, 374–376

New Toolbar dialog box, custom toolbars, 775
newspaper columns, versus tables, 252
newspapers, first line indents, 415
newspaper-style columns, column formatting, 286–291
nonadjacent files, selection methods, 196
nonbreaking hyphens, uses, 161
noncontiguous items, selection methods, 52
nonprinting characters, displaying, 39, 42–43
non-uniform tables, drawing, 255–258
Normal paragraph style, described, 93
Normal style
    captions, 502
    described, 369
Normal template
    described, 29–30, 391
    global template, 391
    User Templates folder, 392
Normal view (Alt+Ctrl+N)
    described, 24
    footnote/endnote separator line editing, 334
    inserting a text box, 481
    returning from Outline view, 626
    splitting windows, 632–633
Norton AntiVirus, 747
note pane, viewing footnotes/endnotes, 331
Notepad, corrupted file recovery, 745
notes, hidden text, 114
notes pane, footnote/endnote separator line editing, 334
nudging, 553
Number button, Formatting toolbar, 277
number conversion, format field switch (*) , 598–599
number field, forms, 612–614
number formats, tables, 279–280
number picture field (\#) switch, uses, 599–601
number sign (#) placeholder, number format, 614
numbered items, cross-reference support, 324
numbered lists
    customizing, 152–153
    editing, 154
    outline numbered lists, 154–156
    removing, 154
    restarting/continuing numbering, 153
    uses, 151–152
    Web page enhancements, 655–656
Numbering button, Formatting toolbar, 277
numbering styles, captions, 503
numbers, line, 299–301

O

Object dialog box
    embedding an existing file, 523–524
    linked objects, 530
    new object embedding, 522–523

OLE supported application display, 521, 522
    sound object insertion, 514
Object Linking and Embedding (OLE)
    Access data, 534–536
    COM (Component Object Model) foundation, 521
    versus copying/pasting data, 520
    CorelDRAW support, 439
    document-centric view, 521
    linked versus embedded objects, 519–521
    object embedding methods, 522–528
    object linking methods, 529–533
    Office application support, 519
    PowerPoint data, 537–538
    shading, 533–534
object scroll buttons, footnote/endnote navigation, 331–332
objects. *See also* graphics
    alignment methods, 463–464
    anchors, 460–461
    callouts, 496–498
    captions, 498–504
    defined, 504
    drawing canvas, 466–467
    drawing positioning, 477–478
    Edit Wrap Points, 458
    Graph Charts, 540
    grouping/ungrouping, 475
    layering, 478–480
    layout positions, 455–457
    linked versus embedded, 519–521
    positioning methods, 459–464
    positioning selections, 462–463
    regrouping, 475
    rotating/flipping, 476–477
    selection methods, 462–463
    text wrapping styles, 457
    types, 504
Office 2003, CD-ROM system requirements, 821
Office Assistant
    displaying/hiding, 18, 34, 35
    IntelliSense technology, 34
Office Clipboard. *See* Clipboard
Office Shortcut bar, Word startup, 4
OLE. *See* Object Linking and Embedding
On My Computer link, template access method, 30
online fax services, 686–687
online help, Microsoft on the Web, 36
Online Meeting toolbar, buttons, 728–729
Open button, 189
Open dialog box
    corrupted file recovery, 745
    Create New Folder button, 196
    Desktop button, 190

Continued

Open dialog box *(continued)*
   file display views, 4–5
   file group operations, 195
   file selection methods, 191, 195–196
   file types display, 191
   file views, 190
   file/folder navigation, 190–191
   My Computer button, 190
   My Network Places button, 190
   My Recent Documents button, 190, 192
   Open shortcut menu commands, 195
   previewing documents, 193–194
   property settings, 193–194
   thumbnails, 193–194
   Webviews, 193
Open shortcut menu, commands, 195
OpenType fonts, 117
operators
   comparison, 579
   defined, 81
   expressions, 593–594
   file search, 219
   form expressions, 616
   Microsoft Equation, 551
   searches, 81–82
Option button, dialog box element, 20
option (radio) buttons, form element, 669–670
optional hyphens, uses, 161
Options dialog box
   backup file copy, 744–745
   Compatibility tab, 761–763
   cut/paste options, 59–60
   default folder path, 743–744
   document related options display, 750
   Edit tab, 755–757
   File Locations tab, 763–764
   General tab, 753–754
   nonprinting character display options, 42
   Print tab, 757–759
   Save tab, 764–766
   Save tab options, 198–200
   Security tab, 767–769
   Spelling & Grammar tab, 766–768
   Spelling & Grammar tab options, 227–229
   Track Changes tab, 759–760
   User Information tab, 761
   View tab, 750–752
   When Selecting, Automatically Select Entire Word, 94
Options tab, Customize dialog box, 778–779
Organization Chart Style Gallery dialog box, 495–496
Organization Chart tool, 494–496

Organizer dialog box
   copying styles between documents, 378–382
   copying/deleting/renaming templates, 401–403
   Macro Project Items tab, 795–796
   moving toolbars between documents/templates, 770
orientation
   page formatting, 295–297
   table text, 270–271
outline fonts, 109
Outline Levels, table of content assembly, 357
outline numbered lists, uses, 154–156
Outline view (Alt+Ctrl+O)
   automatic style application, 378
   described, 25, 26, 625–627
   selection methods, 630
   splitting windows, 632–633
   table of contents use, 351
outlined text, character formatting, 101
outlines
   copying, 633
   globally promoting/demoting headings, 630
   heading style integration, 625
   keyboard shortcuts, 631–632
   moving headings, 631
   new outline creation, 627–629
   Outline view (Alt+Ctrl+O), 625–627
   printing, 632
   promoting/demoting levels, 629–631
   rearranging, 630–632
   style viewing, 629
   uses, 625–626
Outlining toolbar
   activating, 626
   buttons, 628–629
   Master Document buttons, 634–635
   promoting/demoting outline levels, 630–631
Outlook. *See* Microsoft Outlook
Outlook address book, mail merges, 570
Overtype (OVR) mode, 17, 43

P
page breaks
   hard versus soft, 272
   inserting, 297
   paragraph formatting, 158–159
   preventing in tables, 271
Page Dn key, Reading Layout view navigation, 25
page formatting
   background repagination, 297–298
   facing pages, 295
   gutters, 295

hard breaks, 297
landscape orientation, 295–296
line numbers, 299–301
margin settings, 292–295
odd/even headers/footers, 310
pagination, 297
paper size/orientation settings, 295–297
portrait orientation, 295–296
soft breaks, 297
units of measurement, 292
vertical alignments, 298–299
Page Layout view
checking your work, 424
header/footer text entry, 307–308
Page Number Format dialog box, 305
page numbers
fields, 306–307
formatting, 304–305
header/footers, 303–304
removing, 304
repositioning, 304
section formatting, 305–307
viewing, 303
Page Numbers dialog box, 303–304
page ranges
index references, 342
printing, 164–165
page selections, printing, 164–165
Page Setup dialog box, margin settings, 292–294
Page Up key, Reading Layout view navigation, 25
page-composition, 412
page-layout, 412
pagination
correction techniques, 423–424
page formatting, 297
paragraph formatting, 158–159
Print Preview mode adjustments, 171–172
Paint Shop Pro
Animation Shop, 513
bitmap graphics, 437
decreasing colors, 510
image editor, 505
image resolution adjustments, 508–509
tiled backgrounds, 511–512
transparent backgrounds, 511–512
paper, size/orientation settings, 295–297
paragraph breaks, 121
Paragraph dialog box
indent settings, 138–139
line breaks, 158–159
line spacing adjustments, 128–129

page breaks, 158–159
paragraph alignments, 125–126
paragraph spacing adjustments, 128
paragraph formatting
alignments, 125–126, 414–415
automatic hyphenation, 159–160
borders, 139–145
border/text spacing, 143
bulleted lists, 148–151
click and type support, 127
fill shading, 145
finding/replacing, 87–90
format duplicating, 123–124
Format Painter button, 123–124
horizontal rules, 147
hyphenation, 159–161
indents, 135–139
justified alignment, 414–415
leading, 127–130
line breaks (Shift+Enter), 124–125
line spacing, 127–130
list styles, 157
manual hyphenation, 160–161
margins, 415
nonbreaking hyphens, 161
numbered lists, 151–156
optional hyphens, 161
outline numbered lists, 154–156
page breaks, 158–159
pagination, 158–159
paragraph information display, 122–123
paragraph spacing, 127–128
pattern shading, 145
removing formats, 124
ruler settings, 16
shading, 139, 145–146
styles, 121
tab settings, 130–135
white space, 127–130, 416
paragraph layout information, template component, 390
paragraph marks
described, 43, 121
displaying/hiding, 121
finding/replacing, 85–87
troubleshooting, 738–739
paragraph spacing, paragraph formatting, 127–128
paragraph styles
application methods, 372–373
copying styles between documents, 380
described, 368
Normal, 93

paragraphs
    beginning with Enter key, 43
    cutting/pasting, 56–57
    default character style, 93
    first line indents, 415
    format checking, 122–123
    resetting to default style format, 373
    style application methods, 372–373
    text entry conventions, 41
    white space uses, 416
parental controls, Research task pane, 248
passive sentences, readability statistics, 235
passwords
    digital signatures, 808–809
    document modification protection, 803–804
    document opening protection, 801–802
    form element, 671
    locking form fields, 622
    naming conventions, 802
Paste button, 55
Paste Options button, 55–56
Paste Special dialog box, 525–527, 530
pattern shading, paragraph formatting, 145
patterns
    background, 312–314
    picture borders, 450–451
PDFMarker.dot template, hiding/displaying Adobe
        Acrobat toolbar, 738
Pencil tool, merging/splitting cells, 272
percentages, zoom magnifications, 28
performance enhancements, 24, 742–743
period (.) character, pressing spacebar twice after, 414
peripheral devices, troubleshooting, 746
Perl, CGI (Common Gateway Interface) scripts, 667, 672
permissions
    document editing control, 816
    document restrictions, 807–808
Person Name Smart Tag menu, 604–605
Personalized Menus, IntelliSense recognition, 778–779
PhotoImpact, image editor, 505
phrases, AutoText entry conventions, 71–72
Picture Bullet dialog box, 150–151
Picture toolbar
    brightness/contrast adjustments, 453
    displaying, 8
    resizing/cropping pictures, 447
    wrapping styles, 457
pictures. See also clip art; graphics; images
    adding to a text box, 481–842
    adjustment methods, 452–454
    aspect ratio, 449
    borders, 449–451

bulleted lists, 150
ClipArt task pane, 441–445
converting to Word picture format, 512
copying/pasting into documents, 446
cropping, 447–449
document insertion methods, 440–441
hiding to speed up performance, 742
hiding while editing documents, 454
inline images, 450
placement troubleshooting, 741
resizing, 447–449
shadow borders, 451
SharePoint service, 718
pilcrows, 738
pixels
    bitmap graphic element, 437
    button image editing, 775
    defined, 553
placeholders
    displaying graphics as, 24
    number format, 614
    pictures, 454
plotter fonts, 110
plug-ins, image editors, 506
PNG (Portable Network Graphics), 507, 510
pointers, mouse shapes, 21
points, font size adjustments, 112–113
Portable Network Graphics (PNG), Web browser
        support, 507
portrait orientation, page formatting, 295–296
POST method, form data submission, 671
postage, envelope printing, 182
postal bar codes, envelopes, 572
POSTNET codes, printing, 180
PostScript Type 1 fonts
    character pair spacing, 107
    size/style adjustments, 108–113
    when to use, 117
PowerPoint. See Microsoft PowerPoint
presentation, linking/embedding data, 537–538
Preview view, file display, 5
Print button, 163
Print dialog box, 164, 172–174
Print Layout view (Alt+Ctrl+P)
    changing margins, 25
    comment balloon display, 699
    footnote/endnote separator line editing
        non-support, 334
    recurring/disappearing text, 740–741
    removing text boxes, 481
    returning from Outline view, 626
    vertical ruler display, 16

viewing page numbers, 303
white space adjustments, 25
Print Preview button, 28
Print Preview mode
    appearance settings, 170–171
    automatic pagination, 171–172
    checking your work, 423
    comment balloon display, 699
    described, 28–29
    document editing, 171
    embedded fonts, 115
    hidden text display, 114
    margin settings, 171
    navigation methods, 170
    previewing documents before printing, 168–172
    vertical ruler display, 16
Print Preview toolbar, screen elements, 168–170
print servers, network document printing, 186–187
Print tab, Options dialog box, 757–759
Printed Watermark dialog box, 315–316
printers
    drivers, 423
    envelope printing, 573
    image resolution adjustments, 508–509
    installation, 163
    print servers, 186–187
    property settings, 185–186
    selecting, 166–167
    troubleshooting, 746
Printers folder, default printer settings, 166
printing
    AutoText contents, 74
    AutoText entries, 166
    bookmark non-support, 319
    color suggestions, 167–168
    comments, 166, 704
    Document Image Writer files, 175
    document information, 166
    drag-and-drop, 166
    electronic postage on envelopes, 819
    envelope graphics, 180–182
    envelope logos, 180–182
    envelope postage, 182
    envelopes, 176–182, 571–573
    to a fax modem, 176
    field codes, 587–588
    to a file, 174–175
    FIMs (Facing Identification Marks), 180
    form data, 185
    forms, 623
    hidden text, 114
    highlighted text issues, 704

image resolution adjustments, 508–509
    keyboard shortcuts, 166
    labels, 176, 182–185
    list of styles, 382
    mailing labels, 573–574
    merge record order, 581–582
    multiple documents, 165
    multiple/collated copies, 165
    network documents, 186–187
    outlines, 632
    page ranges, 164–165
    page selections, 164–165
    POSTNET codes, 180
    previewing documents, 168–172
    Print Preview mode, 168–170
    printer selections, 166–167
    reverse order, 165
    styles, 166
    text selections, 164–165
    updating linked objects, 532
    watermarks, 315–316
privacy, Customer Service Improvement Program
        settings, 34
problem solving. See also troubleshooting
    bookmarks, 323–324
    dictation taking, 430–431
    master document naming conflicts, 636
profiles, speech recognition, 428
Programs menu, Word startup, 3
Progressive JPEG, versus JPEG, 510
proofreading
    AutoCorrect, 236–239
    checking your work, 422–424
    correcting spelling/grammar after working, 224–229
    spelling/grammar errors as you type, 223–224
    word translations, 243–244
properties
    documents, 166, 210–212
    frame configuration, 650–652
    Open dialog box, 193–194
Properties dialog box, 210–212, 669
Properties view, file display, 5
proportional fonts, 44
Protect Document button, Options dialog box, 804
Protect Document task pane, document editing, 816
Protect Form button, locking form fields, 622
protections. See also security
    data encryption, 802–803
    document modification, 803–804
    editing restrictions, 806
    formatting restrictions, 805–806
    levels, 804–807

Continued

protections *(continued)*
 passwords, 801–802
 person/section exceptions, 806–807
 style locking, 815
 unprotecting multiple document areas, 807
publishing, Web pages, 659–660
pull quotes, 168, 421
PWS (Microsoft Personal Web Server), Web Folders,
 658–659

Q

queries
 merge records, 578–581
 Microsoft Query, 534
Query Options dialog box, merge queries, 578–582
Quick Launch, Word startup shortcut, 4
quotes, pull, 168

R

radio (option) buttons, form element, 669–670
random numbers, merge accuracy enhancement, 807
ransom-note desktop publishing, described, 411
rasterizing, 509
RC4 encryption, Word version limitations, 803
Read button, Reading Layout view access, 712
readability
 bold text, 421
 colored text, 421
 document design element, 412–413
 image issues, 421–422
 italic text, 421
 serif versus sans serif typefaces, 417–418
 typesetting characters, 419–420
 underline text, 421
 white space enhancement, 416
Readability Statistics dialog box, 235
Reading Layout view
 comment balloon display, 699
 document navigation, 25–26, 712–713
 text editing, 714
 text sizing, 714
Reading Mode Markup toolbar, 712
Reading Mode toolbar, 712
Read-Only Recommended, document modification
 protection, 804
REC indicator, status bar display, 787
REC (record) mode, status bar display, 17
Recently Used File List, changing default settings, 5
Recheck Document button, spelling/grammar, 236
Record Macro dialog box, recording macros, 787–788
record (record) mode, status bar display, 17

records, merge queries, 578–581
recovery, files, 207–210
Recycle Bin, emptying, 747
Redo button, 54
reference marks, footnotes/endnotes, 331
reference sources, Research task pane, 247–248
references, object captions, 498–504
registration, activating, 34
regular text field, forms, 612, 613
remarks, macro application, 794
Repeat (Ctrl+Y/F4) command, 23
Research button, Research task pane access, 240
Research task pane
 access methods, 240
 adding/updating/removing services, 248
 dictionary, 242–243
 display options, 247
 encyclopedia search, 245
 information search enhancements, 818
 Internet searches, 244–245
 navigation techniques, 240–241
 parental controls, 248
 reference sources, 247–248
 stock quotes, 245–247
 thesaurus, 242–243
 translations, 243–244
 uses, 239–241
Reset button, form element, 672
Reset Toolbar command, 12
Reset Window Position button, side-by-side document
 comparison, 711
resolutions
 bitmap versus vector graphics, 437–438
 image adjustments, 508–509
 monitor display settings, 507–508
 scanned image guidelines, 446
 task pane viewing enhancements, 814
restricted characters, document naming conventions, 32
result fields, 590
Resume Wizard, 407–408
reveal codes, Word versus WordPerfect, 38
 accessing, 371
 character formatting display, 102–104
 described, 38
 paragraph information display, 122–123
reverse order printing, uses, 165
Review AutoFormat Changes dialog box, 385
reviewer initials, comments, 698
reviewers
 automatically saving new file versions, 206
 comparing/merging comments, 710–711

Reviewing pane
    comment editing, 701–702
    comment navigation, 702
    comment selections, 700
    inserting comments, 698
    printing comments, 704
    reviewing comments, 702–703
Reviewing toolbar
    accepting/rejecting changes, 706–707
    change views, 705–706
    displaying, 8
    uses, 698–699
revision marks
    AutoFormat, 386
    comparing/merging, 710–711
    customizing, 708–709
    highlighting text, 704
    uses, 705
Rich Text Format (RTF) file format, 527
right alignment, table positioning, 259
Right Indent marker, 137
right margin, object positioning, 460
right-aligned tabs, 131
right-alignment, paragraph formatting 125–126
right-click shortcut menus, 22–23
Rights Management, document protections, 817
routing, e-mail documents, 690–692
Routing Slip dialog box, 691–692
row titles, Datasheet window element, 540–541
rows
    chart data exclusion, 546–547
    copying/moving, 264–265
    Datasheet window element, 540–541
    height adjustments, 265, 269
    inserting in Datasheet window, 543
    inserting/deleting, 263–264
    spacing adjustments, 269
    table headings, 272
    table limitations, 253
RTF (Rich Text Format) file format, 527
rulers
    changing margins in Print Layout view, 25
    column width adjustments, 265–267
    displaying/hiding, 16
    indent markers, 137
    margin settings, 294–295
    Move Table Column markers, 265–266
    paragraph formatting, 16
    row height/spacing adjustments, 269
    tab settings, 130, 132–133
    table tab stops, 273–274
    units of measurement, 16

rules
    grammar/writing style, 234
    merge query, 579–581

S

sans serif typefaces
    Arial, 417–418
    heading text advantages, 417–418
    Verdana, 418
Save As dialog box (Ctrl+S)
    Create New Folder button, 196
    described, 32–33
    file format converters, 201–202
    renaming a file when saving, 200–201
    saving a document as a Web page, 203–204
Save tab, Options dialog box, 198–200, 764–766
Save Version dialog box, 204–205
scalable fonts, 109
scanners
    picture insertion method, 446
    resolution guidelines, 446
    troubleshooting, 746
Schema Library dialog box, 680
schemas, XML document, 679–681
scraps, document, 61
ScreenTip help, toolbar buttons, 8
Scribble tool, drawing freeform lines/shapes, 473
Script Editor. *See* Microsoft Script Editor
scripts
    adding to a Web page, 672–675
    CGI (Common Gateway Interface), 672
    Perl, 667
    rollover, 673–675
    Web forms, 667
scroll bars
    displaying/hiding, 48
    document navigation method, 16
    insertion point navigation, 47–49
scroll box, document navigation method, 16
scrolling text banners, Web pages, 677
Scrolling Text button, adding banners to a
    Web page, 677
Scrolling Text dialog box, 677–678
Search Browse Object button, searches, 83
searches
    adding text to replacement text, 87
    Advanced File Search task pane, 217–218
    bookmarks, 320–321
    comments, 702–703
    directions, 79–80
    fields, 586–587
    file indexes, 217

Continued

searches *(continued)*
    File Open dialog box, 218–219
    File Search task pane, 214–218
    files, 214–219
    Find command, 77–81
    finding versus highlighting, 79
    finding/replacing formats, 87–90
    finding/replacing special characters, 85–87
    finding/replacing word forms, 85
    footnotes/endnotes, 332
    Go To What list, 50
    help system, 36
    highlighted text, 106
    horizontal lines, 147
    Internet, 244–245
    match case criteria, 80
    merge records, 578–581
    Microsoft Clip Organizer, 443–445
    Microsoft Encarta, 245
    operators, 219
    replacing found text, 83–90
    Research Task pane, 818
    SharePoint hosting services, 717
    Smart Tags, 604–607
    sounds like, 82–83
    stock quotes, 245–247
    text entry conventions, 78
    text selections, 80
    text strings, 81
    thesaurus, 241–242
    whole words, 80
    wildcard characters/operators, 81–82
    wildcards, 219
    word translations, 243–244
section breaks
    copying, 285
    inserting, 284–285
    page numbers, 305–207
    pasted text issues, 62–63
    removing, 286
    showing/hiding, 284
section formatting
    copying section breaks, 285
    different first-page header/footer, 309–310
    headers/footers, 309
    inserting section breaks, 284–285
    page numbers, 305–307
    pasted text issues, 62–63
    removing section breaks, 286
    when to use, 283
sections, 17

security. *See also* protections
    collaboration protection methods, 801–807
    digital signatures, 808–809
    document modification protection, 803–804
    document opening protections, 801–802
    document protection levels, 804–807
    encryption, 802–803
    macro methods, 810
    passwords, 801–802
    permission restrictions, 807–808
    RC4 encryption, 803
Security tab, Options dialog box, 767–769
Select Browse Object button
    field navigation, 586–587
    Find command search, 77–78
    footnote/endnote navigation, 331–332
Select Certificate dialog box, digital signatures, 808–809
Select Multiple Objects dialog box, 462
selection bar, text selections, 51
semicolon (;) placeholder, number format, 614
Send To Exchange Folder dialog box, 731–732
separators, footnote/endnote, 333–334
serial comma, 234
serif typefaces, 417–418
Set Target Frame dialog box, frame links, 654
Set Transparent Color button, backgrounds, 454
Settings, Taskbar and Start menu command, 737
shading
    application methods, 146
    described, 139
    field code display, 586–587
    fill versus pattern, 145
    linked and embedded objects, 533–534
    tables, 273
    Tables and Borders toolbar, 146
    Web page enhancements, 655–656
shadow borders, pictures, 451
Shadow button, picture borders, 451
Shadow Setting toolbar, 451
Shadow Style button, drop shadows, 451
shadowed lines/shapes, drawing, 473–474
shadowed text, character formatting, 101
shapes
    AutoShapes menu, 470–471
    bulleted lists, 148
    drawing methods, 469–474
    freeform, 472–473
    removing, 477
    resizing, 476
    shadowed, 473–474
    WordArt, 492

shared documents. *See* documents
shared workspaces, SharePoint enhancements, 818
SharePoint
    access methods, 717
    bookmarks, 724
    Document Library page, 720–724
    document workspaces, 724–725
    document-management workspaces, 718
    file sharing, 718–720
    hosting services, 717–718
    index workspace, 718
    library check-out system, 722–723
    meeting workspace, 718
    My Network Places, 727–728
    online meetings, 728–731
    shared workspace enhancements, 818
    uploading files, 722
    versions, 723–724
    Web discussions, 725–727
Shift key
    adjacent file selections, 195
    automatic macro run prevention, 792
    column width adjustments, 265
    constraining tool, 471
    text selections, 52
Shift+Tab keys, dialog box navigation method, 19
shortcut keys. *See also* keyboard shortcuts
    versus character codes, 65
    character formats, 89
    character formatting uses, 94
    command selection method, 22
    finding/replacing special characters, 85–87
    font size adjustments, 112
    line spacing, 129
    macro assignment, 788
    paragraph alignments, 126
    restoring to default, 783
    special characters, 65–66
    styles, 377
    template component, 391
shortcut menu (Shift+F10)
    editing, 777
    moving/copying selections, 57
    right-click access, 22–23
Shortcut Menus toolbar, editing shortcut menus, 777
shortcut-menu key, PC keyboards, 57
shortcuts
    adding a document to the desktop, 192–193
    deleting, 4
    placing on the desktop, 4
    starting Word from, 3–4

Web Folder, 658–659
Word startup switches, 6
Show, Comments command, 699
Show/Hide button (Ctrl+Shift+*)
    described, 113–114
    displaying/hiding paragraph marks, 121
    nonprinting character display, 39, 42
    showing/hiding section breaks, 284
Show/Hide Document Text button, Headers and
        Footers toolbar, 308
side headings, text boxes, 487
side margins, default settings, 414
signatures, e-mail, 693
slot, Microsoft Equation assembly box, 551
Small Caps (Ctrl+Shift+K), character formatting, 99
Small Icons view, file display, 5
Smart Documents, XML content reliance, 819
Smart Tags
    AutoCorrect dialog box, 605–607
    ESPN, 607
    FedEx, 607
    LexisNexis, 607
    MSNBC, 607
    Person Name Smart Tag menu, 604–605
snaking columns. *See* column formatting
snapshots, automatically saving new file versions, 206
soft breaks, page formatting, 297
soft returns. *See* line breaks (Shift+Enter)
software, CD-ROM applications, 822–827
Sort button, Tables and Borders toolbar, 276
Sort dialog box, table data sort, 276–277
sorts
    bookmarks, 320
    merge records, 581–582
    table data, 276–277
    tabular text, 277
Sound button, adding sounds to a Web page, 676–677
sound cards, speech recognition requirement, 426
sound clips
    editing embedded objects, 528
    Web pages, 657
sound objects, embedding, 514
Sound Recorder, voice comments, 700–701
sounds
    adding to a Web page, 676–677
    audio clips, 514
    background, 514
    supported audio types, 514
    voice comments, 700–701
sounds like search, 82–83
source code, HTML, 652–653, 664–665

source file, linked objects, 519–520
spacebar
    pressing twice after period (.) character, 414
    text alignment concerns, 44
    text entry conventions, 41
spacing
    character, 106–107
    character pairs, 107
    column formatting, 289–290
    justified text, 414–415
    leading, 127
    line, 127–130
    Microsoft Equation, 552
    paragraph, 127–128
    row adjustments, 269
    table cell adjustments, 267–268
    versus tabs, 130
    between text and border, 143
    toolbar buttons, 772
    WordArt, 493–494
Spacing control, character spacing, 106–107
Spacing dialog box, 552–553
speakers, speech recognition requirement, 426
special characters
    bulleted lists, 150
    field codes, 590
    finding/replacing, 85–87
    inserting, 63–67
    typesetting characters, 419–420
special effects
    embossed text, 100
    engraved text, 100
    outlined text, 101
    shadowed text, 101
    text animation, 101–102
Special menu, special characters, 85–87
speech recognition
    adding/deleting words, 431
    described, 425
    hardware requirements, 426
    Language bar, 426–433
    microphone volume settings, 426–427
    problem solving, 430–431
    taking dictation, 429–432
    user profiles, 428
    voice commands, 430
    voice training, 427–429
spell checker
    adding AutoCorrect entries, 237
    checking your work, 422
    correcting after working, 224–229
    correcting as you type, 223–224

custom dictionary, 229–231
    disabling to speedup performance, 742
    exclude dictionary, 231
    rechecking documents, 235–236, 423
    skipping selected text, 226–227
    supported languages, 227
Spelling and Grammar button, 224
Spelling and Grammar dialog box, 224–226, 232–234
Spelling & Grammar tab, Options dialog box,
        227–229, 766–768
Spike (Ctrl+F3/Ctrl+Shift+F3), multiple cut/paste
        operations, 61–62
split bar, splitting windows, 16
split box, document window, 45–46
Split Cells dialog box, 272
split views, Normal/Outline views, 632–633
spreadsheets, versus datasheet, 542
Standard toolbar
    adding Find command to, 79
    buttons, 9–12
    combining/separating with Formatting toolbar, 8
    display settings, 736–737
    zoom magnifications, 28
Start menu, Word startup, 3
Startup folder, starting Windows with Word open, 4
stationery, e-mail, 693
status bar
    displaying/hiding, 17
    document information display, 17
    EXT (Extend Mode) display, 262
    form field help text display, 619–620
    mode indicators, 17
    OVR (Overtype) mode, 43
    REC indicator, 787
    spelling/grammatical status information display, 224
    TRK box display, 705
stock photography, sources, 439–440
stock quotes, information display, 245–247
strikethrough text, character formatting, 100
stroke fonts, 110
Style and Formatting task pane
    modifying styles, 376–377
    viewing style information, 373
Style Area
    outline viewing, 629
    style name display, 381–382
style creep, prevention methods, 805
Style dialog box, 346–347, 373
Style drop-down list box, 369, 376
Style Gallery button, 396
Style Gallery dialog box, 380–382, 396
style guides, form versus function issues, 412–413

styles
    adding to a template, 375
    AutoFormat, 383–388
    automatic application, 378
    automatically updating, 377
    captions, 502–503
    character, 368
    copying between documents, 378–382
    custom views, 371–372
    defined, 121, 367
    deleting, 376–377
    versus direct formatting, 367
    finding/replacing, 87–90
    footnotes/endnotes, 332
    formatting integration, 368
    formatting tools, 376
    heading, 351, 352–354, 369
    HTML, 652–653, 665
    index, 346–347
    information views, 373
    keyboard shortcut support, 782–783
    keyboard shortcuts, 781–782
    lists, 157, 368
    locking/unlocking, 815
    modifying, 376–377
    new, 374–376
    Normal, 369
    Organizer, 378–379
    paragraph formatting, 121, 368, 372–373
    previewing in a template, 396
    printing, 166, 382
    removing paragraph formats, 124
    renaming, 382
    selection methods, 374
    shadow borders 451
    shortcut keys, 377
    Style Area name display, 381–382
    style creep prevention, 805–806
    Style Gallery, 380–382
    table, 368
    table of figures, 358–360
    template relationship, 368–369
    theme relationship, 368–369
    types, 368
    view methods, 369–374
Styles and Formatting task pane, viewing styles, 370
subdocuments, master documents, 638–641
subentries, index entry marking, 341, 343
Submit button, form element, 671–672
subscript text (Ctrl+=), character formatting, 97–98
substitutions, unavailable fonts, 116–117

summary, documents, 212–214
superscript text (Ctrl+Shift+=), character formatting, 97–98
surveys, SharePoint service, 718
switches
    date-time picture field (\@), 601–603
    defined, 344
    field instruction element, 595–596
    format field (*), 597–599
    locking/unlocking fields, 603–604
    number picture field (\#), 599–601
    Word startup, 6
Symbol dialog box, 63–67
Symbol fonts, supported types, 109
symbols
    ANSI character set, 63–64
    bulleted lists, 148
    character code insertion, 64–65
    document naming restricted characters, 32
    finding/replacing special characters, 85–87
    inserting, 63–67
    keyboard shortcut support, 782
    Microsoft Equation, 551
    typesetting characters, 419–420
Synchronous Scrolling button, side-by-side document comparison, 711
synonyms, thesaurus uses, 242–243
system crash, AutoRecover, 207–210
system date/time, document insertion, 44–45
system requirements, CD-ROM, 821
system tray, sound display, 426
systems, information display, 34

T

tab characters, showing/hiding, 752
Tab key
    dialog box navigation method, 19
    tab stop settings, 130–135
    table navigation, 260
tab leaders, uses, 134
tab marks, finding/replacing, 85–87
tab stops. *See also* tabs
    changing/clearing, 133–135
    modifying default settings, 135
    ruler settings, 130, 132–133
    tables, 273–274
Table, AutoFit command, 267
Table, Convert, Table to Text command, 276
Table, Convert, Text to Table command, 275
Table, Delete, Cells command, 263
Table, Delete, Columns command, 264

Table, Delete, Rows command, 264
Table, Delete, Table command, 264
Table, Distribute Rows Evenly command, 269
Table, Draw Table command, 257
Table, Formula command, 278
Table, Heading Rows Repeat command, 272
Table, Hide Gridlines command, 273
Table, Insert, Cells command, 263
Table, Insert, Table command, 252
Table, Insert command, 263
Table, Merge Cells command, 271
Table, Select command, 261
Table, Show Gridlines command, 273
Table, Sort command, 276
Table, Split Cells command, 272
Table, Split Table command, 270
Table, Table AutoFormat command, 254
Table, Table Properties command, 258, 268
Table AutoFormat dialog box, 254–255
Table label, captions, 502
Table menu (Alt+A)
    column width adjustments, 266
    opening, 8
table of contents
    automatic style application, 378
    compiling, 352
    custom style assembly process, 354–355
    document preparation, 351–352
    frames, 351
    heading styles, 352, 352–354
    hidden text, 114
    hyperlinks, 351, 353
    Outline Levels assembly, 357
    selection marking, 351
    TC field, 351, 355–357
    TOC field, 351
    updating, 357–358
    viewing field codes, 354
table of contents (TC) field, 351
table of contents (TOC) field, 351
Table of Contents link, help system, 36
Table of Contents Options dialog box, 355
table of figures, compiling, 358–360
Table Options dialog box, 268
Table Positioning dialog box, 259
Table Properties dialog box, 258–259, 266–267
table styles, described, 368
tables
    adding to documents, 252–259
    alignments, 271
    of authorities, 360–363
    AutoFormat, 254–255

bookmarks, 280
borders, 273
calculations, 278
captions, 280–281
cell numbering, 277
cell spacing adjustments, 267–268
chart conversion, 549
column limits, 253
column width adjustments, 265–267
column/row headings, 272
concordance file, 338–340
copying cells/rows/columns, 264–265
data sorts, 276–277
deleting cells/rows/columns, 263–264
document positioning, 258–259
drawing, 255–258
of figures, 358–360
form addition, 621
formulas, 278–279
gridlines, 273
inserting cells/rows/columns, 263
insertion methods, 252–254
layout modifications, 262–270
merging/splitting cells, 271–272
moving cells/rows/columns, 264–265
navigation techniques, 260
nesting, 255–256, 258
versus newspaper-like columns, 252
non-uniform, 255–258
number formats, 279–280
page break prevention, 271
positioning, 271
repeating commands, 252
resizing, 262
row height adjustments, 265
row height/spacing adjustments, 269
row limits, 253
shading, 273
splitting, 270
tab settings, 273–274
templates, 254–255
text alignments, 270
text conversion, 274–276
text entry conventions, 260
text formatting, 270
text orientation, 270–271
text selection methods, 261–262
text wrapping, 259
text/graphics positioning, 274
undoing mistakes, 252
Web pages, 655

Tables and Borders toolbar
    buttons, 140–141
    shading application, 146
    uses, 252, 257–258
tables of authorities, compiling, 360–363
Tablet PCs, described, 712
tabs. *See also* tab stops
    bar, 131–132
    center-aligned, 131
    decimal, 131
    dialog box element, 20
    leader tabs, 134
    left-aligned, 131
    paragraph formatting, 130–135
    right-aligned, 131
    versus spacing, 130
    tables, 273–274
Tabs dialog box, 130–131, 133–135
tabular text, sorting, 277
tags
    attributes, 663–664
    HTML conventions, 663–665
    XML, 680–681
Target Frame button, frame links, 654
task lists, SharePoint service, 718
task panes
    described, 14–15
    displaying available, 14
    moving between open, 15
    New Document, 30, 31
    opening/closing, 15
    sizing, 15
    viewing available, 813–814
taskbar
    hiding/displaying, 737
    organizing displayed components, 737
    resizing, 737
    sound display, 426
    switching between open documents, 737
    Word startup shortcut placement, 4
TC (table of contents) field
    comment non-support, 701
    described, 351
    table of contents assembly, 355–357
    table of figures, 359
technical support, system information display, 34
Temp folder, saved file limitations, 747
Template folder, template storage, 392
template macros, storage, 786
templates
    access methods, 392–395
    accessing from On My Computer link, 30

    adding a style to, 375
    attachments, 397
    AutoText entries, 391, 400–401
    Blank Document, 391
    boilerplate text, 390
    components, 390–391
    copying, 401–403
    copying components between, 401–402
    copying styles between documents, 380
    copying/moving macros between, 795–796
    creating from another template, 397
    custom creation, 396–397
    defined, 29, 369, 389
    deleting, 401–403
    deleting components, 403
    document design issues, 413
    document links, 397–399
    document/text layout information, 390
    dot file extension, 392
    field codes, 390
    fields, 395
    folder storage path, 392
    form creation method, 610
    local to global conversion, 399
    local versus global, 391
    macros, 391, 400
    menu bars, 391
    menus, 400
    Microsoft Equation, 551
    moving toolbars between, 770
    naming conventions, 392
    Normal, 29–30, 391
    opening as actual template, 395
    opening global automatically, 400
    PDFMarker.dot, 783
    previewing styles, 396
    renaming, 401–403
    renaming components, 403
    restoring default shortcut key assignments, 783
    saving a document as, 395–396
    saving a form as, 622
    shortcut keys, 391
    starting a new document from, 30
    tables, 254–255
    toolbars, 391, 400
    uses, 390
    Web page, 644–645
Templates and Add-Ins dialog box, 397–398
Templates dialog box, 30, 393–394
Templates on Office Online button, online templates, 393–394
temporary files, AutoRecover, 207–208

text
 field instruction element, 595
 highlighting, 704
text alignments
 described, 44
 tables, 270
text area
 form element, 671
 insertion point, 7
text blocks, finding/replacing with Clipboard, 87
Text Box toolbar, 481, 485
text boxes. *See also* frames
 callouts, 496–498
 column placement, 487–488
 copying/moving, 483
 desktop publishing techniques, 486–489
 dialog box element, 20
 flowing text between, 484–485
 form element, 670
 inserting, 480–481
 internal margins, 482
 removing, 481
 repeating text/graphics, 488–489
 resizing, 483–484
 selection methods, 482–483
 side headings, 487
 switching to a frame, 486
 text directions, 486
 text formatting, 484–486
 text/drawing object addition, 481–482
Text button, inserting frames, 480
Text Direction dialog box, 270–271
Text Direction - Text Box dialog box, 486
text editing
 AutoCorrect, 67–71
 AutoText, 71–74
 changing found search text, 80–81, 83–90
 character code insertion, 64–65
 checking spelling/grammar as you type, 223–224
 column conventions, 288–289
 cutting/copying/pasting text, 55, 62–63
 date/time insertion, 44–45
 deleting text, 53–54
 displaying/hiding text, 113–114
 document scraps, 61
 drag-and-drop technique, 60–61
 extended selections, 52–53
 inserting/overtyping text, 43
 last editing location return (Shift+F5), 49–50
 line breaks (Shift+Enter), 43–44
 manual line breaks, 43
 moving/copying text, 54–63

 new paragraph (Enter key), 43
 nonprinting character display, 42–43
 Reading Layout view, 714
 recurring/disappearing text, 740–741
 special characters, 63–67
 Spike (Ctrl+F3/Ctrl+Shift+F3) operations, 61–62
 splitting document window, 45–46
 style application methods, 372–373
 substituting unavailable fonts, 116–117
 symbols, 63–67
 table conversion, 274–276
 table entry conventions, 260
 text alignments, 44
 text entry conventions, 41
 text selections, 51–53
 WordArt text/letters, 493
text editors, 652–653, 664–665
text encoding, file conversions, 191
text fields, forms, 612–617
Text Form Field Options dialog box, 612–613
text formatting
 adding text to replacement text, 87
 clearing, 369
 comments, 701–702
 editing text when performing a search, 80–81
 Find command search, 77–81
 finding versus highlighting items, 79
 finding/replacing special characters, 85–87
 finding/replacing styles, 87–90
 finding/replacing word forms, 85
 footnotes/endnotes, 332
 index entries, 344
 retaining when cutting/pasting, 55–56
 search criteria conventions, 78
 sounds like search, 82–83
 tables, 270
 text boxes, 484–486
 text search markers, 78
text layer, layering drawing objects, 478–480
text layout information, template component, 390
text lines, borders, 143
text markers, Find command search uses, 78
text orientation, tables, 270–271
text selections
 printing, 164–165
 skipping when spell checking, 226–227
text services, described, 426
text strings, 81
text wrap, table positioning, 259
Text Wrapping button, Edit Wrap Points, 458
textures, backgrounds, 313–314
Theme dialog box, 409, 654–655

themes
    defined, 369, 389
    FrontPage, 409
    uses, 408–409
    Web page enhancements, 655–656
thesaurus, 242–243
Thumbnail pane, sizing, 29
thumbnails
    document views, 29
    Open dialog box, 193–194
Thumbnails view, file display, 5
tick marks, chart element, 544
tiled images, described, 511–512
times, document insertion, 44–45
Times New Roman, serif typeface, 417–418
titles
    charts, 547
    Datasheet window column/row, 540–541
    Web pages, 646
TOC (table of contents) field, described, 351
toolbar buttons, ScreenTip help, 8
toolbars
    adding commands to, 79
    adding/removing buttons, 12
    Adobe Acrobat, 738
    AutoShapes, 470
    AutoText, 73
    button addition methods, 771–772
    button editing, 773–775
    button spacing adjustments, 772
    Canvas, 466–467
    combining/separating, 8
    custom, 775–776
    Customize dialog box options, 770–771
    customizing, 8
    Database, 534
    deleting buttons, 772
    display settings, 736–737
    displaying, 8–9
    drag bar, 9
    Drawing, 8, 467–469
    Equation, 550–551
    floating/anchoring, 9
    Formatting, 8, 12–13
    Forms, 611–612
    Frames, 649
    Graph Formatting, 544
    Header and Footer, 307–308
    macro assignment, 402, 788
    Media Player, 515–516
    moving between documents/templates, 770
    moving/copying buttons, 772

    Online Meeting, 728–729
    Organization Chart, 494–495
    Outlining, 626–629
    Picture, 447
    Print Preview, 168–170
    Reading Mode, 712
    Reading Mode Markup, 712
    removing unnecessary, 738
    repositioning, 737
    resetting default buttons, 12
    restoring to default, 773
    Reviewing, 8, 698–699
    Shadow Setting, 451
    Shortcut Menus, 777
    Standard, 8, 9–12
    Tables and Borders, 140–141, 252, 257–258
    task panes, 14–15
    template component, 391, 400
    Text Box, 481, 485
    3-D, 473–474
    Visual Basic Editor, 799
    Web, 658
    Web Tools, 514, 666–667
    Word Count, 817
    WordArt, 491–492
    WordMail, 689
Toolbars tab, Customize dialog box, 770–771
Tools, Add/Delete Word(s) command, 431
Tools, AutoCorrect command, 67, 236
Tools, AutoCorrect Options command, 68, 419
Tools, AutoSummarize command, 212
Tools, Compare and Merge Documents command, 710
Tools, Customize command, 8, 736, 770
Tools, Envelopes and Labels command, 177
Tools, Folder Options command, 191
Tools, Language, Hyphenation command, 159, 423
Tools, Language, Set Language command, 226
Tools, Language, Thesaurus command, 240
Tools, Language, Translate command, 240
Tools, Letters and Mailings, Mail Merge Wizard
        command, 561
Tools, Letters and Mailings, Show Mail Merge toolbar
        command, 568
Tools, Macro, Macros command, 788
Tools, Macro, Record New Macro command, 787
Tools, Macro, Stop Recording command, 788
Tools, Online Collaboration, Meet Now
        command, 728
Tools, Options command, 5, 42
Tools, Protect Document command, 622, 804
Tools, Research command, 14, 240, 818
Tools, Save Version command, 205

Tools, Shared Workspaces command, 818
Tools, Speech command, 426, 429
Tools, Spelling and Grammar (F7) command, 224
Tools, Templates and Add-Ins command, 378, 738
Tools, Training command, 431
Tools, Unprotect Document command, 622
Tools, Word Count command, 212, 817
top/bottom margins, default settings, 414
topics, multilevel indexes, 343
Torricelli's Equation, described, 552
Track Changes dialog box, customizing revision
          marks, 708–709
Track Changes tab, Options dialog box, 759–760
Track Changes/Reviewing
    accepting/rejecting changes, 706–707
    comparing/merging comments/revisions, 710–711
    comparing/merging documents, 709–711
    custom revision marks, 708–709
    revision marks, 705
    side-by-side document comparison, 711
    viewing changes, 705–706
track (TRK) mode, status bar display, 17
translations, uses, 243–244
transparent backgrounds, images, 453–454, 511–512
TRK box, status bar display, 705
TRK (track) mode, status bar display, 17
troubleshooting. *See also* problem solving
    AutoCorrect, 739–740
    AutoFormat, 739–740
    bookmark problems, 323–324
    cannot save a file, 747
    CD-ROM installation, 827
    corrupted files, 745
    detecting/repairing missing or corrupt files, 745–746
    dictation taking, 430–431
    disappearing images, 455
    disk error messages, 747
    display drivers, 746
    file backup/recovery, 744–746
    font display, 741
    hard disk free space, 747
    install on demand, 735–736
    macro viruses, 746–747
    master document naming conflicts, 636
    missing menu components, 736–737
    paragraph marks, 738–739
    peripheral devices, 746
    picture placement, 741
    printers, 746
    recurring/disappearing text, 740–741
    scanners, 746
    taskbar clutter, 737

TrueType fonts
    character pair spacing, 107
    display troubleshooting, 741
    Fonts Control Panel, 117–119
    shared documents, 114–117
    size/style adjustments, 108–113
    when to use, 117
TrueType Symbol font (Ctrl+Shift+Q), 111
trusted sources, macro security, 810
TWAIN protocol, image scanning, 446
type, field element, 591
typefaces (fonts), 417–419
typesetting characters, 419–420

U

ULead
    GIF Animator, 513
    PhotoImpact, 505
unavailable (dimmed) command display, 21
unavailable fonts, substituting, 116–117
Underline button (Ctrl+U), character formatting, 96–97
underlined text
    character formatting, 96–97
    document design guidelines, 421
Undo button, undoing actions, 23, 54
Undo (Ctrl+Z) command, 23
Unicode encoding, font troubleshooting, 741
Unicode text file format, 527
units of measurement
    page formatting, 292
    points, 112–113
    rulers, 16
Update Table of Contents dialog box, 358
UpdateFields macro, uses, 791
URL encoded data, forms, 667
user information, reviewer initials, 698
User Information tab, Options dialog box, 761
user permissions, document editing controls, 816
user profiles, speech recognition, 428
User Templates folder, Normal.dot storage, 392

V

vector fonts, 110
vector graphics, versus bitmap graphics, 437–438
Vector Markup Language (VML), described, 506
Venali Inc. online fax service, 687
Verdana, sans serif typeface, 418
version number, program information display, 34
versions
    automatically saving, 206
    deleting, 205
    document save method, 204–206

saving as a separate file, 205–206
SharePoint documents, 723–724
sharing documents with previous Word
versions, 206
viewing multiple copies of same document, 205
Versions dialog box, 204–206
vertical alignments, page formatting, 298–299
vertical lines, column formatting, 289
vertical ruler
changing top/bottom margins in Print Layout
view, 25
displaying, 16
margin settings, 294–295
row height/spacing adjustments, 269
vertical scroll bar
document navigation, 16
moving insertion point when scrolling, 47–49
Search Browse Object button, 83
Select Browse Object button, 77
split box, 45–46
VGA monitors, resolution/color settings, 508
video clips
adding to a Web page, 675–676
editing embedded objects, 528
inserting, 515–516
Web pages, 657
View, Datasheet command, 542
View, Document Map command, 27
View, Footnotes command, 331
View, Full Screen command, 28
View, Header and Footer command, 303
View, HTML Source command, 652, 664
View, Markup command, 699
View, Normal command, 24
View, Outline (Alt+Ctrl+O) command, 625
View, Print Layout command, 303
View, Reading Layout command, 712
View, Ruler command, 16
View, Thumbnails command, 29
View, Toolbars, AutoText command, 73
View, Toolbars, Customize command, 770
View, Toolbars, Database command, 534
View, Toolbars, Formatting command, 93
View, Toolbars, Forms command, 611
View, Toolbars, Picture command, 447
View, Toolbars, Reviewing command, 698
View, Toolbars, Task Pane command, 14
View, Toolbars, Web command, 658
View, Toolbars, Word Count command, 212
View, Toolbars command, 8
View, Web Layout command, 25, 645, 657
View, Zoom command, 28, 814
View Datasheet window, 542

View menu (Alt+F)
displaying, 28
Document Map view, 27
Full Screen view, 27–28
Normal view, 24
Outline view, 25, 26
Print Layout view, 25
Print Preview view, 28–29
Reading Layout view, 25, 26
Web Layout view, 25
View tab, Options dialog box, 750–752
views
Document Map, 27
file display, 5
Full Screen, 27–28
Normal, 24
Outline, 25, 26
Print Layout, 25
Print Preview, 28–29
Reading Layout, 25, 26
thumbnails, 29
Web Layout, 25
virus checkers, importance of, 810
viruses, macro, 746–747, 790
Visual Basic
ANSIValue macro code display, 797–799
development history, 796
macro writing, 799
versus WordBasic, 796–797
Visual Basic Editor, macro editing techniques, 792–794
Visual Basic Editor toolbar, 799
VML (Vector Markup Language), described, 506
Voice Command button, Language bar, 429, 432
voice comments, uses, 700–701
Voice Training Wizard, 427–429

W
watermarks
image protection method, 513
print guidelines, 168
uses, 315–316
wbk (backup) file extension, 210, 745
Web browsers
HTML coding issues, 643
Microsoft on the Web help, 36
Office on Microsoft.com access, 34
supported image file formats, 506–507
viewing a Web page, 204
Web Discussions toolbar, buttons, 725–727
Web documents. *See also* documents
htm/html file extension, 32, 33
Web Layout view, 25
Web Embedding Fonts Tool (WEFT), 116

Web Folders, server shortcuts, 658–659
Web Layout view
    accessing, 25
    comment balloon display, 699
    previewing Web pages, 657–658
    viewing documents as a Web document, 645
Web Page Preview, previewing Web pages, 657–658
Web page template, access methods, 644–645
Web pages
    background sound considerations, 514
    changing title when saving, 646
    copyright protection methods, 513
    filtered Web page file format, 646
    form elements, 668–672
    forms, 667–672
    frame-definition document, 649–650
    frames, 648–652
    framesets, 649
    FrontPage, 646–648
    htm/html file extension, 645–646
    HTML coding problems, 643
    HTML filters, 647
    HTML styles, 652–653
    hyperlinks, 653–655
    image dragging, 440, 441
    mht/mhtml file extension, 645
    multimedia elements, 656–657
    online template library, 645
    performance enhancements, 743
    previewing, 645, 657–658
    publishing to the Web, 659–660
    rollover scripts, 673–675
    sans serif typeface advantages, 418
    saving a document as, 33, 203–204
    saving documents as HTML format, 645–646
    script addition, 672–675
    scrolling text banners, 677
    sound insertion, 676–677
    sounds, 657
    tables, 655
    templates, 644–645
    themes, 408–409
    video clips, 516, 657, 675–676
    viewing in a Web browser, 204
    visual enhancements, 655–656
    Web Folders, 658–659
    when to use, 644
    Word shortcomings, 643–644
    Word Text Effects non-support, 656
    WYSIWYG presentation, 643

Web Publishing Wizard, Web page publishing, 660
Web servers, Web Folders, 658–659
Web sites
    Adobe, 505
    Adobe Acrobat, 174
    ANSI character set information, 64
    CD-ROM support, 827
    Clip Art on Microsoft.com, 445
    commercial images, 440
    CuteFTP, 660
    Digimarc, 513
    fax services, 687
    file converters, 202
    Fireworks, 506
    hosting-directory, 660
    HTML filters, 647
    McAfee ViruScan, 747
    Microsoft, 439
    Microsoft's Web page template library, 645
    Norton AntiVirus, 747
    Office on Microsoft.com, 34
    Stamps.com, 182
    Thawte, 808
    themes, 409
    VeriSign, 808
    Web Publishing Wizard, 660
    WEFT (Web Embedding Fonts Tool), 116
    Windows Media Player, 516
    Windows Rights Management system
        information, 817
    XML tutorials, 679
Web Tools toolbar
    background sound insertion, 514
    buttons, 666–667
    Internet Explorer integration, 658
Webviews, Open dialog box, 193
WebVise Totality, Auto FX, 513
WEFT (Web Embedding Fonts Tool), 116
What You See Is What You Get (WYSIWYG),
        24, 25, 507
white space
    appearance/readability enhancement, 416
    border/text, 143
    paragraph formatting, 127–130
    Print Layout view adjustments, 25
    snake concerns, 414
whiteboards, Microsoft NetMeeting, 729–730
whole word search, 80
width adjustments, column formatting, 265–267, 289–290
wildcard characters, searches, 81–82, 219

Window, Arrange All command, 60, 339
Window, Compare Side by Side With command, 711
Window, Remove Split command, 632
Window, Split command, 632
windows
    drag-and-drop editing, 60–61
    splitting, 16, 45–46
Windows Explorer
    displaying file extensions, 191
    dragging a document shortcut to the desktop, 193
    opening documents from, 6
Windows Metafile file format, 527
Windows Recycle Bin, recovering files, 196
Windows system
    CD-ROM system requirements, 821
    font management, 117–119
    font smoothing, 117
    starting with Word open, 4
    starting Word from document list, 192
Windows XP, fax setup, 685
Windows XP Table PC Edition, 712
wiz (Wizard) file extension, 392
wizards
    Add Network Place, 727
    Batch Conversion, 203
    Calendar, 403–404
    creating documents from, 30–32
    defined, 389
    Envelope, 573
    Fax, 685–686
    Letter, 30–32, 404–407
    Mail Merge, 561–568
    Microphone, 427
    Resume, 407–408
    Voice Training, 427–429
    Web Publishing, 660
    wiz file extension, 392
Word. *See* Microsoft Word 2003
Word Count dialog box, uses, 212
Word Count toolbar, collaboration enhancement, 817
word forms, finding/replacing, 85
Word hyperlink file format, 527
word processors, versus desktop publishing, 411–412
Word Text Effects, Web page non-support, 656
word wrap
    disappearing images, 455
    table positioning, 259
    text entry conventions, 41

WordArt
    access methods, 490–491
    graphic editing, 491–492
    kerning, 493–494
    lengthening text/letters, 493
    spacing, 493–494
    text alignments, 493
    text shaping, 492
WordArt Gallery dialog box, 490
WordArt toolbar, buttons, 491–492
WordBasic, versus Visual Basic, 796–797
WordMail toolbar, buttons, 689–690
WordML file format, saving XML as, 682
WordPerfect Help, accessing, 34, 38–39
words
    adding to a custom dictionary, 231
    adding to AutoCorrect, 237
    adding/deleting in speech recognition, 431
    automatic selections, 51
    AutoText entry conventions, 71–72
    translations, 243–244
    whole word search, 80
workgroups, Exchange folders, 731–732
workspaces
    shared, 818
    SharePoint document-management, 718
wrapping styles, object positioning, 457
writing styles, grammar checking, 234
WYSIWYG (What You See Is What You Get)
    described, 24, 25, 507
    Web page presentation, 643

X

XE (index entry) field, 337, 340, 344–345, 701
Xenofex, special-effect filter, 506
XML. *See* Extensible Markup Language

Y

Yahoo!
    commercial clip art/stock photography, 440–441
    locating SharePoint hosting services, 717

Z

zero (0) placeholder, number format, 614
Zoom dialog box, zoom magnifications, 28
zoom magnifications, document display, 28
zooming, task pane viewing enhancement
        command, 814

Wiley Publishing, Inc.
End-User License Agreement

READ THIS. You should carefully read these terms and conditions before opening the software packet(s) included with this book "Book." This is a license agreement "Agreement" between you and Wiley Publishing, Inc. "WPI." By opening the accompanying software packet(s), you acknowledge that you have read and accept the following terms and conditions. If you do not agree and do not want to be bound by such terms and conditions, promptly return the Book and the unopened software packet(s) to the place you obtained them for a full refund.

1. **License Grant.** WPI grants to you (either an individual or entity) a nonexclusive license to use one copy of the enclosed software program(s) (collectively, the "Software," solely for your own personal or business purposes on a single computer (whether a standard computer or a workstation component of a multi-user network). The Software is in use on a computer when it is loaded into temporary memory (RAM) or installed into permanent memory (hard disk, CD-ROM, or other storage device). WPI reserves all rights not expressly granted herein.

2. **Ownership.** WPI is the owner of all right, title, and interest, including copyright, in and to the compilation of the Software recorded on the disk(s) or CD-ROM "Software Media." Copyright to the individual programs recorded on the Software Media is owned by the author or other authorized copyright owner of each program. Ownership of the Software and all proprietary rights relating thereto remain with WPI and its licensers.

3. **Restrictions On Use and Transfer.**

    (a) You may only (i) make one copy of the Software for backup or archival purposes, or (ii) transfer the Software to a single hard disk, provided that you keep the original for backup or archival purposes. You may not (i) rent or lease the Software, (ii) copy or reproduce the Software through a LAN or other network system or through any computer subscriber system or bulletin-board system, or (iii) modify, adapt, or create derivative works based on the Software.

    (b) You may not reverse engineer, decompile, or disassemble the Software. You may transfer the Software and user documentation on a permanent basis, provided that the transferee agrees to accept the terms and conditions of this Agreement and you retain no copies. If the Software is an update or has been updated, any transfer must include the most recent update and all prior versions.

4. **Restrictions on Use of Individual Programs.** You must follow the individual requirements and restrictions detailed for each individual program in the About the CD-ROM appendix of this Book. These limitations are also contained in the individual license agreements recorded on the Software Media. These limitations may include a requirement that after using the program for a specified period of time, the user must pay a registration fee or discontinue use. By opening the Software packet(s), you will be agreeing to abide by the licenses and restrictions for these individual programs that are detailed in the "About the CD-ROM" appendix and on the Software Media. None of the material on this Software Media or listed in this Book may ever be redistributed, in original or modified form, for commercial purposes.

5. Limited Warranty.

    (a) WPI warrants that the Software and Software Media are free from defects in materials and workmanship under normal use for a period of sixty (60) days from the date of purchase of this Book. If WPI receives notification within the warranty period of defects in materials or workmanship, WPI will replace the defective Software Media.

    (b) WPI AND THE AUTHOR(S) OF THE BOOK DISCLAIM ALL OTHER WARRANTIES, EXPRESS OR IMPLIED, INCLUDING WITHOUT LIMITATION IMPLIED WARRANTIES OF MERCHANTABILITY AND FITNESS FOR A PARTICULAR PURPOSE, WITH RESPECT TO THE SOFTWARE, THE PROGRAMS, THE SOURCE CODE CONTAINED THEREIN, AND/OR THE TECHNIQUES DESCRIBED IN THIS BOOK. WPI DOES NOT WARRANT THAT THE FUNCTIONS CONTAINED IN THE SOFTWARE WILL MEET YOUR REQUIREMENTS OR THAT THE OPERATION OF THE SOFTWARE WILL BE ERROR FREE.

    (c) This limited warranty gives you specific legal rights, and you may have other rights that vary from jurisdiction to jurisdiction.

6. Remedies.

    (a) WPI's entire liability and your exclusive remedy for defects in materials and workmanship shall be limited to replacement of the Software Media, which may be returned to WPI with a copy of your receipt at the following address: Software Media Fulfillment Department, Attn.: *Word 2003 Bible*, Wiley Publishing, Inc., 10475 Crosspoint Blvd., Indianapolis, IN 46256, or call 1-800-762-2974. Please allow four to six weeks for delivery. This Limited Warranty is void if failure of the Software Media has resulted from accident, abuse, or misapplication. Any replacement Software Media will be warranted for the remainder of the original warranty period or thirty (30) days, whichever is longer.

    (b) In no event shall WPI or the author be liable for any damages whatsoever (including without limitation damages for loss of business profits, business interruption, loss of business information, or any other pecuniary loss) arising from the use of or inability to use the Book or the Software, even if WPI has been advised of the possibility of such damages.

    (c) Because some jurisdictions do not allow the exclusion or limitation of liability for consequential or incidental damages, the above limitation or exclusion may not apply to you.

7. U.S. Government Restricted Rights. Use, duplication, or disclosure of the Software for or on behalf of the United States of America, its agencies and/or instrumentalities "U.S. Government" is subject to restrictions as stated in paragraph (c)(1)(ii) of the Rights in Technical Data and Computer Software clause of DFARS 252.227-7013, or subparagraphs (c) (1) and (2) of the Commercial Computer Software - Restricted Rights clause at FAR 52.227-19, and in similar clauses in the NASA FAR supplement, as applicable.

8. General. This Agreement constitutes the entire understanding of the parties and revokes and supersedes all prior agreements, oral or written, between them and may not be modified or amended except in a writing signed by both parties hereto that specifically refers to this Agreement. This Agreement shall take precedence over any other documents that may be in conflict herewith. If any one or more provisions contained in this Agreement are held by any court or tribunal to be invalid, illegal, or otherwise unenforceable, each and every other provision shall remain in full force and effect.

Where can you find the best information on Microsoft Office 2003?

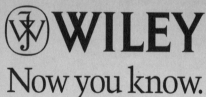

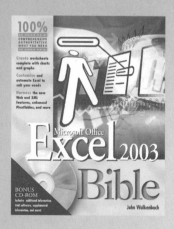

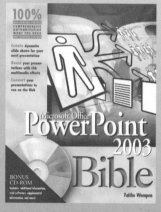